Vessel-Source Marine Pollution

Analysing the regulation of vessel-source pollution from the perspective of the political interests of key players in the ship transportation industry, Alan Khee-Jin Tan offers a comprehensive and convincing account of how pollution of the marine environment by ships may be better regulated and reduced. In this timely study, he traces the history of regulation at the International Maritime Organization (IMO) and investigates the political, economic and social forces influencing the IMO treaties. Also examined are the efforts of maritime states, shipowners, cargo owners, oil companies and environmental groups to influence IMO laws and treaties. This is an important book which uncovers the politics behind the law and offers solutions for overcoming the deficiencies in the regulatory system. It will be of great interest to professionals in the shipping industry as well as practitioners and students.

ALAN KHEE-JIN TAN is an Associate Professor in the Faculty of Law at the National University of Singapore.

CAMBRIDGE STUDIES IN INTERNATIONAL AND COMPARATIVE LAW

Established in 1946, this series produces high-quality scholarship in the fields of public and private international law and comparative law. Although these are distinct legal subdisciplines, developments since 1946 confirm their interrelation.

Comparative law is increasingly used as a tool in the making of law at national, regional and international levels. Private international law is now often affected by international conventions, and the issues faced by classical conflicts rules are frequently dealt with by substantive harmonisation of law under international auspices. Mixed international arbitrations, especially those involving state economic activity, raise mixed questions of public and private international law, while in many fields (such as the protection of human rights and democratic standards, investment guarantees and international criminal law) international and national systems interact. National constitutional arrangements relating to 'foreign affairs', and to the implementation of international norms, are a focus of attention.

The Board welcomes works of a theoretical or interdisciplinary character, and those focusing on the new approaches to international or comparative law or conflicts of law. Studies of particular institutions or problems are equally welcome, as are translations of the best work published in other languages.

General Editors James Crawford SC FBA
Whewell Professor of International Law, Faculty of Law, and Director, Lauterpacht Research Centre for International Law, University of Cambridge
John S. Bell FBA
Professor of Law, Faculty of Law, University of Cambridge

Editorial Board Professor Hilary Charlesworth *University of Adelaide*
Professor Lori Damrosch *Columbia University Law School*
Professor John Dugard *Universiteit Leiden*
Professor Mary-Ann Glendon *Harvard Law School*
Professor Christopher Greenwood *London School of Economics*
Professor David Johnston *University of Edinburgh*
Professor Hein Kötz *Max-Planck-Institut, Hamburg*
Professor Donald McRae *University of Ottawa*
Professor Onuma Yasuaki *University of Tokyo*
Professor Reinhard Zimmermann *Universität Regensburg*

Advisory Committee Professor D. W. Bowett QC
Judge Rosalyn Higgins QC
Professor J. A. Jolowicz QC
Professor Sir Elihu Lauterpacht CBE QC
Professor Kurt Lipstein
Judge Stephen Schwebel

A list of books in the series can be found at the end of this volume.

Vessel-Source Marine Pollution

The Law and Politics of International Regulation

Alan Khee-Jin Tan

CAMBRIDGE UNIVERSITY PRESS
Cambridge, New York, Melbourne, Madrid, Cape Town,
Singapore, São Paulo, Delhi, Tokyo, Mexico City

Cambridge University Press
The Edinburgh Building, Cambridge CB2 8RU, UK

Published in the United States of America by
Cambridge University Press, New York

www.cambridge.org
Information on this title: www.cambridge.org/9780521853422

© Alan Khee-Jin Tan 2006

This publication is in copyright. Subject to statutory exception
and to the provisions of relevant collective licensing agreements,
no reproduction of any part may take place without the written
permission of Cambridge University Press.

First published 2006

A catalogue record for this publication is available from the British Library

Library of Congress Cataloguing in Publication data

ISBN 978-0-521-85342-2 Hardback

Cambridge University Press has no responsibility for the persistence or
accuracy of URLs for external or third-party internet websites referred to in
this publication, and does not guarantee that any content on such websites is,
or will remain, accurate or appropriate. Information regarding prices, travel
timetables, and other factual information given in this work is correct at
the time of first printing but Cambridge University Press does not guarantee
the accuracy of such information thereafter.

To my parents, Keat Seng and Kim Heoh,
my friend and wife, Sun,
and my daughter, Kai Ryn

Contents

Foreword	page xv
Preface	xvii
Table of Conventions	xix
Table of European Union Instruments	xxiv
Table of IMO Resolutions and Guidelines	xxvi
Table of Miscellaneous Instruments	xxix
Table of Domestic Legislation	xxx
Table of Cases (International Courts and Tribunals)	xxxi
Abbreviations	xxxii

Part A The Regulation of Vessel-Source Pollution in its Eco-Political Context

1 Vessel-Source Pollution, the Ecological Imperative and the Compliance Problem   3
  1 Overview   3
  2 Regulating the Sources of Marine Pollution   10
  3 Whither the Freedom of Navigation?   17
  4 Technical Issues and Jurisdiction over Ships   19
  5 Outline of Analysis   25

2 The Dynamics of the Law-Making Process: Actors, Arenas and Interests   29
  1 Overview   29
  2 Key Actors in the Decision-Making Process   34
    2.1 The Maritime Interests   34
      2.1.1 The Shipowners and Operators   34
      2.1.2 The Cargo Owners and Charterers   38
      2.1.3 The Protection and Indemnity (P&I) Clubs and the Marine Insurers   40

		2.1.4 The Classification Societies	43
		2.1.5 The Military Interests	46
		2.1.6 The Flag States and Open Registries	47
		2.1.7 States with Maritime Interests	62
	2.2	The Coastal/Environmental Interests	67
		2.2.1 The Environmental Non-Governmental Organisations	67
		2.2.2 Public Opinion and Media Reaction	69
		2.2.3 States with Coastal Interests	71
	2.3	The Developing Countries	73
3	Major Arenas for Decision-Making		75
	3.1	International Fora: The International Maritime Organization (IMO)	75
		3.1.1 IMO's Initial Years	75
		3.1.2 The Constitutive Structure of IMO	76
		3.1.3 IMO and Maritime Conventions	77
	3.2	International Fora – United Nations Bodies and Specialised Agencies	80
	3.3	Regional Fora	83
		3.3.1 Legal and Political Developments in Europe	83
		3.3.2 Memoranda of Understanding (MOUs) on Port State Control	90
	3.4	Domestic Fora – Agitation Within States	94
4	Marine Pollution Regulation and the Interplay of Interests		98
	4.1	The Relative Capacities of the Relevant Actors	98
	4.2	The Contemporary Political Dynamics at IMO	102

Part B Vessel-Source Pollution and the International Legislative Process

3	Vessel-Source Pollution and Regime Formation		107
	1	Pollution Control Standards and Reception Facilities	107
		1.1 Early Regulatory Efforts	107
		1.2 The OILPOL Regime and the Load-On-Top (LOT) System	110
		1.3 MARPOL 73	126

		1.3.1	Annex I and Segregated Ballast Tanks (SBTs)	126
		1.3.2	Annexes II to V	132
	1.4	MARPOL 73/78 and Crude Oil Washing (COW)		133
	1.5	The Double Hull Requirement		139
		1.5.1	The *Exxon Valdez* and the 1992 Amendments	139
		1.5.2	The *Erika* and the 2001 Amendments	147
		1.5.3	The *Prestige* and the 2003 Amendments	150
2	Air Pollution from Ships			155
3	Anti-Fouling Systems and Tributyl Tin (TBT) Contamination			162
4	Harmful Aquatic Organisms and Ballast Water Management			169
5	Conclusion			174

4 Jurisdiction over Vessel-Source Marine Pollution — 176
  1 The Concept of 'Jurisdiction' in Marine Pollution — 176
  2 Early Attempts to Extend Coastal State Jurisdiction — 181
  3 Jurisdiction under the MARPOL Regime — 184
    3.1 Prescriptive Jurisdiction under MARPOL 73 — 184
    3.2 Enforcement Jurisdiction under MARPOL 73 — 187
    3.3 The 1978 MARPOL Protocol — 191
  4 The 1982 UN Conference on the Law of the Sea (UNCLOS III) — 192
    4.1 The Law of the Sea Convention (LOSC) and Part XII on the Marine Environment — 192
    4.2 The Allocation of State Jurisdiction under the LOSC — 201
      4.2.1 Flag State Jurisdiction — 201
      4.2.2 Coastal State Jurisdiction — 204
      4.2.3 Port State Jurisdiction — 217
  5 Conclusion — 222

5 Implementation and Compliance — 230
  1 Overview — 230
  2 Ratification, Incorporation into Domestic Law and Implementation — 232

		3	The Enforcement Obligations of States	236
			3.1 Pollution Control Standards and State Enforcement Records	236
			3.1.1 Discharge vs. Equipment Standards	236
			3.1.2 State Enforcement of Pollution Control Standards	239
			3.2 The Provision of Waste Reception Facilities in Ports	251
			3.3 Reporting on Implementation Activities	269
			3.3.1 Reporting on the Provision of Reception Facilities	269
			3.3.2 Reporting on Enforcement Action	273
		4	Conclusion	282
6	Liability and Compensation			286
	1	Overview		286
	2	The 1969 Civil Liability Convention (CLC 69)		288
		2.1 Developments Preceding CLC 69		288
		2.2 The 1969 Brussels Conference		293
	3	The 1971 Fund Convention (FUND 71)		300
		3.1 Developments Preceding FUND 71		300
		3.2 The 1971 FUND Conference		302
	4	Amendments to TOVALOP/CRISTAL and CLC/FUND		309
		4.1 Revising the Industry Initiatives		309
		4.2 Developments Preceding the 1984 Conference		311
		4.3 The 1984 IMO Conference		313
		4.4 Further Revision of TOVALOP and CRISTAL		315
	5	Liability and Compensation in the United States		318
		5.1 The *Exxon Valdez* and Developments Preceding OPA-90		318
		5.2 Implications of OPA-90		322
	6	The 1992 Protocols to the CLC and FUND Conventions		327
	7	Pollution by Hazardous and Noxious Substances (HNS)		334
	8	Pollution by Bunker Fuel Oils		339
	9	The Liability and Compensation Regimes: Concluding Analysis		342

Part C The Future of Regulation
7 Challenges and Prescriptions   347
  1 Improving Institutional Responses   347
    1.1 Pro-active Rule-Making by IMO   348
    1.2 Prompt Entry into Force for Conventions   351
    1.3 Ensuring Effective Enforcement and
        Compliance   355
        1.3.1 Market Discrimination Against
             Sub-standard Shipping   356
        1.3.2 Liability of Non-Owner Interests   358
        1.3.3 Return of the Developed State Flags   363
        1.3.4 Tightening Flag State Obligations   365
        1.3.5 Enhancing Port State Control   367
    1.4 Enforcement Powers for IMO   369
  2 Enhancing Equity in Representation and
    Responsibilities   373
    2.1 Reforming IMO   374
        2.1.1 Institutional and Financial Equity   374
        2.1.2 Discipline in Agenda-Setting   376
    2.2 States and the Provision of Reception
        Facilities   378
    2.3 The Cargo Interests and Burden-Sharing   379
    2.4 Shipowners and Intra-Industry Co-operation   381
  3 Final Thoughts   383

Bibliography   385
Index   404

Foreword

I am very pleased to write the foreword to this book, because of its important content and because the author is a colleague at the National University of Singapore's Faculty of Law, where I had the privilege of serving as Dean in the early 1970s.

Coastal states are justifiably concerned about pollution, caused by ships, to their coastal and marine environment. The international regulatory system has had to craft policy responses that seek to balance such concerns with the freedom of navigation for ships. It has been over 50 years since efforts began to regulate vessel-source pollution on a comprehensive scale. Much has changed during that period – from the size of polluting ships and the nature and hazards of pollutants involved, to the growing interest of states and citizens in the environment.

One of the dramatic changes is the rise of the environmental movement, which has led to unprecedented scrutiny being placed on the activities of economic enterprises, including the shipping industry. As a result, the traditional right of freedom of navigation has become increasingly qualified. The international organisations tasked with the role of regulating shipping – principally the International Maritime Organization (IMO) – have had to grapple with a host of increasingly complex issues. Regulating these issues involves a delicate balancing of the interests of states, industry and civil society groups, with the aim of creating a just and equitable system for the use of the oceans.

The author has done an excellent job in analysing these complex issues. He has ably charted the history of regulation, identified the forces energising the regulation of pollution from ships and prescribed remedies for the regulatory system's shortcomings. In the process, this book brings out the key political, social and economic forces which underpin the international regulation of modern shipping. The interplay between shipowners and cargo owners is analysed, as is the problem of 'sub-standard' or irresponsible shipping. The author makes the point that international legal rules are often shaped by the political interests of states. The interests of states are, in turn, determined by the contest of competing interest groups and policy preferences. This phenomenon was especially evident during the Third UN Conference on the Law of the Sea, and continues to feature in the contemporary politics of ocean use. In this regard, I remain optimistic about the capacity of international law to reconcile the competing aspirations of states and their citizens, and to bring about not only equity but sustainability in the use of the oceans.

The sea is close to my heart and that of my country. I am confident that this book will make a significant contribution to international law and legal scholarship. I have great pleasure in commending the book to all those who are interested in the law of the sea.

Professor Tommy Koh
Ambassador-at-Large, Republic of Singapore
President, Third UN Conference on the Law of the Sea
Chairman, Preparatory Committee for and the Main Committee
of the 1992 UN Conference on Environment and Development

Preface

This book analyses the regulation of vessel-source pollution from the perspective of the interest politics underlying the major actors' positions. In essence, it investigates the political, economic and social forces that energise and influence rule-making at international fora, principally the International Maritime Organization (IMO). In the process, the book identifies deficiencies within the shipping industry as well as the international regulatory system that affect the effectiveness of pollution control rules and standards. The book then suggests prescriptions to overcome or reduce the impact of these deficiencies.

I am infinitely grateful to many good people whose support made this book possible and the effort that went into it so worthwhile. First, I wish to thank the National University of Singapore for granting me leave and supporting my studies. To Michael Reisman at Yale Law School, thank you for your encouragement and belief in me. I am also grateful to Daniel Esty, Carol Rose, Judy Couture, Barbara Safriet, Toni Davis, Cina Santos and my good friends from the Yale LLM/JSD Class of 2001–02. Special thanks to Deans Chin Tet Yung and Tan Cheng Han at the Faculty of Law of the National University of Singapore, Robert Beckman, Tommy Koh and the Maritime and Port Authority of Singapore. In London, where the bulk of the research was done, I thank and recall with fondness the International Maritime Organization, its delegates and staff (particularly Rouba Ruthnum and the IMO librarians), the Institute of Advanced Legal Studies, and, our home away from home, the London Goodenough Trust. I also thank the many state, industry and NGO representatives who took time to talk to me.

This book first took form almost seven years ago when Sun and I moved to London after our marriage. While Sun was busy with her own studies and thesis, I made many a visit to the IMO at Albert Embankment, attending numerous meetings, interviewing delegates and spending long, lonely hours at the library scrutinising decades-old documents. Two years later, we moved to New Haven, where I was to finalise the text at Yale Law School. Upon our return home to Singapore in 2001, the effort began to find a publisher and to revise the work substantively. The final product bears little resemblance to the original thesis that inspired it. So many new developments had occurred in the interim that I practically rewrote the bulk of the chapters. Looking back, it is gratifying to know that this book was born not just out of effort, but also in between reflection and rest, from moody rainy days at William Goodenough House in London and impulsive Eurostar trips to meaningful friendships made at Yale and frequent driving distractions around New England.

Finally, my gratitude and love to my dear parents in Penang, who raised my brother and me so well, and to Sun, whose companionship made this surely one of the most fulfilling journeys of our lives. Not to mention an intellectually rewarding honeymoon.

The law is stated as at 1 January 2005.

Alan Khee-Jin Tan, Kent Ridge, Singapore
February 2005

Table of Conventions

1948 Convention on the Inter-Governmental Maritime Consultative Organization, 289 UNTS 3 (in force 17 March 1958), amended and renamed the Convention on the International Maritime Organization, 34 UST 497 (in force 22 May 1982), 75
  art 1(b), 75
  art 28, 52
1954 International Convention for the Prevention of Pollution of the Sea by Oil (OILPOL 54), 327 UNTS 3 (in force 26 July 1958), 111
  art III(b), 124
  art III(c), 115
  art VIII, 111, 116
  art IX, 112
  art IX(5), 217
  art X, 112
  art X(2), 274
  art XI, 112, 184–5
  art XII, 274
1957 International Convention relating to the Limitation of Liability of Owners of Seagoing Ships (LLMC 57), 52 UKTS Cmnd 3678 (1968) (in force 31 May 1968), 289
1958 Geneva Convention on the High Seas, 450 UNTS 82 (in force 30 September 1962), 50
  art 5(1), 50
  art 24, 115
1958 Geneva Convention on the Territorial Sea and the Contiguous Zone, 516 UNTS 206 (in force 10 September 1964), 211
1969 Bonn Agreement for Co-operation in Dealing with Pollution of the North Sea by Oil, 704 UNTS 3; 9 ILM 359 (1970) (in force 9 August 1969), 84, 85

1969 International Convention on Civil Liability for Oil Pollution Damage (CLC 69), 973 UNTS 3, 9 ILM 45 (1970) (in force 19 June 1976), as amended by the 1976 Protocol to the 1969 Convention, 16 ILM 617 (1977) (in force 8 April 1981), 42, 181–3, 217
  art I(1), 298, 305
  art I(5), 298
  art I(6), 298
  art I(8), 299
  art II, 299
  art III, 358
  art III(1), 304
  art III(2), 297
  art III(3), 297, 304
  art III(4), 296
  art III(5), 296
  art V(1), 298
  art V(2), 298
  art V(3), 298
  art VII(1), 305
  art VII(8), 297
  art VII(11), 300
  art IX(1), 298
  art XI(1), 299
  Protocol 1976, 298
1969 International Convention relating to Intervention on the High Seas in Cases of Oil Pollution Casualties (Intervention Convention), 77 UKTS Cmnd 6056 (1975) (in force 6 May 1975), as amended by the 1973 Protocol relating to Intervention on the High Seas in Cases of Marine Pollution by Substances Other than Oil, 13 ILM 605 (1974) (in force 30 March 1983), 70, 182, 217, 223
  art 1(1), 217
  Protocol, 70

1971 International Convention on the
   Establishment of an International
   Fund for Compensation for Oil
   Pollution Damage (FUND 71), 1110
   UNTS 57, 11 ILM 284 (272) (in force 16
   October 1978), as amended by the 1976
   Protocol to the 1971 Convention, 16
   ILM 621 (1977) (in force 22 November
   1994) (ceased operation 24 May 2002),
   42, 302-9
  art 1(2), 305
  art 3, 358
  art 4(1)(b), 305
  art 4(1)(c), 306
  art 4(2), 304
  art 4(2)(a), 303
  art 4(2)(b), 305
  art 4(3), 304
  art 4(4)(a), 303
  art 4(4)(b), 304
  art 5(3), 307
  art 10(1), 303, 358
  art 43, 330
  Protocol 1976, 298
1971 Nordic Agreement concerning
   Co-operation in Measures to Deal with
   Pollution of the Sea by Oil, 822 UNTS
   311 (in force 16 October 1971), 84
1972 London Convention on the Prevention
   of Marine Pollution by Dumping of
   Wastes and Other Matter, 1046 UNTS
   120, 11 ILM 1294 (1972) (in force 30
   August 1975), as amended by the 1996
   Protocol to the 1972 Convention, 36
   ILM 1 (1997) (not in force), 84
1972 Oslo Convention for the Prevention of
   Marine Pollution by Dumping by Ships
   and Aircraft, 119 UKTS Cmnd 4984
   (1975), 11 ILM 262 (1972) (in force
   7 April 1974), 84, 85
1973 International Convention for the
   Prevention of Pollution from Ships
   (MARPOL 73/78), 12 ILM 1319 (1973), as
   amended by the 1978 Protocol to the
   1973 Convention, 1341 UNTS 3, 17 ILM
   546 (in force 2 October 1983), 8, 70, 78,
   126-39, 184-92
  art 3(3), 46
  art 4, 185, 232
  art 4(2), 189, 205
  art 5(1), 188
  art 5(2), 188, 189, 190, 204, 218, 219, 221
  art 5(4), 197, 204
  art 6(2), 189, 190, 218
  art 6(3), 189
  art 6(5), 189, 218
  art 7, 188
  art 8, 188
  art 8(3), 189
  art 9(3), 185
  art 11, 269, 274
  art 11(1), 274
  art 11(1)(d), 273
  art 12(5), 273
  art 13G, 239
  art 19(2)(h), 207
  art 23, 208
  art 25(1), 207
  art 34(1), 209
  art 42(1)(b), 209
  art 42(2), 209
  art 42(3), 209
  art 220, 207
  art 220(6), 206
  art 221(1), 208
  Part III, 209
  Annex I, 126-32, 353
    reg 1(26), 137
    reg 4, 188
    reg 5, 188
    reg 9(1)(a)(v), 131
    reg 10, 264
    reg 10(2), 132
    reg 11, 264
    reg 12, 253, 263
    reg 12(1), 132
    reg 13, 134
    reg 13(1), 137
    reg 13(6), 137
    reg 13(7), 137
    reg 13B, 137
    reg 13E, 137, 148
    reg 13F, 144-6
    reg 13F(4), 145
    reg 13F(5), 146
    reg 13G, 144, 145-7, 148-50, 151
    reg 13G(3)(a), 146
    reg 13G(4), 145
    reg 13G(5), 146
    reg 13G(8)(b), 151
    reg 13H, 151
    reg 13H(8)(b), 151
    reg 14(1), 131
    reg 14(3), 131
    regs 15-19, 131
  Annex II, 133, 138, 257, 353
    reg 7, 263
  Annex III, 133
  Annex IV, 133, 197, 353
    reg 10, 263
  Annex V, 133
    reg 7, 263
  Annex VI, 160, 161, 353-4
    reg 17, 263

TABLE OF CONVENTIONS

1974 Helsinki Convention on the Protection of the Marine Environment of the Baltic Sea Area, 13 ILM 546 (1974) (in force 3 May 1980), 85, 156
1974 Paris Convention for the Prevention of Marine Pollution from Land-Based Sources, 13 ILM 352 (1974) (in force 6 May 1978), 14, 85
1976 Barcelona Convention for the Protection of the Marine Environment against Pollution, 15 ILM 290 (1976) (in force 12 February 1978), 68, 82
1976 Convention on the Limitation of Liability for Maritime Claims (LLMC 76), 13 UKTS Cm 7035 (1990), 16 ILM 606 (1977) (in force 1 December 1986), as amended by the 1996 Protocol to the 1976 Convention, 35 ILM 1433 (1996) (in force 13 May 2004), 314
    art 4, 314, 328
1976 International Labour Organization Convention No 147 concerning Minimum Standards on Merchant Ships, 1259 UNTS 335 (in force 28 November 1981), 82, 90
1978 IMO Convention on Standards of Training, Certification and Watchkeeping for Seafarers (STCW), 1361 UNTS 2 (in force 28 April 1984), as amended by the 1995 Protocol, 1969 UNTS (in force 1 February 1997), 82
    Protocol, 55, 370
1978 Kuwait Regional Convention for Co-operation on the Protection of the Marine Environment from Pollution, 17 ILM 511 (1978) (in force 1 July 1979), 82
1978 Protocol to the International Convention for the Prevention of Pollution from Ships, 1341 UNTS 3, 17 ILM 546 (1978) (in force 2 October 1983), 138
1979 UN-ECE Convention on Long-Range Transboundary Air Pollution (LRTAP) 1392 UNTS 217, 18 ILM 1442 (1979) (in force 16 March 1983), 156
1981 Abidjan Convention for Co-operation in the Protection and Development of the Marine and Coastal Environment of the West and Central African Region, 20 ILM 746 (1981) (in force 5 August 1984), 83
1981 Lima Convention for the Protection of the Marine Environment and Coastal Areas of the South-East Pacific, 20 ILM 696 (1981) (in force 19 May 1986), 83

1982 Jeddah Regional Convention for the Conservation of the Red Sea and the Gulf of Aden Environment, 22 ILM 219 (1983) (in force 20 August 1985), 83
1982 United Nations Convention on the Law of the Sea, UN Doc A.Conf 62/122 (1982), 21 ILM 1261 (1982) (in force 16 November 1994), 31
    art 1(4), 3, 172
    art 2, 179
    art 2(1), 23
    art 19, 177, 207, 208–9
    art 19(2)(h), 152, 208
    art 21(2), 205
    art 21(3), 152, 205
    art 21(6), 172
    art 22, 205
    art 24, 205
    art 25(2), 152, 172
    art 33, 211
    art 38(3), 210
    art 39(2), 210
    art 41, 209
    art 52(1), 211
    art 53(12), 211
    art 56, 223
    art 56(1), 23
    art 56(1)(a), 212
    art 56(1)(b)(iii), 212
    art 57, 212, 223
    art 77, 223
    art 91, 18, 23, 34, 53
    art 92(1), 18, 23
    art 94, 34, 202
    art 94(1), 53
    art 105, 212
    art 109, 212
    art 194, 11
    art 196, 172
    art 196(2), 172
    art 211, 53, 223
    art 211(1), 225
    art 211(2), 179, 195, 202
    art 211(3), 204, 218
    art 211(5), 195, 204, 212
    art 211(6), 172, 195, 212, 215, 227
    art 211(6)(a), 215–16, 216
    art 211(6)(c), 216, 217
    art 214(4), 205
    art 217, 53
    art 217(1), 202
    art 217(2), 202
    art 217(3), 202
    art 217(4), 202
    art 217(5), 202
    art 217(6), 202
    art 217(7), 202

1982 United Nations Convention (cont.)
  art 217(8), 202
  art 218, 53, 218-19, 219, 220
  art 219, 204, 219
  art 220, 53, 206, 208, 210, 214, 216, 223
  art 220(1), 205
  art 220(2), 206, 207, 213
  art 220(3), 206, 213, 214
  art 220(5), 206, 213, 214
  art 220(6), 213, 214
  art 220(7), 214, 218, 220
  art 220(8), 216
  art 221, 223
  art 221(1), 182, 213, 217
  art 226(1), 195
  art 226(1)(b), 218
  art 228, 214, 221
  art 228(1), 203
  art 232, 220
  art 233, 210, 211, 214
  art 234, 200, 212, 215
  art 236, 46, 214
  art 237, 195
  art 237(1), 225
  Part III, 199
  Part IV, 211
  Part XI, 194
  Part XII, 192-201, 211
  Part XV, 214
  Annex, reg C-1(3), 172
  Annex VIII, 202
1983 Bonn Agreement for Co-operation in Dealing with Pollution of the North Sea by Oil and Other Harmful Substances, Cm 9104 (in force 1 September 1989), 84
1983 Cartagena Convention for the Protection and Development of the Marine Environment of the Wider Caribbean Region, 22 ILM 221 (1983) (in force 30 March 1986), 82
1985 Nairobi Convention for the Protection, Management and Development of the Marine and Coastal Environment of the Eastern African Region, 1986 OJ C253, 10 (in force 29 May 1996), 83
1985 Vienna Convention on the Ozone Layer, 26 ILM 1529 (1987) (in force 22 September 1988), 168
1986 Noumea Convention for the Protection and Development of the Natural Resources and Environment of the South Pacific Region, 26 ILM 41 (1987) (in force 22 August 1990), 83

1986 United Nations Convention on Conditions for the Registration of Ships (UNCCRS), 26 ILM 1229 (1987) (not in force), 23, 53-5
  art 7, 54
  art 8, 54
  art 9, 54
  art 9(2)(a-c), 54
  art 9(3), 54
1987 Montreal Protocol on Substances that Deplete the Ozone Layer, 26 ILM 1550 (1987) (in force 1 Janaury 1989), 168
1989 Basel Convention on the Control of Transboundary Movement of Hazardous Wastes and their Disposal 28 ILM 652 (1989) (in force 5 May 1992), 377
1989 International Convention on Salvage, 93 UKTS 8, Cm 3458 (1996) (in force 14 July 1996), 70
1990 Convention on Oil Pollution Preparedness, Response and Co-operation (OPRC), 30 ILM 733 (1991) (in force 13 May 1995), 71, 352
1992 Convention for the Protection of the Marine Environment of the North-East Atlantic (OSPAR), 32 ILM 1069 (1993) (in force 25 March 1998), 14, 85
1992 Convention on Biological Diversity, 31 ILM 818 (1992) (in force 29 December 1993), 11
1992 Framework Convention on Climate Change, 31 ILM 848 (1992) (in force 21 March 1994), 378
1992 Helsinki Convention on the Protection of the Marine Environment of the Baltic Sea Area, UN Law of the Sea Bulletin No 22, reprinted in 8 International Journal of Marine and Coastal Law 215 (1993) (in force 17 January 2000), 14, 68, 85, 156
1992 International Convention on Civil Liability for Oil Pollution Damage (CLC 92), 1953 UNTS 255 (in force 30 May 1996), 217, 327-34
  art I(5), 328
  art I(6), 315
  art I(8), 315, 329
  art II(1)(ii), 314
  art II(b), 315, 329
  art III(4), 328, 329, 343, 359
  art III(4)(c), 358
  art III(5), 359
  art V(2), 314, 328

1992 International Convention on the Establishment of an International Fund for Compensation for Oil Pollution Damage (FUND 92) 87 UKTS Cm 3433 (1996) (in force 30 May 1996), 327–34
  2003 Protocol, 358
  art 3(a)(ii), 314
  art 4(2), 304
  art 4(3), 304
  art 4(4)(a), 313
  art 4(4)(b), 304, 305
  art 10(1), 358
1992 Treaty on the European Union, 31 ILM 247 (1992) (in force 1 November 1993)
  art 130R, 68
1993 FAO Agreement to Promote Compliance with International Conservation and Management Measures by Fishing Vessels on the High Seas, 33 ILM 968 (1994) (in force 24 September 2003), 56
1995 Agreement for the Implementation of the Provisions of the UN Convention on the Law of the Sea relating to the Conservation and Management of Straddling Fish Stocks and Highly Migratory Fish Stocks, 34 ILM 1542 (1995) (in force 11 December 2001), 56
1996 International Convention on Liability and Compensation for Damage in Connection with the Carriage of Hazardous and Noxious Substances by Sea, 35 ILM 1406 (1996) (not in force), 42, 336–9, 353–4
  art 1(5), 336
  art 4(3), 336
  art 5(1), 338
  art 7(2)(d), 337
  art 7(5), 358
  art 7(6), 359
  art 9(1), 338
  art 10, 358
  art 46, 339
1998 Kyoto Protocol to the Convention on Climate Change, 37 ILM 22 (1998) (in force 16 February 2005), 377
2001 Convention on the Control of Harmful Anti-Fouling Systems on Ships (AFS Convention), IMO Doc AFS/CONF 26 (2001) (not in force), 167–8, 352
2001 International Convention on Liability and Compensation for Bunker Oil Spills, IMO Doc LEG/CONF 12/19 (2001) (not in force), 341, 352
2004 International Convention for the Control and Management of Ships' Ballast Water and Sediments (BWMC), IMO Doc. BWM/CONF/36 (2004) (not in force), 172–4
  art 2(3), 172
  art 5, 173
  art 7, 173
  art 9, 173
  art 18, 172
  Annex
    reg B-3, 172
    reg B-3(7), 173
    reg B-4, 173
    reg C-1(5), 172
    reg D-1, 173
    reg D-2, 172

Table of European Union Instruments

Regulations
  417/2002/EC on the accelerated placing of double hull or equivalent design requirements for single hull oil tankers, 2002 OJ L64 1, amended by Regulation 1726/2003 (EC), 2003 OJ L 249, 147, 150
  1406/2002/EC of the European Parliament and Council Establishing a European Maritime Safety Agency (EMSA), 88
  2099/2002 of the European Parliament and of the Council establishing a Committee on Safe Seas and the Prevention of Pollution from Ships (COSS), 2002 OJ L234, 1, 150

Directives
  79/116 Concerning Minimum Requirements for Certain Tankers Entering or Leaving Community Ports, 1979 OJ L33, 33, as amended by Directive 79/1034, 1979 OJ L315, 16, 87
  94/57 on Common Rules and Standards for Ship Inspection and Survey Organisations and for the Relevant Activities of Maritime Administrations (Directive on Classification Societies), 1994 OJ L319, 20, as amended by Directive 97/58, 1997 OJ L274, 8 and Directive 2001/105/EC, 2002 OJ L19, 9, 87
  94/58 on the Minimum Level of Training for Seafarers, 1994 OJ L319, 28, as amended by Directive 98/35, 1998 OJ L172, 1, 87
  95/21 Concerning the Enforcement in Respect of Shipping Using Community Ports and Sailing in the Waters under the Jurisdiction of the Member States, of International Standards for Ship Safety, Pollution, Prevention and Shipboard Living and Working Conditions (Directive on Port State Control), 1995 OJ L157, 1, as amended by Directive 98/25, Directive 98/42, Directive 99/97 and Directive 2001/106, 87, 92-3
  98/8 Concerning the Placing of Biocidal Products on the Market (Directive on Biocides), 1998 OJ L123, 1, 164
  99/32/EC, 1999 OJ L121, relating to a reduction in the sulphur content of certain liquid fuels and amending Directive 93/12/EEC, 1993 OJ L74, 161
  2000/59 on Port Reception Facilities for Ship-Generated Waste and Cargo Residues, 2000 OJ L332, 81, 87, 266-7
    art 8(1), 266
  2001/105/EC, 2002 OJ L19, 9 amending Directive 94/57 on Common Rules and Standards for Ship Inspection and Survey Organisations and for the Relevant Activities of Maritime Administrations, 1994 OJ L 319, 20, 148, 357, 361
    art 6, 362
    art 15, 45
  2001/106, 2002 OJ L19, 17, amending Directive 95/21, 92, 148
    art 7, 92
  2002/59/EC of the European Parliament and of the Council of 27 June 2002 establishing a Community vessel traffic monitoring and information system, 2002 OJ L208, 10 and repealing Council Directive 93/75/EEC, 87, 218

Resolutions
  Council Resolution on a Common Policy for Safe Seas, 1993 OJ C271, 8 June 1993, 87

Communications
  Commission Communication on action to deal with the effects of the Prestige disaster, COM(2003) 105 final, 150, 152, 153, 225
  Communication from the Commission to the European Parliament and the Council on improving safety at sea in response to the Prestige accident, COM(2002) 681 final, 150, 223, 239, 363
  Communication from the Commission to the European Parliament and the Council on the Safety of the Seaborne Oil Trade, COM(2000) 142 final (Erika 1 package), 149
  Communication from the Commission to the European Parliament and the Council on a Second Set of Community Measures on Maritime Safety Following the Sinking of the Oil Tanker Erika, COM(2000) 802 final (Erika II package), 147
  Communication on a Common Policy on Safe Seas, COM(93) 66 final, 87

Commission Proposals
  For a Directive on ship-source pollution and on the introduction of sanctions, including criminal sanctions, for pollution offences, COM(2003) 92 final, 152, 153, 154, 219
  For a Regulation of the European Parliament and of the Council amending Regulation 417/2002/EC on the accelerated phasing in of double hull or equivalent design requirements for single hull oil tankers and repealing Council Regulation 2978/94/EC, COM(2002) 780 final, 150

Table of IMO Resolutions and Guidelines

A.500(XII) (1981) on Objective of the Organization in the 1980s, 235
A.720(17) (1991) on Guidelines for the Designation of Special Areas and the Identification of Particularly Sensitive Sea Areas, 226
A.739(18) (1993) on Guidelines for the Authorization of Organizations Acting on Behalf of Administrations (updated by Resolution A.789(19)), 44
A.741(18) (1993) on the International Management Code for the Safe Operation of Ships and Pollution Prevention (International Safety Management Code), 55
A.774(18) (1993) on International Guidelines for Preventing the Introduction of Unwanted Aquatic Organisms and Pathogens from Ships' Ballast Water and Sediment Discharges (revoked by Resolution A.868(20)), 171
A.777(18) (1993) on the Work Methods and Organisation of Work in Committees and Their Subsidiary Bodies, 235
A.787(19) (1995) on Procedures for Port State Control, as amended by Resolution A.882(21) (1999), 4, 91
A.789(19) (1995) on Specifications on the Survey and Certification Functions of Recognised Organizations Acting on Behalf of Administrations, 44
A.847(20) (1997) on Guidelines to Assist Flag States in the Implementation of IMO Instruments, as bolstered by Resolutions A.912(22) (2001) and A.914(22) (2001), 282
A.868(20) (1997) setting out Guidelines for the Control and Management of Ships' Ballast Water to Minimise the Transfer of Harmful Aquatic Organisms and Pathogens, 171
A.885(21) (1999) on Procedures for the Identification of Particularly Sensitive Sea Areas and the Adoption of Associated Protective Measures and Amendments to the Guidelines Contained in Resolution A.720(17), 227
A.900(21) (1999) on the Objectives of the Organization in the 2000s, 235
A.909(22) (2001) on Policy Making in IMO Setting the Organization's Policies and Objectives, 235
A.913(22) (2001) on Revised Guidelines for the Implementation of the ISM Code, 371
A.923(22) (2001) on Measures to Prevent the Registration of 'Phantom' Ships, 37, 62
A.927(22) (2001) on Guidelines for the Designation of Special Areas and for the Identification and Designation of Particularly Sensitive Sea Areas, 54, 226, 228
A.944(23) (2003) on the Strategic Plan for the Organization for the Period 2004-10, 235
A.946(23) (2003) on the Voluntary IMO Member State Audit Scheme, 371
A.949(23) (2003) on Guidelines on Places of Refuge for Ships in Need of Assistance, 218
A.962(23) (2003) on Guidelines on Recycling of Ships, 377
A.963(23) (2003) on IMO Policies and Practices on GHG Emissions from Ships, 378

MEPC 46(30) (1990) Containing Measures to Control Potential Adverse Impacts

Associated with the Use of TBT
Compounds in Anti-fouling Paints, 163
MEPC 83(44) (2000) on Guidelines for
Ensuring the Adequacy of Port Waste
Reception Facilities, 272, 273
MEPC 102(48) (2002) on Guidelines for
Survey and Certification of Ships' Anti-
Fouling Systems, 167

Guidelines on the Organisation and
Method of Work of MSC and MEPC and
their Subsidiary Bodies, MSC/Circ 816
and MEPC MEPC/Circ 331, as revised by
MSC/Circ 931/MEPC/Circ 366 and MSC/
Circ 1099/MEPC/Circ 405, 101

IMO Council - Submissions and Reports
Report of the 82nd Session, Council Doc
C/82/11 (1999), 14, 15

Secretariat, Council Docs C88/13/2 (2002),
C88/13/3 (2002) and C88/13/4 (2002), 371

**IMO Marine Environment Protection
Committee - Submissions and Reports**
Australia, MEPC Doc 40/21 (1997), 165
Australia, Singapore and Vanuatu, MEPC
Doc 39/6/9 (1997), 159
Austria, Bahrain, India, Mexico, Singapore,
Solomon Islands, Vanuatu and
Venezuela, MEPC Doc 37/13/21
(1995), 157

Bahrain, MEPC Doc 39/6/17 (1997), 159
Belgium, Denmark, France, Germany,
Norway, the Netherlands, Sweden and
the UK, MEPC Doc 38/14 (1996), 166
BIMCO, MEPC Doc 36/INF 4 (1994), 257
BIMCO, MEPC Doc 41/11 (1998), 257
BIMCO, MEPC Doc 41/11/1 (1998), 257
BIMCO, MEPC Doc 49/16/7 (2003), 154
Brazil, MEPC Doc 48/18/12 (2002), 376
Brazil, MEPC Doc 50/2/10 (2003), 151

CEFIC, MEPC Doc 38/14/4 (1996), 164
CEFIC, MEPC Doc 38/INF 8 (1996), 164
CEFIC, MEPC Doc 41/INF 6 (1998), 164
CEFIC, MEPC Doc 42/5/3 (1998), 164
CEFIC, MEPC Doc 42/5/8 (1998), 166
CEFIC, MEPC Doc 42/INF 13 (1998), 164

Denmark, Germany, Japan, the
Netherlands, Norway, Sweden, France,
the UK, Liberia, Panama and Greece,
MEPC Doc 32/J/9 (1992), 145

European Communities Commission,
MEPC Doc 29/21 (1990), 256

European Communities Commission,
MEPC Doc 49/16/1 (2003), 150, 239
Expert Group on Impact Assessment of the
Proposed Amendments to MARPOL
Annex 1, Third Report, MEPC Doc 50/
INF 4 (2003), 6

France, MEPC Doc 32/7/11 (1992), 142
Germany, MEPC Doc 27/16 (1989), 263
Greece, China, France, Liberia, Mexico,
Romania, South Korea, and USSR,
MEPC Doc 31/21 (1991), 142

ICS, MEPC Doc 30/INF 30 (1990), 257
ICS, MEPC Doc 37/13/14 (1995), 158
ICS, MEPC Doc 41/7/6 (1998), 265
INTERTANKO, MEPC Doc 27/5/4 (1989), 256
INTERTANKO, MEPC Doc 31/21 (1991), 263
INTERTANKO, MEPC Doc 32/10 (1992), 256, 263
INTERTANKO, MEPC Doc 32/12/2 (1992), 157
INTERTANKO, MEPC Doc 34/12 (1993), 256
INTERTANKO, MEPC Doc 34/INF 26 (1993), 264
INTERTANKO, MEPC Doc 35/INF 23 (1994), 256
INTERTANKO, MEPC Doc 36/13/1 (1994), 256
INTERTANKO, MEPC Doc 37/16/1 (1995), 256, 264
INTERTANKO, MEPC Doc 38/INF 22 (1996), 256
INTERTANKO, MEPC Doc 50/2/11 (2003), 151
INTERTANKO, MEPC Doc 52/9 (2004), 256
Italy, Malta, Cyprus and Poland, MEPC Doc
50/3 (2003), 151

Kuwait, MEPC Doc 29/18/5 (1990), 157

Netherlands, MEPC Doc 48/INF 4 (2002), 54
Norway, MEPC Doc 41/10/2 (1998), 166

OCIMF, MEPC Doc 34/INF 36 (1993), 157

Paris Commission, MEPC Doc 26/24/4
(1988), 163
Report of the MEPC's 32nd session, MEPC
Doc 32/20 (1992), 146
Report of the MEPC's 44th session, MEPC
Doc 44/20 (2000), 354
Report of the MEPC's 46th session, MEPC
Doc 46/23 (2001), 148, 278
Report of the MEPC's 49th session, MEPC
Doc 49/22 (2003), 5, 159, 268, 378
Report of the MEPC's 51st session, MEPC
Doc 51/22 (2004), 272

Report of the MEPC's 52nd session, MEPC Doc 52/24 (2004), 228

UK, MEPC Doc 32/7/9 (1992), 143
UK, MEPC Doc 38/9/7 (1996), 159

IMO Legal Committee – Submissions and Reports
Brunei, LEG Doc 67/3/9 (1992), 338
Indonesia, LEG Doc 66/4/5 (1992), 338
Indonesia, LEG Doc 67/3/11 (1992), 338
International Group of P&I Clubs, LEG Doc 80/4/2 (1999), 329
International Group of P&I Clubs, LEG Doc 81/4/2 (2000), 329
Malaysia, LEG Doc 67/3/8 (1992), 338
Malaysia, LEG Doc 68/4/13 (1993), 338
United Kingdom, LEG Doc 85/INF 2 (2002), 350
United Kingdom, LEG Doc 86/7 (2003), 339
Report of the Legal Committee's 84th Session, LEG Doc 84/14 (2002), 37

IMO Flag State Implementation Sub-Committee – Submissions and Reports
Netherlands, FSI Doc 7/INF 7 (1999), 246
Netherlands, FSI Doc 8/10/2 (2000), 246
New Zealand, FSI Doc 11/6/2 (2003), 282
UK, Australia and Canada, FSI Doc 6/3/3 (1998), 370
United States, FSI Doc 9/6/5 (2001), 368
Report of the FSI's 10th session, FSI Doc 10/17 (2002), 62, 246
Report of the FSI's 11th session, FSI Doc 11/23 (2003), 167, 272, 273

Secretariat, FSI Doc 12/8/1 (2004), 78
Secretariat, FSI Doc 12/8/4 (2004), 282

Diplomatic Conferences – Submissions
Belgium, Denmark, Finland, Germany, Ireland, Netherlands, Spain, Sweden and UK, LEG/CONF 10/CONF 10/CW/WP 13 (1996), 336
ICS, MP/CONF 3/17 (1997), 158
International Group of P&I Clubs, LEG/CONF 14/12 (2003), 332
OCIMF, LEG/CONF 14/13 (2003), 333

Submissions to the International Oil Pollution Compensation (IOPC) Fund
Australia, Canada, Finland, France, Netherlands, Russia and UK, Doc 92FUND/WGR 3/19/1 (2004), 333
Australia, Canada, Finland, France, Netherlands, Russia and UK, Doc 92FUND/WGR 3/20 (2004), 333, 334
Korea, Doc 92FUND/WGR 3/23 (2004), 333, 334
Report on the 7th Meeting of the IOPC Fund's Third Inter-Sessional Working Group, *Review of the International Compensation Regime*, Doc 92FUND/WGR 3/20 (2004), 333
Report on the 8th Meeting of the IOPC Fund's Third Inter-Sessional Working Group, *Review of the International Compensation Regime*, Doc 92FUND/WGR 3/23 (2004), 333

Table of Miscellaneous Instruments

1969 Tanker Owners' Voluntary Agreement on Liability for Oil Pollution (TOVALOP), 8 ILM 497 (1969) (ceased operation 20 February 1997), 291-3, 309-10
  Supplement, para 3(C)(3), 317
1971 Contract regarding an Interim Settlement of Tanker Liability for Oil Pollution (CRISTAL), 10 ILM 137 (1971) (ceased operation 20 February 1997), 301-2, 310-11
1972 Stockholm Action Plan for the Human Environment, 11 ILM 1421 (1972), 126
1972 Stockholm Declaration on the Human Environment, UN Doc A/CONF 48/14/Rev 1, 11 ILM 1416 (1972), 126
1982 Paris Memorandum of Understanding on Port State Control in Implementing Agreements on Maritime Safety and Protection of the Marine Environment, 21 ILM 1 (1982) (in force 1 July 1982), 70, 90, 153, 356, 367
1985 Montreal Guidelines for the Protection of the Marine Environment against Pollution from Land-Based Sources, 14 ENVTL POL & L 77 (1985), 14
1992 Rio de Janeiro Declaration on Environment and Development, UN Doc A/CONF 151/26 (Vol I) (1992) 31 ILM 874 (1992)
  Principle 15, 68
1993 Noordwijk Guidelines for Integrated Coastal Zone Management, in World Bank, World Coast Conference, Noordwijk, Netherlands 1-5 November 1993 (1993), 14
1995 Washington Declaration and Global Programme of Action on Protection of the Marine Environment from Land-Based Activities, UNEP (OCA) LBA/1G 2/7, 26 ENVTL POL & L 37 (1996), 14

Table of Domestic Legislation

Canada
Arctic Waters Pollution Prevention Act 1971, 9 ILM 543 (1970), 72, 183

United States
Clean Water Act 1977, 319
Comprehensive Environmental Response, Compensation and Liability Act (CERCLA) 1980, 42 § USC 9601–9675, 319

Deepwater Ports Act 1975, 319

Federal Water Quality Improvement Act 1970, 319

Maritime Security Transportation Act 2002, 94
Merchant Marine Act 1920 (Jones Act) 46 USC app § 883 (2000) 46 CFR § 67.3 (1999) § 27, 65

Oil Pollution Act 1990, USC §§ 3703a, 39, 65, 71, 96, 140, 148, 201, 320–7, 358
  § 1006(d)(1)(B), 324
  § 1018(a)(1), 322
  § 2702(b)(2)(A), 343
  § 2718(a)(1), 326
Outer Continental Shelf Lands Act (OCSLA) 1953, 319

Ports and Waterways Safety Act 1972 USC §§ 1221–1227, 46 USC § 3703(a) (2000), 96, 110
Presidential Proclamation 5030, 33 USC § 270(8), 22 ILM 464 (1983), 192, 194

Trans-Alaskan Pipeline Authorization Act (TAPAA) 1973, 43 USC §§ 1651–1656, 140, 319

Table of Cases (International Courts and Tribunals)

Constitution of the Maritime Safety Committee of IMCO Case, 1960 ICJ 150, 52
Grand Prince Case (Belize v France), 2001 ITLOS 8, 58
Muscat Dhows (France v Great Britain), Hague Ct Rep 93 (Perm Ct Arb 1916), 47
MV Saiga (No 2) (St Vincent & Grenadines v Guinea), 1999 ITLOS 2, 79; 38 ILM 1323 (1999), 47, 51, 57
Nottebohm Case (Liechtenstein v Guatemala), 1955 ICJ 4, 50
SS Lotus (France v Turkey) (1927) PCIJ (Series A) No 10, 212
Trail Smelter Arbitration (US v Canada) 3 R INTL ARB AWARDS 1911 (1938); 33 AM J INTL L 182 (1939), 3 R INTL ARB AWARDS 1938 (1941); 35 AM J INTL L 684 (1941), 31

European Court of Justice
C-221/89, R v Secretary of State for Transport, ex parte Factortame Ltd, 1991 ECR I-3905, 52
C-246/89, Commission v UK, 1991 ECR I-4585, 52
C-280/89, Commission v Ireland, 1992 ECR I-6185, 52
C-286/90, Anklagemyndigheden v Peter Michael Poulsen and Diva Navigation Corp, 1992 ECR I-6019, 52
C-62/96, Commission v Greece, 1997 ECR I-6725, 52, 58

Domestic Courts
Aegean Sea Traders Corp (Aegean Sea) v Repsol Petroleo SA [1998] Lloyd's Rep 39, 325
Alaska Native Class v Exxon Corp (Exxon Valdez), 104 F 2d 1196, 1997 AMC 940 (9th Cir 1997), 71

Barracuda Tanker Corp, Re (Torrey Canyon), 409 F 2d 1013 (2d Cir 1969), 288
Lauritzen v Larsen, 345 US 571 (1953), 47
The Nicholas H, Re (1995) 2 Lloyd's Rep 299 (HL), 360
Oil Spill by the Amoco Cadiz, Re, 954 F 2d 1279, 1992 AMC 913 (7th Circ 1992), 312
Oil Spill by the Amoco Cadiz off the Coast of France on 16 March 1978, Re, 1984 AMC 2123 (ND III, 1984); [1984] 2 Lloyd's Rep 304, 312
Puerto Rico v SS Zoe Colocotronis, 628 F 2d 652 (1st Cir 1980), 324
Ray v Atlantic Richfield Co, 435 US 151 (1978), 96
Sundance Cruises Corp v American Bureau of Shipping (Sundancer), 7 F 3d 1077 (2nd Cir 1993), (1994) 1 Lloyd's Rep 183, 360
United States v Locke, 529 US 89 (2000), 96

Abbreviations

AFS	Anti-Fouling Systems
BIMCO	Baltic and International Maritime Council
CDEM	Construction, Design, Equipment and Manning
CEFIC	European Council of Chemical Manufacturers' Federations
CERCLA	Comprehensive Environmental Response, Compensation and Liability Act of 1980 (US)
CLC	International Convention on Civil Liability for Oil Pollution Damage
CMI	Comité Maritime International
COFRs	Certificates of Financial Responsibility
COW	Crude Oil Washing
CRISTAL	Contract Regarding an Interim Settlement of Tanker Liability for Oil Pollution
dwt	deadweight tons
ECOSOC	United Nations Economic and Social Council
EEZ	Exclusive Economic Zone
EU	European Union
FOEI	Friends of the Earth International
FSI	Flag State Implementation
FUND	International Convention on the Establishment of an International Fund for Compensation for Oil Pollution Damage
GAIRS	Generally Accepted International Rules and Standards
GESAMP	IMO/FAO/UNESCO/WMO/WHO/IAEA/UN/UNEP Joint Group of Experts on the Scientific Aspects of Marine Environmental Pollution

grt	gross registered ton
H&M	Hull and Machinery
HELCOM	Helsinki Commission
HNS	Hazardous and Noxious Substances
HNSC	1996 International Convention on Liability and Compensation for Damage in Connection with the Carriage of Hazardous and Noxious Substances by Sea
IACS	International Association of Classification Societies
ICNT	Informal Composite Negotiating Text
ICS	International Chamber of Shipping
IGOs	Inter-Governmental Organisations
ILO	International Labour Organization
IMCO	Inter-Governmental Maritime Consultative Organization
IMDG Code	International Maritime Dangerous Goods Code
IMO	International Maritime Organization
INTERTANKO	International Association of Independent Tanker Owners
IOPC Fund	International Oil Pollution Compensation Fund
IOPPC	International Oil Pollution Prevention Certificate
ISM	International Safety Management
ISO	International Organization for Standardization
ITOPF	International Tanker Owners Pollution Federation
IUMI	International Union of Marine Insurers
LLMC	International Convention Relating to the Limitation of Liability of Owners of Seagoing Ships
LOSC	1982 United Nations Convention on the Law of the Sea
LOT	Load on Top
LRTAP	1979 UN-ECE Convention on Long-Range Transboundary Air Pollution
MARPOL 73/78	1973/78 International Convention for the Prevention of Pollution from Ships
MEPC	Marine Environment Protection Committee
MOU	Memorandum of Understanding
MSC	Maritime Safety Committee
NGOs	Non-Governmental Organisations
NIEO	New International Economic Order
NLS	Noxious Liquid Substances

NRDA	Natural Resource Damage Assessment
OCIMF	Oil Companies International Marine Forum
ODS	Ozone Depleting Substances
OECD	Organisation for Economic Co-operation and Development
OILPOL 54	1954 International Convention for the Prevention of Pollution of the Sea by Oil
OPA-90	Oil Pollution Act of 1990 (US)
OPEC	Organization of the Petroleum Exporting Countries
OPRC	1990 Convention on Oil Pollution Preparedness, Response and Co-operation
ORB	Oil Record Book
OSPAR	1992 Convention for the Protection of the Marine Environment of the North-East Atlantic
P&I Clubs	Protection and Indemnity Clubs
PSC	Port State Control
PSSA	Particularly Sensitive Sea Area
RSNT	Revised Single Negotiating Text
SBTs	Segregated Ballast Tanks
SDRs	Special Drawing Rights
SIGTTO	Society of International Gas Tanker and Terminal Operators
SIRE	Ship Inspection Report Exchange
SNT	Single Negotiating Text
SOLAS 74	1974 Convention on the Safety of Life at Sea
SO_x	Sulphur Oxides
STCW	1978 IMO Convention on Standards of Training, Certification and Watchkeeping for Seafarers
TBT	Tributyl Tin
TOVALOP	Tanker Owners' Voluntary Agreement on Liability for Oil Pollution
TSPP	1978 International Conference on Tanker Safety and Pollution Prevention
ULCC	Ultra Large Crude Carrier
UNCCRS	1986 United Nations Convention on Conditions for the Registration of Ships
UNCED	1992 United Nations Conference on Environment and Development

UNCLOS III	1982 United Nations Conference on the Law of the Sea
UNCTAD	United Nations Conference on Trade and Development
UNEP	United Nations Environment Programme
VLCC	Very Large Crude Carrier
WWF	World Wide Fund for Nature

PART A

The Regulation of Vessel-Source Pollution in its Eco-Political Context

1 Vessel-Source Pollution, the Ecological Imperative and the Compliance Problem

1. Overview

The protection of the marine environment has become one of the most important ecological issues of modern times. Indeed, it forms part of that general emergence of environmental consciousness which has captured world attention in the past five decades or so and which figures so prominently in the politics of international discourse today. The sources of human-induced marine pollution[1] are numerous – these include discharges from land-based sources, ships, atmospheric deposition, ocean dumping and offshore oil and gas installations.[2] This work is concerned with the regulation of vessel-source marine pollution,

---

[1] A commonly accepted definition of 'marine pollution' or 'pollution of the marine environment' is 'the introduction by man, directly or indirectly, of substances or energy into the marine environment, including estuaries, which results or is likely to result in such deleterious effects as harm to living resources and marine life, hazards to human health, hindrance to marine activities, including fishing and other legitimate uses of the sea, impairment of quality for use of sea water and reduction of amenities', see art. 1(4), United Nations Convention on the Law of the Sea, U.N. Doc. A/CONF.62/122 (1982), 21 I.L.M. 1261 (1982) (hereinafter 'LOSC'). This is also the definition adopted by the Joint Group of Experts on the Scientific Aspects of Marine Environmental Protection (GESAMP), see GESAMP, IMPACT OF OIL AND RELATED CHEMICALS AND WASTES ON THE MARINE ENVIRONMENT, REP. STUD. GESAMP No. 50 (1993) (hereinafter GESAMP No. 50). Established in 1969, GESAMP is a scientific advisory body comprising experts nominated by a number of inter-governmental sponsoring agencies. It is currently undergoing a revamp of its operational and financing structure.

[2] Land-based pollution typically involves discharges of organic and industrial effluents into riverine and oceanic systems, while vessel-source pollution arises from operational and accidental discharges of oil and other harmful substances from ships into the sea. Atmospheric pollution involves mainly deposition of pollutants originating on land, and is thus part of land-based pollution. Dumping entails loading wastes from land on board ships for deliberate disposal at sea. It is thus to be distinguished from vessel-source pollution, which does not involve disposal of land wastes.

i.e. pollution of the sea emanating from both deliberate as well as accidental discharges by ocean-going ships.[3]

In the past few decades, international, regional and national regulation over shipping matters such as navigational safety, vessel-source pollution and maritime security have grown to such an extent that the global shipping industry today faces a litany of costly regulatory rules. Consequently, the shipowner's traditional right of free navigation is presently qualified by important imperatives such as the protection of the marine environment and the promotion of maritime safety. In particular, the emphasis on marine pollution control by concerned coastal and port states has come to substantially erode the traditional right of free navigation accruing to maritime states and their shipping interests.

Despite the proliferation of regulations over shipping, many international instruments which prescribe pollution control measures are still not effectively enforced and adhered to. Indeed, the most obvious weakness of the regulatory system appears to be its failure to ensure effective enforcement of and compliance with the relevant rules and standards.[4] Consequently, many 'sub-standard', low-cost ships run by irresponsible operators still ply the oceans today, posing significant risks to human lives and the marine environment.[5] This has led coastal and port states to impose more stringent regulations on ships entering or coming near their waters.

A central tenet of this work is the argument that deficiencies in the regime formation process and the peculiar features of the shipping

---

[3] The terms 'vessel' and 'ship' are used interchangeably, as in the LOSC. For vessel-source pollution generally, see D. W. ABECASSIS, THE LAW AND PRACTICE RELATING TO OIL POLLUTION FROM SHIPS (1978); D. W. ABECASSIS & R. JARASHOW, OIL POLLUTION FROM SHIPS (1985); G. TIMAGENIS, II INTERNATIONAL CONTROL OF MARINE POLLUTION (1980); and K. HAKAPÄÄ, MARINE POLLUTION IN INTERNATIONAL LAW: MATERIAL OBLIGATIONS AND JURISDICTION (1981).

[4] P. S. Dempsey, *Compliance and Enforcement in International Law – Oil Pollution of the Marine Environment by Ocean Vessels*, 6 NW.J. INT'L L. & BUS. 459, 541 (1984). For enforcement in international law generally, see e.g. W. M. Reisman, *Sanctions and Enforcement*, in 3 CONFLICT MANAGEMENT: THE FUTURE OF THE INTERNATIONAL LEGAL ORDER 273 (C. Black & R. Falk eds., 1971).

[5] A 'sub-standard' ship or operation is one that is 'substantially below' the relevant IMO requirements, see IMO Assembly Resolution A.787(19) (1995) on Procedures for Port State Control, as amended by Resolution A.882(21) (1999). In addition, there are ships which do the barest minimum needed to comply with standards. These are technically (though minimally) in compliance and pose significant risks as well, see ORGANIZATION FOR ECONOMIC CO-OPERATION AND DEVELOPMENT (OECD), MARITIME TRANSPORT COMMITTEE REPORT ON THE REMOVAL OF INSURANCE FROM SUBSTANDARD SHIPPING 23–24 (2004) (hereinafter 'REMOVAL OF INSURANCE'), *available at* http://www.oecd.org/dataoecd/58/15/32144381.pdf (last accessed 29 Nov. 2004).

industry have led to a general lack of incentives for compliance with safety and pollution control rules. Thus, in spite of the retreat of the doctrine of free navigation and the growth in regulation over shipping, transgressions of safety, environmental and security rules by sub-standard ships remain all too common. The phenomenon of sub-standard shipping is rampant in many parts of the globe, involving cost-conscious operators who are indifferent to safety and pollution control rules.[6] Thus, many of these operators' ships are old, ill-maintained and operated in a manner falling far below or only minimally above the requirements set out by regulatory instruments.[7] This is to the great detriment of responsible operators, who face distinct competitive disadvantages compared to their low-cost, low-standard rivals.[8]

In recent years, the frequent occurrences of ship pollution incidents, both intentional and accidental, have raised questions as to why these incidents continue to occur despite the existence of numerous rules and practices relating to proper surveys by flag states and delegated classification societies, ship vetting by the oil industry, supervision by insurers and inspections by port state control authorities.[9] The inescapable conclusion appears to be that the prevailing international rules and standards, principally those enacted by the International Maritime Organization (IMO), have not been adequately enforced and complied with.

What is clear is that the contemporary structural realities within which the maritime trading system operates leave great room for inadequate implementation and enforcement of the relevant pollution control rules. Arising from the extremely competitive nature of the shipping business, a significant number of shipowners and operators continue to collude with indulgent flag states, classification societies and insurers to overlook safety and pollution standards so as to reduce

---

[6] L. Goldie, *Environmental Catastrophes and Flags of Convenience – Does the Present Law Pose Special Liability Issues?*, 3 Pace Y. B. Int'l L. 63, 89–90 (1991).

[7] *Supra* note 5.

[8] See generally Organisation For Economic Co-operation and Development (OECD), Cost Savings Stemming from Non-compliance with International Environmental Regulations in the Maritime Sector, DSTI/DOT/MTC(2002)/8/final (hereinafter 'Cost Savings'), *attached to* submission of OECD to the 49th session of IMO's Marine Environment Protection Committee (MEPC), MEPC Doc. 49/INF.7 (2003). The figure '49' denotes a submission to MEPC's 49th session – further references to IMO Committee documents should be understood in similar vein.

[9] See generally H. Ringbom, *The Erika Accident and Its Effects on EU Maritime Regulation*, in Current Marine Environmental Issues and the International Tribunal for the Law of the Sea 265 (M. H. Nordquist & J. N. Moore eds., 2001).

operating costs.[10] Thus, the very actors whose task it is to supervise and regulate the owners are effectively compelled to compete for the latter's patronage. Moreover, the generally secretive and fragmented nature of the shipping industry, together with clandestine efforts to use one-ship companies to shield owners' true identities and the reluctance among owners to co-operate and share information, all add to a lack of compliance incentives.[11]

In relation to the 'human element' of shipping, cost-cutting operators are known to hire cheap and ill-trained seafarers. This often results in low crew morale, high turnover and, more dangerously, overwork, fatigue and increased risks of negligence and accidents. On their part, cargo owners and charterers such as the oil companies often favour low-cost sub-standard vessels. Indeed, the chartering departments of major oil corporations are known to prefer cheaper, 'spot' market tonnage in order to enjoy lower freight rates.[12] This commonly drives freight rates down, to the advantage of the sub-standard operators.

At the same time, other actors in the maritime industry are susceptible to cost-cutting pressures. The marine insurers, for instance, compete intensely for shipowners' business, often forgoing higher premia and deductibles for riskier ships.[13] Meanwhile, shipbuilders respond to the cost-conscious culture by using cheaper high-tensile steel which renders ships lighter but more vulnerable.[14] Shipyards have also been known to impose pressure on classification societies keen on their business to lower certification standards.[15] In addition, banks, mortgagees and ship financiers may neglect to press for higher operational standards.

For their part, many ports worldwide are unable or unwilling to conduct thorough inspections on visiting ships due to the expenses and delays involved. Not uncommonly, port inspectors may even be in complicity with classification societies to gloss over deficiencies in the

---

[10] COST SAVINGS, *supra* note 8, at 44.   [11] These issues are elaborated upon in Ch. 2.

[12] Lloyd's List, *Oiling the Wheels of Misfortune*, 27 Jan. 2000. About half of the Very Large Crude Carrier (VLCC) market trades on the 'spot' market at any one time, see Third Report of the Expert Group on Impact Assessment of the Proposed Amendments to MARPOL Annex I, MEPC Doc. 50/INF.4 (2003).

[13] In fact, operators of whatever quality can find coverage if they look hard enough, and at prices which cause them little pain, see REMOVAL OF INSURANCE, *supra* note 5, at 65–6.

[14] In addition, shipowners are known to demand standard quality ships to be delivered fairly quickly at the lowest price, see INTERTANKO, TANKER TRENDS AND ECONOMICS 26 (2002).

[15] Lloyd's List, *A Ship for Whose Convenience?*, 12 Mar. 2001.

interest of faster 'turn-around' of ships. Overall, the whole emphasis in the shipping industry on cost-cutting and short-term profitability has led to a discernible decline in safety and pollution prevention standards.[16] This exerts a general downward pressure on freight rates to the detriment of the quality operator.

The above account of maritime trading realities, albeit simplified, goes to the heart of why proper compliance with the relevant rules and standards is often absent in the ship transportation industry. Whenever any actor tries to maintain safety and pollution prevention standards, he is faced with the prospect of losing business to cheaper competitors. At the same time, the proliferation of new rules and regulations actually confers a further competitive advantage on the sub-standard operator, who does not have to contend with the ever-increasing costs of compliance.[17] Overall, adequate incentives for compliance are lacking. In the result, a cycle of competition and lowering of standards is created, typically resulting in a 'race to the bottom' phenomenon.[18]

The situation is markedly worse in regions of the world where trading practices are less transparent, maritime administrations under-developed and port state control lacking. As such, it is market wisdom that many sub-standard ships engage in regional trades, rarely venturing into US or European waters where port state enforcement is known to be stricter.[19] Thus, as the competitive nature of the shipping industry continues to erode the effective enforcement of regulations, political pressure grows on legislators worldwide to impose ever more stringent laws on ship operators. Such pressure is especially evident in the aftermath of politically charged events such as vessel accidents causing massive ocean and coastal pollution.

That said, the maritime world comprises a diversity of actors, many of whom are perfectly responsible operators. Therefore, one needs to be

---

[16] See generally REMOVAL OF INSURANCE, *supra* note 5, at 23 and COST SAVINGS, *supra* note 8, at 44.
[17] COST SAVINGS, *supra* note 8, at 6.
[18] L. Goldie, *Recognition and Dual Nationality – A Problem of Flags of Convenience*, 39 BRIT. Y. B. INT'L L. 220, at 221 (1963). On trade policy, regulatory competition and the 'race to the bottom', see e.g. D. VOGEL, TRADING UP: CONSUMER AND ENVIRONMENTAL REGULATION IN A GLOBAL ECONOMY (1995) and REGULATORY COMPETITION AND ECONOMIC INTEGRATION: COMPARATIVE PERSPECTIVES (D. Esty & D. Geradin eds., 2001).
[19] For the view that intransigent owners may still trade among developing countries with limited resources for port state inspections, see H. E. Anderson III, *The Nationality of Ships and Flags of Convenience: Economics, Politics and Alternatives*, 21 TUL. MAR. L. J. 139, at 168 (1996).

discriminating before painting the whole industry with the same broad brushstroke. However, it remains true that even the most reputable of actors – states and industry alike – often experience commercial pressures and are susceptible to lapses of judgment or even outright transgressions. Hence, it is not uncommon for respectable owners, charterers, classification societies or insurers to compromise on regulatory standards in the face of tight schedules, severe competition and unprofitable market conditions.[20] This is borne out by the fact that a good number of ships which have been involved in serious accidents or detained by port state control authorities in recent years have been registered in and owned, operated, chartered, classed, insured or inspected by fairly reputable actors.

The challenge of eradicating sub-standard shipping and of ensuring safer ships and cleaner oceans will thus have to be met with greater enforcement rigour. The problem is largely due to the fact that the international regime formation process which generates the relevant regulations often fails to lay down optimum conditions for compliance and effectiveness. In particular, the regulatory process at the International Maritime Organization (IMO) – the primary global forum for regulating ship safety and pollution issues – often omits to address the ship operators' lack of *incentives* to install or practise adequate safety and pollution control features.

Similarly, in laying down obligations for states to provide port reception facilities for ship wastes, the relevant IMO treaties such as MARPOL 73/78[21] do not adequately address most states' lack of incentives to do so. As far as the system for reviewing implementation is concerned, IMO procedures for reporting compliance and analysing state reports are lacking. In general, the treaties tend to emphasise the technical features of safety and pollution control measures without going to the root causes of sub-standard shipping, *viz.* the absence of incentives for compliance and the lack of enforceability of measures. Hence, the scenario of proliferating rules with inadequate implementation is all too pervasive in the maritime sector, be it at the international, regional or national levels.

Such regime deficiencies are themselves the direct result of features in the ship transportation industry which actively impede implementation

---

[20] COST SAVINGS, *supra* note 8, at 51.
[21] 1973 International Convention for the Prevention of Pollution from Ships, as amended by the 1978 Protocol thereto, 1341 U.N.T.S. 3; 17 I.L.M. 546 (1978) (in force 2 Oct. 1983). See Ch. 3 for details.

of and compliance with rules. As analysed later, the nature of the industry and the dynamics of interaction among its various actors frequently lie at the root of sub-standard shipping practices. In this regard, the present work aims to assess the systemic compliance challenges faced not only by the international regime formation system (comprising, *inter alia*, IMO and the state actors), but also by the ship transportation industry itself. Among the issues to be analysed are the cost-conscious nature of the industry, its lack of incentives for responsible behaviour and the conflict of interests facing actor-regulators like IMO, flag and port states, private classification societies and marine insurers.

Within the maritime sphere, the systemic deficiencies in the international regulatory system are often met by states or group of states resorting to unilateral or regional laws and stringent port state control action.[22] This is particularly common in the aftermath of ship pollution incidents which attract huge media and political attention. In recent years, incidents such as the *Amoco Cadiz*, *Exxon Valdez*, *Erika* and, lately, the *Prestige*, have pressured states to impose ever more stringent regulation on the shipping industry. In this regard, unilateral and regional action going beyond internationally agreed standards are often less than desirable as they undercut the ideals of uniformity and certainty which the multilateral process seeks to uphold. Yet, in the face of continued intransigence by sub-standard ship operators, unilateral and regional action have become preferred political options for environmentally conscious states which view multilateral decision-making to be too slow and encumbered.

Overall, the shortcomings of marine pollution regulation can be explained by the quartet of variables expounded by the scholars E. B. Weiss and H. Jacobson in their study of compliance with international treaty requirements. These factors are: the nature of the accord in question, the nature of the activity being regulated, the international environment within which regulation takes place, and features peculiar to individual state parties to treaties.[23] While these factors are frequently

---

[22] See generally J. Hare, *Port State Control: Strong Medicine to Cure a Sick Industry*, 26 GA. J. INT'L & COMP. L. 571 (1997); A. Clarke, *Port State Control or Sub-Standard Ships: Who is to Blame? What is the Cure?*, LLOYD'S MAR. & COMM. L. Q. 202 (1994); G. C. KASOULIDES, PORT STATE CONTROL AND JURISDICTION: EVOLUTION OF THE PORT STATE REGIME (1993); and Z. O. ÖZÇAYIR, PORT STATE CONTROL (2004).

[23] See ENGAGING COUNTRIES: STRENGTHENING COMPLIANCE WITH INTERNATIONAL ACCORDS 4 (E. B. Weiss & H. Jacobson eds., 1998). See also THE IMPLEMENTATION AND EFFECTIVENESS OF INTERNATIONAL ENVIRONMENTAL COMMITMENTS: THEORY AND PRACTICE (D. Victor et al. eds., 1998); and R. Mitchell

interconnected in any analysis of environmental regulation, it will become apparent that in the specific realm of vessel-source marine pollution, the ship transportation industry's resistance or equivocation toward regulation is a major factor impeding compliance with and effectiveness of the relevant regulatory regimes.

In view of the diversity, influence and differing interests of target actors in the marine pollution arena, their behaviour in affecting compliance with rules and regulations merits special consideration. Thus, it will be argued in this work that the peculiarities of the ship transportation industry substantially affect the nature and effectiveness of the relevant accords, particularly in relation to the lack of incentives among state parties and industry actors to implement these accords. Consequently, prescriptive efforts to enhance the regulation of vessel-source pollution should be directed toward influencing changes within the shipping industry itself. Since this factor can be identified as the root cause of the compliance problem, it should ideally be the most suitable (though not necessarily susceptible) candidate for 'manipulation'.[24]

Ostensibly, such a strategy would be the most cost-effective means of fostering behavioural change among the relevant actors, thereby providing optimal incentives for compliance with safety and pollution control regimes. Prescriptions for achieving this goal are elaborated upon in this work. These include the inculcation of a culture of compliance throughout the ship transportation industry, the broadening of regulatory measures to encompass non-shipowner actors such as the cargo owners and classification societies, and the promotion of pro-active rule-making, legislative discipline and stakeholder equity within international regulatory agencies.

2. Regulating the Sources of Marine Pollution

In economic parlance, all forms of pollution can be considered externalities of economic growth, the costs of which cannot be adequately internalised into the operator's cost-benefit analyses. Human-induced marine pollution exhibits the core features of the commons tragedy:[25]

---

et al., *International Vessel-Source Oil Pollution, in* THE EFFECTIVENESS OF INTERNATIONAL ENVIRONMENTAL REGIMES: CAUSAL CONNECTIONS AND BEHAVIORAL MECHANISMS 33 (O. Young ed., 1999).

[24] Weiss & Jacobson eds., *supra* note 23 at 4–5.
[25] See G. Hardin, *The Tragedy of the Commons*, 162 SCI. 1243 (1968); and G. HARDIN, EXPLORING NEW ETHICS FOR SURVIVAL 254 (1972).

it is in large part introduced by economic activities accompanying growing human populations and changing consumption patterns, the negative costs of which fail to be incorporated into the operator's reckoning and are left to be shouldered by all participants in the societal system. Thus, economically rational shipowners and operators are led to engage in activities such as discharging wastes into the oceans and neglecting safety standards to the point of introducing risks of marine accidents – typical cases illustrating the tragedy of the commons.

It is trite knowledge that two-thirds of the earth's surface is made up of water and that the oceans form the very foundation of life itself. Half of the global human population live in coastal areas and are highly dependent on the sea for food, transportation and general livelihood. Human political and social development over the ages owed a great deal to the growth of maritime trade and commerce. Today, 95 per cent of world trade, by weight, continues to be conducted by sea.[26] Hence, in view of the crucial importance of the oceans to life, the pollution of the marine environment and its effects require serious attention.

The deleterious impact of marine pollution has been widely documented. In general, the degradation of the marine environment is most pronounced in coastal areas where rapid population growth, urbanisation and industrialisation have resulted in serious habitat loss and deterioration in the quality and productivity of the marine ecosystem.[27] Given the importance of the oceans to planetary ecology, the preservation of the oceans' environmental health has become a critical concern for the global community. To this end, the state parties to the United Nations Convention on the Law of the Sea (LOSC) are obliged to take measures that are necessary to prevent, reduce and control pollution of the marine environment from any source.[28] Numerous instruments ranging from multilateral conventions to 'soft law' pronouncements such as Agenda 21[29] have also reiterated the importance of marine environmental protection.

---

[26] R. R. CHURCHILL & A. V. LOWE, THE LAW OF THE SEA 255 (1999).
[27] For the effects of marine pollution generally, see D. BRUBAKER, MARINE POLLUTION AND INTERNATIONAL LAW: PRINCIPLES AND PRACTICE (1993); R. CLARK, MARINE POLLUTION (1997); and J. BURGER, OIL SPILLS (1997). For resource protection issues, see C. Joyner, *Biodiversity in the Marine Environment: Resource Implications for the Law of the Sea*, 28 VAND. J. TRANSNAT'L L. 635 (1995).
[28] LOSC, art. 194.
[29] U.N. Doc. A/CONF.151/26/Rev. 1 (Vol. I) (1992), see particularly Ch. 17. See also the 1992 Convention on Biological Diversity, 31 I.L.M. 818 (1992), particularly its 1995 'Jakarta Mandate' on Marine and Coastal Biological Diversity, U.N. Doc. UNEP/CBD/COP/2/19.

It should be noted at the outset that the biggest contributor to marine pollution is acknowledged to be land-based sources. Pollution from ships (excluding dumping, which entails the deliberate disposal at sea of wastes originating on land) constitutes a relatively smaller – albeit still significant – fraction of the overall marine pollution problem. A much-quoted scientific study[30] attributes 44 per cent of all human-induced marine pollution to land-based sources, 33 per cent to atmospheric sources (much of this originating from land as well) and only 12 per cent to maritime transportation.

As regards pollution by oil alone (by far the most conspicuous and heavily regulated of marine pollutants), a 1990 study estimates that 50 per cent of oil released annually into the oceans comes from land-based sources.[31] This compares to a 24 per cent contribution from marine transportation and 13 per cent from atmospheric sources. A more recent study claims that less than 13 per cent of oil spills come from the transport of petroleum products, and that nearly 70 per cent of petroleum pollution in the oceans comes from land-based industries, small pleasure craft and natural seepage.[32]

Despite the far greater contribution of land-based pollutants, the bulk of international regulatory attention has traditionally been paid to vessel-source pollution. In many ways, this is understandable, even though it may appear to be a case of misplaced priorities. By their very nature, ships traverse the world and affect the interests of coastal states when they come within the latter's jurisdiction. As such, it can be wholly expected that these states would wish to control ship activities that are deemed prejudicial to their interests, particularly if the ships are foreign-owned or -operated.[33] At the same time, though, there arise competing interests in the form of maritime actors who wish to

---

[30] GESAMP, THE STATE OF THE MARINE ENVIRONMENT, REP. STUD. GESAMP No. 39, at 88 (1990) (hereinafter 'GESAMP No. 39').
[31] NATIONAL ACADEMY OF SCIENCES, PETROLEUM IN THE MARINE ENVIRONMENT (1990), attached to MEPC Doc. 30/INF.13 (1990).
[32] NATIONAL ACADEMY OF SCIENCES, OIL IN THE SEA III: INPUTS, FATES AND EFFECTS (2002). This report updates two earlier reports published in 1975 and 1985 (as updated in 1990, supra note 31).
[33] The coastal state's claim for jurisdiction has traditionally been based on the protective principle. In modern times, the assertion of jurisdiction beyond the territorial sea is based on the 'effects' doctrine, on the grounds that pollution may have adverse effects on the coastal state or threaten its security, see generally C. Mooradian, Protecting 'Sovereign Rights': The Case for Increased Coastal State Jurisdiction Over Vessel-Source Pollution in the Exclusive Economic Zone, 82 B.U. L. REV. 767 (2002).

preserve free navigation and commerce by minimising coastal state interference with shipping. There thus arises a potential conflict between the maritime interests' ideals of free navigation and the coastal states' desire for security and protection.

In this regard, regulation through negotiated *international* agreements has emerged as the preferred means of reconciling the divergent aspirations of the coastal and maritime interests. The international nature of shipping means that a ship may be owned, chartered, managed and manned by nationals of different countries, thus creating potential problems of conflicts of laws and jurisdiction.[34] Without international uniformity, unilateral laws that differ from one state to another can be expected to present serious impediments to global shipping and commerce.[35] Harmonised international regulation is also instrumental in establishing a level playing field for commercial actors. Ship operators will then not be economically disadvantaged by strict pollution control rules applying to them but not to their competitors from other countries. It can thus be appreciated that the motivations for regulating vessel-source pollution at a global level arise not only from environmental factors but also from fundamental commercial, security and political considerations.[36]

In contrast, there has been much less of an impetus to regulate land-based pollution on an international scale. Marine pollution emanating from land typically affects coastal areas and rarely threatens the interests of other states in a direct and tangible manner. In any event, the slow, localised seepage of industrial effluents into riverine systems carrying pollutants to the sea does not conjure up the catastrophic images that a foundering oil tanker would. The costs of controlling land-based pollution are also incalculable. The numerous actors in

---

[34] D. W. Abecassis, *Marine Oil Pollution Laws: The View of Shell International Marine Limited*, 8 INT'L BUS. L. 3 (1980), citing the *Torrey Canyon* incident to illustrate the multi-jurisdictional issues involved in a pollution incident. See also J. C. Sweeney, *Oil Pollution of the Oceans*, 37 FORDHAM L. REV. 115, at 156 (1968).

[35] S. A. Meese, *When Jurisdictional Interests Collide: International, Domestic and State Efforts to Prevent Vessel-Source Oil Pollution*, 12 OCEAN DEV. & INT'L L. 71, at 86–7 (1982).

[36] For the standard view that concerted international action is needed to tackle marine pollution, see e.g. Meese, *supra* note 35 and T. A. Mensah, *International Environmental Law: International Conventions Concerning Oil Pollution at Sea*, 8 CASE W. RES. J. INT'L L. 110, at 111–12 (1976). See, however, the literature on regulatory competition which questions the assumption that harmonisation is always better, e.g. Esty & Geradin eds., *supra* note 18. The present work adopts the IMO view that harmonised, international regulation is preferable.

the land-based pollution arena are often extremely diffused and well-concealed behind the curtains of national sovereignty, rendering it difficult to identify and regulate them on a global basis. The political reality is that land-based pollution continues to be viewed by many states as a wholly domestic issue that is much less susceptible to international regulation.[37] Consequently, no global convention or agreement on land-based pollution has to date been adopted.[38]

In the case of vessel-source pollution, however, there exist readily identifiable actors who can be easily subjected to regulation and control. Regulatory attention to shipping is thus facilitated by the presence of a discrete and concentrated group of maritime actors (viz. shipowners, cargo owners and associated interests) that is often, fairly or otherwise, a convenient target for politicians and environmentalists. The international nature of shipping thus facilitates its own regulation, enabling multilateral fora to be established to regulate what is essentially a trans-jurisdictional industry. Therefore, as a matter of political and functional reality, it is understandable why the international regulation of land-based pollution remains at its infancy whereas vessel-source pollution continues to be subjected to rigorous international discipline.

With the intense regulation over shipping, the amounts of oil and other pollutants entering the oceans from maritime transportation have reportedly fallen by nearly 75 per cent during the period from 1973 to 1989[39] and generally, by about 60 per cent since the 1970s.[40]

---

[37] CHURCHILL & LOWE, supra note 26, at 379. For land-based pollution, see e.g. Q.-N. MENG, LAND-BASED MARINE POLLUTION (1987); B. Kwiatkowska, Marine Pollution from Land-Based Sources: Current Problems and Prospects, 14 OCEAN DEV. & INT'L L. 315 (1984); and A. E. Boyle, Land-Based Sources of Marine Pollution: Current Legal Regime, 16 MARINE POL'Y 20 (1992).

[38] To date, only non-binding, 'soft-law' instruments have been adopted. In 1985, the UN Environment Programme (UNEP) released its Montreal Guidelines for the Protection of the Marine Environment against Pollution from Land-Based Sources, reprinted in 14 ENVTL. POL. & L. 77 (1985). Following Agenda 21's call to revise the Guidelines, UNEP adopted the 1995 Washington Declaration and Global Programme of Action on Protection of the Marine Environment from Land-Based Activities, UNEP(OCA)LBA/IG.2/7, reprinted in 26 ENVTL. POL. & L. 37 (1996). Although no international convention exists as yet for land-based pollution, regional instruments are in place, e.g. the 1974 Paris Convention, the 1992 OSPAR Convention and the 1992 Helsinki Convention, see Ch. 2. For efforts to deal with land-based pollution through coastal zone management, see the World Bank's Noordwijk Guidelines for Integrated Coastal Zone Management, in WORLD BANK, WORLD COAST CONFERENCE, NOORDWIJK, THE NETHERLANDS, 1–5 NOVEMBER 1993 (1993).

[39] GESAMP No. 50, supra note 1.

[40] IMO Secretary-General's comments at the IMO Council's 82nd session, Council Doc. C/82/11 (1999). See also ORGANISATION FOR ECONOMIC CO-OPERATION AND DEVELOPMENT, REPORT ON

Thus, 99.988 per cent of all oil transported over the oceans is delivered safely to its ports of destination.[41] Moreover, there appears to have been a dramatic reduction in ship losses and tonnage in the past few decades, despite the increase in the volume of sea trade.[42] It has also been suggested that over 80 per cent of tanker tonnage is operated within the framework of high operational safety standards.[43] With the stringent measures adopted in recent years to phase out aging tankers, the world tanker fleet today is greatly modernised, with 62 per cent of tankers having been built between 1990 and 2002.[44]

There is thus a strong belief within the shipping industry that ever-increasing regulation is unnecessary. Indeed, the shipowning interests feel that the emphasis should now turn away from the enactment of new rules to the *implementation* of existing ones. Without doubt, such arguments are inspired by resistance to the high costs of new regulatory efforts in view of the diminishing benefits of additional regulation. Moreover, it has often been pointed out – quite legitimately – that the majority of ship operators are responsible actors and that it is only a minority of rogue operators who are committing transgressions of safety and pollution control rules.

Yet it is precisely because of the continued presence of these substandard operators that coastal states deem tighter regulation to be absolutely necessary. In the past few decades, the growth of the environmental agenda in the developed economies has led to increasing intolerance for the activities of polluting industries. Within the maritime world, the continuing occurrence of highly publicised tanker pollution incidents such as the *Exxon Valdez*, *Erika* and *Prestige* has led to regulators in the US and Europe demanding ever more stringent

---

SHIP SCRAPPING 138–52, OECD Doc. DSTI/DOT/MTC(2001)12 (2001), *attached to* MEPC Doc. 48/INF.2 (2002). However, other sources feel that even after decades of regulation, the reality is that the objectives of pollution control instruments such as MARPOL 73/78 have not been achieved, see e.g. the report of Lord Donaldson, HER MAJESTY'S STATIONERY OFFICE, SAFER SHIPS, CLEANER SEAS – REPORT OF LORD DONALDSON'S INQUIRY INTO THE PREVENTION OF POLLUTION FROM MERCHANT SHIPPING, Cm. 2560 (1994) (hereinafter 'DONALDSON REPORT').

[41] IMO Secretary-General's comments at the IMO Council's 86th session, Council Doc. C/86/10 (2001).
[42] IMO Secretary-General, Council Doc. C/82/11 (1999), *supra* note 40, quoting sources from the Institute of London Underwriters and the International Association of Dry Cargo Shipowners (INTERCARGO).
[43] *Ibid.*
[44] INTERTANKO, *supra* note 14, at 12. The situation is not as rosy in the developing countries. The average age of the Chinese tanker fleet, for instance, is eighteen years, well above the world average of fourteen years, *ibid.* at 62.

regulation over the shipping industry. The fact that the vast majority of ship operators are responsible citizens and that the bulk of sea-borne cargo is delivered safely to their destinations has failed to convince governments more keen on appeasing domestic political demands for stringent action. The occasional vessel accident is thus seen emotively as 'one incident too many'.

New rules and regulations are also viewed to be necessary to keep up with the changing circumstances and challenges of vessel-source marine pollution. In recent times, new forms of pollution from ships have emerged, some of them with biological, as opposed to physical impact. Examples include the effects of non-native aquatic species spread by ballast water, the harm posed by certain paints used to coat the hulls of ships and air pollution caused by the combustion of fuel oil. At the same time, human error arising from lack of skills and training continues to form a major cause of accidental and operational pollution.[45] There is thus a continuing need to ensure adequate training, certification and communication skills for seafarers, particularly those from the developing countries.

One major reason why vessel-source pollution remains a huge concern is the age and condition of cargo-carrying vessels, particularly in the developing world. Without uniform rules to phase out old ships, the average age of the world fleet will progressively rise. Of course, age alone is not determinative; maintenance remains a critical factor. Indeed, well-maintained older tankers can still be sturdy and safe. In general, however, there is evidence to suggest that older tankers experience more accidents, particularly those due to fires, explosions and structural failures.[46]

In addition, a consequence of tanker economics is that ships tend to fall into the hands of less scrupulous owners as they age.[47] The progressive phasing out of older tankers in the developed regions of the world also raises concerns that these vessels will be deployed to developing regions where government and industry controls are less stringent. Taken together with the fact that the overall rate of compliance with

---

[45] DONALDSON REPORT, *supra* note 40, at 141.
[46] See REMOVAL OF INSURANCE, *supra* note 5, at 24, for the view that older ships tend to be more prone to insurance claims, both of the hull and liability types. However, there is only a weak correlation between quality of ship operator and claims, making it difficult to conclude that quality operators are paying more for their insurance because of claims from sub-standard operators, *ibid.* at 45.
[47] Goldie, *supra* note 6, at 89.

existing regulations is still unsatisfactory, and that violations by 'substandard' operators continue to occur worldwide, the pressure for more stringent regulation continues to be exerted by concerned states and their environmental interests.

Presently, the oceans remain the primary viaduct for the conduct of world trade. In the long term, the global reliance on oil as the primary source of energy will result in ever-increasing volumes of this commodity being transported by super-tankers across the oceans.[48] At the same time, greater amounts of non-oil pollutants such as hazardous chemicals and nuclear materials are being transported. With the growth of environmental consciousness in the modern age and the corresponding expectation that industry undertake greater environmental obligations, governments worldwide have become increasingly sensitive to the prospect of large-scale pollution of their coasts and waters. This explains why the need to maintain vigilance in preventing and controlling pollution from ships remains as compelling today, if not more so, as several decades ago.

Overall, the fact that increasing regulation has led to declining levels of casualties and pollution incidents has failed to impress national regulators precisely because a significant minority of sub-standard vessels continues to operate. Viewed in this light, the continuing attention to vessel-source pollution cannot be said to be misplaced; indeed, it is a testimony to the efforts of the international community to improve upon a regulatory regime which appears to be working but is as yet far from perfect. At the same time, it is natural to expect that more resources be directed toward tackling the pernicious problem of land-based pollution. There are hopeful, albeit fledgling, signs that land-based pollution will be more meaningfully addressed in the years to come. Until then, the regulation of vessel-source pollution will continue to be pursued with an intensity that has come to characterise the expectations of the modern ecological age.

3. Whither the Freedom of Navigation?

Much of the resistance against the regulation of shipping stems from the maritime interests' traditional perception that shipping must be free and

---

[48] World oil demand grew substantially in the 1990s, even though growth slowed from 2000 to 2002, see INTERTANKO, *supra* note 14, at 47–9. For the view that maritime oil pollution can be directly traced to the prominence of petroleum in the industrialised world's economies, see B. Shaw et al., *The Global Environment: A Proposal to Eliminate Marine Oil Pollution*, 27 NAT. RESOURCES J. 157 (1987).

unhindered. The popular legal doctrine of the 'freedom of the oceans' was first formulated by the eminent Dutch jurist, Hugo Grotius, in the seventeenth century.[49] In Grotius's view, the oceans were open to unlimited common use by the world's inhabitants and could not be appropriated by any nation. This view formed the genesis of the doctrines of free navigation and flag state primacy. According to these doctrines, flag state jurisdiction over vessels was absolute and exclusive – states other than the flag state had no business inquiring into the activities on board vessels.[50] Freedom of navigation and flag state jurisdiction thus became the twin policy pillars of the great maritime powers.

Transposed to modern conditions, however, the concept of flag state jurisdiction cannot adequately address contemporary maritime concerns, including those relating to marine environmental protection. The fundamental weakness of flag state jurisdiction is the fact that most flag states – whose vessels rarely venture into their own waters – have never had the incentive to regulate the activities of these vessels which cause harm to or affect the interests of other states. In essence, the traditional primacy accorded to the freedom of navigation and flag state control dates from an age when environmental problems, as we recognise them today, were virtually non-existent. For one thing, the volume of vessel traffic in the merchant days of yore was tiny in comparison with the huge fleets plying the oceans today. The coastal states then never had to endure pollution problems of such magnitude as to compel them to claim jurisdiction over foreign vessels polluting the oceans. At that time, the maritime powers were singularly more concerned with preventing interference to international trade by coastal states seeking to impose tariffs or other impediments upon passing merchant vessels.

As the global population expanded and the level of human development increased, the marine environment came under severe strain from the continuous injection of pollutants into the oceans.[51] In due time, the protection of the oceans from further degradation became a pressing international concern. Under present global circumstances, the major legal regime that has grown to personify free navigation,

---

[49] H. GROTIUS, THE FREEDOM OF THE SEAS (1608) (R. Van Deman Magoffin trans., J. B. Scott ed., 1916). See also R. Lapidoth, *Freedom of Navigation – Its Legal History and Its Normative Basis*, 6 J. MAR. L & COM. 259 (1975).
[50] The flag state is the state whose flag the ship flies, i.e. the state whose nationality the ship bears, see LOSC, arts. 91 and 92(1). For details, see Chs. 2 and 4.
[51] See Y. L. Tharpes, *International Environmental Law: Turning the Tide on Marine Pollution*, 20 U. MIAMI INTER-AM. L. REV. 579, at 581 (1989).

namely flag state jurisdiction, can no longer claim the primacy and exclusivity it once enjoyed. At the same time, the freedom of navigation can no longer be viewed to embrace the freedom to pollute the oceans.[52]

The present study thus seeks to assess how modern political imperatives for the protection of the marine environment are chipping away at the traditional notion of free navigation over the oceans. In this regard, the whole history of marine pollution regulation over the past 80 years or so has essentially been a chronicle of the gradual retreat of exclusive flag state control and the concomitant expansion of coastal and port state jurisdiction. Indeed, the whole general corpus of laws relating to maritime regulation today, be it in the field of anti-competitive practices, liner shipping, illegal fishing, navigational safety, environmental protection or security against terrorism, can be reduced into one common recurring theme: the progressive erosion of the concepts of free navigation and exclusive flag state control.

That being said, flag state jurisdiction is hardly dead. Far from it; it remains very much a central doctrine in maritime affairs, consistent with the notion of state sovereignty. The difference today lies in the fact that flag states now share their once-exclusive jurisdiction, in well-defined circumstances, with other actors such as the coastal and port states. What interests us presently is how the balance between the flag and coastal and port states has shifted in recent years.[53] At the same time, the roles of private, non-state actors such as the shipowners and operators, cargo owners, classification societies and insurers as well as the media and environmental groups must also be assessed for their impact on the regulatory process.

4. Technical Issues and Jurisdiction over Ships

At this juncture, it is opportune to appreciate the technical intricacies of the vessel-source pollution problem. Pollution from vessels entails either

---

[52] See generally E. MOLENAAR, COASTAL STATE JURISDICTION OVER VESSEL-SOURCE POLLUTION 42 (1998) and L. Legault, *The Freedom of the Oceans: A License to Pollute?*, 21 U. TORONTO L. J. 39 (1971).

[53] On coastal state practice staking out enhanced jurisdiction over adjacent waters and the effects on the UNCLOS III balance and its ongoing recalibration, see e.g. VESSEL-SOURCE POLLUTION AND COASTAL STATE JURISDICTION: THE WORK OF THE ILA COMMITTEE ON COASTAL STATE JURISDICTION RELATING TO MARINE POLLUTION (1991–2000) (E. Franckx ed., 2001); J. A. ROACH & R. W. SMITH, EXCESSIVE MARITIME CLAIMS (1994); B. CICIN-SAIN & R. KNECHT, THE FUTURE OF U.S. OCEAN POLICY: CHOICES FOR THE NEW CENTURY (2000); E. Franckx, *Coastal State Jurisdiction with Respect to Marine Pollution – Some Recent Developments and Future Challenges*, 10 INT'L J. MARINE & COASTAL L. 253 (1995); and MOLENAAR, *ibid*. Flag, coastal and port state jurisdiction will be examined in Ch. 4.

the discharge of pollutants from the routine operation of vessels used for ocean transportation ('operational' pollution) or the release of pollutants arising from vessel accidents ('accidental' pollution). Historically, the subject of regulatory attention has been commercial ships, particularly cargo-carrying vessels transporting oil and its derivatives. It is contended, however, that if the environmental health of the oceans is to be considered a policy-making imperative in the modern era, all classes of vessels carrying all forms of potential pollutants need to be subjected to international regulation. While the *de minimis* principle can justify leaving small coastal vessels and pleasure craft to be regulated by national rules, there is no good reason why international regulation should be confined to commercial shipping.

Thus, the time-hallowed exemption accorded to public vessels such as warships and government-owned vessels is outmoded and should be re-assessed. As it stands, the international regulatory regime confers sovereign immunity to all public vessels from international pollution control requirements even if such vessels do contribute to significant pollution of the oceans. With the end of the Cold War and the growing pre-eminence of ecological concerns, the blanket exemption of public vessels from international scrutiny must be re-considered.[54]

As stated above, the primary source of pollution of the oceans has traditionally been oil and its derivatives. Despite the sensational media prominence accompanying accidental oil spills, marine casualties account for only 20 per cent of total vessel-source oil pollution.[55] Yet, regulation over vessel-source pollution has consistently been driven by high-publicity oil spill accidents such as the *Exxon Valdez*, and lately the *Erika* and the *Prestige*. Thus, one of the most significant trends to emerge in the field of maritime regulation is the ever-tightening net of rules designed to prevent accidental pollution, even though accidents remain a small source of marine pollution in the aggregate. This can be traced to the fact that spectacular oil spills accompanying vessel accidents invariably evoke strong political responses from governments, particularly in the developed world.

By far, the biggest source of oil pollution from ships is the intentional discharge of oil and oily wastes associated with the *routine* commercial operation of ships.[56] This is what is commonly referred to as 'operational' pollution. Such pollution includes discharges of bilge, engine and fuel oil

---

[54] For elaboration, see Ch. 2.   [55] National Academy of Sciences, *supra* note 31.
[56] *Ibid*. See also Abecassis & Jarashow, *supra* note 3, at 7 and Molenaar, *supra* note 52, at 19.

wastes, oily water from the ballasting process and cargo tank washings. Bilge oil pollution arises from the disposal of oil used for the lubrication and smooth operation of engines, machinery spaces and equipment on board tankers and non-tankers alike. Instead of discharging the oily bilge wastes into shore reception facilities, ship operators typically release them into the sea.

On its part, ballasting is a process that occurs after a ship has discharged its cargo. For its return journey to the loading port, the empty ship requires seawater in its cargo or fuel tanks to 'weigh' it down to ensure stability. As far as ballast-related pollution is concerned, the biggest problem relates to tankers. The seawater ballast that is pumped into a tanker's empty cargo tanks mixes with oily remnants and settled residues, resulting in contaminated ballast water. Upon nearing the loading port, this oily mixture is typically discharged into the sea. Of course, this practice would be unnecessary if ports possessed suitable facilities to receive contaminated ballast. However, as will be examined later, many ports lack the incentive to provide adequate reception facilities because of their high costs. Hence, overboard discharge of dirty ballast water becomes all too common.

Another major source of operational pollution is tank washings. After the initial load of oily ballast is discharged at sea, oil tankers often conduct tank cleaning to remove residual oily clingage before a fresh load of ballast is taken on. This cleaning operation produces dirty tank washings, which like oily bilge and ballast water, are conveniently discharged into the sea prior to the tanker entering the loading port. In the aggregate, even though the occasional tanker accident spills large volumes of oil into localised areas and elicits huge media and public alarm, it is the cumulative and clandestine discharge of operational wastes such as machinery bilges, dirty ballast water and tank washings which constitutes the bulk of oil pollution from ships.

In this regard, it must be borne in mind that pollution from vessels is not confined to oil discharges from tankers alone. The risk of accidental discharges of oil, for instance, is borne by tankers and non-tankers alike. Thus, during a collision or grounding, non-tankers such as bulk carriers, passenger ships and warships may spill large volumes of bunkers from their fuel tanks into the sea, albeit in smaller quantities than when a laden tanker spills its cargo.[57] As regards operational pollution, *all*

---

[57] However, bunker fuel is often of lower grade and higher density and can thus cause more serious environmental damage, see Ch. 6.

ships – be these tankers, cargo vessels, passenger liners, fishing vessels or warships – contribute their fair share of oily bilge wastes.

Nor are pollution risks confined to oil. For chemical tankers and ships built to transport hazardous or noxious materials, there is always the risk of the ship spilling its cargo during accidents. Such ships also face operational pollution problems with their wastes and cargo residues. Nuclear-powered warships present their own peculiar accident risks. In addition, ships of all types and sizes produce sewage and garbage as long as they carry a human complement. Furthermore, the burning of fuel oil by all kinds of ships has been identified as a contributing cause of air pollution, acid rain and global climate change. The ballasting process also introduces a biological scourge – the intake and discharge of ballast water by ships have been shown to facilitate the introduction of non-indigenous marine organisms into bodies of water around the world. These organisms may then pose a threat to native marine populations. At the same time, contamination from anti-fouling paints used to coat the hulls and bottoms of ships has become a major contemporary concern.[58]

The relevant pollution control instruments adopted by IMO typically lay down technical standards to prevent, reduce or control the different forms of vessel-source pollution described above, whether operational or accidental. In general, the standards can be grouped into three categories: discharge; navigation; and construction, design, equipment, and manning (CDEM) standards. Discharge standards regulate the permissible amount of pollutants released operationally into the marine environment. An example of such a standard is the 'parts per million' (ppm) requirement, which measures the maximum permitted ratio of oil to water in an oily discharge.

Navigation standards prescribe ship routeing measures, traffic separation schemes and other general safety measures. In this regard, the object of ship safety rules is primarily to avert accidents at sea and to protect the lives of mariners. However, to the extent that such rules enhance the safety of shipping and lower the risks of accidents and accompanying spills, there will always be a close relationship between ship safety and pollution control ideals. CDEM standards generally relate to the seaworthiness and structural qualities of a vessel as well as the competence of the crew. Like navigation standards, these standards play an indirect but critical role in reducing instances of vessel-source pollution. The

---

[58] See Ch. 5.

substantive content of all these pollution standards will be detailed in Chapters 3–5.

To reconcile the divergent interests of the various participants over the use of the oceans, international law has developed specific rules seeking to allocate jurisdiction over vessels traversing the sea. Thus, the pollution control standards mentioned in the preceding paragraph may be prescribed and enforced by any one or more of three state actors – the flag state, coastal state and port state. Here, the international law of the sea purports to lay down precise rules ascertaining whether a particular vessel falls within the purview of the flag, coastal or port state. This determination invariably depends on the specific area or zone of the ocean the vessel is navigating in at any relevant time.[59]

In the nomenclature of the law of the sea, the 'flag state' refers to the state with whom a vessel is registered or whose flag the vessel flies. For all purposes, the ship becomes the national or bears the 'nationality' of that state.[60] The 'coastal state' refers generally to the state that claims jurisdiction over its surrounding waters.[61] In relation to pollution from a particular vessel, the coastal state is the state in one of whose maritime zones the vessel has committed a violation. The 'port state' is the state whose ports and internal waters a vessel sails into.

Except where international law provides for jurisdiction to be exercised by the coastal and port states, the primary jurisdiction over vessels resides with the flag states. This is a reflection of the traditional emphasis accorded by international law to flag state control and the freedom of navigation. Thus, flag states generally enjoy unlimited competence to prescribe rules and standards for their vessels. In fact, marine pollution regulations often empower flag states, if they should so desire, to prescribe standards that are more stringent than those which are internationally accepted. At the same time, flag state rules and standards must at least be as stringent as internationally accepted rules.

---

[59] See Ch. 4.
[60] LOSC, arts. 91 and 92(1). The LOSC does not explicitly define a 'flag state', although conventions like the 1982 UNCCRS, *infra* note 138, define it as 'a state whose flag a ship flies and is entitled to fly'.
[61] LOSC, art. 2(1) provides that the sovereignty of a coastal state extends beyond its land territory and internal waters and, in the case of an archipelagic state, its archipelagic waters, to an adjacent belt of sea described as the territorial sea. Further, art. 56(1) provides for the coastal state to exercise sovereign rights over natural resources in the exclusive economic zone. For details, see Ch. 4.

In contrast, coastal states can only enact or prescribe laws that give effect to prevailing internationally accepted rules and standards.[62] In very select circumstances, the coastal state is allowed limited authority to prescribe national measures which are more stringent than internationally accepted rules. In other words, internationally accepted measures represent the minimum and maximum allowable levels for flag and coastal state jurisdiction respectively. The port state is to act as an alternative to coastal state jurisdiction and is also generally constrained to adopt internationally accepted measures as a maximum.

As will be examined below, coastal states have every incentive to impose stringent pollution control rules and standards on ships while flag states generally do not. By establishing internationally accepted criteria as minimum and maximum levels for flag and coastal state jurisdiction respectively, the international regulatory system seeks a balance which maintains flag state accountability while restraining coastal state exuberance for regulating foreign vessels. The international regulatory process thus seeks to ensure the uniformity and reasonableness of national pollution control laws worldwide.

In practice, flag states typically lack the incentive to exercise their powers in controlling the activities of vessels flying their flags. This is largely because many ships fly the flags of 'convenience' registries, which have no real connection with the ships apart from the nominal act of registration.[63] Thus, the vessels of such registries rarely, if ever, sail into the waters of their flag states. Consequently, these states maintain little interest in ensuring their vessels' compliance with pollution control rules in other states' waters. This effectively defeats the aims of the various pollution control standards laid down by the international treaties.

In response, the coastal states have become increasingly more assertive in claiming greater control over foreign-flagged ships in their waters. With the growing political importance attached to environmental protection in recent years and the frequency of pollution incidents by ships, particularly the massive oil tankers, the coastal interests are increasingly questioning the traditional primacy of flag state jurisdiction. Hence, coastal states (or regional groupings of such states) are either resorting to unilateral measures going beyond those permitted by international law or dictating the development of new international regulations which accord them greater powers to deal with pollution

---

[62] See Ch. 4. [63] See Ch. 2.

and safety matters.⁶⁴ In sum, these developments are contributing to the progressively tighter regulation faced by the shipping industry today and the corresponding erosion in the industry's traditional freedom of navigation.

5. Outline of Analysis

The regulation of shipping activities has historically been dominated by a select group of players who typically resisted impediments to navigational freedom and increased costs for shipping. These actors have traditionally been the developed, affluent maritime states and the commercial and military interests which they represent – the shipowners, cargo owners, insurers, financiers, shipbuilders, shipbrokers, naval forces and defence agencies. As a whole, the conservatism toward environmental regulation of the developed maritime states has evolved into much greater liberalism in recent decades. This change has been driven largely by the powerful environmental consciousness arising within the developed pluralist democracies. To such extent, the traditional notion of free navigation has progressively been eroded in Europe, North America and Australia by the acceptance and encouragement of greater regulation over shipping activities.

In the realm of marine pollution regulation, the most prolific law-making and regulatory body is the London-based International Maritime Organization (IMO), the United Nations specialised agency tasked with the mandate of regulating maritime safety and marine environmental protection. While IMO has grown in stature and productivity in recent years, the drive for its activism has arisen largely from the national capitals of its most endowed developed member states. To such extent, any meaningful appraisal of the factors dictating IMO's pollution control agenda must take into account the pervasive role of domestic environmental politics in certain key states and regions of the world.

In the following chapters, this work will assess the political powers and interests behind the existing as well as proposed new regulations for vessel-source pollution. The contemporary dynamics of influence-wielding and decision-making, together with the interplay of interests

---

⁶⁴ On recent trends favouring coastal state claims, see J. A. Roach, *Salient Issues in the Implementation of Regimes under the Law of the Sea Convention: An Overview*, in ORDER FOR THE OCEANS AT THE TURN OF THE CENTURY 435 (D. Vidas & W. Østreng eds., 1999).

among the relevant actors, will be examined for their impact on the regime formation process.[65] Along the way, an appreciation of the larger extra-institutional forces at work will be attempted. In addition, this study seeks to assess the extent to which the relevant regulatory regimes fulfil modern environmental imperatives and to identify the modalities through which international regulation can be made more responsive to contemporary environmental concerns. Thus, the impediments to compliance with and effectiveness of regulations will be analysed, and solutions thereto prescribed.

The chapters that follow will provide the historical backdrop to the regulatory stage and introduce the main cast of actors and their concerns. This will throw some light on the relevant interests within the ship transportation industry and how they impinge upon the decision-making process as well as the implementation of and compliance with regulatory regimes. The legal, jurisdictional and constitutional context provided by the United Nations Conferences on the Law of the Sea will also be considered, specifically in relation to Part XII of the 1982 UN Convention on the Law of the Sea, which deals with the protection of the marine environment.

Within each chapter, the relevant political and economic interests of the key actors will be examined together with their impact on the regime formation and compliance processes. Several recurring and interlocking themes will appear as central tenets of this work. First, the behaviour of state actors in negotiating and prescribing treaty rules for the issue at hand, and in subsequently accepting these for ratification and actual implementation on the domestic front, are conditioned upon their own unique perceptions of their national interests. Second, it is only the interests of a powerful minority of actors that *effectively*

---

[65] See generally M. S. McDougal et al., *The World Constitutive Process of Authoritative Decision*, in THE FUTURE OF THE INTERNATIONAL LEGAL ORDER 73 (C. Black & R. Falk eds., 1969); M. S. MCDOUGAL & W. T. BURKE, THE PUBLIC ORDER OF THE OCEANS: A CONTEMPORARY INTERNATIONAL LAW OF THE SEA (1962); and TOWARDS WORLD ORDER AND HUMAN DIGNITY: ESSAYS IN HONOR OF MYRES S. MCDOUGAL (W. M. Reisman & B. H. Weston eds., 1976). A similar approach was adopted in the seminal work on ship pollution, R. M. M'GONIGLE & M. W. ZACHER, POLLUTION, POLITICS AND INTERNATIONAL LAW: TANKERS AT SEA (1979). See also J. W. KINDT, MARINE POLLUTION AND THE LAW OF THE SEA (1986); 3 NEW DIRECTIONS IN THE LAW OF THE SEA (R. R. Churchill et al. eds., 1973–5); E. D. BROWN, THE LEGAL REGIME OF HYDROSPACE (1971); THE ENVIRONMENTAL LAW OF THE SEA (D. Johnston ed., 1981); THE 1982 CONVENTION ON THE LAW OF THE SEA (A. W. Koers & B. H. Oxman eds., 1984); D. P. O'CONNELL, THE INTERNATIONAL LAW OF THE SEA, Vol. I (1982), Vol. II (1984); W. M. Ross, OIL POLLUTION AS AN INTERNATIONAL PROBLEM (1973); and H. SILVERSTEIN, SUPERSHIPS AND NATION STATES: THE TRANSNATIONAL PROBLEM OF OIL POLLUTION (1972).

dictate the trend and pace of regulation at the multilateral level. Often, the larger forces which propel law-making are situated *outside* the relevant regulatory bodies, with such bodies merely serving as institutional endorsers of political *fiat* decreed elsewhere by powerful state and industry interests.[66]

Third, the effective implementation of existing regulations remains a monumental challenge. The majority of states in the world are ill-equipped to translate international regulations into any meaningful effect on the domestic stage. In this regard, the compliance records of the less developed countries are unlikely to improve until a higher level of economic, social and administrative sophistication is achieved domestically. Yet, the onset of new environmental challenges invariably dictates that the pace of international regulation will have to be maintained, if not quickened.

Overall, this work posits that while the growth in environmental regulation has substantially eroded the traditional right of free navigation, at least in as far as regime formation is concerned, the actual implementation of and compliance with the relevant rules remain lacking. This is due in large part to the competitive and profit-driven nature of the shipping industry and the lack of incentives among state and private actors to ensure the effectiveness of environmental rules and regulations. In turn, this leads back to and reinforces the inherent regime deficiencies which have long afflicted international marine pollution control and inhibited subsequent compliance with the associated rules.

As the concluding chapter will argue, the solutions to the vessel-source marine pollution problem lie with creating incentive-enhancing measures which foster more accountability, transparency and burden-sharing equity among the ship transportation industry's myriad actors.[67] These measures include the promotion of compliance incentives and the distribution of costs, not only among shipowners but industry-wide among cargo owners, insurers, classification societies and financiers as well as flag, coastal and port states. Such measures can be introduced either at the regime formation stage, at which point they can seek to avoid regime deficiencies, or at the post-formation

---

[66] See Ch. 2.
[67] On burden-sharing among maritime actors, see generally ORGANISATION FOR ECONOMIC CO-OPERATION AND DEVELOPMENT, SAFETY AND ENVIRONMENTAL PROTECTION: DISCUSSION PAPER ON POSSIBLE ACTIONS TO COMBAT SUBSTANDARD SHIPPING BY INVOLVING PLAYERS OTHER THAN THE SHIPOWNER IN THE SHIPPING MARKET, OECD Doc. DSTI/DOT/MTC(98)10/final (1998).

implementation stage, where they may overcome or ameliorate the impact of regime deficiencies.[68] At the same time, IMO needs to play a more pro-active role in ensuring effective implementation of pollution control rules. Only through such wide-ranging and concerted efforts can a culture of compliance be cultivated within the ship transportation industry and the goals of a safer and cleaner marine environment be achieved.

---

[68] An example of a regime formation deficiency would be the oil industry's insistence in 1997 for a generous cap on sulphur content in bunker fuels, see Ch. 3. Post-regime mechanisms such as pro-active port state control which targets not only shipowners but other relevant actors may reduce the impact of such deficiencies, albeit in a remedial manner, see Chs. 5 and 7. Thus, the avoidance of regime deficiencies at the outset must remain a priority. On commercial interests influencing regime formation, see M'GONIGLE & ZACHER, *supra* note 65, at 260-3 and R. MITCHELL, INTENTIONAL OIL POLLUTION AT SEA – ENVIRONMENTAL POLICY AND TREATY COMPLIANCE 110-11 (1994).

2 The Dynamics of the Law-Making Process: Actors, Arenas and Interests

1. Overview

The regulation of vessel-source pollution fittingly illustrates the roles of law and power in reconciling the interests of diverse political actors. By virtue of its inherently global nature, ocean transport entails the confluence of a number of political, commercial and civic forces, each striving to advance its own agenda. Among the competing interests are the maritime and military actors intent on maintaining freedom of navigation and trade on the oceans; governmental interests seeking to regulate vessel traffic for security, economic and environmental purposes; shipowning, cargo-owning and other shipping-related interests which consistently resist the increased costs of regulation; and domestic lobbies – including the media, environmental groups, local governments, politicians and even individual activists – which campaign for enhanced regulation over shipping.

The interested actors are not necessarily aligned with the states from where they operate or with whom they identify. In other words, the interests of the non-state entities are generally independent of and distinguishable from those of their state hosts even though both parties may try to recruit each other to advance their respective claims. In spite of the non-state actors' increasing influence, states have traditionally been and remain the principal participants in the formal arenas of international decision-making. As such, the instrumentality of the state is invariably used by non-state actors as a means to espouse their demands when their interests coincide with or even dictate those of the state.

Any analysis of vessel-source marine pollution must consider the political dynamics between two groups of state actors representing the maritime and coastal interests respectively. The former group – known generally as the 'maritime states' – comprises those states with significant military and commercial navigation interests. Consistent with their desire to maintain unhindered navigation and commerce over the oceans, maritime states and their associated industries traditionally subscribe to the principle of freedom of navigation for all vessels. The 'coastal states', as the term suggests, are shoreline states that seek to regulate the movement and activities of foreign vessels in or near the waters adjacent to their coasts. Such regulation would traditionally be for security purposes even though this extends in modern times to marine environmental protection.

At the global level, the regulation of vessel-source pollution is thus manifested in a political contest between coastal states seeking to protect their waters and shores by adopting strict environmental controls over their own vessels and those of other states, and maritime states which perceive coastal state regulation to be inimical to the traditional freedom of navigation.[69] As with any discourse involving competing interest groups, the international regulatory system has had to craft negotiated compromises to balance the different groups' demands. While several interest-balancing efforts have produced satisfactory outcomes, significant differences still exist between the economic, commercial and military interests on the one hand, and marine environmental protection interests on the other.

It must be noted that the regulation of marine pollution cannot be considered in isolation from the general context of public international law, particularly the norms relevant to international environmental protection. To the extent that shipping is an international venture impinging upon the relations among states and the use of navigational waterways falling either within or totally outside state jurisdiction, the customary principles of the law of the sea and international environmental law must be expected to prevail upon and govern the conduct of relevant actors.

Yet, customary rules alone are inadequate to deal with the complex problems of marine pollution.[70] The traditional principles of state responsibility for transboundary pollution, for instance, are premised upon the establishment of a clear obligation of states not to allow injury

---

[69] See HAKAPÄÄ, *supra* note 3, at 68 and D. M. Bodansky, *Protecting the Marine Environment from Vessel-Source Pollution: UNCLOS III and Beyond*, 18 ECOLOGY L. Q. 719, at 720 (1991).

[70] CHURCHILL & LOWE, *supra* note 26, at 333.

to another state.⁷¹ Such principles make little provision for the responsibility of non-state actors like shipowners, nor for recourse action by non-state victims. In addition, the maritime practice of registering ships under 'flags of convenience'⁷² renders it practically difficult to attach customary responsibility and liability on the flag state for damage caused by a ship.

These are among the reasons why the regulation of marine pollution is conducted today primarily through multilateral conventions or treaties negotiated under IMO auspices.⁷³ At the same time, while conventions form the primary tools in IMO's regulatory arsenal, many of the norms and obligations prescribed by these instruments can be traced to non-conventional customary sources or principles. As far as marine pollution is concerned, the overlap between convention and custom is significant. Indeed, much of the customary law of the sea evolved over the centuries through state practice has today been enshrined in conventions, particularly the 1982 UN Convention on the Law of the Sea (LOSC). Thus, many of the LOSC principles can be viewed as declaratory of existing customary international law.

It must be noted that the popular expressions 'maritime state' and 'coastal state' are largely terms of convenience. While they may have served their purpose in the past by classifying states according to their shipping or coastal inclinations, they are far from being mutually exclusive today. Underlying the apparent mélange of state interests is a more sophisticated reality confronting the modern regulatory system. The majority of states today have maritime *as well as* coastal interests. Diverse lobby groups – maritime or otherwise – arise within most political entities. As a result, the proclivities of state actors cannot be so easily reduced into one category or another in the scheme of political preferences.

To illustrate, states with traditionally strong maritime interests such as the United States, the European countries and Japan are invariably cross-pressured by their domestic environmental lobbies. Conversely, even traditionally non-maritime coastal states like Canada and Australia

---

[71] See e.g. *Trail Smelter Arbitration* (US v. Can.), 3 R. INT'L ARB. AWARDS 1911 (1938), *reprinted in* 33 AM. J. INT'L L. 182 (1939); 3 R. INT'L ARB. AWARDS 1938 (1941), *reprinted in* 35 AM. J. INT'L L. 684 (1941). On state responsibility generally, see THE INTERNATIONAL LAW COMMISSION'S ARTICLES ON STATE RESPONSIBILITY: INTRODUCTION, TEXT AND COMMENTARIES (J. Crawford ed., 2002).
[72] See Ch. II.
[73] The terms 'treaty', 'convention' and 'agreement' are used interchangeably.

have large export-oriented economies highly dependent upon maritime trade. At the same time, the terms 'maritime state' and 'coastal state' cannot be taken to be synonymous with developed and developing states respectively. Many environmentalist states, such as Canada and Australia, are developed countries. There are then the developing states with huge shipping interests, including Panama, Liberia, China or Brazil, which may just as accurately and comfortably be termed 'maritime states'.

In the result, it is the intercourse among interest groups arising within states rather than simply pure inter-state politics that more accurately describes the power fluxes characterising the international regulation of vessel-source pollution. Often, varied sectoral interests emerge within states depending on the nature of the pollutant being regulated, the associated costs of regulation to individual actors, the relative influence of the industry or environmental protagonists involved, the force of domestic public opinion and the stake which the state ultimately holds in supporting or resisting regulation over particular pollutants or practices.

From this perspective, the 'state' becomes little more than an agglomeration of issue-specific interests – public and private, political and commercial. It follows that while multilateral agreements still commonly refer to states as the sole repositories of jurisdiction and competence, the final positions that states adopt at international negotiations will invariably be a compromise or composite response to domestic interest tensions. Hence, the regulation of vessel-source pollution derives its energy not so much from state-centric or institution-based discourse as from interest group politics operating fairly independently of states and international bodies. This is entirely consistent with one of the great phenomena of contemporary international law – the emergence of the non-state actor. Often, the influence of non-state interests over their state proxies may turn out to be far more determinative of policy outcomes than these interests' own direct participation in the rule-making process.

It is also critical to appreciate the role played by individuals whose temperaments, personal traits and preferences may substantially influence the decision-making and regime formation processes. Multilateral negotiations have commonly witnessed how the personalities of actors such as conference chairpersons, working group leaders, secretariat staff and individual delegates may determine outcomes. At the national level, the backgrounds, inclinations and biases of individual politicians, civic leaders or public interest agitators all play a crucial role in influencing domestic policy. Where appropriate, this work will identify the personalities who have had tremendous influence – tangible or otherwise – in shaping the outcome of national and international decision-making processes.

It follows that, just as there is a multitude of actors whose interests impinge upon vessel-source pollution, there exists an equally diverse array of arenas – domestic, regional and global – for the relevant actors to espouse their causes. At the most fundamental level, the process of reconciling the demands of the maritime and coastal interests must take place within national boundaries. Typically, it is only when a composite position is achieved within state entities that the next level of discussions is entered into – regional or international decision-making. As such, while major policy prescriptions may be formulated and approved at global institutionalised levels, it is critical to appreciate that the genesis for such prescriptions often lies in domestic fora.

Transposed to the realm of vessel-source pollution, what this means is that while there exists a primary global decision-making arena in the form of IMO, the policy prescriptions emanating therefrom will invariably have been dictated by external forces. These include domestic political demands, pressure from regional groupings of states, media agitation in reaction to maritime catastrophes, the sectoral interests of powerful participants and international developments such as wars, hostilities and price fluctuations in world commodity markets. Even then, the Secretariat of IMO may, under certain circumstances, emerge as a relevant actor in its own right. This could happen, for instance, when the interests of the relatively weaker developing states demand some form of collective representation.

Examples abound to illustrate how vessel-source pollution issues have largely been energised by extrinsic factors. Pollution control measures adopted by IMO in the 1970s were initiated at the behest of the US, seeking to placate domestic outrage over vessel accidents in its coastal waters. During the period of high crude oil prices in the 1970s, hitherto resisted pollution control measures came to be embraced by the oil industry due to their ability to reduce oil wastage. In the 1990s, the move to curb air pollution from ships resulted directly from the North Sea states' concern with sulphur deposition and acid rain. In recent years, the US and the EU have demonstrated willingness to legislate (or to threaten to legislate) national and regional rules relating to vessel safety and the environment, thereby challenging IMO's decision-making competence. In response, IMO has had little choice but to accede to the demands of these interests for more stringent pollution control measures.

The following section will proceed to identify the key actors relevant to the marine pollution debate and assess how their interests impinge upon the international regulation of vessel-source pollution.

2. Key Actors in the Decision-Making Process

2.1 *The Maritime Interests*

2.1.1 The Shipowners and Operators

This first group of relevant actors comprises the individuals, companies and state-owned enterprises which own, manage and operate the commercial shipping fleets of the world. In maritime parlance, they are collectively referred to as 'shipowners', even though professional ship operators and managers are often distinct from their owner-clients. In order to operate, all ships are customarily registered with a state registry (the flag state), thereby assuming that state's nationality and enjoying its protection.[74] The flag state's laws thus apply to the ship in question with regard to all operational aspects such as taxation, the registration of mortgages and the hiring of crew.[75] The entity that appears in the registry as the 'owner' is taken to be the ship's registered legal owner.

Within the maritime world, controversial arrangements exist whereby a ship can be owned by a company incorporated with the sole and explicit purpose of owning that ship. By virtue of the recognition of companies as separate entities in most legal systems, these so-called 'one-ship' or 'two-dollar' companies – the latter term referring to the typical minimum amount placed as shareholding in a company owning no other assets – effectively shields the 'real' beneficial owner(s) from liability to third parties arising from the operation of the ship. Such liability includes obligations to compensate for pollution damage caused to third party interests.

The beneficial owners of ships are typically individuals, companies or mortgagees in the developed countries, particularly in Western Europe,

---

[74] LOSC, art. 91. On registration generally, see SHIP REGISTRATION: LAW AND PRACTICE (R. Coles & N. Ready eds., 2002).
[75] LOSC, art. 94.

the US and Asia.⁷⁶ These interests have traditionally embraced the concepts of free navigation and flag state control, eschewing any interference from external actors such as coastal states or international regulatory agencies. Many owners typically register their ships under low-cost 'flags of convenience' or open registries. This essentially reflects the commercial motivations of the shipowning industry and the flags they use, namely minimal costs and maximum profits.⁷⁷

A further trait of the shipowning industry is its highly fragmented and competitive nature. The global merchant fleet is owned and operated by thousands of companies competing vigorously for market share. Vessel ownership structures are typically multi-layered and shrouded in secrecy, often involving, as mentioned above, 'one-ship' companies set up to limit exposure to liability and to conceal the true beneficial owner's identity. Many owners are not averse to operating sub-standard (meaning poor quality and ill-maintained) ships to save on costs. In essence, these are the very features of the industry that earn it so much odium among politicians and environmentalists following any catastrophic vessel accident.

In the past few decades, the shipowning industry has been increasingly compelled to accept the need for harmonised vessel regulation through international agreement. The industry itself has realised that international rules are needed in order to prevent coastal states from imposing differing safety and environmental standards on visiting ships. At the same time, shipowners have been wary of the competitive distortions arising from the imposition of rules by certain flag states but not by others. Initially, considerations for protecting the marine environment did not feature quite so highly in the shipowners' minds. In modern times, however, the benefits of positive public relations that accompany environmental responsibility have provided further motives for ship operators to support international pollution control standards.

Even then, the shipowning industry typically resists high standards, lobbying instead for minimally invasive lowest common denominators. However, with the declining influence of shipping lobbies in the developed states, the shipowners' efforts to oppose high standards are increasingly proving to be futile. Consistent with the 'polluter pays'

---

⁷⁶ See Table 2-2.
⁷⁷ R. Payne, *Flags of Convenience and Oil Pollution: A Threat to National Security*, 3 Hous. J. Int'l L. 67, at 69 (1980).

principle, shipowners are now regarded as the primary polluter in the maritime transport sector. As the following chapters will show, states have generally sought to shift the costs of environmental compliance to industry.[78] Thus, more emphasis is placed, for instance, on ships installing waste minimisation technology and pollution control equipment than on ports providing waste reception facilities. Such developments are powerful indicators of how modern environmental imperatives have significantly eroded the owner's traditional right to free and unhindered navigation.

In the wake of the terrorist attacks of September 2001, it will be interesting to see how the beneficial owners can possibly uphold their tradition of secrecy. During an IMO Conference on Maritime Security convened in December 2002,[79] the US floated proposals to curb the excesses of ownership secrecy, principally those relating to beneficial owners. Preliminary discussions at IMO saw the US demanding a radical change to the understanding of the terms 'ownership' and 'control' such that details of beneficial ownership could be made more readily transparent to reveal the real owners behind the corporate veil.

The proposal came up against strong objections from the shipowning interests, which argued that the identity of those responsible for the effective management, control and operation of ships is far more pertinent than details of their ownership for purposes of ensuring maritime security and eradicating terrorism. In the shipowners' view, information on vessel ownership is practically irrelevant, since many shareholders are simply passive investors of one form or another with no management involvement.

In reality, uncovering the beneficial shareholder may be next to impossible on a complete or consistent basis. This is especially so in a system where the corporate veil is already thick and multi-layered, where multiple or corporate ownership is the norm, where shares are held on behalf of third parties by institutions or trusts, or where a bank might hold shares as security for a loan. Thus, it is unlikely that attempts to compel transparency will work, given the major legal changes that will be required in various individual states. In addition, an argument can be made for leaving the corporate veil in place, the

---

[78] See COST SAVINGS, *supra* note 8, at 43–6, for an assessment of the costs of compliance with pollution control measures.
[79] The Conference adopted amendments to SOLAS 74 in the form of Chapter XI-2 on Special Measures to Enhance Maritime Security and a new International Ship and Port Facility Security (ISPS) Code. These entered into force on 1 July 2004.

contention being that opening the book on vessel ownership represents an infringement on the right to financial privacy.[80]

These arguments were not lost on the US and its allies, themselves the biggest beneficial owners of ships. IMO eventually achieved general consensus on the desirability of focusing on the effective management and operation of ships, as opposed to beneficial ownership thereof.[81] Although the concept of 'beneficial ownership' survives, the effort to redefine its meaning may well herald in an age of increasing willingness to dismantle the traditional primacy of flag state control and the secrecy which pervades ship ownership and operation. This may have profound effects not only on security issues, but also on the safety and pollution prevention responsibilities of shipowners and managers. While it is currently too early to assess the impact on the pollution control aspects of regulation, it is at least clear that maritime security concerns have triggered an important momentum to re-assess the less transparent workings of the shipowning world.[82]

At international regulatory fora, the most vocal representatives of the shipowning community include the International Chamber of Shipping (ICS), the International Association of Independent Tanker Owners (INTERTANKO) and the Baltic and International Maritime Council (BIMCO), all of whom enjoy consultative status at IMO. Established in London in 1921, ICS is a voluntary organisation of more than forty national shipowners' associations from thirty countries. It represents some 50 per cent of global merchant tonnage and is dominated by members from the developed countries.

The Oslo-based INTERTANKO was formed in 1971 to defend the interests of the independent tanker owners vis-à-vis the major oil companies. It has some 240 members from more than forty countries worldwide,

---

[80] All these concerns are detailed in Lloyd's List, *USCG Dismisses Pleas for Secrecy*, 27 Mar. 2002.

[81] Report of the IMO Legal Committee's 84th session, LEG Doc. 84/14 (2002). See also Lloyd's List, *IMO Buries Ownership Check*, 1 May 2002. IMO also committed itself to eradicating the registration of 'phantom' ships, i.e. ships of obscure provenance which could be the target of unlawful acts or could be used as weapons to commit such acts: see IMO Assembly Resolution A.923(22) (2001) on Measures to Prevent the Registration of 'Phantom' Ships.

[82] The Organisation for Economic Co-operation and Development (OECD) is also probing covert ownership and control of ships: see e.g. OECD, THE COST TO USERS OF SUBSTANDARD SHIPPING (2001), *available at* http://www.oecd.org/dataoecd/27/18/18273888.pdf and OECD, OWNERSHIP AND CONTROL OF SHIPS (2003), *available at* http://www.oecd.org/dataoecd/53/9/17846120.pdf (last accessed 29 Nov. 2004).

representing 160 million dwt of tanker tonnage, or about 70 per cent of the independent world tanker fleet. Norwegian, Greek and Japanese owners form a substantial proportion of INTERTANKO membership. On its part, BIMCO is the largest private shipping organisation in the world. Established in 1905 and based in Denmark, BIMCO groups together shipowners, brokers, agents, P&I Clubs and other commercial actors from over 120 countries. Its members currently control around 65 per cent of the global merchant fleet.

2.1.2 The Cargo Owners and Charterers

The next major group of maritime actors consists of the owners or shippers of goods carried on board ships. In relation to vessel-source pollution control, the shipowner has traditionally been the primary target of regulation by virtue of his direct operational role in transporting cargoes that are potential pollutants. At the same time, regulators have tried to impose responsibility on cargo owners based on the argument that the owners of polluting cargoes must share in the costs of preventive and remedial action as well as of compensation to pollution victims.

While this logic is perfectly sound, cargo owners have traditionally been very successful in deflecting the bulk of regulatory costs onto the shipowners. This is largely due to the stronger influence of the cargo owners, particularly the oil companies. By their nature, cargo owners are extremely diffused in number and locality, given the huge variety and amounts of cargoes shipped throughout the world. Imposing responsibility on the cargo owners would thus present an administrative quagmire, save perhaps for bulk cargoes like oil for which the owners, shippers or receivers are relatively easy to identify.[83] In contrast, shipowners are a discrete, identifiable group that can more practicably be subjected to regulation.

At first glance, the interests of shipowners and cargo owners coincide substantially. Both industries typically resist expensive pollution control measures since these tend to result in higher transportation costs reflected in higher freight and consumer prices. However, this is where the similarity ends. While the bulk of world oil tanker tonnage is owned by the so-called 'independent' owners,[84] the rest are owned by states,

---

[83] Even where the cargo owners are identifiable, they have managed to shift a large part of costs onto other actors such as shipowners: see Chs. 3 and 6.

[84] The majority of these are nationals of developed maritime states such as Greece, Norway, Japan, Denmark and the US: see Table 2-2.

state-linked concerns and private oil companies. Thus, the oil companies (both state owned and private) are concurrently shipowners as well, using their own tankers and those chartered from the independents.[85]

In order to project a positive public image, the oil 'majors' (as the large oil companies are known) had acted from an early stage to adopt environmentally responsible corporate profiles. With their vast oil revenues, they could well afford to subsidise the costs of pollution abatement. However, the oil companies have skilfully insisted on assuming regulatory costs in their capacity as tanker owners only, *not* cargo owners. This way, regulatory costs can be shared with the independents. Owing to their unique dual capacity, the oil companies effectively enjoy a measure of flexibility not possessed by the independents. This often compromises the independents' bargaining position at multilateral negotiations.

For instance, the oil majors – with their huge influence over national economies – were able in the 1960s and 1970s to persuade states to back the imposition of regulatory costs onto owners of tankers. And so it turned out that a variety of pollution-related regulations – ranging from preventive and remedial measures to compensation for oil pollution victims – was imposed upon tanker owners as a whole.[86] On their part, the independents lacked the political and economic muscle to resist these measures. For one thing, most influential maritime states had, by the 1980s, begun to identify more closely with their cargo-owning interests. The migration of tanker owners from the registries of the traditional maritime states to those of the cheaper 'open' registries also weakened the owners' leverage with the former states. With no alternative revenue to subsidise pollution control costs, the independents felt the strain of increasing regulation, particularly during periods of weak freight markets.

The chasm between the independents and the oil companies widened further in the late 1980s and early 1990s, when the latter began to divest themselves of tanker ownership. Divestment was brought about by the mounting financial risks and liabilities being imposed on tanker operation by new regulations, particularly the US Oil Pollution Act of 1990. Thus, the vast majority of tanker owners today are independents left to shoulder the bulk of high pollution control costs.

---

[85] The oil companies' share of tanker ownership has progressively fallen over the years, and is today only about 20 per cent of the global fleet.
[86] See Chs. 3 and 6.

The volatile freight rates of the past few decades have also encouraged oil companies to shun long-term, fixed-price time charters and to use 'spot' charters instead. This necessarily entails scouting the market for the cheapest available rates at any one time, thereby tending to favour the sub-standard operator. In any event, most chartering today is conducted by smaller independent charterers or private oil traders who are not as easily identifiable for regulation. Compared to the oil majors, these actors are far less scrupulous in their choice of vessels for charter. Indeed, their penchant for 'spot' fixtures is well known in the industry.[87] Such chartering practices bear negative effects for the shipowners, particularly the quality operators. Consequently, any effort to address the vessel safety and pollution control problems must take into account the behaviour of the cargo interests.

The oil companies are represented at international regulatory fora by the Oil Companies International Marine Forum (OCIMF). OCIMF was formed in 1970 by the oil majors to address public concerns over the spectacular spills of the 1960s, including the *Torrey Canyon* disaster of 1967. For a time, the oil companies were represented through ICS but the divergent interests of the oil companies and the shipowners soon saw the former establishing OCIMF to advance their interests separately. Today, OCIMF represents more than 40 major oil companies from all over the world, even though it continues to be dominated by the American and British majors.

2.1.3 The Protection and Indemnity (P&I) Clubs and the Marine Insurers

Shipowners customarily insure their operations against two types of risks – hull and machinery (H&M) and third party liability risks. H&M coverage protects a shipowner against losses to his own ship and its equipment resulting from collisions, groundings and other accidents. In contrast, third party liability coverage indemnifies an owner against claims by third parties for damage incurred to their interests arising from the operation of the ship. Such parties include other owners whose ships may have been damaged by the insured ship during a collision, port authorities whose installations suffer damage or victims of pollution caused by the insured ship.

---

[87] Personal interviews.

Third party liability insurance is normally taken out with the so-called Protection and Indemnity (P&I) Clubs.[88] These are associations of shipowners that have banded together on a mutual basis to indemnify themselves against all forms of third party claims including those arising from vessel-source pollution. While the Clubs are distinct from the underwriting syndicates of the marine insurance industry, they customarily enter into reinsurance contracts with the latter to spread out the relevant risks. In relation to oil pollution and nuclear incident claims, there exist special policies that enable the Clubs to protect themselves by means of reinsurance against catastrophic claims. Currently, the Clubs cover oil pollution damage up to a maximum of US$1 billion with the aid of reinsurance. In practice, this limit is rarely reached since a shipowner is invariably entitled to limit his liability.[89]

The largest P&I Clubs can presently be found in the UK, Norway, Japan and the US. In the late nineteenth century, a number of these Clubs formed the International Group of P&I Associations. Today, members of the International Group cover between them some 90 per cent of world shipping tonnage. The remaining 10 per cent of tonnage (if insured at all) is covered by competitors such as non-International Group P&I Clubs and fixed premium insurance providers, as well as small domestic insurers. The International Group represents the interests of the major P&I Clubs at various international fora, including at IMO where it wields considerable influence due to its expertise in insurance matters. The Group is invariably consulted on whether particular liability and compensation provisions are realistic in the light of insurance market capacity.

On its part, the commercial insurance industry is represented at IMO by the International Union of Marine Insurers (IUMI). IUMI comprises some 50 national associations of hull and cargo insurers from all over the world. The marine insurance industry is dominated by the London-based Lloyd's syndicates of insurance underwriters. Together with the other major insurance body, the Institute of London Underwriters (ILU), Lloyd's virtually controls the setting of insurance rates for the global maritime industry. As mentioned above, the underwriters' role in oil pollution coverage is usually to act as re-insurers for the P&I Clubs. The underwriters' interest in safe and clean shipping stems from the fact that their business entails the assessment of trading risks associated with the

---

[88] See M. Tilley, *The Origin and Development of the Mutual Shipowners' Protection and Indemnity Associations*, 17 J. Mar. L. & Com. 261 (1986).
[89] On the shipowner's right to limitation, see Ch. 6.

condition and operation of ships. Thus, insurance premia are typically structured to reflect the level of risk presented by a particular ship.

Despite their close co-operation, the P&I Clubs compete vigorously among themselves and with fixed premium insurers for shipowners' business.[90] The same holds true for the marine underwriting industry in general. What this means is that it is still possible for the most substandard ships to obtain insurance coverage, often from the less discriminating clubs and insurers.[91] This remains a major weakness of the marine insurance industry.

As the effective alter ego of the shipowners where insurance matters are concerned, the P&I Clubs have been constantly battling to stave off greater liability costs for the owners. Often, their efforts have been unsuccessful. Thus, in 1969, a civil liability regime crafted to respond to victims' claims for compensation arising from oil pollution damage imposed substantial first-tier strict liability on the shipowners.[92] In this regard, the oil companies succeeded in ensuring that cargo owners such as themselves would pay for oil pollution claims only when compensation was either unobtainable from the shipowner or where the claim amounts exceed the maximum limits payable by the shipowner.[93]

In the result, the scheme ensured that the cargo owners' second-tier liability would only be triggered in the most catastrophic of pollution incidents.[94] A broadly similar regime was adopted in 1996 in relation to pollution by hazardous chemicals.[95] This time, the major chemical manufacturers were at the forefront of resisting costs for cargo owners. The result of these manoeuvres by the cargo interests has been the imposition of substantial first-tier costs on shipowners and their P&I insurers.

Another source of P&I Club discontent has been the erosion of the hallowed principle of indemnity in marine insurance law. Customarily,

---

[90] P. BOISSON, SAFETY AT SEA – POLICIES, REGULATIONS AND INTERNATIONAL LAW 422 (D. Mahaffey trans.) (1999).
[91] H. Payer, *Insurer and Class and Marine Accidents*, in Nordquist & Moore eds., *supra* note 9, at 296 and REMOVAL OF INSURANCE, *supra* note 5, at 65-6.
[92] 1969 International Convention on Civil Liability for Oil Pollution Damage, 973 U.N.T.S. 3; 9 I.L.M. 45 (1970) (in force 19 June 1975). For details, see Ch. 6.
[93] See Ch. 6.
[94] The second-tier system was set out by the 1971 International Convention on the Establishment of an International Fund for Compensation for Oil Pollution Damage, 1110 U.N.T.S. 57; 11 I.L.M. 284 (1972) (in force 16 Oct. 1978). This Convention is now defunct and has been replaced by a new instrument adopted in 1992, see Ch. 6.
[95] 1996 International Convention on Liability and Compensation for Damage in Connection with the Carriage of Hazardous and Noxious Substances by Sea, 35 I.L.M. 1406 (1996) (not in force).

this principle obliges the insurer to compensate the insured only after the latter has paid off the claimants (the so-called 'pay-to-be-paid' rule). Otherwise, the insurer generally owes no obligation to third party claimants. Also, where the shipowner has breached a term in his contract with the insurer (such as failure to pay the insurance premium), the latter is generally not liable to pay compensation.

As regards oil pollution liability, however, the civil liability regime adopted in 1969 dramatically eroded the principle of indemnity by according pollution victims the right of 'direct action' against P&I Clubs in the latter's capacity as the shipowners' insurer. In addition, the Clubs cannot plead as a defence that the insured has breached a relevant contractual term. The net result of these developments has been the imposition of significant pollution insurance costs on the shipowners in the form of higher P&I as well as reinsurance premia. This has formed yet another significant qualification to the shipowner's traditional right to free and unhindered navigation.

2.1.4 The Classification Societies

Closely linked to the P&I Clubs and the marine insurance industry are the classification societies. The oldest of these were established in the eighteenth century to provide 'class rating' services to insurance underwriters and cargo owners wishing to obtain information on the seaworthiness of a ship. In particular, ship insurers relied on the information provided by classification societies to assess the risks associated with a particular ship and to compute the relevant insurance premium. The leading classification societies are those found in the established maritime states. In 1968, seven major societies banded together to form the International Association of Classification Societies (IACS).

Members of IACS certify between them some 95 per cent of current world shipping tonnage. IACS represents the interests of its members at regulatory fora such as IMO and aims to promote the development of standardised certification procedures even as its members compete for market share. More than 50 other classification societies currently exist outside IACS, mainly in the developing countries, where they cater primarily to national flag fleets with small ships.[96]

---

[96] There is apparently a higher percentage of sub-standard vessels in non-IACS societies than there are in IACS societies, see Payer, *supra* note 91, at 295 (note that Mr Payer is a former Chairman of IACS).

From a private commercial service provided to facilitate maritime trade, the role of classification societies has expanded in modern times to cover the public function known as statutory certification. Pursuant to the numerous safety and pollution control standards laid down by national law, international conventions and private industry groups, classification societies conduct surveys on ships and issue certificates testifying to the ships' compliance with these statutory regulations.[97]

Technically, the responsibility to inspect and certify ships in this manner lies with the national maritime administrations of the flag states. However, almost all flag states delegate such functions to recognised classification societies largely because of their own lack of resources, expertise or interest. Thus, classification according to each society's internal rules is now accompanied by statutory certification pursuant to externally imposed standards. These twin functions form the crux of classification societies' work today.

In recent years, the societies have been severely criticised for their alleged laxity in surveying ships for compliance with the relevant standards. Given that shipowners contract directly with the society of their choice for certification services, allegations have arisen of bias, lack of objectivity and outright neglect on the part of societies. The common perception is that some classification societies have failed to meet expectations with respect to the enforcement of vessel standards, particularly regarding the conduct of unannounced inspections or surveys and the extension of prescribed intervals between periodic surveys.[98]

The problem resides mainly in the way the classification and certification functions have coalesced, as well as the commercialisation of what were originally meant to be governmental statutory functions. In essence, the fact that the societies have become the commercial clients of shipowners may render them less than objective or independent in performing statutory certification (i.e. public control functions) on the

---

[97] IMO has guidelines for its member states on the appointment of classification societies, see IMO Assembly Resolution A.739(18) (1993) on Guidelines for the Authorization of Organizations Acting on Behalf of Administrations, as updated by Resolution A.789(19) (1995) on Specifications on the Survey and Certification Functions of Recognized Organizations Acting on Behalf of Administrations. These Resolutions have mandatory effect through SOLAS reg. XI/1.

[98] See generally P. F. Cane, *The Liability of Classification Societies*, 3 LLOYD'S MAR. & COM. L. Q. 363 (1994); C. B. Anderson & C. de la Rue, *Liability of Charterers and Cargo Owners for Pollution from Ships*, 26 MAR. LAW. 42 (2001); and J. D. Gordan III, *The Liability of Marine Surveyors and Ship Classification Societies*, 19 J. MAR. L. & COM. 301 (1988).

same ships.[99] In addition, the classification societies may come under severe pressure from shipyards to accept standard designs and approve construction plans.[100] The confidentiality agreements typically signed between yards and classification societies also contribute to a lack of transparency.

In this regard, it is not only the role of the classification societies which has evolved. The paymasters of these societies have also shifted from the underwriters and cargo owners to the shipowners, flag states and shipyards. This invariably creates a situation of conflict of interests.[101] The problem is made worse by the fact that survey reports are typically the confidential property of the shipowners. This arises from the privileged relationship between owners and their societies. A lack of transparency is thus endemic in the system, since it is often impossible for insurers or any other party to obtain access to the records of sub-standard ships.

The practice of hiring local, non-exclusive surveyors at ports of call also leads to a dilution in standards – these surveyors are never fully imbued with the values of the relevant society. More often than not, the surveyors retain close connections with the desires and expectations of the local shipowning community. Continued cost-cutting has also led to societies hiring less qualified and cheaper staff. In recent years, cynicism over the efficacy of classification societies has grown due to the rampant practice among shipowners to transfer class to other societies (known as 'class-hopping' or 'class-shopping') whenever a society is no longer deemed to be 'co-operative' or indulgent.[102] This exerts pressure on classification societies to turn a blind eye to their clients' shortcomings and to resist expelling them lest they move their business to less rigorous competitors.[103]

---

[99] See generally H. Honka, *The Classification System and its Problems with Special Reference to the Liability of Classification Societies*, TUL. MAR. L. J. 1, at 5 (1994) and R. Harling, *The Liability of Classification Societies to Cargo Owners*, 1 MAR. & COM. L. Q. 1, at 7–8 (1993).
[100] Lloyd's List, *Rule Out the Culture to Cut Corners*, 26 Apr. 2001.
[101] Payer, *supra* note 91, at 294.
[102] Harling, *supra* note 99, at 7. To counter criticisms against this practice, IACS has developed a Transfer of Class Agreement (TOCA) among its members to prevent abuse of transfers. Thus, the society which the ship is transferring out from (the 'losing' class) must provide the 'gaining' class with a complete history file of the vessel. Pursuant to the *Erika* I package, *infra* note 377, the transfer of class requirements has been made mandatory in Europe by art. 15, Directive 2001/105/EC, 2002 OJ (L 19) 9, amending Directive 94/57 (Directive on Classification Societies), *infra* note 237.
[103] In response to criticisms of the classification system, some P&I Clubs have begun using their own surveyors while some hull insurers consult the inspections conducted by oil companies, see REMOVAL OF INSURANCE, *supra* note 5, at 37.

2.1.5 The Military Interests

The departments or ministries of defence in states with significant naval capabilities have traditionally been staunch supporters of the right to free navigation. From their perspective, this right affords military vessels exemption or immunity from the jurisdiction of any state apart from the flag state. This position has existed for centuries, and is often justified on security grounds. The military interests were extremely active at the negotiation of the LOSC in the 1970s, with many delegations having strong participation by their defence ministries.[104] Not only were these interests adamant that sovereign immunity be upheld for military and government vessels, they were actively engaged in discussions to secure a general right of free navigation for all vessels across the high seas, the exclusive economic zones, straits used for international navigation and archipelagic waters.[105]

With regard to vessel-source pollution, the military interests succeeded in exempting their vessels from *any* pollution control rules enacted by coastal states even if these rules are consistent with the international conventions to which the vessel's flag state is party. Thus, the LOSC, together with the relevant IMO conventions, explicitly accord sovereign immunity to all military vessels in relation to pollution control.[106] In this regard, the only obligation on flag states is to ensure that their military vessels act in a manner consistent, *so far as is reasonable and practicable*, with the LOSC.[107] Hence, the flag state's application of pollution control rules to their military vessels is a matter of voluntary compliance and good faith. Consequently, such vessels have an effective licence to pollute, and many in fact do engage in intentional marine pollution.[108]

---

[104] On military interests and the sea, see generally R. A. SHINN, THE INTERNATIONAL POLITICS OF MARINE POLLUTION CONTROL 88 (1974) and D. P. O'CONNELL, THE INFLUENCE OF LAW ON SEA POWER (1975).
[105] See Ch. 4. [106] LOSC, art. 236 and MARPOL 73/78, art. 3(3).
[107] LOSC, art. 236 (emphasis added).
[108] See e.g. A. KISS & D. SHELTON, INTERNATIONAL ENVIRONMENTAL LAW 451 (2000); J. S. Dehner, *Vessel-Source Pollution and Public Vessels: Sovereign Immunity v. Compliance – Implications for International Environmental Law*, 9 EMORY INT'L L. REV. 508, at 510 (1995); and W. L. Schachte, Jr., *The Value of the 1982 UN Convention on the Law of the Sea: Preserving Our Freedoms and Protecting the Environment*, in THE MARINE ENVIRONMENT AND SUSTAINABLE DEVELOPMENT: LAW, POLICY AND SCIENCE 105 (A. Couper & E. Gold eds., 1993). On warships and pollution generally, see B. H. Oxman, *The Regime of Warships Under the United Nations Convention on the Law of the Sea*, 24 VA. J. INT'L L. 809 (1984). On the US Navy's compliance practice, see F. J. Yuzon, *Full Speed Ahead: International Law Concerning Marine Pollution and the United States Navy – Steaming Towards State Responsibility and Compliance*, PACE INT'L L. REV. 57, at 97 (1997).

Given modern ecological expectations, the sovereign immunity of military vessels from pollution control rules appears to conflict with the critical need to protect and preserve the marine environment. The relevant international pollution control rules should thus be made applicable to all military vessels even if a coastal state's competence actually to enforce these rules remains unestablished. In other words, the principle of sovereign immunity should be re-assessed in modern times so as to impose international pollution control obligations upon military vessels. While the time may not yet be ripe to endorse coastal state *enforcement* of such standards, the flag states of military and government vessels must at least bear a mandatory (as opposed to voluntary) obligation to prescribe and enforce international standards vis-à-vis these vessels.[109]

2.1.6 The Flag States and Open Registries

The Open Registry Debate. One traditional aspect of the freedom of navigation is the owner's unfettered right to choose whichever flag to sail his ship under. Correspondingly, each state has the right to determine its own requirements by which a vessel may be registered in its registry and fly its flag.[110] In this regard, many states open up their ship registries to foreign-owned vessels in order to earn registration revenue. Some states maintain a completely free registry for any shipowner (be this an individual or a body corporate) to register his/its vessel regardless of the owner's nationality or links with that state; hence the term 'open registry'. In turn, a 'flag of convenience'[111] has been defined as the 'the flag of any country allowing the registration of foreign-owned

---

[109] See generally Kiss & Shelton, *supra* note 108 at 451 and Dehner, *supra* note 108 at 522-3.

[110] This was affirmed by the Court of Permanent Arbitration in Muscat Dhows (Fr. v. Gr. Brit.) Hague Ct. Rep. 93 (Perm. Ct. Arb. 1916). See also the US Supreme Court decision in *Lauritzen v. Larsen*, 345 US 571 (1953) and the International Tribunal for the Law of the Sea (ITLOS) decision in *The M/V 'Saiga' (No. 2)* Case (St. Vincent v. Guinea), 1999 ITLOS No. 2, 79; 38 I.L.M. 1323 (1999). On choice of flag and conflict of laws, see W. Tetley, *The Law of the Flag, 'Flag Shopping' and the Choice of Law*, 17 Tul. Mar. L.J. 175 (1992).

[111] The terms 'open registry' and 'flag of convenience' are used interchangeably. On this topic generally, see the classic works H. Meyers, The Nationality of Ships (1967); B. A. Boczek, Flags of Convenience: An International Legal Study (1962); R. P. Carlisle, Sovereignty for Sale: The Origins and Evolution of the Panamanian and Liberian Flags of Convenience (1981); R. Rienow, The Test of Nationality of a Merchant Vessel (1937); E. D. Naess, The Great PanLibHon Controversy – The Fight over the Flags of Shipping (1972); and N. Singh, Maritime Flag and International Law (1978). See also Organization for Economic Co-Operation and Development, OECD Study on Flags of Convenience (1973), *reprinted in* 4 J. Mar. L. & Com. 231 (1973).

and foreign-controlled vessels under conditions which for whatever the reasons, are convenient and opportune for the persons who are registering the vessels'.[112]

At the other end of the spectrum are the closed registries, which typically register only vessels owned and manned by flag state nationals.[113] In between the extremes, there exist gradations of systems allowing registration based on varying degrees of 'linkage' between the shipowner and the registry in question.[114] Due to domestic political and social factors, the developed maritime states customarily operate closed or semi-closed registries with stringent laws relating to taxation, crew employment conditions and safety and pollution standards. Taken together, these factors substantially raise the overall costs of vessel operation in these states.[115] This led directly to the popularity of open registries among Western shipowners, particularly during the recession that followed the OPEC oil crisis in the 1970s.

What is characteristic about most open registries is the fact that they maintain neither real links with, nor control over, their registered vessels, apart from the purely nominal fact of registration. A large proportion of fleets flagged in open registries today are owned by one-ship companies controlled by interests in the developed countries.[116] From the perspective of shipowners, open registries offer myriad benefits including liberal registration of vessels, low taxes, favourable double taxation arrangements, solid mortgage registration laws, reduced expenditure on safety and environmental standards, access to cheap foreign labour, low crew or wage standards, absence of trade union pressures, corporate confidentiality or anonymity for shipowning interests and general freedom from the control of flag states.[117]

---

[112] BOCZEK, *supra* note 111. See also the definition provided by the Rochdale Report, *infra* note 117.

[113] An example is the US, which has the most stringent registration requirements of any maritime nation, see Anderson, *supra* note 19, at 151.

[114] Some writers use the categories 'open', 'closed' and 'compromise' registries, the last being registries which are intermediate between closed and open registries, see K. X. Li & J. Wonham, *New Developments in Ship Registration*, 14 INT'L J. MARINE & COASTAL L. 137 (1999).

[115] G. K. Sletmo & S. Holste, *Shipping as the Competitive Advantage of Nations: The Role of International Ship Registers*, 20 MAR. POL'Y MGMT. 243, at 245 (1993).

[116] See Table 2-2.

[117] Some of these characteristics are used in the definition of 'flags of convenience' by an influential UK document known as the 'Rochdale Report', HER MAJESTY'S STATIONERY OFFICE, REPORT OF THE COMMITTEE OF INQUIRY INTO SHIPPING, Cmnd. 4337 (1970). The Report refers to characteristics such as ownership and manning by non-nationals, easy access

Among these factors, lower manning and taxation costs remain the primary motivations for 'flagging out'.[118]

The repercussions flowing from the use of liberal open registries are manifold: weak safety records, poor pollution control, unsatisfactory training and crewing conditions and low wages.[119] The lack of flag state supervision over safety and pollution standards is often identified to be a main cause of accidental collisions involving open registry fleets.[120] Equally alarming is the high rate of intentional discharge violations committed by such fleets and their frequent detention by port state control authorities.[121] In this regard, the non-observance of international rules and standards has been shown to translate into concrete competitive advantages for open registry fleets.[122]

Some open registry states are not parties to international instruments governing maritime safety and pollution control. Even if they are parties, these states typically possess little incentive to enforce safety and pollution standards diligently. Due to their significant dependence on registry income, it is often unrealistic to expect these registries – many of them located in developing countries – to prevent and punish violations committed by their clients.[123] Even if these states were pre-disposed

---

to and transfer of registry, low and non-locally levied taxes, favourable revenue for the state of registry, and the lack of power and administrative capacity to impose regulations on flag ships. A state need only satisfy some, and not all, of these characteristics to be considered a 'flag of convenience', see E. Duruigbo, *Multinational Corporations and Compliance with International Regulations Relating to the Petroleum Industry*, 7 ANN. SURV. INT'L & COMP. L. 101, at 112 (2001).

[118] Manning appears to be largest cost item, see M. WILLINGALE, SHIP MANAGEMENT 44–9 (1998).

[119] E. GOLD, MARITIME TRANSPORT: THE EVOLUTION OF INTERNATIONAL MARINE POLICY AND SHIPPING LAW 268 (1981). See also E. Osieke, *Flags of Convenience Vessels: Recent Developments*, 73 AM. J. INT'L L. 604 (1979) and E. DeSombre, *Flags of Convenience and the Implementation of International Environmental, Safety, and Labor Standards at Sea*, 37 INT'L POL. 213 (2000).

[120] The correlation between open registry flags and casualty/pollution rates is demonstrated by works such as B. N. METAXAS, FLAG OF CONVENIENCE: A STUDY OF INTERNATIONALISATION (1985) and S. R. TOLOFARI, OPEN REGISTRY SHIPPING: A COMPARATIVE STUDY OF COSTS AND FREIGHT RATES (1989). See, however, the view that many open registries have modern, well-maintained fleets complying with IMO safety rules, M. McConnell, '... *Darkening Confusion Mounted Upon Darkening Confusion': The Search for the Elusive Genuine Link*, 16 J. MAR. L. & COM. 365, at 368 (1985). Not all serious vessel accidents have involved convenience flags, e.g. the US-flagged *Exxon Valdez*: see D. F. Matlin, *Re-evaluating the Status of Flags of Convenience Under International Law*, 23 VAND. J. TRANSNAT'L L. 1017 (1991).

[121] See Ch. 5.

[122] ORGANIZATION FOR ECONOMIC CO-OPERATION AND DEVELOPMENT (OECD), NON-OBSERVANCE OF INTERNATIONAL RULES AND STANDARDS: COMPETITIVE ADVANTAGES, OCDE/GD(96)4 (1996), attached to MSC Doc. 66/12/1 (1996).

[123] See e.g. Ademuni-Odeke, *Port State Control and UK Law*, 28 J. MAR. L. & COM. 657 (1997).

to doing so, most vessels flying open registry flags never even sail into or near their flag states. This is because such states are seldom located on major shipping routes or may not have significant ports.[124] Such are the states which have been described as having 'neither the power nor the administrative machinery effectively to impose any government or international regulations'.[125]

Efforts to Phase Out Open Registries. As states possess sovereign immunity from being held liable before the jurisdiction of other states, the international legal system has largely been powerless in taking action against recalcitrant open registries. In the early 1970s, however, some attempts were made to phase out these registries. To this end, the maritime interests in the developed states argued that the open registry system was not in accord with international law, in particular the 1958 Geneva Convention on the High Seas.[126] This convention had required states effectively to exercise jurisdiction and control in administrative, technical and social matters over ships flying their flags based on the existence of a 'genuine link' between the registry and the vessel.[127]

What a 'genuine link' meant was left vague by the Geneva Convention. In particular, it was unclear whether the exercise of effective jurisdiction and control by the flag state was an indispensable element of the 'genuine link', or whether it was independent of the latter.[128] That these uncertainties were left unresolved was not surprising, since the elucidation of the 'genuine link' concept was severely resisted by the open registries, which saw it primarily as an effort to impose nationality requirements on the owning and crewing of ships. In their view, such motives to link the vessel's registration to the nationality of its owners and crew were purely political, designed to

---

[124] See A. V. Lowe, *The Enforcement of Marine Pollution Regulations*, 12 SAN DIEGO L. REV. 624 (1975), P. S. Dempsey & L. Helling, *Oil Pollution by Ocean Vessels – Environmental Tragedy: The Legal Regime of Flags of Convenience, Multilateral Conventions and Coastal States*, 10 DENV. J. INT'L L. & POL'Y 37, at 63 (1980) and Dempsey, *supra* note 4, at 526.

[125] Rochdale Report, *supra* note 117.   [126] 450 U.N.T.S. 82 (in force 30 Sept. 1962).

[127] *Ibid.*, art. 5(1). The concept of a 'genuine link' can be traced to the *Nottebohm* Case (Liech. v. Guat.), 1955 I.C.J. 4, which held that a state could not have legal standing to bring an action on behalf of an individual with whom it had no genuine connection of existence, interests and sentiments.

[128] R. R. Churchill, *The Meaning of the 'Genuine Link' Requirement in Relation to the Nationality of Ships*, A Report for the International Transport Workers' Federation, at 20 (2000), *available at* http://www.oceanlaw.net/hedley/pubs/ITF-Oct2000.pdf (last accessed 2 Nov. 2004).

curb the re-flagging of ships from the more costly registries of the traditional maritime states to the open registries.

In the years that followed the 1958 Geneva Conference, state practice and scholarly opinion on the conditions necessary for the granting of nationality to ships proved to be extremely diverse, with little consensus emerging on the meaning of a 'genuine link'. That said, most writers agree that a mere administrative act such as registration is, in itself, insufficient to constitute a 'genuine link'.[129] There is also agreement that the effective exercise of jurisdiction and control constitutes an essential, though not the sole, criterion of a 'genuine link'.[130] At the same time, there is strong authority for the view that a vessel's lack of a 'genuine link' with a flag state does not entitle another state to refuse recognition of the vessel's nationality and the validity of its registration.[131] In fact, such entitlement to refuse recognition for lack of a 'genuine link' had been proposed by the International Law Commission's draft articles for the 1958 Convention, but the relevant provision was ultimately omitted in both the 1958 and 1982 Conventions.[132]

Whatever the meaning and content of the 'genuine link' requirement and the consequences of its absence for flag states, there is evidence to suggest that the requirement has, since the days of its inception, become progressively side-stepped and inconsequential. In an advisory opinion given in 1960, the International Court of Justice (ICJ) ruled that

---

[129] See e.g. conclusion of Churchill, *ibid.* at 69, after surveying the literature. For the view that the sole test of a vessel's nationality is its registration and that any attempt to define a 'genuine link' would only impede competition and create instability in the shipping industry, see e.g. McDougal & Burke, *supra* note 65, Boczek, *supra* note 111 and M. S. McDougal et al., *The Maintenance of Public Order at Sea and the Nationality of Ships*, 54 Am. J. Int'l L. 25 (1960).

[130] Churchill, *supra* note 128 at 38 and 70.

[131] M/V 'Saiga' (No. 2), *supra* note 110; G. Walker & J. Noyes, *Definitions for the 1982 Law of the Sea Convention*, 32 Cal. W. Int'l L. J. 343, at 381 (2002); M. Tomczak, *Defining Marine Pollution: A Comparison of Definitions Used by International Conventions*, 8 Marine Pol'y 311 (1984); and S. W. Tache, *The Nationality of Ships: The Definitional Controversy and Enforcement of Genuine Link*, 16 Int'l Lawyer 301, at 305 (1982). Note, however, the view that non-recognition is not necessarily prohibited, and that the burden of proving that the link is not genuine lies on the state refusing recognition, see Meyers, *supra* note 111, at 282. For the view that some consequences must follow in the absence of a genuine link, lest the requirement in the LOSC serves no purpose, see Churchill, *supra* note 128. at 39 and 51.

[132] Churchill, *supra* note 128. at 20, citing the opposition of Liberia, Panama, the US and West Germany to the provision's inclusion. The proponents of a stringent 'genuine link' test included Norway, the Netherlands and the UK.

in determining which states were the 'largest shipowning nations' for the purpose of election to IMCO bodies, an objective test based on pure registered tonnage was to be used, as opposed to factors suggestive of a 'genuine link' such as beneficial ownership by nationals of a state.[133] This decision greatly favoured the open registry system and was widely interpreted as signalling a major shift away from the 'genuine link' requirement.[134]

In the 1970s, following several catastrophic accidents involving open registry fleets, the maritime states invited the Secretariat of the United Nations Conference on Trade and Development (UNCTAD) to look into the matter, a step which these states were to regret later. UNCTAD, apparently quick to recognise a fruitful new area of work for itself, agreed that the open registry system should be dismantled as it adversely affected shipowners – especially those in the developing countries – who did not enjoy the benefits of that facility.[135]

By the mid-1970s, however, the onset of the OPEC-induced oil crisis had led to a severe oversupply of tonnage, depressed freight rates and increased bunker and operational costs. 'Flagging out' to less costly registries became even more attractive to shipowners in the developed states and by extension, their respective governments. Hence, the brakes were swiftly applied on the momentum to phase out open registries. On its part, however, UNCTAD was not to be deterred. The 1970s was an unsettling period during which the Group of 77 (G77)

---

[133] Constitution of the Maritime Safety Committee of IMCO Case, 1960 I.C.J. 150. The advisory opinion was sought after Liberia and Panama failed to be elected to the Maritime Safety Committee (MSC). The majority of the IMCO Assembly had felt that these two states' registered tonnage alone did not qualify them to be considered as 'largest shipowning nations' under art. 28 of the IMCO Convention, which laid out the criteria for election to the MSC. However, the ICJ felt differently. For a critique, see K. R. Simmonds, *The Constitution of the Maritime Safety Committee of IMCO*, 12 INT'L & COMP. L. Q. 56, at 83–6 (1963).

[134] McConnell, *supra* note 120, at 378 and H. W. Wefers Bettink, *Open Registry, the Genuine Link and the 1986 Convention on Registration Conditions for Ships*, 18 NETH. Y.B. INT'L L. 68, at 87 (1987). In a series of decisions involving fisheries quota-hopping between flags, the European Court of Justice has also swung away from the 'genuine link' concept by emphasising instead the state in which the vessel is registered, see e.g. Case C-221/89, *R v. Secretary of State for Transport, ex parte Factortame Ltd.*, 1991 E.C.R. I-3905; Case C-246/89, *Commission v. United Kingdom*, 1991 E.C.R. I-4585; Case C-286/90, *Anklagemyndigheden v. Peter Michael Poulsen and Diva Navigation Corp.*, 1992 E.C.R. I-6019; Case C-280/89, *Commission v. Ireland*, 1992 E.C.R. I-6185 and Case C-62/96, *Commission v. Greece*, 1997 E.C.R. I-6725. On these cases, see Churchill, *supra* note 128, at 27–33.

[135] On UNCTAD's interest in the issue, see I. M. Sinan, *UNCTAD and Flags of Convenience*, 18 J. WORLD TRADE L. 95 (1984).

caucus of developing countries had launched scathing attacks on the inequities of the prevailing global order. Sovereignty over natural resources was being pursued at the UN General Assembly and a great battle was emerging over deep seabed and other ocean resources at the Third UNCLOS Conference. The majority of developing countries which did not benefit from open registries were thus adamant in phasing them out.

After more than a decade of protracted discussions, the UN General Assembly, dominated as it was by the developing states, decided to convene a conference of governments in 1986 to consider the adoption of a multilateral instrument on the matter. By that time, though, a change of mood had become discernible. In particular, the rhetoric of the radical developing states had subsided together with their fervent call for a New International Economic Order (NIEO). Developing states were beginning to embrace market policies for greater integration into the global economic theatre.

On its part, the 1982 LOSC had been successfully negotiated. The 'genuine link' concept was duly reaffirmed in the convention but again, without the benefit of a workable definition.[136] By this time too, the focus had clearly shifted from the nationality of ships and the 'genuine link' between vessels and states to the actual, substantive duties of flag states to exercise effective jurisdiction and control over their ships. Hence, the rights and duties of the flag states were highlighted by the LOSC, as were those of the coastal and port states.[137] The 'genuine link' requirement thus became increasingly sidelined.

Amidst these changes, the zeal for the complete phasing out of open registries gradually dissipated. As a result, the conference which met to adopt the 1986 UN Convention on Conditions for the Registration of Ships (hereinafter 'UNCCRS')[138] failed to make headway in clarifying

---

[136] LOSC, arts. 91 and 94(1). The formulation in the 1982 LOSC differed only in respect of the 'effective exercise of jurisdiction and control' clause being separated from art. 91's 'genuine link' and shifted to art. 94(1) (which outlines the duties of the flag state). Academic opinions suggest that this alteration effected no legal change to the meaning of the 'genuine link', see e.g. Churchill, *supra* note 128, at 46-7 and 55 and McConnell, *supra* note 120, at 381-2. See also 3 UNITED NATIONS CONVENTION ON THE LAW OF THE SEA 1982: A COMMENTARY (S. N. Nandan et al. eds., 1995), at 108, 144 and 150.

[137] LOSC, arts. 211, 217, 218 and 220.

[138] 26 I.L.M. 1229 (1987) (not in force). For critiques, see e.g. G. C. Kasoulides, *The 1986 United Nations Convention for the Conditions for the Registration of Vessels and the Question of Open Registry*, 20 OCEAN DEV. & INT'L L. 543 (1989); G. Marston, *The UN Convention on Registration of Ships*, 20 J. WORLD TRADE L. 575 (1986); M. McConnell, *'Business as*

the concept of a 'genuine link'. The convention itself shied away from defining a 'genuine link' but instead enumerated compromise criteria for the ownership and manning of a vessel by the registering state's nationals.[139]

The fact that flag states had great latitude under the UNCCRS to determine the extent of involvement by their nationals in ownership and manning represented a significant watering-down of the convention. In particular, states are free under the UNCCRS to determine the 'level of participation' by its nationals in the equity ownership of vessels.[140] In addition, only a '*satisfactory* part of [the vessel's] complement' need be nationals of the flag state.[141] Furthermore, states could choose to comply with either one (and not necessarily both) of the twin requirements of ownership and manning.[142] In relation to manning, states are also permitted to have regard to limiting factors such as the availability of qualified seafarers from these states and the sound and economically viable operation of their ships.[143] Moreover, compliance with the crew nationality requirement need not even be ship-specific, i.e. the ratio of nationals to non-nationals can be adhered to on an overall company or fleet basis.[144] In sum, these provisions effectively meant that many vessels could *still* be owned and manned by foreign non-flag state nationals.

These in-built weaknesses represented significant pathologies in the UNCCRS's regime-building process. In essence, the proponents of the open registry system succeeded in implanting a wide measure of flexibility for flag state registration, thereby defeating efforts to entrench a proper link between ships and their flag states. In effect, the convention ended up legitimising the concept of an open registry by spelling out the conditions for its regulation.[145] What was telling was that there was absolutely no mention of eliminating or phasing out open registries.

As of July 2005, the UNCCRS was still not in force. Indeed, it does not appear likely that the convention will ever enter into force, since so few states have shown interest in it. In retrospect, the convention can be

---

Usual': An Evaluation of the 1986 UNCCRS, 18 J. Mar. L. & Com. 435 (1986); and S. G. Sturmey, *The United Nations Convention on Conditions for Registration of Ships*, Lloyd's Mar. & Comm. L. Q. 97 (1987).

[139] UNCCRS, arts. 8 and 9, on ownership and manning respectively.
[140] UNCCRS, art. 8.   [141] UNCCRS, art. 9 (emphasis added).
[142] UNCCRS, art. 7, providing that states can choose to comply with either art. 8 or art. 9.
[143] UNCCRS, art. 9(2)(a)–(c).   [144] UNCCRS, art. 9(3).
[145] McConnell, *supra* note 138, at 449.

assailed as having been a failure.[146] Clearly, despite repeated efforts to restrict or regulate their activities, open registries persist up to this day. In fact, they remain hugely popular and show few signs of retreat, reflecting the continuing desire of the shipping community for low operating costs and flexible regulation.

Rather than reiterating the 'genuine link' requirement, recent regulatory developments have instead turned on tightening the obligations of flag states to prescribe and enforce regulations for their flag vessels, as well as enhancing port state control procedures.[147] On the whole, these efforts promise more effective exercise of jurisdiction and control over ships than do attempts to define the nebulous 'genuine link' between vessels and flags.[148] Through this broader approach, a wider array of flexible policy instruments can be fashioned to respond to the diverse individual issues posed by the open registry system such as safety, pollution control, security and fisheries management.[149]

Thus, the emphasis on the jurisdiction of flag, coastal and port states in the LOSC, taken together with developments such as the establishment of the Flag State Implementation (FSI) Sub-Committee[150] within IMO, the introduction of the International Safety Management (ISM) Code,[151] the advent of numerous port state control arrangements worldwide[152] and the adoption of IMO's 'White List' certification system for vessel crewing standards[153] have all turned the international community's attention away from the troublesome nationality requirements to the substantive challenge of overcoming sub-standard shipping and the lack of enforcement. Recent legal instruments relating to

---

[146] Sturmey, *supra* note 138, at 106, KASOULIDES, *supra* note 22, at 75 and McConnell, supra note 138.

[147] J. A. Roach, *Alternatives for Achieving Flag State Implementation and Quality Shipping*, in CURRENT MARITIME ISSUES AND THE INTERNATIONAL MARITIME ORGANISATION 151 (M. H. Nordquist & J. N. Moore eds., 1999).

[148] Commentary by Noyes, *in* Walker & Noyes, *supra* note 131, at 381-2.

[149] A. G. Oude Elferink, *The Genuine Link Concept: Time for a Post Mortem?*, Netherlands Institute for the Law of the Sea Paper (1999), *available at* http://www.uu.nl/content/genuine%20link.pdf (last accessed 2 Nov. 2004).

[150] The FSI meets annually and is charged with assessing governments' implementation of IMO conventions for safety and pollution prevention. The analysis on compliance in Ch. 5 draws substantially from state reports to FSI.

[151] The Code was adopted by IMO Assembly Resolution A.741(18) of 4 November 1993 and made mandatory under Chapter IX of SOLAS 74. It came into effect in stages – the initial phase covering certain classes of ships became effective on 1 July 1998, and the final phase on 1 July 2002.

[152] See Ch. 5.

[153] Pursuant to the 1995 Protocol to the 1978 STCW Convention, *infra* note 213.

fisheries management also support a trend toward imposing detailed obligations on flag states of fishing vessels to exercise regulation over their vessels, as opposed to spelling out conditions to be satisfied for the registration of fishing vessels and the 'genuine link' between vessels and their registries.[154]

These developments are to be welcomed. The reality of the matter is that the open registry issue is not a simple juridical problem which can be wished away by a legal formula such as the 'genuine link' requirement. Rather, it is a complex political and economic phenomenon which has its roots in the underlying dynamics of the global maritime trading system. To the extent that shipowners, charterers and cargo owners persist in employing cheaper ships registered in open registries to save on costs, the problem with such registries will never fully be eradicated. Neither is it realistic to expect the open registry system to be abolished. The issue thus goes far beyond the lack of a 'genuine link' between vessels and states of registry. Indeed, the solution to the vessel safety and marine pollution problems is not the phasing out of open registries, but the creation of market disincentives for sub-standard shipping through the tightening of flag state and port state enforcement obligations.[155]

That said, continued criticism has actually led to pressure being imposed on operators and registries to improve on standards, particularly in relation to safety and pollution control.[156] Similarly, cargo owners have been pressured to adopt a more responsible attitude toward chartering vessels. The oil industry actors, for instance, have adopted a voluntary policy of inspecting vessels at their terminals pursuant to the Ship Inspection Report Exchange (SIRE) vetting programme. The stated aim of the oil industry is to refrain from chartering black-listed vessels flagged in questionable registries.

Classification societies are also under tremendous pressure to tighten their survey and certification procedures. On their part, the marine

---

[154] See the 1993 Food and Agriculture Organization (FAO) Agreement to Promote Compliance with International Conservation and Management Measures by Fishing Vessels on the High Seas, 33 I.L.M. 968 (1994) (in force 24 Apr. 2003) and the 1995 UN Agreement for the Implementation of the Provisions of the UN Convention on the Law of the Sea relating to the Conservation and Management of Straddling Fish Stocks and Highly Migratory Fish Stocks, UN Doc. A/CONF.164/37, 34 I.L.M. 1542 (1995) (in force 11 Dec. 2001). At FAO, efforts to concentrate on registration and the 'genuine link' were abandoned after the Organization realised the minefield that this could pose, see Churchill, *supra* note 128, at 64.
[155] See Ch. 7.   [156] McConnell, *supra* note 120, at 368.

insurers are being urged to charge higher premia for less reputable owners and to refrain from insuring sub-standard vessels. Given the current attention being paid to maritime security, there is every indication that whatever improvements effected in terms of increased ship-owning transparency may lead to incidental positive effects for vessel safety and marine pollution control. In any event, the issue of open registries is nowadays highlighted not so much by international organisations such as IMO or UNCTAD, but by national port state control authorities and seafarers' unions such as the International Transport Workers' Federation (ITF).[157]

Overall, the emphasis in recent years – even that of ITF – has shifted from flags of convenience to sub-standard shipping *in general*, irrespective of the flags which vessels fly. This is timely given that many sub-standard ships are today registered in national registries such as Albania, Algeria and Bolivia. In any case, most flags in the world today, including those of the developed countries, allow foreign ownership to some extent or other. In that sense, most flags can be regarded as offering 'convenience', the difference being only one of degree. Hence, the distinction today ought simply to be between responsible and sub-standard flags.

Where then does that leave the concept of the 'genuine link'? Given the enduring popularity of open registries, state practice in the last few decades does not support the proposition that a genuine link (whatever its meaning) is a precondition for a state's registration of a vessel.[158] Neither does the absence of a 'genuine link' (or a perceived lack of effective exercise of jurisdiction and control) lead to a loss of nationality or entitle other states to withhold recognition of the vessel's nationality.[159] Rather, what the 'genuine link' requirement amounts to is a

---

[157] On ITF and convenience shipping, see H. R. NORTHRUP & R. L. ROWAN, THE INTERNATIONAL TRANSPORT WORKERS' FEDERATION AND FLAG OF CONVENIENCE SHIPPING (1983) and H. R. Northrup & P. B. Scrase, *The International Transport Workers' Federation Flag of Convenience Shipping Campaign: 1983-95*, 23 U. DENV. TRANSP. L. J. 369 (1996). ITF regularly boycotts ships flagged in open registries in order to force owners to accept agreements (evidenced by so-called 'Blue Certificates') which guarantee ITF wage stipulations and other conditions of employment. Some observers feel that ITF policies ignore the comparative cost advantages of developing countries and will only price the labour supply of these countries out of the international market, see Anderson, *supra* note 19, at 166.

[158] See M/V Saiga (No. 2), supra note 110.

[159] *Ibid.* at para. 83, where the ITLOS concluded that the purpose of the genuine link requirement is to secure more effective implementation of flag state duties, and 'not to establish criteria by reference to which the validity of the registration of ships in a flag

duty of supervision and implementation of standards *resulting from* the grant of nationality,[160] the breach of which must entail some *other* form of legal consequence.

In other words, an obligation arises to exercise effective jurisdiction and control over flag vessels subsequent to, and independent of, registration. A flag state must thus be in a position to exercise effective jurisdiction and control over a ship at the time that it grants nationality to that ship.[161] A breach of this obligation invites *neither* a nullification of registration nor non-recognition by other states, but a host of other consequences such as flag state responsibility, IMO admonition and even a possible denial of flag state enjoyment of rights or benefits.[162] That flag state responsibility is, in practice, difficult to invoke and seek reparation for in event of a breach are separate matters for which the international community is still devising remedies, e.g. more responsive flag state action, IMO action through the FSI Sub-Committee, market differentiation of quality flags and port state inspections and detentions.

The Changing Face of Ship Registration. What is striking today is how the open registry phenomenon has achieved far greater sophistication than in the past. The attractiveness of maintaining a cheaper off-shore fleet is every bit as relevant today as it was in the 1970s. In the face of the backlash against the traditional open registries, many developed states created new forms of registries: the so-called 'off-shore', 'dependent' or 'captive' registries. These are commonly located in small overseas territories, possessions or colonies of the parent country. Examples are the Canary Islands and Bermudan registries operated by Spain and the UK respectively.

Vessels on an off-shore registry typically fly the same flag as the parent country or a local variant of it but come under the favourable maritime laws and taxation framework of the off-shore registry.

---

state may be challenged by other states'. See also the ITLOS decision in the '*Grand Prince*' Case (Belize v. Fr.), 2001 ITLOS No. 8.

[160] See *Commission v. Hellenic Republic, supra* note 134, opinion of Advocate General Tesauro, at para. 13.

[161] Churchill, *supra* note 128, at 72.

[162] *Ibid.* at 56 and 72, citing B. H. Oxman & V. Bantz, *Case Note on the Saiga Case*, 94 AM. J. INT'L L. 140, at 149 (2000) for the proposition that there is an emerging tendency to link the enjoyment of rights to the performance of related duties. Thus, a flag state's failure to comply with its duty to ensure a genuine link between itself and its ships would have the consequence of denying that state the right to exercise rights in respect of such ships, including, for instance, the right to exercise diplomatic protection.

Usually, these registries are reserved for the exclusive use of ships owned by nationals of the parent country. They may also be open to ships owned abroad, in which case they function no differently from open registries except that they are not registries of independent states.

Another variant of the open registry theme relates specifically to ships on bareboat charters. Such charters allow a ship to fly the flag of another state temporarily (typically, a cheaper flag of the charterer's choice) while remaining on its original registry. This flexibility is consistent with the nature of a bareboat charter, which accords the charterer maximum control over the operation of the ship. Critically, such parallel or dual registration arrangements allow the bareboat charterer to enjoy the economic advantages of operating under the cheaper temporary flag while retaining the owner's benefits associated with the original flag, such as registration of mortgages.[163] In such situations, registries offering parallel registration to bareboat charterers are mostly indistinguishable from open registries.

Another common phenomenon similar to off-shore registries is the arrangement known as the 'second', 'internal' or 'international' registries. These are typically found in the developed countries and are maintained as a subset of the national registry. Ships on the second registry fly the same flag and enjoy the same nationality as those on the national registry. However, they are subject to a wholly separate regime of maritime laws including the all-critical lower taxation structure and more liberal rules on employing foreign crew. Frequently, these registries allow foreign ownership, in which case they function no differently from the open registries.

In essence, the second registries aim to stem the flight of national vessels to open registries elsewhere (or to entice them back) as well as to attract foreign-owned vessels. At the same time, they seek to preserve the waning maritime heritage of the developed states. The Norwegian, Danish and German International Ship Registers, Kerguelen (France), Madeira (Portugal), Luxembourg (for Belgian ships) and the Isle of Man (UK) are among the notable examples of such registries or variants thereof.

By and large, the 'second' registries have not allowed themselves to be patronised by sub-standard ships. The objectives of such registries and the states which created them have been clear from the outset: lower taxation and crewing costs but not lax safety and pollution control

---

[163] See generally ADEMUNI-ODEKE, BAREBOAT CHARTER (SHIP) REGISTRATION (1998).

measures. Yet, despite their relatively good safety and pollution records, 'second' registries have been frequently criticised for their liberal crew employment policies. In this regard, merchant fleets from the developed states have long encountered problems of high costs relating to crew wages, highly unionised labour and dwindling pools of seafaring nationals.[164] The instrumentality of the second registry is thus meant to offer the operator the facility to hire seafarer labour from developing countries at non-OECD rates. Of course, this has incurred the displeasure of maritime unions in the developed states which have gone as far as to call for boycotts on vessels registered under second registries.

In the past decade or so, there have been indications that the developed maritime states are actively seeking to entice tonnage back to their main national registries over and above promoting their second registries. Thus, countries such as Norway, the Netherlands, Germany and the UK have adopted favourable tonnage-based taxation regimes in order to encourage 're-flagging' to the national flag. Preliminary results have been encouraging – several owners have returned to their national flags with more promising to do the same. The return of ships to developed state registries has its benefits for shipowners, since it means that the developed states would henceforth have greater incentives to advance shipowner interests at international regulatory fora. Hitherto, the small size of national registries in the developed states has meant that owners wielded little influence over the policies of developed state governments as compared to the environmentalists.

In terms of tonnage registration, the largest of the open registries today are Panama, Liberia, the Bahamas, Malta and Cyprus.[165] Panama alone accounts for over 20 per cent of global tonnage. In the past decade, the traditional giants – Panama and Liberia – have been progressively losing market share to new entrants such as the Bahamas, Malta, Cyprus, the Marshall Islands, Vanuatu and Belize. What is astonishing is the increasing number of unlikely states peddling their services as open registries. These include landlocked states, such as Bolivia and Mongolia, as well as states with little maritime history or capacity, such as Mauritius, Cambodia, the Seychelles, Samoa and Equatorial Guinea.

---

[164] It has been estimated that a ship flying the US flag faces 70 per cent higher operating costs, 90 per cent higher labour costs and 100 per cent higher repair costs compared to one flying a flag of convenience, see M. Boos, *The Oil Pollution Act of 1990: Striking the Flags of Convenience?*, 2 COLO. J. INT'L ENVTL. L. & POL'Y 407, at 411 (1991).

[165] See Table 2-1.

Their level of vigilance in supervising flag vessels remains highly questionable.[166]

In terms of interest politics, the open registry states are generally united in their promotion of freedom of navigation and their resistance to increased regulation. In addition, these states frequently campaign against the perceived discriminatory practices of port state control inspectors who traditionally target ships registered in open registries. The behaviour and positions of open registry states at international fora are invariably dictated by the profile of their shipowning clientele. Thus, the Liberian flag typically reflects the interests of its large American shipowning base, just as Cyprus and Malta customarily espouse Greek shipowning views. On their part, Panama has a high proportion of Japanese-owned ships while the Bahamas counts Greek, Norwegian and American interests as its largest clients.

Due to the increasing environmental emphasis in the shipping world, open registry states have generally been compelled to tighten supervision over their flag vessels.[167] Thus, the biggest of these registries such as Panama, Liberia and the Bahamas have publicly agreed that flag states must lead the campaign against sub-standard shipping. The pressure to exhibit greater environmental responsibility has come from the shipowners themselves, many of whom recognise the perils of negative publicity in the event that their ships are involved in gross accidents or pollution incidents.

That said, it is to be noted that ships registered in the open registries continue to feature highly on the lists of port state control detentions worldwide.[168] The correlation between low standards and open registries continues to be made, with some studies showing that a flag state with the worst accident record suffers more than 100 times more losses than a flag state with the best record.[169] In essence, enough substandard owners and operators exist to continue providing business to the less scrupulous registries. The problem is greatly exacerbated by the

---

[166] See the detention statistics of the various Port State Control MOUs, Ch. 5.
[167] McConnell, *supra* note 120, at 368. For the view that many open registries are today efficient and vigilant in ensuring compliance with rules, see N. Howe, *ITLOS – A Practitioner's Perspective, in* Nordquist & Moore eds., *supra* note 9, at 159.
[168] See Ch. 5 and the tables therein analysing the performance of the open registries. See also D. M. Dzidzornu, *Coastal State Obligations and Powers Respecting EEZ Environmental Protection Under Part XII of the UNCLOS: A Descriptive Analysis*, 8 Colo. J. Int'l Envtl. L. & Pol'y 283, at 310 (1997), maintaining that these states continue to be recalcitrant or ineffective in enforcing anti-pollution standards.
[169] 3 IMO News 1 (1993).

fact that owners can freely engage in 'flag-hopping' and change their vessels' nationality at any time.[170]

The problem of open registries has also manifested itself in the fisheries industry. The effectiveness of many international and regional fisheries management agreements is currently being undermined by the practice of owners flagging vessels in states (usually open registries) which are not parties to such agreements. In this way, these vessels, which are typically owned and controlled by interests within state parties to the agreements, are able to circumvent whatever fishing quotas that are otherwise applicable to them.[171] The problem is currently being tackled by the Food and Agriculture Organization (FAO), which has approached it from the broader perspective of illegal, unreported and unregulated (IUU) fishing.[172]

In the aftermath of the terrorist attacks of 11 September 2001, the issue of maritime security has become a huge priority in the shipping world. In particular, there have been moves to re-assess the role of flags of convenience and to investigate if these flags may be used to disguise the commercial operations of terrorist groups. There are also moves to prevent the registration of 'phantom ships' – ships which are registered on the basis of false or inaccurate information and which are often implicated in ship hijack, piracy and armed robbery cases.[173] Plans are also afoot to tighten the procedures relating to a ship's transfer of flag and class.[174] There are thus indications that the use of flags of convenience or open registries will once again come under international scrutiny, even though the prospects for their total elimination remain unlikely.

Tables 2-1 and 2-2 below reflect the largest merchant fleets in recent times based on flag and nationality of owner.

2.1.7 States with Maritime Interests

The developed states have traditionally dominated the ship transportation industry through their vast interests in the shipowning, cargo-owning,

---

[170] Matlin, *supra* note 120, at 1021–40.
[171] See generally P. Birnie, *Reflagging of Fishing Vessels on the High Seas*, 2 RECIEL 270 (1993) and CHURCHILL & LOWE, *supra* note 26, at 260.
[172] See B. Vukas & D. Vidas, *Flags of Convenience and High Seas Fishing: The Emergence of a Legal Framework*, in GOVERNING HIGH SEAS FISHERIES: THE INTERPLAY OF GLOBAL AND REGIONAL REGIMES 53 (O. Stokke ed., 2001) and D. Warner-Kramer, *Control Begins at Home: Tackling Flags of Convenience and IUU Fishing*, 34 GOLDEN GATE U. L. REV. 497 (2004).
[173] IMO Assembly Resolution A.923(22) (2001), *supra* note 81.
[174] See Report of the FSI Sub-Committee's 10th session, FSI Doc. 10/17 (2002).

Table 2-1. *Top Ten Merchant Fleets by Flag (million grt, covering ships of not less than 100 grt)*

1965		1975		1985		1995	
UK	21.7	Liberia	65.7	Liberia	54.4	Panama	62.5
Liberia	18.4	Japan	37.9	Panama	40.4	Liberia	57.4
Norway	15.5	UK	32.1	Japan	37.4	Greece	29.9
Japan.	11.9	Norway	25.8	Greece	29.1	Cyprus	22.8
USA	11.4	Greece	22.4	USSR	17.2	Bahamas	22.6
Italy	8.2	Panama	13.3	USA	16.7	Japan	20.6
USSR	5.9	USSR	12.3	UK	11.9	Norway	19.8
Greece	5.7	USA	11.4	China, PR	10.8	Malta	15.4
Germany	5.4	France	10.3	Norway	10.3	China, PR	14.9
France	5.0	Italy	9.9	Cyprus	9.4	USA	13.2
World	159	World	325	World	386	World	451
2000		2001		2002		2003	
Panama	114.4	Panama	122.4	Panama	124.7	Panama	125.7
Liberia	51.4	Liberia	51.8	Liberia	50.4	Liberia	52.4
Bahamas	31.4	Bahamas	33.4	Bahamas	35.8	Bahamas	34.8
Malta	28.1	Greece	28.7	Greece	28.8	Greece	32.2
Greece	26.4	Malta	27.1	Malta	26.3	Malta	25.1
Cyprus	23.2	Cyprus	22.8	Cyprus	23.0	Singapore	23.2
Singapore	21.5	Singapore	21.0	Singapore	21.1	Cyprus	22.1
Norway	18.7	Norway	19.0	Norway	18.4	Hong Kong	20.6
Japan	16.5	China, PR	16.7	China, PR	17.3	China, PR	18.4
China, PR	15.3	Japan	14.6	Hong Kong	16.2	Marshall Islands	17.6
World	558	World	575	World	585	World	605

insurance underwriting, classification, shipbuilding and other maritime-related industries. To varying degrees, these states include the US, Japan and most Western European countries, particularly the UK, Norway, Germany, the Netherlands, Greece, Italy, France, Sweden and Denmark.

The US is a dominant player by virtue of its economic might. As a primary producer, importer and consumer of petroleum,[175] the US also has the majority of the world's biggest oil-producing companies. Hence, in terms of cargo-owning interests, US influence is unparalleled. Given its size and complexity, the US is an extremely diverse entity with varied domestic interests and public opinions constantly jostling for the

---

[175] The US alone accounts for some 25 per cent of world oil consumption, see INTERTANKO, *supra* note 14, at 53.

Table 2-2. Top Twenty Merchant Fleets by Nationality of Owner (million grt, covering ships of not less than 1000 grt)

1999		2000		2001		2002		2003	
Greece	80.8	Greece	84.9	Greece	86.7	Greece	89.5	Greece	91.1
Japan	70.6	Japan	69.2	Japan	71.6	Japan	73.3	Japan	77.1
Norway	38.3	Norway	39.7	Unknown	41.6	Norway	39.6	Norway	36.7
USA	35.9	USA	31.9	Norway	41.5	USA	30.7	Germany	36.4
China, PR	26.9	China, PR	26.5	USA	30.9	Germany	30.5	USA	34.5
Germany	23.2	Germany	25.1	Germany	28.6	China, PR	28.6	China, PR	30.6
Hong Kong	20.0	Hong Kong	20.1	China, PR	27.2	Hong Kong	21.4	Hong Kong	17.5
Korea, Rep.	17.5	Korea, Rep.	17.4	Hong Kong	20.4	Korea, Rep.	17.1	Korea, Rep.	16.8
UK	15.5	UK	14.6	Korea, Rep.	17.1	UK	15.1	Taiwan	15.3
Russia	15.4	Russia	13.8	UK	15.2	Taiwan	15.0	UK	15.2
Taiwan	13.4	Denmark	13.6	Taiwan	14.8	Russia	13.8	Singapore	14.4
Singapore	12.7	Singapore	13.2	Russia	13.4	Denmark	12.8	Russia	13.9
Denmark	11.8	Taiwan	13.0	Denmark	13.0	Singapore	12.0	Denmark	12.8
Sweden	10.8	Italy	9.7	Singapore	11.1	Italy	10.1	Italy	10.7
Italy	10.4	Sweden	8.0	Italy	10.2	India	6.4	India	7.4
India	7.6	India	7.2	India	7.1	S. Arabia	6.1	Malaysia	7.3
Turkey	6.7	S. Arabia	5.9	Sweden	6.7	Sweden	6.1	Switzerland	6.7
S. Arabia	6.5	Turkey	5.6	Turkey	5.9	Turkey	5.8	S. Arabia	6.7
Panama	6.2	Switzerland	5.3	S. Arabia	5.7	Malaysia	5.6	Turkey	5.6
Brazil	5.2	Netherlands	4.8	Malaysia	5.5	Netherlands	5.5	Sweden	5.5

Source for Tables 2-1 and 2-2: LLOYD'S REGISTER, WORLD FLEET STATISTICS, various years

attention of policy-makers. Many of these interests give rise to lobbies which commonly expound conflicting goals at both the state and federal levels. These include the oil producers, the manufacturing and mining industries and the environmental groups, to name but a few. As such, it would be inaccurate to label the US as a maritime or coastal state alone – often, it is all of these and more.

Due to its unique position, the US is possibly the only country which can afford to impose unilateral laws on ships visiting its ports or even laws with extra-territorial effect without substantially hurting its own interests. Indeed, the propensity for unilateralism has been exhibited on several occasions, leading to the enactment of laws outside the aegis of international agreement. One prominent example is the enactment of the Oil Pollution Act of 1990 (OPA-90) following domestic outcry over the *Exxon Valdez* incident in Alaska. This led directly to the US staying out of the international regime for the compensation of oil pollution victims. Periodic episodes of US unilateralism (or threats thereof) continue to be sources of concern for IMO and other countries.

US shipowning interests used to be large but as with the trend in other developed countries, shipowners have long fled the US flag to register in countries where taxation, manning and other costs are cheaper.[176] The majority of tonnage registered in open registries such as Liberia and the Bahamas are American owned. Hence, even though *direct* US shipowning interests are no longer significant, the US is still very much a dominant shipowning force when beneficial ownership of foreign-flagged vessels is considered. In any event, the domestic US fleet remains substantial for purposes of coastal trade within the US, such trade being exclusively reserved for US-flagged and -crewed vessels under domestic cabotage law.[177]

For its part, the UK retains tremendous influence in the shipping world through its provision of maritime services. The City of London, while having lost its port services a long time ago, retains its historical status as the premier maritime hub for the insurance underwriting industry as well as for dispute settlement services. A great deal of commercial operations relating to the carriage of goods, brokerage, admiralty and insurance continue to be transacted through London, as had been done for centuries.

---

[176] Matlin, *supra* note 120, at 1050.
[177] Section 27, Merchant Marine Act of 1920 (the Jones Act), 46 U.S.C. app. § 883 (2000), 46 C.F.R. § 67.3 (1999).

The presence of IMO in London also accords the UK some prestige and allows it to send large delegations to negotiations, thereby maintaining its influence over maritime matters. Indeed, many of IMO's treaties continue to be initiated by the UK government. In terms of shipowning tonnage, the UK national registry has declined along with those of the other developed countries and no longer features among the top ten in the world. Nevertheless, the continued influence of the City of London and the forces of tradition associated with hallowed institutions such as Lloyd's of London underline the enduring maritime relevance of the UK.

Japan's role in world shipping is significant in view of the size of its economy and the strength of its industrial production. Due to its lack of natural resources, Japan relies heavily on the import of raw materials, much of which is carried by sea.[178] Oil is imported in large volumes from the Middle East and the majority of tankers plying the Indian and Pacific Oceans through the Straits of Malacca and Singapore service the Japanese market. Along with South Korea, Japan is home to a massive shipbuilding industry, which has constructed many of the oil supertankers.[179] With the absence of the US from the international regime for oil pollution liability and compensation, Japan is by far the biggest contributor to the regime's compensatory system based on its proportion of oil receipts. Due to these factors, Japan wields substantial influence at IMO.

Unlike the other developed countries, Japan has maintained its position as one of the largest shipowning states. Apart from the Japanese, an increasing number of major shipowners are today found in Asia, particularly in Taiwan, South Korea, China, Singapore, Hong Kong and India. This has prompted observations that the shipowning world's centre of gravity is gradually shifting to Asia. The Asian owners, together with their home states, are widely known to be discontented by the Eurocentric nature of shipping regulation.[180] Yet these countries have generally not done enough to improve the quality and intensity of their participation at global fora such as IMO. Indeed, Asian influence at IMO remains weak compared with that of the European countries.

The Norwegians continue to be among the world's largest shipowners. In particular, a substantial proportion of the global independent tanker

---

[178] Japan is the world's second largest consumer of oil, see INTERTANKO, *supra* note 14, at 60.
[179] The South Koreans are the world's largest shipbuilders, followed by Japan and China, *ibid.* at 21–5.
[180] Personal interviews.

fleet is owned by Norwegian interests, as are major P&I Clubs such as Gard and Skuld. The Nordic countries are also home to significant maritime industries and services, including the shipbuilding, ship repair and classification sectors. Hence, despite their relatively small size and populations, Norway, Denmark, Sweden and Finland have consistently wielded considerable influence at IMO. The fact that the Nordic states tend to co-ordinate and adopt common positions further strengthens their influence at international fora.

Other influential maritime state actors include Greece, Germany, France, Italy, the Netherlands and Spain. Greek individuals and companies form the largest shipowners in the world, controlling some 20 per cent of the global fleet and 55 per cent of the fleet registered in the European Union.[181] Fifty-five per cent of the entire Greek-owned fleet is flagged in open registries.[182] On their part, the Germans, French and Italians retain considerable influence by virtue of the size of their economies and their cargo-owning interests.

2.2 The Coastal/Environmental Interests

2.2.1 The Environmental Non-Governmental Organisations

In the past few decades, non-governmental organisations (NGOs) with environmental causes have emerged as powerful forces in domestic and international politics. The momentum for environmental activism has grown ever stronger following the convening of the watershed UN Conference on Environment and Development (UNCED – the Rio Summit) in 1992. No government today, particularly in the liberal democracies, can afford to ignore the demands of environmental NGOs. Indeed, the Green parties in Western countries and the votes they command have transformed environmentalism into a potent political force.

In contrast to the environmental groups, the shipowning industry has long lost its political leverage in the developed countries. This is mainly due to the few votes which the industry controls, its lingering reputation as a polluter and the declining ship registries of the developed countries. Not surprisingly, states which at one time identified strongly

---

[181] At the same time, the Greeks are alleged by ITF to be among the most exploitative of owners, see Lloyd's List, *ITF Says Greek Owners Are Among Most Exploitative*, 4 Dec. 1997. For the Greeks' response, see Lloyd's List, *Greek Owners Set to Reject ITF Claims*, 5 Dec. 1997.

[182] Lloyd's List, *Greek Owners Set to Reject ITF Claims*, ibid.

with the corporate maritime cause have now assumed a more proenvironment stance. These states – primarily the Western European countries, the US and Japan – are essentially the politically relevant actors with the resources and expertise to demand effective changes at international regulatory fora.

Together with traditional coastal advocates such as Canada and Australia, these states are currently driving efforts to incorporate more environmental considerations into global maritime regulation. A change in mood is thus discernible at IMO as regime formation processes become increasingly 'greened' by ecological imperatives.[183] For their part, the environmental NGOs have been particularly adept at translating new environmental protection concepts into laws and policies. Several of these concepts have entered the mainstream of contemporary international law and politics; they include the notions of sustainable development, the precautionary approach and the 'polluter pays' principle.

The precautionary approach, as contained in Principle 15 of the Rio Declaration,[184] has been particularly influential in advancing the environmentalist cause. The approach prescribes that where threats of serious or irreversible environmental damage exist, the lack of full scientific certainty shall not be used as a reason for postponing cost-effective measures to prevent environmental degradation. In view of the strong emphasis given by states to the precautionary approach (and the 'polluter pays' principle), it is hardly surprising that the shipping industry is facing intense regulation over its polluting activities. As mentioned earlier, environmental regulation of shipping has moved beyond the traditional issues relating to oil and chemical pollution to concerns such as ship-generated air pollution, ocean dumping, ballast water organisms, anti-fouling paints and ship recycling. In each of these cases, environmentalists seeking regulatory action have succeeded in

---

[183] See generally K. Stairs & P. Taylor, *Non-Governmental Organisations and the Legal Protection of the Oceans: A Case Study*, in THE INTERNATIONAL POLITICS OF THE ENVIRONMENT: ACTORS, INTERESTS AND INSTITUTIONS 110 (A. Hurrell & B. Kingsbury eds., 1992).

[184] UN Doc. A/CONF.151/26 (Vol. I) (1992), 31 I.L.M. 874 (1992). See also para. 17.21 of Agenda 21 and art. 130R of the European Union Treaty, 31 I.L.M. 247 (1992) (in force 1 Nov. 1993). The precautionary approach has also been reflected in regional treaties such as the Helsinki (Baltic) Convention, *infra* note 231 and the amended Barcelona (Mediterranean) Convention, *infra* note 214. On the precautionary approach generally, see THE PRECAUTIONARY PRINCIPLE AND INTERNATIONAL LAW: THE CHALLENGE OF IMPLEMENTATION (D. Freestone & E. Hey eds., 1995).

invoking the precautionary approach to overcome the lack of scientific evidence relating to the seriousness of the problems.

Four major environmental NGOs have been accorded consultative status at IMO. These are Friends of the Earth International (FOEI), Greenpeace International, the World Wide Fund for Nature (WWF) and the International Union for the Conservation of Nature (IUCN). The NGOs are particularly active at the Marine Environment Protection Committee (MEPC), the Legal Committee and the diplomatic conferences convened by IMO. They are usually represented by interested scientists, academics or volunteer experts who aim to contribute environmental perspectives to discussions which they perceive to be otherwise dictated by purely commercial or industrial concerns. Due to their lack of financial and manpower resources, however, the NGOs have had to be issue-selective in their participation at IMO meetings. This has compromised their effectiveness to a fair extent.

2.2.2 Public Opinion and Media Reaction

Closely aligned to NGO activism is media reporting of catastrophic ship pollution incidents. Many marine pollution initiatives undertaken at international fora have been the direct result of domestic reaction to specific pollution incidents.[185] In almost all cases, popular opinion has been shaped by adverse media reports and images of spilled pollutants, contaminated beaches and soiled seabirds and wildlife. In some instances, media reporting has been sensational and lacking in accuracy and objectivity. This is largely due to the lack of specialist shipping correspondents in the mainstream media who are familiar with the nature of the shipping trade or the technical consequences of oil spills. Thus, the media often neglects to report that only a minuscule percentage of oil carried by sea ends up being spilled in accidents or that the environmental effects of many spills may only be temporary.

At the same time, less attention seems to have been paid to the loss of non-tanker merchant ships such as bulk carriers, often with crew casualties.[186] Such are the unfortunate realities in an environment where domestic concerns often take priority over events occurring elsewhere and affecting 'other people'. In sum, public perceptions are

---

[185] See E. Gold, *Learning from Disaster: Lessons in Regulatory Enforcement in the Maritime Sector*, 8 RECIEL 16 (1999), MITCHELL, *supra* note 68, at 108 and Hare, *supra* note 22, at 573.

[186] Hare, *ibid.* at 574–5. A large proportion of seamen serving on board merchant ships today are from developing countries such as the Philippines and India, see WILLINGALE, *supra* note 118, at 203–11.

all-powerful in the modern environmental age, particularly within a domestic political context. Hence, it can only be in the interest of states and industry to manage public opinion to their advantage and to present a responsible face to an increasingly pro-environment world populace.

The first tanker catastrophe to capture public attention through media agitation was the grounding of the *Torrey Canyon* off the coast of Cornwall, UK in 1967. The huge damage claims which arose out of the accident were unparalleled. A large proportion of the claims could not be settled and this resulted in the widespread belief that an international compensatory scheme had to be urgently crafted to deal with similar accidents in the future. These concerns led to the creation of IMO's Legal Committee and the adoption of global instruments on liability and compensation for oil pollution victims.[187] The UK's aerial bombing of the *Torrey Canyon* wreck also inspired the adoption of a convention which permitted coastal states to take action against foundering vessels on the high seas under clearly defined situations.[188]

Other examples abound of regulatory measures being undertaken as direct political responses to pollution incidents. The grounding of the *Amoco Cadiz* in 1978 led France to demand tough new regulatory measures including the recognition of salvor efforts to protect the environment. This resulted in IMO adopting a convention on salvage matters in 1989.[189] The *Amoco Cadiz* incident, together with the sinking of yet another vessel – the *Tanio* – off France in 1980, also inspired the establishment of the 1982 Paris Memorandum of Understanding on Port State Control,[190] the introduction of improved steering gear systems on board tankers and the development of port state jurisdiction in the LOSC.[191] The adoption of MARPOL 73/78 was itself a result of US reaction to several vessel accidents off its Atlantic coast in the 1970s.

---

[187] See Ch. 6.
[188] 1969 International Convention relating to Intervention on the High Seas in Cases of Oil Pollution Casualties, 77 U.K.T.S. Cmnd. 6056 (1975) (in force 6 May 1975). The convention is limited to incidents causing or threatening pollution by oil. A 1973 Protocol extended coastal state intervention powers to non-oil substances, see 1973 Protocol relating to Intervention on the High Seas in Cases of Marine Pollution by Substances Other than Oil, 13 I.L.M. 605 (1974) (in force 30 Mar. 1983).
[189] 1989 International Convention on Salvage, 93 U.K.T.S. Cm. 3458 (1996) (in force 14 July 1996).
[190] *Infra* note 246.   [191] See Ch. 4.

The *Exxon Valdez* spill in 1989 was another turning point in the history of vessel-source pollution regulation.[192] As a result of domestic public and media outrage over the incident, the US was compelled to demand the double hull requirement for tankers and to enact the Oil Pollution Act of 1990 (OPA-90). The *Exxon Valdez* was also in part responsible for the adoption of the 1990 Convention on Oil Pollution Preparedness, Response and Co-operation (OPRC).[193] This largely uncontroversial convention imposes obligations on state parties to maintain a national system for prompt and effective response to oil pollution incidents.[194]

In more recent times, the *Erika* disaster in December 1999 off the coast of France served to catalyse further rule-making at IMO. This time, it was the turn of the European Commission to threaten unilateral action in order to extract responses at IMO such as accelerating the phasing out of single-hull tankers.[195] The more recent sinking of the oil tanker *Prestige* off the Galician coast of Spain in November 2002 has energised the European Commission all over again in its efforts to regulate the shipping industry to a higher degree. The fact that Loyola de Palacio – the outspoken Transport Commissioner of the Commission at the time – was from Spain probably led the Commission to push for even more stringent regulation of the tanker industry.[196]

It has often been said that many of IMO's regulatory initiatives have been ill-considered knee-jerk reactions to catastrophic vessel pollution incidents. Whether or not this is the case, such reactions amply reflect the power and influence of domestic public opinion over the international decision-making process. Invariably, what lies as a conduit between public opinion and regulatory reaction has been the instrumentality of the NGOs and the media, working their way through state and inter-governmental bureaucracies to exert influence on the law-making process. The influence of these actors will be assessed in detail in the following chapters.

2.2.3 States with Coastal Interests

States with minimal maritime interests but significant coastal resources or coastlines have traditionally been the prime initiators of environmental

---

[192] On the litigation aspects of the case, see *Alaska Native Class* v. *Exxon Corp.* (The *Exxon Valdez*), 104 F.2d 1196, 1997 A.M.C. 940 (9th Cir. 1997).
[193] 30 I.L.M. 733 (1991) (in force 13 May 1995).
[194] A protocol extending the OPRC to non-oil hazardous noxious substances was adopted in 2000 but is currently still not in force.
[195] See Ch. 3.   [196] Personal interviews.

regulation over shipping. The main actors in this regard have been Australia, Canada and to a smaller extent, New Zealand and Ireland. Canada, in particular, has had a history of claiming jurisdiction over its adjacent waters for purposes of regulating foreign vessels.[197] Here, the Canadians have never been motivated by environmental considerations alone. Canada's claims for increased powers over adjacent waters have long been dictated by its interest in the vast maritime resources lying off its shores, particularly fisheries. Hence, there have been frequent conflicts with foreign fishing vessels attempting to fish in waters claimed by Canada.

For a period in the 1960s and 1970s, Canada's policy stance on jurisdiction over foreign vessels and adjacent seas was at odds with the free navigation interests of its closest ally, the US. Canadian foreign policy in this regard even led to the enactment of unilateral legislation in the form of the Arctic Waters Pollution Prevention Act in 1970[198] and the outright rejection of IMO's oil pollution compensatory regime for imposing too low a protection level for coastal state victims. At the UNCLOS negotiations in the 1970s, Canada led a coastal state coalition comprising mainly developing countries to claim exclusive jurisdiction over wide ocean areas for natural resource exploitation and marine environmental protection.

On their part, the Australians have also been extremely adept at advancing their interests at IMO. Largely a non-maritime state with negligible shipowning interests, Australia has consistently advocated stringent regulation over vessels traversing its waters. The fact that Australia is a primary exporter of bulk commodities ensures a constant stream of foreign-owned vessels to its shores. In turn, this leads to high pollution risks. Ever mindful of the sensitivity of its vast marine ecosystems, particularly in the Great Barrier Reef, Australia has recently led efforts to address the problem of non-indigenous organisms introduced into local waters by the discharge of ballast water. Like the Canadians, Australia's prominence at international fora owes much to its ability to send delegations to influence IMO negotiations.

Traditional coastal states such as Canada and Australia have today been joined by other developed states which place environmental

---

[197] See generally OCEANS LAW AND POLICY IN THE POST-UNCED ERA: AUSTRALIAN AND CANADIAN PERSPECTIVES (L. Kriwoken, et al. eds., 1996).

[198] 9 I.L.M. 543 (1970) (in force 2 Aug. 1972). The Act sought to impose controls over foreign ships navigating off the Canadian Arctic coast, see Ch. 4.

protection as a political priority. Thus, formerly pro-maritime states such as the US and the Western European countries are espousing increasingly environmentalist agendas. One can observe how the regulatory mood at IMO has moved from an almost exclusively pro-shipping and environmentally conservative stance to a much more liberal outlook. This shift has evidently been at the behest of an elite group of state actors which share common characteristics of being developed, pluralist democracies.

For these states, the motivation for international regulation is provided not only by the growing force of environmental consciousness in their domestic constituencies but also the corresponding decline of their maritime interests. At the same time, these states are also moved by the desire to prevent unilateral, non-uniform coastal state regulation and to avoid competitive distortions. To some extent, market opportunities for providing pollution control technologies help to ease the political and economic costs inherent in the transition toward greater environmental liberalism.

2.3 The Developing Countries

Depending on the specific issue at stake, developing countries exhibit varying degrees of commitment toward maritime or coastal policies. Indeed, the sheer number and diversity of developing countries makes it almost impossible to generalise their political preferences. In the past, however, developing countries tended to display environmental inclinations as far as vessel-source pollution was concerned. This was because many of these states had substantial coastlines but no major shipowning or shipping-related interests. Thus, the great majority of developing states assumed coastal state positions at the UNCLOS negotiations in the 1970s.

Unlike the developed coastal states, the developing states' motives had less to do with domestic public interest pressures but more with the need to exercise control over resources in adjacent seas and along with that, foreign vessels engaged in pollution. In any event, the stakes during the UNCLOS negotiations were high and most states deemed it necessary to identify with one interest group coalition or another. As far as the developing states were concerned, it was convenient to rally against the developed states and their demands for free navigation. This may explain the generally pro-coastal tendencies of the developing states at the time and their preference for wide coastal state jurisdiction over natural resources and foreign ships. The great exception to this general position was the open registry states. In addition, there were several developing states which had long been cross-pressured by their own maritime interests. These included China, Brazil, Argentina and India – large states with significant state-owned or private shipowning interests.

Today, the deliberations at international regulatory fora are no longer as polemical. Indeed, the developed–developing state dynamics underlying much of international discourse in the 1970s have largely dissipated. The more relevant tussle at IMO today is one between coastal and port states seeking greater control over foreign ships and maritime states seeking to uphold the freedom of navigation. This bifurcation of interests cuts across traditional economic development profiles with many pro-maritime policies being advocated not by the developed states but by the open registries. Conversely, as mentioned above, the developed states are much more pro-environment today. As for the developing states, most appear not to have a clear position on issues, that is if they turn up for IMO meetings to begin with! Many of these states display intermittent activism depending on whether a particular proposal impacts directly on their national interests. At other times, they remain ambivalent.

On balance, it is accurate to say that the developing countries are largely sympathetic to the shipowners' arguments that their industry is over-regulated. With the increasing load of legal instruments being adopted globally, almost all developing states find the pace of regulation punishing. The general inability to implement existing rules, coupled with the alarm at the proliferation of new rules, have persuaded many a developing state to view environmental activism with trepidation. Moreover, developing states are easily convinced that their indirect interest in maintaining low freight rates and competitive prices for their exports should militate against the high costs of environmentalism.

In any event, the developing states often find it difficult to identify with modern concerns such as the transfer of harmful marine organisms even if these problems are occurring in their own waters. Until scientific knowledge and public opinion in these states are sufficiently advanced to raise the status of these concerns, developing states will continue to be indifferent. Consequently, while it would be excessive to describe developing states as being 'maritime' inclined, it is fair to say that their support for greater environmental liberalism is often equivocal at best.

3. Major Arenas for Decision-Making

3.1 International Fora: The International Maritime Organization (IMO)

3.1.1 IMO's Initial Years

No analytical account of shipping regulation is complete without examining the work of IMO, which is the international regulatory body entrusted with overseeing and co-ordinating matters relating to maritime safety and the prevention of vessel-source pollution. The international convention establishing IMCO had been adopted as early as 1948 but did not receive sufficient ratifications for entry into force until 1958.[199] The delay was largely due to the suspicion of the maritime interests toward IMCO and its role. In particular, there was concern over the IMCO Convention's provision for the Organization to exercise jurisdiction not only with respect to technical matters but also commercial matters such as the discriminatory practices of shipping firms. The shipping interests in the maritime states opposed these provisions as they viewed the involvement of inter-governmental agencies in trade and competition matters to be unwarranted interference with their freedom to operate.

Thus, the very inclusion of the word 'consultative' within IMCO's name was meant to restrict the new agency's competence to purely advisory and technical matters.[200] Despite the resistance of the maritime interests, IMCO's broader economic role remained in its constitution and was never formally ousted. Nevertheless, a tacit understanding emerged subsequently to the effect that IMCO's role would be strictly limited to technical matters. Consequently, IMCO/IMO has never been allowed to exercise its full economic mandate. This remains so up to this day.

During the initial years of IMCO's existence, it was virtually impossible to separate the interests of the shipping industries and those of the

---

[199] Convention on the Inter-Governmental Maritime Consultative Organization, 289 U.N.T.S. 3 (in force 17 Mar. 1958). The IMCO Convention was later amended and renamed the Convention on the International Maritime Organization, 34 U.S.T. 497 (in force 22 May 1982). IMCO was correspondingly renamed IMO. On IMCO/IMO generally, see e.g. S. Mankabady, The International Maritime Organization (1986); K. R. Simmonds, The International Maritime Organization (1994); L. Juda, *IMCO and the Regulation of Ocean Pollution from Ships*, 26 Int'l & Comp. L. Q. 558 (1977); C. P. Srivastava, *The Role of the International Maritime Organisation*, 14 Marine Pol'y 243 (1990); A. Sielen & R. McManus, *IMCO and the Politics of Ship Pollution*, in Environmental Protection: The International Dimension (D. Kay & H. Jacobsen eds., 1983); and M. Valenzuela, *IMO: Public International Law and Regulation*, in The Law of the Sea and Ocean Industry: New Opportunities and Restraints 141 (D. Johnston & N. Letalik eds., 1984).

[200] IMO Convention, art. 1(b).

developed maritime states where these industries were primarily owned and located. This led to the frequent accusation of IMCO being a 'shipowner's club'. With the advent of decolonisation and the emergence of the newly independent states, IMCO's membership grew significantly. Today, the developing states heavily outnumber the developed states at IMO, as is the case in all UN agencies.

Nevertheless, the developed maritime states continue to maintain their dominance at IMO through their influence in the governing IMO Council. More significantly, these states retain power and influence through their leadership of and participation in the committees, sub-committees, working groups and other subsidiary bodies of IMO where the substantive policies of the Organization are actually determined.

3.1.2 The Constitutive Structure of IMO

In its early years, IMCO was principally occupied with matters pertaining to safety at sea and efficiency of navigation. To the extent that safety procedures and precautions prevented accidents at sea, the risks of vessel-source pollution were lowered correspondingly. Explicit pollution control functions did not appear in IMCO's original 1948 constitution, although this was formally rectified by amendments adopted in 1975. This amply demonstrates how pollution concerns were virtually non-existent during IMCO's early years. Following the *Torrey Canyon* incident in 1967 and the subsequent emergence of environmentalism in the developed states, a new and important role was to be found for IMCO in its regulation of shipping activities.

The internal structure of IMO reflects its evolving mandate. At its inception, IMCO was made up of the Assembly, the Council and the Maritime Safety Committee (MSC). Over the years, three more committees were established: the Legal Committee, the Marine Environment Protection Committee (MEPC) and the Technical Co-operation Committee (TCC).[201] In addition, there is also the Facilitation Committee, which is not a full-fledged organ of IMO but a subsidiary body of the Council. Its task is to harmonise shipping procedures and to eliminate unnecessary bureaucratic paperwork and 'red tape' in international shipping.[202]

---

[201] These main committees have various sub-committees within them. Together, the work of these bodies make up the bulk of IMO's regulatory agenda.

[202] An amendment adopted in 1991 had sought to institutionalise the Facilitation Committee, but this has yet to enter into force.

As of December 2004, IMO had 164 member states and 3 associate members. In addition, there are some 100 inter-governmental and non-governmental organisations which have observer status. These organisations represent a wide variety of commercial, industrial, political and environmental interests. They are composed primarily of shipping-related associations and environmental groups as well as agencies of the UN and other regional bodies. The activities of IMO are co-ordinated by the Secretariat, which comprises the Secretary-General and a team of international civil servants based in the Organization's London headquarters.[203]

The Assembly is the highest governing body of the Organization and consists of all member states. It meets once every two years and is responsible for electing the Council and approving the work programme, budget and financial arrangements of the Organization. The Council is composed of 40 member states elected for two-year terms by the Assembly to carry out the bulk of governing functions.[204] Council members are elected to represent the different interests within the Organization – ten states with the largest interest in providing international shipping services (Category A), ten states with the largest interest in international seaborne trade (Category B) and the remaining twenty members not elected under the first two categories being states with special interests in maritime transport and navigation and whose election will ensure the representation of all major geographic areas of the world (Category C). Financial contributions by member states are currently calculated based on two components: the tonnage of the merchant fleet (87.5 per cent) and the state's ability to pay as determined by a general UN formula (12.5 per cent).

3.1.3 IMO and Maritime Conventions

IMO is today responsible for some fifty international conventions and protocols, forty of which are in force or due to enter into force shortly. A significant part of IMO's functions include adopting new conventions as well as amending existing ones. In recent years, technical amendments have been expedited by employing the so-called 'tacit

---

[203] To date, seven individuals have held the post of Secretary-General: Ove Nielsen (Denmark), William Graham (UK), Jean Roullier (France), Colin Goad (UK), C. P. Srivastava (India), William O'Neil (Canada) and the incumbent, Efthimios Mitropoulos (Greece).

[204] When originally constituted, the Council had just sixteen members. Its size increased progressively to 18 in 1967, 24 in 1978, 32 in 1984, and 40 in 2002.

acceptance' procedure. This entails the entry into force of such amendments within a fixed period after their adoption unless a specified number of states register their objection thereto.[205] Table 2-3 below sets out the key IMO conventions.

Apart from legally binding conventions, IMO also produces a vast array of codes, guidelines, resolutions and recommendations pursuant to its legislative mandate. While the majority of these are only recommendatory in nature, several codes have been given mandatory effect through incorporation into binding instruments.[206] On their part, IMO Assembly resolutions are not legally binding but contain strong moral force representing the will of all member states. Customarily, states which are keen to initiate the adoption of conventions begin the process by first having their concerns recognised in the form of guidelines, recommendations or Assembly resolutions. These concerns may then eventually be raised to the status of a convention through discussions and negotiations and, often, the sheer persistence of the sponsoring states.

The adoption of a convention marks the conclusion of only the initial stage of a lengthy process. Before the convention enters into force and becomes legally binding, it must be formally acceded to or ratified by individual states. All international conventions, including those adopted by IMO, stipulate specific conditions which have to be fulfilled for entry into force. To this end, the IMO instruments typically require the acceptance of a minimum number of states accounting for not less than a certain percentage of world shipping tonnage. Thus, for instance, MARPOL 73/78 provides for entry into force upon the ratification by fifteen states whose combined merchant fleets represent not less than 50 per cent of world gross tonnage.

A requirement to this effect ensures that the convention will be applied to the maximum number of ships possible. Otherwise, the convention remains a dead letter if the largest maritime states with the greatest number of ships choose to remain outside its orbit. Such

---

[205] The procedure has been so successful that the frequency and volume of amendments have become burdensome for many states, see CHURCHILL & LOWE, *supra* note 26, at 272. See also the challenges outlined by the IMO Secretariat in FSI Doc. 12/8/1 (2004).

[206] Examples include the International Safety Management (ISM) Code which has been made mandatory through the SOLAS Convention, *supra* note 151. On 'soft law' IMO instruments, see P. W. Birnie, *The Status of Environmental 'Soft Law': Trends and Examples with Special Focus on IMO Norms*, in COMPETING NORMS IN THE LAW OF MARINE ENVIRONMENTAL PROTECTION – FOCUS ON SHIP SAFETY AND POLLUTION PREVENTION 31 (H. Ringbom ed., 1997).

Table 2-3. *Status of Selected IMO Conventions (as at 30 November 2004)*

Convention	Date of Entry into Force	Number of Contracting States	Percentage of World Tonnage
IMO Convention	17 March 1958	164	98.56
SOLAS 1974	25 May 1980	153	98.52
SOLAS Protocol 1978	1 May 1981	107	94.99
COLREG 1972	15 July 1977	146	97.60
STCW 1978, as amended 1995	28 April 1984	147	98.49
MARPOL 73/78 (Annexes I & II)	2 October 1983	130	97.07
MARPOL 73/78 (Annex III)	1 July 1992	115	92.99
MARPOL 73/78 (Annex IV)	27 September 2003	100	54.35
MARPOL 73/78 (Annex V)	31 December 1988	119	95.23
MARPOL Protocol 1997 (Annex VI)	19 May 2005	18	59.92
London Convention 1972	30 August 1975	81	69.85
London Convention Protocol 1996	*Not in force*	21	12.02
Civil Liability (CLC) 1969	19 June 1975	45	4.81
Civil Liability (CLC) Protocol 1992	30 May 1996	104	93.44
FUND 1971	*Ceased existence*	–	–
FUND Protocol 1992	30 May 1996	92	88.39
FUND Protocol 2000	27 June 2001	–	–
FUND Protocol 2003	*Not in force*	7	9.04
Salvage 1989	14 July 1996	47	36.33
OPRC 1990	13 May 1995	82	60.28
OPRC/HNS Protocol 2000	*Not in force*	10	15.67

Table 2-3. (cont.)

Convention	Date of Entry into Force	Number of Contracting States	Percentage of World Tonnage
HNS Convention 1996	Not in force	7	1.73
Anti-Fouling (AFS) Convention 2001	Not in force	9	9.06
Bunkers Convention 2001	Not in force	5	0.45
Ballast Water Management 2004	Not in force	–	–

requirements confer substantial power on the largest shipowning states, whose participation determines the very success of a convention. In recent years, the profile of ship registration has changed dramatically with the open registries and developing states now forming the upper echelons of shipowning states.[207] Consequently, the prompt entry into force of newer, pro-environment conventions may possibly be held back given that not all the top shipowning states accord priority to shipping-related ecological concerns.[208] In response to this development, IMO has recently begun to employ less stringent entry into force requirements for its newer conventions.[209] This is meant to ensure that the conventions will enter into force expeditiously.

3.2 International Fora – United Nations Bodies and Specialised Agencies

Apart from IMO, the functions of several other UN specialised agencies and bodies impinge upon the issue of marine pollution regulation. These entities include the UN Conference on Trade and Development (UNCTAD), the International Labour Organization (ILO), the UN Environment Programme (UNEP), and to lesser extents, the Food and

---

[207] See Table 2-1.
[208] J. Angelo, *The International Maritime Organization and Protection of the Marine Environment*, in Nordquist & Moore eds., *supra* note 147, at 105.
[209] See Ch. 7 for a critique of this approach.

Agriculture Organization (FAO) and the World Meteorological Organization (WMO).

The formation of UNCTAD in December 1964 to deal with global issues of equity in trade and development had presented the developing states with the opportunity to advance their shipping-related concerns. To this end, a permanent Committee of Shipping was established by UNCTAD in 1965 to deal with the commercial and economic aspects of shipping. This was a significant victory for the developing states which had seen their efforts to get IMCO to discuss these matters repeatedly thwarted by the developed countries. Among the major issues raised at the UNCTAD Shipping Committee were the activities of liner conferences, the development of merchant marines in the Third World and the protection of cargo interests. Underlying all these issues was the political desire of the developing countries for greater equity in their trading relations with the developed world.

By the late 1980s, however, the confrontation between the developed and developing countries had waned, together with the latter's push for a New International Economic Order (NIEO). Many developing states lost interest in group politics and began to pursue individual national interests. Several states embraced the concept of free and open markets as the way forward for national reconstruction and economic growth. This mood extended to shipping as well. Before long, it was perceived that there was no longer any need for the UNCTAD Shipping Committee. In 1992, the Committee was disbanded and shipping was placed under a new Standing Committee on Developing Services Sectors. With that, UNCTAD's effectiveness in dealing with maritime matters was irreversibly curtailed.[210]

On its part, ILO was founded in 1919 with its main objectives being the protection of workers' welfare and the alleviation of social injustices in employment. These concerns were manifested in various forms, ranging from working hours to minimum wage levels and workplace conditions. ILO's operational structure is unique among UN agencies; its constituent bodies are tripartite in nature, being made up of representatives not only from governments but also employers' associations and workers' unions. The Organization's General Conference meets annually to adopt conventions or recommendations in areas of labour practice.

---

[210] Whatever residual competence over shipping is today exercised by the Division for Services Infrastructure for Development and Trade Efficiency (SITE).

In the maritime context, ILO has been especially active in improving working conditions for seafarers.[211] Accidents at sea are increasingly attributed to fatigue, carelessness or lack of training among seafarers – the so-called 'human element'. In this regard, ILO has co-operated with IMO to adopt various standards relating to the recruitment, wages, hours of work and working conditions of seafarers. Two significant conventions relevant to the training and working conditions of seafarers are in force. These are the ILO Convention No. 147[212] and the 1978 IMO Convention on Standards of Training, Certification and Watchkeeping for Seafarers (STCW).[213] Efforts are currently being undertaken to consolidate the various ILO conventions on seafarer working standards into a single comprehensive Maritime Labour Convention.

The UN Environment Programme (UNEP) was established in the wake of the landmark 1972 Stockholm Conference on the Human Environment. Among UNEP's main objectives are the reconciliation of development and environmental needs and the protection of the human environment, especially in the developing countries. UNEP is not a specialised UN agency but is entrusted with the role of co-ordinating and streamlining the activities of all UN agencies in relation to environmental protection.

In the first few years following its inception, UNEP actively promoted its Regional Seas Programme. Hence, regional pollution agreements were adopted for the protection of the marine environment in several parts of the world, including the Mediterranean,[214] the Persian Gulf and the Gulf of Oman,[215] the Caribbean,[216] the African West

---

[211] See generally E. Osieke, *The International Labour Organization and the Control of Sub-standard Merchant Vessels*, 30 INT'L & COMP. L. Q. 497 (1981).

[212] 1976 ILO Convention No. 147 Concerning Minimum Standards on Merchant Ships, 1259 U.N.T.S. 335 (in force 28 Nov. 1981). See particularly art. 2(3) laying out the obligation of flag states to ensure that seafarers on board their flag vessels are properly qualified or trained for the duties for which they are engaged. On seafarer welfare, see e.g. J. M. Ng, *International Maritime Conventions: Seafarers' Safety and Human Rights*, 33 J. MAR. L. & COM. 381 (2002).

[213] 1361 U.N.T.S. 2 (in force 28 Apr. 1984), as amended by the 1995 Protocol, 1969 U.N.T.S. 41 (in force 1 Feb. 1997). See G. Sperling, *The New Convention on Standards of Training, Certification and Watchkeeping: What, if Anything, Does it Mean?* 22 TUL. MAR. L. J. 595 (1998).

[214] 1976 Barcelona Convention for the Protection of the Marine Environment against Pollution, 15 I.L.M. 290 (1976) (in force 12 Feb. 1978).

[215] 1978 Kuwait Regional Convention for Cooperation on the Protection of the Marine Environment from Pollution, 17 I.L.M. 511 (1978) (in force 1 Jul. 1979).

[216] 1983 Cartagena Convention for the Protection and Development of the Marine Environment of the Wider Caribbean Region, 22 I.L.M. 221 (1983) (in force 30 Mar. 1986).

Coast,[217] the South-East Pacific,[218] the Red Sea and the Gulf of Aden,[219] the East African region[220] and the South Pacific.[221] The UNEP Regional Seas instruments adopt a uniform format of laying down only general obligations drawn from the LOSC with detailed provisions being elaborated upon in separate protocols to the relevant conventions.

The UN-convened Conferences on the Law of the Sea have also been critical in facilitating legislative consensus on vessel-source pollution matters. Three such conferences have been convened to date, with the most recent and celebrated being the Third UNCLOS Conference. UNCLOS III culminated in the adoption of the UN Convention on the Law of the Sea (LOSC) in 1982. The UNCLOS process has been instrumental in laying down agreement over the jurisdiction of states to prescribe and enforce pollution control rules over foreign ships. At the same time, the LOSC established a constitutive framework governing far wider issues relating to the use and exploitation of the oceans in general. The UNCLOS process as it relates to vessel-source pollution will be examined in Chapter 4.

3.3 Regional Fora

3.3.1 Legal and Political Developments in Europe

Regional initiatives have also played a crucial role in efforts to protect the marine environment.[222] As mentioned above, UNEP has established

---

[217] 1981 Abidjan Convention for Co-operation in the Protection and Development of the Marine and Coastal Environment of the West and Central African Region, 20 I.L.M. 746 (1981) (in force 5 Aug. 1984).

[218] 1981 Lima Convention for the Protection of the Marine Environment and Coastal Areas of the South-East Pacific, 20 I.L.M. 696 (1981) (in force 19 May 1986).

[219] 1982 Jeddah Regional Convention for the Conservation of the Red Sea and the Gulf of Aden Environment, 22 I.L.M. 219 (1983) (in force 20 Aug. 1985).

[220] 1985 Nairobi Convention for the Protection, Management and Development of the Marine and Coastal Environment of the Eastern African Region, *available at* http://www.unep.ch/seas/main/eaf/eafconv.html (in force 29 May 1996) (last accessed 4 Nov. 2004).

[221] 1986 Noumea Convention for the Protection and Development of the Natural Resources and Environment of the South Pacific Region, 26 I.L.M. 41 (1987) (in force 22 Aug. 1990). A glaring exception to these efforts is the Asia–Pacific, where no regional instrument exists. This is due to a lack of political will among regional governments. On marine issues in the Asia–Pacific, see THE LAW OF THE SEA IN THE ASIAN PACIFIC REGION (J. Crawford & D. Rothwell eds., 1995).

[222] See generally P. H. SAND, TRANSNATIONAL ENVIRONMENTAL LAW: LESSONS IN GLOBAL CHANGE 175 (1999).

regional agreements for the protection of the marine environment in several regions of the world. At IMO, the impetus for regulation has often been provided by the experiences and demands of regional interests. In particular, developments in Western Europe have led the world in crafting regulatory responses to the marine pollution problem.

One of the earliest European initiatives was the 1969 Bonn Agreement for Co-operation in Dealing with Pollution of the North Sea by Oil.[223] The Agreement was essentially a regional response by the North Sea states to the *Torrey Canyon* incident.[224] Early efforts also arose at the sub-regional level among like-minded states seeking to address issues of common concern. One such effort was the 1971 Nordic Agreement Concerning Co-operation in Measures to Deal with Pollution of the Sea by Oil.[225]

In the 1970s, regulatory activities reached new levels of institutional sophistication when permanent commissions were established to administer the relevant conventions. Thus, the 1972 Oslo Convention for the Prevention of Marine Pollution by Dumping by Ships and Aircraft[226] established the Oslo Commission to oversee implementation matters. The Oslo Convention was limited to regulating dumping activities; its coverage included the North Sea, the Arctic Ocean and the Northeast Atlantic but excluded the Baltic and Mediterranean Seas. The Oslo Convention pioneered the use of the 'black' and 'grey' lists of substances and the 'prior consent' approach which were later adopted by instruments such as IMO's 1972 London Convention on Dumping.[227]

---

[223] 704 U.N.T.S. 3; 9 I.L.M. 359 (1970) (in force 9 Aug. 1969).
[224] In 1983, a revised version of the Bonn Agreement was adopted to extend regulation to non-oil harmful substances, see 1983 Bonn Agreement for Co-operation in Dealing with Pollution of the North Sea by Oil and Other Harmful Substances, *available at* http://www.bonnagreement.org/eng/html/welcome.html (last accessed 4 Nov. 2004) (in force 1 Sept. 1989)
[225] 822 U.N.T.S. 311 (in force 16 Oct. 1971). The parties which signed the Agreement were Denmark, Finland, Norway and Sweden.
[226] 119 U.K.T.S. Cmnd. 4984 (1975); 11 I.L.M. 262 (1972) (in force 7 Apr. 1974).
[227] 1972 London Convention on the Prevention of Marine Pollution by Dumping of Wastes and Other Matter, 1046 U.N.T.S. 120; 11 I.L.M. 1294 (1972) (in force 30 Aug. 1975), as amended by the 1996 Protocol to the 1972 Convention, 36 I.L.M. 1 (1997) (not in force). The 1996 Protocol replaced the 1972 Convention's 'black' and 'grey' lists of prohibited substances with a 'reverse' list of substances (i.e. only listed materials may be dumped; anything not listed may *not* be dumped). The 1996 Protocol also formally introduced

In 1974, the Paris Convention for the Prevention of Marine Pollution from Land-Based Sources[228] was adopted, covering land-based pollution within the same geographical area as that of the Oslo Convention. Like its Oslo counterpart, the Paris Convention was administered by a Commission comprising representatives of the contracting parties. The legal framework of the Oslo and Paris Conventions has since been amalgamated and modernised by the 1992 Convention for the Protection of the Marine Environment of the North-East Atlantic (hereinafter OSPAR).[229] With OSPAR's entry into force in 1998, the Oslo and Paris Conventions have ceased to operate. A new OSPAR Commission has since been formed to administer the OSPAR Convention.

The Bonn Agreement, together with the Oslo and Paris Conventions, attempted to address *specific* sources of marine pollution rather than the problem of pollution in its entirety. The first regional agreement to deal comprehensively with the pollution problem *in general* was the 1974 Helsinki Convention on the Protection of the Marine Environment of the Baltic Sea Area.[230] The convention was substantially based upon the provisions of MARPOL 73 but contained several improvements to the latter. Regulatory efforts under the 1974 Convention were actively pursued by the national representatives to the convention's institutional administrator, the Baltic Marine Environment Protection Commission (better known as the Helsinki Commission or HELCOM). The 1974 Helsinki Convention was extremely influential in laying out the framework for the subsequent adoption of the UNEP Regional Seas conventions. In addition, it provided a useful basis for the negotiations at UNCLOS III. The convention has since been strengthened and modernised by the 1992 Helsinki Convention on the Protection of the Marine Environment of the Baltic Sea Area.[231]

Quite apart from the regional conventions and their commissions, mention must be made of important political fora which serve to energise law-making processes in Europe. Among the most influential of

the precautionary approach and 'polluter pays' principle and banned incineration at sea. On dumping generally, see CHURCHILL & LOWE, *supra* note 26, at 363–70.

[228] 13 I.L.M. 352 (1974) (in force 6 May 1978).
[229] 32 I.L.M. 1069 (1993) (in force 25 Mar. 1998). For details, see E. Hey et al., *The 1992 Paris Convention for the Protection of the Marine Environment of the North-East Atlantic: A Critical Analysis*, 8 INT'L J. MARINE & COASTAL L. 1 (1993).
[230] 13 I.L.M. 546 (1974) (in force 3 May 1980).
[231] Reprinted in UN Law of the Sea Bulletin No. 22; 8 INT'L J. MARINE & COASTAL L. 215 (1993) (in force 17 Jan. 2000). See generally P. Ehlers, *The Helsinki Convention: Improving the Baltic Sea Environment*, 8 INT'L J. MARINE & COASTAL L. 191 (1993).

these are the International Conferences on the Protection of the North Sea, widely known as the North Sea Conferences.[232] First held in 1984, the Conferences are convened periodically every few years at ministerial levels to discuss contemporary marine pollution problems and to find effective means of addressing them. The North Sea Conferences are essentially political in nature and complement the treaty-based mandates of the Oslo/Paris and OSPAR Commissions. The Ministerial Declarations issued at the Conferences, although not legally binding, typically contain policy directions which drive national and regional action. For instance, efforts at IMO to reduce air pollution from ships originated with acid rain concerns first expressed at the North Sea Conferences.

It will be appreciated in the following chapters that the numerous environmental initiatives undertaken at international fora such as IMO have often derived inspiration from activities at the local and regional levels, particularly in Western Europe and North America. In this regard, local and regional decision-makers have always had an interest in extending regulation beyond their shores. European regulators, for instance, are sensitive to the fact that stringent regional regimes tend to disadvantage their own industries, ports and other maritime interests. There is also the fundamental realisation that environmental concerns like marine pollution recognise no political boundaries. Thus, regional standards can be severely compromised if actors outside the region continue to ignore the problem. In addition, industry interests such as shipowners themselves recognise that uniform global standards are necessary, lest states or regions embark on unilateral standard-setting.

Regional activism in Western Europe cannot be properly understood without an appreciation of the political dynamics of the European Union (EU) institutions. The political philosophy of the EU revolves crucially around the division of competence between the member states on the one hand, and Community institutions such as the Council of Ministers, the Commission and the European Parliament on the other. With the ever closer integration being forged among the EU member states, supra-national institutions like the European Commission are increasingly assuming an activist stance.

It has been widely observed that the Commission is seeking to repose in itself greater competence to initiate legislation for the

---

[232] See generally, THE NORTH SEA: PERSPECTIVES ON REGIONAL ENVIRONMENTAL CO-OPERATION (D. Freestone & T. IJlstra eds., 1990).

Community. In the vessel-source pollution arena, where the EU and its member states share competence, a great number of shipping-related matters are today governed by Community Regulations, Directives, Decisions and Recommendations.[233] Member state competence in such matters is correspondingly being displaced. Thus, the Commission has initiated legislation and policies relating to matters as diverse as tanker reporting requirements,[234] a common policy on safe shipping,[235] rules for vessel traffic monitoring,[236] rules governing the conduct of classification societies,[237] seafarer training,[238] reception facilities[239] and port state control.[240] In the wake of the

---

[233] See A. Nollkaemper & E. Hey, *Implementation of the LOS Convention at Regional Level: European Community Competence in Regulating Safety and Environmental Aspects of Shipping*, 10 INT'L J. MARINE & COASTAL L. 281 (1995).

[234] Directive 79/116 Concerning Minimum Requirements for Certain Tankers Entering or Leaving Community Ports, 1979 OJ (L 33) 33, as amended by Directive 79/1034, 1979 OJ (L 315) 16.

[235] Communication on a Common Policy on Safe Seas, COM(93) 66 final and Council Resolution of 8 June 1993 on a Common Policy for Safe Seas, 1993 OJ (C 271). For commentaries, see H. Ringbom, *Preventing Pollution from Ships – Reflections on the 'Adequacy' of Existing Rules*, 1 RECIEL 21 (1999) and L. Pineschi, *The EEC, Safety of Navigation and Vessel-Source Pollution*, in THE LAW OF THE SEA: NEW WORLDS, NEW DISCOVERIES 526 (E. Miles & T. Treves eds., 1993).

[236] Directive 2002/59/EC of the European Parliament and of the Council of 27 June 2002 establishing a Community vessel traffic monitoring and information system, 2002 OJ (L 208) 10 (in force 5 Feb. 2004). The Directive is part of the post-*Erika* measures and requires, *inter alia*, ships bound for Community ports to make advance notification and ships passing EU waters to be monitored. The Directive also added requirements on mandatory automatic identification systems ('transponders') and vessel data recorders ('black boxes') on board all EU-bound ships. It further provides for member states to draw up plans to provide places of refuge for vessels in distress within waters under their jurisdiction.

[237] Directive 94/57 on Common Rules and Standards for Ship Inspection and Survey Organisations and for the Relevant Activities of Maritime Administrations (Directive on Classification Societies), 1994 OJ (L 319) 20, as amended by Directive 97/58, 1997 OJ (L 274) 8 and Directive 2001/105/EC, 2002 OJ (L 19) 9. The latest amendment by Directive 2001/105/EC was part of the *Erika I* package of reform measures to tighten regulation over classification societies, *infra* note 378.

[238] Directive 94/58 on the Minimum Level of Training for Seafarers, 1994 OJ (L 319) 28, as amended by Directive 98/35, 1998 OJ (L 172) 1.

[239] Directive 2000/59/EC on Port Reception Facilities for Ship-Generated Waste and Cargo Residues, 2000 OJ (L 332) 81.

[240] Directive 95/21/EC of 19 June 1995 Concerning the Enforcement, in Respect of Shipping Using Community Ports and Sailing in the Waters under the Jurisdiction of the Member States, of International Standards for Ship Safety, Pollution Prevention and Shipboard Living and Working Conditions (Directive on Port State Control), 1995 OJ (L 157) 1, as amended by Directive 98/25, 1998 (L 133) 19; Directive 98/42, 1998 (L 184) 40; Directive 99/97, 1999 OJ (L 331) 67 and Directive 2001/106, 2002 OJ (L 19) 17.

Erika and *Prestige* incidents, stronger rules on single-hull tankers, classification societies and port state control have been put into place, and a European Maritime Safety Agency has been established.[241] In addition, the European Community harbours plans to become a full member of IMO to ensure that its member states' positions are co-ordinated.[242]

Despite the proliferation of Community instruments, the European states are generally still viewed as being supportive of IMO. Compared to the US, the European states have had a stronger tradition of upholding multilateral decision-making processes at IMO. For one thing, the shipping-related interests are far more entrenched in Europe than they are in the US. Indeed, several European countries such as Greece, Norway, the UK, Cyprus and Malta continue to have strong shipping interests. Consequently, by virtue of the greater variety of interests at stake, the European outlook appears to be more balanced in reconciling the competing demands of the shipping and environmental interests.

That said, the maritime world hardly doubts the EU's ability to pursue unilateral action on maritime safety and environmental protection matters. In this regard, the shipowners are well aware that the Western European region is a significant economic force with a consumer base exceeding even that of the US. Shipowners rely heavily on the Western European trade and can scarcely afford the costs of European unilateralism. In addition, the shipping community is left in no doubt as to the European Commission's power and inclination to enact binding Community-wide legislation and to even take action against member states for contravening Community laws. Consequently, any European threat to adopt unilateral action is taken very seriously.

In recent years, impatience with the IMO system has grown in Europe, particularly in the wake of several major vessel pollution incidents. This has paved the way for aggressive unilateralist posturing by European governments and the Commission to drive the agenda at IMO. Thus, in the aftermath of the sinking of the *Erika* off the coast of France in December 1999, the European Commission's Directorate-General in

---

[241] Regulation (EC) 1406/2002 of the European Parliament and Council Establishing a European Maritime Safety Agency (EMSA). The Executive Director of EMSA was appointed on 29 Jan. 2003.

[242] See the European Commission's proposal of 9 April 2002 *vide* IP/02/525.

charge of transport matters (DG VII) publicly threatened to initiate unilateral regulation over shipping outside the aegis of IMO.[243]

No doubt, such attitudes were fanned by the French presidency of the EU in the latter half of 2000. Sentiments such as these are also fuelled by reactionary forces within Europe which believe that stringent regulatory measures adopted by the US must be accompanied by equally strong responses from Europe, lest sub-standard ships move their operations from the US to European waters. In this regard, the recent sinking of the *Prestige* off the coast of Spain in November 2002 further bolstered the Commission's commitment to ban single-hull tankers from European waters and to regulate the shipping industry in a more robust manner. Intense European pressure subsequently compelled IMO to adopt new global regulations accelerating the phasing out of older tankers.[244]

The increasingly federalist nature of decision-making in Europe also helps to explain the tremendous influence of supra-national bodies and processes such as the European Commission, the North Sea Conferences and even smaller outfits such as the Helsinki and OSPAR Commissions. In this regard, it can be seen that the European countries are moving toward greater integration in environmental policy-setting and are developing a discernibly 'pro-coastal' Community posture.[245] States with large shipping interests such as Greece have thus been compelled to go along with stricter regulation over ships.

Even powerful actors with strong maritime traditions like the UK have had to submit to Community demands in a variety of matters. By the same token, new EU member states such as Cyprus and Malta, both of which operate large open registries, have also had to adopt more stringent regulation over shipping to align their policies with those of the Community. Overall, the impact of Community legislation and policies on member states is significant. By extension, this activism invariably finds its way into the decision-making processes at international fora such as IMO, where the European states retain tremendous influence.

---

[243] The Council also committed itself to proceed with European measures if IMO failed to act, see Ringbom, *supra* note 9, at 282.
[244] See Ch. 3.   [245] Ringbom, *supra* note 9, at 284.

3.3.2 Memoranda of Understanding (MOUs) on Port State Control

In January 1982, just months before the conclusion of UNCLOS III, the maritime authorities of fourteen Western European countries signed a Memorandum of Understanding on Port State Control[246] in Paris to co-ordinate and enhance port state control over ships visiting European waters. At that point, the UNCLOS negotiations were close to reaching agreement on the jurisdictional aspects of port state control.[247] Procedures for port state control had hitherto been established by instruments such as SOLAS 74 and MARPOL 73/78, but the level of their enforcement differed considerably among states.

The general objective of the Paris MOU was to bring about a uniform approach to port state control on a regional level based on the overarching provisions of the LOSC and the IMO instruments. In particular, the MOU aimed to ensure compliance by ships with all applicable IMO regulatory requirements pertaining to matters such as safety, pollution control, manning and security. To this end, the national maritime authorities would exercise the power to board vessels, inspect documentation and physical conditions and, where appropriate, detain vessels until the relevant deficiencies were remedied.

As conceived, the Paris MOU did not bear the characteristics of a formal legal convention entered into by state parties. Instead, it was designed simply as an administrative agreement among the various maritime authorities to harmonise port state control activities in Western Europe. The concept of a regional arrangement for port state control had first emerged in March 1978 when an MOU was signed in The Hague to unify enforcement of shipboard living and working conditions pursuant to the ILO's Convention No. 147. Shortly after the Hague MOU was signed, the disastrous *Amoco Cadiz* oil spill occurred off the coast of France. The resultant political outcry led to demands for a new and more stringent port state control MOU designed to enforce regulations pertaining not only to shipboard working conditions but to maritime safety and pollution prevention as well.[248]

---

[246] 21 I.L.M. 1 (1982), http://www.parismou.org. For commentaries, see KASOULIDES, *supra* note 22 and R. Legatski, *Port State Jurisdiction over Vessel-Source Pollution*, 2 HARV. ENVTL. L. REV. 448 (1977).

[247] See Ch. 4.

[248] See generally H.-G. Nagelmackers, *Aftermath of the Amoco Cadiz – Why Must the European Community Act?*, 4 MARINE POL'Y 3 (1980).

The Paris MOU came into effect on 1 July 1982, comprising a main section and several annexes laying out procedures for port state inspections and detentions. At present, maritime administrations from twenty countries are participating in the arrangement. In essence, the MOU parties undertake to conduct port state enforcement of IMO conventions relating to maritime safety and the prevention of pollution, principally SOLAS 74, MARPOL 73/78, STCW 78/95, COLREG 72, Load Lines 1966 and ILO Convention No. 147. MOU inspections are meant to target all aspects of the ship's safety, pollution and crewing standards, including operational requirements relating to the crew's familiarity with essential shipboard procedures.[249]

Member maritime administrations are expected to inspect 25 per cent of all vessels entering their ports.[250] This has resulted in almost 90 per cent of vessels using European ports being inspected.[251] Since its adoption, the Paris MOU has been amended several times to accommodate new rules and requirements. One of the most important changes was the introduction in 1993 of a 'targeting factor' designed to facilitate the identification of sub-standard ships for more stringent inspections. This amendment was introduced at the behest of the UK following the Donaldson Report's inquiry into the *Braer* incident.[252]

Pursuant to MOU inspections, the profiles of the most deficient ships and their flag states are generated in order to facilitate the targeting of ships for future inspections. In particular, three-year rolling average tables of the flag states with the most frequently inspected and detained ships are published by the MOU Secretariats.[253] The information on inspections, target profiles and detentions is shared among MOU members through a sophisticated computer network. Most importantly, such information is published and disseminated so that ship brokers, insurers and charterers worldwide know which the sub-standard

---

[249] Pursuant to amendments made to SOLAS 74 and MARPOL 73/78, see e.g. SOLAS 74, reg. XI/4. IMO's port state control policy is laid out in IMO Assembly Resolution A.787(19) (1995) on Procedures for Port State Control, as amended by Resolution A.882(21) (1999).
[250] Proposals are currently being made to increase the inspection rate to 100 per cent (full coverage).
[251] G. Kiehne, *Investigation, Detention and Release of Ships under the Paris MOU on Port State Control: A View from Practice*, 11 INT'L J. MARINE & COASTAL L. 217, at 219 (1996).
[252] *Supra* note 40.
[253] These statistics are analysed in Ch. 5 in relation to compliance.

vessels and operators are.[254] The targeting regime has recently been extended to the identification of classification societies and charterers.

In addition to the IMO instruments, the Paris MOU parties seek to enforce the contents of various EU Directives pertaining to maritime safety and vessel-source pollution.[255] The main instrument in this regard is Directive 95/21/EC (the Directive on Port State Control), which makes the Paris MOU requirements mandatory within member state ports.[256] From July 2003, the Directive introduced a strengthened 'blacklist' system which empowers member states to ban altogether ships posing the greatest safety and pollution threats. Thus, entry into EU ports will be refused when a ship either flies the flag of a state appearing in the black-list and has been detained more than twice in the preceding twenty-four months in an MOU state, *or*, flies the flag of a state categorised as 'very high risk' or 'high risk' in the black-list, and has been detained more than once in the preceding thirty-six months.[257]

Mandatory expanded inspections will also be conducted on certain classes of ships which are considered high risk, such as older gas and chemical tankers, bulk carriers and oil tankers.[258] In addition, the name of the charterer will be made public together with ship detention data. More transparency will be imposed on, and between, port state inspectors, classification societies and flag states through mandatory information exchange. In 2004, further amendments were adopted to provide the legal basis for port state control over security matters.

---

[254] Publication was initially resisted due to the threat of legal action by shipowners, see Hare, *supra* note 22, at 580. However, publication has become the norm today, and statistics can be found on the MOU websites.

[255] *Supra* notes 236–41.

[256] *Supra* note 240. For details, see R. Salvarani, *The EC Directive on Port State Control: A Policy Statement*, 11 INT'L J. MARINE & COASTAL L. 225 (1996) and E. Molenaar, *EC Directive on Port State Control in Context*, 11 INT'L J. MARINE & COASTAL L. 241 (1996). The Directive was adopted to make port state control mandatory after several port authorities displayed reluctance in complying with the Paris MOU, see T. Keselj, *Port State Jurisdiction in Respect of Pollution from Ships: The 1982 United Nations Convention on the Law of the Sea and the Memorandum of Understanding*, 30 OCEAN DEV. & INT'L L. J. 127, at 143–8 (1999). Even then, considerable disparity persists in relation to the degree of diligence exercised by port state administrations.

[257] Directive 2001/106/EC, *supra* note 240, art. 7b. This is the so-called 'three strikes and out' provision, in force since 22 July 2003. See generally EUROPEAN COMMISSION DIRECTORATE GENERAL FOR ENERGY AND TRANSPORT, MEMORANDUM: ERIKA – TWO YEARS ON (2001), at http://europa.eu.int/comm/transport/library/erika-en.pdf (last accessed 15 Dec. 2004).

[258] Directive 2001/106/EC, *supra* note 240, art. 7.

Overall, the Directive imposes legal obligations on the EU member states to conduct port state control where none existed before under the terms of the Paris MOU. Hence, the European Commission is now empowered to bring member states before the European Court of Justice for failing to adhere to the Directive's requirements.[259] This is an example of how regulatory efforts relating to pollution from ships have gradually been taken over by the formal organs of the EU. Naturally, this development was not welcomed by shipowners who had initially supported the Paris MOU precisely because it was a non-mandatory arrangement independent of governments.

Since its inception, the Paris MOU has had considerable success in its attempt to curb sub-standard shipping within Western European waters. Based on its experience, similar regional arrangements have been instituted in various other parts of the world, namely the Asia-Pacific, the Mediterranean, the Caribbean, the Indian Ocean, Latin America, West and Central Africa and the Black Sea.[260] Among these, the seventeen-member Tokyo MOU for port state control in the Asia-Pacific is the most active. Since 1994, the US Coast Guard has maintained its own port state control system over visiting ships, implementing various IMO and domestic US laws. Like the Paris and Tokyo MOUs, the US system targets sub-standard ships for inspection and detention using a demerit points matrix built on information relating to owners, flags, vessel type, classification societies and previous boarding history.[261] The lists of owners, flags and classification societies which have bad inspection records are then published. A limited list of targeted charterers and ship management companies

---

[259] For example, in 2001, the Commission considered taking action against Luxembourg, Belgium, the Netherlands, Greece, Germany and the UK for failing to comply with port state control legislation, see Lloyd's List, *Court Threat to EU States over Safety*, 19 Jul. 2001.

[260] The other regional MOUs are the 1992 Latin-America (Viña del Mar) Agreement; the 1993 Asia-Pacific (Tokyo) MOU; the 1996 Caribbean MOU; the 1997 Mediterranean MOU; the 1998 Indian Ocean MOU; the 1999 West and Central African (Abuja) MOU; and the 2000 Black Sea MOU. A Persian Gulf Region MOU is currently under development. For more on port state control, see e.g. KASOULIDES, *supra* note 22, P. B. Payoyo, *Implementation of International Conventions Through Port State Control: An Assessment*, 18 MARINE POL'Y 379 (1994) and P. B. PAYOYO, PORT STATE CONTROL IN THE ASIA-PACIFIC: AN INTERNATIONAL LEGAL STUDY OF PORT STATE JURISDICTION (1993).

[261] See D. L. Bryant, *Port State Control as Practised by the US Coast Guard*, 10 INT'L MAR. L 303 (1997). See Ch. 5 for an analysis of port state control enforcement, including by the US Coast Guard.

and last ports of call has also been released, primarily in relation to safety and security violations.²⁶²

Overall, the various port state control arrangements have greatly made up for the failure of flag states to exercise effective control over their vessels. The overall reduction in vessel-source pollution worldwide has also been partly attributed to enhanced port state controls.²⁶³ From a systemic perspective, the uniformity imposed upon inspection and detention activities has been beneficial. Apart from safety and environmental gains, harmonised port state control serves to prevent a distortion in competition among ports.²⁶⁴ Indeed, without uniformity of action – the very *raison d'être* of port state control MOUs – a 'port shopping' phenomenon may conceivably arise within and between regions, fuelling business for the less stringent ports.²⁶⁵

3.4 Domestic Fora – Agitation Within States

Other cases of activism can be seen in the domestic political processes of certain key states. This has been particularly evident in the US, both at the federal and state levels. Thus, while the US is invariably a key actor at international decision-making arenas, it is a major forum in its own right (like the EU) in relation to enacting regulations over ships. Due to its economic position and the inevitable need of tankers to enter its ports, it has never been doubted by the shipping industry that the US can afford to act unilaterally in pursuing its vessel regulation policies. This leverage enables the US to influence and dictate international decision-making to its liking, a point not lost on Washington legislators.

For a long time, US interests were clearly aligned with its shipowning lobbies and strategic naval interests. However, a series of tanker accidents occurring within US waters in the 1970s unleashed strong responses against vessel-source pollution. It was increasingly felt in the US that oil pollution from tankers was too urgent a problem to await the initiation of regulatory action at IMCO. On its part, IMCO was then still predominantly controlled by the maritime interests which showed little sensitivity to ecological concerns. The US thus moved to dictate IMCO's regulatory agenda and to threaten unilateral

---

²⁶² US port state control activities are now very much dictated by security considerations against terrorism, see the provisions of the 2002 Maritime Security Transportation Act, implementing the ISPS Code. For details, see http://www.uscg.mil/hq/g-m/pscweb/ (last accessed 4 Nov. 2004).
²⁶³ E. Gold, GARD Handbook on Marine Pollution 317 (1997).
²⁶⁴ Keselj, *supra* note 256, at 143-8. ²⁶⁵ *Ibid.*

action if the rest of the international community refused to accede to its demands.²⁶⁶

The relative weakness of American commitment to the international regulatory process has very much to do with the division of federal state powers in the US. Within the US, the individual states with coastlines have always felt that a uniform international regime inhibited them from enacting their own regulatory laws with regard to visiting ships. In this respect, state autonomy within a federal system remains a cherished principle in the US. As such, the various states have a propensity for jealously guarding their competence vis-à-vis federal agencies. Under the federal system, any competence that is not expressly reserved for the federal government must reside with the states. Since any international agreements entered into by the federal government would necessarily trump state competence on the same subject matter, political support from the states for harmonised IMO standards has often been lacking, particularly if these standards are viewed to be inadequate.

On a more fundamental level, there have always been inward-looking forces within the US which believe that national sovereignty should never be compromised by foreign dictates, including those of multilateral organisations. This suspicion of foreign motives is regularly exploited by influential state Governors, Congressmen and Senators, as well as media and environmental groups seeking to galvanise populist sentiments for preserving state discretion over coastal pollution matters.²⁶⁷ Often, such sentiments are clouded by extraneous concerns such as the protection of shipbuilding and seafaring jobs,²⁶⁸ issues which can easily be used to fan hostility toward foreigners. As in Europe, the fact that the US national ship registry has diminished considerably means that visiting ships are often foreign-flagged. This can only encourage intense campaigns against shipping, an industry with a negligible domestic constituency.

Amidst such political undercurrents, stringent state laws have frequently been enacted in the US. Some of these laws continue to exist alongside federal laws, while others have been struck down by the courts following challenges by federal authorities or interested

---

[266] See e.g. Ch. 3 for the way in which the US influenced the adoption of MARPOL 73 and MARPOL 73/78.
[267] For example, see *infra* note 269, in relation to the state of Washington's port regulations.
[268] *Infra* note 364, in relation to the double hull issue.

parties.²⁶⁹ In most cases, the principal reason for challenging these state laws would be their alleged inconsistency with federal laws in areas where the latter are meant to be supreme. The unilateral enactment of OPA-90 and the US withdrawal from the international compensation schemes for oil pollution damage are direct results of such domestic tensions. Ultimately, it can be appreciated how political forces impacting upon domestic arenas such as the US Congress and the various state legislatures may have profound impact on regulatory efforts at the international level. This aspect of US influence on regime formation at IMO is a factor that cannot be ignored.

The UK government has also recently demonstrated a robust environmental posture. Traditionally a strong proponent of maritime interests, the UK has experienced major policy swings in the last few decades. This has been due to the government being continuously cross-pressured by its domestic shipping, oil and environmental interests. At the same time, the UK's policy choices have also been affected by its political commitment to Europe, even if this is often ambivalent.

A clear emphasis on environmental protection has emerged in London in recent years, consistent with the mood in other developed countries. Contemporary UK policy on shipping matters is heavily influenced by a report released by the inquiry into the sinking of the oil tanker *Braer* in 1993. The inquiry, chaired by the prominent maritime expert Lord Donaldson, produced a voluminous report entitled 'Safer Ships, Cleaner Seas',²⁷⁰ containing 103 wide-ranging

---

[269] See e.g. *United States v. Locke*, 529 US 89 (2000), where the US Supreme Court unanimously struck down several aspects of the state of Washington's regulations designed to impose stricter requirements than would be necessary under federal law. These had been challenged by INTERTANKO as well as the US federal government for being more stringent than the 1972 Ports and Waterways Safety Act (PWSA), 33 U.S.C. §§ 1221-1227. The state of Washington subsequently repealed the regulations in September 2000. See also the earlier case of *Ray v. Atlantic Richfield Co.*, 435 US 151 (1978). For federalism issues and the shipping industry, see generally C. H. Allen, *Federalism in the Era of International Standards: Federal and State Government Regulation of Merchant Vessels in the United States (Part III)*, 30 J. Mar. L. & Com. 85 (1999) and G. Mitchell, *Preservation of State and Federal Authority Under the Oil Pollution Act of 1990*, 21 Envtl. L. 237 (1991).

[270] Donaldson Report, *supra* note 40. The UK government's response to the report can be found in Cm. 2766 (1995), see also G. Plant, *A European Lawyer's View of the Government Response to the Donaldson Report*, 19 Marine Pol'y 453 (1995) and M. Wallace, *Safer Ships, Cleaner Seas: The Report of the Donaldson Inquiry into the Prevention of Pollution from Merchant Shipping*, Lloyd's Mar. & Comm. L. Q. 404 (1995).

recommendations on how accidental and operational pollution from merchant shipping could be prevented and abated.

The UK government subsequently agreed to adopt all but four of the report's recommendations. Among those accepted were the tightening of the port state control system, the provision of reception facilities in ports and the undertaking of improvements to the liability and compensation system. The implementation of these recommendations was also recognised to be of international concern. Consequently, the UK has been extremely active at IMO in proposing new regulatory initiatives, many of which can be directly traced to the Donaldson Report and the UK government's commitment to pursue its recommendations.

A comparable development arose earlier in Australia, where a parliamentary committee was established to inquire into the loss in close succession of six bulk carriers off the Western Australian coast between January 1990 and August 1991.[271] Pursuant to the Committee's deliberations, two documents known as the 'Ships of Shame' reports were released.[272] The reports contained several recommendations aimed at eradicating sub-standard shipping and preventing future occurrences of shipping mishaps and pollution incidents. The recent emergence of the Australian delegation as a strong proponent of greater environmental regulation over shipping can be directly linked to its government's commitment to implement the 'Ships of Shame' recommendations.

Another country where political agitation has been evident in relation to vessel incidents is France. Owing to the numerous accidents affecting French waters over the years such as the *Torrey Canyon, Amoco Cadiz, Tanio* and *Erika*, the French Assemblée Nationale and Sénat have been extremely influential in directing the tenor of European Commission policies at international regulatory fora. Indeed, in the wake of the *Erika* incident, France used its presidency of the EU to demand tough action at the regional and international levels. In the aftermath of the *Prestige* incident in November 2002, Spain has now

---

[271] Of these, the most infamous was the pollution incident caused by the Greek-flagged tanker *Kirki* in 1991. Her condition was particularly sub-standard, leading to the spill of nearly 18,000 tons of crude oil into Western Australian waters.

[272] PARLIAMENT OF THE COMMONWEALTH OF AUSTRALIA, SHIPS OF SHAME: INQUIRY INTO SHIP SAFETY (1992). The Chairman of the Committee, Peter Morris, recently chaired another body, the International Commission on Shipping, which looked into general issues relating to sub-standard ships. Its report is provocatively entitled 'Ships, Slaves and Competition', *infra* note 980.

joined the list of countries agitating for more stringent regulation of the shipping industry.[273]

Like the Donaldson Report, the Australian, French and Spanish initiatives have an impact going far beyond domestic shores in view of their influence over other technically advanced administrations which can be expected to draw inspiration from them for their own submissions to IMO. In this sense, the efforts of like-minded actors at IMO are often complementary in the way they mutually reinforce each other's policy goals. Consequently, it can be appreciated how domestic political developments within key state actors can hugely influence multilateral action. This is especially so when democratically elected governments have publicly committed to accept recommendations for international action put forward by official inquiries into relevant vessel accidents.

4. Marine Pollution Regulation and the Interplay of Interests

4.1 The Relative Capacities of the Relevant Actors

Notwithstanding the roles of organisations such as UNCTAD, ILO and UNEP and the regional and national arenas such as Europe and the US, the epicentre of maritime regulation – especially in the public law field – is still very much at IMO. However, consistent with the historical restriction of IMO competence to advisory and technical matters, the IMO Secretariat customarily receives instructions from member states and rarely initiates policy decisions on its own. In addition, IMO possesses no power to enforce compliance with its rules or to impose sanctions on member states for non-compliance. This has led to frequent criticisms of IMO as being bureaucratic, slow and ineffective in responding to contemporary challenges as well as lacking 'teeth' in ensuring compliance.[274]

As observed above, the developed states continue to retain tremendous influence at IMO despite their being outnumbered by the developing countries. This is primarily due to the developed states possessing the capacity to send sizeable delegations with the requisite expertise to influence IMO negotiations, particularly at the sub-committee and working group levels. Individual personalities also exert substantial influence – many delegates from the developed countries have

---

[273] See Ch. 3.   [274] See Ch. 7 for recommendations to address these concerns.

been attending IMO meetings for years and have accumulated vast experience in their areas of expertise. Consequently, they command great deference and respect and are able to influence IMO proceedings in significant ways. Hence, through their superior manpower and financial resources, the developed countries maintain their long-standing influence at IMO.

Table 2-4 below provides a general assessment of the delegations which the present author has observed to wield the greatest influence at IMO. The determinants of influence comprise myriad factors including the size of the national economy, the amount of tonnage flying the national or associated registry's flag, beneficial ownership of global shipping tonnage by nationals, share of world trade carried by maritime shipping, membership in the IMO Council, size of delegations sent to IMO meetings and the competence, standing and leadership skills of delegates. Of these, the effectiveness of individual delegates is perhaps the single most important determinant of overall influence.

In stark contrast to the developed states, the developing countries are often unable to influence IMO decision-making owing to inadequate expertise and finances. To begin with, the vast majority of developing states do not have the resources to send large delegations to IMO. Travel costs to London alone compel governments to keep delegations small. Often, the sole delegates from the developing countries are representatives from their respective embassies in London. These are frequently Foreign Service officers with little working knowledge of shipping matters relevant to IMO.

Even when the developing countries are represented, small delegations are unable to attend the numerous Working and Drafting Group meetings which often meet simultaneously during Committee sessions. As plenary meetings of the IMO Committees are suitable only for general policy discussions, smaller groups are invariably entrusted to prepare texts of regulations which are then submitted for approval by the plenary. Consequently, substantive decision-making is commonly conducted within the smaller groups.

Moreover, preparatory work and even in-principle decisions may be undertaken in advance of Committee meetings through informal sessions or correspondence through electronic means. Typically, developing countries do not participate in such preparatory efforts. Even when they do attend meetings, developing state delegates do not normally voice their opinions, often due to a lack of understanding of the issue or the fact that their superiors in the national capitals may not have had the

Table 2-4. State Delegations with Significant Influence at IMO (in Alphabetical Order) and Determinants of Influence

	Size of National Economy	Tonnage in Associated Registries	Nationals' Ownership of Tonnage	Share of Maritime Trade	Size of Delegation to IMO	Delegates' Leadership & Influence	Council Membership 2003–5
Argentina	✓						✓
Australia	✓					✓	✓
Bahamas		✓					✓
Brazil	✓			✓			✓
Canada	✓		✓	✓✓			✓
China, PR	✓	✓✓	✓	✓✓	✓	✓	✓
Cyprus			✓				✓
Denmark	✓		✓	✓		✓✓✓	✓
France	✓	✓	✓✓	✓✓			✓
Germany	✓		✓✓	✓✓			✓
Greece	✓		✓✓	✓✓			✓
India	✓			✓			✓
Italy	✓			✓		✓	✓
Japan	✓	✓✓	✓✓	✓	✓	✓✓	✓
Liberia		✓✓					✓
Netherlands	✓	✓✓	✓✓	✓			✓
Norway	✓	✓✓	✓✓	✓✓		✓	✓
Panama		✓✓	✓✓	✓✓			✓
Rep. of Korea	✓			✓			✓
Russian Fed.	✓		✓✓				✓
Singapore	✓		✓✓	✓	✓✓	✓	✓
Spain	✓						✓
Sweden	✓					✓	✓
UK	✓	✓		✓		✓✓	✓
USA	✓			✓	✓✓	✓	✓

opportunity to study the matter. Often, non-English-speaking delegations do not enjoy the benefit of translation during Working Group sessions outside plenary meetings. For all these reasons, the influence of the developing countries at Working Group discussions remains negligible.

In recognition of the problem, IMO has adopted guidelines providing that no more than five groups (e.g. three Working Groups and two Drafting Groups) can meet simultaneously during each Committee's session.[275] In addition, when a Working Group has finalised its tasks and has been terminated, no other Working Group should be convened in its place during the same session. Inter-sessional Working Groups are also to be avoided unless absolutely essential. These guidelines seek to balance the developing states' capacity concerns with the ever-pressing need to enact new rules to meet contemporary challenges.

Unfortunately for the developing states, the existence of these guidelines has not wholly stopped IMO Working and Drafting Groups from meeting outside plenary hours. The reality is that so many issues arise for IMO's consideration that the Committees find it unavoidable to delegate work to sub-committees. The convening of inter-sessional working groups has also become more common, as exemplified by the discussions on ballast water management and anti-fouling paints.[276] It is arguable that these practices go against the spirit of the IMO guidelines which is to prevent developing states from being disadvantaged by a proliferation of meetings.

The developing countries which are consistently active at IMO are mainly the open registry states. These often speak out to defend their flag state interests. In the past, major developing states like India, Brazil and Argentina used to place the establishment of national shipping lines as a top priority and thus speak out on behalf of the developing states. However, such activism has since ebbed and developing state participation and influence have generally become weak. More often than not, these states only speak up when specific national interests are at stake. In recent years, increasing participation has been demonstrated by emerging states such as Brazil, China, the Republic of Korea, Singapore and the Philippines. By and large, however, IMO decision-making remains in the hands of the dominant developed states.

---

[275] Guidelines on the Organisation and Method of Work of MSC and MEPC and their Subsidiary Bodies, MSC/Circ. 816 and MEPC/Circ.331, as revised by MSC/Circ. 931, MEPC/Circ. 366 and MSC/Circ.1099-MEPC/Circ.405.
[276] See the complaints of the Brazilian delegation in this regard, Council Doc. C89/SR.6 (2002).

Apart from the member states, the participation of numerous transnational public and private interest groups adds to the depth and complexity of IMO deliberations. As mentioned above, there are numerous inter-governmental (IGOs) and non-governmental organisations (NGOs) enjoying consultative status at IMO. These include representatives from the shipping and industry bodies. True to the competitive and dispersed nature of the maritime industries, the shipping-related actors do not often speak with one voice. Indeed, as will be analysed later, the industry is hardly monolithic and united. In contrast, the other major non-state observers – the environmental NGOs – are typically more coherent and single-minded in their quest for greater protection for the oceans. However, they do not always have co-ordinated positions either, particularly when each has specific priority issues to address.

Whilst not conferring voting rights, consultative status affords the non-state entities the opportunity to speak, participate and influence proceedings at formal meetings. Their participation lends a more democratic flavour to international decision-making. The non-state actors typically seek alliances with member governments to pursue, defeat or modify policy alternatives impinging on their interests. Through their local chapters or branches, several of these entities would have had prior access to decision-makers in their respective national capitals. At the IMO meetings proper, the non-state actors frequently attempt to explain the implications of proposed policies and regulations in the practical world. These are often realities which may be far removed from the deliberations of government bureaucrats.

4.2 The Contemporary Political Dynamics at IMO

The dynamics at IMO today reflect less of the state-centred jurisdictional conflicts prevalent in the 1970s. Instead, the more relevant contemporary discourse is one between commercial shipping interests and flag states resisting increasing regulation on the one hand, and coastal and environmental interests seeking greater control over the polluting activities of ships on the other. While this is not altogether novel, the fundamental difference lies in the fact that the commercial shipping interests do not presently enjoy the full and unwavering support of their traditional maritime state allies.

In large measure, the shift in maritime state policy has been due to the progressive decline of these states' shipping registries.[277] In addition,

---

[277] See Table 2-1.

many associated industries such as the shipbuilding, ship management and shipbreaking sectors have moved to the more cost-effective developing countries. Ships are also increasingly being manned by the nationals of developing countries.[278] In general, the centre of gravity of shipping operations has moved away from the traditional maritime states toward the developing world, at least in as far as shipping registration is concerned.

The progressive diminution of the maritime industry's relevance in the developed states has thus enabled these states to champion environmental causes to greater degrees. As a result, strong enforcement systems predicated upon greater inspection powers for coastal and port states have been established, particularly in Western Europe and North America. Cumulatively, these developments represent a significant retreat of those traditional bulwarks of maritime commerce – the time-hallowed concepts of free navigation and flag state primacy.

It is with these factors in mind that we are able to locate the current trends of decision-making at IMO. To the extent that developed state delegations with the capacity to influence outcomes are increasingly dictated by environmental pressures, the prevailing mood at IMO is one of partiality to stringent regulation. The cynics would maintain that IMO and its bureaucrats, having largely exhausted the regulation of oil pollution, have moved on to other pastures such as regulation over chemicals and alien organisms in ballast water in order to justify their continued existence.[279] This allegation is not altogether fair, since it is the member states who have always determined the direction of IMO activities, not the Secretariat.

It would be more accurate to explain the current legislative intensity as being propelled by the interests of a minority of influential states wishing to use IMO as a platform to advance coastal state concerns and to 'internationalise' what could arguably be called localised problems. An example would be the initiative to regulate ballast water discharge from ships. This initiative is being led by Australia and the US, two countries with sensitive marine ecosystems threatened by non-indigenous harmful organisms.

On their part, the commercial shipping interests, for so long accustomed to an alliance of interests with the developed states, have had to adjust to the changing regulatory atmosphere. To some extent, the shipping interests have turned to the open registry states to advance

[278] WILLINGALE, *supra* note 118, at 203–11.   [279] Personal interviews.

their interests at IMO. These states, however, have neither the capacity nor influence to act as effective proxies. Meanwhile, most shipping interests have acknowledged, albeit reluctantly, that increased regulation is now inevitable. In any event, the shipowners concede that harmonised regulation at the international level is far more preferable to the dislocations arising from unilateral or regional action by states. In the result, the shipping community has been progressively compelled to accept the case for greater international controls over sea-going ships.

As argued earlier, the primary determinants affecting the regulation of vessel-source pollution are the intrinsic nature of the ship transportation industry and the dynamics of competitive interaction among its members. In the next few chapters, the problems thrown up by the industry and the means of overcoming them will be analysed, particularly in Chapter 5, where the specific challenge of compliance is considered. The substantive regulatory instruments and the history behind their adoption will also be examined. In the process, a chronological assessment of the various instruments is provided, detailing how the interest politics of the relevant state and non-state actors have come to influence the regime formation process and its effectiveness in dealing with the vessel-source pollution problem.

PART B

Vessel-Source Pollution and the International Legislative Process

3 Vessel-Source Pollution and Regime Formation

1. Pollution Control Standards and Reception Facilities

1.1 Early Regulatory Efforts[280]

One of the most important concepts employed in the regulation of vessel-source pollution is that of controlled discharges within ocean zones. The concept can be traced back to the early part of the twentieth century when political pressure in the UK and the US led to regulation over oily waste discharges (mainly by non-tankers) beyond the traditional three-mile territorial waters limit. Subsequently, international agreement was sought on the matter, and a conference was convened in Washington DC in June 1926 for this purpose. For the UK and the US, international agreement was needed to avert unilateral action by other states and to avoid competitive disadvantages for their own merchant fleets.

At the Washington conference, the UK and the US were able to persuade other states to adopt pollution control zones of up to 50 nautical miles from shore.[281] Within these zones (which states could declare at their discretion), ship discharges beyond 500 parts per million (ppm) of oil to water were prohibited. This formed the genesis of the 'ppm' discharge standard and the 'prohibition zone' concept so widely prescribed in later conventions.[282] In advocating a zonal approach, the UK and the US had to assure the other states that international law remained

---

[280] The historical account of developments in the twentieth century up to the 1970s is derived largely from S. Z. PRITCHARD, OIL POLLUTION CONTROL (1987), M'GONIGLE & ZACHER, *supra* note 65 and personal interviews conducted by the author.
[281] The width of the zones could be extended to 150 miles under exceptional circumstances.
[282] PRITCHARD, *supra* note 280, at 18.

unaltered and that flag states retained jurisdiction over their vessels, even within the prohibition zones. For the first time, a pollution control measure was to be introduced beyond territorial limits in areas then considered to be high seas. As such, there was great trepidation among the maritime interests which feared coastal state interference with their vessels on the high seas.

In retrospect, and from an environmental perspective, the concession to flag state jurisdiction was the major flaw of the zonal system. This is because flag states – then and now – lack the incentive to control the polluting activities of their flag vessels in other states' waters. Under the Washington proposal, coastal states possessed no enforcement (as opposed to prescriptive) authority over foreign-flagged vessels outside the three-mile limit. As such, coastal states did not have the power to board and inspect vessels outside that limit for suspected violations.

In any event, it was never seriously contemplated in the 1920s that coastal states had the practical means to enforce discharge standards beyond three miles from shore. Consequently, prohibition zones beyond the three-mile limit were highly unrealistic from an enforcement and compliance perspective. In addition, the zonal approach only served to transfer the problem farther out to sea – outside the zones, ships could discharge as they pleased. Depending on factors such as tidal and wind conditions, persistent oily discharges could still make their way to shore.

Recognising these shortcomings, the US had actually proposed during the Washington Conference to introduce stricter requirements for shipboard retention and separation of oily wastes. As opposed to the zonal approach, this measure would have imposed an *ocean-wide* prohibition on discharges beyond a certain concentration – this became known as the 'total prohibition' measure. At the same time, the US assiduously deflected any proposal for reception facilities to be provided in ports. This was primarily due to the high costs of reception facilities. Despite its merits, the 'total prohibition' proposal was ultimately defeated by maritime powers such as Germany and the Netherlands which objected to its high costs.

In any event, the draft convention produced by the 1926 Conference never came to be formally adopted. In the years following the Conference, UK and US government officials became largely apathetic to oil pollution concerns.[283] Little support for the draft convention

---

[283] *Ibid.*

came from the other countries, the majority of which did not view operational pollution to be a serious problem. With the onset of the Great Depression in the late 1920s, world trade collapsed and oil pollution became the farthest concern in the minds of states and shipowners.

Another attempt to lay down pollution control standards arose in the 1930s. In the wake of the Washington Conference, environmental groups in the UK had condemned the zonal approach as a mere palliative and had called for the adoption of total prohibition instead.[284] Unilateral claims by states for expanded power over the high seas were also increasing. Wary of its first failed attempt at international agreement, the UK began to contemplate action within the League of Nations. However, the common feeling at that time was that the major maritime states could not accept total prohibition.

The eventual League Draft Convention thus maintained the system of 50-mile zones in normal circumstances and 150-mile zones for special coastal configurations. Jurisdiction over ships in the zones would remain with the flag state. During the negotiations, a French proposal for exclusive coastal state jurisdiction over the zones was expectedly rejected. The same fate befell a British proposal for concurrent or dual jurisdiction of flag and coastal states. The League Draft Convention thus suffered from the same structural deficiencies found in the 1926 Washington Draft Convention. In particular, the reliance on flag state enforcement authority undermined both instruments' potential efficacy.

In place of total prohibition, British and League experts sought to insert an obligation on ports to provide reception facilities instead. However, this proposal was rejected by a group of states led by the US. The US was especially averse to obligatory reception facilities because its ports were either privately owned or came within the jurisdiction of the various states and not the federal government. In the result, a compromise was reached to leave the provision of port reception facilities as a mere recommendation. In any event, the equivocation of the Axis powers and the onset of the Second World War eventually shelved plans for a League conference to adopt a formal instrument on the matter. In retrospect, while the failure of the League's efforts has commonly been blamed on the Axis powers, some fault can also be attributed to the lack of interest demonstrated by other maritime states, not least the US and the UK themselves.

[284] *Ibid.*

1.2 The OILPOL Regime and the Load-On-Top (LOT) System

Following the war, the rapidly growing world economy triggered a massive demand for energy resources. It became clear by this time that tankers posed a more serious threat to the marine environment than non-tankers. In 1948, the UN convened a Maritime Conference in Geneva. The Conference resulted, *inter alia*, in the establishment of the Inter-Governmental Maritime Consultative Organization (IMCO), the precursor to IMO. However, IMCO faced a troubled start due to the maritime powers' suspicion toward its broad competence.[285] In the meantime, British officials had to consider if the new body could be used to initiate fresh attempts at oil pollution control. In this regard, the UK was seeking to preserve its influence over maritime matters and was extremely wary of being pre-empted by the UN bodies.

During this period, the increasingly serious problem of oil discharges led to heightened public concern, particularly among UK environmentalists.[286] By this time, too, the shipowning interests in the UK had begun to warm up to the inevitability of growing regulation over oil pollution. There were, however, lingering concerns over the risk of unilateral state action as well as the competitiveness of the UK fleet vis-à-vis those of the other states. A Committee was thus established under the direction of Lord Faulkner to look into the desirability of global measures to harmonise regulatory action. As with the situation before the war, the motivation for international action arose as much from commercial considerations as it did from genuine environmental concerns.

Among its recommendations, the Faulkner Committee resurrected the British interest in a complete ocean-wide prohibition of discharges, both by tankers and non-tankers alike. There was acknowledgment that the main problem related to tankers – it was thus proposed that these could utilise slop tanks to separate the oil and water components of tank washings and dirty ballast. At the same time, the UK sought to make port reception facilities mandatory. In May 1954, a diplomatic conference was duly convened in London to negotiate a convention on the matter. At its conclusion, the conference produced the first ever multilateral agreement on oil pollution control, the International

---

[285] In fact, IMCO did not begin operations until 1958.
[286] Bird and animal welfare groups were among the first to lobby for regulation over vessel-source pollution.

Convention for the Prevention of Pollution of the Sea by Oil (hereinafter 'OILPOL 54').[287]

OILPOL 54 adopted the familiar zonal formula of a 50-mile coastal prohibition zone within which discharges by oil tankers beyond 100 ppm were illegal. Ships under 500 gross tons were exempted. However, these were to comply with the convention 'as far as was reasonable and practicable'. On its part, the provision of reception facilities for tankers failed to be made a binding obligation. Instead, it was only included as a recommendatory conference resolution, and even then, only for oil company terminals and shipyards but not governments.[288]

Despite this setback, the UK succeeded in making the provision of *non-tanker* reception facilities obligatory. In this regard, OILPOL 54 laid down an obligation for contracting states to 'ensure the provision' of these facilities without causing undue delay to ships.[289] At the same time, the UK proposal for separators on board non-tankers was relegated to the status of a conference resolution.[290] Given the wide scope of the prohibition zones and the lack of support for obligatory separators on board non-tankers, it was inevitable that these ships would need shore reception facilities to dispose of their oily discharges. This probably helped to convince a majority of states to accept reception facilities in their ports for non-tankers. In any event, most states knew that compliance with this costly requirement would prove problematic; consequently, many states went along quietly with its adoption.[291]

The effective result of OILPOL 54 was that no prohibition whatsoever was to be prescribed for most parts of the oceans. Thus, vessels were essentially free to discharge whatever amounts of oily wastes they pleased so long as they did so *outside* the prohibited coastal zones. In any case, whatever zonal prohibitions adopted would apply only to tankers; non-tankers were free to continue discharging within prohibition zones if they were headed for ports which had no reception facilities. Given that most ports had no such facilities, this effectively meant that non-tankers came under no regulation. Of course, there was the new obligation on states to construct reception facilities for non-tankers.

---

[287] 327 U.N.T.S. 3 (in force 26 Jul. 1958). [288] OILPOL 54, Final Act, Resolution 4.
[289] OILPOL 54, art. VIII.
[290] Separators were needed to separate oil and water components in an oily mixture. During the conference, the UK arranged to demonstrate the efficacy of separators on board one of its ships. The demonstration failed miserably, effectively killing the proposal for compulsory separators for non-tankers, PRITCHARD, *supra* note 280, at 91.
[291] PRITCHARD, *supra* note 280.

However, as demonstrated in later years, this provision was never adhered to by most state parties. Moreover, its very inclusion deterred many states from ratifying OILPOL 54.

As regards enforcement, state parties to OILPOL 54 had the right to inform another party when the latter's ships violated any of the convention's provisions. In this regard, the primacy of flag state jurisdiction was affirmed.[292] The flag state so informed shall investigate the matter. If satisfied that sufficient evidence exists, it shall institute proceedings against the vessel.[293] Any contravention of OILPOL 54 shall be an offence punishable under the law of the flag state. State parties were also obliged to report all penalties imposed to IMCO.[294]

Coastal and port states had no concrete enforcement powers save for inspecting the vessel's Oil Record Book (ORB) in port.[295] Under OILPOL 54, the coastal states could 'take measures *within its jurisdiction* in respect of any matter to which the Convention relates'.[296] However, the extent and content of this 'jurisdiction' remained vague. It was clear (at least to the maritime states) that coastal state jurisdiction could *not* be exercised beyond the three-mile territorial waters limit.

Indeed, the 100-ppm standard within the 50-mile prohibition zones, whilst directly benefiting the coastal states around which the zones were declared, entailed no actual transfer of prescriptive or enforcement jurisdiction to these states. As long as a vessel was outside the three-mile territorial sea (or twelve-mile, for some states), effective jurisdiction remained with the flag state *even if* the vessel was within a prohibition zone. In this regard, the maritime states were careful to ensure that the right of free navigation continued to accrue to their shipping interests.

In any event, most coastal states had little practical experience and capacity in enforcing pollution control standards, especially beyond their territorial seas. The effective enforcement of the 100-ppm standard proved to be excessively technical, requiring skilled expertise as well as expensive equipment well beyond the capacity of most states. In fact, the technology for accurate measurement of oil content on board ships was not even available in the 1950s. Physical detection of discharges beyond a threshold level would have entailed the commitment of

---

[292] For enforcement issues and the unsatisfactory aspects of flag state jurisdiction, see Ch. 4.
[293] OILPOL 54, art. X.   [294] IMCO's operation was anticipated in the coming years.
[295] The ORB was required to be maintained aboard every oil tanker and vessel using oil as fuel so that all oil transfers and ballasting operations could be recorded, see OILPOL 54, art. IX.
[296] OILPOL 54, art. XI (emphasis added).

massive resources, especially aerial surveillance in the open seas. Most state parties to OILPOL 54 thus conducted monitoring of oil discharges, if at all, only within their internal waters and territorial seas.

Even where violations outside the territorial sea could be proven against a particular vessel, coastal state action under OILPOL 54 was limited to informing the flag state of the violation. In this regard, the traditional reluctance of flag states to prosecute offending vessels effectively removed whatever incentives the coastal state had to conduct surveillance and detection. As for the port states, enforcement was restricted to non-invasive techniques such as inspections of the ORB as opposed to inspections of the ship's holds or outright prosecution.

Since ORB accuracy depended upon the diligence of crew members to incriminate themselves, there was naturally little to be gained from its inspection. More often than not, the ORB was easily falsified.[297] Many loading ports had no incentives to conduct ORB inspections, particularly because these had to be done without causing the vessel any delay. Beyond ORB inspections, the only other action coastal states could take was to report certain matters to IMCO. Even then, there was no provision for IMCO to act upon such reports.

OILPOL 54's enforcement system was thus fraught with inadequacies. Its main enforcement tool was the self-reporting system, which in turn relied on inspection rights which were either heavily circumscribed or ineffective. In retrospect, the UK was probably over-optimistic in advocating strict pollution control measures at a time when most other states were indifferent to the problem. Indeed, the UK's failure to canvass support from the other maritime powers – particularly the US – was a key factor in many of the proposals' rejection.

In reinforcing flag state authority and restricting the obligatory provision of reception facilities to non-tankers only, the OILPOL regime formation process had effectively compromised the new convention's enforceability from the outset. Thus, there was never any real possibility for meaningful compliance with the convention. Yet, despite OILPOL 54's structural defects, the fact that it was even adopted was a significant development in itself. Indeed, most states were indifferent to oil pollution given the incipient state of environmental awareness at the time. The maritime interests' pre-occupation with costs and free navigation thus won out over environmental concerns.

---

[297] Personal interviews.

Table 3-1. Summary of OILPOL 54 Provisions

Type of Ship	Discharge limits Within Zones	Discharge limits Outside Zones	Max. Total Discharge	Reception Facilities	Enforcement
Tankers > 500 tons	<100 ppm, <50 miles + special areas	None	None	Voluntary at oil terminals and shipyards	Coastal state, if within ports and territorial sea; flag state for all other situations
Non-tankers > 500 tons	Upon entry into force, as far as practicable from land	None	None	Mandatory in ports within 3 years of entry into force	
	3 years after entry into force, <100 ppm, <50 miles + special areas, when heading for port with reception facilities	None	None		

Adapted from: E. MOLENAAR, COASTAL STATE JURISDICTION OVER VESSEL-SOURCE POLLUTION (1998)

OILPOL 54 came into force on 26 July 1958, by which time the convention establishing IMCO had itself entered into force. The UK government, which had hitherto exercised depositary responsibilities over OILPOL 54, transferred these powers over to IMCO in 1959. The need to amend and improve upon OILPOL 54 was soon manifested. Global demand for oil was increasing and ever larger tankers were being constructed. Yet, it was clear that compliance with OILPOL 54 was severely lacking, given the regime deficiencies.

By this time too, the first and second UN Conferences on the Law of the Sea had taken place in 1958 and 1960 respectively. The question of marine pollution, however, did not feature highly on their agenda.[298] Like OILPOL 54, the four conventions which arose out of the 1958 Conference effected little change to the jurisdictional *status quo*. Within the contiguous zone extending up to twelve miles from the coast, the 1958 Conventions accorded the coastal states limited powers to prescribe and enforce regulations for 'sanitation' purposes, which arguably covered pollution control.[299] For the first time, there was thus a recognised possibility that coastal states could enjoy actual jurisdiction in a functional zone beyond its territorial sea to deal with marine pollution. While this was an improvement over OILPOL 54, few specific powers were granted.

In response to growing calls to amend OILPOL 54, IMCO convened a diplomatic conference in London in 1962. A total of thirty-nine countries were in attendance, several of them developing states responding to the oil pollution problem for the first time. Not surprisingly, the conference was dominated by the Western maritime nations and the Soviet bloc. The UK was able to secure acceptance for total prohibition of discharges by *new* ships over 20,000 gross tons (grt).[300] In this regard, France and Italy – the two major Mediterranean powers – supported the UK in a reversal of their 1954 position. This was largely because the North Atlantic prohibition zone established earlier by OILPOL 54 had

---

[298] Art. 24 of the High Seas Convention, 450 U.N.T.S. 82 (in force 30 Sept. 1962), contained a vague provision requiring states 'to draw up regulations to prevent pollution of the sea by discharges of oil from ships ... taking account of existing treaty provisions on the subject'. Nothing was added beyond a reference to 'existing treaty provisions', which presumably meant OILPOL 54.
[299] One observer views this interpretation to be possible only 'with some stretch of the imagination', see Y. Dinstein, *Oil Pollution by Ships and Freedom of the High Seas*, 3 J. MAR. L. & COM. 363, at 367 (1972).
[300] OILPOL 54/62, art. III(c).

the result of forcing ships to discharge oily slops in the Mediterranean (near the French and Italian coasts) before entering the Atlantic.

Several other states which accepted the British proposal did so probably because they expected it to be futile.[301] This was because the proposal's restriction to *new* ships effectively meant that the majority of global vessel tonnage remained subject to the less stringent zonal approach.[302] Thus, the 50-mile prohibition zone and the 100-ppm discharge maximum continued to apply to all existing tankers as well as new vessels less than 20,000 grt. Meanwhile, a Canadian proposal to extend the standard width of zones to 100 miles was rejected. Most delegations felt that such wide zones could not be practically enforced. Moreover, the UK, among other states, feared that a widening of zones might lead to states legislating 100-mile zones without bothering to ratify OILPOL. However, the conference did agree to enlarge prohibition zones to 100 miles for certain 'special areas' prone to higher risks of pollution. These included the Mediterranean and Adriatic Seas, the Persian Gulf, the Red Sea and the coasts of Australia and Madagascar.

The shipping interests agreed to all these measures, probably reckoning that the enforcement of discharge measures would be effective, if at all, only within the territorial sea. Indeed, it was widely known that states had little capacity to enforce the prohibition zones beyond waters close to shore. For its part, the oil industry accepted the amendments without much protest. BP and Shell, which were dominated by British interests, supported the UK proposals largely out of goodwill.[303]

In relation to non-tanker reception facilities, the OILPOL 54 obligation in Article VIII to 'ensure' the provision of such facilities was replaced in 1962 by a weaker provision for states to 'take all appropriate measures to promote' reception facilities. This step backward was driven by US insistence that ports could not be compelled to provide facilities.[304] The US then offered to broaden the ambit of this amended (but weakened) article to include not only facilities for non-tankers, but

---

[301] See generally M'GONIGLE & ZACHER, *supra* note 65, at 91–6.

[302] Even then, the US, Japan, Norway and the Netherlands voted against the proposal. In addition, these states made clear their understanding that the provision of reception facilities in ports and terminals was the responsibility of industry, not governments.

[303] It subsequently transpired that the oil industry was represented at the 1962 Conference by junior officials who apparently did not fully appreciate the consequences of industry accepting responsibility for providing reception facilities, see M'GONIGLE & ZACHER, *supra* note 65, at 95.

[304] At the 1962 Conference, the UK had even proposed to delete art. VIII altogether because its presence had reportedly deterred many states from ratifying OILPOL 54.

for tankers at ports, oil-loading terminals and shipyards as well. Thus, for the first time, reception facilities for tankers became included within the convention's main provisions, albeit in non-obligatory language. It was the hope of many delegations that the relaxed provision on reception facilities would make the convention more attractive to non-contracting states.

The 1962 Conference also included a requirement for vessels over 20,000 dwt to report discharges exceeding the maximum level to their flag states for onward transmission to IMCO. In addition, penalties would be imposed for discharge violations recorded in the ORB. As expected, the ORB provision continued to be futile given its unrealistic expectation of crew members' readiness to incriminate themselves. Other changes under the 1962 amendments obliged flag states to impose penalties 'adequate in severity' to deter violations and to report on inadequate reception facilities in ports which their vessels visited. Again, such faith on flag state diligence was misplaced given these states' lack of incentives to conduct stringent enforcement.

In essence, the 1962 Conference failed to make improvements to enforcement where it mattered. The maritime interests continued to resist efforts to strengthen the enforcement system if these meant imposing new burdens on their industries and eroding the right of free navigation. Thus, a UK proposal to give port states the right to inspect any vessel on which incriminating evidence had been received failed to gain support. This was effectively the first form of port state control to have been proposed at an international forum. In this regard, France had gone even further to propose that such powers be given in relation to *any* vessel in port. This was roundly rejected by the maritime interests at the 1962 Conference.

As regards prosecuting powers,[305] the flag states had all along held the prerogative to initiate proceedings against offending vessels and to impose penalties. This was one aspect of enforcement over which coastal states had traditionally little or zero authority. A UK proposal at the 1962 Conference to shift the burden of proof to the master to show that he did *not* commit an alleged violation was rejected by the continental European countries for being incompatible with their legal systems.[306] With this rejection, it became clear that no meaningful

---

[305] This was the adjudicative component of 'enforcement jurisdiction', see Ch. 4.
[306] M'GONIGLE & ZACHER, *supra* note 65, at 222.

enforcement of the 100-ppm standard or prosecution of violations could be achieved.

Another measure which was rejected was the UK proposal to require OILPOL parties to inform IMCO as well as the flag states of suspected violations. The maritime interests felt that this would impose undue pressure on the flag states to investigate the allegation. More importantly, it was perceived that the proposal would allow IMCO to interfere with the flag state's legal system on behalf of other states. Again, the desire to protect the flag state's sovereignty and its legal autonomy, coupled with a distrust of IMCO and coastal state action, thwarted improvements to the prosecution process. Finally, proposals to establish minimum penalties pegged to an international standard or to impose these directly on the master and crew without resort to the flag state were rejected, again for their perceived interference with national legal systems.

Ultimately, the 1962 amendments effectively ensured that reception facilities would not be built and that vessels could continue to flout the 100 ppm discharge maximum. In the result, although the UK had scored an in-principle victory for total prohibition, most states knew fully well that the essential preconditions for a general prohibition – effective oily water separators on board ships and reception facilities in oil-loading ports – simply did not exist. In addition, the fact that separators were not made compulsory on board non-tankers meant that these vessels could continue to discharge oily wastes, even close to shore. The widespread absence of reception facilities also meant that the new total prohibition measure for new ships above 20,000 grt could not be adequately enforced.

Overall, the reliance on flag states to enforce OILPOL 54/62 meant that the prospect for the amended convention's effective implementation appeared bleak. Indeed, it was clear that compliance would again be seriously hampered by the failure of the regime formation process to address the actual problem, which was states' lack of capacity and incentives to conduct proper enforcement.

Following the Suez crisis of 1956, the oil-importing states saw a need for alternative routes to transport oil from the Middle East to Europe and North America.[307] To this end, the longer route around the southern tip of Africa would prove economical only if tankers of much greater

---

[307] See generally E. J. Ellis, *International Law and Oily Waters: A Critical Analysis*, 6 COLO. J. INT'L ENVTL. L. & POL'Y 32, at 35–8 (1995).

Table 3-2. Summary of the 1962 Amendments to OILPOL 54

Type of Ship	Age of Ship	Discharge limits		Max. Total Discharge	Reception Facilities	Enforcement
		Within Zones	Outside Zones			
Tankers > 150 tons	Existing	<100 ppm, <50 miles + special areas	None	None	States to take all appropriate steps to promote the provision of facilities	Flag states to impose penalties 'adequate in severity' and to report inadequate reception facilities in ports which their vessels visit
	New, <20,000 grt	<100 ppm, <50 miles + special areas	None			
	New, >20,000 grt	<100 ppm				
Non-tankers > 500 tons	Existing	Upon entry into force, as far as practicable from land	None	None		
		3 years after entry into force, <100 ppm, <50 miles + special areas	<100 ppm			
	New, <20,000 grt	<100 ppm, <50 miles + special areas	None			
	New, >20,000 grt	<100 ppm				

Adapted from: E. Molenaar, Coastal State Jurisdiction over Vessel-Source Pollution (1998)

capacity were employed. Together with increasing oil consumption in the industrialised countries, the Cape voyage stimulated demand for ever larger tankers. By the early 1960s, the Japanese shipyards were producing tankers well over 100,000 deadweight tons (dwt). In time, the so-called Very Large Crude Carriers (VLCCs) of over 200,000 and 300,000 dwt came into service. The early 1970s witnessed the advent of the Ultra Large Crude Carriers (ULCCs), supertankers of over 400,000 dwt.

With their increasing size, it was only a matter of time before one of these tankers caused pollution of unprecedented severity. On 18 March 1967, the fateful shipping disaster which was to change the landscape of marine pollution control occurred. On that day, the Liberian-registered oil tanker, the *Torrey Canyon*, carrying 120,000 tons of crude oil, grounded on the high seas off the Scilly Isles near the British coast. Though not a VLCC, the *Torrey Canyon* caused the largest single oil spill ever recorded up to that time. Amidst fears of accidents involving even larger tankers, efforts began at IMCO in 1969 to revise the OILPOL 54/62 regime.

This time round, the negotiations witnessed greater involvement by the shipping and oil industries. The major oil companies which displayed little interest in the 1962 Conference had by now realised how expensive it could be if they were forced to construct reception facilities at their Middle Eastern loading terminals. Even though the OILPOL requirement on reception facilities had been watered down considerably in 1962, there was still concern that the provision of facilities may yet be made obligatory at some point.

There was little doubt that the oil companies were highly sensitive to the growing calls for more effective measures to control oil pollution. They soon resolved to pursue a measure known as the load-on-top (LOT) system to stave off the more costly reception facilities. LOT was premised upon contaminated ballast water settling down during an oil tanker's return voyage to the loading port. As the oil and water components separated, the heavier water could be decanted from the tank bottoms and discharged. The remaining slop would then be retained on board while a fresh shipment of oil was 'loaded-on-top' at the loading port. Thus, LOT avoided the necessity of washing tanks to prepare for fresh shipments of oil and reduced the amounts of slop discharged into the sea. Very importantly, it appeared to reduce the demand for reception facilities in loading ports as well.

With the increasing amounts of oil being transported, the oil companies also recognised the economic incentive of conserving oil (albeit slops) through LOT instead of discharging these overboard. Of course, such motivations came to matter even more in the 1970s when world oil prices spiralled following the OPEC-induced crisis. Indeed, the oil price hike during the crisis may have had a greater effect in reducing overall ship discharges than the legal conventions ever did.[308]

LOT had been developed by the Shell Oil Company as early as 1953. However, the process did not prove popular with the oil refineries then because it resulted in a high salt content in tanker-transported crude oil. By the 1960s, however, major companies like Shell had 'discovered' techniques for adjusting their tanker and refinery operations to employ LOT. There was widespread belief at the time that the oil companies had known of LOT's feasibility all along but had kept this 'under wraps' until they recognised that the high costs of reception facilities actually rendered LOT an attractive proposition.

Shell had little trouble persuading the other oil companies, including those in the US such as Exxon, to agree to using LOT on board their tankers.[309] At the time, the oil companies still owned a large number of tankers. Nonetheless, they needed also to convince the European independent tanker owners to retain slop wastes instead of discharging these overboard. During that time, a major disincentive for retaining slop on board was the fact that the Egyptian government charged levies for unclean tankers passing through the Suez Canal.[310] There was thus every motivation for ship operators to engage in slop discharge. Moreover, if ports refused to accept retained slop, the independent shipowner stood to lose out because of the ship's decreased capacity for fresh oil shipments.

To provide the requisite incentive, the oil companies promised to reimburse the independents for any additional expenses incurred in employing LOT. In particular, the oil majors were prepared to pay freight on slops as if these were cargo. Charterparty clauses were thus drafted to give effect to the LOT practice.[311] It was clear that the oil companies were extremely eager to claim a high adherence rate to LOT among tanker operators. In their reckoning, the deeper LOT was

---

[308] W. G. WATERS II ET AL., OIL POLLUTION FROM TANKER OPERATIONS – CAUSES, COSTS, CONTROLS 182 (1980).
[309] The principal person credited with the successful promotion of LOT was John Kirby, marine co-ordinator at Shell Marine International, see M'GONIGLE & ZACHER, *supra* note 65, at 96.
[310] M'GONIGLE & ZACHER, *supra* note 65, at 98.
[311] P. VALOIS, TANKERS – AN INTRODUCTION TO THE TRANSPORT OF OIL BY SEA 51 (1997).

entrenched in practice, the easier it would be to resist port reception facilities.

The fact that LOT was developed, promoted and adopted independent of governments and in a relatively short time demonstrated how successful the oil companies were in presenting states with what was effectively a *fait accompli*.[312] In promoting LOT, the oil industry had openly conceded that the technique actually led to discharges exceeding 100 ppm, especially in the final stages of decanting when the water near the water/oil interface was being discharged. In this regard, only proper oily water separators and interface detection meters could have effectively ensured compliance with the 100-ppm measure. However, such on-board equipment was not yet available at the time.

Consequently, tankers employing LOT on short-haul or rough voyages would have flagrantly breached OILPOL 54/62's 100-ppm standard in the prohibition zones given that there would inevitably have been inadequate separation of oil and water. Similarly, there would have been equally serious breaches by new tankers over 20,000 grt which were prohibited from discharging beyond 100 ppm *anywhere at sea* under the 1962 amendments. In essence, LOT could never guarantee discharges below 100 ppm even in the best of conditions. Moreover, LOT did not obviate the need for tank washings completely – reception facilities were still needed when incompatible cargoes were carried or when ships had to be dry-docked for repairs.

The result of LOT's effective adoption by industry ahead of the 1969 amendments was that the 100-ppm measure became irrelevant and sidelined. In large measure, the only reason why the oil companies were so successful in undermining OILPOL 54/62 was because compliance with its obligations was so poor, particularly in ocean areas beyond the territorial sea. This helped to ensure quick acceptance of industry proposals worldwide. Indeed, several states – including the UK and Sweden – even legislated the use of LOT in open contravention of their prevailing obligations under OILPOL 54/62.

Plans to revise OILPOL 54/62 and to legitimise LOT formally were thus set in motion. By this time, UK policy had become more sensitive to its shipping and oil interests. Scientific tests conducted in the UK began to focus not on the concentration of oil in the discharge (the basis of the 'ppm' standard), but on the amount of oil released over a distance traversed by the vessel. The tests concluded that an

---

[312] M'GONIGLE & ZACHER, *supra* note 65, at 98.

instantaneous rate of discharge of 60 litres per nautical mile would produce a sheen on the water surface which would disperse within two to three hours.

In other words, this quantity of oil could be so well dispersed by the ship's wake such that tar balls would not be expected to result from a properly operated LOT process.[313] Used in conjunction with LOT, the litre/mile standard would henceforth allow ships to discharge the decanted water component of contaminated ballast without worrying about the precise oil concentration therein. This conveniently got around the 'ppm' standard. Scientific development of the litre/mile standard had thus greatly aided a deliberate policy shift toward a new pollution control standard.

Together with France, the UK threw its weight behind LOT. However, the US, the USSR, Japan and Germany actively opposed sacrificing the 100-ppm standard and the coastal prohibition zone. In effect, the US and the UK had reversed positions since the 1950s; the US was now leading the environmental cause, while the UK was more inclined toward its maritime and oil interests. On its part, the USSR had its own peculiar reason to resist LOT. Whereas LOT needed ballast voyages of at least two days to enable oil and water to separate properly, most of the Soviet tankers operated only on short-haul routes.[314] Thus, employing LOT would be meaningless for the Soviet fleet. As for the Japanese, their reservations over LOT had to do with the fact that their refineries were still resistant to oil with a high salt content.

By the end of 1968, amidst intensive lobbying by the oil industry, the opponents of LOT agreed to a compromise. LOT would be acceptable provided that the 60 litre/mile standard was accompanied by a restriction on the *total* volume of oil discharged during the ballast voyage. This cap would be expressed as a fraction of the ship's total cargo-carrying capacity. It was thus agreed that the total amount of oil discharged pursuant to the litre/mile standard could not exceed 1/15,000 of the tanker's total capacity.

In addition, complete prohibition zones would be retained within 50 miles of *all* shores. Within such zones, tankers would be permitted to discharge only 'clean ballast' as opposed to oily mixtures below 100 ppm. This new 'clean ballast' provision rested upon a simple visual determination of whether a vessel's discharge left a sheen of oil on the water surface. If a sheen was visible, the vessel could be presumed

---

[313] *Ibid.* at 99.   [314] *Ibid.* at 100.

to have breached the provision.³¹⁵ These proposed standards spelled the end for the 'ppm' standard as well as the 'total prohibition' concept in so far as these related to tankers.

The oil companies initially opposed the 1/15,000 total discharge limit, arguing that it could not be complied with during short voyages or rough weather. In such situations, it was contended, the oil and water components in an oily mixture would not separate properly and *any* discharge would breach the 'clean ballast' requirement and the 1/15,000 discharge maximum. More importantly, the 1/15,000 limit was resisted because for the first time, violations could actually be detected by port state inspectors. If the amount of slops brought in by a vessel was too small, the inescapable inference must be that the vessel had discharged more than the permitted volume of oil at sea.

Eventually, as a price for securing LOT and abolishing the 'ppm' standard, the industry interests compromised and accepted the 'clean ballast' measure, the 50-mile zone limit, the 1/15,000 total discharge limit as well as an improved version of the ORB.³¹⁶ In essence, these were the new provisions adopted by the 1969 amendments to OILPOL 54/62. As for the non-tankers, discharges anywhere on the oceans must not exceed 60 litres/mile as well. The 100-ppm standard continued to apply to non-tankers exceeding 20,000 grt, although such vessels were rare. In general, non-tanker discharges below 60 litres/mile or 100 ppm were to be made 'as far as practicable from land'. This formula thus dispensed with the old zonal prohibition. In effect, it meant that all non-tankers would have to be fitted with oily water separators.

In this regard, however, no improvements were made by the 1969 amendments. In fact, the continued non-availability of monitoring, recording and oil separating equipment meant that no objective investigation could be made of the events surrounding an alleged discharge. Thus, any allegation of an illegal discharge by tankers or non-tankers could only be backed up by examining the relevant circumstances surrounding the event. This necessarily raised problems of proof, since the crew would invariably have their own version of relevant events.

Overall, in view of the prevailing mood at IMCO, the 1969 amendments which revised OILPOL 54/62 went only as far as introducing new

---

[315] The visible sheen test can be traced back to the US position at the 1926 Washington Conference.
[316] OILPOL 54/69, art. III(b).

discharge standards. No substantive improvements were made to the compliance, enforcement or prosecution regimes. Whatever improvements made to the enforcement system in 1969 were entirely incidental and flowed from the inherent nature of the new discharge standards themselves. Thus, even though the 1/15,000 total discharge limit effectively facilitated the loading port state in inspecting tankers for compliance, no explicit right of port state inspection or enforcement was conferred.[317] Even if the 1/15,000 standard could raise a presumption of discharge, prosecution was *still* entirely in the hands of the flag state.

In relation to port state powers, the French delegation had boldly proposed at the 1969 meeting that *all* states be *required* to inspect *all* vessels in their ports for discharge violations.[318] In addition, all states should be allowed to board vessels in their coastal zones to inspect for possible violations. As expected, these proposals were rejected. Among the objections raised were that the proposals would cause unwarranted delays to innocent ships; they were too expensive and technically difficult to implement; allowing coastal states to board ships in mid-ocean was highly dangerous; and perhaps most forcefully, the proposals interfered with the balance of coastal and flag state jurisdiction and were outside IMCO's mandate.[319]

The French proposals, radical as they were, went to the heart of the malaise which was afflicting OILPOL's self-reporting enforcement system. In retrospect, the proposals were ahead of their time, given that jurisdictional innovations were largely abhorred at IMCO during that period. There was an unstated philosophy, not only among the maritime states but several coastal states as well, that jurisdictional changes were best left to the upcoming UNCLOS to settle. It was thus up to the UK to advance a more modest proposal which allowed port states to inspect vessels only after receiving evidence of a violation. This was the very proposal that had been rejected earlier at the 1962 Conference. Perhaps as a concession to the political capital expended by the French on the matter, the UK proposal was accepted at the 1969 meeting, albeit only as a non-binding Assembly resolution.

---

[317] See Ch. 4.
[318] France, whose Normandy coast had been badly affected by the *Torrey Canyon* spill, was the only overtly pro-environmental delegation at the 1969 meeting. However, French exuberance for the environment did not last. By 1970, her commercial interests had brought France firmly back onto the maritime track, M'GONIGLE & ZACHER, *supra* note 65, at 224 and 268.
[319] M'GONIGLE & ZACHER, *supra* note 65, at 224.

With the regulatory system settling for an imperfect LOT mechanism and weak coastal and port state enforcement, meaningful prevention of oily discharges remained effectively unattainable. Industry had thus won the battle to defeat the potentially costly measures introduced by the 1962 amendments, i.e. oily water separators and reception facilities. Nonetheless, the LOT system was still enforceable to *some* extent and could be expected to reduce some vessel discharges. In addition, port authorities could check the volume of residues left in a vessel's tanks to determine if the total discharge limit had been breached. The limit to total discharge was also innovative since it attempted, for the first time, to regulate and reduce the actual quantity of oil discharged into the sea.[320]

1.3 MARPOL 73

1.3.1 Annex I and Segregated Ballast Tanks (SBTs)

The early 1970s marked a significant epoch in the history of environmental consciousness. During this period, the developed Western states experienced intense domestic pressure to enhance regulation over polluting activities. In June 1972, the landmark UN Conference on the Human Environment was convened in Sweden. The Conference adopted the Stockholm Declaration on the Human Environment[321] together with an Action Plan for the Human Environment.[322] In addition, the Conference established the momentum for the creation of a specialised UN agency for environmental protection – the United Nations Environment Programme (UNEP).

As regards the marine environment, the Stockholm Conference highlighted the weaknesses of OILPOL 54, particularly the fact that the convention's scope was limited to oil.[323] By 1972, the 1969 amendments to OILPOL were still not in force, leaving the 1962 amendments to be the legally effective standards.[324] As explained above, LOT was the

---

[320] The 'ppm' and litre/mile standards merely regulated the concentration and rate of discharges respectively. Without limits to total discharge, ship operators would still be able to legally dispose of vast quantities of oily wastes.

[321] UN Doc. A/CONF.48/14/Rev.1, 11 I.L.M. 1416 (1972). See L. B. Sohn, *The Stockholm Declaration on the Human Environment*, 14 Harv. Int'l L. J. 423 (1973).

[322] 11 I.L.M. 1421 (1972).

[323] See generally O. Schachter & D. Serwer, *Marine Pollution Problems and Remedies*, 65 Am. J. Int'l L. 84 (1971) and A. Mendelsohn, *Ocean Pollution and the 1972 United Nations Conference on the Environment*, 3 J. Mar. L. & Com. 385 (1972).

[324] Further amendments in 1971 had introduced limits to cargo tank sizes such that oil outflow during accidents would be reduced.

Table 3-3. Summary of the 1969 Amendments to OILPOL 54/62

Type of Ship	Age of Ship	Discharge limits		Max. Total Discharge	Enforcement
		Within Zones	Outside Zones		
Tankers	All	Clean ballast, <50 miles	<60 litres/mile	<1/15,000 of total cargo capacity	Port states could inspect for 1/15,000 requirement, but prosecution remains with flag states. Overall, no change to enforcement and prosecution regimes.
Non-tankers	All	As far as practicable from land, <60 litres/mile, <100 ppm for ships >20,000 grt	<60 litres/mile, <100 ppm for ships >20,000 grt	None	

Adapted from: E. MOLENAAR, COASTAL STATE JURISDICTION OVER VESSEL-SOURCE POLLUTION (1998)

preferred practical tool being employed by tankers, yet its use frequently breached the 1962 'ppm' standards. As such, an anomalous situation had arisen whereby many vessels professed to adhere to the 1969 amendments which were not in force while few vessels complied with the binding prohibition in OILPOL 54 (for existing vessels) and its 1962 amendments (for new vessels above 20,000 grt).

In the meantime, the US was experiencing an unprecedented surge in ecological consciousness. The Environmental Protection Agency (EPA) had been created in 1970 and in the same year, the Nixon Administration called for more effective standards to regulate tanker operations. At IMCO, the US openly criticised LOT, barely a year after it had been adopted. Among the criticisms were the frequently inadequate separation of water and oil, the reliance on manual discretion as to when to decant and the inapplicability of LOT to short or rough voyages. Most notably, LOT was assailed for failing to ensure compliance by non-diligent crew members.[325]

The US subsequently moved to revise the existing regulatory regime. To this end, it espoused a pro-active port enforcement system coupled with the requirement for segregated ballast tanks (SBTs) and double hulls for tankers. As conceived, the SBT was an equipment standard which entailed the construction of tanks dedicated to the exclusive carriage of ballast. As such, SBTs did away with the carriage of ballast water in cargo tanks and the attendant oil-water mixes and discharges. On its part, the double hull standard entailed the construction of a ship with two protective layers encasing the hull. This minimised the risks of oil outflow during collisions.

In addition to these measures, the US called for non-tankers to be designed and constructed such that they would never need to use fuel tanks for ballast. Most importantly, the US signalled to IMCO that it was prepared to act unilaterally and enact legislation imposing SBTs as a condition for entry into its ports regardless of whether international action was taken on the matter. The US zeal for more stringent anti-pollution measures greatly unsettled the European states, especially those with strong oil and shipping lobbies. The gauntlet had thus been thrown to the industry interests: LOT had to be improved, or else costly equipment standards would be imposed unilaterally.

---

[325] See e.g. S. Z. Pritchard, *Load on Top – From the Sublime to the Absurd*, 9 J. Mar. L. & Com. 185 (1978).

The oil companies were put on the defensive and quickly recognised that with mounting US pressure, the halcyon days of LOT and flexible enforcement were over. Subsequently, the US-based oil companies spearheaded a shift in industry policy toward accepting SBTs. Before long, most other oil multinationals abandoned their resistance to SBTs, with only the French and Japanese holding out.[326] The US companies, far from being dictated by altruistic environmental goals, realised that they had no choice but to be on the good side of their government. From this negotiating position, they sought to persuade the US to drop the percentage of tanks it demanded to be designated as SBTs.

The oil companies also calculated that by supporting SBTs, they could potentially stave off US demands for double hulls which were monumentally more expensive. In any event, the global tanker boom had by then subsided. The oil companies thus reckoned that any SBT requirements on *new* tankers alone were unlikely to have immediate economic impact given that few fresh orders were being placed.

Arising from US pressure, IMCO duly convened the International Conference on Marine Pollution in October 1973. The Conference was attended by 71 nations with the developing states forming the majority of participants for the first time. By then, preparatory work for the Third UNCLOS had also commenced and the world was deeply polarised between power blocs. Hence, the group divisions appearing at the UNCLOS negotiations – principally the maritime states, coastal states, G77 developing states and the Soviet bloc – were replicated at the 1973 IMCO Conference.

The result of the 1973 Conference was a new instrument, the International Convention for the Prevention of Pollution from Ships (popularly referred to as MARPOL 73).[327] The new convention effectively superseded the regime established by OILPOL 54 and its amendments.[328] In contrast to OILPOL 54 which dealt only with oil, MARPOL 73 covered all technical aspects of pollution from ships save for the disposal of wastes by dumping. It applied to all ships but not to pollution arising out of the exploration and exploitation of seabed mineral resources.

The operational aspects of MARPOL 73 were laid out in five annexes dealing with pollution by oil, noxious liquid substances carried in bulk,

---

[326] M'GONIGLE & ZACHER, *supra* note 65, at 110. [327] 12 I.L.M. 1319 (1973).
[328] A small number of states are still parties to OILPOL, but their fleets account for only a small proportion of global shipping tonnage.

harmful substances carried in packages, sewage and garbage respectively. Two Protocols were also adopted, dealing with Reports on Incidents involving Harmful Substances and Arbitration respectively. The most significant and controversial provision introduced by MARPOL 73 was Regulation 13 of Annex I which mandated SBTs for all new tankers over 70,000 dwt.[329]

During the Conference negotiations, the SBT standard was strenuously resisted by the independent tanker owners – particularly the Scandinavians – due to its high construction costs. However, as stated above, the oil companies were prepared to support SBTs in order to avert more costly requirements like double hulls. In this regard, the oil companies' greater willingness to accept SBTs severely undermined the independent owners. Other actors which saw benefits in SBTs were the major oil-exporting states in the Middle East. Not only would SBTs increase environmental protection for these states, the costs of SBTs would not fall on them. More importantly, SBTs did away with the need for these states to provide reception facilities.

The majority of developing states obtained little direct benefit from the imposition of SBTs. Like the maritime interests, several developing states opposed SBTs for the direct construction costs that these would impose on their fledgling fleets. The introduction of SBTs would also generally raise the costs of shipping and imports. Given that most developing states imported oil using foreign vessels, even a deliberate choice not to ratify MARPOL would not have saved them from these indirect costs.

Eventually, however, most developing states ended up supporting SBTs, a peculiar outcome given that they had relatively few oil pollution problems and a much greater concern for economic development.[330] For its part, the USSR was amenable to new regulations because it had little interest in the global maritime transportation industry. In any event, it appeared that the Cold War détente made it possible for US–Soviet co-operation to be maintained. The Soviets also had an environmental interest in stringent vessel-source pollution standards because many

---

[329] New vessels were those for which the building contract was placed after 31 December 1975, or whose keels were laid after 30 June 1976 or were delivered after 31 December 1979. The 1978 MARPOL Protocol later extended the SBT requirement to new vessels over 20,000 dwt.

[330] M'GONIGLE & ZACHER, *supra* note 65, at 115. It appeared that many developing states followed the Egyptian lead in supporting SBTs. Egypt was one of those states which steadfastly resisted reception facilities.

semi-enclosed seas came within their territory, jurisdiction or control.[331]

Ultimately, the shipping interests relented, consoled by the fact that SBTs would be required only of new tankers. In this regard, the prevailing glut in the tanker market meant that new orders would not be fulfilled for some time. Hence, the shipowners were convinced that the *status quo* would effectively remain for years. More importantly, the US proposal for double hulls had been averted. As for the non-tankers, SBTs were not required at all. However, Regulation 14(1) achieved a similar result by prohibiting all new non-tankers over 4,000 grt and all new oil tankers over 150 grt from using fuel tanks to carry any ballast.[332]

As for discharge standards, MARPOL 73 required ships to comply with measures substantially similar to those established by the 1969 OILPOL amendments. Thus, the LOT process was reaffirmed, as were discharge standards for cargo tank washings and machinery space bilges first laid down by OILPOL 54/69. Several new features were added, including regulations mandating the installation of oil discharge, monitoring and control systems and oily-water separating and oil-filtering systems.[333]

In addition, MARPOL 73 required that any residues not meeting the relevant standards would have to be retained on board for subsequent disposal to shore reception facilities. Hence, for the first time, a concrete legal obligation was laid down to install shipboard technology for retaining slops. This is in contrast to OILPOL 54/69 which merely required shipowners to ensure the provision of such equipment. For new oil tankers, the 1/15,000 total discharge limit was replaced by a new and more stringent limit of 1/30,000 of the vessel's capacity.[334]

Apart from the standard 50-mile coastal zones, MARPOL 73 also established new 'special areas' within which no discharge of oil or oily mixtures by any oil tanker or by a non-tanker of above 400 grt would be permitted, except for 'clean ballast'. Thus, no ship or tanker may discharge any oil in a special area with the exception of non-tankers

---

[331] On Soviet maritime policies, see e.g. THE LAW OF THE SEA AND INTERNATIONAL SHIPPING: ANGLO-SOVIET POST-UNCLOS PERSPECTIVES (W. E. Butler ed., 1985) and R. E. Bradshaw, *The Politics of Soviet Maritime Security*, 10 J. MAR. L. & COM. 411 (1979).
[332] Reg. 14(3) further provided that 'all other ships' shall comply with reg. 14(1) as far as reasonable and practicable.
[333] MARPOL 73, Annex I, regs. 15–19.   [334] MARPOL 73, Annex I, reg. 9(1)(a)(v).

under 400 grt in restricted circumstances.[335] The 'special area' concept was not entirely new, having found expression in OILPOL 54/69 in the form of prohibited coastal zones. However, MARPOL 73's special areas were considerably more stringent and amounted to a total prohibition on discharges.

In any event, the maritime interests were not too perturbed with this development since effectively functioning special areas had to have port reception facilities. To the extent that these were not readily available, many delegations at the 1973 Conference believed that the 'special area' regime would not be a practical reality for years to come. The Conference thus proceeded to designate several 'special areas' – for oil pollution under Annex I, these were the Mediterranean Sea, the Black Sea, the Baltic Sea, the Red Sea and the Persian Gulf.[336]

As for reception facilities, MARPOL 73 succeeded in laying down a requirement for such facilities in all ports where tankers and non-tankers would have to discharge oil residues. To this end, MARPOL 73 reverted to the original formula in OILPOL 54 which required states to 'undertake to ensure the provision' of such facilities.[337] However, this provision was interpreted by many states at the 1973 Conference to be not legally binding. In fact, several developing states accepted the provision on the explicit condition and understanding that it was not obligatory.[338] Meanwhile, some other states approved of it knowing full well that they would never ratify the convention. Even those states, including the UK, which considered the provision to be legally binding felt that it was up to industry, and not governments, to bear the costs of reception facilities.[339] On the whole, these qualifications largely negated the value of the provision.

1.3.2 Annexes II to V

During the 1973 Conference, Annex I issues relating to oil pollution were the most contentious. However, the other pollutants raised

---

[335] MARPOL 73, Annex I, reg. 10(2).
[336] The Gulf of Aden, the Antarctic and the Northwest European Waters were designated as Annex I special areas in later years. The Oman area of the Arabian Sea has recently been approved as the latest Annex I special area. Under Annex II (relating to noxious liquid substances), the Baltic Sea, the Black Sea and the Antarctic have been designated 'special areas'. Annex V 'special areas' relating to garbage disposal have been designated in the Mediterranean, Baltic, Black, Red and North Seas as well as the Persian Gulf, the Antarctic and the Wider Caribbean.
[337] MARPOL 73, Annex I, reg. 12(1). [338] M'GONIGLE & ZACHER, *supra* note 65, at 116.
[339] Ibid.

problems of their own. Annex II, in particular, dealt with chemical wastes derived from noxious liquid substances (NLS) carried in bulk. Such wastes originated mainly from tank washings, and could potentially be more toxic to the marine environment than oil. To address this concern, Annex II imposed NLS discharge controls that were dependent on factors such as distance from land, nature and concentration of effluents and minimum ocean depth at the place of discharge. More stringent restrictions applied to 'special areas' designated under Annex II. In addition, prohibited chemical discharges had to be retained on board for disposal at shore reception facilities. To this end, MARPOL 73 obliged governments to ensure the provision of facilities for the reception of NLS residues.[340]

In contrast to the compulsory Annexes I and II, Annexes III, IV and V were made optional for MARPOL 73 parties. Annex III contains requirements for preventing pollution by harmful substances carried in packaged form, or in freight containers, portable tanks or road and rail tank wagons. Annexes IV and V regulate the disposal of sewage and garbage respectively. They provide rules relating to the distances from land where these wastes may be disposed of, the specific manner of disposal as well as requirements for reception facilities.

Given that MARPOL 73 provided a common architecture for the prescription and enforcement of discharge standards, the same regime deficiencies encountered by Annex I can be found in the other annexes as well. Thus, compliance depended largely upon the ship's crew to ensure proper practices and to maintain discharge record books. Like in Annex I, the reliance on flag state enforcement was problematic, as was the requirement to ensure the provision of reception facilities. There was also pessimism over the effectiveness of Annexes II and V 'special areas' due to the lack of reception facilities. Moreover, arising from the numerous types of NLS, compliance with Annex II required sophisticated discharge monitoring equipment – these were either unavailable at the time or prohibitively expensive. Overall, Annexes II to V suffered from the same shortcomings afflicting Annex I, primarily the non-availability of shipboard equipment and the over-reliance on flag state enforcement.

1.4 MARPOL 73/78 and Crude Oil Washing (COW)

During the mid-1970s, oil tanker operators were still effectively adhering to the 1969 OILPOL amendments. The MARPOL 73 regime was beset

---

[340] Annex II, reg. 7.

with problems since much of the technology it called for – separators, monitoring systems and reception facilities – were still not in existence.[341] In addition, the fact that Annexes I and II were 'coupled' together and made compulsory for state parties introduced huge challenges, particularly because the many types of chemicals falling under Annex II made it extremely difficult to implement. All these factors deterred ratification of and compliance with MARPOL 73.

As for the SBT requirement, the major criticism of Regulation 13 of Annex I had been the fact that it required SBTs of new tankers only. With the prevailing surplus of tankers following the OPEC crisis and the resultant slow-down in new constructions, it was clear that SBTs could not become as widespread as originally hoped. Hence, MARPOL 73's insistence on SBTs appeared to be compromised by tough economic realities. In the event, calls were soon made for MARPOL 73 to be amended so that SBTs could be extended to *existing* tankers as well. This proposal did not spring as much from environmental concerns as it did from commercial realities surrounding the slump in the tanker trade. The spiralling oil prices had led to decreased global demand for oil and overcapacity in the already weak tanker market. As a result, large numbers of tankers were laid up, with their owners reeling from severe losses.

The major independent tanker owners in Norway, Greece and Italy swiftly recognised the potential of SBTs in stimulating demand for their laid-up tankers.[342] Since SBTs reduced the oil-carrying capacity of tankers, their installation would lead to more tankers being needed to transport the same amount of oil. Hence, the independents began to campaign for SBTs to be imposed on *existing* tankers. Their efforts were largely supported by the Mediterranean countries which feared increasing pollution off their coasts as well as several oil-exporting states which were keen to stave off reception facilities.

At about the same time, the Organization for Economic Co-operation and Development (OECD) became convinced that retrofitting existing tankers was one way to stimulate the depressed shipping sector. Predictably, the major oil companies and the developing states with shipping interests expressed strong reservations over the costs involved. The US, in the meantime, was conducting its own study on

---

[341] J. B. Curtis, *Vessel-Source Oil Pollution and MARPOL 73/78: An International Success Story?*, 15 ENVTL. L. 679, at 695 (1985).
[342] M'GONIGLE & ZACHER, *supra* note 65, at 123–4.

the matter and remained conspicuously silent. In the event, a vote was taken at MEPC in December 1976 on the issue; the proposal to extend SBTs to existing tankers was roundly rejected by a majority of states.

The US position was soon to change. A spate of some fifteen vessel accidents during the winter of 1976-7, particularly the *Argo Merchant* disaster off the Massachusetts coast, ignited public fury and forced a reconsideration of US policy on the matter. At the same time, the US Coast Guard came under attack for being too conservative in its pollution control efforts. The incoming Carter Administration also saw the Department of Transportation – under which the Coast Guard was constituted – undergoing leadership changes. The new Secretary of Transportation, Brock Adams, was a native of the State of Washington which was (and still is) well known for its strong environmental stance, particularly on tanker pollution.[343]

The Carter Administration subsequently produced a set of initiatives in March 1977 promising action to prevent further vessel accidents. Known as the 'Carter Initiatives', these measures proposed, *inter alia*, the installation of SBTs for all new *and* existing tankers above 20,000 dwt as well as US ratification of MARPOL 73. At the same time, the Carter Initiatives proposed changes to the international standards for tanker construction and equipment and for the inspection and certification of tankers by the US Coast Guard. To such ends, co-operation with the international community was pledged, even though it was made clear that the US would act alone if it had to.

Ultimately, the threat of US unilateralism proved so great that the IMCO Council was compelled to agree to a new marine pollution conference. The International Conference on Tanker Safety and Pollution Prevention (TSPP) was thus convened from 6 to 17 February 1978. Its main purpose was to consider and adopt instruments to modify MARPOL 73 as well as the 1974 International Convention on the Safety of Life at Sea (SOLAS 74). The Conference eventually produced two new Protocols – one improving on MARPOL 73, the other on SOLAS 74.

As expected, preparatory work for the 1978 Conference was very much dictated by US demands. During this preliminary phase, the US proposal for double hulls was deflected. As a compromise measure, it was agreed that all future SBTs would be 'protectively located' at the

---

[343] On developments in the US at this time, see M'GONIGLE & ZACHER, *supra* note 65, at 122–30 and A. W. Anderson, *National and International Efforts to Prevent Traumatic Vessel Source Oil Pollution*, 30 U. MIAMI L. REV. 985 (1976).

sides or wings of tankers, so as to absorb the first collision impact and to prevent cargo tanks from being breached. This measure was considered to be a logical extension of MARPOL 73's provisions which had recognised the benefits of segregated ballast in reducing operational pollution but were silent in respect of secondary benefits to be derived from proper placement of SBTs.

MARPOL 73 had only required SBTs of all new tankers above 70,000 dwt. The US thus pressed the 1978 Conference to require SBTs on board *all* vessels – new and existing – over 20,000 dwt. This drew objections from most delegations, particularly over the high costs of retrofitting existing tankers. In response, the oil industry, together with maritime states such as the UK, proposed an alternative system of tank washing in place of SBTs for all tankers above 70,000 dwt. Known as crude oil washing (COW), this method employed high pressure jets of crude oil instead of water to dissolve residues on cargo tank walls, thereby avoiding oil-water mixes and discharges. The residues could ultimately be pumped ashore together with the cargo without necessitating any discharges.

Like LOT a decade earlier, COW was a testimony to the oil industry's nimbleness in adapting to changing political and economic circumstances. COW had been in existence since the 1960s and was developed not as an environmental measure but simply as a means to prevent wastage of oil which would otherwise have been washed away. Originally, the amount of oil saved from COW was too small to render the operation commercially profitable. However, the oil price shocks of the 1970s immediately rendered COW attractive for the larger tankers, particularly if its adoption could stave off expensive SBT requirements for existing tankers. Hence, the oil industry was quick to tout COW's environmental and cost advantages and to lobby for its inclusion in place of SBTs on existing tankers.

The 1978 Conference was thus left to choose between COW and retrofitted SBTs. The participants at the 1978 Conference were deeply polarised – on the one end were the oil companies which had agreed to SBTs on new tankers in 1973 only because the tanker glut meant that the prospect for new tankers was far off. Now that the US was proposing to retrofit existing tankers, the oil companies were suitably alarmed, apparently even promising to pay for reception facilities in the Arab states if the US proposal was defeated.[344] To this end, the oil companies were staunchly supported by the UK, which was sympathetic to its oil interests.

---

[344] M'Gonigle & Zacher, *supra* note 65, at 134, citing an unnamed delegate at the Conference.

At the other end of the divide were the US and the states representing the shipbuilding and tanker-owning interests, principally Norway, Sweden and Greece. The US Coast Guard, though not primarily involved in the Carter Initiatives, was by now leading the US delegation. In contrast to the UK, the various interests were more evenly represented within the US delegation. Hence, the Coast Guard was acutely aware of the need to secure a package balancing the demands of the US Congress and the environmental lobbies with their own conception of what was technically realistic. In addition, it had to take into account the conservative cost demands of the US Treasury which militated against extensive retrofitting.[345]

After intense negotiations, a compromise package emerged and was adopted unanimously by the Conference. All *new* crude oil tankers over 20,000 dwt were to install *both* SBTs *and* COW.[346] The US-proposed 20,000 dwt requirement was a significant change from the old 70,000 dwt limit imposed by MARPOL 73. This resulted in more tankers falling under the new regulations. In addition, the SBTs must be protectively positioned to minimise oil outflow during collisions or groundings.[347] The concept of protectively located SBTs was accepted in place of a mandatory installation of double hulls and bottoms. This effectively addressed US concerns over accidental pollution.

The SBT requirement was also imposed on all new product (i.e. non-crude oil) carriers above 30,000 dwt.[348] As far as new tankers were concerned (for both crude oil tankers and product carriers),[349] the US obtained virtually all it wanted. As for the *existing* tankers, those crude oil tankers above 40,000 dwt would have a choice of installing *either* SBTs or COW.[350] This effectively allowed shipowners to opt for the cheaper COW alternative. On their part, existing product carriers above 40,000 dwt were made to undergo compulsory SBT retrofitting. In reality, however, this made little difference since most product carriers were below that size.

In the result, the US emerged generally satisfied with the compromise package.[351] Most other states were relieved that no mandatory retrofitting of SBTs had been imposed on *existing* tankers. The states resisting

---

[345] *Ibid.* at 135.   [346] MARPOL 73/78, Annex I, regs. 13(1), 13(6) and 13B.
[347] MARPOL 73/78, Annex I, reg. 13E.   [348] MARPOL 73/78, Annex I, reg. 13(1).
[349] 'New' tankers were defined as those tankers for which the construction contracts were agreed to after 1 June 1979, or in the absence of a building contract, for which the keel was laid after 1 January 1980 or the vessel delivered after 1 June 1982, see MARPOL 73/78, Annex I, reg. 1(26).
[350] MARPOL 73/78, Annex I, regs. 13(7) and 13B.
[351] M'GONIGLE & ZACHER, *supra* note 65, at 140-2.

port reception facilities were also relieved, since the adoption of SBT and COW would greatly reduce oily ballast discharges and hence, the pressure for reception facilities. In actuality, however, reception facilities continued to be needed in situations such as when SBTs were eroded by seawater or contaminated by oil in adjacent cargo tanks or when cargo tanks had to take in additional ballast during bad weather. Of course, such concerns were glossed over during the negotiations.

The 1978 MARPOL Protocol adopted by the Conference also took the important step of decoupling the problematic Annex II on NLS from the operation of Annex I. Since the changes envisaged by the 1978 Conference related primarily to oil, the Conference decided to defer the implementation of Annex II for three years after the date of entry into force of the MARPOL Protocol.[352] It was hoped that by that later date, the technical problems with Annex II would have been resolved. At the same time, the Annex II delay would not be allowed to affect the entry into force of the Annex I regulations. A linkage was also established between the 1978 Protocol and the parent MARPOL 73 Convention such that these could be ratified as a single instrument. This measure, along with the deferred implementation of Annex II, aimed to facilitate ratification by states and to expedite the entry into force of the composite instrument, henceforth known as MARPOL 73/78.[353]

Overall, the Conference was a testimony to the powerful bargaining positions of the US and other influential interests. Evidently, the threat of US unilateralism proved too compelling to ignore. Yet, the oil and shipping interests were able to moderate US demands for SBTs to a significant degree. In essence, industry was well aware, as were the state actors, that the US was more capable of threatening unilateralism than actually undertaking it.[354] This was because unilateral action would cause severe political and economic dislocations, particularly since the European states still wielded substantial maritime power.

As was the case at the 1973 Conference, it is ironic how the most controversial issue at the 1978 Conference – SBT retrofitting – was primarily an *operational* pollution measure when the real motivation for the Conference was accidental pollution arising out of the December 1976

---

[352] The MARPOL Protocol entered into force on 2 October 1983, two years later than the recommended target of June 1981. The effective date for Annex II's implementation was thus deferred to 2 October 1986.

[353] 1978 Protocol to the International Convention for the Prevention of Pollution from Ships, 1341 U.N.T.S. 3; 17 I.L.M. 546 (1978) (in force 2 Oct. 1983).

[354] M'GONIGLE & ZACHER, *supra* note 65, at 142.

incidents in the US. It is also interesting to note that environmental leadership had, since the early days of OILPOL 54, passed from the UK to the US. Overall, it can be appreciated how the political forces arising out of the divergent interest groups and state caucuses came to be reconciled to produce a composite international response. In the process, the 1978 Conference succeeded in energising MARPOL 73, which had hitherto been stagnating and lacking in state support. Indeed, within five years of the 1978 Conference, MARPOL 73/78 had entered into force.

1.5 The Double Hull Requirement

1.5.1 The *Exxon Valdez* and the 1992 Amendments

In the early 1990s, significant new policy initiatives were pursued at IMO, catalysed in large part by the furore over the *Exxon Valdez* incident of 1989.[355] One such initiative was the introduction in 1992 of the double hull requirement for new and existing tankers. As explained earlier, the shipping interests had successfully resisted this requirement during the 1970s. However, with the frequent occurrence of serious pollution incidents and the political costs which they exacted, it soon became clear that double hulls could no longer be opposed. The adoption of this costly design/equipment standard proved to be extremely contentious. To this day, it represents one of the most vivid examples of how IMO's legislative process is often driven by external political forces.

At this point, it is useful to appreciate the concept of the 'double hull'. Some tankers are built with a feature known as the 'double bottom', which protects the tanker's bottom against rupture in the event of groundings. In addition, the tanker may have 'wing ballast' tanks, which reduce the impact of side collisions. Cumulatively, the double bottom and wing tank features extending the entire cargo tank length of the ship are referred to as the 'double hull' design. In essence, the design entails the construction of the hull such that minimum distances or spaces are provided between the cargo tank boundaries and the bottom plating and ship sides. Such spaces protect the cargo tanks and minimise the risk of oil outflow following groundings or collisions. While protectively located SBTs required under Regulation 13E protect

---

[355] The US-flagged tanker ran aground in Alaska in March 1989, spilling more than 37,000 tonnes of oil and causing severe pollution to the sensitive environment around Prince William Sound.

about a third of the cargo, double hulls are expected to provide total protection since they run the entire length of the ship.

As with earlier design changes introduced by MARPOL 73 and its 1978 Protocol, the double hull amendments were very much dictated by domestic developments in the US. Following the *Exxon Valdez* incident, the US Congress had swiftly enacted the Oil Pollution Act of 1990 (hereinafter 'OPA-90').[356] Under this Act, all new and existing tank vessels visiting US ports or transiting US waters (including the EEZ) had to be fitted with double hulls by the year 2015 based on a phase-out schedule that took into account vessel size, configuration and construction date.

It will be recalled that during the 1978 TSPP Conference, US efforts to introduce mandatory SBTs for existing tankers as well as double hulls had been rejected by the other states. Nevertheless, the US had emerged fairly satisfied with the package it obtained. In the decade following the 1978 Conference, however, public opinion in the US became heavily influenced by a series of tanker accidents occurring within US waters, culminating in the *Exxon Valdez* in 1989. The US Congress subsequently came to believe that such accidents could have been prevented if the tankers in question had had their cargoes shielded by protective spaces or double hulls.

Since design and constructional changes could be readily appreciated by an anxious public, such measures took precedence over operational and manning improvements whose benefits were not so immediately tangible. The US was thus determined to resurrect its double hull proposal even though it remained questionable whether such hulls could have prevented accidents like the *Exxon Valdez* in the first place. Within the US, proposals for double-sided and double-hulled barges had actually been made by the Coast Guard as early as the 1970s, long before the *Exxon Valdez* incident. At that time, several public interest groups had also filed suits before the US courts seeking to compel the relevant authorities to consider designs such as the double hull.

In the meantime, following the discovery of oil in Alaska, promises had been made to environmentalists that the transport of oil from Alaska to the US West Coast by sea would be accompanied by stringent vessel standards such as double hulls. Subsequently, the 1973 Trans-Alaskan Pipeline Authorization Act (TAPAA)[357] became approved, but only narrowly and after further promises had been made to ensure

---

[356] Oil Pollution Act, 1990, Pub. L. No. 101–380, 104 Stat. 484 (1990), § 4115 (codified at 46 U.S.C. § 3703a).
[357] 43 U.S.C. §§ 1651–1656.

stringent environmental protection. Ultimately, these promises were never fulfilled even as oil began to flow from Alaska. The inland barge industry's strong opposition to the costly double hull standard, coupled with the standard's rejection at both the 1973 and 1978 IMCO Conferences, had effectively led the Coast Guard to abandon its double hull proposals. Eventually, only the SBT requirement came to be mandated at IMCO. Since then, there had been frustration among US legislators and environmentalists that even after so many years, the double hull issue had yet to be conclusively settled.

The stage was thus set for a swell of public outrage against the oil and shipping industries following the *Exxon Valdez*. The fact that the incident polluted the pristine waters of Alaska was all the more galling given the history of unfulfilled promises relating to the transport of Alaskan oil. The mood 'to get tough' with shipping became even stronger in February 1990 when another tanker – the *American Trader* – caused pollution in waters off California. This helped to persuade influential Californian legislators of the need for swift political action. Under such circumstances, double hulls could no longer be resisted.[358] The shipping industry's protests that standards should only be adopted at IMO were virtually ignored. By this time, there was considerable disdain in the US for the IMO system, for it was at IMO that earlier US proposals for double hulls had been rejected.

With the passage of OPA-90 and the threat of US unilateralism on the matter, IMO was compelled to commence immediate discussions on tanker designs and the adoption of double hull requirements at the international level. Even before work began on the issue, it was clear that any proposed extension of new design standards to *existing* tankers would be particularly contentious. Proponents of double hulls such as the US, the Netherlands and the Scandinavian countries were adamant that if double hulls were to be required at all, the existing tankers should be made to install them. These states pointed out that a large proportion of the existing tanker fleet was only equipped with COW and had not even installed SBTs pursuant to MARPOL 73/78. It will be recalled that the 1978 MARPOL Protocol had stopped short of mandating SBTs for *existing* tankers. Instead, these tankers were given a choice between SBT and COW. The result was that most tanker owners opted for the cheaper COW alternative.

---

[358] See T. M. Alcock, *'Ecology' Tankers and the Oil Pollution Act of 1990: A History of Efforts to Require Double Hulls on Oil Tankers*, 19 ECOLOGY L. Q. 97 (1992).

At IMO, a sizeable number of countries supported the principle that new tanker designs should now be made applicable to both new and existing tankers as a single 'package', not least because the environmental benefits of the new measures would be limited if they were to be confined to new tankers alone. After all, it was the modification of *existing* tankers which would have the largest impact in reducing accidental spills. Some states also felt that the application of measures to new tankers alone would place these vessels at a competitive disadvantage vis-à-vis existing tankers. This might have the undesirable effect of encouraging owners to delay new constructions and to continue prolonging the lifespan of older existing tankers. Consequently, several states proposed that a schedule be drawn up for existing tankers to be upgraded to the standards of new tankers. The ultimate aim was to ensure that *all* existing tankers eventually upgrade to double hulls (or an acceptable equivalent) within a certain time period or face the prospect of complete 'phasing out'.

As the deliberations progressed, strong opposition to double hulls for existing tankers emerged among industry interests and the developing countries.[359] At the same time, scientific opinion relating to the technical merits of double hulls remained divided.[360] Apart from the cost issue, the industry interests were concerned over safety in view of the fact that experience with double hulls was lacking. Some of the doubts expressed related to leakages, corrosion, stress distribution and greater structural damage in high-energy groundings. In particular, there were concerns that double hull spaces could not be easily accessed for inspection, maintenance and repair work.[361]

In relation to contact accidents, the industry interests emphasised that double hulls were only effective in protecting against low-energy impacts. In high-energy collisions, it was argued, the inner hull containing the cargo would have been breached in any case. In this regard, it was contended that large incidents such as the *Exxon Valdez* would almost certainly have caused significant pollution *whatever the ships' design*. In any event, contact accidents were often caused by human

---

[359] The states resisting double hulls for existing tankers included Greece, China, France, Liberia, Mexico, Romania, South Korea and the USSR, see MEPC Doc. 31/21 (1991). France was particularly concerned over the unresolved safety implications of double hulls, see submission of France, MEPC Doc. 32/7/11 (1992).

[360] See e.g. REPORT OF IMO COMPARATIVE STUDY ON OIL TANKER DESIGNS, *attached to* MEPC Docs. 32/7/15 (1992) and 32/7/17/Add.1 (1992).

[361] Submission of France, *supra* note 359.

factors and not deficiencies in design and construction. Therefore, it was contended that the double hull requirement failed to address the nub of the issue which was the need for increased *operational* vigilance against human error. In industry's opinion, all these uncertainties tended to balance, or even override, the additional environmental protection afforded by double hulls.

Amidst such resistance, agreement could not be reached on installing double hulls on the existing tankers. The industry interests *were* prepared, however, to consider double hulls for new tankers, although this was clearly meant to be a leverage to resist double hulls for existing tankers. The industry representatives proceeded to argue that the prevailing global shipyard and ship repair capacity would be insufficient to handle the huge demand for double hulls in *both* new and existing ships. Neither would the shipyards be capable of handling the demand for interim SBT upgrades.

With nearly 70 per cent of operational VLCCs having been constructed between 1973 and 1977, it was true that any age-related phasing-out scheme would abruptly remove a large proportion of existing tankers within a five-year period in the following few years.[362] Assuming continued growth in global oil demand, a drastic jump in new tanker deliveries would have to be ensured at the relevant time to replace the retired tonnage. The shipping interests argued that this could not possibly be done given that the shipbuilding industry had by then contracted dramatically since the 'boom' years of the early 1970s.

At this stage, it became generally accepted by most actors that any time scale for upgrading and phasing out existing single-hull ships had to be linked to prevailing transportation demands in the world market as well as to shipyard capacity to provide replacement tonnage. Otherwise, a massive distortion in the supply of tankers and the transportation of oil could be expected. Arising from the wide-ranging debates, MEPC was finally able to agree on a principle for the upgrading and phasing out of existing tankers, spread out over time based on the age of the ships.[363]

---

[362] Submission of the UK, MEPC Doc. 32/7/9 (1992).
[363] This approach had been advocated by Denmark, Germany, Japan, the Netherlands, Norway, Sweden, the UK and the US, but with resistance by France, Greece, Liberia, Panama, Romania, Spain, ICS and INTERTANKO.

Having opted for this approach, MEPC proceeded to consider several alternative drafts of what would eventually become Regulation 13G, the provision dealing with existing tankers. By this time, a compromise understanding had emerged that if existing tankers were to be made subject to the new requirements at all, alternative designs to double hulls must be considered. In this regard, several countries with shipbuilding interests, primarily Japan, Norway and France, had lobbied IMO to accept alternative designs to double hulls which promised *equivalent protection* against oil outflow.

IMO eventually came to approve the 'mid-deck' tanker design as an alternative to double hulls. This was a design which utilised double sides as opposed to double bottoms. The approval of the 'mid-deck' design was essentially a concession to the Japanese, who were its inventors. Most other delegations, including the industry representatives, supported the design because it apparently promised greater cost-effectiveness. However, the US remained fervently opposed to any design other than double hulls. By that time, political opinion in the US had settled on double hulls as the *only* acceptable solution. In large part, this was because double hulls had already been promised to an American public clamouring for a swift and easily understood response to *Exxon Valdez*.

The US Congress was also under tremendous pressure from domestic shipbuilding interests to accept only the double hull design.[364] In the event, although the OPA-90 legislation anticipated subsequent Congressional approval of alternative designs, the US Coast Guard felt unable to recommend the approval of such alternatives to Congress. At MEPC, the US and the Friends of the Earth International (FOEI) delegations stood alone in their staunch opposition to mid-deck tankers. In the face of US resistance, MEPC ultimately moved to approve mid-deck tankers as an alternative to double hulls. It was also provided that other alternative designs would be acceptable if they could be shown to provide 'equivalent protection' against oil pollution.

Two new Regulations were thus adopted in Annex I of MARPOL 73/78 to introduce the double hull requirements – Regulation 13F for new tankers, and Regulation 13G for existing tankers. The relatively

---

[364] US politicians even alleged that Japan's advocacy of 'mid-deck' tankers was a plot to bolster its own shipbuilding industry at the expense of American shipyard jobs: see Drewry Shipping Consultants, Safer Ships (1992) and Lloyd's List, *Scathing Attack on SCA Article*, 24 Feb. 1992. In the opinion of industry watchers, this was simply an episode of Japan-bashing by a hopelessly uncompetitive US shipbuilding industry.

uncontroversial Regulation 13F required all new oil tankers[365] over 5,000 dwt to comply with the double hull requirement, i.e. double bottoms and wing tanks extending the entire cargo tank length of the tanker and measuring at least one metre in width. Under Regulation 13F(4), the double hull measure may be dispensed with if the tanker applies an alternative feature known as the 'hydrostatic balance' method.[366] On their part, new tankers between 600 and 5,000 dwt shall be fitted with double bottoms of at least 0.76 metres in width and be provided with cargo tanks which capacity does not exceed 700 cubic metres each. Tankers below 600 dwt would be exempted altogether from Regulation 13F.

From among the initial drafts presented by MEPC and several states, a joint compromise version prepared by a group of maritime countries eventually emerged as the approved Regulation 13G.[367] Pursuant to this Regulation, *existing* crude oil tankers above 20,000 dwt and product carriers above 30,000 dwt which had not been constructed according to the requirements of the 1978 MARPOL Protocol[368] (the so-called 'pre-MARPOL' tankers) were required to comply with Regulation 13F not later than twenty-five years after their delivery. However, if these tankers are retrofitted with wing tanks or double bottom spaces protecting at least 30 per cent of their side or bottom shell area, compliance with Regulation 13F would be required not later than thirty years after delivery.[369] Thus, a five-year deferral period was afforded to such tankers. Alternatively, these tankers may gain a five-year reprieve if they are retrofitted with the 'hydrostatic balance' method.

As for existing tankers which *had* been built to the 1978 MARPOL Protocol's specifications, these received a straightforward exemption from the requirements of Regulation 13F until they reached thirty years

---

[365] These are defined as crude oil tankers or product carriers which are ordered on or after 6 July 1993, or whose keels are laid on or after 6 January 1994 or which are delivered on or after 6 July 1996.

[366] 'Hydrostatic balance' works on the principle of ensuring water inflow, or at least, limited cargo outflow, following an accident. This is achieved by restricting the tanker's amount of cargo such that the hydrostatic pressure of the cargo is maintained below that of the surrounding seawater.

[367] Submission of Denmark, Germany, Japan, the Netherlands, Norway, Sweden, France, the UK, Liberia, Panama and Greece, MEPC Doc. 32/J/9 (1992).

[368] See Section 1.4 above.

[369] MARPOL 73/78, Annex I, reg. 13G(4). For an overview of the 1992 amendments, see A. Griffin, *MARPOL 73/78 and Vessel Pollution: A Glass Half Full or Half Empty?*, 1 IND. J. GLOBAL LEGAL STUD. 489, at 490 (1994).

of age.³⁷⁰ Under Regulation 13G, all existing tankers are also to be subject to enhanced inspections and surveys.³⁷¹ As alternative arrangements, *both* new and existing tankers would be allowed to adopt other protective designs if these ensure equivalent levels of protection against oil pollution.³⁷² Specifically, these alternatives include the 'mid-deck' tanker concept.

The US subsequently reserved its position on Regulations 13F and 13G.³⁷³ This came as a severe blow to the delicate compromise reached by MEPC on the matter. To this day, the US is not a party to the 1992 amendments, even though it had got its way in demanding double hulls for existing tankers. In essence, the acceptance of alternative designs had been meant as a *quid pro quo* for the imposition of double hulls on existing tankers. For the other countries, the US refusal to accept Regulations 13F and 13G is all the more aggravating given that it was on the US's account that the issue had been brought for international regulation in the first place.

As it turned out, even though the proponents of alternative designs such as Japan can claim victory for having secured their in-principle acceptance, no such design has since proven to be commercially viable. To avoid problems with US authorities, shipowners trading to the US have had no choice but to ensure that their ships are equipped with double hulls. A non-double-hull tanker would also have little resale value if it could not trade to the US market. Since most major shipowners engage in the lucrative US trade, the practical effect today is a near-complete reliance on double hulls to achieve compliance with tanker design standards.

However, this is only true for those shipowners who operate to the US, almost all of whom can be considered as reputable. Elsewhere, the reality is less promising. Single-hull tankers (and more importantly, the ill-maintained, sub-standard ones) continue to operate in flagrant breach of the relevant IMO regulations. This is one crucial indication of how implementation of and compliance with IMO regulations remain far from being uniform.³⁷⁴

An interesting point to note is that the fears over shipyard capacity to meet the double hull requirements have proven to be unfounded. By the

---

[370] MARPOL 73/78, Annex I, reg. 13G(5). [371] MARPOL 73/78, Annex I, reg. 13G(3)(a).
[372] MARPOL 73/78, Annex I, reg. 13F(5).
[373] As did Indonesia, see Report of MEPC's 32nd session, MEPC Doc. 32/20 (1992).
[374] See Ch. 5 for details.

late 1990s, there was actually a surplus of global shipyard capacity. Mainly due to expectations for increased demand, shipyards worldwide – particularly in South Korea and China – had rushed to expand their capacity following the 1992 amendments.[375] The fact that sudden 'peaks' in demand have not arisen can also be attributed to Regulation 13G's successful spreading out of vessel retirement over a longer period.

1.5.2 The *Erika* and the 2001 Amendments

The 'double hull' story does not end with the *Exxon Valdez*. It is a fact that the international regulation of vessel-source pollution has historically been driven by political reactions to catastrophic vessel accidents. In spite of efforts by agencies such as IMO to adopt a more pro-active – rather than reactive – approach to problem-solving, the reality is that without an accident to galvanise public opinion, far-reaching measures are seldom pursued in as expeditious a manner. That this remains so in today's regulatory climate is borne out by the sinking of the tankers *Erika* and the *Prestige* off the coasts of France and Spain in December 1999 and November 2002 respectively.

Following the *Erika* incident,[376] the threat of European unilateralism forced IMO to accede to key French and European Commission demands for more stringent international action. To that end, three major initiatives were proposed to strengthen the regulatory system – these related to the accelerated phasing out of single-hull tankers, greater control over classification societies and a more stringent port state control mechanism.[377] The first of these measures was pursued at IMO within

---

[375] Such increased capacity has often been alleged to arise from massive government subsidies, a continuing issue of great contention between the EU and South Korea.

[376] The *Erika* was a Maltese-flagged tanker which sank in the Bay of Biscay off France in December 1999 and spilled approximately 20,000 tonnes of heavy fuel oil.

[377] This is the so-called *Erika* I package, see Regulation (EC) 417/2002 on the accelerated phasing in of double hull or equivalent design requirements for single hull oil tankers, 2002 OJ (L 64) 1 (as amended after the *Prestige* incident by Regulation (EC) 1726/2003, 2003 OJ (L 249) 1). Some elements of the *Erika* II package (entailing the creation of a European maritime safety agency, promotion of greater safety in maritime traffic and prevention of ship pollution, and improvements to the liability and compensation schemes) have also been developed, see Communication from the Commission on a Second Set of Community Measures on Maritime Safety Following the Sinking of the Oil Tanker *Erika*, COM(2000) 802 final. For an assessment, see M. Baldwin et al., *Recent Developments: A Review of Developments in Ocean and Coastal Law 1999-2000*, 5 OCEAN & COASTAL L. J. 367 (2000). A raft of controversial new maritime safety initiatives, officially referred to by European staff as the 'Maritime Safety Package 2004', but commonly dubbed *Erika* III, is being proposed. It includes further matters such as seafarer

only a few months of the *Erika* incident, while the second and third have been enacted through EU legislation.[378]

Under the US OPA-90, all non-double-hull tankers would be barred from US waters from the year 2015. Under IMO's 1992 amendments, however, single-hull tankers could technically operate until well past 2015. This was where there were still differences between the IMO and OPA-90 regimes. In the aftermath of the *Erika*, environmental interests in Europe raised the spectre of sub-standard ships being excluded from the US by OPA-90 and visiting European waters instead. It was thus felt that Europe needed an equally stringent regime to bring forward the phasing out of single-hull tankers, lest it becomes inundated with sub-standard ships turned away by the US.

In April 2001, following intense EU pressure, Regulation 13G was amended at IMO to bring forward the 1992 schedule for the phasing out of single-hull tankers. The amendments, which entered into force by tacit acceptance on 1 September 2002, were primarily based upon a compromise package crafted by Denmark, the Netherlands and the UK.[379] The compromise was formulated with several familiar concerns in mind, principally the need to avoid clustered 'peaks' in ship scrapping and replacement schedules as well as a shortage in available tonnage. The negotiators were also keen to ensure that whatever action taken did not affect the global availability and price of fuel.

Pursuant to the amendments, the group of tankers known as the pre-MARPOL ('Category 1') tankers[380] would be progressively phased out between 2003 and 2007 depending on the date of their delivery. As for the post-MARPOL ('Category 2') tankers, these would be phased out between 2003 and 2015, again based on their delivery dates. Similarly,

standards, a review of port state control procedures and new measures on the investigation of accidents and EU flag state standards.

[378] Directive 2001/105/EC, 2002 OJ (L 19) 9, amending Directive 94/57 (Directive on Classification Societies), *supra* note 237, and Directive 2001/106, 2002 OJ (L 19) 17, amending Directive 95/21/EC (Directive on Port State Control), *supra* note 240.

[379] The states demanding stringent action included France, Belgium, Germany, Spain, the UK, Sweden, the Netherlands and Denmark. Reservations came from Brazil and Thailand and a host of Latin American developing countries, see Report of MEPC's 46th session, MEPC Doc. 46/23 (2001). During the discussions, the US (with some irony) took the position that action should be taken multilaterally by IMO, and not unilaterally by the EU. On the US position generally, see J. Angelo, *Erika Aftermath: Developments at IMO on Double Hulls (a US Perspective)*, in Nordquist & Moore eds., *supra* note 9, at 309.

[380] These are the oil tankers above 20,000 dwt carrying crude oil, fuel oil, heavy diesel oil or lubricating oil as cargo, and those above 30,000 dwt carrying other oils, which do not comply with the requirements for protectively located SBTs pursuant to MARPOL 73/78, reg. 13E.

the 'Category 3' group of tankers (i.e. those above 5,000 dwt but below the tonnage specified for Categories 1 and 2) will be phased out between 2003 and 2015. In sum, the principal cut-off date for single-hull tankers was brought forward to 2007 for Category 1 tankers and 2015 for Categories 2 and 3 tankers. This was a compromise which was more lenient than the European Commission's initial demand of 2005, 2007 and 2015 for the three categories respectively.[381]

In earlier negotiations, the shipping interests had fought for a deferred 2017 deadline for Category 2 tankers. This was to cater primarily to those Category 2 tankers which would still be relatively youthful at the time of their scheduled phase-out. Ultimately, MEPC settled on a compromise which retained the 2015 phase-out date but which gave flag state administrations the discretion to permit newer single-hull Category 2 tankers conforming to certain technical specifications to continue trading until their twenty-fifth year.[382] To balance this flag state prerogative, port states were given the discretion to deny entry of any of these tankers into their ports or offshore terminals after communicating their intention to do so to IMO. As an additional precautionary measure, a Condition Assessment Scheme (CAS) would be applied to all Category 1 vessels continuing to trade after 2005 and all Category 2 vessels after 2010.

The 2001 amendments bear dramatic implications not only for the issue of single-hull tankers but more fundamentally, the right of port states to deny entry to certain ships. At MEPC, the member states of the EU, together with Cyprus and Malta (the two then-aspiring EU states with large ship registries), voiced their intention to deny entry to all single-hull tankers after 2015. This raised concern with the shipping industry, which foresaw that the major open registries would invariably certify Category 2 tankers for operation beyond 2015, only to have the European port states deny entry to these very vessels.

In this regard, a uniform worldwide prohibition would have been preferable. Ultimately, however, it is clear that the emphasis given to the matter had been motivated by the political demands of the European states. In the process, considerations relating to the wisdom

---

[381] Communication on the Safety of the Seaborne Oil Trade, COM(2000) 142 final.
[382] These compromises arose as a result of the insistence of countries such as Brazil, which feared possible disruption to their oil supplies, see INTERTANKO, *supra* note 14, at 30.

and costs of accelerated phasing out were glossed over, as were concerns that sub-standard vessels turned away by Europe will only be dispatched to some other region of the world.[383]

1.5.3 The *Prestige* and the 2003 Amendments

Barely had the 2001 amendments been adopted when another major pollution disaster occurred in Europe, bringing with it a fresh new wave of regulatory fervour. In November 2002, the Bahamas-flagged tanker *Prestige* sank off the coast of Spain, causing severe pollution damage to coastal and shore interests. The *Prestige* had developed trouble in heavy weather off Galicia. After the Spanish authorities refused it permission to enter port, it sank and spilled 77,000 tonnes of heavy fuel oil, a large quantity of which washed up on the coasts of Spain and also Portugal and France.

In its aftermath, more politically driven measures have been pursued, both at the regional European level as well as at IMO. In particular, the European Commission proposed to tighten its package of responses adopted after the *Erika*, demanding that IMO accelerate *further* the phasing out of single-hull tankers and of sub-standard ships in general.[384] Here, the Commission felt vindicated that its original post-*Erika* proposals – watered down at IMO in 2001 – should have been adopted to begin with. It thus resurrected the proposal to phase out Categories 1, 2 and 3 tankers according to much earlier deadlines than what IMO had agreed upon in April 2001.[385]

Under intense pressure, IMO convened a meeting in December 2003 and duly revised Regulation 13G to bring forward the final phasing out date for 'Category 1' tankers to 2005 from 2007, and for 'Category 2' and

---

[383] Lloyd's List, *Asia-Pacific Alert on Substandard Ships*, 9 Mar. 2001. See also Anderson, *supra* note 19, at 168 and Sinan, *supra* note 135, at 103.

[384] Commission Proposal for a Regulation of the European Parliament and of the Council amending Regulation (EC) 417/2002 on the accelerated phasing in of double hull or equivalent design requirements for single hull oil tankers and repealing Council Regulation (EC) 2978/94, COM(2002) 780 final. This eventually resulted in Reg. 1726/2003, amending Reg. 417/2002, *supra* note 377. For the initial reaction after the *Prestige*, see Commission Communication on improving safety at sea in response to the *Prestige* accident, COM(2002) 681 final and Commission Communication on action to deal with the effects of the *Prestige* disaster, COM(2003) 105 final. See also Regulation (EC) No. 2099/2002 establishing a Committee on Safe Seas and the Prevention of Pollution from Ships (COSS), 2002 OJ (L 324) 1.

[385] *Supra* note 381. The document presenting the proposal to IMO was jointly submitted by the EU states and the Commission, see MEPC Doc. 49/16/1 (2003).

'Category 3' tankers to 2010 from 2015.[386] At the same time, the Condition Assessment Scheme (CAS) is to apply to all single-hull tankers of fifteen years or older, irrespective of design.[387] These amendments were successfully pushed through despite the resistance of delegations such as Brazil, India and INTERTANKO, which felt it wholly inappropriate to alter rules which had only recently been changed after the *Erika*.[388] As in 2001 and earlier in 1992, familiar arguments were made relating to the industry's lack of capacity to cope with a sudden retirement of single-hull tankers. In part due to the shipbuilding industry's demonstrated capacity to meet increased demand, these arguments failed to persuade the Europeans.

A new Regulation 13H was also adopted to ban the carriage of heavy grades of oil (HGO) in single-hull tankers of 5,000 dwt and above after 5 April 2005,[389] and in single-hull tankers of 600 to 5,000 dwt, not later than the anniversary of their delivery date in 2008. This ban will have significant impact on the oil transport industry, as cargo owners will no longer be able to charter single-hull tankers for carrying HGO. It is noteworthy that even before Regulation 13H was adopted at IMO, a ban to the same effect had entered into force in Europe in October 2003.[390] At that time, two European states, namely Spain and Italy, had already enacted national laws prohibiting single-hull tankers carrying heavy fuel from entering their ports.

---

[386] Nevertheless, the flag state administration may authorise the continued operation of certain classes of Categories 2 and 3 tankers beyond the relevant date under certain conditions.

[387] Hitherto, CAS applied only to all Category 1 vessels trading after 2005 and all Category 2 vessels after 2010.

[388] See e.g. submissions of Brazil and INTERTANKO, MEPC Docs. 50/2/10 (2003) and 50/2/11 (2003) respectively. Brazil was particularly critical of the phasing out of Categories 2 and 3 tankers which were still relatively youthful and well maintained.

[389] This is the date that regs. 13G and 13H will enter into force by tacit amendment. Under reg. 13H, the technical definition of HGOs is based on their nature, density and viscosity. The flag state may authorise the continued carriage of HGO by certain tankers beyond 5 April 2005 under certain conditions, but no later than when the ship reaches twenty-five years after its delivery. Also exempted are certain tankers operating exclusively in domestic trade or as floating storage units. However, under regs. 13G(8)(b) and 13H(8)(b), state parties have the right to deny entry into their ports and terminals of single-hull, HGO-carrying tankers authorised for extended operation under regs. 13G and 13H. The EU states have clearly indicated their intention to deny such entry, see statements of Italy, Malta, Cyprus and Poland at the December 2003 meeting, MEPC Doc. 50/3 (2003).

[390] Reg. 1726/2003 (in force 21 Oct. 2003), *supra* note 377.

In addition, France, Spain and Portugal had gone even further to ban such tankers from transiting their EEZs and territorial seas, and to have military ships escort those which had entered out of the EEZs.[391] Such action clearly breached the right of free navigation under the LOSC and international law, particularly if the vessels were merely transiting the EEZs. Even if the vessels were within the territorial sea, the right of innocent passage persists and the coastal state cannot impose restraints, except where the vessel is *en route* to a port of the state concerned.[392]

At the same time, the EU Parliament, as well as the Commissioner for Transport and Energy, had also called for the LOSC's explicit revision to permit coastal states to take action, including expulsion of ships, within the EEZ.[393] These actions served to further increase the pressure on IMO member states to accede to European demands when these were presented to the Organization in December 2003.

As part of the broad range of post-*Prestige* measures to deal with vessel-source pollution, the European Commission has further proposed that the illegal discharge of polluting substances (as well as the participation in and the instigation of such discharge) be regarded as *criminal* offences when committed intentionally or by gross negligence within EU waters. To this end, a new Directive on criminal sanctions has been proposed.[394] The sanctions will extend to the participation in and instigation of illegal discharges by *any* person, i.e. not only the shipowner but also the cargo owner, the classification society or any other person involved. The penalties extend to deprivation of liberty of persons, even though for the most part, monetary fines are prescribed.[395] The criminal sanctions are designed to go beyond the CLC/FUND regime for civil liability, which is viewed to possess insufficient deterrent value since the shipowner's liability can always be capped by his/its right to limitation.[396]

---

[391] Lloyd's List, *French Tanker Ban Stays until IMO Deal*, 1 May 2003.
[392] LOSC, arts 25(2) and 211(3). As to whether the right of innocent passage is lost, it is questionable whether a single-hull tanker carrying HGO and which is in a sub-standard condition and posing a threat to the marine environment can be said to have lost this right if it was merely transiting the territorial sea without having committed an actual act of 'wilful and serious' pollution, see LOSC, art. 19(2)(h). For discussions, see Ch. 4.
[393] COM(2003) 105, *supra* note 384, at 11.
[394] Commission Proposal for a Directive on ship-source pollution and on the introduction of sanctions, including criminal sanctions, for pollution offences, COM(2003) 92 final (hereinafter 'Commission Proposal for a Directive on Sanctions'): see particularly art. 6.
[395] Under the proposed Directive, the fines imposed cannot be insured.
[396] See Ch. 6.

While the criminal sanctions are clearly targeted at intentional or grossly negligent operational discharges, it will ostensibly apply to accidents as well if it can be shown that pollution arose out of damage to the ship or its equipment which can be traced to gross negligence in operation or maintenance.[397] In this regard, there is division among EU member states – Spain, for instance, wants the law to cover cases of negligence on the part of the owner and the master, but the UK, Denmark, and particularly Greece, Cyprus and Malta, believe that the EU should not go beyond MARPOL 73/78, which does not anticipate sanctions following accidental or non-intentional pollution.[398] In the first place, there appears to be no consensus that criminal sanctions should be applied, and opinions remain divided as to whether the European Commission has competence to propose penal sanctions in the first place.[399] In any event, any sanctions are bound to be controversial if they are to be prescribed and enforced beyond the internal waters and territorial sea.[400]

In the wake of the *Prestige* incident, the Commission has also made various other proposals, including the tightening of port state inspection procedures in Europe pursuant to the Paris MOU, the creation of a third tier compensation fund at IMO and the overhaul of the CLC/FUND civil liability regime.[401] As regards the latter, there are proposals to remove the charterer's immunity and to ensure that cargo interests desist from chartering old vessels and carrying heavy fuel on single-hull tankers.[402] In addition, the Commission has proposed that proof of gross negligence be enough to break the shipowner's right to

---

[397] Commission Proposal for a Directive on Sanctions, *supra* note 394, at 8. It should be noted that the Directive contemplates polluting substances extending beyond oil.

[398] The P&I Clubs are also concerned. While they exclude deliberate spillage from cover, they would generally pay for accidental ones, see REMOVAL OF INSURANCE, *supra* note 5, at 18. If even accidental spillages are deemed criminal under the new Directive, the Clubs will face the dilemma of whether or not they can continue, or afford to cover such claims, see Lloyd's List, *Time Behind Bars: A New Barrier for Those Earning a Living at Sea*, 10 Aug. 2004.

[399] As of December 2004, deliberations were still ongoing in the EU organs (the Council of Ministers and Parliament) on the scope of the Directive. The term 'serious negligence' appears to be preferred over 'gross negligence'.

[400] See Ch. 4.

[401] The third tier has since been created, while the CLC/FUND overhaul is being studied, see Ch. 6.

[402] COM(2003) 105, *supra* note 384, at 8.

limitation.⁴⁰³ These proposals are currently being studied at IMO and the IOPC Funds.⁴⁰⁴

In yet another post-*Prestige* move, the European states successfully lobbied IMO in October 2004 to establish a Particularly Sensitive Sea Area (PSSA) around a large tract of their Atlantic coasts.⁴⁰⁵ Among the protective measures proposed to be adopted is a forty-eight-hour reporting rule for ships carrying certain cargoes entering the area. The European states also proposed the Western European Tanker Reporting System (WETREP), a form of mandatory ship reporting system for the PSSA. An earlier proposal to ban carriage of HGO in single-hull tankers in the PSSA was abandoned, presumably due to the realisation that this would be inconsistent with the LOSC and international law.

Overall, the reaction to the *Prestige* incident has been extremely politicised, even more so than for the *Erika*. While the December 2003 meeting at IMO reached broad consensus on the further phasing out of single-hull tankers, the bigger controversy appears to be the EU's plans to impose criminal penalties for illegal discharges that go beyond the member states' obligations under MARPOL 73/78 and international law. Just as the political response to the *Exxon Valdez* failed to address the root cause of the accident (i.e. human navigational error), the reactions to the *Erika* and *Prestige* incidents have similarly accorded disproportionate emphases on structural and equipment matters at the expense of more relevant issues relating to poor supervision, maintenance, repair and operation of vessels.

Indeed, regulators in Europe and elsewhere have constantly ignored evidence that ill-fated vessels such as the *Erika* and *Prestige* sank due more to structural failure caused by poor maintenance and human error than the fact that they were single-hulled.⁴⁰⁶ Such reactions can be explained by the fact that short-term construction and equipment changes are more readily appealing to politicians and the general public. At the same time, systemic problems such as the enduring competitiveness of sub-standard shipping remain unredressed.⁴⁰⁷ Again, such deficiencies in the international regulatory process can be traced to

---

⁴⁰³ Commission Proposal for a Directive on Sanctions, *supra* note 394, at 6.
⁴⁰⁴ See Ch. 6.
⁴⁰⁵ For PSSAs, see Ch. 4.
⁴⁰⁶ Shipping bodies like BIMCO have argued that the real issue with incidents such as the *Prestige* was not single hulls, but structural failure caused by placing heated cargo tanks next to uncoated ballast tanks, see MEPC Doc. 49/16/7 (2003).
⁴⁰⁷ See Chs. 1 and 2.

the realities of political governance in many states today where the impatient public is more swiftly mollified by short-term political responses rather than a fundamental re-assessment of the underlying global maritime trading system.

The results are ever-increasing regulation over the shipping industry and an obsession with 'age' as the determinant of quality. These have severe cost repercussions for those responsible operators who maintain their vessels diligently. In addition, stringent regional (as opposed to multilateral) rules have significant effects on other regions of the world. It is wholly conceivable that vessels turned away from Europe and the US will now find their way to Asia, Latin America and Africa, less developed regions which can scarcely afford to deal with the sub-standard shipping problem. In the years to come, international and regional regulators will clearly have to meet such problems as a matter of priority.

2. Air Pollution from Ships

Another example of how the regime formation process is driven by the interests of select actors is in the realm of air pollution by ships. Here, certain actors in the ship transportation industry, particularly the oil companies, have again been able to influence the effectiveness of treaty rules and obligations. For the past few decades, global concern had arisen over the effects of ozone-depleting substances (ODS) such as halons and chlorofluorocarbons (CFCs) and 'greenhouse' gases such as carbon dioxide. Even before these issues had captured international attention, the largely localised acid rain problem was already raising concern in Europe and North America. In particular, questions arose in the 1980s over the contribution of shipping to the air pollution and acid rain problems, even though it was clear that land-based sources contributed the bulk of such pollution.[408]

The combustion of sulphur-containing fuel was considered to be a major cause of acid rain. On the regional front, Norway raised the issue of regulating the content of sulphur in marine bunker fuel at the Second International Conference on the Protection of the North Sea (the so-called 'North Sea Conferences' process) held in 1987.[409]

---

[408] Atmospheric sources account for 33 per cent of total marine pollution, but much of these originate from land, see GESAMP No. 39, *supra* note 30.
[409] On the North Sea Conferences, see Ch. 2. For a background of the air pollution control efforts, see B. Okamura, *Proposed IMO Regulations for the Prevention of Air Pollution from*

The deliberations at the North Sea Conferences led directly to the issue being raised at IMO. Meanwhile, other advocates of regulation emerged, including the Baltic Sea states as well as environmental NGOs like FOEI. In addition, the European parties to the 1979 UN-ECE Convention on Long-Range Transboundary Air Pollution (LRTAP)[410] and its various protocols also supported the sulphur content initiatives.

At IMO, member states acknowledged that the most effective solution was to ensure the use of low-sulphur fuel on board ships. It was thus proposed that a new annex to MARPOL 73/78 be adopted to restrict or 'cap' the content of sulphur in marine bunker fuels. This would then reduce sulphur oxide (SO_x) emissions, the main contributor to acid rain. At that time, the prevailing global standard prescribed by the International Organization for Standardization (ISO) for marine fuel oil imposed a maximum sulphur content of 5 per cent. The concerned states thus proposed that IMO adopt a substantially lower cap.

Apart from the content of the proposed regulations, there was also the issue of their geographical coverage. In this regard, the Western European states favoured a *global* solution, particularly the states bordering the semi-enclosed Baltic Sea, who were ever conscious of their region's sensitivity to acid rain. Due to the prohibitively high costs of desulphurisation, sulphur caps imposed solely in Europe would have affected European competitiveness in supplying the bunkers market. This compelled the Europeans to champion the reduction of sulphur levels on a global scale, as opposed to a regional one. As might be expected, the motives were not entirely environmental.

However, initial proposals for a universal solution encountered resistance, primarily from the shipping and oil industries as well as the developing oil-producing states. Subsequently, the Baltic states decided to concentrate on a regional approach. To this end, they were anxious to introduce the concept of air pollution 'special areas' pursuant to which the entire Baltic Sea region could be established as a special area where stricter rules on ship-source atmospheric pollution would apply.[411]

Ships, 26 J. Mar. L. & Com. 183 (1995). Note that Annex VI lays down controls for other pollutants such as nitrous oxides (NO_x) and volatile organic compounds.

[410] 1302 U.N.T.S. 217; 18 I.L.M. 1442 (1979) (in force 16 Mar. 1983). See generally A. Rosencranz, *The ECE Convention of 1979 on Long-Range Transboundary Air Pollution*, 75 Am. J. Int'l L. 975 (1981).

[411] Under the 1974 and 1992 Helsinki Conventions, *supra* note 231, regulations on air pollution were already in place. However, these were only applicable to ships from contracting parties. Consequently, the Baltic states wanted a 'special area' status for the Baltic Sea which could be applied against ships of all flags.

This did not mean, however, that the proponents of a *global* solution were prepared to back down. The Europeans proposed that outside special areas, a global sulphur cap would still have to be imposed – albeit a less stringent one than in special areas. Hence, two major issues arose for discussion at IMO: the precise substantive measure to be adopted and the geographical reach of its application. In the ensuing negotiations, these two issues crystallised around the following questions: the delineation and size of special areas, the sulphur cap within such areas, and the cap, if any, to be imposed outside special areas.

The benefits of using low-sulphur fuel were obvious – these included reduced SO_x emissions, higher calorific (energy) value of fuel, reduced sludge formation and disposal concerns, less wear and tear on engines and increased savings in overall maintenance costs. However, the economic consequences of a sulphur cap were high, primarily because the desulphurisation process that lowered sulphur content in fuels was costly. For the shipping industry, bunkers accounted for at least 30 per cent of ship operational costs.[412] Consequently, a sulphur cap would invariably raise the price of bunker fuel, resulting in higher freight rates and decreased competitiveness vis-à-vis other modes of transport. In addition, classification societies and tanker crews would have to bear the burden of analysing fuel deliveries and ensuring purchase of appropriate fuels.[413]

From the oil producers' perspective, a sulphur cap would severely affect countries whose crude oil resources contained high sulphur levels. Oil refineries in such countries would have to invest heavily in desulphurisation plants. These would increase production costs significantly and result in higher freight charges and increased costs for consumers.[414] As expected, the countries with high-sulphur crude reserves, such as the Persian Gulf states, actively opposed the proposed cap. At the same time, it was obvious that a cap benefited countries which produced low-sulphur crude oil, among them the North Sea states. In the result, the oil industry, together with the shipping interests and several interested states, opposed a global cap.

In the meantime, the proposal for a 'special area' regime for sulphur emissions quickly gained currency. Largely to stave off demands for a

---

[412] Submission of OCIMF, MEPC Doc. 34/INF.36 (1993).
[413] Submission of INTERTANKO, MEPC Doc. 32/12/2 (1992).
[414] Submissions of Kuwait, MEPC Doc. 29/18/5 (1990) and of Austria, Bahrain, India, Mexico, Singapore, Solomon Islands, Vanuatu and Venezuela, MEPC Doc. 37/13/21 (1995).

strict global cap, the oil industry decided to support the adoption of stringent standards in special areas where the air pollution problem was demonstrably more acute. In this regard, a preliminary proposal for a 1.5 per cent cap within special areas received general support. On their part, however, the shipping industry and the major flag states were less enamoured of the 'special area' concept. This was a situation in which the interests of the shipowners and the oil companies diverged sharply.

In particular, shipowner organisations such as ICS had problems with the idea of ships having to change fuel in order to enter special areas. It was pointed out that ships which entered such areas only occasionally would have to be burdened with storing different grades of fuel, thereby reducing their cargo capacity substantially. In addition, the use of different grades of fuel on board ships could lead to engine breakdown at critical moments.[415] On a broader level, ICS expressed concern over the prospect of states declaring special areas unilaterally and the distortion this would have on market competition.

The environmental NGOs also rallied strongly against special areas, but for separate reasons. In their view, a regime of higher standards in special areas would simply not be enforceable. This was because the use of different grades of fuel depending on whether the ship was in a special area effectively meant that enforcement, if any, could take place only at sea. Naturally, at-sea enforcement would be highly impractical, ineffective and costly. It was further contended that an unenforceable regime would only encourage unscrupulous operators to violate the sulphur cap by burning high sulphur fuel in special areas, thus gaining an unfair commercial advantage.

Despite these reservations, consensus was reached fairly quickly on the need for special areas and a 1.5 per cent cap within such areas. However, the question of the size of these areas was not as easily resolved. The oil industry, together with major flag states such as the Bahamas, Liberia and Panama, could accept the establishment of special areas but wanted their geographical reach to be as restricted as possible. After further negotiations, the oil industry accepted the need to be flexible – the industry probably strategised that if a strong 'special area' regime were created, proposals for a strict global cap outside such areas could be more easily resisted. Moreover, it appeared that

---

[415] Submission of ICS, MEPC Doc. 37/13/14 (1995). See also the ICS submission to the Conference of Parties, MP/CONF.3/17 (1997).

many states were willing to concede a large geographical reach for special areas.

Hence, by the time the diplomatic conference commenced in 1997, it had already been decided at MEPC that the SO_x Emission Control Area – as the 'special area' concept came to be known – would be rather generous. With the in-principle acceptance of the concept, the opponents of a global cap argued that there was no longer a need for a cap outside special areas.[416] For these interests, the standard outside special areas should remain at the prevailing ISO *status quo* of 5 per cent. However, the developed European states were adamant that a global cap had to be imposed. As noted above, these states were concerned that their competitiveness in the bunkers market would be affected if low-sulphur levels were to be applicable only to Europe.[417]

Given the insistence of the European states, it became clear that a global cap could not be resisted. The only question was the strictness of such a cap. The major oil-exporting and -refining states swiftly proposed a generous maximum cap of 5 per cent, a figure which subsequently appeared in preliminary drafts of the new annex. Even though the global average for sulphur levels in bunker fuel was in the range of 2.8 to 3.5 per cent,[418] many oil-exporting states produced or supplied bunker fuel with more than 4 per cent sulphur content. For these states, any cap of less than 5 per cent would have had a damaging effect on their exports.

On its part, the oil industry had much to lose from a stringent sulphur cap on marine fuel. This was because terrestrial markets were already being compelled by national governments to move to low-sulphur fuel for environmental purposes. As such, shipping remained one of the few remaining markets for high-sulphur products. The oil industry was thus keen to protect its traditional market for low-quality high-sulphur fuel. To the environmentalists, however, a lenient 5 per cent standard

---

[416] Submissions of Australia, Singapore and Vanuatu, MEPC Doc. 39/6/9 (1997), and of Bahrain, MEPC Doc. 39/6/17 (1997).

[417] European states even reminded IMO that discussions were already under way in Europe to adopt a Directive on liquid fuel sulphur which would cap sulphur content at 3.5 per cent, see submission of the UK, MEPC Doc. 38/9/7 (1996). No doubt, this veiled threat to resort to regionalism was meant to influence the outcome of the negotiations.

[418] The current average level is about 2.7 per cent, see submission of the Netherlands, MEPC Doc. 48/INF.4 (2002) and Report of MEPC's 49th session, MEPC Doc. 49/22 (2003).

rendered the whole idea of a cap nugatory since most fuels in actual use fell below that level.

The debate over the cap carried into the Conference of Parties to MARPOL 73/78, which was convened at IMO in September 1997. After lengthy discussions, the Conference adopted the Protocol of 1997 which amended the 1978 MARPOL Protocol and laid out the new Annex VI on the Regulations for the Prevention of Air Pollution from Ships. As regards the actual level of the global cap, it was not until the very last day of the Conference – 25 September 1997 – that a consensus was finally reached. On that day, agreement was achieved on a compromise global cap of 4.5 per cent of sulphur in marine fuels.

Owing to the powerful objections of the oil industry as well as the oil-producing and -refining states, agreement on a more stringent cap could not be obtained. In this regard, the desire of a majority of states to set a global cap that was higher than the prevailing average sulphur content of fuel was widely attributed to the oil companies' influence on domestic economies. For the environmentalists, the 4.5 per cent cap was a huge disappointment, even though the acceptance of SO_x Emission Control Areas came as some consolation.

As in many other maritime negotiations, it is the shipowner who appears to have drawn the shortest straw. The shipping interests are presently concerned that states unhappy with the lenient global cap will be driven to establish SO_x Emission Control Areas. A proliferation of controlled areas can only be a burden for shipowners as it is they who will have to bear the direct costs and inconvenience of storing different grades of fuel when entering such areas. In this regard, the shipping interests such as ICS are concerned that the regime established by the 1997 Protocol will actually lead to an increase in unilateral and regional action.

From the perspective of many states, the outcome of the 1997 Conference was unsatisfactory. In fact, many delegations with environmental interests consider the 4.5 per cent cap to be one of the lowest points in IMO's recent law-making history.[419] Indeed, the 1997 Protocol is an aberration in the series of pro-environment instruments which had been successfully negotiated at IMO in the past two decades. In the immediate years following its adoption, many developed state governments which favoured stringent caps found it politically difficult to

---

[419] Personal interviews.

accept the Protocol simply because the 4.5 per cent cap was meaningless for them.

Nevertheless, there is now increasing support for the Protocol, even within the developed countries. Annex VI entered into force on 19 May 2005, having attracted ratifications by the requisite number of fifteen states accounting for 50 per cent of world shipping tonnage. Among these are developed as well as open registry states, including Germany, Norway, Spain, the UK, Singapore, the Bahamas, Greece, Liberia, Vanuatu and Panama. At the same time, the EU states have made it clear that their acceptance of Annex VI does not preclude them from enforcing a more stringent cap within EU waters. In fact, MEPC has already approved amendments to Annex VI to establish a North Sea SO_x Emissions Control Area, with a view to adoption once the annex enters into force. Together with the already designated Baltic Sea area, this will bring substantial bodies of European waters within the specialised regime.[420]

The 1997 amendments amply illustrate how politically influential actors like the oil industry can implant a deficiency within a regime such that the resulting agreement becomes less than effective. In the result, even if the developed states do end up ratifying the Protocol, it would be for the express purpose of legitimising SO_x Emission Control Areas, and not the implementation of the general sulphur cap proper. A resulting patchwork of such controlled areas worldwide could be a costly affair for the shipowners. In addition, it would not bring about the uniformity needed to reduce global sulphur emissions effectively. On their part, the majority of developing countries and oil-producing states continue to find little incentive to ratify the Protocol.

Meanwhile, it may be time for the oil industry to consider the voluntary adoption of caps below 4.5 per cent. This appears to be a practical, though legally unsatisfactory, response to the conundrum thrown up by the 1997 Protocol. Given their huge influence over the oil-producing states, the major oil companies should have little difficulty in persuading these states to agree to a lower cap. Hence, the shipowning and environmental interests, together with the relevant states and the IMO Secretariat, should spare no effort in convincing the oil industry that it

---

[420] See Directive 99/32/EC, 1999 OJ (L 121) relating to a reduction in the sulphur content of certain liquid fuels and amending Directive 93/12/EEC, 1993 OJ (L 74). Directive 99/32/EC lays down a 0.2 per cent sulphur cap for marine diesel and gas oils, but not for heavy fuel oils. There have been proposals for the 0.2 per cent cap to be extended to all fuels used within port areas, including heavy fuel oils.

must lead renewed efforts to revisit the sulphur cap and to bring about a more realistic regime for air pollution control.

To this end, the oil industry must find the incentives to develop cheaper desulphurisation methods and to abandon its traditional market for low-quality, high-sulphur fuel. Here, the increasing number of expected SO_x Emission Control Areas could lead to a greater all-round demand for low-sulphur fuel. Such market-driven factors, together with the public relations benefits accompanying 'green' policies, should hopefully work to convince the oil companies of the merits of a lower sulphur cap.

3. Anti-Fouling Systems and Tributyl Tin (TBT) Contamination

In recent years, several new environmental issues have arisen which previously received little attention from regulators. One of these is the problem posed by the use of anti-fouling paints to coat the hulls and bottoms of ships. Anti-fouling paints containing organotin compounds known as tributyl tin (TBT) have long been applied to ships to retard the attachment and growth of barnacles, algae, shellfish and other marine organisms on the ships' outer surfaces. TBT paints work on the basis of their gradual dissolution or leaching into the seawater by a process known as hydrolysis. Acting as biocides, the released TBT compounds kill organisms which may otherwise cling to and foul the hulls and bottoms of ships.

Fouling by marine organisms typically results in increased drag, slower ship movement and increased fuel consumption for the ship to maintain its desired speed. Consequently, fouling increases the costs of transportation. At the same time, air pollution from increased fuel combustion is a major side effect. By preventing the attachment of marine organisms onto ships' structure, TBT compounds reduce friction between ship surfaces and the water and contribute to greater vessel speed and fuel efficiency. Apart from being used on ships, anti-fouling organotin compounds are also frequently employed in coastal mariculture to prevent submerged equipment such as nets from being fouled by marine organisms. TBT also plays an important role in preventing the transfer and spread of unwanted aquatic organisms which attach to the bottoms of ships.[421]

---

[421] See Section 4 below.

In theory, fouled ships can be cleaned at regular intervals. This entails the physical removal of the attached organisms by methods such as underwater cleaning by divers. However, this process involves frequent maintenance of ships and high associated costs. In contrast, the use of anti-fouling paints has proven to be more cost-effective, resulting in greater savings in vessel operation and maintenance expenses. However, despite their obvious advantages, anti-fouling paints containing TBT compounds have in recent years been assailed by environmentalists. Owing to its non-discriminating nature, TBT has been shown to affect non-target species. Thus, in several countries, shellfish mortality and deformation have been attributed to TBT accumulation in water columns and sediments. More significantly, TBT has been claimed to cause imposex in certain marine organisms, i.e. the development of hermaphrodite or dual-sex tendencies with resulting sterility. TBT has also been alleged to pose serious risks to human health and wildlife through contamination of the food chain.

Concerns over the detrimental effects of TBT thus led to the negotiation of a convention to phase out its use. The problem had first been raised at IMO in 1988 by the Paris Commission to the Convention for the Prevention of Marine Pollution from Land-Based Sources.[422] In 1990, following the adoption of an MEPC resolution on the matter,[423] governments were urged to eliminate the use of anti-fouling paints containing TBT compounds which had an average release rate of more than 4 microgrammes of organotin per square centimetre per day. It was also recommended that the use of TBT be banned on all non-aluminium hulled vessels of less than 25 metres in length. These measures were intended to be interim responses pending consideration of a total prohibition.

In the meantime, laws were enacted in several countries to regulate the use of TBT. France, Japan and the Netherlands were among the first countries to introduce measures to regulate the production, import and use of organotin compounds. Similar measures were also imposed in the UK, New Zealand, the US, Australia and Norway. On its part, the EU

---

[422] Communication from the Secretary of the Paris Commission to the IMO Secretary-General, *attached to* MEPC Doc. 26/24/4 (1988). The Paris Commission has now been reconstituted as the OSPAR Commission, *supra* note 229.
[423] Resolution MEPC.46(30) (1990) Containing Measures to Control Potential Adverse Impacts Associated with the Use of TBT Compounds in Anti-fouling Paints.

issued a Directive on Biocides to regulate anti-fouling products in the European market.[424]

As far as large seagoing ships were concerned, the absence of a suitable alternative to TBT made it difficult to ban the use of TBT on such ships. Consequently, domestic bans had been limited to small pleasure craft operating close to shore. Studies soon revealed, however, that the effects of TBT were beginning to be felt outside harbour areas at dump sites for dredged materials as well as in highly trafficked sea lanes. A case could thus be made for a global ban on the use of TBT on *all* ocean-going vessels. The impetus for global regulation extending to all ships also arose from competitive pressures. The shipyards in the developed countries were concerned that an exclusively regional ban would drive shipowners to maintain and repair their ships in other countries where cheap TBT products were available. As with the air pollution and sulphur content problems, these fears compelled the European states to lobby for a global and comprehensive ban.

The numerous national and regional moves to ban TBT eventually resulted in pressure to take harmonised action at the global level.[425] The developed countries which had banned TBT domestically, together with the representatives of the paint manufacturers, emerged at IMO as the main proponents of a global ban. In particular, Japan forcefully advocated the benefits of copper-based paints developed by its paint industry. Such alternatives to TBT seek to achieve comparable anti-fouling results while producing apparently less harm to marine organisms.

Other ways of preventing fouling have also been investigated. These include the use of super-smooth or non-stick coatings on ships. Such coatings employ compounds such as silicone-based materials which are not meant to leach out and act as biocides but simply prevent organisms from clinging onto ship hulls. Research has also been conducted into natural biocides derived from marine sponges. There have also been

---

[424] Directive 98/8 Concerning the Placing of Biocidal Products on the Market (Directive on Biocides), 1998 OJ (L 123) 1. A Community-wide ban on organotin-based anti-fouling systems came into force in the EU on 1 January 2003.

[425] The initial results of national and regional bans have been encouraging – monitoring programmes in Europe, Japan and the US have shown declining levels of TBT and its negative impacts in coastal waters, see submissions of the European Council of Chemical Manufacturers' Federations (CEFIC), MEPC Docs. 38/INF.8 (1996), 38/14/4 (1996), 41/INF.6 (1998), 42/5/3 (1998) and 42/INF.13 (1998).

calls on ships to rely on regular physical cleanings to remove fouling organisms.

Unfortunately, none of these proposed alternatives have been found to be practicable. This was the principal reason why a consensus on banning TBT globally had been so elusive. First and foremost, conclusive scientific evidence as to the efficacy of TBT alternatives was felt to be lacking. It was widely believed that copper- and silicone-based alternatives were nowhere as long-lasting and effective in preventing fouling by marine organisms. Similarly, the natural biocides being tested were not long-lasting enough to be of commercial value. Consequently, it was projected that ships using less effective TBT-free paints would have to be re-coated at shorter intervals, thereby necessitating more frequent dry-dockings and interruptions to service. This would entail a significant cost burden on shipowners and operators.

In any event, the environmental soundness of the alternatives was uncertain. In this regard, some states expressed fears that alternative paints may themselves be equally, if not more damaging to the marine environment. Copper toxicity, for instance, remains a major problem in many localised coastal areas. In such circumstances, the shipowners were concerned that the hasty acceptance of any alternative paints may prove to be costly if these very paints should have to be regulated in the future.

The use of less effective biocides also increases the risks of introducing harmful aquatic organisms into sensitive local waters. In this regard, TBT represented a classic instance of an agent which was both environmentally beneficial and destructive. States concerned about the harmful aquatic species problem were thus wary about a complete ban on TBT.[426] The negative effects of physical scrubbing of ship hulls were also not fully appreciated. Apart from unwittingly scraping off old coats of paint containing anti-fouling biocides, scrubbing could introduce harmful alien species into coastal environments. From an air pollution perspective, the loss of fuel efficiency resulting from less effective paints would increase exhaust emissions. For all these reasons, it was feared that the elimination of one environmental problem might simply lead to the introduction of new ones.

Above all, there was the important issue of costs. TBT-free paints, having been newly developed, cost more than TBT compounds.[427]

---

[426] Comment by Australia, *reproduced in* MEPC Doc. 40/21 (1997).
[427] It was estimated that the annualised additional cost to the global fleet of bulkers, container vessels and large tankers would be in the order of $500 million if a thirty-month tin-free self-polishing polymer was substituted for a 60-month TBT-containing equivalent, see Lloyd's List, *TBT Manufacturers Lobby Diplomats Against Ban*, 1 Oct. 2001.

Other alternatives which showed promising results such as non-stick silicone-based systems were also prohibitively expensive. Of course, proponents of TBT-free techniques hoped that the increased demand for their products would rapidly ensure greater cost-effectiveness and lower prices. As such, there was much effort by paint manufacturers to espouse the virtues of TBT-free systems and to secure the swift removal of TBT compounds from the market.

Indeed, the paint manufacturing industry – through its main representative, the European Council of Chemical Manufacturers' Federations (CEFIC) – emerged as an ardent supporter of a global ban. To a large extent, the paint manufacturing industry stood to gain from increased demand for alternative products even as demand for TBT fell. In any event, it was in the paint manufacturers' interest that any ban was global in scale and uniformly enforceable. Otherwise, a distortion in competition might arise among paint manufacturers in different countries.[428]

On their part, the shipping interests had grave reservations over a global ban.[429] Apart from doubts over the effectiveness and safety of alternative paints, there was the concern that the phasing out of TBT and the repainting of ships involved dry-docking entire fleets and putting ships out of service for long intervals. As with the issue of alien organisms in ballast water, the shipowning interests believed that there was insufficient scientific proof to attest to the cost-effectiveness of phasing out TBT completely.

Despite these reservations, IMO eventually decided that a global ban on TBT was inevitable. Proponents of regulation, including the North Sea states, Japan and the environmental NGOs, reasoned that a ban was the only effective way to compel industry into generating a market for TBT-free alternatives.[430] At the same time, it was felt that a global ban was needed to prevent competitive distortions in the global shipping, shipbuilding and ship repair markets. The ban was also bolstered by the European states' willingness to threaten regional action under the aegis of the EU.[431]

---

[428] Submission of CEFIC, MEPC Doc. 42/5/8 (1998).
[429] States which resisted a global ban were primarily those with significant fleets and open registries, including the Bahamas, Bangladesh, Barbados, Brazil, China, Egypt, India, Liberia, Malta, the Marshall Islands, Saudi Arabia and Vanuatu.
[430] Submission of Belgium, Denmark, France, Germany, Norway, the Netherlands, Sweden and the UK, MEPC Doc. 38/14 (1996).
[431] See the Ministerial Declaration at the 4th North Sea Conference, referred to in the submission of Norway, MEPC Doc. 41/10/2 (1998).

In October 2001, IMO duly adopted the Convention on the Control of Harmful Anti-Fouling Systems on Ships (hereinafter 'AFS Convention')[432] to prohibit the application of TBT paints by 2003 and to completely prohibit the presence of TBT on ships by 2008. In adopting a precautionary approach, IMO also recognised the need to develop a mechanism for anti-fouling systems other than organotin-based ones to be assessed for their efficacy and environmental effects. Other features of the new convention include a restricted list of controlled anti-fouling systems and a procedure for evaluating further additions to the list. A regime for surveys and the issuance of international anti-fouling systems certificates was also instituted.

Violations are to be prohibited under the law of the flag state with port states being allowed to inspect certificates and conduct thorough inspections and detentions if necessary.[433] Requests for inspection by the port state may be made by any state party with the necessary evidence of a violation. Regrettably, no provision is made for port state prosecution of offences. Reliance will thus have to be placed on flag states for this purpose, which is unlikely to be effective. This weakness of the convention was evidently a *quid pro quo* for the shipping interests' acceptance of a far-reaching ban.

Overall, the new convention does not depart appreciably from the familiar provisions of MARPOL 73/78 in its reliance on flag state enforcement. To such extent, the new convention can be expected to suffer from the same enforcement problems faced by the regulation of oil discharges. Given the current global emphasis on environmental protection, it is unfortunate that IMO did not venture beyond the conservative provisions of MARPOL 73/78 to exercise allowance for stronger port state enforcement. It will thus be up to the regional port state control MOUs to pay special attention to the TBT enforcement issue to make up for the convention's shortcomings.

The TBT episode illustrates yet another situation where the shipping and open registry interests have been unsuccessful in resisting ever stricter environmental regulation over the industry. In fact, the shipping interests have had no choice but to support proposals for global regulation, perceiving this to be a lesser evil than national or regional

---

[432] IMO Doc. AFS/CONF.26 (2001).
[433] Guidelines for Survey and Certification of Ships have been adopted, see Resolution MEPC.102(48) (2002). Guidelines on sampling and inspections are being developed, the latter to be implemented as part of port state control, see FSI Doc. 11/23 (2003).

unilateral action. Notably, the new convention will have the effect of imposing the bulk of regulatory costs on the shipowners ('polluter pays') with little burden-sharing by other actors such as states or charterers.

The fear of slow entry into force has also been somewhat ameliorated. At the October 2001 Conference, the environmentalist states inserted a provision which sought to reduce the influence of the shipowning states in bringing about the AFS Convention's entry into force. Thus, the convention will enter into force after being ratified by twenty-five states representing among them 25 per cent of global shipping tonnage. This hard-won provision is a significant departure from the traditional MARPOL 73/78 formula which conditions entry into force upon the acceptance of states representing at least 50 per cent of global shipping tonnage.

Despite the less stringent requirements, the convention has faced problems in fulfilling its entry into force requirements by the 1 January 2003 phase-out deadline, when its provisions were slated to take effect. By December 2004, only nine states had ratified the convention, accounting for just 9 per cent of world shipping tonnage. Other obstacles abound, primarily enforcement and compliance problems in those areas of the world where TBT compounds are still widely available. The fact that fully effective alternatives to TBT are not yet globally available means that the use of TBT will continue to be widespread in the years to come.

The future success of the TBT phase-out regime is likely to depend more on the availability of alternatives and the corresponding market obsolescence of TBT rather than the wide acceptance of the regime by states and shipowners. In this regard, the TBT regime is likely to resemble the Montreal Protocol[434] system of phasing out ozone-depleting substances which has witnessed market and industry forces playing a hugely significant role. Consequently, there is every likelihood that reliance will be placed not so much on compliance by shipowners to phase out the use of TBT, but rather, on the gradual removal and obsolescence of the compound in the global market.

---

[434] 1985 Vienna Convention on the Ozone Layer, 26 I.L.M. 1529 (1987) (in force 22 Sept. 1988) and the 1987 Montreal Protocol on Substances that Deplete the Ozone Layer, 26 I.L.M. 1550 (1987) (in force 1 Jan. 1989).

4. Harmful Aquatic Organisms and Ballast Water Management

Another recent concern in maritime shipping relates to the problem posed by harmful aquatic organisms and pathogens transmitted by the carriage of ballast water. When ships such as tankers and bulk carriers take in ballast water, living aquatic organisms contained in the seawater are invariably taken into their tanks or holds. The ballast water and its sediments are subsequently discharged into the sea as the ships approach their loading ports. In the process, harmful organisms, disease-carrying vectors and contaminants are released into the marine environment.[435]

The effects of such release have been shown to be devastating, particularly in coastal areas. The alien organisms may encounter no natural predators in their new environment and proceed to displace indigenous species, thereby disrupting the ecological balance in the area. There may also be negative economic effects due to reduced aquaculture and fishing yields. Human health concerns have also arisen, particularly over the impact of toxic dinoflagellates which cause diseases such as paralytic shellfish poisoning.

The problem of harmful aquatic organisms was first highlighted to IMO in the 1980s by Canada and the US after foreign organisms started appearing in the Great Lakes region.[436] The issue has since been driven by states such as Australia, the US and Norway. Australia's interest in the matter arises particularly from its geographical uniqueness as well as the vulnerability of its native fauna and flora to alien organisms. As a major commodities exporter, empty bulk carriers typically return to Australia with ballast water in their holds after delivering their cargoes. Consequently, Australia ends up 'importing' substantial amounts of ballast water. Many of the alien species brought into Australian coastal areas originate from Asian waters. This is not surprising given that the majority of bulk carriers returning to Australia take in ballast in East Asia where Australia's major export markets lie.

---

[435] It is estimated that about 10 billion tonnes of ballast water, with 10,000 species of marine organisms, are transferred each year, see Lloyd's List, *Shipboard Solution 'the Only Option' for Ballast Contamination*, 8 Nov. 2001.

[436] The European zebra mussel is the most prevalent alien species in the Great Lakes and has inflicted nearly US$500 million of damage in the Lakes' maritime industry. For an assessment, see D. Bederman, *International Control of Marine 'Pollution' by Exotic Species*, 18 Ecology L. Q. 677 (1991).

The scale of the problem has compelled Australian, US and other national administrations to impose strict controls over the discharge of ballast water in their coastal waters. Such controls typically take the form of national quarantine regulations. In recent years, mandatory ballast water management techniques have been employed in Australia and the US state of California. Voluntary guidelines are also in effect in other countries including Canada, Israel and Argentina. These national guidelines typically encourage ships to undergo a voluntary process of ballast water exchange before they enter the internal waters of states or sensitive coastal areas.

The problem with harmful aquatic organisms is a universal one, even though it would appear that the majority of concerned states are in the developed world. With their scientific expertise and financial capacity, it is only the developed states which have consistently managed to produce studies highlighting the scale of the problem. At present, research into the matter is driven not only by ecological considerations but by commercial incentives as well. Indeed, the inventor of an effective remedy can expect to market it profitably. However, given that none of the proposed measures to eliminate harmful aquatic organisms have to date been shown to be cost-effective, it would appear that a viable solution remains elusive. For now, reliance is generally placed on the ballast water exchange technique.

The process of ballast water exchange essentially entails the ship exchanging its load of ballast, together with whatever harmful organisms contained therein, with a fresh intake of ballast some distance away from shore. The perceived efficacy of this process rests on scientific studies showing that near-coastal organisms released into the deep sea, and correspondingly, oceanic organisms released into coastal waters, do not generally survive. Thus, when a ship which has undergone ballast water exchange discharges its ballast (of deep sea origin) in the coastal waters of the destination port, it is expected that whatever marine organisms contained therein would be less likely to survive and cause damage.

Notwithstanding its apparent ecological merits, the safety aspects of ballast water exchange remain the principal obstacle to its widespread and mandatory adoption at the global level. The process of exchanging ballast in mid-sea renders the ship unstable and subjects it to undue stress, particularly in bad weather. Extreme caution is especially needed when the tanks are deballasted and refilled in sequence since the sloshing action of water in partially filled tanks may destabilise a ship greatly. Ballast water exchange also raises doubts among shipowners because of the considerable delays and costs entailed. In addition, the process consumes substantial amounts of energy – ships would have to burn vast amounts of fuel, thereby contributing to atmospheric pollution. Ultimately, ballast water exchange remains but a short-term solution since it is capable only of minimising – not preventing – the introduction of alien species.

Various other physical, chemical and biological measures have been proposed to IMO to treat ballast water before overboard discharge. However, none of these measures has yet to be proven effective, economically viable or environmentally sound. For instance, measures such as heat treatment and filtration, even if effective, can be expected to consume large amounts of energy and contribute to air pollution. In the absence of fully effective alternative measures, it has been recognised at IMO that despite its attendant weaknesses, mid-ocean ballast water exchange represents the best currently available solution. At the same time, it is recognised that continued scientific research is needed to find effective alternative strategies particularly as new information on organisms becomes available.

At IMO, international guidelines on dealing with the problem of harmful aquatic organisms and pathogens were first adopted in 1993.[437] Under the leadership of the Australian delegation, MEPC subsequently began developing draft regulations on ballast water management with a view to incorporating them into a mandatory legal instrument. In the meantime, while re-affirming its commitment to the IMO process, Australia reserved the right to introduce unilateral legislation. In 1997, a revised set of IMO guidelines was issued.[438] Governments were urged to apply the revised guidelines as a basis for any national measures pending the development of mandatory regulations. In this way, it was hoped that any national measure taken would be consistent with emerging international norms.

Recent negotiations at IMO have succeeded in achieving broad consensus on the issue. A diplomatic conference convened in February 2004 produced the International Convention for the Control and Management

---

[437] IMO Assembly Resolution A.774(18) (1993) on International Guidelines for Preventing the Introduction of Unwanted Aquatic Organisms and Pathogens from Ships' Ballast Water and Sediment Discharges.

[438] IMO Assembly Resolution A.868(20) (1997) setting out Guidelines for the Control and Management of Ships' Ballast Water to Minimise the Transfer of Harmful Aquatic Organisms and Pathogens.

of Ships' Ballast Water and Sediments (hereinafter 'BWMC').[439] The convention – which has yet to enter into force[440] – is divided into main articles and an annex containing technical standards for the control and management of ballast water and sediments. Overall, the BWMC is premised upon a two-tiered approach. The first tier of standards subjects all ships – new and existing – to baseline requirements for ballast water management at all times throughout the world. This universally applicable first tier is complemented by second-tier rules, allowing state parties to designate special ballast water discharge control areas within which additional measures can be imposed.[441] At the same time, coastal states retain the discretion to take more stringent measures where these are consistent with international law.[442]

Based on the ship's construction date and its ballast water capacity, the first-tier standards[443] prescribe a final date after which the ship must adhere to a ballast water performance standard specified in Regulation D-2.[444] Before that date, ships may elect either to perform

---

[439] IMO Doc. BWM/CONF/36 (2004).
[440] The BWMC will enter into force twelve months after ratification by thirty states, representing 35 per cent of world merchant shipping tonnage: see art. 18. Like the AFS Convention, this is a relaxation of the traditional MARPOL 73/78 formula requiring 50 per cent of world tonnage. As of December 2004, there are no state parties yet.
[441] Such 'special area' measures must not compromise the ship's safety and security or contradict any applicable conventions, see BWMC, Annex, reg. C-1(5). Other requirements include consultation with adjoining states and timely communication to IMO. IMO's approval is necessary if required by customary international law as reflected in the LOSC, see reg. C-1(3). This latter provision is rather vague, and while art. 211(6) of the LOSC (requiring IMO approval for special measures, *infra* note 616) is probably inapplicable to harmful alien species, *infra* note 442, the safest route for coastal states designating BWMC special areas may still be to go through IMO, particularly if these extend beyond the territorial sea.
[442] BWMC, art. 2(3). This would be for areas falling within national sovereignty such as internal waters and territorial seas, and as conditions for entry into port, see also LOSC, arts. 25(2) and 196. Note that harmful aquatic organisms and pathogens do not explicitly fall under the LOSC's definition of 'pollution' under art. 1(4). The only LOSC reference to alien species is in art. 196, which provides that control measures on alien species do not affect the provisions relating to the protection of the marine environment, see art. 196(2). Hence, it would appear that the LOSC's Part XII provisions, including art. 211(6) on special measures, do not apply to harmful aquatic organisms and pathogens. The BWMC and associated state practice will thus become authoritative on the subject.
[443] BWMC, Annex, reg. B-3.
[444] Reg. D-2 provides that ships shall discharge less than ten viable organisms per cubic metre greater than or equal to 50 micrometres in minimum dimension and less than ten viable organisms per millilitre less than 50 micrometres in minimum dimension and greater than or equal to 10 micrometres in minimum dimension. In addition, ships shall not discharge certain harmful indicator microbes beyond specified concentrations. These microbes include *Vibrio cholerae*, *Escherichia coli* and Intestinal Enterococci.

ballast water exchange as a temporary measure[445] or to adopt the Regulation D-2 standard outright. Thus, for instance, ships constructed before 2009 and possessing a ballast water capacity of between 1,500 and 5,000 cubic metres have until 2014 before Regulation D-2 becomes mandatory. All ships constructed after 2012 will have to meet the Regulation D-2 standard. Alternative methods of ballast water management may be accepted, provided that they ensure at least the same level of protection to the environment, human health, property or resources, and are approved in principle by MEPC.[446]

All ships must carry a Ballast Water Management Plan approved by the flag state administration. Like the AFS Convention, enforcement procedures will be consistent with MARPOL 73/78, which means that flag states remain the primary enforcers while coastal and port states possess enforcement powers only for violations occurring within their jurisdiction. A survey and certification mechanism will be in place,[447] with compliant ships being issued with an International Ballast Water Management Certificate. Port state control officers may verify the ship's certificate, inspect the Ballast Water Record Book, take samples of ballast water and, if needed, conduct detailed inspections and take steps to prevent discharges.[448] State parties also undertake to ensure the provision of sediment reception facilities in ports or terminals where cleaning or repair of ballast tanks occur.[449]

While recognising the interim nature of ballast water exchange, the BWMC addresses the need to drive research into more effective methods of ballast water management. In the meantime, MEPC has begun work on developing detailed guidelines relating to ballast water exchange, sampling and reception facilities. The future implementation of the BWMC is expected to throw up significant (and familiar) challenges, among them the expected reluctance of states to provide sediment reception facilities, the primary reliance on flag state enforcement, the difficulties in policing illegal discharges, the uncertainty over coastal states' discretion to impose more stringent rules and the possible proliferation of ballast water discharge control areas. At the same time, the continuing lack of a cost-effective method for controlling the

---

[445] Reg. B-4 imposes conditions on ballast water exchange such as the distance from land and depth of water where the technique is performed, taking into account the relevant IMO Guidelines. Reg. D-1 stipulates ballast water exchange performance standards such as the requirement for 95 per cent volumetric exchange.
[446] BWMC, Annex, reg. B-3(7). [447] BWMC, art. 7. [448] BWMC, art. 9.
[449] BWMC, art. 5.

transfer of harmful aquatic organisms will mean that the problem is likely to persist for many more years.

In general, what is intriguing about the harmful aquatic organisms and anti-fouling systems issues is the fact that regulatory controls are now demanded not only for environmental damage with direct impact on human interests (such as oil pollution) but also damage involving less tangible biological effects such as the displacement of native organisms or the occurrence of mutated species. Indeed, the 'greening' of shipping appears to have attained a more sophisticated level now that less anthropogenic concerns are being aired. Also, the AFS and Ballast Water Management Conventions are noteworthy for their reliance on the precautionary approach to justify action where scientific evidence may still be inconclusive. Such developments would have been unheard of three decades ago.

5. Conclusion

The contemporary regulation of vessel-source marine pollution illustrates a major assertion of this work that policy initiatives at IMO and other decision-making fora are often catalysed by domestic and regional political agitation. Furthermore, the events at such fora illustrate how modern environmental sensibilities such as the 'polluter pays' principle and the precautionary approach have penetrated the mainstream of political consciousness to such an extent that industry actors are now much less able to resist environmental regulations. The increasing invocation of the precautionary approach has also meant that new (and some would say esoteric) environmental concerns such as the threat of alien organisms and anti-fouling paints are now easier brought to the negotiating table without awaiting scientific proof as to their impact.

Yet, within the relevant actors' power hierarchy, some are more able than others to deflect or evade the growing burdens of environmental regulation. Thus, as the regime formation process relating to double hulls, sulphur content in crude oil, anti-fouling systems and harmful aquatic organisms have shown, the shipowners have consistently ended up with the lion's share of regulatory costs in their capacity as the 'polluters' of the oceans. Meanwhile, more influential actors such as the oil companies and cargo interests have been largely successful in resisting the costs of environmental regulation and in moulding the regulatory regimes to their favour. A case in point is the ability of the oil interests to oppose a stringent cap on the level of sulphur in crude oil, thereby preserving their revenue streams from the sale of high-sulphur crude.

To the extent that the shipowners represent a limited pool of resources to spread out the burden of environmental regulation, an optimal level of protection for the marine environment remains elusive. The situation is exacerbated by the competitive nature of the ship transportation industry, its continuing emphasis on low costs and its spawning of sub-standard operators. It is thus imperative for the regulatory process to effect a more equitable distribution of environmental costs and burden-sharing among industry actors. Otherwise, the multifaceted and complex problem of sub-standard shipping will never be fully eradicated.

Ultimately, the other relevant actors in the safety and environmental chains, primarily the cargo owners and the state interests, should be made to assume a larger share of environmental liability and responsibility. In this regard, the following chapters will consider the related issues of state jurisdiction, implementation and compliance, and civil liability. In the process, it will be assessed how the costs of compliance can be more equitably apportioned among the relevant interests in the ship transportation industry so as to improve substantially on the marine environmental protection effort.

4   Jurisdiction over Vessel-Source Marine Pollution

1. The Concept of 'Jurisdiction' in Marine Pollution

The previous chapter has dealt with the substantive rule-making process in relation to vessel-source pollution and how this is influenced by the relevant actors' interests. A related issue is how international regulation shapes the *jurisdiction* of states to prescribe the substantive rules and to bring them to bear upon relevant target actors. Having examined the substantive content of the international rules and standards, it is imperative to appreciate how the jurisdiction to prescribe and enforce these rules is allocated among the different state actors.

The notion of state 'jurisdiction' over a particular event, its effects and/or its perpetrator(s) is one of the central tenets of international law. In the context of marine pollution regulation, 'jurisdiction' refers to the competence of states to prescribe and enforce legislation against vessels engaged in pollution. Thus, 'prescriptive' or 'legislative' jurisdiction relates to the state's competence to enact or promulgate substantive pollution control standards. These standards are often internationally agreed upon (e.g. at IMO as discussed in the previous chapter), even though international law may also endorse the prescription of national standards under certain circumstances.

The jurisdiction to prevent or punish the actual violation of the relevant standards would be termed 'enforcement jurisdiction', while 'adjudicative jurisdiction' is the power of national courts or tribunals to adjudicate prosecutions against a vessel or a person for transgressions of prescribed standards. International agreements such as the UN Convention on the Law of the Sea (LOSC) and the IMO instruments do not always draw clear distinctions between enforcement and adjudicative jurisdiction. This work will thus treat the term 'enforcement jurisdiction' as encompassing the adjudicative authority of states.[450]

In order to attain an equitable balance between the maritime and coastal interests, the regime formation process has generally sought to allocate among the relevant state actors varying degrees of jurisdiction to prescribe and enforce pollution control rules under various circumstances. This chapter will thus examine the manner in which jurisdiction has been allocated, particularly from the perspective of the interest politics which have influenced the evolution of flag, coastal and port state competence. Thus, the gradual expansion of coastal and port state jurisdiction, together with the continuing prominence of flag state jurisdiction, will be traced through events leading up to and subsequent to the adoption of the LOSC.

Under international law, the two pertinent features relating to a state's prescriptive jurisdiction are the *extent* and *content* of jurisdiction respectively.[451] 'Extent' relates to the physical or geographical area within which prescriptive jurisdiction may be exercised. On its part, 'content' determines what substantive standards may be prescribed, i.e. whether the standards should be internationally agreed standards or unilateral national ones.

States generally enjoy unfettered prescriptive jurisdiction within their own territories, including their internal waters and territorial seas. Thus, in relation to marine pollution control, states may generally prescribe their own (i.e. national) discharge standards for their internal waters and territorial seas, subject only to the general right of ships to innocent passage in the latter.[452] Beyond the territorial sea, however, prescriptive jurisdiction must be specifically conferred by international law, both in relation to extent and content.

The other critical aspect of jurisdiction relates to the capacity of states to *enforce* prescribed standards, be these national or international standards. The two fundamental questions relevant to enforcement jurisdiction are: who is to enforce the prescribed legislation; and by what means

---

[450] Several writers also treat enforcement jurisdiction as encompassing adjudicative jurisdiction, see e.g. M. N. Shaw, International Law 572 (5th ed., 2003). *Cf.* Restatement (Third) of the Foreign Relations Law of the United States 401 (1987), identifying three categories of jurisdiction – prescriptive, enforcement and adjudication. Other writers categorise enforcement jurisdiction into the competence to arrest (arrest jurisdiction) and the competence of judicial organs to deal with alleged breaches of the law (judicial jurisdiction), see Churchill & Lowe, *supra* note 26, at 344.

[451] See generally M'Gonigle & Zacher, *supra* note 65, at 207.   [452] LOSC, art. 19.

this is to be done. The first question is often settled under international law by defining clearly which state or states have the authority for enforcement. In the maritime context, enforcement jurisdiction, like prescriptive jurisdiction, may be conferred on one or more of the flag, coastal or port state actors.

Once the identity of the enforcing state is determined, the second inquiry arises as to the specific means by which enforcement is to be carried out. This relates directly to the question of capacity since the means for optimal enforcement may be beyond the capability of the competent enforcing state. In this regard, three major types of enforcement provisions have generally been employed by IMO instruments: inspection of ships, action against violations and reporting of compliance.[453]

Ultimately, whenever a vessel discharges pollutants into the sea, be it operationally or accidentally, two over-arching inquiries arise which relate to prescriptive and enforcement jurisdiction respectively. First, which state's laws govern the ship's conduct? Related to this inquiry is the *substance* of the relevant prescribed laws – are these national laws or internationally agreed ones as pre-determined by IMO? Second, which state or states possess the jurisdiction to *enforce* the relevant laws against the offending vessel and to prosecute it for violations? The response of the maritime powers to these questions (and thus, the default position in international law) has traditionally been that flag states should *exclusively* prescribe *and* enforce generally accepted *international* standards against their own flag vessels.

Hence, under the regime established by OILPOL 54 and MARPOL 73/78, state parties are required to undertake a host of obligations such as prescribing internationally accepted standards for flag vessels, inspecting ships to ensure compliance with the relevant standards and instituting proceedings against delinquent vessels, regardless of where the violation occurred. Thus, an offending vessel's actions are assessed primarily according to the laws of the flag state, which should have incorporated the relevant international standards into its corpus of laws. Thus, the IMCO treaties leading up to the LOSC clearly favoured the interests of the maritime states by subjecting vessels to both the prescriptive *and* enforcement jurisdiction of the flag state. As examined below, the LOSC generally reaffirmed this position.

As for the *substance* of what flag states may prescribe and enforce, it has been stated above that these states are generally required by the

---

[453] See Ch. 5 for state compliance with these obligations.

various conventions to incorporate into their domestic laws the relevant international standards adopted by IMCO/IMO. However, it is typically expressed that flag state laws shall 'at least have the same effect' as the international standards.[454] This means that the international standards merely represent the *minimum* threshold for the flag states, which may thus prescribe standards that are more stringent.

The flag state's prerogative to prescribe more stringent rules going beyond the international standard is entirely consistent with the concept of state sovereignty over nationals. In this case, the flag state is accorded jurisdiction based on the fact that vessels flying its flag assume its nationality. In practice, however, there has been no proliferation of stringent and non-uniform flag state laws. The reality is quite the opposite, for flag state laws typically display a tendency to dip below international standards due to these states' general lack of incentives to regulate their vessels.

For many flag states, especially the open registries, flag vessels seldom sail into their ports. Hence, any potential damage caused by these vessels would be to the marine environment of the high seas or of areas under the jurisdiction of other states. Moreover, many of the developing flag states lack the requisite manpower and financial resources to enforce standards rigorously. Often, the only interest the flag state has is the registration revenue obtained from ships flying its flag.[455] In essence, the lack of flag state incentives to prescribe and enforce pollution control measures is the very reason why a minimum standard has had to be imposed on the flag states by the various regulatory instruments, including MARPOL 73/78 and the LOSC.

The converse is true for the coastal states. These actors typically possess the incentive and inclination to regulate shipping in their waters, particularly if the ships are foreign-flagged. Since vessel-source pollution may affect the waters and shores of coastal states together with the marine resources contained therein, coastal states have a natural interest in prescribing and enforcing more stringent standards to combat vessel-source pollution effectively. Under international law, the protection of internal waters and the territorial sea could justifiably be based on the sovereignty which coastal states enjoy over these waters.[456] As for pollution occurring *beyond* the territorial sea, wider coastal state jurisdiction has often been asserted on the ground that

---

[454] LOSC, art. 211(2).   [455] See Ch. 2.   [456] LOSC, art. 2.

pollution may have adverse effects on the coastal state or threaten its security.[457]

At the same time, it has been recognised that broad coastal state jurisdiction extending beyond the territorial sea may potentially interfere with the right of free navigation. Without some form of harmonisation of permissible legislation, there arises the unwelcome prospect of coastal states prescribing and enforcing an array of unilateral and potentially differing standards over ships. Indeed, the idea of ships having to adhere to different discharge or construction, design, equipment or manning (CDEM) standards whilst traversing the waters of different countries is eminently unreasonable. This would almost certainly have the effect of impeding efficient movement of commercial and military vessels worldwide.[458]

To avoid this scenario, the international regulatory process has generally circumscribed the authority of coastal states to prescribe unilateral national measures beyond their territorial seas. As will be examined below, the LOSC and IMO's marine pollution instruments generally provide that coastal states cannot go beyond enacting laws which give effect to the prevailing *internationally accepted* rules and standards. Thus, these standards represent the *maximum* level permitted for coastal state prescription beyond the territorial sea. Only in exceptional circumstances can coastal states prescribe national measures beyond the territorial sea which are more stringent than internationally accepted rules. These include special measures for the protection of ecologically sensitive sea areas like ice-covered regions and 'special areas'.[459]

In addition to the flag and coastal states, the LOSC and the IMO instruments have also recognised the role of a third group of states – the port states. Port state jurisdiction is intended to act as a countervailing force against the potential excesses of coastal state jurisdiction, and was designed to address the coastal states' clamour for increased jurisdiction.[460] In establishing the division of prescriptive and enforcement powers among the relevant state actors, the LOSC adopted a formula based on spatial demarcation of authority over the oceans. Thus, the jurisdictional zones of the ocean – internal waters, territorial

---

[457] See e.g., Bodansky, *supra* note 69, at 737, detailing the operation of such an 'effects' doctrine.
[458] Dzidzornu, *supra* note 168, at 301.   [459] *Infra* notes 613-19.
[460] Lowe, *supra* note 124, at 642.

sea, contiguous zone, exclusive economic zone and high seas – are functionally used to allocate the prescriptive and enforcement powers of the flag, coastal and port states respectively.

The demarcation of jurisdiction among the various states will be examined in detail below. Suffice it to mention here that the general principle is that the coastal state enjoys greater jurisdiction over the ocean zones closer to shore, while the flag states' jurisdiction increases concomitantly as one proceeds farther out from the coast. In this manner, the international regulatory process seeks to balance the interests of the maritime states against those of the coastal states.

2. Early Attempts to Extend Coastal State Jurisdiction

The inadequacies of the OILPOL 54/69 regime have been examined in the previous chapter. In sum, the regime suffered from a misplaced reliance on flag state enforcement and on non-existent reception facilities and oily water separating technology. At the time, developments were also unfolding in relation to the issues of coastal state intervention and compensation. Following the *Torrey Canyon* incident in 1967, discussions at IMCO had led to the adoption of the 1969 Intervention and Civil Liability (CLC 69) Conventions,[461] both of which had some impact on the question of state jurisdiction.

In relation to CLC 69, no significant jurisdictional or enforcement issues were involved save for new provisions on pollution liability insurance. At the behest of the maritime states, CLC 69 provided that all contracting states could require full insurance of *any* ship entering their ports regardless of whether the ship's flag state was a party to the convention. This was not so much an enforcement provision against contracting states as it was a disincentive against non-contracting states which may have otherwise felt it beneficial to remain outside the convention and to enjoy insurance exemption and competitive advantages.

In any event, this provision demonstrated how the maritime states were prepared to secure a jurisprudentially significant concept when their commercial and competitive interests demanded it.[462] After all, the ability of a coastal or port state to enforce the provisions of a convention against vessels from non-parties was an entirely novel

---

[461] *Supra* notes 92 and 188. For more on CLC, see Ch. 6.
[462] M'GONIGLE & ZACHER, *supra* note 65, at 226. The following account of negotiations up to the late 1970s is derived from M'GONIGLE & ZACHER and personal interviews.

concept in shipping law during the time of CLC 69's adoption. The fact that adopting this provision involved IMCO in a jurisdictional, non-technical matter did not appear to have troubled the maritime states.

The adoption of the 1969 Intervention Convention proved to be a major boost for enlarged coastal state authority beyond the territorial sea. The convention dramatically recognised the right of coastal states – albeit under exceptional circumstances – to prescribe and enforce unilateral measures on the high seas to deal with incidents threatening their interests, e.g. the UK aerial bombing of the *Torrey Canyon* wreck.[463] Whilst commonly perceived to be a public law convention enacted to deal with a highly unusual situation, a case can be made that the Intervention Convention merely codified what was already an *existing* customary right for coastal state action.[464] Otherwise, IMCO would simply not have had the authority to prescribe a new jurisdictional right on the high seas where none previously existed.[465] The fact that the aerial bombing was conducted by the UK – an influential maritime state at the time – clearly helped the 'intervention' cause.

Yet, the mood was generally a cautious one. This was the period running up to UNCLOS III and there was a general wariness toward creating jurisdictional precedents. Accordingly, a proposal which would have made the Intervention Convention applicable to the territorial sea of a coastal state was rejected at IMCO. Such a move would have introduced restrictions to the coastal state's rights in an area over which it hitherto enjoyed generally unlimited powers. Even though such a restriction of coastal state rights favoured the maritime states and their shipping interests, the long-term implications of broadening IMCO's mandate in this manner and direction were uncertain. In essence, the maritime states recognised that empowering IMCO with jurisdictional competence would be a double-edged sword which could well work against them in the future.

---

[463] The Intervention Convention must today be taken to extend to the EEZ, a concept not yet developed during its inception. If this were not the case, a state would enjoy more extensive powers in the high seas than in its EEZ, which would be absurd. For an analysis of the convention, see Dinstein, *supra* note 299.

[464] See e.g. T. L. McDorman et al., The Marine Environment and the Caracas Convention on the Law of the Sea 10 (1981).

[465] See e.g. M'Gonigle & Zacher, *supra* note 65, at 203. Other writers take the view that the UK's action, coupled with its acceptance by other states, formed an emerging rule of customary law later confirmed by the Intervention Convention and art. 221(1) of the LOSC, see Churchill & Lowe, *supra* note 26, at 355.

In the same vein, certain other proposals submitted in relation to CLC 69 were rejected. Coastal states such as Canada had insisted on CLC compensation to be payable for pollution damage occasioned *beyond* the territorial sea.[466] Such a proposal would have entailed a major jurisdictional revolution at the time given that coastal state prescriptive jurisdiction beyond the territorial sea was as yet undefined.[467] What motivated Canada was its pursuit of greater rights over adjacent waters for jurisdictional, resource conservation and ecological purposes. Domestically, the Canadian federal government was seeking to establish its right to regulate Canada's continental shelf over that of the provincial governments. At the same time, Canada was concerned that the oil industry was proposing to transport oil from Alaska to the eastern coast of the US through the sensitive waters of the Canadian Northwest Passage.[468]

Following its failure to entrench greater coastal state rights under CLC 69, Canada unilaterally prescribed its Arctic Waters Pollution Prevention Act on 5 June 1970.[469] This controversial Act established a 100-mile pollution control zone in the Canadian Arctic regions and had the effect of extending the Canadian fisheries zone well beyond its territorial sea. Quite expectedly, the Act met with strong formal protests from the maritime powers, including the US and the UK.[470] The Act effectively signalled coastal state dissatisfaction with flag state jurisdiction, and it was clear that the seeds had been sown for the issue of wider coastal state jurisdiction to be re-opened.

Yet another early attempt at enlarging coastal state jurisdiction failed at IMCO. This was the proposal to require all ships in the territorial sea, including those exercising innocent passage, to carry insurance coverage pursuant to CLC 69. Resistance came not only from the maritime

---

[466] The EEZ concept was not existent at the time, and any extension of jurisdiction beyond the territorial sea would have impacted the high seas. Today, CLC compensation is obtainable for pollution occasioned in the EEZ, see Ch. 6.
[467] See discussion on OILPOL 54, art. XI, *infra* note 473.
[468] This concern was especially heightened following the voyage of the US tanker *Manhattan* in 1969 through Canadian Arctic waters and the pollution caused by the oil tanker *Arrow* in 1970.
[469] 9 I.L.M. 543 (1970) (in force 2 Aug. 1972). For critiques, see e.g. J. Beesley, *Rights and Responsibilities of Arctic Coastal States: The Canadian View*, 3 J. Mar. L. & Com. 1 (1972); R. Bilder, *The Canadian Arctic Waters Pollution Prevention Act: New Stresses on the Law of the Sea*, 69 Mich. L. Rev. 1 (1970); and L. Henkin, *Arctic Anti-pollution: Does Canada Make or Break International Law?*, Am. J. Int'l L. 131 (1971).
[470] See Shinn, *supra* note 104, at 77–9.

states which were concerned with shipping costs but also from those states which had security and political concerns over foreign interference in shipping.[471] In any event, the majority of developing states with shipping interests were not keen to impose additional costs upon their fleets or import bills. Thus, expanded coastal state jurisdiction in this matter was rejected even by the developing coastal states. The cumulative impact of these developments was to keep IMCO strictly within the confines of its mandate during the late 1960s.

3. Jurisdiction under the MARPOL Regime

3.1 Prescriptive Jurisdiction under MARPOL 73

By the early 1970s, concerns had arisen over the inadequacies of OILPOL 54, as amended. As examined previously, the 1969 amendments were not in force while compliance with OILPOL 54/62 remained unsatisfactory. There was also widespread dissatisfaction with the LOT method introduced in 1969. These concerns led to the convening of the 1973 IMCO Conference.[472] In addition to proposing improvements to the substantive rules on vessel-source pollution, the Conference also anticipated the adoption of new jurisdictional mechanisms to improve upon the prescription and enforcement of pollution control standards.

Nevertheless, with preparations for UNCLOS well in motion by then, there was great reluctance among states to create jurisdictional precedents at IMCO. Given that MARPOL 73 was meant to supersede the OILPOL regime, the maritime states were particularly uneasy over what would replace Article XI of OILPOL 54/62. This was the provision which accorded coastal states the power to 'take measures *within its jurisdiction* in respect of any matter to which the Convention relates' (emphasis added). Hitherto, flag state jurisdiction was recognised to be paramount under the OILPOL regime and the scope of coastal state 'jurisdiction' under Article XI remained extremely vague.

At IMCO, the coastal states insisted on a replacement for Article XI which would grant them clearer and greater powers to prescribe stringent standards in their coastal zones.[473] Controversy thus arose not only over the *content* of coastal state prescriptive jurisdiction (in relation to

---

[471] For instance, Israel feared that expanded coastal state jurisdiction would allow the Arab states to interfere in its shipping, see M'GONIGLE & ZACHER, *supra* note 65, at 205.
[472] See Ch. 3.
[473] The issue became known as the 'special measures' controversy.

what standards could be prescribed), but also the geographical *extent* of that jurisdiction. As regards *extent*, the maritime states such as the US wanted it made clear that Article XI's 'jurisdiction', whatever its content, was to be geographically confined to the territorial sea. On the other hand, the coastal state coalition led by the so-called 'Territorialist states'[474] wanted both the extent and content of coastal state jurisdiction to be determined by state practice such as their own unilateral proclamations.

Consequently, leaving Article XI unchanged was not good enough for both sides. This would have left the term 'jurisdiction' to be determined by the vagaries of customary international law or the uncertainties of the upcoming UNCLOS. In reality, there was little doubt that the issue was rightly one for UNCLOS to decide. In the end, the final compromise at the 1973 IMCO Conference was suitably vague – under MARPOL 73, the flag state was to prohibit violations 'under the law of the Administration' (i.e. the flag state) while the coastal state would prohibit violations 'within the jurisdiction' of the state.[475] The term 'jurisdiction' remained undefined, even though it was provided that it would be construed 'in the light of international law in force at the time of application or interpretation of [MARPOL]'.[476] These provisions effectively left the limits of coastal state jurisdiction to UNCLOS to resolve. Hence, the result at IMCO effected no change whatsoever to the OILPOL jurisdictional regime.

What was a more germane argument was the *content* of coastal state prescriptive jurisdiction. The maritime states had hitherto found the vague formulation in Article XI to be tolerable but sensing the growing mood on the eve of UNCLOS for increased coastal state jurisdiction, decided that an equivocal wording was not good enough.[477] For the maritime interests, the substantive content of coastal state jurisdiction, particularly beyond the territorial sea, had to be explicitly circumscribed.

On their part, the coastal states too, felt that Article XI lacked clarity. These states would have wished it to legitimise wider coastal state authority – better still, if this authority could be unilaterally proclaimed! In seeking international endorsement for its 1970 Arctic

---

[474] These were mainly Latin American countries such as Argentina, Chile, Ecuador, Mexico, Peru and Uruguay, as well as African states like Tanzania.
[475] MARPOL 73, art. 4.   [476] MARPOL 73, art. 9(3).
[477] M'GONIGLE & ZACHER, *supra* note 65, at 206–7.

waters legislation, Canada had earlier proposed at IMCO that coastal states should be accorded full legislative (prescriptive) authority for marine environmental protection in waters under their jurisdiction. If accepted, this proposal would have settled the question of substantive *content* by leaving it wholly to coastal state determination, i.e. coastal states could unilaterally prescribe whatever content they wanted while the question of *extent* could be left to UNCLOS to settle.

The Canadian proposal drew extensive support in the run-up to the 1973 IMCO Conference. However, maritime state resistance was great. A compromise was necessary and this was swiftly provided by a group of maritime states during the opening days of the conference. The maritime states proposed to recognise *some* coastal state powers, provided such powers would not cause major navigational impediments. Specifically, coastal states would be allowed the power to set stricter discharge standards in waters under their jurisdiction, but *not* stricter construction, design, equipment or manning (CDEM) standards.[478] The latter prohibition would apply in *any* area of the sea – even in internal waters and the territorial sea – except where the environment was 'exceptionally vulnerable'.

The Canadians, long the lynchpin of coastal state activism, were suitably placated by the 'exceptionally vulnerable' exception which nicely addressed their Arctic concerns. However, the compromise formula left the more radical coastal states less than satisfied. Meanwhile, the US, despite its new-found environmental zeal, was opposed to any measure which had the slightest potential of interfering with free navigation.[479] At the same time, the US found the prohibition on unilateral CDEM standards within internal waters and the territorial sea to be an infringement of its own sovereignty. In this respect, the prohibition would have undermined the 1972 US Ports and Waterways Safety Act (hereinafter PWSA),[480] which imposed certain unilateral design and construction standards on visiting ships.

For these reasons, the US moved to defeat the proposal. The more radical coastal states needed little persuasion that the prohibition

---

[478] The rationale for this distinction was, of course, the fact that unilateral CDEM standards were much more obstructive to shipping than discharge standards.
[479] This particular concern of the US Department of Defense illustrated the cross-pressures facing the US delegation.
[480] U.S.C. §§ 1221-1227. This Act, together with OPA-90, *supra* note 356, constitute examples of unilateral legislation prescribing CDEM standards going beyond international standards.

against CDEM requirements denied them the full jurisdiction they desired. On the other hand, the US reinforced the maritime states' fears that the proposal threatened their bargaining position on free navigation at the upcoming UNCLOS. The US strategy 'to play both ends against the middle'[481] was made entirely possible by the inherent contradictions within the proposal – it expanded coastal state authority, and yet curtailed unilateral action on CDEM standards. At the same time, the US was campaigning on a third front by threatening unilateral imposition of SBT equipment standards unless these were accepted by the Conference.[482]

Ultimately, despite having won approval at the preliminary stage, the Canadian proposal was defeated at the plenary of the 1973 Conference. Six of the proposal's original supporters withdrew their support at the plenary vote, including two key maritime states – the UK and the Netherlands – and three major coastal states – Brazil, Iran and Uruguay.[483] The USSR, which had originally supported the Canadians on the compromise, abstained during the plenary vote.[484] The Soviet abstention, although surprising, was generally viewed as a deferential gesture to US–USSR détente.[485]

With no substitute for Article XI of OILPOL 54/62, *both* jurisdictional extent and content had to await clarification at UNCLOS. As mentioned above, MARPOL 73 was eventually left with a suitably vague provision requiring the flag state to prohibit violations 'under the law of the Administration', while the coastal state would prohibit such violations 'within the jurisdiction' of the state, whatever 'jurisdiction' meant.

3.2 *Enforcement Jurisdiction under MARPOL 73*

By 1973, it was patently clear that the existing enforcement system under the amended OILPOL 54/62 regime was simply not functioning. With the 100-ppm standard being effectively ignored and the new

---

[481] In the words of M'GONIGLE & ZACHER, *supra* note 65, at 210.
[482] See Ch. 3.   [483] The sixth was Ireland.
[484] Like Canada, the Soviets had supported the proposal for their own Arctic interests. As a naval superpower, the USSR also welcomed measures which restricted coastal state unilateralism. On Soviet interests generally, see N. D. Koroleva & V. A. Kiesev, *Soviet Marine Pollution Legislation: Prevention of Pollution from Ships and the LOS Convention*, 15 MARINE POL'Y 49 (1991).
[485] M'GONIGLE & ZACHER, *supra* note 65, at 218. This was, after all, the height of the Cold War. Moreover, the 1973 Conference took place amidst Arab-Israeli hostilities during the Yom Kippur War.

litre/mile standard not yet in force, there effectively existed an enforcement vacuum, particularly for undetectable violations in the open seas. During this period, the self-reporting obligation under OILPOL 54/62 was almost universally ignored.[486]

As the initiator of the 1973 Conference, the US was in a delicate situation. Whilst genuinely desirous of improving the prescription and enforcement of pollution control rules, it remained opposed to excessively broad jurisdictional changes, particularly in the field of enforcement. The result of this caution was a MARPOL 73 which effected only modest changes to enforcement jurisdiction. Thus, the convention retained the familiar OILPOL reporting provisions[487] which had long been recognised to be deficient.

In addition, the flag states would enforce compliance with the new SBT equipment standard. Flag states were also obliged to inspect their vessels at regular intervals and to issue relevant certificates of compliance.[488] In this regard, MARPOL 73 introduced the concept of the International Oil Pollution Prevention Certificate (IOPPC). Such certificates would be conclusive evidence of compliance and were not to be challenged by port states unless there were 'clear grounds' for believing that the condition of the ship did not correspond substantially to the certificates or that the certificates were invalid.[489] In such situations, the inspecting port state shall take such steps as will ensure that the ship shall not sail until it can proceed to sea without presenting an unreasonable threat of harm to the marine environment. In sum, a right of port state inspection was recognised even though this was restricted to checking the veracity of certificates and Oil Record Books (ORBs).

These provisions were opposed by the coastal states and environmentalists who pounced on the unsatisfactory record of flag state enforcement and the fact that certificates could either be easily falsified or awarded by lenient classification societies. However, the maritime states, together with the Soviet bloc, were unrelenting in resisting greater coastal state enforcement powers. In fact, the maritime states even went one step further and extracted a coastal state obligation to provide compensation for any undue delays caused by inspecting CDEM violations.[490]

---

[486] See Table 5-16, Ch. 5.   [487] MARPOL 73, art. 8 and Protocol I.
[488] MARPOL 73, art. 5(1) and Annex I, regs. 4 and 5.
[489] MARPOL 73, art. 5(2). The 'clear grounds' provision was meant to protect against capricious coastal state action. In recent years, however, port state inspections have become more stringent and tended to go beyond certificates, *infra* note 642.
[490] MARPOL 73, art. 7.

Inspection rights over discharge standards were separately handled. The Conference was able to agree on a *general* right of inspection for port state authorities, either on their own initiative or at the request of another contracting party which had evidence of a discharge contravention. Thus, port states may inspect a ship for the purpose of verifying whether it had discharged any harmful substances in violation of the convention.[491] This was a significant achievement in view of the previous failure of France and the UK to introduce similar port state control provisions.[492] For the first time, some form of port state inspection procedure had been explicitly recognised for discharge standards. However, its status as a right, not an obligation, meant that it would be entirely up to coastal state discretion to pursue an effective inspection regime.

As for the prosecution of violations, the coastal states managed to secure some powers, even obligations. As stated above, coastal states were obliged in relation to CDEM violations to prevent a ship from sailing if it presented an unreasonable threat to the marine environment unless it was heading to a repair yard.[493] Coastal states were also obliged to report violations outside their jurisdiction[494] to flag states. For violations occurring within their jurisdiction, coastal states shall either initiate proceedings in accordance with their own laws or transmit information and evidence to the flag state for further action.[495]

In this atmosphere of greater sympathy toward coastal state enforcement powers, the US, Canada and Japan attempted to advance an innovative 'port state enforcement' regime with greater *prosecutorial* powers. Coastal state powers to prosecute violations had hitherto been restricted to their internal waters and territorial seas, with flag state authority being exclusive on the high seas.[496] This strict demarcation of authority was beginning to unsettle the coastal states. In an attempt to broker a compromise, the US proposed that a power to arrest and prosecute could be conferred on *port* states instead. In essence, a port state could initiate proceedings against any vessel *while it was in port* for any violation committed *anywhere at sea*.

---

[491] MARPOL 73, arts. 6(2) and 6(5). The port state will usually inspect the slop tanks for compliance with the total discharge limits of 1/15,000 or 1/30,000 of tanker capacity.
[492] See Section 1.2 above.
[493] MARPOL 73, art. 5(2). See also SOLAS 74, reg. I/19, as amended.
[494] Again, it was unclear what exactly 'jurisdiction' entailed.
[495] MARPOL 73, art. 4(2). See also arts. 6(2), 6(3) and 8(3).
[496] The high seas at the time started seaward of the territorial sea.

The US, Japan and the oil industry clearly strategised that by legislating port state enforcement at IMCO, they would subsequently be able to legitimise it at UNCLOS and thus resist even more radical coastal state demands. The proposal was premised upon the maritime states' belief that port state enforcement was inherently safer and more predictable than coastal state enforcement, the former being conducted in port as opposed to the open sea. The proposal was to be subsequently entrenched at UNCLOS as a major jurisdictional innovation. For now, however, it was flatly rejected at IMCO by a variety of interests for their own peculiar reasons.

In general, most states were unwilling to commit to any solution ahead of the impending UNCLOS. Even though port state enforcement would have allayed fears of mid-sea inspections by over-zealous coastal states, it was nonetheless viewed by some maritime interests as being too radical in its erosion of flag state primacy. Moreover, the European tanker-owners were concerned about discriminatory treatment in port by the oil-exporting Arab states.[497]

On their part, the developing maritime and open registry states feared discrimination by ports (both in developing countries as well as developed ones) against their vessels. The Soviet bloc clung to its traditional suspicion of foreign interference with its state-owned vessels. Meanwhile, the coastal states, including Canada,[498] feared that accepting the proposal would be a premature sacrifice of their greater ambitions at UNCLOS. In the result, MARPOL 73 was only able to lay down a *general* right of inspection (but not prosecution) for port states in relation to CDEM and discharge violations.[499] The traditional separation of flag state and coastal/port state prosecuting authority would remain unaltered.

Overall, the achievements at the 1973 Conference were modest in as far as jurisdictional and enforcement measures were concerned.[500] The new discharge standards – the 60 litre/mile standard and the 1/15,000 total limit – were accompanied by *some* improved port state inspection

---

[497] M'Gonigle & Zacher, *supra* note 65, at 232.
[498] This was an about-turn for Canada, which had originally supported the scheme. Even though Canada eventually voted for the proposal, it apparently signalled to others that it would be unwise for them to do so, see M'Gonigle & Zacher, *ibid.* at 234.
[499] MARPOL 73, arts. 5(2) and 6(2). Note, however, that port states are increasingly using administrative sanctions such as detention, as opposed to judicial measures. This has been made possible with the advent of the various Port State Control MOUs, see Ch. 5.
[500] On enforcement generally, see e.g. Lowe, *supra* note 124 and P. W. Birnie, *Enforcement of the International Laws for the Prevention of Oil Pollution from Vessels*, in The Impact of Marine Pollution 95 (D. J. Cusine & J. P. Grant eds., 1980).

rights. However, these rights were mainly illusory since coastal and port state *prosecution* powers remained weak. In effect, MARPOL 73 reaffirmed the dependence on flag state prosecution which showed no promise of improvement. In relation to CDEM standards, port state enforcement authority was effectively restricted to inspecting IOPP Certificates. As for the new discharge standards, effective enforcement relied heavily on state incentive and technical capacity to monitor, neither of which existed for most states.

3.3 The 1978 MARPOL Protocol

The unfinished debate over jurisdictional claims was subsequently brought over to UNCLOS. This will be examined in the next section. By the time the 1978 Tanker Safety and Pollution Prevention (TSPP) Conference was convened, jurisdictional and enforcement issues were no longer as prominent. Hence, the imposition of more stringent construction and equipment standards such as SBTs and COW was accompanied by fairly docile provisions for the enforcement of these standards. In this regard, the 1978 MARPOL Protocol adopted several new regulations for vessel surveys and certification, all of which fell on the flag states to implement. In particular, a new form of the IOPP Certificate was introduced.

At the 1978 Conference, the US also secured the acceptance of more frequent or 'intermediate' surveys for older tankers. In addition, several new enforcement measures relating to CDEM standards were adopted, principally to be implemented by nationally appointed surveyors. Flag states were also obliged to transmit to IMCO all information regarding the identity and responsibilities of appointed surveyors.[501] These improvements accompanied the new COW requirement introduced by the 1978 MARPOL Protocol.

The LOT system which COW replaced had been largely ineffective because of its reliance on oil-loading ports to conduct enforcement.[502] In contrast, the enforcement of COW rested with the ports of discharge. These were invariably located in the developed oil-importing states which had the requisite political will, incentives and capacity to carry out enforcement. Thus, the introduction of COW effected some improvement to the enforcement process. In addition, the US demand for the ability to implement the 1978 MARPOL and SOLAS Protocols ahead of their entry into force bolstered the prospects of early ratification and enforcement by states.

---

[501] These would invariably be the classification societies.   [502] See Ch. 3.

In sum, the 1978 Conference effected significant changes to the substantive content of pollution control regulations but only modest improvements to the associated enforcement regime, particularly that of the coastal and port states. As seen in Chapter 3, the bulk of the improvements related to new construction and equipment standards. Like the earlier LOT measure, the new SBT and COW standards led to incidental improvements in enforcement only by virtue of their inherent nature and not because coastal or port state enforcement powers were specifically enhanced. On the whole, jurisdictional questions remained side-stepped given that the UNCLOS negotiations were by then underway. It is to UNCLOS that we now turn.

4. The 1982 UN Conference on the Law of the Sea (UNCLOS III)

4.1 The Law of the Sea Convention (LOSC) and Part XII on the Marine Environment

The obligations of states relating to the protection of the marine environment are to be found not only in the IMO conventions but also in the LOSC. While the IMO instruments deal more with technical issues relating to substantive pollution control standards, the LOSC provides a broad jurisdictional framework within which the regulation of marine pollution can be located. As an all-encompassing legal document, the LOSC seeks to govern the conduct of states in every aspect of ocean use. In effect, the LOSC is a 'constitution for the oceans'[503] which seeks to reconcile the diverse claims of global players over the exploitation of the sea and its resources.

The LOSC was a product of more than a decade's worth of difficult negotiations, often involving intense bargaining and trading of interests. Earlier attempts at securing agreement among states on the uses of the oceans[504] had failed to resolve crucial jurisdictional issues such as

---

[503] The phrase is attributed to Ambassador Tommy Koh of Singapore, President of UNCLOS III, speaking at the final session of the Conference, see T.T.B. Koh, *A Constitution for the Oceans*, in THE LAW OF THE SEA – UNITED NATIONS CONVENTION ON THE LAW OF THE SEA, U.N. Pub. Sales No. E.83. V.5 xxiii (1983).

[504] These were the First and Second UN Conferences on the Law of the Sea, held in 1958 and 1960 respectively. In part, these Conferences sought to respond to the challenges posed by President Truman's Proclamation of 1945 which claimed sovereign rights for the US over its continental shelf, primarily for oil exploration purposes. This was the first major expansion of coastal state jurisdiction over the ocean and unleashed a

the delimitation of the territorial sea, the right of coastal states to declare exclusive fishing zones adjacent to the territorial sea and the width of the outer continental shelf. By the late 1960s, a new contentious issue had emerged. The deep seabed under the high seas had been discovered to contain nodules with significant manganese and other mineral deposits. The issue of ownership of these resources, together with the rules governing how they were to be exploited, soon led to calls for the convening of a new UN Conference.[505]

By this time, too, there was renewed impetus to re-open discussions on the jurisdictional issues relating to the breadth of the territorial sea and the fishing rights of coastal states. In this regard, several states with long coastlines had begun to agitate for increased rights over their adjacent seas and shelves and the resources contained therein. In the meantime, other associated issues became added to the proposed UNCLOS agenda – these included navigation through international straits, protection of the marine environment, marine research and settlement of disputes. Hence, the wheels were put into motion to convene what was to emerge as the largest and most complicated diplomatic conference ever to be undertaken by the United Nations.

Years of negotiations ensued in the form of preparatory meetings and sessions.[506] Even from a fairly early stage, the negotiations became radicalised by the emergence of several developing country participants who sought to rectify what they perceived to be inequities in the global economic order.[507] One of the early contentious issues to arise involved voting procedures. Given that the majority of states were from the developing world, the outnumbered developed states insisted on a 'consensus approach' which would ensure that they were not outvoted in the adoption of decisions.[508]

---

series of claims by other states, see E. D. Brown, The International Law of the Sea 8-19 (1994).

[505] This followed calls made by Ambassador Arvid Pardo of Malta to study the matter. It was subsequently decided that the drafting of the new convention would not be left to the International Law Commission, as had been the case at UNCLOS I and II, but would be subjected to a broader political process involving not just lawyers but diplomats, politicians, scientists and other experts.

[506] For an analysis of the preparatory sessions, see E. L. Miles, Global Ocean Politics: The Decision Process at the Third United Nations Conference on the Law of the Sea, 1973-1982 (1998).

[507] See generally J. W. Kindt, *The Effect of Claims by Developing Countries on LOS International Marine Pollution Negotiations*, 20 Va. J. Int'l L. 313 (1980).

[508] See e.g. J. Sibenius, Negotiating the Law of the Sea (1984) and B. Buzan, *Negotiating by Consensus: Developments in Technique at the United Nations Conference on the Law of the Sea*, 75 Am. J. Int'l L. 324 (1981).

At the same time, the Conference adopted a 'package deal' approach to the emerging convention. This necessarily entailed furious trading and bargaining among the various interests in relation to different parts of the deal. The result was that no issue could be deemed to be formally resolved until all other inter-related issues had been addressed. After more than ten years' work, the Conference finally succeeded in producing a convention. The LOSC was formally adopted and opened for signature in 1982, and entry into force was achieved on 16 November 1994, one year after the sixtieth ratification was received. As at December 2004, there were 146 state parties to the LOSC.

The controversy over the deep seabed mining provisions in Part XI of the LOSC had originally caused the advanced industrialised countries to withhold their ratification of the convention. These states had felt that the decision-making process in the relevant organs created by Part XI did not accord them sufficient influence, that exploitation policies were not in accord with free market principles and that provisions for mandatory transfer of private technology disadvantaged their commercial interests. Since then, these issues have been substantially renegotiated, culminating in agreement in 1994.[509] With the exception of Switzerland and the US, all the developed countries have since become parties to the LOSC.[510]

Within the jurisdictional context of marine pollution control, the LOSC's interest-balancing effort is primarily effected by demarcating the respective states' jurisdiction over the zones of the sea which are recognised under contemporary international law: the internal waters, the territorial sea, the contiguous zone, the exclusive economic zone (itself

---

[509] 1994 Agreement Relating to the Implementation of Part XI of the United Nations Convention on the Law of the Sea, G.A. Res. 263, U.N. GAOR, 48th Sess., 33 I.L.M. 1309 (1994) (in force 28 July 1996). The 1994 Agreement essentially overhauls Part XI and calls on all states to ratify the LOSC. On Part XI and the 1994 Agreement, see e.g. S. MAHMOUDI, THE LAW OF DEEP SEA BED MINING (1987), J. I. Charney, *U.S. Provisional Application of the 1994 Deep Seabed Agreement*, 88 AM. J. INT'L L. 705 (1994) and L. D. M. Nelson, *The New Deep Seabed Mining Regime*, 10 INT'L J. MARINE & COASTAL L. 189 (1995).

[510] Congressional politics – particularly in the Senate – continues to hinder US ratification of the LOSC. The doubts relate primarily to the provisions on deep seabed resources and compulsory dispute settlement. Even with the changes introduced by the 1994 Agreement, the LOSC's opponents maintain that the deep seabed provisions continue to favour the developing states. This issue aside, the US has consistently declared its understanding that the LOSC represents customary international law, see Proclamation 5030, 33 U.S.C. § 2701(8), *reprinted in* 22 I.L.M. 464 (1983) and RESTATEMENT (THIRD) OF THE FOREIGN RELATIONS LAW OF THE UNITED STATES 514 (1987). See also B. H. Oxman, *United States Interests in the Law of the Sea*, 88 AM. J. INT'L L. 167 (1994) and ROACH & SMITH, *supra* note 53, at 113–15.

an LOSC creation) and the high seas.⁵¹¹ Thus, each of these zones has a specific allocation of jurisdiction among the coastal, port and flag state actors, with the underlying theory being that as one proceeds farther out to sea, the coastal state's interest in protecting its environment decreases while the maritime state's interest in navigational freedom increases. In adopting this segmented approach, the UNCLOS negotiators rejected early proposals by states such as Canada which would have allowed coastal states an all-encompassing pollution control zone.

As regards the prescription of specific pollution control measures, the LOSC avoided enumerating new standards for particular forms of pollution. Instead, it proclaims a general regime of powers and duties which builds upon the codification and development of existing and future pollution control conventions.⁵¹² Thus, the LOSC incorporates by reference those existing as well as future instruments to be adopted under IMO auspices. In this regard, the convention is riddled with terms of reference such as 'applicable international rules and standards', 'internationally-agreed rules', 'international rules' and 'generally accepted international rules and standards'. These rules of reference have the advantage of automatically incorporating the technical standards set by IMO as these are continuously adopted and amended to keep up with changing circumstances. At the same time, the fact that these rules and standards are referred to by the LOSC ensures their pre-eminence over national laws and regulations.

There has been much uncertainty over the precise meaning of the rules of reference, particularly 'generally accepted international rules and standards' (commonly truncated as GAIRS).⁵¹³ At the very least, most writers agree that in the context of vessel-source pollution, these

---

⁵¹¹ For the UNCLOS interest-balancing process, see e.g. CHURCHILL & LOWE, supra note 26, MILES, supra note 506; J. I. Charney, Entry into Force of the 1982 Convention on the Law of the Sea, 35 VA. J. INT'L L. 381 (1995); J. R. Stevenson & B. H. Oxman, The Future of the United Nations Convention on the Law of the Sea, 88 AM. J. INT'L L. 488 (1994); and J. I. Charney, The Marine Environment and the 1982 United Nations Convention on the Law of the Sea, 28 INT'L LAW. 879 (1994). For an assessment of UNCLOS III's interaction with the 1992 UNCED, see e.g. R. Falk & H. Elver, Comparing Global Perspectives: The 1982 UNCLOS and the 1992 UNCED, in Vidas & Østreng eds., supra note 64, at 145 and A. E. Boyle et al., Marine Environment and Marine Pollution, in AGENDA 21 AND THE UNCED PROCEEDINGS 1207 (N. Robinson ed., 1992).
⁵¹² LOSC, art. 237. See also A. E. Boyle, Marine Pollution under the Law of the Sea Convention, 79 AM. J. INT'L L. 347, 350 (1987). As noted earlier, MARPOL 73/78 anticipated the advent of UNCLOS and was carefully designed so as not to contradict the principles established by the latter, see Dempsey, supra note 4, at 541.
⁵¹³ This phrase appears throughout Part XII in arts. 211(2), 211(5), 211(6) and 226(1). See generally B. Vukas, Generally Accepted International Rules and Standards, in IMPLEMENTATION OF THE LAW OF THE SEA CONVENTION THROUGH INTERNATIONAL INSTITUTIONS 405 (A. Soons ed., 1990).

phrases must refer to IMO's principal instrument on marine pollution control, MARPOL 73/78.[514] As for other possible instruments, however, some writers take a restrictive view, limiting GAIRS to rules which have become customary international law.[515] Others link GAIRS to IMO conventions which are in force, whether or not the state concerned (flag or coastal) is itself a party to the particular convention.[516]

Both views seem overly restrictive – in the first place, the rule of reference would be rendered redundant if it referred only to customary rules or rules contained in conventions in force for the parties concerned. In such situations, the relevant rules would have been binding on the state in any case. By accepting the LOSC, states should be taken to have accepted a rule of reference that could have the effect of extending their obligations to rules which they are ordinarily not bound to observe.[517] The situation is analogous to IMO's widely used 'tacit acceptance' procedure,[518] which, as a method of law-creation duly accepted by states, operates to bind states to obligations which they have not explicitly accepted.

Thus, as long as it can be established that a specific rule or standard enjoys sufficiently general state practice in a particular field of regulation, the rule of reference ought to extend to that rule or standard notwithstanding that it may have been expressed in a convention that the relevant states are not parties to, or that has yet to enter into force,

---

[514] See e.g. 2 UNITED NATIONS CONVENTION ON THE LAW OF THE SEA 1982: A COMMENTARY, at 21.11 (S. N. Nandan et al. eds., 1993); M. Valenzuela, *Enforcing Rules Against Vessel-Source Degradation of the Marine Environment: Coastal, Flag and Port State Jurisdiction*, in Vidas & Østreng eds., *supra* note 64, at 485–8; MOLENAAR, *supra* note 52; at 140 and Bodansky, *supra* note 69, at 760. For the view that MARPOL 73/78 represents customary international law, see P. BIRNIE & A. E. BOYLE, INTERNATIONAL LAW AND THE ENVIRONMENT 363 (2002).

[515] See e.g. HAKAPÄÄ, *supra* note 3, at 120, KASOULIDES, *supra* note 22, at 38–41; and W. van Reenen, *Rules of Reference in the New Convention on the Law of the Sea, in Particular in Connection with the Pollution of the Sea by Oil Tankers*, 12 NETH. Y.B. INT'L L. 3, at 25 (1981).

[516] E.g. CHURCHILL & LOWE, *supra* note 26, at 346 and TIMAGENIS, *supra* note 3, at 605. This is also the position taken by member states of the Paris MOU on Port State Control, with no apparent protests from flag states, see Franckx ed., *supra* note 53, at 46.

[517] This is the view of scholars who feel that the GAIRS formula is less strict than suggested by the earlier two groups, see e.g. B. H. Oxman, *The Duty to Respect Generally Accepted International Standards*, 24 N.Y.U. J. INT'L L. & POL. 109 (1991); L. B. Sohn, *'Generally Accepted' International Rules*, 61 WASH. L. REV. 1073, at 1074 and 1080 (1986); L. B. Sohn, *Implications of the Law of the Sea Convention Regarding the Protection and Preservation of the Marine Environment*, in THE DEVELOPING ORDER OF THE OCEANS 106 (R. Krueger & S. Riesenfeld eds., 1985); and R. Wolfrum, *IMO Interface with the Law of the Sea Convention*, in Nordquist & Moore eds., *supra* note 147, at 223.

[518] See Ch. 2.

or is in force with limited state acceptances, or even in a non-binding instrument such as an IMO resolution. The critical element is the *sufficiently general acceptance* of that rule or standard, not the general acceptance of the legal instrument in which the rule or standard appears.[519]

As for the phrase 'applicable international rules and standards', it would appear that, in order to distinguish it from GAIRS, 'applicable' must be taken to be a broader concept referring to a set of rules and standards which the relevant states have specifically accepted, including those which are not GAIRS.[520] Here, a case-by-case analysis is warranted, for what rules and standards are 'applicable' in a specific case (particularly for enforcement purposes) would depend on what has been accepted by the flag, coastal and port states concerned in a particular dispute or matter. An exercise to determine which rules and standards have been mutually accepted by the states concerned would have to be conducted to determine 'matching' rights and obligations for these states. This is particularly so if the relevant rules and standards are not encapsulated in customary law but in treaties requiring explicit acceptance.

Overall, the UNCLOS deliberations were divided along the lines of two dominant packages. The first, negotiated in Committee I, was the seabed regime which witnessed intense deliberations. The major protagonists here were the advanced industrialised countries which had the technology and the finances to harvest the deep seabed resources and the Group of 77 (G77) developing countries which sought to turn the issue into an ideological struggle for a more equitable world order. The other package, negotiated within Committees II and III, consisted of

---

[519] Franckx ed., *supra* note 53, at 29 and 112. Examples of such rules and standards include those relating to the phasing out of tributyl tin (TBT) on ships (found in IMO's 2001 Anti-Fouling Systems Convention, *supra* note 432, not in force) and the rules on the discharge of sewage (found in MARPOL 73/78's Annex IV, in force but with less than widespread state acceptance).

[520] Franckx ed., *supra* note 53, at 41 and van Reenen, *supra* note 515, at 12. It follows that within coastal state enforcement situations, GAIRS are always 'applicable' (this being the broader concept) as between states. This is because customary international law, as evidenced by state practice, allows coastal states to apply GAIRS in their maritime zones irrespective of the flag of the ship, see Franckx ed., *ibid.* at 54–5 and the 'no more favourable treatment' rule under MARPOL 73/78, art. 5(4). This would mean that whether a flag state has accepted the LOSC or not is strictly irrelevant, since it would have been obliged to conform to GAIRS in any case. Of course, a flag state's acceptance of the LOSC and its rules of reference would strengthen the case for coastal state enforcement of GAIRS. On relations between parties and non-parties to the LOSC, see L. T. Lee, *The Law of the Sea Convention and Third Parties*, 77 AM. J. INT'L L. 541 (1983).

jurisdictional issues pertaining to the territorial sea, straits used for international navigation, the exclusive economic zone, archipelagos, the continental shelf, the landlocked states, the marine environment, marine scientific research and the transfer of technology.[521] The contest here was between the maritime states seeking to preserve the freedom of navigation and the coastal states which were claiming increased jurisdiction over ocean resources.

As averred to earlier, any assessment of the outcome of UNCLOS III, as reflected in the constituent portions of the LOSC, must necessarily take into account the negotiation of the other parts of the convention. In effect, the whole convention is a series of compromises. Within the package crafted by Committees II and III, the fundamental trade-off was between resources and navigation. Thus, the coastal states were awarded a grand bounty comprising a twelve-mile territorial sea, a 200-mile exclusive economic zone (encompassing the territorial sea) within which sovereignty may be exercised over all living and non-living resources, sovereignty over the continental shelf to 200 miles (or beyond under certain conditions) and straight baselines connecting the outermost points of the outermost islands for archipelagic coastal states. Taken together, these provisions represented a dramatic expansion of coastal state jurisdiction never before witnessed in the history of international law and diplomacy.[522]

In exchange for these entitlements, the coastal states were made to recognise new concepts guaranteeing the freedom of navigation in the form of special transit rights over straits used for international navigation and archipelagic waters. In particular, the specialised 'transit passage' regime was crafted to maintain the freedom of navigation and overflight through narrow straits which would otherwise have been

---

[521] The latter three issues were specifically dealt with in Committee III. Some jurisdictional questions relating to the marine environment were also discussed in Committee II.

[522] The cumulative impact of the coastal states' extension of jurisdiction over their adjacent waters was the surrender to these states of exclusive control over an estimated additional 35 to 36 per cent of the planet's territory, see MILES, *supra* note 506, at 23. See, however, CHURCHILL & LOWE, *supra* note 26, at 179, for the view that the EEZ victory is more a psychological gain than a material one for developing countries. This is because the EEZ scheme effected little change to the distribution of oil and gas resources, as these already belonged to coastal states under the continental shelf regime. As for fish, many of the states which gained larger EEZs were actually developed states. The biggest beneficiaries were the US, France, Indonesia, New Zealand, Australia, Russia, Japan, Brazil, Canada and Mexico.

subsumed by the expanded twelve-mile territorial sea covering these straits.[523]

Apart from the specific straits and territorial sea issues, the superpowers were keen to limit – on a general basis – any trend in expanding coastal state jurisdiction (also known as 'creeping jurisdiction') they could detect.[524] This position was to colour the negotiation of all the other substantive issues, including those relating to the marine environment discussed in Committee III.[525] Hence, numerous constraints ended up being imposed upon coastal state authority to regulate marine pollution.

This brings us presently to Part XII of the LOSC, the component on the protection of the marine environment.[526] The only problematic aspect of Part XII related to vessel-source pollution; agreement on this topic hinged largely upon the related discussions in Committee II. During early negotiations, the prevailing regime of flag state jurisdiction over vessels had been challenged by a coalition of developed and developing coastal states with minimal shipping interests. It will be recalled that the 1970s was the period during which the open registry system came under attack by UNCTAD and developing countries in general.[527] On the other hand, the maritime interests were labouring under the increased operating costs brought about by the OPEC crisis. Hence, these interests saw every reason to ensure the continued relevance of open registries and the primacy of flag state jurisdiction.

The OPEC-imposed embargo had also convinced the oil companies and the developed states of the utmost necessity to curb future coastal state interference with oil tanker movements. Moreover, a multiplicity of diverse coastal state pollution laws raised the spectre of unwelcome regulation and delays. In any event, superpower security interests were

---

[523] LOSC, Part III. The regime of innocent passage within the territorial sea would not have included the right of overflight and the right for submarines to traverse submerged.
[524] See B. Kwiatkowska, *Creeping Jurisdiction Beyond 200 Miles in the Light of the 1982 Law of the Sea Convention*, 22 Ocean Dev. & Int'l L. 153 (1991).
[525] This Committee was chaired by Ambassador Yankov of Bulgaria, and was essentially created to satisfy Soviet bloc demands for a committee leadership post.
[526] For analyses of Part XII, see e.g. J. I. Charney, *The Protection of the Marine Environment by the 1982 United Nations Convention on the Law of the Sea*, 7 Geo. Int'l Envtl. L. Rev. 731, at 731–5 (1995); R. P. Lotilla, *The Efficacy of the Anti-Pollution Legislation Provisions in the 1982 Convention on the Law of the Sea*, 41 Int'l & Comp. L. Q. 137 (1992); L. Kimball, *The Law of the Sea Convention and Marine Environmental Protection*, 7 Geo. Int'l Envtl. L. Rev. 745 (1995); and J. Hargrove, *Environment and the Third Conference on the Law of the Sea*, in Who Protects the Oceans? 191, at 206–7 (J. Hargrove ed., 1975).
[527] See Ch. 2.

anxious that pollution control measures would not be abused and used as a pretext by coastal states seeking to interfere with navigation.

For all these reasons, the maritime interests fought hard at UNCLOS – as they did earlier at IMCO – to resist unilateral coastal state regulation over vessel-source pollution. In their minds, the prescription of pollution control rules had to be harmonised at the international level by IMCO. In addition, coastal state enforcement of these rules had to be strictly controlled. To these ends, the maritime states were supported by the Soviet bloc, the developing maritime states as well as the landlocked and geographically disadvantaged states, all of whom had an interest in preserving free navigation and resisting enhanced coastal state jurisdiction. In addition, the maritime states sought to subject a large part of Part XII to the compulsory dispute settlement procedure of Part XV.[528] Their eventual success in doing so had the result of 'internationalising' pollution control issues, thereby curbing coastal state jurisdiction and preserving a large portion of the right to free navigation.

The final outcome of the negotiations, as enshrined in section 5 of Part XII (Articles 211 and 217 to 233), reflects the triumph of the maritime actors. In essence, these interests prevailed not only because of their powerful bargaining position but also because the opposing coastal state coalition was weakened by internal divisions. The coalition had been made up primarily of G77 developing countries but was effectively led by Canada and Australia, the two developed coastal states. As was the case at IMCO, it became clear that the Canadians were really only interested in protecting their Arctic waters.[529] Once that concern had been effectively met by a special LOSC provision on ice-covered areas,[530] Canada was suitably neutralised. This concession to the Canadians came at little cost to the maritime interests since negligible shipping movements occurred through ice-covered areas.

At the same time, many of the open registries which were G77 members broke ranks and campaigned openly to maintain flag state supremacy. Several developing countries with emerging merchant fleets

---

[528] The Conference established the International Tribunal for the Law of the Sea (ITLOS) to form part of the LOSC's dispute settlement mechanism. On ITLOS and dispute settlement generally, see e.g. CURRENT MARINE ENVIRONMENTAL ISSUES AND THE INTERNATIONAL TRIBUNAL FOR THE LAW OF THE SEA (M. H. Nordquist & J. N. Moore eds., 2001); S. Oda, *Dispute Settlement Prospects in the Law of the Sea*, 44 INT'L & COMP. L. Q. 863 (1995); and A. E. Boyle, *Dispute Settlement and the Law of the Sea Convention: Problems of Fragmentation and Jurisdiction*, 46 INT'L & COMP. L. Q. 37 (1997).

[529] MILES, *supra* note 506, at 53.   [530] LOSC, art. 234, *infra* notes 613-15.

were also concerned that their vessels might face discriminatory treatment in foreign ports. More importantly, the majority of developing states were persuaded by the maritime state argument that it was entirely within their interest, as users of shipping, to keep costs and freight rates down. Hence, there was considerable convergence of interests among both developed and developing states to resist unilateral coastal state regulation.[531]

Moreover, the impetus to expand coastal state jurisdiction over pollution beyond the territorial sea was really little more than an incidental component of the larger EEZ issue. Once the 200-mile EEZ claim was recognised along with sovereign rights over the resources therein, many coastal states lost interest in the marine pollution issue.[532] Not surprisingly, what *really* mattered to most were rights over resources, not the marine environment. As a result, coastal state authority over polluting vessels emerged significantly curtailed, particularly in relation to enforcement. The flag state would thus remain as the primary repository of prescriptive and enforcement jurisdiction.

This is not to say that the developed maritime states were ignoring the problem of marine pollution. Far from it; the US and UK were busy initiating pollution control efforts at IMCO at about the same time that the LOSC was being negotiated. As seen above,[533] these efforts attempted to control pollution by tightening flag state responsibilities and developing the alternative of port state jurisdiction. The strategy of the maritime interests was simple – effective control over marine pollution, but only through international agreement and decidedly *not* through coastal state autonomy.[534]

4.2 The Allocation of State Jurisdiction under the LOSC

4.2.1 Flag State Jurisdiction

With the negotiating history at UNCLOS and IMCO in mind, the specific outcome of the UNCLOS deliberations over the issue of jurisdiction becomes more readily appreciable. In reinforcing flag state obligations, the LOSC incorporates by reference those international standards for the protection of the marine environment established by the

---

[531] MILES, *supra* note 506, at 93.
[532] M'GONIGLE & ZACHER, *supra* note 65, at 246.   [533] See Ch. 3.
[534] Of course, the fact that states like the US later embarked on unilateral law-making (in the form of OPA-90) testified to the growing influence of the environmental agenda and the corresponding weakening of shipping interests in the developed states.

'competent international organisation'[535] or 'general diplomatic conference' which have become 'generally accepted'. Specifically, flag states are required to enact legislation that 'shall at least have the same effect as' that of generally accepted international rules and standards.[536] Thus, flag states may apply higher standards should they so desire since international standards only form a *minimum* threshold for them.[537]

Pursuant to the LOSC, flag states have an obligation not only to prescribe but also to enforce the legislation which gives effect to international standards. Thus, flag states are to ensure compliance with applicable international rules and standards by their vessels.[538] To this end, they 'shall' adopt laws and regulations and take other measures necessary for the implementation and effective enforcement of such rules.[539] Flag states shall also take appropriate measures to ensure their vessels' compliance with international CDEM standards and to prohibit vessels from sailing unless these standards have been complied with.[540]

With regard to certification, flag states must ensure that their vessels carry certificates required by the international rules and that these certificates accurately reflect the vessel's condition.[541] Periodic inspections shall be conducted to ensure the accuracy of these certificates. Other states are to accept the certificates as evidence of the vessel's condition unless there are clear grounds for believing that the vessel's condition does not correspond to the certificate.[542] Flag states must also investigate alleged violations committed by their vessels including violations alleged by another state,[543] institute proceedings for violations of international rules and standards regardless of where these occur[544] and impose penalties adequate in severity to deter violations wherever they occur.[545]

---

[535] This phrase is commonly understood to refer to IMO, see e.g. CHURCHILL & LOWE, *supra* note 26, at 346 and Bodansky, *supra* note 69, at 740. Interestingly, IMO is never once mentioned in the main articles of the LOSC – instead, it is referred to only in Annex VIII relating to the resolution of disputes. For IMO's synergy with the LOSC, see S. Rosenne, *The International Maritime Organization Interface with the Law of the Sea Convention*, in Nordquist & Moore eds., *supra* note 147, at 251.
[536] LOSC, art. 211(2). Note also the general duties of flag states enumerated in LOSC, art. 94.
[537] Note the far less stringent obligations on states (i.e. only to the extent of 'taking into account' international rules and standards) in relation to pollution from land-based sources and the atmosphere, see arts. 207 and 212 respectively.
[538] LOSC, art. 217(1). [539] *Ibid.* [540] LOSC, art. 217(2).
[541] LOSC, art. 217(3). [542] *Ibid.* [543] LOSC, art. 217(6).
[544] LOSC, arts. 217(4), (5), (6), (7). [545] LOSC, art. 217(8).

Therefore, in relation to jurisdictional issues, the LOSC does not depart appreciably from MARPOL 73/78 in its entrenchment of flag state primacy. If properly adhered to, the obligations outlined above can conceivably enhance the effectiveness of flag state jurisdiction, particularly in remedying the recalcitrance of open registry vessels. However, the reality remains that flag states have never had (and continue not to have) the incentive to prescribe and enforce pollution control rules diligently.[546] Thus, by not providing for any review of flag state enforcement or for concrete penalties to be taken against flag states which fail to comply with their obligations, the LOSC essentially perpetuates the unsatisfactory *status quo*.

The situation is exacerbated by provisions in the LOSC which accord the flag state a right to pre-empt coastal and port state action. Under Article 228, any coastal state proceedings to impose penalties for pollution offences committed beyond the territorial sea shall be suspended if the flag state steps forward to institute its own proceedings. The only exceptions are for violations which cause major damage to the coastal state, or where the flag state has not instituted proceedings within six months of the coastal/port state's taking action, or where the flag state has 'repeatedly disregarded its obligation to enforce effectively' the applicable international rules and standards.[547]

Pre-emption does not apply to coastal state proceedings for territorial sea offences or port state proceedings for offences in the port state's own territorial sea. It *does* apply, however, to all coastal state proceedings over violations committed in their EEZs and indeed, over any violation 'committed by a foreign vessel beyond the territorial sea'. As such, the pre-emption power is extremely wide and can effectively negate or usurp coastal and port state jurisdiction.[548] The problem remains that once a flag state claims jurisdiction under Article 228, there is no way to ensure that it will render an effective or satisfactory judgment. In this regard, the LOSC does not significantly improve upon the regulatory regime.[549] Consequently, recourse will still have to be sought in coastal or port state jurisdiction.

---

[546] See Ch. 2.
[547] LOSC, art. 228(1). On the difficulty of determining what constitutes 'repeated disregard', see Dzidzornu, *supra* note 168, at 311.
[548] T. L. McDorman, *Port State Enforcement: A Comment on Article 218 of the 1982 Law of the Sea Convention*, 28 J. Mar. L. & Com. 305, at 322 (1997).
[549] One writer views art. 228(1) as potentially making a 'mockery' of port and coastal state enforcement, see J. Bernhardt, *A Schematic Analysis of Vessel-Source Pollution: Prescriptive*

4.2.2 Coastal State Jurisdiction

The LOSC adopts a comprehensive approach in reconciling the competing interests of coastal and maritime states. In addition to reinforcing flag state obligations, the convention attempts to bolster pollution control effectiveness by enhancing the jurisdiction of coastal and port states, albeit in limited circumstances. Coastal state jurisdiction is assessed as follows in relation to the different jurisdictional zones of the sea:

Internal Waters. Traditionally, a coastal state enjoys unfettered prescriptive and enforcement authority in its internal waters. It may thus require vessels entering its internal waters or ports to comply with international CDEM and discharge standards or impose national standards if it pleases.[550] On the basis of the 'no more favourable treatment' rule, the coastal state may also inspect vessels for compliance with international CDEM standards regardless of whether the vessel's flag state is party to the conventions setting out these standards.[551] Under MARPOL 73/78, a state may even detain unseaworthy vessels in port until repairs are effected, notwithstanding the impact this may have on the vessel's freedom of navigation.[552] The LOSC does little to change these rules.

One significant innovation effected by the LOSC relates to a coastal state's enforcement jurisdiction in its internal waters and ports for incidents occurring *beyond the territorial sea*. Prior to UNCLOS, coastal states could not institute proceedings against vessels in port for pollution incidents occurring beyond their territorial sea. Under the LOSC, however, coastal states possess the authority to prescribe international discharge and CDEM standards for their EEZs.[553] In this regard, an offending vessel discharging pollutants illegally in a coastal state's

---

and *Enforcement Regimes in the Law of the Sea Conference*, 20 Va. J. Int'l L. 265, at 307 (1980). See, however, McDorman, *supra* note 548, at 318 and Churchill & Lowe, *supra* note 26, at 351, for the view that the port state retains jurisdiction until any proceedings in the flag state are concluded. Thus, the flag state's failure to conclude proceedings allows the port state to continue with its own case. Moreover, the port state need not transmit to the flag state any bond or posted financial security until the flag state concludes its proceedings. McDorman thus concludes that art. 228 notwithstanding, port states *can* still effectively pursue prosecution.

[550] LOSC, art. 211(3).   [551] MARPOL 73/78, arts. 5(2) and 5(4).
[552] MARPOL 73/78, art. 5(2), LOSC, art. 219.
[553] LOSC, art. 211(5), *infra* note 597.

EEZ (and of course, the territorial sea) may find itself prosecuted if and when it voluntarily enters the state's ports.[554]

The Territorial Sea. Within the territorial sea, a coastal state is generally sovereign, possessing prescriptive and enforcement authority subject only to the vessel's right of innocent passage. Even prior to UNCLOS III, a coastal state could prescribe and enforce vessel-source pollution standards 'within [its] jurisdiction'.[555] As regards the 'extent' of jurisdiction, it was at least clear that 'jurisdiction' included internal waters and the territorial sea.

However, it was uncertain whether the 'content' of jurisdiction was restricted to the prescription of international standards only or whether the coastal state may also prescribe more stringent national standards. The LOSC established a compromise by authorising coastal states to prescribe national discharge and navigation standards, but *only* international CDEM standards in their territorial seas.[556] It will be recalled that this was the very proposal which had failed to attract agreement earlier at the 1973 IMCO Conference.[557] Further limitations imposed by the LOSC include the requirements that the territorial sea regulations be duly publicised, non-discriminatory and not hamper innocent passage of foreign vessels.[558]

The limitation on CDEM standards was clearly meant to accommodate the maritime interests. Unilateral national CDEM standards were considered particularly onerous to shipping, and the maritime interests were envisaging the huge costs and operational dislocations involved if each state were to unilaterally impose separate construction or design specifications for ships transiting its territorial sea without even going into port. Thus, while national CDEM standards would be tolerable in ports and internal waters, they were unacceptable in the territorial sea. It also appears to be the case that even if there were no international rules governing a particular CDEM matter, coastal states are not allowed to prescribe any corresponding national measure for the territorial sea.[559]

---

[554] LOSC, art. 220(1).
[555] MARPOL 73/78, art. 4(2). See generally Bodansky, *supra* note 69, at 749 and discussion above, *supra* note 473.
[556] LOSC, art. 21(2). See J. Schneider, *Something Old, Something New: Some Thoughts on Grotius and the Marine Environment*, 18 VA. J. INT'L L. 147, 158 (1977).
[557] *Supra* text accompanying notes 478–85.
[558] LOSC, arts. 21(3), 24 and 211(4). Under art. 22, the coastal state may designate sea lanes and traffic separation schemes for regulation of passage through the territorial sea. In doing so, it shall take into account the recommendations of IMO.
[559] TIMAGENIS, *supra* note 3, at 627.

As for enforcement jurisdiction, coastal state authority in the territorial sea is subjected to numerous conditions under Article 220 of the LOSC. The coastal state may undertake physical inspection of the offending vessel and may undertake the full range of enforcement measures, including instituting proceedings and detaining the vessel, but only if there are 'clear grounds for believing' that the vessel has violated the applicable national laws or international rules while navigating in the territorial sea.[560] These enforcement powers relate to violations of both the applicable discharge and CDEM standards within the territorial sea.

Where there exist clear grounds for the belief that a violation of applicable international rules has occurred in the EEZ, and the vessel is then found in the territorial sea (or EEZ), the coastal state may require the vessel to provide information regarding its identity, flag, ports of last and next call and other relevant information.[561] In addition, the coastal state is authorised to undertake physical inspections on a vessel navigating in the territorial sea (or EEZ) where there are clear grounds for believing that the vessel has committed a violation (in the EEZ) resulting in a 'substantial' discharge causing or threatening 'significant' pollution, *and* the vessel has refused to give information or the information provided is manifestly at variance with the factual situation.[562]

Where there is clear objective evidence of a violation in the EEZ resulting in a discharge 'causing major damage or threat of major damage to the coastline or related interests of the coastal state, or to any resources of its territorial sea or exclusive economic zone', the coastal state may institute proceedings including detaining or arresting the vessel, where that vessel is found in the territorial sea (or EEZ).[563] The LOSC is silent on enforcement action in the converse situation, i.e. where an earlier violation occurs in internal waters or the territorial sea but the vessel is now out in the EEZ. In principle, there is no reason why the same 'gradations' in enforcement powers described above should not apply, since the coastal state must surely

---

[560] LOSC, art. 220(2). See generally D. M. Dzidzornu & B. M. Tsamenyi, *Enhancing International Control of Vessel-Source Oil Pollution Under the Law of the Sea Convention, 1982: A Reassessment*, 10 U. Tasm. L. Rev. 270 (1991) and I. Shearer, *Problems of Jurisdiction and Law Enforcement Against Delinquent Vessels*, 35 Int'l & Comp. L. Q. 320 (1986).

[561] LOSC, art. 220(3).   [562] LOSC, art. 220(5).   [563] LOSC, art. 220(6).

have a larger interest in violations occurring in its internal waters and the territorial sea than in the EEZ.[564]

The above powers may be exercised against all non-military vessels, even those which are in innocent passage through the territorial sea. Indeed, violations committed by a ship may not be serious enough to render passage non-innocent. For such ships, the coastal state is limited to the powers conferred under Article 220, as examined above. For ships in *non*-innocent passage, the LOSC provides an additional recourse – the coastal state may take the necessary steps to prevent the passage of the relevant ship.[565] This is taken to encompass the power to exclude or expel the ship from the territorial sea.

In this regard, Article 19 of the LOSC enumerates a list of acts which would be considered prejudicial to the peace, good order or security of the coastal state, thereby rendering a vessel's passage non-innocent. With regard to pollution, passage is non-innocent if the vessel, while in the territorial sea, engages in 'any act of wilful *and* serious pollution contrary to th[e] Convention'.[566] In such a case, the coastal state is empowered to exercise its right to exclude the vessel from the territorial sea. Of course, it may choose to invoke the powers of boarding and detention under Article 220(2), which, as mentioned above, may be used against all non-military ships, whether in innocent passage or not.[567]

The formulation of the phrase 'wilful and serious pollution' is problematic. While most operational discharges are deliberate and therefore 'wilful', they are seldom 'serious' when considered on an individual basis.[568] Conversely, a vessel involved in an accidental discharge may be engaged in a 'serious' act but this cannot possibly be considered 'wilful'. Moreover, it appears that non-innocence arises only when serious damage is actually inflicted, but not when a threat (even a

---

[564] See generally Franckx ed., *supra* note 53, at 94–5, and Hakapää, *supra* note 3, at 243. Where the violation occurs in the territorial sea and the vessel is found in the territorial sea, the provisions of art. 220(2) apply, *supra* note 560. As far as CDEM violations are concerned, these tend to 'stay' with the ship. Hence, once a vessel with CDEM violations enters the territorial sea from the EEZ, art. 220(2) becomes applicable. If that vessel remains in the EEZ, only a request for information can be made (under art. 220(3)) if no actual discharge has occurred, *infra* note 600.
[565] LOSC, art. 25(1).
[566] LOSC, art. 19(2)(h) (emphasis added).
[567] Note, though, that art. 220 does not confer the power to exclude vessels.
[568] Boyle, *supra* note 512, at 359. While this provision may be ineffective in curbing routine operational discharges of oil, it would clearly cover the deliberate dumping of wastes. Also, a wilful operational discharge of wastes into protected sensitive areas, no matter how small the quantities, should be regarded as 'wilful and serious'.

major one) is posed. Thus, it is doubtful if a ship which is in violation of CDEM requirements and/or is carrying hazardous cargoes and/or is limping along in a dangerous, sub-standard condition through the territorial sea is engaging in a 'wilful and serious' act of pollution justifying exclusion.[569]

In sum, the conjunctive requirement of 'wilful *and* serious' pollution in Article 19(2)(h) effectively hampers coastal state jurisdiction in the territorial sea instead of enhancing it. Together with the prohibition against national CDEM standards and the strict conditions for exercising enforcement jurisdiction under Article 220, the restrictive nature of Article 19(2)(h) represents a significant curtailment of coastal state jurisdiction within its own territorial sea. This can hardly be satisfactory, particularly if a situation arises where a grave threat of pollution is being posed in the territorial sea over which the state enjoys sovereignty.

Indeed, in situations of a maritime casualty posing a serious threat of pollution, the coastal state must possess the right to take measures to protect its interests before damage actually materialises.[570] Even when there is as yet no casualty but the passage is highly risky due to the hazardous nature of the cargo,[571] the sub-standard condition of the ship and/or the violation of international CDEM standards,[572] the coastal state must arguably retain the right to exclude passage in the territorial sea, subject to the conditions of necessity and proportionality.

This contention is bolstered by the fact that Article 19's list of activities permitting exclusion of passage does not appear to be exhaustive.

---

[569] See generally Franckx ed., *supra* note 53, at 57 and 126. In such situations, the coastal state may only resort to the powers under art. 220(2), which do not include expulsion.

[570] This right is not explicitly provided for in the LOSC. However, art. 221(1) accords states the right to take protective measures beyond the territorial sea in relation to maritime casualties. This confirms the right of intervention granted by the 1969 Intervention Convention, *supra* note 188. There must thus exist an equal or more extensive (albeit implicit) right in the territorial sea. For the view that coastal states enjoy broad enforcement powers over vessels in non-innocent passage consistent with its full sovereignty in the territorial sea, see B. Smith, *Innocent Passage as a Rule of Decision: Navigation v. Environmental Protection*, 21 COLUM. J. TRANSNAT'L L. 49, at 66–84 (1983).

[571] See J. M. Van Dyke, *Sea Shipment of Japanese Plutonium and International Law*, 24 OCEAN DEV. & INT'L L. 399, at 408 (1993) and L. Pineschi, *The Transit of Ships Carrying Hazardous Wastes Through Foreign Coastal Zones*, *in* INTERNATIONAL RESPONSIBILITY FOR ENVIRONMENTAL HARM 299 (F. Francioni & T. Scovazzi eds., 1991). Note also the special precautions to be taken in the territorial sea by nuclear-powered ships and ships carrying nuclear or other inherently dangerous substances, LOSC, art. 23.

[572] State practice provides ample evidence of the so-called 'leper' ships being denied entry into the territorial sea of coastal states, see Franckx ed., *supra* note 53, at 58 and 88.

In any case, state practice indicates that few states have explicitly incorporated the 'wilful and serious' limitation into their legislation.[573] Indeed, some states take the view that expulsion from or denial of entry into the territorial sea is not exclusively limited to cases where passage has been characterised as non-innocent under the limbs of Article 19.[574] In the wake of the *Prestige* incident, it appears that moves by coastal states to ban sub-standard ships from entering their ports (wholly legitimate under international law) may progressively extend even to denying passage through the territorial sea, even if the ship is ostensibly still in innocent passage and is merely transiting and not headed for the coastal state's port. These trends, if legitimised, may well render the requirement of 'wilful and serious' pollution, and indeed the distinction between innocent and non-innocent passage, superfluous.

Straits Used for International Navigation. Where the territorial sea consists of straits used for international navigation, the specialised regime of transit passage applies to foreign vessels.[575] At the same time, transit passage does not, in other respects, affect the legal status of the waters forming the straits or the sovereignty of the bordering states over such waters.[576] The coastal states bordering a strait used for international navigation may prescribe pollution regulations, but only if these give effect to 'applicable international regulations regarding the discharge of oil, oily wastes and other noxious substances in the strait'.[577] Such regulations must be duly publicised, non-discriminatory and not hamper transit passage of foreign vessels.[578] In relation to the safety of navigation and the regulation of maritime traffic, coastal states may designate sea lanes and prescribe traffic separation schemes that conform to generally accepted international regulations, in consultation with IMO and after agreement with other states bordering the straits.[579]

As for enforcement measures, the LOSC provides that the legal regime of straits used for international navigation will not be affected by any

---

[573] *Ibid.* at 69. [574] *Ibid.* at 88-9.
[575] See LOSC, Part III. For pollution in straits and archipelagic waters, see B. H. Oxman, *Environmental Protection in Archipelagic Waters and International Straits – The Role of the International Maritime Organization*, 10 INT'L J. MARINE & COASTAL L. 467 (1995). On straits generally, see J. N. Moore, *The Regime of Straits and the Third United Nations Conference on the Law of the Sea*, 74 AM. J. INT'L L. 77 (1980); W. M. Reisman, *The Regime of Straits and National Security: An Appraisal of International Lawmaking*, 74 AM. J. INT'L L. 48 (1980); and S. N. Nandan & D. H. Anderson, *Straits Used for International Navigation: A Commentary on Part III of the United Nations Convention on the Law of the Sea 1982*, 60 BRIT. Y.B. INT'L L. 159 (1989).
[576] LOSC, art. 34(1). [577] LOSC, art. 42(1)(b).
[578] LOSC, arts. 42(2) and 42(3). [579] LOSC, art. 41.

prescriptive or enforcement jurisdiction of the coastal state.[580] On their part, ships in transit passage shall comply with generally accepted international regulations, procedures and practices for safety at sea and the prevention, reduction and control of pollution from ships.[581] The coastal state may thus take 'appropriate enforcement measures' if a foreign vessel commits a violation of the relevant international rules prescribed by the coastal state, but only when 'major damage to the marine environment of the straits' is caused or threatened.[582] Here, the precise 'appropriate' measures which can be taken are undefined but at the very least, they must include the boarding and detention powers conferred under Article 220 for violations in the territorial sea.

On this score, it can be further argued that ships which are in violation of the relevant rules will lose their right of transit passage, and by extension, their right of innocent passage as well.[583] This will then attract the coastal state's power to exclude these ships. Although the LOSC is hardly explicit on this point, it must be the case that whatever serious circumstances that would render a ship liable to be expelled from the territorial sea would produce a similar result in relation to the right of transit passage through straits used for international navigation.[584] Thus, 'wilful and serious' acts of pollution caused in straits must attract the same expulsion power conferred under the regime of innocent passage.

However, if major damage is merely threatened *but not yet caused*, the 'appropriate enforcement powers' envisaged by Article 233 arguably extend to boarding and detention only, but not expulsion. By the same token, and in contrast with the territorial sea, it does not appear that expulsion powers can be exercised in straits used for international navigation where no major damage is caused or threatened, but where passage is simply risky due to the hazardous nature of the cargo or the sub-standard condition of the ship.[585] This is due to the

---

[580] LOSC, art. 233. [581] LOSC, art. 39(2). [582] LOSC, art. 233. [583] LOSC, art. 38(3).
[584] See Franckx ed., *supra* note 53, at 90–3, citing some state practice to this effect, particularly the position taken by Indonesia, Malaysia and Singapore in relation to the Straits of Malacca and Singapore.
[585] *Cf.* Franckx ed., *supra* note 53, at 91, for a contrary view. It is conceivable, though, that if a ship traversing a strait used for international navigation is in such serious breach of international CDEM standards and is in such deplorable and unseaworthy condition as to threaten likely major damage to the marine environment, a right of expulsion should be available to the coastal state.

significantly higher level of protection accorded to shipping by the transit passage regime in straits used for international navigation.

Archipelagic Waters. Foreign vessels enjoy a right of innocent passage in archipelagic waters.[586] In addition, vessels enjoy a broader right of archipelagic sea lanes passage through designated archipelagic sea lanes, or where these have yet to be designated, through 'the routes normally used for international navigation'.[587] Although Part XII of the LOSC does not mention archipelagic waters explicitly, the full range of provisions and safeguards in Part XII relevant to vessel-source pollution in the territorial sea should be extended to archipelagic waters.[588] Similarly, the lack of any explicit provisions for enforcement powers in archipelagic sea lanes can be overcome by the cross-reference to the regime of transit passage in straits used for international navigation.[589]

Consequently, archipelagic states should be able to exclude vessels which cause serious pollution and which have lost their right of archipelagic sea lanes passage (and by implication, innocent passage). In addition, these states should be able to exercise the boarding and detention powers granted under Article 220 within their archipelagic waters. In sum, the rights of archipelagic states in their archipelagic waters and archipelagic sea lanes in relation to vessel-source pollution should be co-extensive with the general right of coastal states in their territorial seas and straits used for international navigation respectively.

The Contiguous Zone. Beyond the territorial sea, coastal state prescriptive and enforcement competence have traditionally been curtailed. In relation to a state's contiguous zone which extends twelve miles beyond the territorial sea, the LOSC effects no change to the regime prescribed by the 1958 Convention on the Territorial Sea and Contiguous Zone.[590] This permits a state to prevent and punish infringement of its customs, fiscal, immigration or sanitary laws and regulations within its territory or territorial sea.[591] It is unclear, though, if 'sanitary regulations' may

---

[586] LOSC, art. 52(1).   [587] LOSC, art. 53(12).
[588] Franckx ed., *supra* note 53, at 92. The lack of cross-referencing between the provisions of Part IV (on archipelagic states) and Part XII (on protection of the marine environment) could have been a legislative oversight, see CHURCHILL & LOWE, *supra* note 26.
[589] Thus, while the enforcement provision in art. 233 lacks a direct reference to archipelagic waters, there is a mention of art. 42 (on straits), which in turn is applicable *mutatis mutandis* to archipelagic sea lanes passage, see art. 54.
[590] 1958 Geneva Convention on the Territorial Sea and the Contiguous Zone, 516 U.N.T.S. 206, art. 24. On the contiguous zone generally, see S. Oda, *The Concept of the Contiguous Zone*, 11 INT'L & COMP. L. Q. 131 (1962).
[591] LOSC, art. 33.

include anti-pollution measures.[592] However, because the LOSC now accords states authority to prescribe and enforce vessel-source pollution standards in the EEZ (which subsumes the contiguous zone), the restrictive nature of the contiguous zone provision can be taken to be overcome.[593]

The Exclusive Economic Zone. The most significant change instituted by the LOSC in relation to expanding the prescriptive and enforcement authority of coastal states pertains to the exclusive economic zone (EEZ). Indeed, the very concept of the EEZ was first crystallised at UNCLOS III.[594] Previously, the waters beyond the territorial sea were considered part of the high seas, and ships in these waters were subject to the exclusive jurisdiction of the flag state.[595] Under the LOSC, the EEZ regime provides for an ocean zone extending up to 200 nautical miles from the baseline of the territorial sea over which coastal states possess exclusive rights to exploit economic resources.[596]

However, coastal state jurisdiction over pollution control in the EEZ remains substantially restricted. This was due to the maritime interests' perception that pollution control was too closely intertwined with shipping to leave it wholly within coastal state prerogative. Thus, all coastal state pollution laws prescribed for the EEZ must conform to and give effect to generally accepted international rules and standards.[597] In essence, coastal states may not prescribe for their EEZ any national CDEM, discharge or navigation standard which exceeds the international standard, save only in 'special' and ice-covered areas.[598]

---

[592] Scholars tend to interpret sanitary regulations as *not* including anti-pollution measures, see e.g. McDorman et al., *supra* note 464, at 9.

[593] Bodansky, *supra* note 69, at 755–6.

[594] The legal status of the EEZ has often been considered to be of a *sui generis* character, situated between the territorial sea and the high seas, see Churchill & Lowe, *supra* note 26, at 166 and Brown, *supra* note 504, at 21.

[595] See generally *SS Lotus* (Fr. v. Turk.) 1927 P.C.I.J. (Ser. A) No. 10. The exceptions to this principle relate to piracy (LOSC, art. 105) and unauthorised broadcasting (LOSC, art. 109). It has been questioned why pollution on the high seas should merit less concern than unauthorised broadcasting or piracy, see Bodansky, *supra* note 69, at 776 and L. A. Teclaff, *International Law and the Protection of the Oceans from Pollution*, in International Environmental Law 104, at 139 (L. A. Teclaff & A. E. Utton eds., 1974).

[596] LOSC, arts. 56(1)(a), 56(1)(b)(iii) and 57. On the EEZ generally, see D. Attard, The Exclusive Economic Zone in International Law (1987) and B. Kwiatkowska, The 200-Mile Exclusive Economic Zone in the New Law of the Sea (1989).

[597] LOSC, art. 211(5).

[598] LOSC, arts. 211(6) and 234, *infra* notes 613–19. Even then, national CDEM standards are allowed only in ice-covered areas. For 'special' areas designated under art. 211(6), only *international* CDEM standards may be prescribed, see art. 211(6)(c).

As outlined earlier,[599] enforcement jurisdiction in the EEZ is restricted to requests for information if the coastal state has 'clear grounds for believing' that a vessel navigating in the EEZ has committed, in the EEZ, a violation of applicable international rules and standards.[600] In addition, physical inspection is permitted only where there are 'clear grounds for believing' that a vessel has committed, in the EEZ, a violation resulting in a 'substantial discharge causing or threatening significant pollution', *and* the vessel has refused to give accurate information or if the information supplied is manifestly at variance with the facts.[601] Hence, physical inspection is permitted only where there has been an actual discharge violation.[602] In practice, the inspection power is meaningless as it is unlikely that a coastal state can ever detect a discharge *and* still be able to board the vessel while it is still in the EEZ.

As for prosecutions, coastal states may only arrest a vessel or institute proceedings if there is 'clear objective evidence' of a violation of international rules in the EEZ resulting in a discharge causing 'major damage or threat of major damage' to the coastal state.[603] Again, no preventative measures are allowed where pollution has not actually occurred but appears likely. Hence, a coastal state cannot take any action (apart from requiring information) against a substandard vessel in the EEZ which is in breach of CDEM standards and is posing a serious threat to the environment but which has not *actually* caused a discharge or become a maritime casualty.[604] Overall,

---

[599] *Supra* text accompanying notes 561-3, in relation to vessels navigating in the territorial sea which had committed violations while in the EEZ. To reiterate, arts. 220(3), (5) and (6) treat all vessels engaging in violations in the EEZ in the same manner, regardless of whether the vessels subsequently encounter coastal state enforcement action in the territorial sea or the EEZ.

[600] LOSC, art. 220(3).   [601] LOSC, art. 220(5).

[602] If the violation relates purely to CDEM infractions, the coastal state may only request information pursuant to art. 220(3). If the ship enters the territorial sea (with its CDEM violations subsisting), the full enforcement powers of art. 220(2) will then apply, *supra* note 564.

[603] LOSC, art. 220(6). The distinction between 'substantial discharge causing ... significant pollution' and 'discharge causing major damage ...' (in arts. 220(5) and 220(6) respectively) is likely to be one of degree. The coastal state would probably retain sole discretion to adjudge the difference until this is subsequently disputed by the flag state.

[604] LOSC, art. 221(1). This is why the practice of several European states in excluding single-hull tankers carrying heavy grades of oil (HGO) from their EEZs was in breach of international law, *supra* note 392. To exclude or expel from the EEZ would require an explicit amendment to the LOSC's enforcement provisions, even with the IMO ban on the carriage of HGO on single-hull tankers, see Ch. 3.

the jurisdiction of the coastal states in their EEZs is only protective, rather than fully territorial in character.[605]

In sum, the conditions imposed on coastal state action are onerous, given that coastal states can contemplate action only in the most deleterious of violations or threats thereof. Even then, the already limited prosecution powers of coastal states were strongly opposed during the UNCLOS III negotiations, particularly by maritime interests such as the UK, the USSR and Greece. In fact, the maritime powers succeeded not only in curtailing the content of coastal state prosecution powers but also in securing the right of flag state pre-emption under Article 228[606] and imposing various other safeguards against coastal state action.[607]

In the result, unless the coastal state is able to fulfil the various conditions for taking action, its only practical recourse is still to refer violations to the flag state.[608] At the same time, state practice on coastal state enforcement jurisdiction within the EEZ remains inconclusive – few states have detailed provisions on EEZ enforcement in their laws. Those which have claimed enforcement jurisdiction do so in general terms, and do not typically incorporate the detailed gradations in enforcement capacity found in Articles 220(3), (5) and (6).[609]

On top of the general restrictions on coastal state authority, the LOSC exempts all warships, naval auxiliary or other vessels or aircraft owned or operated by states and used on government non-commercial service from the operation of the above provisions.[610] Moreover, nothing in Part XII was to affect the legal regime of straits used for international navigation.[611] Parties to the LOSC are also obliged to settle disputes concerning the application or interpretation of the articles in accordance with the dispute settlement provisions of the convention.[612] From the perspective of the coastal states, all these restrictions represent a significant erosion of sovereignty. Ultimately, the LOSC's recognition of

---

[605] Boyle, *supra* note 512, at 365.   [606] *Supra* notes 547–9.
[607] See LOSC, art. 220(7) (arrangements for bonding or other financial security) and section 7 safeguards in arts. 223 to 233 (e.g. non-discrimination, time bars and rights of the accused).
[608] Indeed, few states have resorted to the exercise of Article 220 powers, and actual cases of coastal state enforcement in the EEZ remain rare, see Valenzuela, *supra* note 514, at 496.
[609] Franckx ed., *supra* note 53, at 95–6. Only a dozen states or so appear to have modelled their legislation on Articles 211 and 220. Even then, not all of them are in conformity with the exact language of these provisions, see CHURCHILL & LOWE, *supra* note 26, at 352.
[610] LOSC, art. 236.   [611] LOSC, art. 233.   [612] LOSC, Part XV.

enhanced coastal state rights over EEZ economic resources is substantially qualified by the circumscribed authority enjoyed over foreign vessels whose polluting activities may well prejudice these very resources.

In relation to 'special' and ice-covered areas within the EEZ, coastal states are allowed a limited authority under Articles 211(6) and 234 to go beyond international standards to prescribe more stringent pollution control measures for these areas. This concession to coastal state prescriptive authority was meant to address special circumstances which may exist in particularly sensitive areas of the EEZ. In particular, the ice-covered area exception under Article 234 was designed to meet Canada's Arctic concerns.[613] Thus, coastal states may prescribe and enforce national rules in their ice-covered EEZ areas, including national CDEM rules extending beyond those which are internationally accepted. These rules need not be adopted in consultation with IMO, and the only limitations are that they must be non-discriminatory in nature and must have 'due regard' to navigation and the protection and preservation of the marine environment based on the best available scientific evidence.[614]

With this concession, Canada effectively withdrew from the debate at UNCLOS III, leaving the coastal state camp without an effective leader.[615] Consequently, the maritime interests moved to restrict the ambit of Article 211(6), which was the other provision governing areas of particular sensitivity. In its final form, Article 211(6)(a) allows coastal states to designate clearly defined areas of their EEZs within which special mandatory measures for pollution prevention can be adopted for recognised technical reasons in relation to the area's oceanographical and ecological conditions, as well as the utilisation or protection of its resources and the particular character of its traffic. In this regard, the 'competent international organisation' (IMO) must be consulted, and no such area can be designated and measures prescribed without IMO concurrence.[616]

The measures that coastal states can prescribe under Article 211(6)(a) would be those international rules and standards or navigational practices that are made applicable, through IMO, for special areas. These would include the measures applicable to the 'special areas'

---

[613] Supra notes 529-30. See M'GONIGLE & ZACHER, supra note 65, at 246 and C.-P. Wang, *A Review of the Enforcement Regime for Vessel-Source Oil Pollution Control*, 16 OCEAN DEV. & INT'L L. 305, at 326 (1986). On art. 234 generally, see D. McRae & D. Goundrey, *Environmental Jurisdiction in Arctic Waters: The Extent of Article 234*, 16 U. BR. COL. L. REV. 197 (1982).
[614] LOSC, art. 234.   [615] See Ch. 3.
[616] This is a requirement not imposed on art. 234.

contemplated by the MARPOL 73/78 annexes, which are not limited to EEZs and can be declared for entire seas or regions. Hence, the LOSC 'special area' concept envisioned here should not be confused with the MARPOL 73/78 'special area', although the latter is one such measure envisaged by Article 211(6)(a). Other measures which can conceivably be employed pursuant to Article 211(6)(a) include the Particularly Sensitive Sea Area (PSSA) concept, with accompanying associated measures such as areas to be avoided, vessel traffic schemes, pilotage requirements and anchoring prohibitions.[617]

Under Article 211(6)(c), a coastal state may propose to adopt in the same area additional measures going beyond those envisaged by Article 211(6)(a). These may be specialised national measures relating to discharges or navigational practices that go beyond any existing international standards. IMO approval is needed here, and presumably, IMO will first have to be persuaded that its pre-existing generally accepted international rules and standards (contemplated by Article 211(6)(a)) are inadequate to meet the coastal state's concerns. The overriding condition here is that no CDEM measures other than generally accepted international rules and standards may be prescribed.

In addition, coastal states are to enjoy no more enforcement powers than already granted under Article 220.[618] Hence, the different levels of enforcement conditions prescribed by Articles 220(3) to 220(6) are equally applicable to the 'special' areas. In the result, even though Article 211(6) went some way toward rectifying the otherwise circumscribed prescriptive authority of coastal states, the maritime interests succeeded in ensuring that coastal state jurisdiction remained strictly controlled by the international community. In practice, states have generally relied on the MARPOL 73/78 'special areas' and the PSSA regime,[619] together with associated IMO navigational measures, to

---

[617] These are pre-existing requirements which have long been adopted by IMO in relation to specific navigational, safety and environmental concerns all over the world.

[618] LOSC, art. 220(8).

[619] Neither of these is restricted to the EEZ – both PSSAs and MARPOL special areas can be established within and beyond the territorial sea. There are other features distinguishing the various concepts, all of which are theoretically distinct. For instance, art. 211(6)(a) of LOSC allows for a broader range of measures and standards than those specified by MARPOL 73/78 for its special areas. Also, the criteria for the designation of art. 211(6)(a) 'special areas' are more expansive than those for MARPOL areas. In turn, the PSSA criteria are much broader than even those expressed in art. 211(6)(a). In addition, the associated protective measures declared under the PSSA can conceivably

give concrete expression to the need for special mandatory measures in sensitive ocean areas.

The High Seas. On the high seas, the traditional principle of exclusive flag state jurisdiction remains unchallenged. If a discharge on the high seas affects the coastal state's territory or waters, the state can take measures under the 1969 Intervention Convention and claim damages under the 1969 or 1992 Civil Liability Conventions (CLC), but only where there has been a maritime casualty.[620] States may thus enforce protective measures proportionate to the actual or threatened damage following upon maritime casualties such as collisions or strandings. Apart from these highly exceptional situations, coastal states enjoy no prescriptive or enforcement authority over vessels on the high seas even though these may potentially harm their shores or coastal waters.[621]

4.2.3 Port State Jurisdiction

While the provisions governing coastal state jurisdiction may have fallen short of giving coastal states effective control over foreign vessels, the enhanced competence of port states appears to promise a strong anti-pollution regime. Prior to UNCLOS III, port states into whose ports the offending vessel has entered only had jurisdiction over violations committed in or affecting the state's own internal waters or territorial sea. For violations occurring beyond the territorial sea, the port state could only inspect the vessel's documents to determine if there had been such a violation.[622] If so, the port state's only recourse was to refer the case to the flag state for further investigation and possible prosecution. This was the position under OILPOL 54/69.

On its part, MARPOL 73/78 effected limited improvements to a port state's competence over discharge violations committed beyond the territorial sea. In addition to discharges within its own waters, the

---

include those envisaged under both arts. 211(6)(a) and 211(6)(c). Under the LOSC, further national measures pursuant to art. 211(6)(c) can presumably be taken only after the international measures contemplated by art. 211(6)(a) are first shown to be insufficient. Note, however, that PSSAs have no conventional bases – they derive their legitimacy purely from IMO Assembly Resolutions, *infra* note 663. Note also that 'special areas' can be designated under several of the conventions adopted under UNEP's Regional Seas Programme, *supra* notes 214–21. Other variants include the Maritime Environmentally Sensitive Area (MESA) broached in Europe and the Marine Environmental High Risk Area (MEHRA) proposed by the Donaldson Report in the UK, *supra* note 40.

[620] LOSC, art. 221(1) and Intervention Convention, art. I(1).
[621] For a critique, see Section 5 below.   [622] OILPOL 54, art. IX(5).

port state may inspect for discharge violations occurring anywhere else, either at its own initiative or at the request of another state.[623] However, the limitation here is that prosecutions can be undertaken *only* by the flag state. At the same time, port states may also inspect vessels of any state – including those of non-parties – for violations of CDEM standards.[624] In this regard, port states may even prescribe and enforce national CDEM standards as conditions for the use of its ports. This is entirely consistent with the sovereign right of states to apply stricter national laws and to impose conditions for entry into ports.[625] A port state need only give due publicity to such conditions and notify IMO of their existence.[626]

At UNCLOS III, as was the case at IMCO, enhanced port state jurisdiction emerged as a preferred solution over the expansion of coastal state jurisdiction. This was primarily because port state action was seen to present less severe impediments to navigation compared to coastal state action. Inspecting a vessel while it is in port imposes little constraint on navigation and can be conducted safely.[627] Even if proceedings were to be brought against a vessel, its freedom to navigate could always be guaranteed upon posting bond.[628] In addition, port states were seen to possess a greater economic interest in the movement of goods through their ports and were thus likely to be more sensitive to maritime interests than would coastal states. The only problem was that international law, as it then stood, did not recognise a port state's jurisdiction over violations which occurred outside its waters.

For these reasons, UNCLOS III came up with the revolutionary Article 218, which effectively extended port states' jurisdiction to cover discharge violations occurring on the high seas or in another state's coastal waters at the request of that state, the flag state or any injured state.

---

[623] MARPOL 73/78, arts. 6(2) and 6(5).   [624] MARPOL 73/78, art. 5(2).
[625] There is no general right of access into ports, i.e. states can deny access to vessels and prescribe whatever conditions for access, even though this is subject to the principle of non-discrimination, see CHURCHILL & LOWE, *supra* note 26, at 63, MOLENAAR, *supra* note 52, at 101; L. de la Fayette, *Access to Ports in International Law*, 11 INT'L J. MARINE & COASTAL L. 1, at 22 (1996); and T. L. McDorman, *Regional Port State Control Agreements: Some Issues of International Law*, OCEAN & COASTAL L. J. 207, at 219 (2000). Denying access may, however, cause even greater safety and environmental risks, for the ships would then be at the mercy of the elements. Arising from the *Prestige* incident, IMO has adopted Guidelines on Places of Refuge for Ships in Need of Assistance, see IMO Assembly Resolution A.949(23) (2003). In Europe, Directive 2002/59/EC, *supra* note 236, lays down equivalent provisions on places of refuge for ships in distress.
[626] LOSC, art. 211(3).   [627] Bodansky, *supra* note 69, at 739.
[628] LOSC, arts. 220(7) and 226(1)(b).

Even in the absence of any detrimental pollution effects on itself, the port state can *prosecute* foreign ships visiting its ports for discharging pollutants in violation of international standards virtually *anywhere at sea*.[629] Thus, the port state may take action where the coastal state is unable to do so or where the vessel is unlikely to ever come within its flag state's jurisdiction.

However, this necessarily amounts only to the port state's *enforcement* jurisdiction of internationally accepted rules, and arguably not to a prescriptive jurisdiction for incidents on the high seas or in another state's waters.[630] As Article 218 makes it clear that only international standards may be enforced, it appears that there is no question of a substantive *prescriptive* authority for port states. In any event, it would be highly anomalous for a port state to enjoy prescriptive authority for events occurring in another state's waters, if not on the high seas.

Port state enforcement competence will conceivably come in useful, for instance, in prosecuting discharge violations occurring within any sensitive marine areas situated on the high seas or in the EEZ of other states. Coupled with the power to prosecute for serious violations in their own EEZs,[631] this represents a major enhancement of overall port state authority. In addition, a port state may also prevent an unseaworthy vessel in its port from sailing until repairs have been made.[632]

---

[629] See generally B. H. Oxman, *The New Law of the Sea*, 69 A.B.A.J. 157 (1983). While art. 218 dispenses with the need for the port state to show 'effects' on its interests before enjoying jurisdiction over events occurring beyond its waters (this would have been the pre-LOSC position for states invoking the 'effects' doctrine), there is a trade-off in that the LOSC imposes limits on port state jurisdiction such as flag state pre-emption under art. 228, see McDorman, *supra* note 548, at 321. Such a limitation would not have applied if it were a pure 'effects' claim for jurisdiction.

[630] See Bodansky, *supra* note 69, at 762, arguing that art. 218 is in section 6 of Part XII, which deals with enforcement jurisdiction, as opposed to section 5 which is on prescriptive jurisdiction. For an opposing view, see McDorman, *supra* note 548, at 315, arguing for port state prescriptive (as opposed to merely enforcement) jurisdiction on the high seas. A related argument is that it is meaningless for an enforcement power to be conferred and exercised without at least an implicit prescriptive basis, see Franckx ed., *supra* note 53, at 43. Meese, *supra* note 35, similarly maintains that port states have prescriptive jurisdiction on the high seas. Even if this is correct, the prescriptive authority must extend only to the prescription of *international* standards. The European Commission Proposal for a Directive on Sanctions, *supra* note 394, may be doing just this in its proposed prescription of international rules such as MARPOL 73/78 for violations on the high seas.

[631] Although this power is subject to flag state pre-emption under art. 228, *supra* note 547.

[632] LOSC, art. 219 and MARPOL 73/78, art. 5(2).

Notwithstanding these gains, there remain limitations. For one thing, port state enforcement is optional rather than mandatory. Thus, a port state need not honour a coastal state's request to investigate discharge violations, particularly if there was insufficient proof linking such a violation to a particular ship. A port state may also wish to proceed cautiously since the shipowner is always entitled to compensation for losses suffered as a result of unlawful or excessive port state action.[633] Moreover, vessels which are internationally bonded against violations are not susceptible to port or coastal state detention.[634] Considering that delays are extremely costly to shipowners and charterers, a significant number of vessels would be indemnified against pollution violations. This may provide shipowners with an undesirable 'escape hatch' and a licence to pollute.

The most compelling reason for a port state to be judicious in exercising its enforcement jurisdiction is perhaps its own viability as a port. No port state would want to acquire a reputation for being an overzealous enforcer of pollution standards, lest it be shunned by international vessel traffic.[635] There may also be logistical problems for ports which receive thousands of ship visits annually.[636] In sum, the interests of port states are still aligned to those of the maritime states, namely the free and unimpeded movement of maritime trade. As such, any port state deference to coastal state requests to prosecute offending vessels is more likely to be a function of international comity than of adherence to treaty rules.

In this regard, state practice appears to confirm that few port states have ever had the incentive to resort to Article 218 in prosecuting violations occurring outside their own waters.[637] For their part, the various MOU port state control administrations have not explicitly

---

[633] LOSC, art. 232. On the port state's lack of incentives to exercise jurisdiction, see S. Boehmer-Christiansen, *Marine Pollution Control: UNCLOS III as the Partial Codification of International Practice*, 7 ENVTL. POL'Y & L. 71, at 73 (1981).

[634] LOSC, art. 220(7). Other limitations include the restriction of penalties to monetary fines generally (art. 230) and notification to flag states (art. 231), *supra* note 607.

[635] McDorman, *supra* note 625, at 207-8.

[636] The fact that port state control could be influenced by improper political biases is also a major problem, see Anderson, *supra* note 19, at 160.

[637] MOLENAAR, *supra* note 52, at 109-10; Bodansky, *supra* note 69, at 763; Valenzuela, *supra* note 514, at 496; and R. R. Churchill, *Levels of Implementation of the Law of the Sea Convention: An Overview*, in Vidas & Østreng eds., *supra* note 64, at 318, 322.

adopted the powers granted under Article 218 to prosecute discharge violations occurring outside their waters.[638] It is thus uncertain if the provisions of Article 218 have become general customary law.[639] In any event, it must be remembered that whatever benefits there are in enhanced port and coastal state jurisdiction can potentially be negated by the flag state's pre-emption powers under Article 228.[640] In this regard, the insertion of Article 228 was a clear *quid pro quo* designed to balance the enhanced jurisdiction of port states.

That port states are generally reluctant to prosecute for discharge violations occurring beyond their waters is not surprising, given the inherently difficult task of proving such violations. This is in stark contrast to CDEM violations, which typically 'stay' with the ship as it enters port and which consequently raise no issues for port state jurisdiction. Hence, the energies of active port state control administrations in Europe, the US and Australia are usually channelled toward inspecting for CDEM deficiencies.

In this respect, there are indications that port states are now prepared to go beyond examining the vessel's certificates, which has long been the standard norm for inspections. To form 'clear grounds'[641] for believing that a ship is sub-standard, stringent inspections are increasingly taking the form of walks through the ship to examine its actual condition.[642] Overall, while many port state control authorities worldwide remain practically unable or unwilling to conduct stringent inspections, there is a clear tendency for those in the developed countries to use inspections and detentions as means of deterring sub-standard shipping, particularly for CDEM violations. In the aftermath of serious pollution incidents such as the *Erika* and *Prestige* and the growing intolerance of sub-standard shipping, it can be expected that port state control and its level of stringency will only increase in the coming years.

---

[638] McDorman, *supra* note 625, at 217 and Keselj, *supra* note 256, at 143. While port state control under the MOUs does extend to inspecting operational aspects of ship operations, most inspections are limited to checking for CDEM violations. This has been rectified to some extent by the advent of the ISM Code, *infra* note 1002 and accompanying text.

[639] See e.g. CHURCHILL & LOWE, *supra* note 26, at 353; McDorman, *supra* note 625, at 217; V. D. Degan, *Internal Waters*, 17 NETH. Y.B. INT'L L. 3, at 22–6 (1986); and T. Clingan, *Vessel-Source Pollution, Problems of Hazardous Cargo and Port State Jurisdiction*, in INTERNATIONAL NAVIGATION: ROCKS AND SHOALS AHEAD? 227 (J. Van Dyke et al. eds., 1988).

[640] *Supra* note 547.   [641] MARPOL 73/78, art. 5(2), SOLAS 74, reg. XI/4.

[642] This is the preferred US approach, see M. Cuttler, *Incentives for Reducing Oil Pollution from Ships: The Case for Enhanced Port State Control*, GEO. INT'L ENVTL. L. REV. 175, at 202 (1995).

5. Conclusion

With its adoption, the LOSC has succeeded in establishing broad consensus among states on the jurisdictional principles governing the exploitation and protection of the oceans. For one thing, the language of prescriptive and enforcement jurisdiction is now spoken in terms of a *duty* for states.[643] What were formerly fragmented pieces of conciliatory efforts have now been redefined into a single comprehensive regime aimed at securing an acceptable political balance among the competing maritime and coastal interests.

This is not to say that the UNCLOS outcome has been wholly satisfactory. To the extent that the emphasis on flag state primacy impedes fully effective pollution control, the LOSC can be assailed as having fallen short of contemporary expectations for a healthy ocean environment.[644] Although the LOSC tightened flag state responsibility by obliging these states to enforce pollution control measures, to investigate alleged violations by their vessels and to impose adequate penalties if there is sufficient evidence, it remains doubtful if the majority of flag states will ever observe these obligations. In any event, what constitutes 'sufficient evidence' will depend on the incentives of individual states to monitor and investigate violations.

From past practice, flag state investigations have often been lengthy and produced too few convictions.[645] Where violators have been found to be guilty, the penalties imposed have been manifestly inadequate.[646] In the result, the reliance on flag state enforcement entrenched by earlier instruments and reaffirmed by the LOSC does little to improve substantially upon the regulation of vessel-source pollution. In addition, IMO's negligible enforcement authority renders it powerless to take meaningful action against recalcitrant flag states.[647] Overall, the LOSC does not adequately remedy the problem of lack of incentives which has long bedevilled flag state enforcement.

On balance, the maritime interests emerged victorious in curtailing coastal state prescriptive and enforcement jurisdiction over pollution by foreign vessels, particularly in relation to *national* measures in ocean zones farther away from shore. As far as the coastal states are

---

[643] See generally Bodansky, *supra* note 69, at 722.
[644] See M'GONIGLE & ZACHER, *supra* note 65, at 241–51, for the view that the LOSC is 'woefully inadequate' from an 'ideal perspective'. See also Bodansky, *supra* note 69, at 767–77, for the view that the LOSC does not adequately reflect the interests of the coastal states.
[645] See Tables 5-3 and 5-4, Ch. 5.   [646] *Ibid.*   [647] See Ch. 7.

concerned, these actors have had their legislative competence reduced in respect of the kind of pollution regulations which may be prescribed, albeit increased in respect of the geographical area to which such (international) regulations may be applied.[648]

On the whole, the LOSC provisions do not extend far enough to enable coastal states to effectively protect their waters and shores from vessel-source pollution.[649] For one thing, the lack of coastal state authority to deal with violations on the high seas is anomalous given that pollution incidents on the high seas have great potential to damage resources in the EEZ and continental shelf.[650] This anomaly is all the more obvious given the importance placed on environmental protection today and the fact that the international community has itself in recent decades recognised the progressive seaward expansion of national jurisdiction over coastal waters and the protection of economic resources.

In particular, state practice has endorsed the sovereign rights of coastal states over the economic exploitation of resources in their EEZs and continental shelves.[651] In this regard, there is little reason why coastal states should be prevented from adopting their own national measures with the explicit aim of protecting their resources in the EEZ. As long as such measures can be carefully scrutinised by IMO to ensure that they are reasonable and do not excessively interfere with navigation, there is no reason to impose a blanket prohibition on national rules.

There is thus a case for coastal state national regulations in the EEZ to be characterised more as *resource protection* as opposed to merely *pollution control* measures.[652] As the notion of national security is constantly

---

[648] CHURCHILL & LOWE, *supra* note 26, at 347.
[649] See COM(2002) 681, *supra* note 384, at 12, where the European Commission complains that the balance in the LOSC, particularly in arts. 211 and 220, leans heavily in favour of the maritime interests, and that this bias toward the freedom of navigation, at the expense of environmental protection, does not reflect the attitudes of today's society.
[650] The coastal state's only recourse in such situations would be to invoke the 1969 Intervention Convention and art. 221 of the LOSC, *supra* note 570. However, the threshold for invoking these instruments is extremely high, requiring the occurrence of a maritime casualty causing or threatening material damage.
[651] LOSC, arts. 56, 57 and 77.
[652] As far as state practice is concerned, the US appears to have adopted this position in claiming jurisdiction to protect coral reefs by regulating ships anchoring in marine sanctuaries lying within its continental shelf. The US contention (with specific reference to the Flower Garden Banks National Sanctuary off Texas and Louisiana) was that the regulations were *resource-motivated* and were not pollution measures falling within the restrictions of art. 211 of the LOSC, see Bodansky, *supra* note 69, at 766 and MOLENAAR, *supra* note 52, at 417. As long as there is strict joint consultation of such

redefined to embrace non-military issues such as ecological concerns, states should be allowed to protect their resources in the territorial sea and EEZ from ship-source pollution activities, including even those occurring on the high seas. This argument is entirely consistent with new ecological principles such as the precautionary approach recognised by the 1992 UN Conference on Environment and Development (UNCED).[653]

The potential for coastal states' abuse of their powers may, of course, be lessened by requiring them to submit their national resource protection measures to IMO for prior approval. In this way, these measures can be assessed and endorsed for prescription only if they do not impede navigation and are shown *bona fide* to be resource-motivated. While prescriptive jurisdiction should be enhanced, enforcement competence may be qualified such that it is conducted only by port states, in consultation with the prescribing coastal state.[654] This will go some way toward maintaining the balance between resource protection and freedom of navigation. Overall, the international community must begin to recognise the principle that a coastal state's jurisdiction to protect its EEZ resources cannot logically be divorced from its jurisdiction to prevent or control pollution in that same body of water.[655]

Another criticism of the LOSC relates to its failure to recognise the ecological unity of the ocean environment. In essence, human conceptions of jurisdictional boundaries can be seen as mere attempts to divide the indivisible oceans. As examined above, the coastal states enjoy progressively decreasing jurisdiction over their adjacent waters as one proceeds farther away from shore. Yet, sensitive ecosystems invariably defy demarcation and may straddle one or more of the ocean zones. Indeed, sensitive marine areas often fall within several layers of coastal state jurisdiction, particularly where the coastline is indented or littered with offshore islands. The bewildered coastal state may thus find its jurisdictional powers varying between different points of an ecologically congruent ocean area.

The situation becomes even more complicated for ecosystems falling within the jurisdiction of more than one coastal state. Hence, the demarcation of ocean zones into units such as the territorial sea, EEZ or high seas can only hinder the effective management and protection of

---

schemes between the coastal state and IMO (akin to the PSSA regime), coastal states should be allowed to establish these measures.

[653] Mooradian, *supra* note 33, at 806.   [654] *Ibid.* at 811.   [655] *Ibid.* at 805.

sensitive marine areas. In the same vein, the continued emphasis on purely oceanic concerns has led to terrestrial-source marine pollution and the land-sea interface being ignored, with the result that too few concrete measures have been taken to deal with land-based pollution.[656]

Given the modern imperative for preserving the health of the oceans, any regulatory initiative which fails to recognise the ecological unity of the oceans and coastal areas must necessarily be inadequate. In this regard, IMO, as the competent international organisation, should establish flexible co-operative arrangements among coastal states with a view to developing uniform principles that can be applied to sensitive ocean areas forming a single ecological unit but straddling several jurisdictional zones. To this end, concepts such as integrated coastal management and the Particularly Sensitive Sea Area (PSSA) regime may be refined and employed. Such practical approaches will go some way toward ameliorating the deficiencies thrown up by the LOSC regime.

Since it is perhaps unrealistic to expect states to amend the LOSC in the near future,[657] the recalibration of the delicate balance struck between the maritime and coastal interests can perhaps be pursued by having IMO (as the competent international organisation) prescribe new and flexible generally accepted international rules and standards (GAIRS). As seen earlier, the GAIRS formula was adopted by the LOSC precisely to imbue the convention with the immutable qualities of a constitutive document, and yet, with the flexibility and dynamism shaped by subsequent development of the law. In this way, the LOSC provisions will not remain static, but can continue to be interpreted and invigorated by the practice of the relevant actors in response to changing circumstances.[658]

Thus, in limiting coastal state prescriptive jurisdiction, the LOSC does not *necessarily* preclude further expansion of coastal state jurisdiction through customary international law, particularly if this is done through GAIRS adopted by the competent international organisation.[659] Enhancing IMO's role in guiding and endorsing coastal state

---

[656] *Supra* note 38.
[657] See e.g. G. Plant, *The Relationship Between International Navigation Rights and Environmental Protection: A Legal Analysis of Mandatory Ship Traffic Systems*, in Ringbom ed., *supra* note 206, at 28 and Walker & Noyes, *supra* note 131, at 367. This has not stopped the European Commission from raising the possibility, see COM(2003) 105, at 11, *supra* note 384.
[658] This is contemplated by the LOSC itself, see arts. 211(1) and 237(1) which envisage that the rules and standards on marine pollution control can be re-examined.
[659] See generally Mooradian, *supra* note 33, at 812 and Bodansky, *supra* note 69, at 772.

prescriptive jurisdiction and developing new GAIRS will also bolster its relevance as a modern international organisation.[660] More importantly, this may help avert damaging unilateral action by coastal states and thus preserve the LOSC's underlying stability.

To a large extent, progressive expansion of coastal state jurisdiction has already been witnessed at IMO in the form of rules governing ship reporting, routeing and vessel traffic movements. In the past decade, IMO has authorised several of these coastal state-designated schemes which are mandatory for foreign ships and which are applicable even beyond the coastal state's territorial sea.[661] In varying degrees, these schemes are premised upon ships being *required* to comply with certain coastal state prescriptions adopted in consultation with IMO. Although these schemes are largely directed at improving vessel safety as opposed to preventing operational discharges, they provide a relevant model for IMO's role in re-casting coastal state prescriptive jurisdiction over vessel activities beyond the territorial sea.[662]

The recently established Particularly Sensitive Sea Area (PSSA) regime represents yet another innovative IMO mechanism which can be employed to recalibrate the balance struck between the maritime and coastal interests without upsetting the underlying UNCLOS III consensus. The PSSA scheme, as conceived at IMO, specifically allows coastal states to propose special *national* measures which may go beyond the prevailing international standards to be applied in ecologically sensitive ocean areas within and outside the territorial sea.[663] However, the need

---

[660] See Ch. 7.
[661] See Plant, *supra* note 657, at 11-12; Mooradian, *supra* note 33, at 807-15; and Franckx ed., *supra* note 53, at 10. For instance, pursuant to a ship reporting system (SRS) scheme made mandatory under SOLAS reg. V/8-1, vessels report certain information to the coastal state maintaining the SRS, including the vessel name, position, speed and course. Ship routeing systems have also been employed, requiring ships to use particular routes designated by the coastal state. In some areas of the world, Vessel Traffic Systems (VTS) are in place, providing two-way communication between vessels and coastal states. In the 1990s, SOLAS regs. V/10 and V/11 began to provide for the mandatory introduction of international routeing and ship reporting systems for the sole purpose of protecting the marine environment, as distinct from improving the safety and efficiency of navigation. SRS schemes may even be applied beyond the territorial sea, although mandatory VTS schemes are currently restricted to the territorial sea, see SOLAS reg. V/8-2. For an analysis of VTS, see G. Plant, *International Legal Aspects of Vessel Traffic Services*, 14 MARINE POL'Y 71 (1990).
[662] Mooradian, *supra* note 33, at 810.
[663] See IMO Assembly Resolution A.927(22) (2001), laying out the new Guidelines for the Designation of Special Areas and for the Identification and Designation of Particularly Sensitive Sea Areas. The Resolution updated and replaced the earlier Resolutions

for such measures must first be justified to IMO, and their content developed in close consultation with other states, before they can be brought into effect.[664] IMO will thus conduct a cost-benefit analysis – in particular, the proposing state's 'associated protective measures' (APMs) may be prohibited if they have a severe impact on navigational freedoms relative to the coastal state's interests, or approved if they have less severe impact and where coastal state interest is high.[665]

Pursuant to the PSSA scheme, IMO has to date promulgated a host of APMs prescribing traffic lanes, compulsory pilotage, ship reporting systems, Vessel Traffic Systems (VTS), Areas to be Avoided (ATBAs), no-anchoring areas and other special measures to be taken by ships when traversing a designated PSSA with sensitive ecological characteristics. Some of these measures will in time, if not already, become generally accepted international rules and standards.[666] What is useful about the PSSA concept is that it seeks practicably to reconcile the coastal state's desire for enhanced prescriptive and enforcement jurisdiction with the international community's interest in avoiding navigational impediments.

In recent years, however, the balance at IMO has tilted excessively in the coastal states' favour, with some PSSA designations being extremely wide in geographic scope or lacking clear justification.[667] The

---

A.720(17) (1991) and A.885(21) (1999) which had provided guidance on the matter. The PSSAs approved to date are the Great Barrier Reef and Torres Straits (Australia), the Sabana-Camaguey Archipelago (Cuba), Malpelo Island (Colombia), the Florida Keys (US), the Wadden Sea (Northern Europe), the Paracas National Reserve (Peru), the Canary Islands (Spain), the Galapagos Islands (Ecuador), the Baltic Sea and the Western European waters.

[664] There are several states with unilateral legislation designating marine areas beyond their territorial seas. Many of these were established without prior consultations with IMO and thus, did not follow the art. 211(6) procedure. Their consistency with the LOSC is thus questionable, see MOLENAAR, *supra* note 52, at 418, citing Bangladesh, Canada, Estonia, Russia and Sri Lanka as examples.

[665] Bodansky, *supra* note 69, at 775. For a detailed assessment of PSSAs, see K. Gjerde & D. Freestone eds., *Particularly Sensitive Sea Areas – An Important Environmental Concept at a Turning Point*, 9 INT'L J. MARINE & COASTAL L. 431 (1994) and G. Peet, *Particularly Sensitive Sea Areas – A Documentary History*, 9 INT'L J. MARINE & COASTAL L. 469 (1994).

[666] E.g. ship reporting systems (SRS), *supra* note 661.

[667] The Western European and Baltic Sea PSSAs, although successfully designated, are extremely controversial. The former arose as part of the political reaction to the *Erika* and *Prestige* incidents, and is particularly contentious owing to its large area of coverage (with potential impacts on navigation), *supra* note 405. Meanwhile, Russia has rejected the Baltic Sea PSSA and excluded its territorial waters from the PSSA's ambit on the grounds that current measures in the Baltic including traffic separation schemes, MARPOL special areas, SO_x Emission Control Area and HELCOM initiatives

possibility of states obtaining in-principle approval for PSSAs well ahead of submitting proposed APMs has also compromised the stringency of the assessment process and effectively created a presumptive expectation for successful designation. The PSSA Guidelines are currently being reviewed at IMO, and it would be desirable for some discipline to be restored to the assessment process and for checks to be imposed on coastal state exuberance. In particular, a clear requirement should be laid down for states to justify their APMs *at the same time* as when they propose PSSAs for designation. Otherwise, an overly permissive PSSA system can only risk undermining the UNCLOS III balance.

Ultimately, it can be readily understood why and how the provisions in Part XII of the LOSC have come to assume their present form. It must be borne in mind that the whole UNCLOS process was characterised by political trade-offs and concessions. In the overall scheme of things, the preservation of the marine environment was seen by the maritime interests to be too inextricably linked to the freedom of navigation. By agreeing to recognise the sovereign rights of coastal states to exploit natural resources extending 200 miles into the sea, a corresponding *quid pro quo* had to be extracted in the form of a coastal state guarantee for unimpeded navigation.

Since pollution control efforts entailed a real risk of tampering with free navigation, the maritime interests had no qualms in resisting coastal state claims for increased authority over polluting vessels. Thus, the Canadian proposal for an outright pollution control zone[668] was rejected in favour of a regime which conditions coastal state jurisdiction upon strict tests such as distance from shore, degree of harm and nature of standards violated. At the same time, the fact that these tests defy the ecological unity of the oceans and rest on wholly subjective verbal formulae such as 'significant', 'substantial' or 'major' damage must testify to the deficiencies in the regime formation process.

In the final analysis, the LOSC can be assessed as having accorded limited recognition to the ideals of 'safer shipping and cleaner oceans' in the context of modern environmental imperatives. It remains to be

---

are all more than sufficient. Russia's concerns relate to the high costs which the PSSA would impose on shipping through its Baltic ports, particularly double hulls for oil exports. The objections to both PSSAs have triggered an ongoing revision of the Guidelines in Resolution A.927(22), see Report of MEPC's 52nd session, MEPC Doc. 52/24 (2004). The perception among the maritime interests is that the Guidelines have been too leniently implemented, thereby fuelling a proliferation of PSSA proposals.

[668] *Supra* note 511.

seen if the ever-growing coastal state demands for resource and environmental protection will lead to a re-assessment of the relevant LOSC provisions. As things stand, there are signs that coastal state agitation is on the rise.[669] While the laws of most states are LOSC-compliant, there is a growing number of coastal states whose laws are possibly inconsistent with the LOSC.[670] Outright violations of the LOSC have also been recorded,[671] and an increasing number of maritime disputes have been brought before international tribunals in recent years.[672] As argued here, one realistic way of addressing these challenges is to allow IMO to develop new and progressive GAIRS which can meet coastal state demands without unravelling the UNCLOS III consensus. Innovations such as the PSSA regime and ship reporting systems must also continue to be fine-tuned by IMO and the international community in general.

---

[669] This is true particularly in Western Europe following the *Erika* and *Prestige* incidents, see Chs. 2 and 3. See also Plant, *supra* note 657, at 11, for the view that since the LOSC's entry into force, there has been little evidence of a reversal of the trend of coastal states increasingly seeking to protect their coasts from vessel-source pollution.

[670] For instance, the laws of some states (e.g. India, Pakistan and Russia) relating to the territorial sea and the EEZ employ terminology which may not be LOSC-consistent, see MOLENAAR, *supra* note 52, at 367-71. There are also possible conflicts between the LOSC and Canadian and US legislation, see e.g. MOLENAAR, *ibid.* at 376-8 and D. VanderZwaag, *Shipping and Marine Environmental Protection in Canada: Rocking the Boat and Riding a Restless Sea*, in NAVIGATIONAL RIGHTS AND FREEDOMS AND THE NEW LAW OF THE SEA 209, at 212 (D. Rothwell & S. Bateman eds., 2000).

[671] Many of these are connected to attempts by countries to extend their jurisdiction beyond what is permitted by the LOSC, see I. K. Kolossovsky, *The Future of the UN Law of the Sea Convention and Maintenance of Legal Order and Peace in the Oceans in the 21 st Century*, in THE ROLE OF THE OCEANS IN THE 21ST CENTURY 321 (S.-Y. Hong et al. eds., 1995).

[672] A. Yankov, *The International Tribunal for the Law of the Sea: Its Place Within the Dispute Settlement System of the UN Law of the Sea Convention*, 37 INDIAN J. INT'L L. 356, at 359 (1997).

5 Implementation and Compliance

1. Overview

The previous chapters have examined how the international regime formation process achieves agreement on the substantive vessel-source pollution standards and the jurisdictional competence of states to prescribe and enforce these standards. As examined earlier, multilateral standard-setting is conducted primarily within the IMO arena where the interests of the relevant actors are advanced and reconciled. Once resultant compromises or outcomes are reached in the form of conventional rules,[673] these are transmitted to the states for ratification and implementation. Thus, where the rule-making competence of IMO ends, the domestic *implementation* of internationally formulated rules begins.

Needless to say, a uniform global regime can be *effective* only when the relevant rules are *implemented* and *enforced* adequately and command a high degree of *compliance* by those 'target actors' at whom they are directed.[674] In this regard, 'implementation' refers to the measures which states adopt at the national level to make relevant treaty rules effective in domestic law. From a broader perspective, 'implementation' is concerned with the state's overall effort to accomplish the objectives of a body of rules. On its part, the related but narrower concept of 'enforcement' entails the direct and immediate bringing into force of rules by states (often, on pain of penalties or sanctions) to compel 'compliance' on the part of target actors.[675]

---

[673] It must be noted that IMO's bodies also issue guidelines, codes, resolutions and other non-binding instruments.
[674] Weiss & Jacobson eds., *supra* note 23, at 4.
[675] The prospect or certainty of enforcement is thus a critical factor in one's decision to comply, see G. Handl, *Controlling Implementation of and Compliance with International*

Compliance thus goes beyond implementation and refers to whether states are putting into effect the measures which they have instituted and whether target actors are in fact adhering or conforming to the rules.[676] Finally, 'effectiveness' is concerned with whether the stated goals or objectives of a body of rules have been met and whether the problems leading to the adoption of the rules have been addressed. In other words, effectiveness entails both behavioural change in the required direction and problem-solving from the point of view of scientific-technical rationality.[677] In this respect, 'effectiveness' is connected to, but not identical with compliance. States and target actors may well be in compliance with treaty rules, but the rules themselves may be ineffective in attaining the relevant objectives.[678]

Indeed, enforcement and implementation do not necessarily produce the desired compliance; neither does compliance guarantee 'effectiveness'. Nevertheless, a properly crafted implementation regime may bring about a higher degree of congruence between compliance and effectiveness. In this vein, strict compliance is not necessarily a prerequisite for an effective regime; an 'acceptable' level of compliance is all that is required. Of course, what is an 'acceptable' level differs in each individual case as this can change over time depending on the type of treaty, the particular context and the specific behavioural change expected of target actors.[679]

As explained in Chapter 1, one reason why 'effectiveness' is so elusive in the regulation of vessel-source pollution is because the regime formation process, influenced as it is by the maritime interests, often contains pathological impediments to enforcement and compliance. These shortcomings (if not inadvertently inserted) would typically have been introduced at the behest of the politically relevant interests dictating the rule-making process. Thus, it has been seen how the

---

Environmental Agreements: The Rocky Road from Rio, 5 COLO. J. INT'L ENVTL. L. & POL'Y 305, at 330 (1994). Some writers feel that inducing compliance is not a matter of enforcement but a process of negotiation, see A. Chayes & A. H. Chayes, *Compliance Without Enforcement: State Behavior Under Regulatory Treaties*, 7 NEGOTIATION J. 311, at 312 (1991). Enforcement is often viewed to be a sufficient, though not a necessary condition for compliance, see O. YOUNG, COMPLIANCE AND PUBLIC AUTHORITY: A THEORY WITH INTERNATIONAL APPLICATION 25 (1979).

[676] MITCHELL, *supra* note 68, at 30. On compliance generally, see A. CHAYES & A. H. CHAYES, THE NEW SOVEREIGNTY: COMPLIANCE WITH INTERNATIONAL REGULATORY AGREEMENTS (1995).

[677] E. L. Miles, *Implementation of International Regimes: A Typology*, in Vidas & Østreng eds., *supra* note 64, at 327.

[678] An instance of just such a rule is the 4.5 per cent sulphur cap, see Ch. 3.

[679] Miles, *supra* note 677, at 329-30.

maritime interests' insistence on flag state jurisdiction – despite the flag states' obvious lack of incentives to conduct enforcement – implants a deficiency in the regime from the outset. Similarly, the fact that no mechanism was laid down to enforce state obligations to provide waste reception facilities in ports continues to impede the proper disposal of vessel wastes. Further examples include the oil companies' successful opposition to a stringent sulphur cap for marine fuels and their insistence upon a secondary and limited burden for pollution liability and compensation.[680]

As will be examined below, the compliance records of states and industry alike are generally unsatisfactory. In large part, this is due to the competitive and cost-conscious nature of the ship transportation industry which leads to a distinct lack of incentives among target actors to comply with vessel-source pollution rules and to ensure the effectiveness of such rules. This, in turn, feeds back on the general lack of state incentives to enforce the relevant rules, further augmenting the regime deficiencies referred to earlier. The result is a mutually reinforcing incentive deficit on the part of both state and industry actors, which presents itself not only at the regime formation stage but at the implementation phase as well. The remainder of this book will explore means to overcome this problem and to create greater all-round incentives for securing compliance with the relevant vessel-source pollution rules.

2. Ratification, Incorporation into Domestic Law and Implementation

Several of the major IMO conventions enjoy a relatively high degree of acceptance by states, including those states which, among themselves, constitute the largest proportion of shipowning nations in the world. Given that the primary authority over ships is reposed in the flag states,[681] it is crucial that the IMO instruments enjoy the acceptance of flag states whose national shipping registries contain the highest amounts of tonnage. From Table 2-3 in Chapter 2, it can be seen that instruments such as SOLAS 74 and Annexes I and II to MARPOL 73/78 enjoy near-universal application to global shipping. In particular, 130 states representing 97.07 per cent of world shipping tonnage have

---

[680] See Ch. 6.
[681] See e.g. MARPOL 73/78, art. 4 and discussion in Chs. 2 and 4.

acceded to or ratified MARPOL 73/78 and are currently parties to Annexes I and II. These include the majority of coastal and port states in the world, as well as the major trading, shipowning and open registry states.

From the perspective of the individual states, the process of accession or ratification[682] is a relatively simple operation. Various constitutional and legal mechanisms exist within states to pave the way for the formal accession to or ratification of international instruments. The exact procedure varies among different countries, but one common feature is that government agencies in charge of maritime transport, environmental protection, economic planning and foreign affairs will typically consult with one another before recommending the accession to or ratification of an IMO instrument. In most countries, the interests represented by the shipping, environmental and other relevant communities will be heard in the domestic consultative process.

States will thus customarily weigh the cumulative costs and benefits of accepting a particular convention. Consistent with the function of self-interest in international politics, individual states will have their own peculiar composite reasons why they should choose to accept or to remain outside the ambit of certain conventions. Of course, there may be innocuous reasons why states do not accept particular conventions – usually, these entail inertia, indifference or the lack of administrative or implementing capacity.

Once a state decides to accept an IMO convention, what usually follows is a decision by the executive branch of government to deposit an instrument of accession or ratification with the Secretary-General of IMO. Following that, an important aspect of the process of implementation is the degree to which states incorporate the obligations of an accepted convention into their domestic laws. Typically, state authorities will have to prepare implementing legislation for this purpose. This is essentially a major feature of the prescriptive jurisdiction of states and forms a critical component of the implementation process.

---

[682] A state ratifies a convention which it has signed (usually at the conclusion of the Conference adopting it), while it would accede to a convention which it had not previously signed. Being a signatory connotes no legal obligations, except for the obligation to refrain from acts which would defeat the object or purpose of the treaty, see art. 18, 1969 Convention on the Law of Treaties, 8 I.L.M. 679 (1969) (in force 27 Jan. 1980). On the other hand, accession or ratification brings forth legal obligations for the state concerned, which becomes a 'contracting party' to the convention. For convenience, this work will use the term 'acceptance' to denote both 'accession' and 'ratification'.

The intricate details of how conventional commitments are incorporated or transplanted into domestic legal regimes need not concern us here. Indeed, procedures vary significantly among countries with different constitutional and legal orders. Suffice to say that, in many countries, the incorporation of international commitments into domestic law may be a complex matter. Counterpart domestic legislation may be vaguely worded, translation difficulties may arise and uncertainties may emerge as to which competent government agency is to implement the treaty commitments, either at the central or provincial levels or both.[683] In particular, the developing countries often experience a serious lack or absence of capacity to oversee the incorporation and compliance processes.[684] These practical problems invariably affect the implementation of and compliance with treaty commitments.

Typically, the biggest challenge for a state's administrative apparatus is the effective enforcement of international treaty commitments once these have been incorporated into domestic law. This entails the enforcement jurisdiction of the state, to be exercised within the confines laid down by international law.[685] Put simply, accession/ratification, incorporation into local laws and the designation of a responsible national administrative agency are relatively straightforward processes. The greater difficulty lies in ensuring that the obligations assumed under the convention(s) are continuously and effectively met by the state and other target actors.

By acceding to or ratifying conventions, states accept not only the rights and obligations which are directed at them *qua* state parties but also those rights and obligations accruing to private actors operating within the state's territory, jurisdiction or control. Hence, a state which becomes a party to MARPOL 73/78, for instance, assumes the obligations to provide reception facilities and to report incidents of ship pollution to IMO. In its capacity as a coastal or port state, the state is accorded the right (as opposed to obligation) to prescribe and enforce the provisions of MARPOL 73/78 against foreign vessels navigating within its waters. On their part, flag states are *obliged* to ensure that the owners of their vessels operating wherever in the world comply with the standards mandated by MARPOL 73/78. The flag state is also obliged to investigate

---

[683] For instance, the division of authority among constituent units in a federal system may pose problems. Inter- and intra-departmental rivalries may also arise. For an analysis, see E. Gold, *From Process to Reality: Adopting Domestic Legislation for the Implementation of the Law of the Sea Convention*, in Vidas & Østreng eds., *supra* note 64, at 375.
[684] See generally CHAYES & CHAYES, *supra* note 676.   [685] See Ch. 4.

allegations of violations committed by its flag vessels and to prosecute offending vessels and their owners where appropriate.[686]

In general, state enforcement of treaty obligations may be lacking for a variety of reasons – these include budgetary constraints, lack of trained manpower or administrative inefficiencies. Indeed, even in the most advanced of national administrations, implementation and enforcement by state authorities are often imperfect. The problem is especially acute in developing countries with long coastlines and insufficient monitoring capabilities. That most states cannot keep up with the proliferation of international regulations is a well-known fact in the shipping world – this has been amply recognised in numerous policy instruments issued by the IMO Assembly.[687]

Yet, arising from the relentless political pressure in the developed states to tighten environmental regulations, IMO has had little choice but to submit to the wishes of its most powerful member states to step up its regulatory momentum. This is an inescapable fact facing states and the shipping industry today. Ensuring the adequate implementation of the numerous international conventions is thus one of the greatest contemporary challenges for states and IMO.

The peculiar difficulties encountered by individual states in implementing IMO instruments are outside the scope of this study. What this work hopes to achieve is to highlight the broad obligations which states assume under the IMO instruments and to analyse how these obligations – in the form in which they have been influenced and crafted during the regime formation process – may themselves affect the extent to which they are complied with by states and industry.[688] Thus, this book seeks to assess how the regulatory process at IMO can anticipate the provision of incentives (and the removal of disincentives) for the effective enforcement of the relevant standards.

Under the major IMO marine pollution instruments such as MARPOL 73/78, three major obligations are imposed on state parties in their respective capacities as flag, coastal or port states. These are the obligations to enforce compliance with the relevant discharge and CDEM standards against all national and foreign ships, to provide reception

---

[686] See Ch. 4.
[687] See e.g. IMO Assembly Resolution A. 500(XII) (1981) on the Objectives of the Organization in the 1980s, as reaffirmed in Resolutions A.777(18) (1993), A.900(21) (1999), A.909(22) (2001) and most recently, A.944(23) (2003) on the Strategic Plan for the Organization for the Period 2004–10.
[688] See Chs. 3 and 4.

3. The Enforcement Obligations of States

3.1 Pollution Control Standards and State Enforcement Records

3.1.1 Discharge vs. Equipment Standards

In general, compliance with treaty obligations can be seen as a function of three factors – legal authority, capacity and incentives.[689] Where there is a confluence of these factors, compliance by target actors is likely to be high. 'Legal authority' refers to the perception by a state that it is empowered by legal norms and precepts to pursue a particular course of action. 'Capacity' refers to the ability of a state to act, taking into account the financial, manpower and other resources it has at its disposal. Finally, 'incentive' refers to the political and economic forces which lead a state to reckon that it has an interest in taking a certain course of action.

Of course, a state would have more incentives to act if it already possessed the requisite legal authority and capacity. Thus, where actors have had a necessary alignment of the political and economic incentives, the practical ability as well as the legal authority to act, it is likely that such states will demonstrate a higher degree of compliance with treaty obligations. For instance, it has been seen how, in relation to discharge standards, the 'parts per million' (ppm) measure introduced by OILPOL 54 largely failed because it relied on the crew's good faith to effectuate compliance.[690] In any event, reliable monitoring equipment and surveillance capacity were not available. Consequently, there was little incentive and practical ability on the part of ship operators to comply, and of states to monitor for compliance.

In contrast, the total discharge limits, the litre/mile instantaneous discharge standard and the associated LOT method elicited higher compliance because they improved the ability of tankers to self-monitor discharges and the capacity of states to verify compliance. Alas, the *ability* to comply was meaningless as it was not accompanied by the *incentive* to do so. The independent tanker owners had few economic

---

[689] The idea of a strategic triangle of compliance involving incentives, capacity and authority in assessing state behaviour for treaty compliance is attributed to R. O. Keohane, see MITCHELL, *supra* note 68, at 11.

[690] See Chs. 3 and 4.

incentives to use LOT or to save on oil discharges as they were typically paid for the amount of oil on-loaded as opposed to the amount delivered. Since a particular shipment would already have been paid for, discharging oily wastes at sea on ballast voyages cost the independents nothing.[691] Moreover, using LOT and retaining slops on board reduced cargo room for fresh shipments.

On their part, the oil-loading OPEC states never had the incentive to inspect returning tankers diligently, despite possessing the authority and ability to do so. This was because the discharge of tanker wastes typically occurred on the high seas or in the waters of other states. In any event, prosecution for discharges beyond the territorial sea still depended on the flag states, which clearly lacked the incentives for such action.[692]

The OILPOL and MARPOL 73/78 discharge standards, in and of themselves, have thus had minimal impact on compliance behaviour. Whatever compliance by industry has arguably not been induced by treaty rules or their enforcement by states, but by external factors such as the impact of rising oil prices or public relations pressure.[693] Consequently, the international regulatory system has had to develop alternative strategies to discharge standards. As we have seen, these arose in the form of construction, design or equipment standards which are, by their very nature, self-enforceable.[694]

Equipment standards such as SBTs and double hulls are typically premised on coercing operators to comply with them from the outset rather than on deterring subsequent violations. Therefore, the compliance system necessarily depends on pre-violation monitoring and control. The fact that equipment standards can be imposed on shipbuilders at the construction stage ensures a high compliance rate among shipowners.[695] At every stage of the transaction, the act of procuring and operating a tanker rests on the knowledge and co-operation of several parties, including shipbuilders, classification societies, insurers and even banks in their role as financiers and mortgagees. In this manner, ships which do not comply with the IMO equipment specifications invariably face difficulties in securing insurance coverage or financial backing.

---

[691] MITCHELL, *supra* note 68, at 225–31.   [692] See Chs 3 and 4.
[693] This is true particularly for the oil companies, see Ch. 3 and MITCHELL, *supra* note 68, at 251–6.
[694] For convenience, this chapter will refer to all these standards as 'equipment' standards.
[695] MITCHELL, *supra* note 68, at 263–7.

Hence, so far as new ship orders are concerned, there is very little ability for industry actors to circumvent design and equipment standards, despite their having the economic incentives to do so. The only real issue for such ships is their proper maintenance once they are operational to ensure that they *continue* to comply with the relevant standards. As for existing ships which have not been constructed with the requisite equipment standards, MARPOL 73/78 provided a schedule for retrofitting or complete phasing out.[696] In this regard, the major challenge lies in ensuring that ships operating in the second-hand market do not escape retrofitting or phasing-out requirements. This concern, together with the challenge of ensuring continuous maintenance for all ships, new and old, form the basis for MARPOL 73/78 and SOLAS provisions relating to survey and certification.

On the whole, equipment standards have proven to be far more effective than discharge standards in eliciting compliance with vessel-source pollution rules. Equipment standards can be enforced by the developed port states which, unlike the flag states, have the confluence of authority, ability as well as incentives for enforcement. In addition, the administrative sanctions of port state detention and denial of entry have greater deterrent effects on shipowners than judicial fines for discharge violations. Detention or denial of entry typically result in costly delays, thereby providing significant disincentives for errant operators. Enforcement of equipment standards also assures increased detection of violations, thereby eliminating competitive advantages for sub-standard fleets. This provides further incentives for operators to comply.

Empirically, the level of industry compliance with MARPOL 73/78 equipment regulations has been high. In 1981, only 45 per cent of tankers built from 1976 to 1981 and only 26 per cent of pre-1976 tankers had SBT or COW. By 1991, 94 per cent of older tankers had installed COW or SBT and almost all post-1982 tankers had done so.[697] On their part, new tankers for which SBTs were compulsory have generally complied with the requirement.[698] Ship scrapping statistics also show that owners were scrapping tankers which had neither SBT nor COW far more frequently in the early 1980s than they scrapped compliant tankers.[699] All these developments support the claim that the equipment regulations were effectively driving behaviour.

---

[696] See Ch. 3.   [697] MITCHELL, *supra* note 68, at 270.   [698] *Ibid.* at 270–4.
[699] *Ibid.* at 270, citing DREWRY SHIPPING CONSULTANTS, THE IMPACT OF NEW TANKER REGULATIONS 21–2 (1981). For a recent assessment, see DREWRY SHIPPING CONSULTANTS, COST OF QUALITY IN SHIPPING: THE FINANCIAL IMPLICATIONS OF THE CURRENT REGULATORY ENVIRONMENT (1998).

As for the double hull standards, about 9 per cent of all crude oil tankers above 10,000 dwt had double hulls at the end of 1993. By the end of 1998, 21 per cent of such tankers had double hulls.[700] At the end of 2002, the proportion (by tonnage) of tankers above 5,000 dwt with double hulls was 51 per cent, with projected compliance rates of 75 and 81 per cent by 2007 and 2010 respectively.[701] In Europe alone, the proportion of double hull tankers rose from 39 per cent in 2000 to 51 per cent by the end of 2002, as the *Erika*-inspired renewals kicked in.[702] The global proportion is expected to increase further following IMO's latest acceleration in December 2003 of the phase-out schedule for single-hull tankers.[703]

On their part, the majority of existing single-hull tankers have either been scrapped or, less commonly, retrofitted with protectively located SBTs or hydrostatic balancing to prolong their operating lives. As an indication of global fleet renewal, 62 per cent of the current world tanker fleet was built in the period 1990 to 2002, signifying that IMO's phasing-out measures have led to a massive retirement or conversion of older tankers.[704] Overall, the new ship orders of the 1990s have greatly modernised the world tanker fleet, and non-SBT tankers built in the 1970s are now only a marginal segment of the fleet.[705]

3.1.2 State Enforcement of Pollution Control Standards

As examined in Chapter 4, the flag, coastal and port states enjoy differentiated levels of enforcement jurisdiction over vessels which violate the relevant discharge and CDEM standards. Port states may inspect ships in port for compliance with certification requirements and may, subject to the conditions laid out in the LOSC and IMO instruments, detain ships, prosecute violations, impose fines or deny ships entry into port. Coastal state enforcement powers are much more circumscribed,

---

[700] See JACOBS & PARTNERS, WORLD OIL TANKER TRENDS 57 (1998); CLARKSON, THE TANKER REGISTER (1994); and JAPAN MARITIME RESEARCH INSTITUTE, IMO REGULATIONS RELATING TO DOUBLE-HULL STRUCTURE AND THEIR EFFECTS ON EXISTING TANKERS, REPORT No. 45 (1993).
[701] INTERTANKO, *supra* note 14, at 13 and the submission of the European states, MEPC Doc. 49/16/1 (2003), *supra* note 385. These estimates do not take into account the effects of the December 2003 amendments at IMO.
[702] COM(2002) 681, *supra* note 384.
[703] See Ch. 3 for developments in the wake of the *Prestige* incident.
[704] INTERTANKO, *supra* note 14, at 12.
[705] *Ibid.* at 13. Industry research has also found that tankers continue to be sold for recycling ahead of their MARPOL reg. 13G phase-out deadline, *ibid.* at 27.

Table 5-1. Port State Inspections Reported to IMO

	1984	1985	1986	1987	1988	1989	1990	1991	1992	1993
No. of reporting port states	5	7	11	9	11	11	10	10	7	15
- OECD states	4	6	8	5	7	7	7	8	4	9
- Non-OECD states	1	1	3	4	4	4	3	2	3	6
Ships inspected	3,602	14,610	21,879	32,332	29,957	27,444	35,243	24,636	21,629	27,040
Ave. inspection per state report	720	2,087	1,989	3,592	2,723	2,495	3,524	2,464	3,090	1,803
Ships detained	71	101	50	44	387	12	30	28	4	117
Ave. detention per state report	14	14	5	5	35	1	3	2.8	0.57	7.8
Detention (as % of inspections)	2.0	0.7	0.2	0.1	1.3	0.1	0.1	0.11	0.02	0.43
IOPPC discrepancies	316	359	534	264	316	244	208	NA	NA	175
- Compliance rate (as % of inspections)	91.2	97.5	97.6	99.2	98.9	99.1	99.4	98	99	99.3
Oil Record Book (ORB) discrepancies	NA	NA	NA	NA	NA	NA	NA	NA	NA	1,167
- Compliance rate (as % of inspections)	NA	NA	NA	NA	NA	NA	NA	98	94.85	95.68
MARPOL 73/78 equipment discrepancies	NA	NA	NA	NA	NA	NA	NA	NA	NA	491
- Compliance rate (as % of inspections)	NA	NA	NA	NA	NA	NA	NA	98	98	98.18

	1994	1995	1996	1997	1998	1999	2000	2001	2002
No. of reporting port states	23	20	22	18	16	13	16	24	20
- OECD states	10	11	8	9	12	6	10	11	7
- Non-OECD states	13	9	14	9	4	7	6	13	13
Ships inspected	52,806	27,179	27,243	44,318	45,021	29,342	35,834	61,158	31,962
Ave. inspection per state report	2,296	1,356	1,238	2,462	2,814	2,257	2,240	2,548	1,598
Ships detained	468	478	240	392	676	251	295	671	656
Ave. detention per state report	20.3	23.9	10.9	21.8	42.3	19.3	18.4	28.0	32.8
Detention (as % of inspections)	0.89	1.76	0.88	0.88	1.50	0.86	0.82	1.10	2.05
IOPPC discrepancies	186	305	191	286	684	311	459	702	902
- Compliance rate (as % of inspections)	99.65	98.88	99.30	99.35	98.48	98.94	98.72	98.86	97.18
Oil Record Book discrepancies	2,928	2,616	1,593	2,116	1,827	1,217	1,388	1,953	1,819
- Compliance rate (as % of inspections)	94.45	90.37	94.15	95.23	95.94	95.85	96.13	96.81	94.31
MARPOL 73/78 equipment discrepancies	658	459	518	764	1,469	1,684	1,172	1,261	965
- Compliance rate (as % of inspections)	98.75	98.31	98.10	98.28	96.74	94.26	96.73	97.94	96.98

Notes:

1. Due to the changing formats of state reports, some information was not consistently solicited over the years.
2. In some years, the figures reflect reports which were submitted late to IMO.
3. Associate members (e.g. Hong Kong) are considered member states for all tabulations. OECD states are classified as such from their dates of entry into that organization.
4. The number of states in this table does not correspond exactly to those submitting mandatory MARPOL 73/78 reports, as reflected in Tables 5-16 and 5-17 below. This is because in some years, several states which submitted MARPOL 73/78 reports did not specifically provide information on port state inspections.

Sources: 1984 to 1990: R. Mitchell, Intentional Oil Pollution at Sea (1994); 1991 to 2002: Mandatory Reports under MARPOL 73/78, as reflected in the annual Flag State Implementation (FSI) Sub-Committee documents.

Table 5-2. Penalties Imposed by Port States (other than detentions) as Reported to IMO[706]

	1991 Information on Reporting States: N.A.		1992 Information on Reporting States: N.A.		1993 Information on Reporting States: N.A.		1994 Information on Reporting States: N.A.		1995 Information on Reporting States: N.A.		1996 Port States Reporting: 7 [OECD: 3; non-OECD: 4]			
	Ave. Fines		Ave. Fines		Ave. Fines		Ave. Fines		Ave. Fines		Fines (GBP)			
	No.	(USD)	No.	(USD)	No.	(USD)	No.	(USD)	No.	(USD)	No.	Max.	Min.	Ave.
1. Illegal Discharge	272	2,178	422	3,892	872	3,762	716	3,484	876	2,029	NA	NA	NA	1,839
2. Oil Record Book	350	1,096	234	211	NA	NA	NA	NA	NA	NA	NA	NA	NA	445
3. IOPP Certificate	49	1,025	415	480	NA	NA	NA	NA	NA	NA	NA	NA	NA	55
4. Others	66	3,546	34	399	295	NA	531	NA	24,111	NA	NA	NA	NA	82

[706] The reports are solicited from states by means of MEPC Circulars, see Section (3a), Part 4, MEPC/Circ.318. For more on port state fines, see COST SAVINGS, supra note 8, at 47-9.

	1997 Port States Reporting: 11 [OECD: 7; non-OECD: 4]				1998 Port States Reporting: 12 [OECD: 8; non-OECD: 4]				1999 Port States Reporting: 7 [OECD: 3; non-OECD: 4]				2000 Port States Reporting: 9 [OECD: 4; non-OECD: 5]				
		Fines (GBP)				Fines (GBP)				Fines (GBP)				Fines (GBP)		
	No.	Max.	Min.	Ave.	No.	Max.	Min.	Ave.	No.	Max.	Min.	Ave.	No.	Max.	Min.	Ave.
1. Illegal Discharge	456	NA	NA	2,990	656	65,000	15	1,845	576	57,114	17	110–7,000	126	1.8 mil.	86	31,441
2. Oil Record Book	441	NA	NA	730	313	8,330	15	751	44	NA	NA	NA	345	50,000	9	852
3. IOPP Certificate	35	NA	NA	343	36	1,500	15	123	4	NA	NA	NA	9	545	364	454
4. Others	55	NA	NA	1,339	202	15,000	15	209	37	NA	NA	NA	131	6,566	18	812

	2001 Port States Reporting: 20 [OECD: 9; non-OECD: 11]				2002 Port States Reporting: 12 [OECD: 5; non-OECD: 7]			
		Fines (GBP)				Fines (GBP)		
	No.	Max.	Min.	Ave.	No.	Max.	Min.	Ave.
1. Illegal Discharge	163	50,000	32	3,323	160	36,758	78	2,736
2. Oil Record Book	303	50,000	10	1,209	195	15,000	31	1,326
3. IOPP Certificate	38	2,392	10	403	2	3,420	600	2,010
4. Others	131	10,417	32	1,048	20	9,567	10	1,891

Sources: Mandatory Reports under MARPOL 73/78, as reflected in annual FSI Sub-Committee documents.

Table 5-3. Penalties Imposed by Flag States as Reported to IMO[707]

	1996 Flag States Reporting: 2 [OECD: 0; non-OECD: 2] Fines (GBP)				1997 Flag States Reporting: 7 [OECD: 4; non-OECD: 3] Fines (GBP)				1998 Flag States Reporting: 8 [OECD: 6; non-OECD: 2] Fines (GBP)				1999 Flag States Reporting: 3 [OECD: 1; non-OECD: 2] Fines (GBP)			
	No.	Max.	Min.	Ave.	No.	Max.	Min.	Ave.	No.	Max.	Min.	Ave	No.	Max.	Min.	Ave.
1. Illegal Discharge	NA	NA	NA	NA	131	4,215	NA	NA	137	9,100	7	737	NA	NA	NA	NA
2. Oil Record Book	NA	NA	NA	NA	91	30	NA	NA	187	3,330	7	50	NA	NA	NA	NA
3. IOPP Certificate	NA	NA	NA	NA	4	NA	NA	NA	8	6,600	15	959	NA	NA	NA	NA
4. Others	NA	NA	NA	NA	146	NA	NA	NA	81	6,000	7	448	NA	NA	NA	NA

	2000 Flag States Reporting: 7 [OECD: 3; non-OECD: 4] Fines (GBP)				2001 Flag States Reporting: 8 [OECD: 3; non-OECD: 5] Fines (GBP)				2002 Flag States Reporting: 9 [OECD: 3; non-OECD: 6] Fines (GBP)			
	No.	Max.	Min.	Ave.	No.	Max.	Min.	Ave.	No.	Max.	Min.	Ave
1. Illegal Discharge	249	50,000	9	1,364	183	50,000	23	1,184	587	28,766	39	1,937
2. Oil Record Book	430	4,444	9	83	490	778	8	102	487	1,167	39	317
3. IOPP Certificate	20	2,222	28	170	48	389	NA	30	27	233	40	79
4. Others	152	946	9	188	178	1,260	23	98	216	25,000	23	349

Sources: Mandatory Reports under MARPOL 73/78, as reflected in annual FSI Sub-Committee documents.

[707] Pursuant to Section (3b), Part 4, MEPC/Circ.318, *ibid*.

Table 5-4. *Flag State Action as Reported to IMO*

	No. of Coastal States Referring Cases	No. of Cases Referred by Coastal State (A)	No. of Flag States Reporting on Referrals	Cases where Action Taken by Flag State (B)	Ratio of (B) to (A) [%]
1991	NA	289	10	40	13.8
1992	NA	258	8	60	23.3
1993	NA	NA	5	NA	NA
1994	NA	NA	3	NA	NA
1995	NA	NA	NA	NA	NA
1996	9	150	NA	NA	NA
1997	8	148	NA	26	17.6
1998	10	134	NA	17	12.7
1999	13	81	NA	5	6.2
2000	7	100	NA	9	9.0
2001	9	78	NA	3	3.8
2002	NA	NA	NA	NA	NA

Notes: No confirmation is available as to whether the cases in which flag state action had been taken related specifically to those cases reported to IMO by coastal states.
Sources: Mandatory Reports under MARPOL 73/78, as reflected in annual FSI Sub-Committee documents.

particularly if the offending vessel is merely transiting through adjacent waters.

In situations where neither the port or coastal state enjoys enforcement jurisdiction, it is up to the flag state to take the requisite action against the offending vessel. In such cases, coastal and port states with information on relevant violations will typically refer the case to the flag state for further investigation and prosecution. Of course, the major stumbling block to successful enforcement of MARPOL 73/78 has been the reluctance and lack of incentives on the part of flag states to take action against their flag vessels.

Tables 5-1 and 5-2 summarise the available data on action taken and penalties imposed by port states against visiting ships for various offences. Tables 5-3 and 5-4 lay out the corresponding data for flag state action.

From Table 5-2, it can be seen that port state enforcement remains uneven throughout the world. The data must be viewed with caution, however, because of the low number of states reporting on the matter.⁷⁰⁸ Since 1990, only a handful of states have provided annual information to IMO on port state control, the majority of them being OECD countries. On average, only around 20 per cent of all MARPOL 73/78 state parties have ever submitted information on port state control to IMO. Indeed, many states which submit the annual mandatory enforcement reports required under MARPOL 73/78 fail to provide specific information on port state control, thereby reducing the returns for this category of enforcement.⁷⁰⁹ One reason suggested for such low reporting rates is the fact that different authorities may be responsible within states for SOLAS and MARPOL matters respectively.⁷¹⁰

It can generally be discerned from Tables 5-1 and 5-2 that more inspections and detentions are being carried out annually by those port states which are diligently reporting on enforcement. Most reported inspections relate to equipment, Oil Record Book (ORB) and International Oil Pollution Prevention Certificate (IOPPC) deficiencies. The compliance rate for each of these categories is reportedly high, often well over 90 per cent.⁷¹¹ Again, due to the low number of returns from state parties, it is impossible to draw accurate and reliable conclusions from the statistics.

That said, one key observation appears incontestable. Table 5-4 suggests, albeit from sketchy responses, that the number of cases referred by coastal states for flag state action exceeds that in which action has been reportedly taken by flag states.⁷¹² It would thus appear that the

---

⁷⁰⁸ See submission of the Netherlands on Deficiency Reports, Detention Statistics and Deficiency Statistics, FSI Docs. 8/10/2 (2000) and 7/INF.7 (1999), highlighting deficiencies in the reporting system such as low returns and incomplete or unclear submissions. All these factors substantially affect the quality of the statistics received.

⁷⁰⁹ The information on port state control is obtained through the same circular used to solicit annual mandatory reports, viz. MEPC/Circ.318, supra note 706. Note that port states typically inspect and detain ships for a variety of factors, chief of which are the safety and manning requirements. The statistics in Table 5-2, however, relate only to enforcement action vis-à-vis pollution control deficiencies as reported by states.

⁷¹⁰ Report of the FSI Sub-Committee's 10th session, FSI Doc. 10/17 (2002).

⁷¹¹ See Table 5-1.

⁷¹² Further evidence of flag state inaction can be found in the results of a study published in 1989, which found that flag states took action in only 17 per cent of referrals by North Sea states, see M. Stoop, Olieverontreiniging door schepen op der Noordzee over de periode 1982–1987: Opsporing en vervolging (1989), cited in Mitchell, supra note 68, at 163. A similar study reported to IMO in 1992 found that during the period 1983 to 1990, flag states reported taking action in only 206 out of 1,077 cases (20 per cent) referred to them for action, G. Peet, Operational Discharges From Ships: An Evaluation of the Application of the Discharge Provisions of the MARPOL Convention by its Contracting Parties (1992).

rate of flag state action following coastal state referrals remains very low. This indicates a low degree of flag state compliance with the relevant IMO requirements.[713]

A more complete and reliable assessment of port state enforcement emerges from the records of the Secretariats to the European and Asia-Pacific Memoranda of Understanding (MOU) on Port State Control and the US Coast Guard. These records reflect a clearer picture of not only enforcement by states, but compliance by industry. In this regard, the MOU and national authorities' records are useful tools for studying the compliance behaviour of the various actors, including shipowners, flag states and classification societies. The data is given in Tables 5-5 to 5-11.

The MOU Secretariats and national port state control authorities such as the US Coast Guard maintain profiles of those flag states whose vessels are most frequently detained. The detentions relate to all forms of deficiencies and not just pollution-related ones such as non-existing or unsatisfactory IOPP Certificates. A three-year rolling average method is typically used to compute the average rate of ship detentions as a percentage of the number of ships entering ports. Flag states for whom detention rates exceed the rolling average are then identified for vessel priority inspections.

In recent years, port state control authorities have begun targeting ships based not only on the performance records of the flags they fly, but also on the records of the classification societies they employ. This is a welcome development which will compel owners to be more discerning with the classification societies they use as well as encourage the societies themselves to upgrade their performance. This trend to target ships using broader criteria should be extended to the managers, insurers, charterers and financiers of ships as well so as to create industry-wide disincentives for sub-standard practices. Indeed, the US Coast Guard now requires ships to submit information on charterer identity as part of its 96-hour Advanced Notice of Arrival. Lists of charterers, ship management companies as well as last ports of call associated with detained ships are now published on the Coast Guard website.[714]

---

[713] One reason for the low flag state response rate could be the time lag between the incident leading to the report and the finalisation of flag state investigations into the matter, see MEPC Doc. 48/12 (2002).

[714] http://www.uscg.mil/hq/g-m/pscweb/index.htm (last accessed 17 Nov. 2004). Charterers began to be targeted from 1 Jul. 2004.

Table 5-5. State Reports to the Paris MOU on Port State Control

	1984	1985	1986	1987	1988	1989	1990	1991	1992	1993
No. of MOU states reporting	14	14	14	14	14	14	14	14	15	15
No. of ships inspected	7,686	7,879	8,721	10,337	8,382	9,164	9,842	10,101	10,455	11,252
Total no. of inspections	**10,227**	**10,417**	**11,740**	**11,451**	**11,224**	**12,459**	**13,955**	**14,379**	**14,783**	**17,294**
Ave. no. of inspections per report	731	744	839	818	802	890	997	1,027	986	1,153
Total no. of IOPPC discrepancies	828	652	572	407	332	265	317	297	353	422
Ave. no. of IOPPC discrepancies per report	59	47	41	29	24	19	23	21	24	28
IOPPC discrepancies as % of ships inspected	10.8	8.3	6.6	3.9	4.0	2.9	3.2	2.9	3.4	3.8
No. of ships delayed/detained (d/d)	**476**	**356**	**307**	**280**	**295**	**344**	**441**	**525**	**588**	**926**
Ave. no. of d/d per report	34	25	22	20	21	25	32	38	39	62
d/d, as % of ships inspected	6.2	4.5	3.5	2.7	3.5	3.8	4.5	5.2	5.6	8.2
d/d, as % of inspections	4.7	3.4	2.6	2.4	2.6	2.8	3.2	3.7	4.0	6.4

	1994	1995	1996	1997	1998	1999	2000	2001	2002	2003
No. of MOU states reporting	16	16	17	18	18	18	19	19	19	19
No. of ships inspected	10,694	10,563	10,256	10,719	11,168	11,248	11,358	11,658	11,823	12,382
Total no. of inspections	**16,964**	**16,381**	**16,070**	**16,813**	**17,643**	**18,399**	**18,559**	**18,681**	**19,766**	**20,309**
Ave. no. of inspections per report	1,060	1,024	945	934	980	1,022	977	983	1,040	1,069
Total no. of IOPPC discrepancies	604	896	888	861	814	852	NA	NA	NA	NA
Ave. no. of IOPPC discrepancies per report	38	56	52	48	45	47	NA	NA	NA	NA
IOPPC discrepancies as % of ships inspected	5.6	8.5	8.7	8.0	7.3	7.6	NA	NA	NA	NA
No. of ships delayed/detained (d/d)	**1,597**	**1,837**	**1,719**	**1,624**	**1,598**	**1,684**	**1,764**	**1,699**	**1,577**	**1,428**
Ave. no. of d/d per report	100	115	101	90	89	94	93	89	83	75
d/d, as % of ships inspected	14.9	17.4	16.8	15.2	14.3	15.0	15.5	14.6	13.4	11.5
d/d, as % of inspections	9.4	11.2	10.7	9.7	9.1	9.2	9.5	9.1	8.0	7.0

Notes: Since 2000, IOPPC discrepancies are no longer listed as a separate deficiency. The figures above are for all ship types, not just tankers.

Sources: Paris MOU Annual Reports, FSI and MEPC documents and R. MITCHELL, INTENTIONAL OIL POLLUTION AT SEA (1994).

Table 5-6. *Paris MOU – Flag States on Black List, based on inspections and detentions and Excess Factor over three-year period from 2001 to 2003* **(poorest performance first)**

	Flags	Inspections 2001-2003	Detentions 2001-2003	Excess Factor 2001-2003
1.	Albania (1)	191	92	12.68
2.	São Tomé & Principe (3)	72	32	10.18
3.	Korea, Dem. People's Rep. (7)	102	43	9.98
4.	Tonga (4)	139	56	9.78
5.	Bolivia (2)	78	32	9.24
6.	Comoros (–)	77	25	7.39
7.	Lebanon (5)	218	66	7.07
8.	Honduras (8)	219	65	6.89
9.	Algeria (6)	204	56	6.14
10.	Georgia (10)	378	96	5.92
11.	Cambodia (9)	989	224	5.50
12.	Turkey (11)	2,463	503	5.03
13.	Syrian Arab Republic (12)	340	66	4.00
14.	St Vincent & Grenadines (16)	2,484	417	3.86
15.	Romania (14)	186	35	3.44
16.	Morocco (17)	197	33	2.87
17.	Belize (15)	368	52	2.43
18.	Ukraine (18)	703	93	2.40
19.	Egypt (19)	182	27	2.26
20.	Panama (20)	5,552	489	1.40
21.	India (22)	171	20	1.33
22.	Bulgaria (23)	284	30	1.26
23.	Iran, Islamic Rep. of (–)	214	23	1.18
24.	Cyprus (25)	3,792	300	1.07
25.	Malta (21)	4,696	364	1.04
26.	Libya (13)	31	5	1.00

Notes: Numbers in brackets denote position in black list for previous three-year period (2000–2). Comoros and Iran are new entrants to the black list. The flags from Syria upwards to Albania (in italics) are considered 'very high risk'.
Sources: Paris MOU Annual Reports, 2002 and 2003.

The Paris and Tokyo MOU and US Coast Guard statistics show that the flag states with the most serious detention records include Albania, Algeria, Belize, Bolivia, Cambodia, Honduras, Lebanon, North Korea, São Tomé and Principe, St Vincent and the Grenadines, Tonga and

Table 5-7. *Paris MOU – Classification Societies with Highest Class-Related Detainable Deficiencies (in detentions as percentage of total inspections), 2003 (poorest performance first)*

1.	Register of Shipping (RS) (Albania)
2.	INCLAMAR (INC) (Cyprus)
3.	International Naval Surveys Bureau (INSB) (Greece)
4.	International Register of Shipping (IRS) (USA)
5.	Hellenic Register of Shipping (HRS) (Greece)
6.	China Corporation Register of Shipping (CCRS) (PR China)
7.	China Classification Society (CCS) (PR China)
8.	Polski Rejestr Statkow (PRS) (Poland)
9.	Turkisch Lloyd (TS) (Turkey)
10.	Bulgarski Koraben Registar (BKR) (Bulgaria)

Notes: Countries in brackets denote location of classification society and not necessarily any connection with the maritime administrations of these countries.
Sources: Paris MOU Annual Report, 2003.

Tunisia.[715] Several of these flags are not major open registries, but emerging registries with substantial proportions of tonnage made up of nationally owned vessels. Such vessels typically operate in developing regions of the world where port state control mechanisms are weak. Moreover, their flag state administrations and classification authorities are often little-known national entities which lack resources to supervise their vessels effectively. It is thus critical for IMO and the shipping community to pay more attention to the performance of these national flags. On their part, several traditional open registries – e.g. Panama, Malta and Cyprus – are showing signs of improved standards on board their flag vessels. This is largely due to the pressure imposed by the port states, IMO and responsible owners themselves.

3.2 *The Provision of Waste Reception Facilities in Ports*

The provision of reception facilities in ports has been a long-standing issue of contention. Successive instruments culminating in MARPOL 73/78 had sought to oblige states to provide reception facilities in ports and loading terminals, particularly those located within the designated

---

[715] See also the shipping industry's own assessment of flags, *infra* note 988, which identifies largely the same flags as the worst performers.

Table 5-8. State Reports to the Tokyo MOU on Port State Control

	1994	1995	1996	1997	1998	1999	2000	2001	2002	2003
Administrations reporting	11	12	15	16	16	17	17	17	17	18
No. of inspections	8,000	8,834	12,243	12,957	14,545	14,921	16,304	17,379	19,588	20,124
Ave. no. per report	727	736	816	810	909	878	959	1,022	1,152	1,118
As % of ship visits into MOU ports	32	39	50	52	60	61	65	71	78	77
No. of detentions	282	524	689	830	1,061	1,071	1,101	1,349	1,307	1,709
Ave. no. per report	26	44	46	52	66	63	65	79	77	95
As % of inspections	3.80	5.93	5.63	6.41	7.29	7.18	6.87	7.76	6.67	8.49

Sources: Tokyo MOU Annual Reports, FSI Sub-Committee documents.

Table 5-9. *Tokyo MOU – Flag States on Black List, based on inspections and detentions and Excess Factor over three-year period from 2001 to 2003 (poorest performance first)*

Flags	Inspections 2001-2003	Detentions 2001-2003	Excess Factor 2001-2003
1. Korea, Dem.People's Rep. (1)	666	367	15.95
2. Mongolia (–)	99	48	11.96
3. Bolivia (2)	85	37	10.15
4. Cambodia (4)	2,747	741	7.20
5. Indonesia (3)	525	139	6.45
6. Belize (5)	1,890	405	5.30
7. Vietnam (6)	446	90	4.38
8. Honduras (7)	390	73	3.86
9. Bangladesh (8)	38	10	3.79
10. Papua New Guinea (13)	45	8	1.83
11. Tonga (–)	83	12	1.59
12. Egypt (–)	78	11	1.45
13. Taiwan (–)	591	57	1.25
14. Russian Federation (10)	1,424	124	1.18
15. Malaysia (9)	1,091	96	1.15
16. St Vincent & Grenadines (12)	1,189	103	1.13
17. Thailand (11)	656	59	1.08

Notes: Numbers in brackets denote position in black list for previous three-year period (2000–2).
Sources: Tokyo MOU Annual Report, 2003.

'special areas'.[716] In this respect, it had been the original intention of the OILPOL and MARPOL negotiators that as a *quid pro quo* for mandating pollution control equipment and practices on board ships, states would provide port facilities for the reception of wastes retained by ships. Quite apart from this political understanding between states and industry, it made logical sense that if wastes were to be prohibited from being discharged overboard, some shore-based facility had to be made available to receive them.

Unfortunately, states have consistently ignored their obligation to provide adequate reception facilities in ports. Instead, their response to growing environmental pressures has been to tighten further the regulations on overboard discharges and to mandate new equipment

---

[716] MARPOL 73/78, Annex I, reg. 12. See Ch. 3 for details.

Table 5-10. Flag States Targeted by US Coast Guard on Account of Detention Ratios (D. R.) Higher than Three-year Overall Average

Flag State	D. R. (%) (1997-1999) 3-year overall ave: 5.08%	Flag State	D. R. (%) (1998-2000) 3-year overall ave: 3.55%	Flag State	D. R. (%) (1999-2001) 3-year overall ave: 2.69%	Flag State	D. R. (%) (2000-2002) 3-year overall ave: 2.41%	Flag State	D. R. (%) (2001-2003) 3-year overall ave: 2.22%
1. Belize	50.56	Bolivia	100.00	Bolivia	42.86	Cambodia	46.15	Cambodia	41.67
2. Honduras	39.06	Cambodia	42.86	Cambodia	30.77	Bolivia	37.50	Bolivia	22.22
3. Venezuela	13.95	Belize	38.20	Belize	23.08	Algeria	21.74	Algeria	20.83
4. St Vincent & Grenadines	11.43	Honduras	25.51	Algeria	18.52	Belize	16.67	Mexico	19.35
5. Turkey	11.41	St Vincent & Grenadines	8.43	Honduras	18.18	Brazil	16.22	Venezuela	18.18
6. India	8.94	Turkey	7.25	Venezuela	14.29	Mexico	13.79	Brazil	14.63
7. Cyprus	8.19	India	7.09	Brazil	12.50	Venezuela	12.90	St Vincent & Grenadines	11.48
8. Vanuatu	7.84	Antigua & Barbuda	5.56	Mexico	12.50	Honduras	10.39	Ukraine	8.70
9. Thailand	7.23	Cyprus	5.42	Latvia	11.11	Lithuania	8.82	Belize	7.55
10. Panama	6.92	Panama	5.17	India	7.58	St Vincent & Grenadines	8.38	Honduras	6.52
11. Malta	6.70	Russia	5.17	Turkey	6.77	Bulgaria	7.41	Turkey	5.71
12. Russia	5.83	Malta	4.75	Portugal	6.67	Turkey	7.20	Lithuania	5.41
13. Antigua & Barbuda	5.59	Philippines	3.59	Lithuania	6.25	India	5.56	Croatia	4.76

Notes: Detention ratios are based on data for successive three-year periods.
Sources: US Coast Guard Port State Control Reports, 1999–2001; FSI Docs. 9/6/4, 10/INF.10, 11/INF.2 and 12/INF.5.

Table 5-11. *Classification Societies Targeted by US Coast Guard for Priority I Inspections in 2002 and 2003, based on performance over three-year periods (2000–2 and 2001–3) (poorest performance first)*

2002 (for period 2000–2002)	2003 (for period 2001–2003)
1. Phoenix Register of Shipping (PHRS)	INCLAMAR (INC) (Cyprus)
2. Panama Ship Register (PSR) (Panama)	Phoenix Register of Shipping (PHRS)
3. INCLAMAR (INC) (Cyprus)	Panama Ship Register (PSR) (Panama)
4. Panama Maritime Surveyors Bureau, Inc. (PMS) (Panama)	Isthmus Bureau of Shipping, S.A. (IBS) (Panama)
5. Isthmus Bureau of Shipping, S.A. (IBS) (Panama)	Panama Maritime Documentation Services (PMDS) (Panama)
6. Honduras International Naval Surveying and Inspection Bureau (HINSB) (Honduras)	International Register of Shipping (IRS) (USA)
7. Panama Maritime Documentation Services (PMDS) (Panama)	Honduras International Naval Surveying and Inspection Bureau (HINSB) (Honduras)
8. Hellenic Register of Shipping (HRS) (Greece)	Panama Register Corporation (PRC) (Panama)
9. Panama Register Corporation (PRC) (Panama)	Hellenic Register of Shipping (HRS) (Greece)
10. International Register of Shipping (IRS) (USA)	Polski Rejestr Statkow (PRS) (Poland)
11. China Corporation Register of Shipping (CCRS) (PR China)	

Sources: US Coast Guard Port State Control Reports, 2002 and 2003.

standards for ships. Indeed, states have generally supported all forms of ship-based measures, as long as these averted the need for shore-based facilities. Yet, reception facilities continue to be needed in a variety of situations. Oily slops and bilges are still being produced in large quantities by non-tankers. On their part, tankers continue to generate slops during short or rough-weather voyages as well as when carrying incompatible successive cargoes or when conducting tank cleanings. Even SBT-equipped tankers produce sludges when undergoing tank cleaning prior to dry-docking.

Despite these problems, states worldwide remain averse to the high costs of reception facilities, preferring instead to deflect the burden onto industry. Apart from direct construction and maintenance costs, states fear that the imposition of charges for the use of reception facilities may affect their ports' commercial competitiveness. This concern would be especially pertinent if neighbouring ports do not require the use of such facilities. Consequently, the uneven provision of reception facilities has raised concern throughout the world – particularly in Europe – over the distortion in competition arising among different ports and shipping companies.[717]

The states' reluctance to construct reception facilities has also been compounded by the realisation that received slops must be treated on land. Without some capacity for recovery, reprocessing and reuse of wastes, the transfer of slops from sea to land only introduces new environmental concerns. Thus, the problem is not just one of reception, but of ultimate disposal as well. Yet, facilities which are capable of recycling slops are prohibitively expensive and are not readily available even in the most developed states.

Where reception facilities are provided, states have commonly sought to pass on the costs to shipowners in the form of high port dues or charges. There have even been allegations of ports which unscrupulously charge for non-existent or inadequate reception facilities. Complaints have also arisen regarding ports which refuse to permit overboard disposal of clean ballast and yet impose high charges for receiving these on shore.[718] Other common complaints relate to ports which require ships to discharge slops on the high seas and to enter port in clean condition and ports which refuse altogether to provide berths for oily ballast discharges.[719]

The shipping industry has consistently raised such problems with IMO. In particular, the industry representatives – INTERTANKO, ICS and BIMCO – have frequently highlighted instances of unavailable, inadequate or exorbitantly priced facilities in ports.[720] The industry also opposes the passing of reception costs to ships in the form of high port dues.[721] Over the years, the shipping interests have presented IMO with numerous surveys on the worldwide availability of reception

---

[717] See e.g. submission of the European Commission, MEPC Doc. 29/21 (1990).
[718] E.g. ports in the Ukraine and the Red Sea region, see submissions of INTERTANKO, MEPC Docs. 36/13/1 (1994) and 37/16/1 (1995).
[719] E.g. Pakistan and the Russian Federation respectively, *ibid*.
[720] *Ibid*. INTERTANKO maintains a compilation of port reception facilities worldwide, see Reception Facilities for Tankers, *attached to* MEPC Doc. 35/INF.23 (1994) (updated in 1996, *attached to* MEPC Doc. 38/INF.22 (1996)).
[721] Submissions of INTERTANKO, MEPC Docs. 27/5/4 (1989), 32/10 (1992), 34/12 (1993), 38/INF.22 (1996) and 52/9 (2004).

facilities. Such surveys are typically conducted by having ship masters make confidential reports on the availability and adequacy of reception facilities in visited ports.[722]

The surveys have consistently revealed that a great number of the world's ports, including major oil exporting and importing terminals, fail to provide adequate facilities for the reception of oily wastes, chemicals and garbage.[723] Such surveys have also found that ports with inadequate facilities are located in both the developed and developing countries. In addition to the industry surveys, IMO itself maintains a list of reception facilities generated through reports submitted by the states themselves.[724] The industry surveys and state reports are reflected in Tables 5-12 and 5-13 respectively.

The tables above reflect only the situation in ports which have been the subject of reports by ship masters and states. Hence, facilities are not necessarily absent or inadequate in non-reported ports, of which there are many. Also, the low number of reporting states in Table 5-13 relative to the total number of MARPOL 73/78 state parties cautions against a generalisation of the situation for all states. In this regard, the industry surveys in Table 5-12 cover a greater number of ports in more countries, thereby reducing the margin of error and improving reliability considerably.

Reporting rates appear to be much higher in the OECD states than in the developing countries. While this may reveal a higher absolute number of absent facilities in the OECD states, it does not necessarily mean that these states have a greater share of ports without reception facilities. In addition, the number of reports has increased over the years with the latest surveys showing a higher number of returns. Consequently, while these reports may show a large number of ports lacking reception facilities, they do not necessarily prove that the provision of facilities has deteriorated over time. In fact, it would appear from

---

[722] INTERTANKO has a Terminal Vetting Database that allows a master to fill out a rating system assessing a terminal's performance while his vessel is alongside.

[723] See the results of a survey conducted by ICS in 1990, *attached to* MEPC Doc. 30/INF.30 (1990). Earlier surveys were presented to IMO in 1983 and 1985. For similar surveys by BIMCO, see Reference Manual on Reception Facilities, *attached to* MEPC Doc. 36/INF.4 (1994). All these surveys are reflected in Table 5-12. See also submissions by BIMCO, MEPC Docs. 41/11 (1998) and 41/11/1 (1998).

[724] The reports are reproduced by MEPC in Circulars MEPC.3/Circ.3, MEPC.3/Circ.4, MEPC.4/Circ.4 and MEPC.4/Circ.5. The latter two relate to reception facilities for noxious liquid substances (Annex II to MARPOL 73/78).

Table 5-12. *Availability of Reception Facilities (RFs) as Reported by Industry Surveys Commissioned in Various Years*

	1983 ICS	1985 ICS	1990 ICS	1994 BIMCO	1996 INTER-TANKO
Worldwide					
- No. of states surveyed	93	82	63	117	81
- No. of ports surveyed	300	328	179	1149	406
- No. of ports without RFs	197	204	110	475	103
- *% of ports without RFs*	**66**	**62**	**61**	**41**	**25**
United States					
- No. of ports surveyed	19	32	23	84	40
- No. of ports without RFs	10	23	12	28	1
- *% of ports without RFs*	**53**	**72**	**52**	**33**	**2.5**
OECD countries (non-US)					
- No. of states surveyed	17	19	15	23	22
- No. of ports surveyed	101	133	63	761	210
- No. of ports without RFs	63	58	29	260	32
- *% of ports without RFs*	**62**	**44**	**46**	**34**	**15**
OPEC countries					
- No. of states surveyed	12	12	9	11	10
- No. of ports surveyed	51	49	24	38	35
- No. of ports without RFs	46	41	19	27	18
- *% of ports without RFs*	**90**	**84**	**79**	**71**	**51**
Non-OPEC/non-OECD countries					
- No. of states surveyed	63	50	38	83	48
- No. of ports surveyed	129	114	69	266	121
- No. of ports without RFs	78	82	50	160	52
- *% of ports without RFs*	**60**	**72**	**72**	**60**	**43**

Notes: Figures for the US and several OECD countries include reports for overseas territories and possessions. States surveyed include those which were not MARPOL 73/78 parties at the relevant time.

Sources: 1996 – MEPC Doc. 38/INF.22 (INTERTANKO); 1994 – MEPC Doc. 36/INF.4 (BIMCO); 1990 – MEPC Doc. 30/INF.30 (ICS); 1985 – MEPC Doc. 22/8/2 (ICS); 1983 – MEPC Doc. 19/5/2 (ICS).

Table 5-13. *Availability of Reception Facilities (RFs) as Reported by States to IMO*

	1956	1964	1973/76	1980/84	1985/93	1994	1995/99	2003
All countries								
- States reporting on RFs	40	31	27	40	37	44	57	58
- Total no. of state parties	65	69	80	113	77	86	109	127
- % of Parties reporting on RFs	**62**	**45**	**34**	**35**	**48**	**51**	**52**	**46**
- Total no. of ports	162	189	353	508	993	NA	1978	2004
- No. of ports without RFs	37	31	37	22	104	NA	445	182
- % of ports without RFs	**23**	**16**	**10**	**4**	**10**	**NA**	**22**	**9**
United States								
- Total no. of ports	14	14	55	39	325	NA	1033	1033
- No. of ports without RFs	0	0	0	0	36	NA	73	73
- % of ports without RFs	**0**	**0**	**0**	**0**	**11**	**NA**	**7**	**7**
OECD countries (excluding US)								
- States reporting on RFs	19	18	17	18	17	17	23	23
- Total no. of state parties	24	24	24	24	20	21	28	28
- % of Parties reporting on RFs	**79**	**75**	**71**	**75**	**85**	**81**	**82**	**82**
- Total no. of ports	121	149	260	390	575	NA	781	752
- No. of ports without RFs	27	22	36	14	48	NA	309	49
- % of ports without RFs	**22**	**15**	**14**	**4**	**8**	**NA**	**40**	**7**
Non-OECD countries								
- States reporting on RFs	20	12	9	21	19	26	33	34
- Total no. of state parties	40	44	55	88	56	64	80	98
- % of Parties reporting on RFs	**50**	**27**	**16**	**24**	**34**	**41**	**41**	**35**
- Total no. of ports	27	26	38	79	93	NA	164	219

Table 5-13. (cont.)

	1956	1964	1973/76	1980/84	1985/93	1994	1995/99	2003
- No. of ports without RFs	10	9	1	8	20	NA	63	60
- % of ports without RFs	37	35	3	10	22	NA	38	27

Notes: The figures are computed to the best of the author's ability, relying on state submissions to IMO. Due to incomplete information in these submissions, the accuracy of the figures cannot be guaranteed. The reports appear to build on state responses solicited from previous exercises. Hence, the latest reports do not necessarily indicate fresh information. For instance, the US figures for 1995/99 and 2003 appear to stem from the same report compiled in September 1990, the (unlikely) assumption being that the situation has not changed in a decade. Also, the list of reporting states in 2003 (Table 5-14 below) mirrors that in 1995/99 very closely, with only one new reporting state appearing in 2003. The figures include reports by a small number of states which were not parties to MARPOL 73/78 at the relevant date but which submitted reports nonetheless. The pre-1984 reports include those submitted by a few OILPOL 54 parties.
Sources: 2003 – MEPC.3/Circ.4; 1995/99 – MEPC.3/Circ.1, MEPC.3/Circ.2, MEPC.3/Circ.2/Add.1, MEPC.3/Circ.3, MEPC.3/Circ.3/Add.1; 1994 – MEPC/Circ.278; 1985/93 – MEPC/Circ. 234, MEPC/Circ.234/Add.1, MEPC/Circ.234/Add.2, MEPC/Circ.234/Add.3; 1956, 1964, 1973/76 and 1980/84 – R. MITCHELL, INTENTIONAL OIL POLLUTION AT SEA (1994) and various IMO documents.

Table 5-13 that the situation has improved considerably between 1999 and 2003, particularly in the developed countries.

Another point of caution relates to how non-availability is assessed. The industry surveys typically request ship masters or states to indicate whether facilities are available to receive not only ballast water, but also other types of wastes such as tank washings, oily mixtures containing chemicals, scale and sludge from tanker cleaning, oily bilge water and sludge from fuel oil purifiers. For many ports, facilities are available for the reception of one or more types of such wastes but *not* necessarily all of them. In such situations, this study treats such ports as having made reception facilities available. In other words, only those ports which are wholly incapable of receiving wastes of *any* form are considered to be lacking in facilities. This assumption is necessary in order to simplify the tabulation of the survey results. However, it is acknowledged that this underestimates the total number of ports lacking facilities of *some* kind or other as well as masks the *inadequacy* of many of these facilities.

Indeed, the surveys summarised above only reflect the availability of reception facilities in ports; they do not testify to the *adequacy* of these facilities or to their *cost-reasonableness*. Yet, the problem facing many shipowners is not so much the availability of facilities but their adequacy and cost. In this regard, often accompanying the ship masters' responses to industry surveys are various personal observations relating to adequacy and cost. Due to their irregular and highly subjective nature, these comments are not analysed here. Suffice it to say that according to these comments, problems of inadequacy and high costs are regularly encountered in both developed and developing countries.

It should also be noted that neither the shipping industry nor IMO has ever subjected their survey results to comprehensive analyses. In all cases, the results had simply been presented in the form of lists sorted according to port, country and availability of facilities. For the shipowners' purposes, such tabulation is all that is necessary given that the industry surveys are meant simply for the ship masters' reference. Whatever analyses employing more meaningful criteria such as geographical distribution, the extent of non-availability and adequacy have only been attempted by observers such as academic writers.[725]

Despite these analytical constraints, it is nevertheless possible to draw several conclusions from the surveys. For one thing, the provision of reception facilities remains unsatisfactory worldwide, particularly in the developing states. A great number of MARPOL 73/78 state parties are clearly failing in their obligation to provide facilities of *any* kind, not to mention adequate ones. The industry surveys reported in Table 5-12, for instance, point to an average of some 40 to 50 per cent of ports worldwide not having reception facilities.

The figure is much lower for the state self-reporting scheme – from Table 5-13, it appears that only 10 to 20 per cent of ports do not have facilities. This apparent discrepancy can be explained by the far smaller number of states surveyed in Table 5-13. Moreover, it is highly probable that the states with the worst records for providing facilities have not submitted reports to IMO. Conversely, the states with good compliance records would have had every incentive to report on this. On balance, these factors render the industry surveys in Table 5-12 to be more accurate and reliable.

Both the industry and state reports conclude that the highest proportion of ports lacking reception facilities are to be found in the

---

[725] E.g. Mitchell, *supra* note 68.

developing countries. In particular, Table 5-12 shows that in the OPEC countries (all of which are developing states), an average of 70 per cent of ports do not have facilities. This is followed by the developing non-OPEC countries, where an average of 60 per cent of ports lack facilities. In general, the developed Baltic and North Sea regions in Europe and the United States appear to have the highest concentration of facilities, even though inadequacies and high charges are frequently encountered in these areas as well.

As shown by the surveys, ports in oil-producing countries are among the most deficient in providing facilities for oily wastes. The lack of reception facilities in the major oil-exporting states is all the more troubling given that it is in their very ports that facilities are most needed for ships terminating their ballast voyages.[726] Indeed, many major oil-producing states are not even parties to MARPOL 73/78. Of the eleven OPEC countries, only Algeria, Indonesia, Iran, Nigeria and Venezuela are MARPOL 73/78 parties. Iraq, Kuwait, Libya, Qatar, Saudi Arabia and the United Arab Emirates are non-parties. Of the Persian Gulf oil producers, only Oman and Iran are parties to the convention.[727]

Nor is the situation any better in MARPOL special areas. In fact, ports located within these areas appear to be no more likely to have reception facilities than ports elsewhere. In the case of the Mediterranean, Black and Baltic Seas, the MARPOL 73 negotiators had originally intended these special areas to take effect from 1 January 1977, the date by which reception facilities would have been required. In contrast, reception facilities were only required 'as soon as possible' in the developing Red Sea and Persian Gulf regions. To date, however, only the Baltic Sea and Northwest European[728] special areas appear to have met the requirement for adequate reception facilities under Regulation 10 of Annex I. The other two original special areas, the Mediterranean and Black Seas, as well as the Red Sea, the Persian Gulf and the Gulf of Aden, continue to demonstrate unsatisfactory compliance with the requirement.[729]

---

[726] The OPEC countries of the Middle East currently produce 23 per cent of the world's oil supply. In addition, the Middle East accounts for 65 per cent of proven oil reserves, see INTERTANKO, *supra* note 14, at 69.
[727] Reportedly, all the countries in the region have started the ratification process, see MEPC Doc. INF.5 (2002).
[728] The Northwest European special area was designated only in 1997 and came into effect in 1999.
[729] Had the 'special area' status been made conditional upon the prior provision of adequate reception facilities, it is arguable that the Mediterranean and Black Seas would not have qualified.

The unanimous conclusion of industry, academic observers as well as of IMO itself has been that a great number of the world's ports fail to provide adequate facilities for the reception of oily wastes. The same is generally true for reception facilities for chemical wastes, sewage and garbage, the provision of which is required under Annexes II, IV and V of MARPOL 73/78 respectively.[730] In fairness to the states, a significant number of shipowners have themselves been recalcitrant in refusing or neglecting to use reception facilities even where these are provided at affordable cost.[731] Ostensibly, ships avoided using such facilities not only because of the direct cost factor but also because visits to the facilities delayed their schedules.

There are also ports which are known to be inefficient or slow in operating reception facilities. Often, these facilities may be inconveniently located away from loading terminals, thereby necessitating a separate and lengthy diversion. At times, there may be great demand by a number of ships or the facilities may simply be unable to receive residues at a rate or in such quantities as to prevent undue delay. In such circumstances, the temptation to discharge wastes illegally into the sea is great. In other instances, problems arise from the practice of charterers inserting contractual clauses which impose tight schedules on tankers arriving in port.[732] The tankers will invariably resort to illegal discharges if a visit to reception facilities will cause delay.

In recent years, the problems with reception facilities have led to a growing tendency for states to shift the responsibility for minimising discharges onto the ships themselves. Hence, regulators have become increasingly enchanted with waste reduction, rather than treatment, schemes. At the same time, requirements for suitably designed and equipped ships have become common, as has the imposition of contractual commitments within charterparties (e.g. the so-called 'clean-seas' clause) to conduct proper waste discharges.

In particular, charterers typically impose the 'clean-seas' clause in areas where loading ports do not maintain adequate reception facilities. Tankers are then required to arrive with clean ballast at loading ports. Yet, compliance with such clauses is virtually impossible for tankers

---

[730] MARPOL 73/78, Annex I, reg. 12; Annex II, reg. 7; Annex IV, reg. 10; Annex V, reg. 7; and Annex VI, reg. 17.
[731] In the 1980s, for instance, a pilot project in Germany to provide reception facilities at no charge to ships attracted only lukewarm response from shipowners, see submission of Germany, MEPC Doc. 27/16 (1989).
[732] See concerns expressed by INTERTANKO in MEPC Docs. 31/21 (1991) and 32/10 (1992).

which are not fitted with SBTs and which only operate in special areas. In addition, if these tankers perform short voyages (as in the Mediterranean, for instance), the operation of LOT would be impossible given the insufficient time for oil and water to separate.[733] In the result, illegal overboard discharges *invariably* occur.[734]

As it turned out, that familiar disagreement between states and the oil companies as to who should pay for shore reception facilities[735] has found a new and practicable solution – waste minimisation and the transfer of costs onto the ship itself. As a result, states continue to avoid their obligation to provide reception facilities, the oil companies (with their increasingly smaller shipowning interests) remain largely indifferent while the independent shipowners end up bearing the bulk of the costs.

Applying the earlier analysis of authority, capacity and incentive to this problem, it can be appreciated that all states possess the legal authority to provide reception facilities. This authority arises from multilateral instruments such as MARPOL 73/78.[736] What is clear, though, is the fact that a great number of states fail to provide facilities for want of *ability* and *incentives*, not authority. Certainly, the majority of developing states lack the financial and manpower resources needed to construct and operate such facilities. At the same time, these actors lack the incentive, particularly if the marine pollution problem is not a priority item on the national agenda. After all, public demands for addressing marine pollution are seldom heard in developing countries which are often more pre-occupied with economic challenges or terrestrial environmental problems.

The major concern is, of course, with the oil-exporting states. These actors not only have the legal authority to provide reception facilities, but clearly the monetary capacity as well. Yet, on account of lack of incentives, compliance is rarely demonstrated. For actors such as the OPEC states, the problem of overboard discharges is literally someone

---

[733] Submission of INTERTANKO, MEPC Doc. 34/INF.26 (1993).
[734] In recent years, shipowners faced with this conundrum have criticised the 'clean-sea' clauses which, in their view, contravene the spirit of MARPOL 73/78 and effectively deter the development of reception facilities, see submission of INTERTANKO, MEPC Doc. 37/16/1 (1995).
[735] See Ch. 3.
[736] Although one may argue that regs. 10 and 12 of Annex I only require state parties to 'undertake to ensure' the provision of facilities. Be that as it may, there are practically no problems in asserting that states have the legal authority to provide reception facilities if they are minded to.

else's – most offending tankers typically arrive in oil-loading ports in a clean condition after having cleaned their tanks and illegally discharged wastes in mid-ocean or in some other state's waters. There is thus little incentive for the oil-exporting states to bear the costs of providing reception facilities in their ports. Consequently, it is no surprise that the special area regimes in the Red Sea, Persian Gulf and Gulf of Aden remain unimplemented.

The statistics available to IMO demonstrate that where reception facilities have been made available, these are mainly to be found in the developed states with the requisite authority, capacity and incentives to provide the facilities. Evidently, environmental consciousness in the wealthy, pluralist democracies provides greater incentives for governments to comply with pollution control requirements. Conversely, the problem is more acute in the developing states precisely because the associated costs often fall on governments with little ability or incentives to provide facilities.

In many ways, the reception facilities problem is not a surprising one; the drafters of MARPOL 73/78 could never have envisioned that they had the authority to accept a duty upon their own ports to provide reception facilities, much less to impose strict requirements on ports in other states. Thus, the requirement that states 'undertake to ensure' facilities 'adequate' to meet the needs of ships has never amounted to more than a hortatory expression by the convention's drafters.[737] Moreover, MARPOL 73/78 was never meant to state clearly who – the states, the ports or the oil companies – should pay for the facilities. This is a classic example of a serious and deliberate deficiency in the regime formation process which has inevitably affected compliance with the treaty.

In contrast, the obligations which were imposed upon ships and their owners to provide on-board pollution control equipment were meant to be specific, tangible and enforceable. Today, more so than ever, the much-invoked 'polluter pays' principle insists that the producer of wastes should shoulder the bulk of pollution costs, consistent with the principle of internalising negative costs or 'externalities'. Modern waste management wisdom also dictates that wastes should be kept to a minimum at source, rather than being generated and then treated.

From this perspective, it is arguable that the substantive MARPOL 73/78 obligations on states to provide reception facilities have been

---

[737] Submission of ICS, MEPC Doc. 41/7/6 (1998).

overtaken by events to such an extent that their applicability in modern times appears unrealistic. In the meantime, shipowners continue to face a litany of differing port regulations around the world, many of which either compel the use of reception facilities at great costs and delay, or effectively prohibit discharges even where no facilities are made available.[738] Shipowners remain most fearful of the latter, that is, the prospect of being hit with stringent enforcement action (especially within special areas), notwithstanding the fact that no reception facilities are available.

Another factor to note is that there is no provision in the IMO conventions for any sanctions to be taken when a state fails to make adequate reception facilities available. Admittedly, the idea of such sanctions is itself novel. Fundamentally, the problem harks back to that common criticism of the international legal system – the lack of an enforcement mechanism against states. Domestically, it is conceivable that municipal law may impose an obligation on port authorities or commercial oil terminals to provide facilities and even introduce sanctions for non-compliance. However, such provisions are rare.

At the regional level, a welcome approach has been adopted by the European Commission in the form of its long-awaited Directive on Reception Facilities.[739] Pursuant to the Directive, EU member states are obliged to provide adequate port reception facilities for ship-generated wastes and cargo residues. Member states are also to develop waste reception and handling plans as well as recover the costs for the facilities. All ships will have to 'contribute significantly' to these costs irrespective of their actual use of the facilities.[740] In this regard, the European Commission has interpreted 'significantly' as a figure of the order of at least 30 per cent of the costs of providing reception facilities.[741]

Crucially, the Directive provides for a reporting system as well as penalties for non-compliance. Thus, shipowners may report instances of unavailable or inadequate facilities, following which the Commission may bring legal proceedings against states whose ports violate the terms of the Directive. Such far-reaching enforcement

---

[738] See the examples of port practices alleged by INTERTANKO to contravene the spirit of MARPOL 73/78, *supra* notes 718-19.
[739] Directive 2000/59/EC on port reception facilities, *supra* note 239.
[740] Directive 2000/59/EC, art. 8(1), *ibid*.
[741] Directive 2000/59/EC, Statement of the Commission, *ibid*.

provisions appear to be the way forward in compelling states to honour their obligations to provide facilities.[742] However, it is only in the EU that such supra-national enforcement measures can be contemplated. Elsewhere, reliance will continue to be placed on municipal law to compel states to provide facilities, itself an unlikely proposition.

On its part, IMO has never felt able to 'blacklist' or bring pressure upon non-compliant states which fail to provide adequate reception facilities. As mentioned above, the IMO surveys reflected in Table 5-13 have never been followed up with comprehensive analyses, let alone concrete punitive action. This is largely due to the fact that IMO was established merely as a consultative organisation and has never been allowed to exercise effective enforcement powers against its members.

In many parts of the developing world, financial incapacity continues to hinder the provision of reception facilities.[743] With the governments of the developed states being reluctant to shoulder the cost of facilities even in their own countries, it is little wonder that financial support for developing countries is sorely lacking. In the past decade, various efforts at IMO to find mechanisms for financing reception facilities in developing countries have failed. Such efforts included a futile attempt to establish a Fund for Reception Facilities (FRF)[744] to be financed by those 'benefiting from economic activities giving rise to the risk of pollution', which presumably included the cargo owners and charterers.

In recent years, several delegations at IMO, particularly the UK, have proposed the adoption of port waste management plans as a means of promoting greater dialogue between the providers and users of reception facilities. The UK's efforts were primarily motivated by the recommendations of the Donaldson Report.[745] Of course, the facilitative process which it advocates pre-supposes that port states are willing to

---

[742] The Directive is not without its problems. Implementation has been inconsistent, particularly because governments leave its enforcement to their various port administrations, see Lloyd's List, *Chorus of Disapproval for EU Directive on Handling Ship Waste*, 30 Apr. 2004. Thus, different European ports have differing interpretations of rules and charging practices.

[743] It has been estimated that the cost of installing waste reception facilities in developing countries for the period from 1993 to 2000 amounted to US$560 million, see MITCHELL, *supra* note 68, at 208.

[744] P. SADLER & J. KING, STUDY ON MECHANISMS FOR THE FINANCING OF FACILITIES IN PORTS FOR THE RECEPTION OF WASTES FROM SHIPS, *attached to* MEPC Doc. 30/INF.32 (1990).

[745] *Supra* note 40.

provide facilities in the first place. Users must also be willing to articulate their needs and report on inadequacies without fear of reprisal from port authorities.

It is currently too early to assess whether the latest initiatives will succeed where others have failed in the past. There is every room for pessimism that as long as a great number of states are unwilling to bear the costs of reception facilities, industry will continue to be saddled with ensuring waste reduction and minimisation. It remains to be seen if strategies such as direct financial incentives can be adopted for those states which might be expected to continue resisting reception facilities in violation of their MARPOL 73/78 obligations.

In sum, relying on industry responsibility alone is clearly inadequate. As has been emphasised repeatedly, the retention of wastes on board ships is meaningful only when there exist shore-based facilities to receive them eventually. Thus, the provision of adequate and affordable facilities on shore appears to be the *sine qua non* for any meaningful control system to be put in place. Only when such facilities are provided can port state control authorities begin to contemplate strong and fair enforcement action against that significant minority of sub-standard operators who continue to engage in illegal discharges.

Concrete incentives must thus be created for states to live up to their bargain to provide reception facilities. One way of doing this is for IMO to create a 'White List' of ports with adequate reception facilities. This would be a first step toward creating a form of certification or recognition for compliant states which will provide incentives for action. Just as there can be a network of 'quality' registers or shipowners, there can also be a similar network of port states possessing the requisite reception facilities. States can also consider pooling resources to provide regional networks of reception facilities.[746] At the same time, innovative ways must be found for cargo owners and charterers to contribute to the costs of providing facilities. This is consistent with the theme of this work, which is that the goal of a safer and cleaner marine environment can be achieved only when the costs of compliance are spread out equitably among state and industry actors, thereby increasing the incentives for each actor to demand compliance of others.

---

[746] There have been proposals to explore regional arrangements in the South Pacific, where individual countries deterred by the high costs of reception facilities have long stayed out of MARPOL 73/78, see Report of MEPC's 49th session, MEPC Doc.49/22 (2003).

3.3 Reporting on Implementation Activities

3.3.1 Reporting on the Provision of Reception Facilities

In common with other environmental treaties, the IMO marine pollution conventions require state parties to report regularly on various compliance matters such as the adequacy of reception facilities and action taken against flag and foreign vessels for alleged violations. Self-reporting requirements such as these form an important mechanism for implementation review, allowing for the assessment and improvement of states' compliance records. They are thus indispensable tools for the evaluation of a convention's effective functioning.

Unfortunately, the failure of states to submit regular reports to IMO is a widespread problem. Comparisons of various countries show that the presence or otherwise of incentives to report and the differing levels of economic development have significant influence on the regularity and accuracy of reports. With regard to reception facilities in their own ports, states are required under Article 11 of MARPOL 73/78 to submit reports to IMO on the availability and adequacy of such facilities. The relevant information has traditionally had to be solicited through questionnaires and surveys sent by IMO to individual states. This practice began in the 1950s when the UN Secretary-General sent a questionnaire to OILPOL 54 state parties on various oil pollution issues, including the availability of reception facilities in ports.

Since then, few states have actually been diligent in sending updated reports on their own volition. IMO has had to continue sending surveys in the form of MEPC Circulars to obtain information on reception facilities. To date, five such periodic exercises have been conducted and their results published. Table 5-13, discussed above, reproduces a summary of these results. The survey findings show that even with the increase in OILPOL and MARPOL 73/78 state parties over the years, the number of survey respondents remained somewhat constant in the vicinity of some thirty to forty states. The records compiled in 1999 show a total of 57 states having submitted information on reception facilities to IMO. This constitutes only 52 per cent of the total number of state parties (109) to MARPOL 73/78 at that time.

Table 5-14 below sets out the states whose records on reception facilities are available with IMO. It must be noted that not all these states updated their records during each survey exercise. Thus, the latest compilation during the period 1995 to 1999 would have recorded a

Table 5-14. *State Reports to IMO on Port Reception Facilities*

	1985/93	1994	1995/99	2003
Argentina	✓	✓	✓	✓
Australia	✓	✓	✓	✓
Barbados	✓	✓	✓	✓
Belgium			✓	✓
Brazil	✓	✓	✓	✓
Canada	✓	✓	✓	✓
Chile			✓	✓
China, PR	✓	✓	✓	✓
Colombia			✓	✓
Croatia		✓	✓	✓
Cyprus	✓	✓	✓	✓
Denmark	✓	✓	✓	✓
Ecuador	✓	✓	✓	✓
Egypt			✓	✓
Estonia		✓	✓	✓
Finland	✓	✓	✓	✓
France	✓	✓	✓	✓
Georgia		✓	✓	✓
Germany, Dem. Rep.	✓			
Germany, Fed. Rep.	✓	✓	✓	✓
Greece	✓	✓	✓	✓
Hong Kong	✓	✓	✓	✓
Iceland			✓	✓
India		✓	✓	✓
Indonesia			✓	✓
Ireland	✓	✓	✓	✓
Israel	✓	✓	✓	✓
Italy	✓	✓	✓	✓
Japan	✓	✓	✓	✓
Korea, Rep. of	✓	✓	✓	✓
Latvia		✓	✓	✓
Lithuania		✓	✓	✓
Malaysia				✓
Maldives	✓	✓	✓	✓
Malta	✓	✓	✓	✓
Mauritius	✓	✓	✓	✓
Mexico			✓	✓
Morocco			✓	✓
Netherlands	✓	✓	✓	✓
New Zealand	✓	✓	✓	✓
Norway	✓	✓	✓	✓
Pakistan			✓	✓

Table 5-14. (cont.)

	1985/93	1994	1995/99	2003
Papua New Guinea			✓	✓
Poland	✓	✓	✓	✓
Portugal	✓	✓	✓	✓
Singapore	✓	✓	✓	✓
Slovenia			✓	✓
South Africa			✓	✓
Spain	✓	✓	✓	✓
Sweden	✓	✓	✓	✓
Trinidad & Tobago	✓	✓	✓	✓
Tunisia	✓	✓	✓	✓
Turkey			✓	✓
Turkmenistan		✓	✓	✓
UK	✓	✓	✓	✓
Ukraine		✓	✓	✓
USA	✓	✓	✓	✓
USSR (later Russian Federation)	✓	✓	✓	✓
Yemen	✓	✓	✓	✓
Total Reports	37	44	57	58
– of which OECD	18	18	24	24
– of which non-OECD	19	26	33	34
State parties to MARPOL 73/78	77	86	109	127
– of which OECD	21	22	29	29
– of which non-OECD	56	64	80	98
Total reports as % of state parties	48	51	52	46

positive entry for a state even if its report had been from earlier exercises and had not since been updated.

From Table 5-14, it can be seen that a large proportion of MARPOL 73/78 state parties (around 50 per cent) have never responded to IMO requests for information. Those states which did respond were more or less equally divided between developed and developing states. However, given that the latter constitute the vast majority of state parties, a higher proportion of the reporting states would have been from the developed world.

As explained earlier, the results cannot justify a conclusion that non-reporting states have no reception facilities. In other words, non-compliance cannot be inferred from non-reporting. Conversely, there were states which had responded in earlier surveys but not in later ones, even though IMO continued to record these states as having submitted information. This shows that even states with reception facilities could have failed to report. Nevertheless, there appears to be some broad correlation between a state's level of economic development and its incentives to report, just as there is that correlation between economic development and incentives to provide reception facilities.

At the 1962 Conference which amended OILPOL 54, the negotiators had removed the original self-reporting requirement and replaced it with one requiring states to report on *other* states' ports with inadequate reception facilities. This provision had been inserted at the behest of the US delegation, which saw it as a useful tool for shaming non-complying states into providing reception facilities. The aim was for tanker captains, through their own governments, to inform IMCO and other governments of non-existent or inadequate facilities in visited ports. This provision was carried over to MARPOL 73/78, which also revived the self-reporting requirement that was deleted in 1962.

It was not until 1978 that MEPC acted upon the 'report on others' requirement and requested responses from states. However, pursuant to IMCO's request for information, only one report was received. Even this was submitted through a shipping company and not through the relevant government. Ostensibly, shipowners were reluctant to make adverse reports to IMCO for fear of losing the goodwill of port authorities.[747] This factor thus dampened the incentive for shipowners and states to submit reports.

A subsequent request for reports in 1984 yielded responses from some twenty-five states. Since then, very few reports have emerged (see Table 5-15 below).[748] Quite evidently, the majority of states were not complying with their obligation to submit reports on reception facilities, be these in their own ports or in other states. Again, reliance

---

[747] Personal interviews.
[748] Information on reception facilities was originally solicited through stand-alone Circulars such as MEPC/Circ.215. From 1996, this became solicited along with general information on enforcement (as required under MARPOL 73/78's annual mandatory reporting system) through MEPC/Circ. 318. In 1998, MEPC/Circ.349 introduced a revised format for reporting alleged inadequacy of reception facilities. These different reporting forms were well-intentioned efforts to improve upon their predecessors, but the resulting confusion left the system with few returns. In August 2000, MEPC adopted Resolution MEPC.83(44) providing guidelines for ensuring the adequacy of port waste reception facilities, reiterating the need to comply with MEPC/Circ.349. There are now proposals to revise MEPC/Circ.349 to cover Annexes IV and VI on sewage and air pollution matters, see MEPC Doc. 51/22 (2004). In the meantime, a questionnaire on low levels of reporting has been circulated to states *vide* MEPC/Circ.417.

Table 5-15. *Information on Action Taken by States on Reception Facilities (RFs)*[750]

Year	No. of States Reporting Alleged Inadequate RFs in Other Countries (including NIL entry)	Number of Alleged Inadequacies	No. of States Reporting Action Taken on Alleged Inadequate RFs in Own Ports (including NIL entry)	Number of Alleged Inadequacies Acted Upon
1991	9	NA	9	NA
1992	2	NA	6	NA
1993	NA	NA	NA	NA
1994	3	NA	0	0
1995	2	NA	0	0
1996	1	2	0	0
1997	0	0	2	4
1998	2	6	1	1
1999	1	2	0	0
2000	1	1	1	1
2001	2	NA	1	NA
2002	3	11	0	0

Sources: FSI Sub-Committee documents.

has had to be placed on the industry surveys. These have elicited far more responses from shipowners probably because they assured the complainants total anonymity. Consequently, the industry surveys have been far more successful than the IMO surveys in capturing information on the state of reception facilities in ports worldwide. In the light of the disappointing reporting rate, IMO is currently looking into reviewing the procedures for states to report on inadequate reception facilities.[749]

3.3.2 Reporting on Enforcement Action

Apart from requiring state parties to report on reception facilities, OILPOL 54 and MARPOL 73/78 contain obligations on state parties to report on general matters dealing with treaty compliance and

---

[749] Report of the FSI Sub-Committee's 11th session, FSI Doc. 11/23 (2003) and MEPC Doc. 51/22 (2004), *ibid.*

[750] Pursuant to MARPOL 73/78, arts. 11(1)(d) and 12(5) and MEPC/Circ.318 and MEPC/Circ.349.

enforcement.[751] The tables in the previous sections have thrown light on the level of *substantive enforcement* by states. At the same time, the tables also provide an indication of the *procedural reporting* of enforcement activities. Obviously, the obligations to enforce and to report on enforcement are separate, even though there is a clear trend for diligent enforcers to report on their activities as well.

Under OILPOL 54, flag states were to report on actions taken on alleged violations referred to them by coastal states. It will be recalled that at the time OILPOL 54 was adopted, coastal and port states enjoyed very little powers over offending vessels found polluting adjacent waters. In most cases, the coastal state's only recourse was to refer such cases to the flag states. In this regard, an early survey undertaken by IMCO in 1961 showed that no flag states receiving coastal state referrals had ever submitted reports on action taken to IMCO.[752] In later years, wider port state enforcement powers have been recognised. Thus, states, in their capacity as port states, have also been required to report on enforcement measures taken against foreign-flagged ships such as inspections, detentions, penalties and denials of entry into port.

It will be recalled that at the 1962 Conference to amend OILPOL 54, the UK and France had attempted to strengthen the reporting requirement by proposing that coastal states which referred cases to flag states provide copies of such referrals to IMCO as well.[753] However, this proposal was dropped after being opposed by states which did not wish to give IMCO increased powers over enforcement matters. A subsequent questionnaire, circulated in 1963, requested general information on enforcement matters from OILPOL state parties. The request was vaguely worded and not surprisingly, only six of the thirty-two responding states referred to enforcement efforts, and even then only in general terms.[754]

Hence, throughout OILPOL's existence, state reporting on enforcement was virtually absent, whether this involved the state's capacity as a flag, coastal or port state. At the 1973 MARPOL Conference, some efforts were taken to strengthen the reporting requirements. MARPOL 73 retained OILPOL 54's reporting provisions and introduced a requirement for an annual statistical report of penalties imposed for infringement of the convention.[755] This was the first time an obligation had been laid down on states to report according to a fixed schedule.

---

[751] OILPOL 54, arts. X(2) and XII, MARPOL 73/78, art. 11.
[752] MITCHELL, *supra* note 68, at 130.   [753] See Ch. 4.
[754] MITCHELL, *supra* note 68, at 130.   [755] MARPOL 73/78, art. 11(f).

In general, MARPOL 73 required states to undertake to communicate information relating to a variety of matters including domestic legislation, reception facilities and enforcement.

In the aftermath of the 1973 Conference, IMCO began requesting compliance and enforcement reports from states on a regular basis. The newly established MEPC also developed a form for reporting penalties and coastal state referrals to flag states. The first annual reports were received in 1975 and a gradual increase in the number of reports followed in successive years. In 1978, MARPOL 73/78 reaffirmed MARPOL 73's reporting requirements without substantive change.

By 1980, MARPOL 73/78 was still not in force. Fewer than one-third of OILPOL parties were submitting reports to IMCO. The majority of states completely ignored the reporting requirement and even those which did report provided little meaningful information.[756] The quality and content of reports varied across countries and even across time for particular countries, making trend analysis difficult. In essence, many state parties knew that OILPOL 54 would soon be superseded by MARPOL 73/78 and thus paid little attention to the former's enforcement.

It was not until 1985 that IMO took some meaningful action toward improving the reporting rate. MARPOL 73/78 had by that time entered into force. A proper standardised format for reporting was introduced in 1985[757] and the reporting rate subsequently improved. Over the next few years, the standard format was revised and reissued several times, principally in 1990[758] and 1993.[759] Despite these efforts, response rates remained unsatisfactory. The low number of reports received simply did not permit an accurate analysis of compliance and enforcement in states worldwide.

At that time, IMO ascribed the low reporting rates to the complex and demanding nature of the reporting format. In 1996, yet another new format was introduced.[760] This required information from states relating to four distinct categories of enforcement – discharge incidents including pollution arising from casualties; coastal state referrals to flag states for alleged discharge violations and the flag state's responses; alleged inadequacy of reception facilities by flag states (as received from masters) and the action taken by the relevant port states; and statistics relating to inspections, detentions and penalties imposed by flag and

---

[756] Dempsey, *supra* note 4, at 484.   [757] The format was circulated by MEPC/Circ. 138.
[758] MEPC/Circ. 228.   [759] MEPC/Circ. 266.   [760] MEPC/Circ. 318.

Table 5-16. *Reporting Rates on OILPOL 54 and MARPOL 73/78 Enforcement (1975 to present)*

Year	Developed States (OECD)			Developing States (Non-OECD)			All States			
	No. of Parties	No. of Reports	Reporting Rate (%)	No. of Parties	No. of Reports	Reporting Rate (%)	No. of Parties	No. of Reports	Reporting Rate (%)	OECD as % of All Parties	OECD Reporting Rate (%)[761]
1975	23	3	13	31	0	0	54	3	6	43	100
1976	23	4	17	35	2	6	58	6	10	40	67
1977	23	6	26	36	3	8	59	9	15	39	67
1978	23	7	30	37	3	8	60	10	17	38	70
1979	24	10	42	38	4	10	62	14	23	39	71
1980	24	9	38	41	7	17	65	16	25	37	56
1981	24	4	17	43	8	19	67	12	18	36	33
1982	24	NA	NA	44	NA	NA	68	NA	NA	35	NA
1983	24	9	38	47	4	9	71	13	18	34	69
1984	23	10	43	48	7	15	71	17	23	32	59
1985	23	15	65	49	15	30	72	30	41	32	50
1986	23	13	56	49	16	32	72	29	40	32	45
1987	23	12	52	49	12	24	72	24	33	32	50
1988	22	17	77	49	15	30	71	32	45	31	53
1989	21	15	71	49	17	34	70	32	45	30	47
1990	22	15	68	47	19	40	69	34	49	32	44
1991	21	10	48	49	7	14	70	17	24	30	59

[761] This is the percentage of total reports accounted for by OECD states.

1992	21	11	52	55	9	16	76	20	26	28	55
1993	22	12	54	60	7	12	82	19	23	27	63
1994	23	11	48	66	13	20	89	24	27	26	46
1995	25	9	36	71	12	17	96	21	22	26	43
1996	28	8	29	70	16	23	98	24	24	29	33
1997	28	13	46	73	12	16	101	25	25	28	52
1998	29	14	48	77	10	13	106	24	23	27	58
1999	29	14	48	83	14	17	112	28	25	26	50
2000	30	14	47	90	13	14	120	27	23	25	52
2001	30	14	47	96	18	19	126	32	25	24	44
2002	30	15	50	96	14	15	126	29	23	24	52

Notes: Figures include numerous reports received late in subsequent years.

Sources: 1991 to 2002 – FSI Sub-Committee documents on Mandatory Reports under MARPOL 73/78; 1975 to 1990 – P. S. Dempsey, *Compliance and Enforcement in International Law – Oil Pollution of the Marine Environment by Ocean Vessels*, 6 Nw. J. Int'l L. & Bus. 459 (1984) and R. Mitchell, Intentional Oil Pollution at Sea – Environmental Policy and Treaty Compliance (1994).

port states. It was hoped that the simplified procedure would encourage more states to submit reports.

Because the reporting format had been changed so often in so short a period and had differing requirements, many states found it a burden to keep up with the reporting system. The frequent changes in format also made it difficult to make coherent comparisons and analyses. A major problem is the fact that many reporting states failed to complete all sections of the relevant report forms, thereby making comparisons across countries and across time more complex. Table 5-16 summarises the reporting rates by state parties from 1975 to the present while Table 5-17 identifies the states which have been submitting annual enforcement reports to IMO.

From Table 5-16, it can be seen that the reporting rate has not improved in the 1990s even with the introduction of simplified formats. On the whole, the reporting rate for all state parties remained in the range of 20 to 30 per cent – a most unsatisfactory level. Thus, about 75 per cent of MARPOL 73/78 state parties fail in their obligation to submit mandatory reports.[762] What is noteworthy is that even countries like France who have been so vocal about marine pollution have never reported; neither have Panama and the Bahamas. Countries which have diligently reported include Australia, China, Estonia, Finland, Germany, Greece, Japan and the UK. Quite evidently, states worldwide were either finding that the reporting requirements were too onerous or that they simply did not consider the reporting obligation to be an important one.

The developed states show higher reporting rates relative to their number. Even then, these rates seldom rise above 50 per cent. On their part, barely 20 per cent of developing states have submitted reports. Table 5-17 shows that only 51 states (of whom 40 per cent are developed states) have ever submitted reports of any form since 1990. This means that more than 60 per cent of the 130 current state parties to MARPOL 73/78 have never submitted a single report in the past decade. That said, it is encouraging to note that several developing and open registry states are among the more consistent providers of reports, including China, Croatia, Estonia, Liberia and Vanuatu.

Like the IMO-collated data reflected in the earlier tables, the MOU figures on port state enforcement presented in Tables 5-5 to 5-11 depend wholly on reports submitted by member national administrations.

---

[762] Report of MEPC's 46th session, MEPC Doc. 46/23 (2001).

Table 5-17. States Submitting Annual Enforcement Reports to IMO

Reporting State	1991	1992	1993	1994	1995	1996	1997	1998	1999	2000	2001	2002
Antigua & Barbuda					✓							
Argentina									✓	✓	✓	✓
Australia	✓	✓	✓	✓	✓	✓	✓	✓	✓	✓	✓	✓
Belgium			✓	✓			✓	✓	✓	✓	✓	✓
Brazil							✓	✓				
Bulgaria		✓	✓	✓								
Canada	✓											
Cape Verde						✓						
Chile												
China, PR	✓	✓	✓	✓	✓	✓	✓	✓	✓	✓	✓	✓
Croatia	✓	✓	✓	✓								
Cyprus		✓										
Denmark		✓					✓		✓	✓	✓	
Egypt										✓		
Estonia			✓	✓	✓	✓	✓	✓	✓	✓	✓	✓
Finland			✓	✓	✓	✓	✓	✓	✓	✓	✓	✓
Germany	✓	✓	✓	✓	✓	✓	✓	✓	✓	✓	✓	✓
Greece	✓	✓	✓	✓	✓	✓	✓	✓	✓	✓	✓	✓
Hong Kong, China	✓											
Iceland	✓											
India	✓	✓										
Italy												
Japan	✓	✓	✓	✓	✓	✓	✓	✓	✓	✓	✓	✓
Korea, Rep. of		✓	✓	✓							✓	
Kuwait												
Latvia									✓		✓	✓

Table 5-17. (cont.)

Reporting State	1991	1992	1993	1994	1995	1996	1997	1998	1999	2000	2001	2002
Liberia	✓										✓	✓
Lithuania											✓	✓
Malta												✓
Marshall Islands				✓								
Mauritius				✓								
Morocco												
Netherlands	✓	✓				✓		✓	✓	✓	✓	✓
New Zealand				✓	✓	✓	✓	✓	✓	✓	✓	✓
Nigeria												✓
Norway	✓	✓	✓	✓	✓		✓	✓	✓	✓	✓	✓
Philippines												✓
Poland					✓	✓						
Portugal			✓	✓	✓	✓						
Russian Federation			✓	✓								
Singapore	✓											
Slovenia												
South Africa											✓	✓
Spain				✓			✓	✓				
Sri Lanka						✓	✓					
Sweden												
Tunisia				✓								
Ukraine												
UK	✓	✓	✓	✓			✓	✓	✓		✓	
USA	✓	✓	✓	✓	✓	✓	✓	✓	✓	✓	✓	✓
Vanuatu	✓	✓	✓	✓	✓	✓	✓	✓	✓	✓	✓	✓
Total	17	20	19	24	21	24	26	25	28	27	32	29
No. of parties	70	76	82	89	96	98	101	106	112	120	126	126
As % of parties	24	26	23	27	22	22	23	22	22	20	25	23

Sources: Various FSI Sub-Committee documents.

Yet, it is interesting to note that the MOU Secretariats receive a far higher and more consistent number of reports than IMO. This can be ascribed to several factors, chief of which is the different reporting systems established by the two organisations.

The MOU system has succeeded in eliciting more reports, primarily because it incorporates the existing standard operating procedures of the enforcing bureaucracies into its reporting requirement.[763] In addition, it processes data in ways that reinforce the reporting authorities' interest and incentive in effectively using their enforcement resources. For example, the common computer databases maintained by the MOU Secretariats are linked to the respective national inspectorates. In this way, member administrations can avoid duplication in inspections and focus their efforts on vessels which are most likely to be in non-compliance. Very importantly, the profiles of the most recalcitrant vessels, flag states and classification societies are disseminated and shared among the MOU inspectorates in order to enhance the likelihood of detecting sub-standard vessels. This is made possible by the fact that reports submitted to the MOU Secretariats are analysed and the results of such analyses are made available to the administrations on a regular basis.

These features of the MOU system provide value to the constituent administrations. In particular, it creates tangible incentives by providing an information tool which renders inspections easier and more effective to operate. In contrast, the IMO reporting system fails to accord those having the ability and authority to inspect and report with any additional incentive to do so.[764] The fact that the information submitted to IMO is rarely analysed and fed back to member states creates a natural lack of incentives to report. Invariably, the IMO reporting system becomes regarded as a bureaucratic 'chore' to fulfil.

Of course, the MOU system elicits greater responses largely because it is premised upon port states' incentives to report on visiting foreign vessels. The problem with flag states lacking the incentives to report on their own performance is still unresolved. Nevertheless, IMO can still derive a useful lesson from the MOU experience, which is that states must perceive a *value* to submitting reports before they will be motivated to do so. IMO should thus re-consider the structural features of its reporting system and adopt the requisite changes to approximate the MOU reporting model. For one thing, it should provide more meaningful analyses and feedback to reporting states so that even the flag

---

[763] MITCHELL, *supra* note 68, at 137–43 and 300.   [764] *Ibid.* at 300.

states may recognise some value in submitting reports. At the same time, IMO should begin to analyse and rationalise the wealth of statistics being submitted by the growing network of port state control MOUs around the world.[765]

IMO's current efforts at MEPC as well as the Flag State Implementation (FSI) Sub-Committee to implement a flag state self-assessment procedure should also be directed at creating value and incentives for flag states to report rather than saddling them with yet another bureaucratic requirement.[766] Providing incentives for states to report should be a priority not only in relation to vessel-source pollution, but also other relevant matters ranging from safety to maritime security. In this regard, incentives for responsible behaviour should be provided, *inter alia*, by the dissemination of a 'White List' of flag states which have diligently submitted self-assessment reports.[767]

4. Conclusion

In general, the compliance record of ships with vessel-source pollution standards is fairly satisfactory, particularly for the equipment standards. Nevertheless, a significant number of sub-standard ships still operate in many parts of the world in blatant disregard of the relevant IMO provisions on both discharge and equipment standards.[768] Hence, while equipment standards in treaties do drive behaviour and have an inherent advantage over discharge standards in reducing incidences of pollution, there is no automatic guarantee that equipment standards will be universally adopted by all shipowners or will effectively overcome vessel-source pollution.

---

[765] See e.g. submission of New Zealand, FSI Doc. 11/6/2 (2003), proposing that MOU reports submitted to IMO should be analysed to provide a holistic picture of port state control.

[766] As at April 2004, only 54 IMO member states (amounting to 79 per cent of world tonnage) had submitted self-assessment forms, see FSI Doc. 12/8/4 (2004). Flag state implementation measures are currently provided for in IMO Assembly Resolution A.847(20) (1997) on Guidelines to Assist Flag States in the Implementation of IMO Instruments, as bolstered by Resolutions A.912(22) (2001) and A.914(22) (2001). There are proposals to enhance Resolution A.847(20) and to possibly turn it into a mandatory Flag State Implementation Code in conjunction with a new audit scheme, *infra* note 1005. While this is encouraging, there is still a problem of creating incentives for compliance with these requirements.

[767] For elaboration, see *infra* text accompanying notes 1006–9.

[768] In 1993, Shell estimated that approximately 20 per cent of the world tanker fleet was sub-standard, Lloyd's List, *Shell Urges Tanker Crackdown*, 21 Jan. 1993.

As examined above, there is practically no problem with imposing equipment standards at the point of a new vessel's construction. What is more difficult is to ensure that existing vessels are retrofitted with the necessary equipment and that all vessels are continuously and adequately maintained to the level of these standards. In the first place, it must be remembered that the imposition of equipment standards *per se* does not address the root causes of many vessel accidents and pollution incidents. Such causes include poor maintenance and operation of vessels as well as negligent navigation, all of which may result in accidents and pollution no matter how stringent equipment standards are.

In short, human-induced causes cannot be rectified by simply mandating equipment standards such as double hulls or SBTs on board ships. Rather, more fundamental measures such as proper inspection, repair and maintenance of vessels, supervision over the operation of vessels, market discrimination against sub-standard vessels in favour of quality operators as well as adequate training for masters and seafarers are needed to address the core problems relating to the human aspects of shipping.

Even if equipment standards were the appropriate prescription for some forms of vessel-source pollution, poor quality ships are still able to slip through the net and avoid retrofitting or maintenance requirements. Often, such ships find new leases of life operating in regions of the world where enforcement mechanisms are weak. For so long as there are charterers willing to cut costs by employing sub-standard ships and flag states willing to accept these ships on their registries, the problem will never fully be eradicated.

The relative success of equipment standards over discharge standards illustrates two major lessons for improving compliance levels among target actors – first, that incentives for compliance must exist, and second, that such incentives can be fostered by having the target actors 'cross-enforce' treaty obligations as against each other.[769] As examined earlier, it is inherently more difficult for equipment standards to be circumvented since these rely, at every stage of the ship procurement and operation process, on a variety of actors for their enforcement. Thus, shipowners, shipbuilders, ship financiers, classification societies and states all have an interest in upholding compliance with equipment standards, at least in the early stages of a ship's life.

---

[769] MITCHELL, *supra* note 68, at 263-7.

The next step is to create adequate incentives for *continuous* compliance, or disincentives for non-compliance, in order to ensure ongoing adherence to equipment as well as discharge and manning standards. This entails vigilance at the operational or maintenance level to ensure that ships continue to uphold the relevant standards as they grow progressively older. Of course, compliance at this stage may be affected by the manner in which deficiencies have been entrenched at the regime formation process. However, even compliance with imperfect regime standards is possible if appropriate incentive-fostering mechanisms are set up for the implementation stage.

One such mechanism is the facility of port state control. As assessed earlier, port state control has been used both at the national and regional levels to target ships based on their previous inspection records and the flags they fly. The recent move to include other targeting factors such as the ship's classification society (and, this should be widely extended to charterers, insurers, financiers and beneficial owners as well) is consistent with the recommendation of this work that regulatory burdens should be spread out among all actors, and not just segments of the industry. This does little to upset the prevailing legal regimes entrenched by MARPOL 73/78 and the LOSC, but strengthens the incentives for non-owner actors to engage in responsible behaviour.

With the increasing transparency that is being demanded of the marine transportation industry, the identities of non-owner interests in a ship must become more readily accessible. Consequently, some regulatory burdens (and legal liability, if this can be proven) should be imposed on the non-owner actors to create incentives for them to behave responsibly. The benefit of such a move is not so much the direct effect of imposing financial burdens on non-owner actors, but the creation of a culture of compliance leading to all interests in the shipping industry possessing the incentives to 'cross-enforce' quality shipping as against each other. In other words, an actor must feel the pressure to comply arising from the actions of other actors.

As a practical measure, the use of port state control targeting is critical because it cannot realistically be expected that all flag states, charterers, classification societies and insurers desist immediately from endorsing sub-standard ships. The reality of the situation is that too many players exist in the market to offer flag, classification and insurance services. Many of these are state-owned enterprises (for instance, the national ship classification services of the numerous countries) which can be expected to raise sovereignty objections should IMO issue a 'black list' of flag states, classification societies or insurers. Thus, it appears that only port state-led market forces can be employed for now to attempt to create a 'quality shipping' culture and to remove the attractiveness of using sub-standard ships.

At the same time, state enforcement efforts against the activities of flag and foreign vessels must be improved. In particular, the incentive for states to report on enforcement activities must be created. This can be done, for instance, by having IMO craft a reporting procedure that not only facilitates reporting but provides value to the reporters in the form of useful analyses. The reluctance of port states to provide shore reception facilities and for ships to use them must also be addressed by instituting greater co-operation and dialogue between providers and users. In particular, cost-effective ways must be found to help developing countries provide and operate such facilities.

6 Liability and Compensation

1. Overview

The previous chapters have dealt with the development of substantive pollution control standards, the allocation of state jurisdiction to prescribe and enforce these standards and compliance by target actors. The next relevant issue is that of liability following the occurrence of vessel-source pollution and the compensation of injured parties, be these states or their private citizens. The inquiry here relates to the *civil* liability of private actors; the questions of *state* liability will not be examined.[770] 'Liability' thus refers to the conventional regime of civil liability facilitating the compensation of pollution damage victims by private, non-state interests, particularly the shipowner and his insurer. The issue of criminal liability under the national laws of states where pollution is suffered falls outside the present inquiry.

This chapter will thus examine the interests which influenced the negotiation of the relevant multilateral liability and compensation instruments, primarily the 1969 International Convention on Civil Liability for Oil Pollution Damage (hereinafter 'CLC 69'),[771] the 1992 Protocol which created the 1992 Civil Liability Convention (hereinafter 'CLC 92'),[772] the 1971 International Convention on the Establishment of an International Fund for Compensation for Oil Pollution Damage

---

[770] On state liability, see B. SMITH, STATE RESPONSIBILITY AND THE MARINE ENVIRONMENT: THE RULES OF DECISION (1988) and G. Handl, *International Liability of States for Marine Pollution*, 21 CAN. Y. B. INT'L. L. 85 (1983).

[771] *Supra* note 92.

[772] 1953 U.N.T.S. 255 (in force 30 May 1996). The abbreviation 'CLC' denotes generally the regime established by the 1969 and 1992 Civil Liability Conventions. Where it is necessary to distinguish between the two conventions, the terms CLC 69 and CLC 92 will be used.

(hereinafter 'FUND 71'),[773] the 1992 Protocol creating the 1992 FUND Convention (hereinafter 'FUND 92')[774] and the 2003 Protocol to FUND 92.[775] The relevant civil liability laws in the US as well as the voluntary compensation schemes developed by the shipping and oil industries will also be analysed. The chapter concludes with a consideration of the newly established civil liability regimes relating to pollution caused by non-oil hazardous noxious substances and bunker fuel.

Several preliminary observations may be made. First, liability and compensation for pollution damage are generally governed by the national laws of the states in whose waters pollution damage is suffered. Most states today are parties to the relevant multilateral conventions relating to marine pollution liability and compensation. Hence, the international CLC/FUND regime for oil pollution is widely reflected in the national laws of the key state players. The major exception is the US, where domestic legislation establishes stricter unilateral regimes of liability and compensation for vessels entering US waters. For most other states, the international conventions form the governing regime, with resort to national law being necessary where claims fall outside the ambit of the conventions.

Second, the liability and compensation laws in most states, be these founded upon international treaties or unilateral prescriptions, have typically replaced the traditional fault-based liability system with a regime of strict, no-fault liability on the part of the shipowner. This is often balanced by the recognition of the concept of 'limitation', whereupon the owner is accorded the right to restrict his liability for third party claims (including for pollution damage) to a certain maximum amount beyond which he is not responsible.

Third, liability and compensation laws typically make it mandatory for visiting ships to take out specialised compulsory insurance for pollution damage up to the relevant limitation level. In this regard, the pollution compensation regimes often nullify the traditional principle of indemnity in insurance law (i.e. the so-called 'pay-to-be-paid' rule)[776] by allowing *direct action* against the insurer or other parties

---

[773] *Supra* note 94.
[774] 87 U.K.T.S. Cm. 3433 (1996) (in force 30 May 1996). The abbreviation 'FUND' denotes generally the regime established by the 1971 and 1992 FUND Conventions. Where necessary, the specific terms FUND 71 and FUND 92 are used to distinguish between the two conventions.
[775] Doc. LEG/CONF.14/20 (2003).
[776] The indemnity principle obliges the insurer to compensate only after the insured party has paid the injured third parties, see Ch. 2.

named in the certificate as guarantor. Fourth, it will be seen that the regimes discussed in this chapter typically impose primary pollution damage liability on the shipowners. The oil and chemical companies, in their capacity as cargo owners, have succeeded in ensuring that they bear only a secondary liability which arises if and when the shipowner's primary liability is unavailable or inadequate to compensate victims.

Overall, there has been a discernible trend to increase the liability of shipowners for pollution damage and the associated compensation payable to victims. This trend has occurred both with the international conventions (and thus in those states subscribing to them) as well as the unilateral state regimes. Taken together, the concepts of strict, primary liability on owners, compulsory insurance, direct action against insurers and increased limitation amounts have imposed significantly higher insurance and operating costs on shipowners and their P&I Clubs. This development forms part of that gradual erosion of the ship transportation industry's traditional right of free and unhindered navigation.

2. The 1969 Civil Liability Convention (CLC 69)

2.1 Developments Preceding CLC 69

The *Torrey Canyon* incident of 1967 revealed a serious gap in the law relating to compensation for oil pollution damage. Within most states at the time, no significant differences existed between the law governing claims for oil pollution damage and that relating to other general claims in tort against a ship or her owners.[777] Enforcement provisions, if any, were mainly penal in nature and were of little relevance to claimants seeking damages in a civil action.

The difficulties inherent in a claim for compensation during this period were reflective of the way the ship transportation industry was structured. To use the example of the *Torrey Canyon*,[778] the Liberian-registered tanker had been owned by a Bermudan corporation called Barracuda which was a corporate subsidiary of the Union Oil Company of California. The vessel had been placed on a bareboat charter to Union Oil itself, which in turn voyage-chartered it to BP, a UK oil company. In

---

[777] See generally, C. DE LA RUE & C. ANDERSON, SHIPPING AND THE ENVIRONMENT: LAW AND PRACTICE 8 (1998).

[778] *In re Barracuda Tanker Corp. (Torrey Canyon)*, 409 F.2d 1013 (2d Cir. 1969). For a comment, see V. P. Nanda, *The Torrey Canyon Disaster: Some Legal Aspects*, 44 DENV. L. J. 400 (1967).

those circumstances, there was great uncertainty as to which jurisdiction or law governed the claims.

There also arose the problem of identifying the appropriate party against whom action could be brought. The Bermudan shipowner was effectively a one-ship company with no assets except for a limited insurance coverage for all its liabilities. This was insufficient to cover the total amount of claims being presented in the UK and France arising from the spill. On its part, the parent company, Union Oil, was a distinct corporate personality against which no action could be brought. There was also no requirement for compulsory insurance or direct action against the insurer.

Even if the proper defendant could have been identified, there arose the substantive problem of establishing its liability. At the time, the traditional basis of liability in most states for maritime cases was the tort standard of 'fault'. This imposed a heavy burden on claimants to prove that the damage arose from the shipowner's fault or negligence. Even if the defendant's liability could be proven, there was still uncertainty as to whether the shipowner could limit his liability, and if so, to what amount.

Indeed, different jurisdictions at the time had different national limits of liability applicable to maritime claims. The only existing international convention which provided some measure of uniformity was the 1957 International Convention Relating to the Limitation of Liability of Owners of Seagoing Ships (hereinafter 'LLMC 57').[779] This convention applied to maritime claims in general, including damage arising from pollution. Prior to CLC 69, no international regime existed to deal exclusively with oil pollution claims. Therefore, any amounts recovered under LLMC 57 had to be shared among general property as well as pollution damage claims.

Overall, it was evident that the prevailing legal principles were wholly inadequate to deal with the consequences of vessel-source pollution. A new regime was clearly needed to redress the problems thrown up by the *Torrey Canyon*.[780] At the behest of the UK, work began within IMCO to deal with the matter,[781] and an *ad hoc* Legal Committee was

---

[779] 52 U.K.T.S. Cmnd. 3678 (1968) (in force 31 May 1968).
[780] In such circumstances, the UK and France were fortunate to have obtained over US$7 million through an out-of-court settlement. Though this was far below the total costs of the damage incurred, it nevertheless exceeded the limitation sum available under LLMC 57.
[781] The following account of events up to the 1970s is derived largely from M'Gonigle & Zacher, *supra* note 65, at 143–99 and personal interviews.

established to consider whether inter-governmental action was needed in the areas of intervention on the high seas and liability and compensation. Most IMCO member states were supportive of a public law convention relating to coastal states' right of intervention on the high seas against ships threatening to pollute the oceans. However, the maritime states were unsettled by the prospect of IMCO encroaching into the realm of private law to discuss issues of civil liability and compensation. In their view, these were issues of commercial significance which were best left to specialised experts such as the Comité Maritime International (CMI).[782]

After a protracted debate and with strong support from the coastal states, IMCO prevailed in establishing its competence over the liability and compensation issue. This victory was not without its price. The major maritime interests which had supported CMI competence, particularly the UK, Norway, France, Germany, Denmark and ICS, ensured that the scope of the proposed new Intervention and CLC Conventions would be restricted to oil. These interests also insisted that primary liability for compensation would be imposed on the shipowners, and not the cargo owners.

Having lost an important element of its competence to IMCO, CMI was quick to capitalise on its great pool of private law expertise to influence the outcome of future discussions. Based on a draft convention which it submitted to IMCO, CMI proposed that CLC liability be based upon fault with a reversed burden of proof falling on the shipowner to show that he was not at fault.[783] This was the most the shipowning interests would concede in accommodating coastal state demands for a total abolition of the traditional 'fault' standard. The shipowners clearly saw the maintenance of 'fault' as a *quid pro quo* for their acceptance of sole owner liability, given that the oil interests were not interested in assuming joint liability.

---

[782] CMI is a private non-governmental organisation whose membership comprises about 50 maritime law associations from developed and developing countries. Based in Belgium, its objectives are the development and unification of the private maritime law aspects of shipping. In recent years, some of CMI's competence has been taken over by IMO, especially after the latter's Legal Committee was established. Nevertheless, CMI continues to participate actively in IMO deliberations pursuant to its consultative status.

[783] For a comparison between the CMI and IMCO drafts, see N. Healy, *The CMI and IMCO Draft Conventions on Civil Liability for Oil Pollution*, 1 J. Mar. L. & Com. 93 (1970) and DE LA RUE & ANDERSON, *supra* note 777, at 14.

Meanwhile, the powerful oil industry worked aggressively to influence the outcome of the Conference. At the initiative of the seven oil 'majors', particularly the dominant US companies, a voluntary compensation scheme for oil pollution claims was swiftly established. Known as the Tanker Owners' Voluntary Agreement on Liability for Oil Pollution (hereinafter 'TOVALOP'),[784] the scheme sought to provide an interim compensation regime ahead of the CLC 69's adoption and entry into force. TOVALOP was an entirely voluntary agreement entered into by participating tanker owners for the benefit of a third party, i.e. the polluted coastal state. It effectively guaranteed governments that their preventive and clean-up expenses following an oil spill would be reimbursed. The scheme would be administered by a new entity created specifically for this purpose, the International Tanker Owners Pollution Federation (ITOPF).

By proposing liability for tanker owners in general, the oil companies deftly sought to spread out the costs of liability among all owners, including the independents who owned the majority of the world tanker fleet. The oil companies' primary objective was to avoid liability being imposed on them in their capacity as cargo owners; this would have placed the costs *wholly* upon their shoulders. In any event, the oil interests were convinced that the independents ought to bear their fair share of the costs particularly since independently owned vessels were commonly alleged to have the worst pollution records.

The oil companies, particularly the US majors, were also keen to improve their battered public image by being seen to be taking action. In essence, the oil interests realised that they could no longer resist coastal state demands for an international liability and compensation regime. Coming so soon before an international conference on the matter, it was reckoned that an effective, functioning TOVALOP would serve not only as a pre-emptive model for the Conference but also to dissuade coastal states from enacting unilateral legislation on the matter.

Not surprisingly, the proposed TOVALOP regime and its compulsory insurance feature were opposed by the independent tanker owners and their mutually constituted P&I Clubs. Ultimately, however, the shipping interests came around to accepting TOVALOP. In essence, the owners and Clubs realised that if they stayed outside TOVALOP, problems of overlap might arise between claims payable under the scheme and

---

[784] 8 I.L.M. 497 (1969). For a critique, see G. Becker, *A Short Cruise on the Good Ships TOVALOP and CRISTAL*, 5 J. Mar. L. & Com. 609 (1974).

those covered by existing legal liabilities insured by the Clubs.[785] In addition, there were recognised benefits to having ITOPF play a technical advisory role in co-ordinating effective responses to oil spills. The Clubs thus agreed to extend their normal insurance coverage to include TOVALOP claims. With this agreement, TOVALOP duly came into effect on 6 October 1969, just one month before the IMCO Conference on the CLC was scheduled to begin.

TOVALOP was able to address some of the legal problems thrown up by the *Torrey Canyon* incident. For one thing, liability under TOVALOP was extended to the bareboat charterer, thus remedying the problem of deceptive corporate barriers encountered with Barracuda and Union Oil.[786] To some extent, this reduced the problem of identifying the appropriate defendant to sue, even though it remained obvious that one-ship companies would continue to flourish. In addition, TOVALOP applied worldwide in any country in whose territory or territorial sea pollution damage was caused as long as the offending vessel was entered with the scheme. It also applied to the escape or discharge of any persistent oil as defined, whether or not carried as cargo, including oil carried as bunkers or slops. Thus, TOVALOP applied to all forms of persistent oil pollution by laden tankers as well as those in ballast. The practical difficulty, however, resided in the requirement that the offending vessel had to be identifiable before compensation was payable. This would continue to pose detection problems in the case of clandestine, operational discharges by anonymous ships.

As for the nature of liability, little innovation was effected. Liability was not in any way strict but would be incurred upon fault with a reversed burden of proof. Only governmental claims would be covered; even then, these were restricted to costs for clean-up and preventive measures. Any losses, expenses or damage incurred by private parties would not be compensated. TOVALOP also excluded any loss or damage which was remote or speculative or which did not result directly from the escape or discharge of oil.

In line with established maritime practice, TOVALOP allowed the tanker owner the right to exercise limitation when his liability could be proven. A US$100 per gross registered ton (grt) limitation would apply, subject to a maximum liability of US$10 million. The US$100 per ton figure was significantly higher than the US$67 per ton limit

---

[785] DE LA RUE & ANDERSON, *supra* note 777, at 15.
[786] M'GONIGLE & ZACHER, *supra* note 65, at 157.

provided under the general LLMC 57 regime. More significantly, the TOVALOP limitation sum applied exclusively to oil pollution claims and would not have to be shared with other property damage claims.

However, the US$10 million overall cap or ceiling was an important qualification to TOVALOP's improvements. This maximum amount effectively restored the limit to the LLMC 57 *status quo* for the larger tankers. For instance, the cap would effectively restore the liability of a tanker of 150,000 tons to approximately US$67 per ton of limitation – the corresponding level under LLMC 57. It followed that the larger the tanker's tonnage, the lower the per unit limitation. This benefited the owners of large tankers tremendously, particularly the oil companies. TOVALOP's idea of an overall cap to limitation subsequently appeared in CLC 69 even though it had not featured in CMI's or IMCO's draft versions of the convention. This was an example of how the oil industry's early initiative to influence the convention paid off handsomely.

Since no state governments were party to TOVALOP, this meant that no difficult questions of jurisdiction would ever arise. This was a major advantage to TOVALOP. However, this also meant that claimant states possessed no legal rights against TOVALOP due to the lack of privity of contract. Thus, states could not require compulsory provision of insurance or other forms of financial responsibility. Since neither the claimants nor the P&I Clubs were party to the arrangement, no direct action could exist against the Clubs. Pursuant to the indemnity principle, the Clubs were thus free to wield contractual defences provided for in the insurance policy. Thus, compensation could be denied the claimants if, for instance, the insured tanker owner had failed to pay premiums in accordance with the insurance policy's contractual terms.

Consequently, despite effecting some improvements, TOVALOP fell short of being as generous as the coastal states had hoped. Ultimately, TOVALOP served to achieve the desired objectives of its oil industry proponents, namely to stave off unilateral coastal state legislation, to spread out liability among all tanker owners (including the independents), to attain public relations benefits for the oil companies and to influence the outcome of CLC 69.

2.2 *The 1969 Brussels Conference*

The International Legal Conference on Marine Pollution Damage was convened in Brussels in November 1969 to adopt the two new conventions relating to the public law issue of high seas intervention and the private law issue of civil liability. The contentious issues relating to CLC fell within three broad inquiries – who should be liable for oil pollution damage, what should be the basis of liability and what should be the limit of that liability. All three questions were inextricably linked and it became clear that a package deal was inevitable.

The policy choices available were relatively straightforward – shipowners or cargo owners could be made liable for pollution damage, or both interests could be jointly liable. Liability could be fault-based, strict or absolute. Finally, limitation could revert to the LLMC 57 level or be increased by CLC 69. Within Committee II of the Conference where CLC 69 was considered, the more radical coastal states like Canada proposed strict or absolute liability to an unlimited amount for both shipowners and cargo owners. These parties would thus be jointly liable for *any* pollution damage occasioned to coastal state interests. This was supported by a number of developing coastal states with long coastlines but minimal shipping interests.

On their part, states like Germany, France, Italy and the US generally agreed with strict liability but wanted this to be borne by the shipowner alone.[787] As major oil importers, these states resisted joint liability because it would significantly increase costs for their oil companies and ultimately, raise oil prices for domestic consumers. By this time too, the US had experienced a decline in its shipping registry and was consequently able to abandon its shipowning lobbies. The US was also encountering strong environmental pressure at home and was keen to support a credible liability and compensation regime so long as this did not affect its oil imports. France, which had taken a strong environmental stance after suffering the effects of the *Torrey Canyon*, took a similar view.

As for the oil companies, these interests felt that even though it was their cargo which was the source of pollution, the problem was mainly an operational one which was wholly within the carrier's control. The oil companies were thus attempting to shift the entire burden onto the shipowners. Militating against this position were the major shipowning states, which insisted upon joint liability based on the fault standard with a reversed burden of proof. Ever protective of their large shipowning and insurance interests, states like Norway, the UK and Japan sought to shift liability, or at least a portion of it, to the cargo owners.[788]

---

[787] *Ibid.* at 170.
[788] *Ibid.* Japan, although possessing a large tanker fleet, was cross-influenced by its huge dependence on imported oil. This differentiated its position somewhat from that of Norway and the UK.

In addition, the shipowning interests wanted to retain the traditional limitation regime of LLMC 57.

To these ends, the maritime interests were supported by the open registries such as Liberia. The USSR, ever resistant to foreign interference with its shipping, adopted a similar position. In addition, Belgium, mindful of its association with CMI, rejected strict liability for being fundamentally inconsistent with traditional maritime principles. To bolster their case, the shipowning interests argued that the prevailing world insurance market capacity would be insufficient to meet the multitude of claims which strict liability and increased limitation could be expected to unleash.[789]

Amidst these debates, an innovative but radical proposal emerged. Originally advanced by Belgium, the idea entailed the establishment of a separate and secondary fund financed by levies on oil imports. As opposed to imposing compulsory insurance upon the cargo owners, the fund would pay for pollution damage directly, although it would retain recourse against any shipowner who caused pollution through his negligence. The proposal drew widespread interest, primarily because governments would not be directly liable under the scheme while the financial burden on the oil industry remained affordable. However, the idea could not be properly considered by the delegates on short notice.

A British-inspired compromise soon emerged to settle the substantive issues. Strict liability would be imposed on the shipowner alone, subject to the usual exceptions to liability. In addition, a limitation of 2,000 Poincare or gold francs (US$134) per ton would apply with an overall ceiling of 210 million francs (US$14 million) per incident. This overall limit had not appeared in the early drafts of the convention nor in LLMC 57 but was clearly inspired by TOVALOP.

The compromise package contained an implicit understanding that an international fund financed by the oil interests would be established as soon as possible. This was considered absolutely necessary since CLC 69, despite its increased limits, could not be expected to cover the most catastrophic accidents. In particular, CLC 69 could not fully cover claims involving the biggest tankers which benefited from the overall limitation ceiling. It was also anticipated that the new fund would return the shipowner's liability to a fault-based regime with limitation amounts effectively restored to the LLMC 57 level.

---

[789] *Ibid.* at 171, citing Lord Devlin, the UK delegate.

Hence, the supplemental fund was meant not only to afford coastal states greater compensation, it would also provide for the oil interests to indemnify the shipowners for part of their burden assumed under CLC 69. This so-called 'roll back' or indemnification provision was deemed necessary because CLC 69 had increased the owner's per ton liability for pollution far beyond that of LLMC 57 for other types of property damage. This promised feature of the fund found great resonance with the independent shipowners who were upset by the way the emerging CLC benefited the oil interests at their expense.

CLC 69's overall limitation ceiling had also placed the Western owners of VLCCs at a great competitive advantage over their developing state counterparts who operated smaller tankers. Thus, the majority of tanker owners in the developing countries were keen to have a second-tier fund which would indemnify them, at least partially, for their first-tier CLC burden. At this stage, however, clearer details regarding the new fund were not available and it was anticipated that another conference would have to be convened to negotiate its creation. Consequently, the shipowners made it clear that their acceptance of the CLC's additional financial burden was conditioned upon the establishment of a second-tier supplementary fund in the near future.

Under CLC 69, liability was 'channelled' solely to the shipowner (or his insurer) in order to simplify the claimants' task of identifying appropriate defendants to sue. Thus, only the owner need take out compulsory insurance, with all claims against other parties for the same damage being unavailable under CLC. Of course, this did not affect the owner's (or his insurer's) right to obtain indemnification from other parties whose wrongful conduct may have caused the pollution incident.[790] Neither did it preclude pollution victims from pursuing claims against non-owner parties under national laws *outside* the CLC regime.

As part of the 'channelling' arrangement, claimants in CLC contracting states would be precluded from pursuing alternative remedies against the owner outside of CLC and independently of its limitation provisions. The owner would thus be protected against oil pollution claims brought in CLC states under alternative regimes such as domestic tort law which may have higher or even unrestricted liability limits. To this end, the liability of the owner's servants or agents under any non-CLC regime was also specifically excluded, these being parties for whose conduct the owner would normally be vicariously liable.[791] As

---

[790] CLC 69, art. III(5).   [791] CLC 69, art. III(4).

stated above, quite apart from the owner and his servants and agents, other parties remained exposed to claims under non-CLC regimes.

In addition to requiring compulsory insurance, CLC 69 also provided for direct action against the insurer, a right hitherto unavailable under TOVALOP. This caused tremendous discomfort among the shipping and insurance interests. As a compromise, some degree of protection was afforded to the insurer. As against third party claims, the insurer would be able to avail himself of any CLC defences which the owner himself would have been entitled to, save for the bankruptcy or the winding up of the owner. In addition, the insurer can avoid liability to third parties if the pollution damage had resulted from the owner's wilful misconduct. This feature of insurance law was critical for a mutuality-based system, since it protected shipowners from the misconduct of their competitors. However, the insurer cannot invoke against third party claims any contractual defence which he might otherwise have been entitled to raise in a claim brought by the owner under the insurance policy.[792]

As regards limitation, the insurer would be allowed to limit his liability to the level afforded to the owner under CLC 69 even if on the facts of the case, the owner himself was guilty of conduct which barred his right to limitation.[793] The insurer's right to limit was deemed to be critical to ensure adequate insurance availability in the market. Nevertheless, CLC 69 did not preclude third party claims in excess of the limitation figure from being brought under national laws governing direct action against insurers. However, it was well known that such claims under national law were commonly subject to stringent restrictions such as the 'pay to be paid' rule.[794]

Having addressed all these fundamental issues, other details of the emerging convention fell into place. The shipowner's strict liability would be subject to the traditional defences such as where damage was caused by acts of war, natural phenomena, intentional acts of third parties, governmental negligence in maintaining navigational aids and intentional or negligent conduct of the party suffering the harm.[795] In recognition of his submission to strict liability, the

---

[792] CLC 69, art. VII(8). Such defences include the insured shipowner's failure to pay insurance premia.
[793] CLC 69, art. VII(8). This remains true for CLC 92.
[794] *Supra* note 776. Thus, the net effect is that claimants' rights to compensation will not materially be improved even if the owner's right of limitation were more easily broken, see Anderson & de la Rue, *supra* note 98, at 57–8.
[795] CLC 69, arts. III(2) and (3).

shipowner would be entitled to limitation in respect of any one incident to an aggregate amount of 2,000 francs (133 SDRs) per ton of the vessel's tonnage. As mentioned above, an overall limit of 210 million francs (14 million SDRs) was imposed.[796] Limitation could be broken if the incident occurred as a result of the owner's 'actual fault or privity'.[797]

To exercise his right to limitation, the shipowner would be obliged to constitute a limitation fund equal to the total amount of his potential liability following an incident.[798] In practice, most shipowners subsequently decided to take out insurance for far larger amounts, usually to the full limit of available P&I cover. This was to enable them to trade to non-CLC states with higher liability limits (principally the US) and to cover CLC risks in the event that limitation was broken.

Under CLC 69, exclusive jurisdiction over compensation claims would be reposed in the courts of a contracting state which suffered the pollution damage.[799] Liability for 'pollution damage' would cover losses and damage outside the ship caused by contamination by oil including clean-up expenses, the cost of preventive measures and further loss or damage caused by preventive measures.[800] Significantly, private claims falling under the definition of 'pollution damage' would be recoverable. Hence, losses such as physical damage to property and consequential economic losses to tourism or fishing facilities could be compensated. These were improvements over TOVALOP, which covered only governmental clean-up and preventive costs.

Compensation under CLC 69 would be restricted to claims arising from pollution by persistent oils such as crude oil, fuel oil, heavy diesel oil, lubricating oil and whale oil.[801] Non-persistent oils such as refined oils and distillates were excluded. Furthermore, CLC 69 only extended to 'ships' which had to be 'actually carrying oil in bulk as cargo'.[802] Hence, all forms of oil pollution emanating from oil tankers would be covered. This included bunker fuel pollution, *but only if* the tanker was laden with oil cargo at the time of the incident. It thus followed that

---

[796] CLC 69, art. V(1). In 1976, one year after CLC 69 entered into force, Protocols to the CLC and FUND Conventions were adopted to alter the unit of account from the Poincare or gold franc to the Special Drawing Right (SDR) as defined by the International Monetary Fund (IMF), see the 1976 Protocol to the CLC 1969, 16 I.L.M. 617 (1977) (in force 8 Apr. 1981) and the 1976 Protocol to the FUND 71, 16 I.L.M. 621 (1977) (in force 22 Nov. 1994). The SDR equivalent of the franc is provided here for comparison. CLC 92 and FUND 92 subsequently adopted the SDR outright.
[797] CLC 69, art. V(2). [798] CLC 69, art. V(3). [799] CLC 69, art. IX(1). [800] CLC 69, art. I(6).
[801] CLC 69, art. I(5). [802] CLC 69, art. I(1).

pollution by oil tankers on ballast voyages would be excluded, as would *any* form of pollution from non-oil tankers, dry cargo ships, passenger ships, warships or other state-owned vessels used, for the time being, only on governmental non-commercial service.[803]

From an environmental perspective, these were regrettable exemptions, since vessels of all categories typically carried bunker oil and waste bilge oils, all of which could cause serious pollution damage. The exclusion of tankers in ballast also made CLC 69 more restrictive than TOVALOP, which covered such tankers.[804] Given that CLC 69 anticipated future supplemental coverage by oil cargo owners, the Conference negotiators clearly felt it unrealistic to expect these interests to cover pollution claims quite apart from those arising from the carriage of their own cargoes. Thus, the prospect of a future oil-financed fund had already influenced the substantive provisions of CLC 69.

As for the convention's geographical scope, it was decided that only damage caused within the territory and territorial sea could be compensated even if the pollution incident occurred outside these areas.[805] This restriction was not well received by coastal states such as Canada, which had sought to extend the shipowner's liability to damage caused beyond the territorial sea such as losses to fishing stocks on adjacent high seas following a devastating oil spill.[806] Unfortunately for these states, the idea that environmental responsibility was not to be constrained by human-imposed jurisdictional boundaries had yet to be fully accepted in international law at the time.[807]

On the other hand, preventive measures taken anywhere – including on the high seas or the territorial waters of other states – with a view to preventing or minimising damage in the territory or territorial sea of a state party could be compensated, as could preventive measures and damage wholly within the territorial sea. In every case, though, the costs of preventive measures can be claimed only if a discharge or escape of oil had *actually* occurred.[808] In this regard, the convention excluded preventive measures taken in the so-called 'pure threat' situation where such measures might have succeeded in preventing any

---

[803] CLC 69, art. XI(1).
[804] CLC 92 and FUND 92 subsequently extended coverage to spills from tankers in ballast, see Section 6 below.
[805] CLC 69, art. II.
[806] The EEZ concept did not then exist, and any ocean areas beyond the territorial sea were high seas.
[807] It is still arguable whether the idea has taken root today.   [808] CLC 69, art. I(8).

subsequent spillage of oil. As stated earlier, no compensation would be payable for any pollution damage caused on or to the high seas or any preventive measures associated with such damage.

Compulsory insurance or equivalent financial security would be required of all ships carrying more than 2,000 tons of oil in bulk as cargo. This requirement would be enforced by each contracting state against any ship, wherever registered, entering or leaving a port in its territory.[809] Thus, even if a vessel's flag state is not a party to CLC 69, the vessel must adhere to the insurance requirement if it wishes to trade with CLC contracting states. These states could henceforth require all visiting ships to be fully insured up to the relevant liability limits. To this end, the Conference introduced a port state control mechanism based upon inspections of the relevant insurance certificates issued by flag state parties to the convention.

The Conference resolution which recommended the establishment of a supplementary fund had also undergone substantive changes by the time CLC 69 was formally adopted. In its final form, the resolution reiterated that the strict liability (as opposed to fault) standard would be applicable and that the fund should in principle, relieve shipowners of the additional financial burden imposed by CLC 69. This vague wording was a result of demands by the US, France and Germany – the major oil importers – that the precise extent of shipowner indemnification be left undecided.[810] Although the resolution was acceptable in principle to both the maritime and coastal states, it was clear that a major conflict between the shipowning and oil industries was forming in the run-up to the 1971 Conference.

3. The 1971 Fund Convention (FUND 71)

3.1 Developments Preceding FUND 71

Encouraged by TOVALOP's impact on CLC 69, the oil companies reckoned that another early initiative on their part would do well to influence negotiations on the supplementary fund. With millions of barrels of oil being transported each day over the oceans, the oil interests were greatly concerned over the costs of the new levy to be imposed under the fund. Pre-emptive action was thus needed not only to dictate future agreement on the topic but also to ward off unilateral coastal state action.

---

[809] CLC 69, art. VII(11).   [810] M'GONIGLE & ZACHER, *supra* note 65, at 175.

As their first step, the oil majors created the Oil Companies International Marine Forum (OCIMF) to represent their interests at international organisations. The oil companies had hitherto been represented at IMCO by ICS but the divergence of interests at the 1969 Conference convinced the oil companies that they needed their own lobby group. As examined earlier, differences had arisen between the two industry groups over the proper apportionment of oil pollution liability. A particular source of annoyance for the oil companies had been ICS's support in 1969 for the Conference resolution which recommended oil pollution liability for the cargo owners.[811]

OCIMF's first mandate was to create a functioning industry fund as a model for the upcoming conference. In January 1971, a new voluntary scheme – the Contract Regarding an Interim Settlement of Tanker Liability for Oil Pollution (CRISTAL)[812] – was concluded among thirty-eight participating oil companies. CRISTAL came into force by April 1971, well ahead of the inter-governmental conference scheduled for November of the same year. A new company – the Oil Companies Institute for Marine Pollution Compensation Ltd (hereinafter 'the Institute') – would administer CRISTAL.

In essence, CRISTAL was designed to supplement TOVALOP compensation for oil pollution claims. Responsibility for paying claims would lie with the Institute with the financial burden being spread out among CRISTAL members in proportion to the quantities of oil which they received by sea transport. In seeking to influence the Conference, CRISTAL completely omitted to deal with the issue of shipowner indemnification.[813] It will be recalled that this had been one of the promised aims of the 1969 Fund resolution. Instead, CRISTAL concentrated on supplementing TOVALOP, under which the shipowner's liability was limited to only US$100 per ton of the vessel. On this score, CRISTAL's main aim was to provide compensation for governments' preventive and clean-up expenses beyond what was available under TOVALOP. In addition, CRISTAL would compensate for private damage claims which had hitherto not been admissible under TOVALOP.[814]

Like TOVALOP, CRISTAL compensated only direct damage and specifically excluded any loss or damage which is remote or speculative or

---

[811] *Ibid.* at 178.   [812] 10 I.L.M. 137 (1971).
[813] M'GONIGLE & ZACHER, *supra* note 65, at 179.
[814] This was not entirely new given that CLC 69 had already recognised all claims, be these governmental or private.

which does not result directly from the escape or discharge of oil. The specific exclusion of remote or speculative claims had never appeared in CLC 69, even though national courts often applied CLC restrictively in the light of general legal principles excluding recovery for such claims. CRISTAL also excluded compensation if alternative domestic arrangements were available to pollution victims. Very significantly, CRISTAL only covered pollution caused by oil owned by a company participating in the scheme *and* even then, only if the ship involved was registered under TOVALOP. The basis of liability would be strict, subject to the same defences applicable under CLC 69. The maximum liability under CRISTAL was US$30 million per incident, inclusive of the sums payable under TOVALOP.

With CRISTAL acting as a supplement, many of TOVALOP's deficiencies were overcome. Pollution damage was now a recognised head of claim together with preventive and clean-up expenses. A larger maximum amount was now available for governmental *and* private claims. In fact, the maximum sum of US$30 million was an improvement not only over TOVALOP but CLC 69 as well. Very significantly, CRISTAL adopted CLC 69's strict liability standard as opposed to TOVALOP's fault standard with a reversed burden of proof. In general, the TOVALOP/CRISTAL scheme would be an effective response to claims exceeding the limits of either TOVALOP or CLC 69. Given that CLC 69 did not enter into force until 1975, the operation of the TOVALOP/CRISTAL regime was critical for coastal states suffering vessel-source oil pollution in the interim.

3.2 *The 1971 FUND Conference*

The 1971 IMCO Conference was convened in Brussels from 29 November to 18 December 1971. The major questions to be settled revolved around the respective contributions of the shipowning and oil industries for oil pollution damage. The familiar divide between the coastal and maritime interests had now been compounded by intra-industry disagreement between the shipowners and oil companies.

The main premise of the creation of a fund was acceptable to all, that is, to have the oil interests provide additional compensation for pollution damage beyond what was recoverable from the shipowner under CLC 69. It was also agreed that the new convention would be designed to complement and to dovetail with CLC 69. Hence, the two conventions would have the same geographical scope, employ the same terminologies and definitions as well as compensate the same kinds of claims, i.e. pollution damage from persistent oils and preventive measures taken to prevent or minimise such damage. It was also agreed that the proposed fund would be administered by a new inter-governmental body – the International Oil Pollution Compensation (IOPC) Fund – to be established with its headquarters in London.

Being inextricably linked to CLC 69, it was also decided that the membership of the IOPC Fund would only be open to states which were already parties to CLC 69. Thus, states which were parties to both CLC 69 and the proposed FUND 71 would enjoy two tiers of compensation in the event of a serious oil spill occurring within their territories or territorial waters. The party against whom initial claims must be brought would be the shipowner and it is only in the event that adequate compensation cannot be recovered from the owner that claims arise against the fund. In addition, it was envisaged that the fund would acquire by subrogation any rights which the compensated person may have against third parties.

The maximum limit of the IOPC Fund's liability was established by the 1971 Conference at a level of 450 million francs per incident (amounting then to about US$35 million). This would be inclusive of any amounts paid by the shipowner or his insurer under CLC 69. A provision was also adopted for the IOPC Fund's Assembly to double this limit if necessary.[815] Although Canada and the US called for unlimited liability at the Conference, there was little support for this position.[816] The IOPC Fund's resources would be constituted by oil receivers in contracting states paying contributions in proportion to the amounts of oil they received by sea. Contributions would be payable only by receivers who in any calendar year received contributing oil exceeding 150,000 tonnes.[817]

The above provisions were adopted by the Conference without much controversy. However, major disagreement arose over the nature of incidents for which the fund would be liable. Under CLC 69, there existed two general situations under which the shipowner would be exonerated from liability – where defences to liability could be raised and where the source of the pollution could not be identified.[818] Major coastal states such as Canada now wanted the IOPC Fund to cover these

---

[815] FUND 71, art. 4(4)(a). [816] M'GONIGLE & ZACHER, *supra* note 65, at 183.
[817] FUND 71, art. 10(1).
[818] Of course, there would be no liability in the first place if the claims fell outside the scope of the convention, e.g. pollution by warships or state-owned vessels, see FUND 71, art. 4.2(a).

situations. This would have effectively abolished all exceptions to liability and to render the IOPC Fund absolutely liable for oil pollution damage. Given that the spirit of the IOPC Fund was to compensate what CLC could not, this argument had some merit to it.[819]

The oil companies which were financing the fund were predictably alarmed. In the ensuing compromise, a few of the exceptions available to the shipowner under CLC 69 were retained for the IOPC Fund while others were totally abolished. Thus, the fund would still be exempted for damage resulting from war, hostilities, civil war or insurrection.[820] In addition, the fund may be exonerated, wholly or in part, if the damage resulted wholly or partially from the intentional or negligent conduct of the party suffering the damage.[821]

The exceptions relating to intentional conduct of third parties and governmental negligence in maintaining navigational aids were abolished, thus rendering the IOPC Fund liable for damage caused by such acts. The fund would also be liable for pollution damage caused by all natural catastrophes. At the insistence of the oil interests, however, the fund's maximum limit of 450 million francs would be available only on the basis of *each* natural disaster irrespective of the number of casualties arising from it.[822] The 'per disaster' formula also had the support of the shipowners and their insurers who were concerned that debilitating claims arising out of calamitous natural events could wipe out the fund's entire resources before these could be applied toward the owner's indemnification.

A major controversy arose in relation to pollution from unknown or unidentified ships passing close to coastal state shores. Operational discharges from such ships have always formed the bulk of vessel-source pollution.[823] Yet, there was little the coastal states could do to redress the problem given the practical difficulties of monitoring vast ocean areas and linking pollution damage to specific ships. As far as CLC 69 was concerned, the shipowner's liability was engaged regardless of whether the discharge of oil was accidental or deliberate, *provided that* the source was identifiable to be an oil-carrying tanker in each situation.[824] In response to this restriction, the coastal states wanted the fund to compensate for *all* pollution incidents of unknown origin.

---

[819] M'Gonigle & Zacher, *supra* note 65, at 184–5.   [820] FUND 71 and FUND 92, art. 4(2).
[821] FUND 71 and FUND 92, art. 4(3). See also CLC 69, art. III(3).
[822] FUND 71 and FUND 92, art. 4(4)(b).   [823] See Ch. 3.   [824] CLC 69, art. III(1).

Due to the high number and magnitude of operational pollution claims, the oil interests resisted the idea of the fund covering such claims. In any event, the oil interests felt that the practice of operational discharges only benefited the shipowners and not the oil industry. Thus, extending coverage to operational pollution would be tantamount to subsidising the shipping industry, particularly the less responsible owners.[825] On their part, the shipowners had little incentive to change the *status quo*, since they were not liable under CLC 69 for unidentified operational pollution to begin with. To agitate for the oil companies to bear these costs would risk resentment and possible retaliation.[826] Accordingly, the owners were indifferent to the matter.

In the result, the coastal states failed to make the IOPC Fund liable for pollution from unidentifiable sources. Thus, any claimant against the fund must still demonstrate that the damage resulted from an incident involving one or more ships actually carrying oil in bulk as cargo.[827] As in CLC 69, this implicitly meant that proof that the offending ship was *an* oil-carrying tanker would be needed, even though the identification of *the* exact ship was strictly unnecessary. The outcome was a blow to the coastal states and the environmentalists who had earlier failed to get CLC 69 to cover damage to areas beyond the territorial sea. The ideal of industry accountability in *all* parts of the ocean for *all* forms of oil discharges would thus remain unrealised. This, unfortunately, was the price for the oil industry's acceptance of FUND 71.

The Conference also provided for fund compensation in situations where the shipowner is liable under CLC 69 but 'is financially incapable of meeting all or part of his obligations, and any financial security provided does not cover or is insufficient to satisfy the relevant claims for compensation'.[828] This provision addressed situations where the owner fails to take out compulsory insurance and has insufficient assets to satisfy the relevant claims. It also dealt with situations where small ships which did not have to carry compulsory insurance became involved in pollution incidents.[829] The final category of claims addressed by FUND 71 related to cases where the owner was liable

---

[825] M'GONIGLE & ZACHER, *supra* note 65, at 185.   [826] *Ibid.*
[827] FUND 71, art. 4(2)(b), read in conjunction with the definition of 'ship' in CLC 69, art. I(1) and FUND 71, art. 1(2).
[828] FUND 71 and FUND 92, art. 4(1)(b).
[829] Under CLC 69, only ships carrying in excess of 2,000 tons of oil in bulk as cargo were required to carry compulsory insurance with the facility of direct action against insurers, see CLC 69, art. VII(1).

under CLC 69 but succeeded in limiting liability.[830] The IOPC Fund would thus compensate claimants in excess of the CLC 69 limits up to the maximum amounts available under the fund. By far, this has been the most common type of claim brought before the 1971 and 1992 IOPC Funds.

Another source of disagreement was the issue of shipowner indemnification. It will be recalled that CRISTAL had neglected to address this very issue. Yet, the IMCO Legal Committee had produced a draft FUND convention in accordance with the 1969 Resolution which clearly recognised the reduction of shipowners' liability as a major function of the IOPC Fund. Hence, the Legal Committee's draft articles provided for the owners' liability to revert effectively to the LLMC 57 limit of 1,000 francs per ton, with the IOPC Fund covering any excess liability.

There were differing views as to whether indemnification should be recognised at all. The US opposed indemnification, as did the UK in a reversal of its 1969 position. In their view, a right to indemnification effectively negated the incentives for safety provided by the fund's higher limitation. In addition, since CLC 69 imposed a limitation of 2,000 francs per ton, indemnification would cover the shipowner's liability for any damage between 1,000 and 2,000 francs per ton, with damage beyond 2,000 francs per ton being fully compensated by the fund *as well*. Therefore, there were concerns that indemnification might actually occur more frequently in practice than compensation beyond 2,000 francs, thus draining the fund's resources substantially.

Some commentators believed that the US anticipated its opposition to the right of indemnification to fail but adopted a tough stance as a bargaining tactic to impose conditions on the right.[831] As expected, the major shipowning states like Liberia and Greece denounced the US position. These states would accept nothing less than a full reversion to the 1,000 francs per ton limit; to deny them this was to renege on the 1969 promise. For its part, the oil industry saw the denial of indemnification, or at least the attachment of conditions thereto, as an effective deterrent for the less responsible shipowners. Of course, denying or restricting indemnification would benefit the oil companies by imposing a larger proportion of liability on the shipowners. Meanwhile, the coastal states were generally indifferent to how the industries apportioned liability among themselves since this would not affect the ultimate level of compensation available to claimants. The more

---

[830] FUND 71, art. 4(1)(c). [831] M'GONIGLE & ZACHER, *supra* note 65, at 187.

environmentally minded coastal states, however, recognised that denying indemnification could provide the incentives for owners to improve on their safety and pollution records.[832]

Ultimately, the Conference brokered a compromise. The IOPC Fund would indemnify a certain portion of the shipowner's liability but only where the owner had demonstrated compliance with four of IMCO's main conventions. These were OILPOL 54 (as amended), SOLAS 1960, the 1966 Load Lines Convention, COLREG 1960 and any subsequent amendments to these conventions. The purpose of this provision was to encourage shipowners, by means of an indirect financial inducement, to conform to the said conventions and to reduce the risks of oil pollution.

At the same time, however, the compromise made it rather difficult to actually deny shipowners their right to indemnification. The shipowner would be so denied only when his non-compliance with any of the four IMCO instruments could be proved to be 'wholly or partially' a cause of the incident.[833] More importantly, the IOPC Fund would only be exonerated from indemnification if it were proven that the ship's non-compliance with the four instruments was 'as a result of the actual fault or privity of the owner and not just the master'.[834] This would be exceedingly difficult to prove given that conventions like OILPOL 54 were so dependent upon the crew's operational diligence that any imputation of fault to the land-based owner was unrealistic.

In the result, it appeared that indemnification would still accrue to the owner in most circumstances. This obviated whatever benefits the conditions to indemnification were meant to confer. In any event, indemnification effectively translated into reimbursing the shipowner's insurer; this would have little deterrent effect on the owner's actual conduct. Be that as it may, the Conference had no choice but to take into account the shipowners' demands. It was thus wholly expected that the oil industry's insistence on conditional indemnification had to be balanced by provisions making the actual denial of indemnification difficult.

Having settled this divisive issue, the negotiations moved on to establish the proper extent of indemnification. The shipowners wanted a

---

[832] *Ibid.* at 189–91.
[833] FUND 71, art. 5(3). In later years, the Fund Assembly interpreted art. 5(3) to encompass MARPOL 73/78 and SOLAS 74 and amendments thereto.
[834] FUND 71, art. 5(3).

'roll-back' to the amount of 1,000 francs per ton – this would have effectively restored their CLC 69 maximum liability from 2,000 francs per ton to 1,000 francs per ton, which was the traditional LLMC 57 level. This proposal drew fire from the oil-importing states and was rejected in an early vote. The oil interests deftly argued that restoration to the LLMC 57 level was no longer reasonable since the owners had already agreed to assume higher limits under TOVALOP.

On this issue, the positions of the key state actors merit some analysis.[835] Long sympathetic to its shipowning and insurance interests, the UK was now convinced that its priority lay with its oil industry. Similarly, net oil importers such as the Netherlands and Germany were persuaded by OCIMF that their oil interests were paramount. After all, the largest tankers in these states were owned by the oil companies, not the independents. As for the US, it was the world's largest oil importer whilst being avowedly pro-environmental. There was thus little sympathy among these delegations for the shipowners' demands for greater indemnification.

As expected, the major shipowning states, including Norway, Greece, Liberia, Denmark and Japan, together with the USSR and France, backed the shipowners strongly. The USSR was predictably supportive of the shipowners given the ongoing expansion of its fleet and its traditional resistance to foreign interference with shipping. The Japanese, despite their huge dependence on oil imports, were cross-pressured by their large shipowning interests. For its part, France appeared to be supporting the shipowners and its relatively modest shipowning industry at rather great costs to its oil-importing interests. The French apparently wanted to reduce the amount of liability for the shipowners and thus the insurance coverage which these owners would have to obtain from the London-dominated insurance market.[836]

It was ultimately left to the Scandinavian countries to broker a compromise. A Norwegian-inspired proposal provided for the IOPC Fund to indemnify the owner for 500 francs per ton, leaving him liable to the tune of 1,500 francs per ton. In other words, indemnification was limited to the upper 50 per cent of the excess over 1,000 francs, that is, the band between 1,500 and 2,000 francs. Despite continued opposition from the shipowning interests, the compromise was eventually accepted by most states. As mentioned above, indemnification was conditional upon the owner complying with the safety and pollution

---

[835] See generally M'GONIGLE & ZACHER, *supra* note 65, at 190–2. [836] *Ibid.* at 190.

standards laid out in the IMCO conventions, with the fund acting as guarantor for the indemnified amount at its sole option. The fund itself would compensate up to a total limit of 450 million francs (30 million SDRs) per incident, inclusive of the indemnified amount as well as the shipowner's liability under CLC 69.

The Conference thus concluded with the adoption of the FUND 71 convention which, like CLC 69 two years earlier, illustrated how the divergent interests of the state, industry as well as environmental actors were reconciled. Seen in this light, the CLC/FUND regime probably represented the best available compromise which the politics of the day would have permitted. In many ways, FUND 71 marked a high point for the coastal state/environmental interests, which now enjoyed the highest level of compensatory protection ever to be recognised by the international legal system for oil pollution damage.

The oil interests, with their nimble manoeuvres and ample resources, were largely able to deflect the costs of regulation onto the shipowning industry. The ultimate losers in the process were thus the shipowners, who witnessed what were arguably only the first few steps toward increased regulation and liability for their industry. In the years which followed, more regulations would be forthcoming as tanker accidents continued to occur and domestic pressure built up within states to enhance regulation over ships and to increase compensation for pollution damage. Whether or not the shipowners realised it, the progressive erosion of the freedom of navigation was well under way.

4. Amendments to TOVALOP/CRISTAL and CLC/FUND

4.1 Revising the Industry Initiatives

The CLC and FUND Conventions did not enter into force until 1975 and 1978 respectively. In the interim, TOVALOP and CRISTAL remained the only operational mechanisms for the compensation of oil pollution claims. When CLC 69 came into force in 1975, the question arose as to whether the two industry schemes were still needed, and if so, how they should be extended. The need for extension was obvious, since many states were still not parties to CLC 69 and would continue to benefit from the industry initiatives. It was also felt that TOVALOP needed to be amended to reflect CLC 69 more closely.

At the same time, the arguments for discontinuing TOVALOP were persuasive. In particular, the continued existence of the industry schemes only discouraged or delayed the ratification of CLC 69 by states. Moreover, if a spill were to occur in a non-CLC (and accordingly, non-FUND) state like the US with high or no limits prescribed under national laws, claimants would be able to obtain voluntary compensation from TOVALOP but there would be nothing to prevent other claimants from seeking further amounts under national law. There would thus be no incentive for non-CLC states to ratify CLC 69. Shipowners would continue to be exposed to strict liability without the accompanying right of limitation.

Fortunately, these problems were overcome by the oil industry's willingness to revise CRISTAL so that it could mirror FUND 71 more closely.[837] Provided a CRISTAL cargo was involved, the oil interests agreed to indemnify the shipowner for any liability incurred under regimes *other than CLC* (e.g. national law) for amounts above the TOVALOP limit. Such indemnity would not be provided if the incident resulted from the owner's wilful misconduct or from unseaworthiness to which he was privy. In addition, the TOVALOP limits would be increased to US$160 per ton, subject to a maximum ceiling of US$16.8 million. Correspondingly, the oil companies agreed to increase the compensation payable under CRISTAL to US$36 million. In sum, this arrangement sought to preserve the incentive for states to accept the CLC/FUND regime.

Another relevant issue was the apportionment of liability for incidents involving small tankers.[838] The low limitation figure arrived at by reference to a small tanker's tonnage was often insufficient to cover the total damage inflicted. This led to CRISTAL bearing a large proportion of the compensation paid in many relatively small incidents. The oil companies sought to redress this situation, arguing that it went against CRISTAL's objective of compensating only the larger, more catastrophic spills. The shipping and oil industries subsequently reached a compromise to the effect that the tanker owners would pay claims up to a minimum of US$500,000 irrespective of the tanker's tonnage. Thus, all spills costing up to this amount would be borne entirely by the shipowner without recourse to CRISTAL. On their part, the oil companies agreed to provide the tanker owners 'indemnification' relief for a portion of their liability resulting from an incident.[839]

---

[837] DE LA RUE & ANDERSON, *supra* note 777, at 29.
[838] The issue of small tankers continues to feature up to this day, *infra* note 910.
[839] This was similar to the indemnification provided under FUND 71, but it would be available whether the tanker owner's liability came under TOVALOP, CLC 69 or any applicable law.

TOVALOP and CRISTAL were thus duly amended and the revisions came into effect on 1 June 1978. With these revisions, the industries' compensation system became broadly similar to the CLC/FUND regime. In October 1978, FUND 71 entered into force – the two-tier compensation system envisaged ten years earlier was now in effect and the IOPC Fund finally began its work. Nevertheless, TOVALOP and CRISTAL continued to meet those claims which could not be pursued under the two multilateral conventions. In order to deter governments from regarding the industry schemes as a substitute for the conventions, their applicability was expressly restricted to a period of three years.

4.2 Developments Preceding the 1984 Conference

Despite the initial success of the industry and inter-governmental instruments, their adequacy was soon called into question. A series of major tanker disasters occurred in the late 1970s, presenting claims which exceeded the maximum amounts available under either the TOVALOP/CRISTAL schemes or the CLC/FUND regimes. In particular, the *Amoco Cadiz* incident off the coast of France in March 1978 gave rise to costs of up to US$100 million. FUND 71 compensation was not available since the casualty occurred before the convention's entry into force. In any event, France had not ratified the convention at that point.

Although CLC 69 was in force in France at the time, the shipowner's liability was limited to a sum amounting to only 15 per cent of the total claims. This was thus the maximum amount recoverable in France unless the shipowner's limitation could be broken by his 'actual fault or privity' in causing the accident. Given the inherent difficulties in proving fault or privity, the French government and other claimants refrained from proceeding against the owner under CLC 69 and instead brought a suit in the US federal district court in Chicago against several defendants who were based there.[840] These defendants included not only the registered owner of the ship, Amoco Transport Corporation, but also several of its associated companies.

The main reason why the US suit could proceed was because CLC 69 never precluded action in tort (under national law) against parties which were not servants or agents of the owner.[841] Neither did CLC 69 confer on such parties the right to limit any liability in non-CLC

---

[840] See generally DE LA RUE & ANDERSON, *supra* note 777, at 31.
[841] Thus, the plaintiffs argued that the other defendants, including the owner's parent company, were not servants or agents of the owner.

proceedings. Moreover, the US legal system did not preclude claims arising from spills occurring outside US waters from being brought in the US under the law of negligence. In the circumstances, the US courts' jurisdiction could be established on the grounds that the defendants were operating out of the US and might thus have committed a relevant tort within the jurisdiction.

In the result, the US court which heard the *Amoco Cadiz* case decided that CLC 69 did not constitute the exclusive legal remedy and did not prohibit claimants in CLC states from bringing an action in tort outside CLC against anyone other than the registered owner or his agents and servants.[842] As a result, CLC 69's channelling provisions could not avail these potential defendants. The case effectively paved the way for oil spill claims arising in CLC contracting states to be litigated in non-CLC states as long as the courts where the action was brought found sufficient grounds to exercise jurisdiction.[843] In this way, the case encouraged forum shopping and enabled claimants to sue in jurisdictions which were less sympathetic toward shipowners' limitation.[844] The case also severely undermined CLC 69's stated goal of promoting a uniform scheme for liability and compensation worldwide.

The *Amoco Cadiz* incident, together with the subsequent *Tanio* spill in March 1980, highlighted the CLC/FUND regime's inadequacy in dealing with catastrophic oil spills. While the majority of incidents were comfortably within the limits of the regime, the occasional large incident proved to be one spill too many. The main problem was that the high inflation rates of the 1970s had severely eroded the real value of the CLC 69 and FUND 71 limits. This had also meant that the IOPC Fund was increasingly being called upon to top up claims, even in relatively small spills. The oil industry was thus greatly concerned, as it had intended the fund to apply only to the occasional major spill. Following pressure from the oil companies and the French government, IMO convened a fresh conference to substantially amend the upper limits of the CLC and FUND Conventions as well as to re-apportion the shipping and oil industries' respective burdens.

---

[842] *In re Oil Spill by the Amoco Cadiz off the Coast of France on 16 March 1978*, 1984 A.M.C. 2123 (N.D. Ill. 1984); [1984] 2 Lloyd's Rep. 304.

[843] After a further trial and subsequent appeals, the case concluded in 1992 with an award to the claimants of some US$61 million plus interest, see *In re Oil Spill by the Amoco Cadiz*, 954 F.2d 1279, 1992 A.M.C. 913 (7th Cir. 1992).

[844] See generally DE LA RUE & ANDERSON, *supra* note 777, at 32 and N. Eskenazi, *Forum Non Conveniens and Choice of Law In re: The Amoco Cadiz Oil Spill*, 24 J. MAR. L. & COM. 371 (1993).

4.3 The 1984 IMO Conference

In April 1984, the International Conference on Liability and Compensation for Damage in Connection with the Carriage of Certain Substances by Sea was convened at IMO to consider the adoption of two new Protocols amending the CLC and FUND Conventions respectively. Once again, the shipowning and oil interests were on opposing sides, particularly as regards the apportionment of financial burdens for spills from relatively small tankers. The other contentious issue was, of course, the new upper limit of the FUND Convention.

All this while, the US had not yet become a party to CLC 69 or FUND 71. As a condition for accepting the conventions, the US demanded a substantial increase in the FUND upper limits from the prevailing 60 million SDRs to 150 million SDRs, with scope for further extension up to 200 million SDRs. While these high figures troubled the other oil-importing countries, particularly Japan, the prospect of participation by the world's largest oil importer attracted broad support for a compromise upper limit of 135 million SDRs, with scope for extension up to 200 million SDRs.[845] The maximum compensation limit would thus be more than doubled from the previous CLC 69/FUND 71 level of 60 million SDRs.

As regards the apportionment of liability between the shipowners and oil companies, the CLC upper limit was increased from 133 to 420 SDRs per ton, with an increase in the shipowner's ceiling from 14 to 59.7 million SDRs. Hence, the shipowners would assume a dramatically higher first-tier liability than they ever did under CLC 69, thereby requiring the IOPC Fund to step in only in the largest spills.

The 'small tanker' problem proved more controversial. OCIMF, with the support of several large oil importers such as Italy and Brazil, had originally argued for a minimum fixed tranche of 50 million SDRs for all ships. This radical formula would have done away altogether with tonnage-pegged liability for sums up to 50 million SDRs. Predictably, OCIMF's proposal encountered resistance from the shipowners. In any event, most states were unwilling to abandon tonnage-based limitation. The issue was ultimately resolved by requiring ships of less than 5,000 tons to bear a limit of not less than 3 million SDRs. This provision was clearly inspired by the TOVALOP revisions of 1978, which had established a similar minimum liability on small tankers.

---

[845] FUND 92, art. 4(4)(a).

Other changes effected by the 1984 Conference included the abolition of the indemnification requirement under FUND 71. With higher CLC and FUND limits being considered, the shipowning interests were now prepared to forgo indemnification. Indeed, most delegations agreed that the balance between shipowners and cargo owners could be better worked out using the new limits. Furthermore, the original aim of indemnification which was to redress the disparity between the CLC 69 and LLMC 57 limits had become less relevant now that the higher limits of the 1976 Convention on the Limitation of Liability for Maritime Claims (hereinafter 'LLMC 76')[846] had been adopted. In any event, indemnification was proving too cumbersome to administer.

Another change introduced by the 1984 Conference was the extension of the CLC and FUND Conventions to include pollution damage or preventive measures taken to prevent or minimise such damage in a contracting state's exclusive economic zone (EEZ) or equivalent designated area.[847] This followed the acceptance of the EEZ concept by the 1982 LOSC. The prevailing 'actual fault or privity' test in CLC 69 which determined whether the shipowner was entitled to limitation was replaced by a stricter one which made it more difficult for limitation to be broken. Thus, the shipowner will be deprived of limitation only if the claimant can prove that the damage resulted from the owner's personal act or omission, committed with the intent to cause such damage, or recklessly and with knowledge that such damage would probably result.[848]

To address the problem thrown up by the *Amoco Cadiz* litigation, liability would be channelled more narrowly toward the shipowner, thereby reducing the scope for recovery under non-CLC regimes against non-owner parties. This provision went far beyond that of CLC 69, which only excluded the liability of the owner's servants or agents.[849] The 1984 Conference also extended the application of the CLC/FUND regime to pollution caused by oil tankers on ballast voyages.

Further, the cost of preventive measures taken in the wake of a casualty threatening grave or imminent risk of pollution would also

---

[846] 13 U.K.T.S. Cm. 7035 (1990); 16 I.L.M. 606 (1977) (in force 1 Dec. 1986), as updated by the 1996 Protocol to the 1976 Convention on the Limitation of Liability for Maritime Claims, 35 I.L.M. 1433 (1996) (in force 13 May 2004).
[847] CLC 92, art. II(a)(ii) and FUND 92, art. 3(a)(ii).
[848] CLC 92, art. V(2). This test originated from art. 4 in LLMC 76. Over the years, national courts had increasingly shown readiness to find 'actual fault or privity', and this had greatly unsettled the shipowners.
[849] For further discussion, see *infra* note 891.

be recoverable under the proposed 1984 Protocols, *even if no actual discharge of oil occurred*.[850] The definition of 'pollution damage' was also clarified to limit compensation for impairment of the environment (other than loss of profit arising from such impairment) to the costs of reasonable measures of reinstatement actually undertaken or to be undertaken.[851] These changes will be elaborated upon below in the discussion on CLC/FUND 92.

The net result of the CLC/FUND amendments in 1984 was to raise the upper limits of compensation for claimants, to make the shipowners pay a greater fraction of the total compensation as well as to ensure that the IOPC Fund would not be called upon to provide compensation save in the most serious spills. Overall, the shipowners were again on the receiving end of increased regulatory costs – not only did they have their limits under CLC increased, their right to indemnification under FUND 71 was abolished and liability would now extend to damage caused to the EEZ. As a *quid pro quo* for these concessions, the shipowners' right to limitation was strengthened by the abolition of the 'actual fault or privity' test.

The entry into force provisions of the two new Protocols were crafted in such a way as to require the participation of the US and at least one other major oil-receiving state. Indeed, throughout the 1984 Conference, the understanding among delegates was that the Protocols' entry into force depended wholly upon US participation. Indeed, there were states which expected not to enact implementing legislation unless and until the US had done so. As it turned out, the eventual refusal of the US to accept the CLC/FUND regime led to the 1984 Protocols never entering into force. As examined below, this development necessitated yet another amendment to the regime in 1992, whereupon the substance of the 1984 Protocols were re-cast in the form of new Protocols.[852]

4.4 *Further Revision of TOVALOP and CRISTAL*

In the mid-1980s, the reticence of the US Congress in approving the 1984 Protocols gave rise to concerns that their entry into force could

---

[850] CLC 92, arts. I(8) and II(b). This is the 'pure threat' situation hitherto unrecoverable under CLC 69, *supra* note 808.
[851] CLC 92, art. I(6). See generally M. Jacobsson & N. Trotz, *The Definition of Pollution Damage in the 1984 Protocols to the 1969 Civil Liability Convention and the 1971 Fund Convention*, 17 J. MAR. L. & COM. 467 (1986).
[852] On the 1984 Protocols and the associated negotiating process, see D. Jacobsen & J. Yellen, *Oil Pollution: The 1984 Protocols and the Amoco Cadiz*, 15 J. MAR. L. & COM. 467 (1984).

take years to achieve.[853] Accordingly, the shipping and oil industries supported a continuing role for TOVALOP and CRISTAL. Unlike the inter-governmental conventions, these agreements were simple contracts between the industry interests which could be easily amended. Thus, it was proposed that TOVALOP and CRISTAL be brought in line with the 1984 Protocols. This would make equivalent compensation quickly available to potential claimants pending the Protocols' entry into force.[854]

There were additional benefits in revising TOVALOP and CRISTAL. Ever since the original CLC/FUND regime became widely adopted, the industry schemes had typically served to re-adjust and fine-tune the burden of claim settlements between the shipowning and oil interests *inter se*. This had been done in 1978, for instance, in relation to the 'small tankers' issue. Readjustment of liabilities did not disturb the total amounts of compensation available to injured third parties under the CLC/FUND conventions; it merely sought to re-distribute the liabilities of the industries as between themselves by way of indemnification.

In the wake of the 1984 Protocols' adoption, some sectors of the oil industry were disgruntled that the shipowners had not been made to assume an even greater proportion of costs.[855] This was despite the fact that the shipowners already bore the burden of increased first-tier limits. In essence, the oil industry felt that the new FUND 84 Protocol's limits exposed it to disproportionately high liabilities. The oil industry thus proposed to revise CRISTAL and to re-adjust the respective industries' liabilities such that the shipowners would now contribute a larger fractional share than required of them under the 1984 Protocols. At the same time, CRISTAL's overall maximum limits could be brought closer to that of the FUND 84 Protocol.

Naturally, the proposal was resisted by the tanker owners. Following protracted discussions,[856] a compromise was eventually reached in 1987. TOVALOP would be split into two versions existing alongside each other. Where a tanker involved in an accident was not carrying

---

[853] See *infra*, Section 5.1.
[854] Since their last revision in 1978, the two industry arrangements had had their duration extended several times, with the latest extension having renewed their lifespan until November 1986. The time was thus ripe for another revision to be considered.
[855] DE LA RUE & ANDERSON, *supra* note 777, at 35.
[856] Early discussions touched on the creation of a revised first-tier voluntary scheme called the Pollution Liability Agreement Among Tanker Owners (PLATO). However, PLATO did not gain the acceptance of the tanker owners, who viewed it as imposing disproportionate burdens on them.

oil belonging to a CRISTAL member, compensation remained available from the shipowner under the prevailing version of TOVALOP last adopted in 1978. This version would henceforth be known as the 'TOVALOP Standing Agreement'. Here, compensation remained limited to US$160 per ton, subject to a maximum ceiling of US$16.8 million.

However, if the vessel was carrying a CRISTAL cargo, the owner's liability would be governed by a new Supplement to TOVALOP. This would provide a new and higher limit of US$3.5 million for tankers of 5,000 tons or less, plus US$493 for each ton in excess of 5,000 tons up to an increased maximum of US$70 million.[857] Beyond this limit, a revised CRISTAL scheme would become applicable, paying additional compensation which likewise depended on the tanker's tonnage. Inclusive of the amount payable under the TOVALOP Supplement, the new CRISTAL limits were set at US$36 million for tankers up to 5,000 tons, plus US$733 for each ton in excess of 5,000 tons up to a maximum of US$135 million.

The new limits were significantly higher than the corresponding amounts under the old versions of the schemes as well as CLC 69 and FUND 71, but were deliberately set slightly lower than the limits of the 1984 Protocols. This was done ostensibly to reiterate the interim nature of the industry arrangements as well as to avoid usurping the Protocols. A new company called Cristal Ltd was incorporated in Bermuda to administer and pay claims under the new scheme (hereinafter 'the CRISTAL Contract').

The new TOVALOP Supplement also provided a benefit for the oil companies should they be liable under the FUND 71 Convention. If an incident were to occur in a state which was party to both CLC 69 and FUND 71, the shipowner would normally be liable to third party claimants up to the CLC limit with the IOPC Fund picking up any excess amounts. However, with the intercession of the TOVALOP Supplement, the shipowner would actually pay up to the *limit of the Supplement* which was higher than that under CLC 69. The net effect of this arrangement – as applied between the industry interests without affecting third party claimants' maximum compensation – was to reimburse the IOPC Fund through CRISTAL the difference between the respective limits of the CLC and the TOVALOP Supplement.[858]

---

[857] TOVALOP Supplement, para. 3(C)(3).
[858] On the revisions generally, see L. Cohen, *Revisions of TOVALOP and CRISTAL: Strong Ships for Stormy Seas*, 18 J. MAR. L. & COM. 525 (1987) and DE LA RUE & ANDERSON, *supra* note 777, at 35-6 and 231-61.

In summary, the 1987 revisions to TOVALOP and CRISTAL were meant to meet the shipowners' concern that the schemes should not be a financial disincentive to the adoption of the 1984 Protocols. At the same time, the revisions re-adjusted burden-sharing between the ship-owning and oil interests to address the latter's concern that it was meeting a disproportionate share of liabilities in cases of major accidents falling under the 1984 Protocols. Throughout the negotiations, the superior bargaining position of the oil companies vis-à-vis the ship-owners was evident.

The new TOVALOP Supplement and CRISTAL Contract thus came into effect for all incidents occurring after 20 February 1987 involving a CRISTAL cargo.[859] In the meantime, the maritime world awaited the long-promised acceptance of the 1984 Protocols by the US. However, for reasons described in the next section below, US ratification of the Protocols never materialised. By 1990, it became clear that the US would not accept the Protocols. Consequently, another IMO Conference had to be convened in 1992 to delete the requirement for US participation in the regime. This is examined in a later part of this chapter.

5. Liability and Compensation in the United States

5.1 *The* Exxon Valdez *and Developments Preceding OPA-90*

Even though the US participated actively at the 1969 and 1971 IMCO Conferences and signed both CLC 69 and FUND 71, the US Senate subsequently refused to ratify both instruments, purportedly because the liability limits were too low. Several other factors explain the luke-warm response to the international regime. To begin with, it was widely felt in the US that oil pollution was too urgent a problem to await international action. Also, due to its strong economic position and the inevitable need of tankers to trade to and from its ports, it was never in doubt that the US could afford to act unilaterally in pursuing its own oil spill policy.[860] It was also felt that a uniform international regime would prevent the individual states of the US from enacting their own liability and compensation laws. In this regard, state autonomy within a federal system is sacrosanct in the US and the various states obviously felt that

---

[859] Following this latest round of revisions, TOVALOP and CRISTAL remained largely intact, with only subsequent minor amendments, up until their termination in 1997.

[860] DE LA RUE & ANDERSON, *supra* note 777, at 22.

they knew best how to deal with oil discharges, and indeed, all environmental matters, within their own jurisdiction.

Until the enactment of OPA-90, oil spill liability and compensation in the US remained governed by a patchwork of federal statutes, the interstices of which were roughly plugged by state legislation and general maritime law.[861] In view of the disparate federal and state regimes and the absence of a uniform national framework, calls were frequently made to enact a comprehensive national oil pollution law. To this end, Congressional debates on a new federal oil pollution regime had begun as early as the mid-1970s. During this time, there appeared to be early consensus on the desirability of a regime adopting strict liability with fairly high limits. There was also agreement over the creation of a consolidated oil fund which would be financed by a per barrel tax on imported oil.

Beyond these broad agreements, however, consensus was lacking on the extent to which state law should be pre-empted by a comprehensive federal regime. While the House of Representatives favoured general pre-emption of state laws, the Senate (with its pro-state inclinations) opposed pre-emption in all but a few areas. Amidst the debate, several major oil spills occurred in or near US waters. In December 1976, the *Argo Merchant* grounded in international waters off Massachusetts. This incident led directly to the Carter Initiatives which effectively compelled IMCO to adopt stricter pollution control standards in the form of the 1978 MARPOL Protocol.[862]

The *Amoco Cadiz* spill in 1978 and the explosion of the *Ixtoc I* exploratory well in Mexico a year later prompted further concerns for marine environmental protection in the US. Subsequently, however, public interest and Congressional attention became distracted by a series of accidents involving non-oil hazardous substances. As a result, the Comprehensive Environmental Response, Compensation and Liability Act (CERCLA) of 1980[863] was enacted to deal with pollution by chemical substances. All this while, the US remained aloof in relation to the CLC 69/FUND 71 oil pollution regimes.

---

[861] Some of the relevant federal statutes at this time included the Federal Water Quality Improvement Act of 1970, the Clean Water Act of 1977, the Outer Continental Shelf Lands Act (OCSLA) of 1953 and its Amendments of 1978, the Trans-Alaska Pipeline Authorization Act (TAPAA) of 1973 and the Deepwater Ports Act of 1975. For analyses of these laws, see DE LA RUE & ANDERSON, *ibid.* at 37–55 and 161–228.

[862] See Ch. 3.   [863] 42 U.S.C. §§ 9601–9675.

Even with the arrival of the Reagan Administration in 1980, oil spill legislation remained neglected. However, a new Bill introduced in Congress in 1983 soon stoked interest in the CLC 69 and FUND 71 Conventions by encouraging the Administration to negotiate more extensive liability and compensation provisions at the international level.[864] Armed with the promise to join the international regime, the US delegation to the 1984 IMO Conference was able to demand the acceptance of major changes such as vastly increased liability limits, compensation for restoration of damaged natural resources, prevention and response measures, the expedition of future increases in liability limits and very crucially, the preservation of state-level oil spill compensation funds within the US. However, the Senate Foreign Relations Committee subsequently refused to approve the 1984 Protocols. To the consternation of the international community, it appeared that the US was not going to accept the Protocols after all.

In the history of marine pollution regulation, nothing catalyses change more dramatically than a huge shipping disaster. And so it was on 24 March 1989, when the US-registered tanker, the *Exxon Valdez*, ran aground in Prince William Sound, Alaska as a result of a navigational error. More than 10 million gallons (37,000 tonnes) of oil were released into the pristine waters of Alaska, fouling one of the most sensitive ecosystems in North America and causing the worst oil spill incident in US history. Media publicity surrounding the event was unparalleled and the political consequences far-reaching. In the months following the *Exxon Valdez*, several other oil spills occurred, triggering further public and media reaction.[865] The US Congress was subsequently galvanised into action to consider a new comprehensive law – the Oil Pollution Act of 1990 (OPA-90).

During the run-up to OPA-90's adoption, powerful state interests within the US Congress vigorously opposed federal pre-emption of state autonomy to enact liability laws and to constitute state compensation funds. Led by Senator George Mitchell of Maine, these interests opposed US acceptance of the 1984 Protocols, primarily because international commitments necessarily pre-empted state laws. In the Reagan Administration's view, however, the benefits of accepting the Protocols

---

[864] The Bill was approved by the House Merchant Marine and Fisheries Committee on 28 June 1983, see H.R. Rep. No. 430, 98th Cong., 1st Sess. (1983).
[865] These were the *World Prodigy* incident off Rhode Island, the *Rachel B* incident at Galveston Bay in Texas, the *Presidente Rivera* incident in Delaware, the *American Trader* incident in California and the *Mega Borg* explosion in the Gulf of Mexico.

far outweighed those to be gained from enacting state laws. These included the availability of foreign shipowners' or insurers' assets against which claims could be brought, the spreading of costs among IOPC Fund member states for pollution incidents in the US and the opportunity for the US to lead and influence international opinion on the matter.

The Administration was also sensitive to the international community's expectation for US participation and leadership in the Protocols. After all, the US had expended much capital dictating the outcome of the 1984 Protocols and any reversion to unilateralism at this stage would decidedly breed resentment. It was also during this crucial period that the Senate had been criticised both at home and abroad for obstructing ratification of the UN Convention on the Law of the Sea.

Within the US, the state interests were supported by the environmental lobby in their resistance to the 1984 Protocols. For the environmentalists, the Protocols were grossly inadequate. For one thing, compensation under the Protocols did not extend to pollution by non-persistent oils, thus rendering the regime less than comprehensive. In addition, it was felt that the range of potential defendants was unnecessarily narrow. This was because the Protocols only channelled liability to the shipowner and did not impose strict, joint and several liability on owners, operators, charterers and pilots.[866]

Moreover, the Protocols entrenched the concept of limitation with limits broken only by proof of intentional or reckless conduct by the owner. While compensation beyond what was recoverable from the shipowner would be provided by the IOPC Fund, this fund maintained an overall limit to liability. The Protocols also restricted the circumstances under which the costs of restoring natural resources could be recovered. In the US environmentalists' view, complete clean-up and compensation had to be effected following an oil spill regardless of the costs involved. Consequently, nothing short of unlimited compensation would suffice.

On their part, the shipowning and oil interests were supportive of a comprehensive federal regime which would pre-empt state laws and impose some much-desired uniformity.[867] The oil interests, in particular, were deeply alarmed over their potentially unlimited liability under federally- or state-constituted funds. Ultimately, however, the powerful sentiments evoked by the US states and their environmental allies

---

[866] DE LA RUE & ANDERSON, supra note 777, at 60.   [867] Ibid. at 59.

prevailed. The popular mood in the US had by that time been swung by media outcry over the general deterioration of the environment and the lack of environmental responsibility shown by corporate interests. As is the norm in US politics, domestic considerations enjoyed far greater currency than international concerns. Thus, the ratification of the 1984 Protocols became relegated to a secondary priority.

As Congress debated the two oil pollution bills presented by the House of Representatives and the Senate respectively, it became clear that federal pre-emption could not be supported.[868] At the same time, the Senate insisted on channelling liability exclusively to the owner or operator of the vessel. Even though the House of Representatives had envisaged some form of liability for the cargo owner, subject to a limit of 50 per cent of total costs, the powerful oil interests succeeded in opposing joint liability. Ultimately, OPA-90 imposed secondary liability on cargo owners in the form of contributions to an Oil Spill Liability Trust Fund.[869] While this provision did impose some costs on cargo owners, it was clear that the bulk of costs would fall on the shipowners, many of whom were foreign controlled. In retrospect, the exoneration of cargo owners from primary liability is regrettable since such liability would have been a stronger disincentive against chartering sub-standard ships.

5.2 Implications of OPA-90

OPA-90 entered into force on 18 August 1990.[870] Almost immediately, its affirmation of the right of individual states to enact rules which could go beyond federal standards raised alarm among shipowners.[871] Moreover, OPA-90's defences to liability were restricted and its limits

---

[868] *Ibid.* at 61–5.

[869] The Fund is administered by the National Pollution Funds Center.

[870] On OPA-90 generally, see e.g. DE LA RUE & ANDERSON, *supra* note 777, at 58–65; J. Morgan, *The Oil Pollution Act of 1990: A Look at its Impact on the Oil Industry*, 6 FORDHAM ENVTL L. J. 1 (1994); M. Marion, *OPA 1990 Revisited*, INT'L J. SHIPPING L. 188 (1997); and J. A. Garick, *Crisis in the Oil Industry – Certificates of Financial Responsibility and the OPA 1990*, 17 MARINE POL'Y 272 (1993).

[871] OPA-90, § 1018(a)(1). For an assessment of the differences between OPA-90 and the IMO instruments, see e.g. A. Ayorinde, *Inconsistencies Between OPA '90 and MARPOL 73/78: What is the Effect on Legal Rights and Obligations of the United States and Other Parties to MARPOL 73/78?*, J. MAR. L. & COM. 55 (1994) and S. T. Smith, *An Analysis of the Pollution Act of 1990 and the 1984 Protocols on Civil Liability for Oil Pollution Damage*, 14 HOUS. J. INT'L L. 115 (1991). On market incentives, see M. de Gennaro, *Oil Pollution Liability and Control under International Maritime Law: Market Incentives as an Alternative to Government Regulation*, 37 VAND. J. TRANSNAT'L L. 265 (2004).

extremely high. Yet, these federal limits could either be overridden by state laws or 'broken' by a relatively low threshold of owner misconduct. Either way, there existed a high potential for unlimited liability falling on owners, thereby rendering the federal limits meaningless. For foreign operators and insurers, the prospect of unlimited liability for tankers calling at US ports was a frightful one.[872] The owners were also deeply unhappy that federal legislators had channelled liability exclusively to them and failed to require greater liability-sharing by the oil industry.

On its part, the International Group of P&I Clubs expressed concern over the insurance market's capacity to absorb the higher liability limits under OPA-90 and the various state laws. In view of the substantially higher risks for tankers trading to the US, the P&I Clubs had to re-assess the relative contributions of tankers and dry cargo vessels as well as those of operators wishing to trade to the US. Subsequently, the Clubs amended their terms and conditions of entry to introduce a so-called Exclusion Clause. This effectively excluded all claims relating to oil pollution in US waters. Tanker owners who needed continued coverage for trading to the US were thus required to request the deletion of the Clause and to submit quarterly declarations of cargo voyages to the US. Of course, these owners were charged a hefty additional premium or surcharge in respect of voyages to or from US ports or transiting the US EEZ. This greatly increased the costs of operating to and from the US.

OPA-90's requirements for Certificates of Financial Responsibility (COFRs)[873] also raised concerns. Under the Act, insurers are required not only to guarantee the shipowners' liabilities up to the maximum statutory limits but to submit to direct action in US federal courts, irrespective of any contractual policy defences the insurer would have enjoyed against a claim by the insured shipowner. This means that the shipowner and his insurer effectively become guarantors for all claimants under the Act for unlimited amounts.

OPA-90's provisions on direct action are also especially severe because unlike the CLC regime's, they do not allow the insurer to raise

---

[872] See generally, DE LA RUE & ANDERSON, supra note 777, at 66–9 and M. K. Cooney, *The Stormy Seas of Oil Pollution Liability: Will Protection and Indemnity Clubs Survive?*, 16 HOUS. J. INT'L L. 343 (1993). It must be remembered that OPA-90 effected changes going far beyond compensation matters – it imposed new regulations for a variety of matters, including tank vessel design (see Ch. 3), manning standards and vessel response plans.

[873] On COFRs generally, see e.g. L. Alcantara & M. Cox, *OPA 90 Certificates of Financial Responsibility*, 23 J. MAR. L. & COM. 369 (1992).

limitation independently of the insured's actual fault or privity or omission. At the outset, the P&I Clubs revolted against these provisions and pronounced that they would not issue COFRs for pollution by oil or other substances to cover potentially unlimited liability under individual state laws. For a while, the controversy threatened to disrupt oil imports into the US but this was eventually redressed when alternative providers of COFRs emerged in the market.

The wide definition of 'damages' under OPA-90 gives rise to its own problems. The Act allows recovery for the cost of restoring or replacing damaged natural resources, the loss of use of these resources pending restoration and the reasonable cost of quantifying such damages.[874] In this regard, the commonly used method of quantification known as Natural Resource Damage Assessment (NRDA) is particularly controversial because it permits the employment of unconventional methods such as computer models, compensation tables and contingency valuation to arrive at damage assessments.[875] To the industry interests, such methods lacked scientific validity, relied on vague and speculative social perceptions of worth and threatened to inflate damage claims beyond any reasonable degree of certainty.

Another irritant is the requirement that owners and operators submit detailed plans for responding to a worst-case oil discharge scenario. The OPA-90 regulations require shipowners to take action such as entering into contracts with clean-up companies, employing spill management teams and carrying on-board pollution response equipment. These provisions are essentially viewed by shipowners as little more than lucrative business opportunities for a host of oil spill response companies, many of whom mushroomed to meet the demands of OPA-90.[876]

Yet another problem relates to the high criminal and administrative penalties imposed by OPA-90. In the past decade or so, there have been frequent reports of coastal states (including the US) resorting to criminal sanctions or threats thereof in order to pressure owners to pay higher amounts in settlement of civil claims. Such tactics are particularly effective since criminal convictions or pleas of guilt tend to affect the defendant's civil case adversely. The increasing trend to criminalise

---

[874] OPA-90, § 1006(d)(1)(B).
[875] The NRDA featured significantly in a 1973 case involving the *Zoe Colocotronis* spill in Puerto Rico, see *Commonwealth of Puerto Rico v. S. S. Zoe Colocotronis*, 628 F.2d 652 (1st Cir. 1980). On NRDAs generally, see e.g. J. T. Smith, *Natural Resource Damages Under CERCLA and OPA: Some Basics for Maritime Operators*, 18 Tul. Mar. L. J. 1 (1993).
[876] Personal interviews.

ship masters and crew in the aftermath of an accident is also cause for concern.[877] These developments are undesirable primarily because they often result in plea bargains which do not reflect the owner's or master's true degree of culpability for a vessel accident.

From the US perspective, few of industry's fears over OPA-90 have materialised. A US government study in 1992 concluded that there was no statistical evidence to suggest that reputable independent owners with a substantial interest in US trade were withdrawing from the market.[878] Indeed, most independents who initially discontinued oil deliveries to US ports have since returned.[879] The response of the major oil companies has been instructive – given that the US market is too lucrative to ignore, they have instead adopted various innovative schemes to avoid liability under the draconian provisions of OPA-90. For one thing, several oil companies sold their tankers and resorted to chartering instead, thereby avoiding primary liability as owners.[880] The passage of OPA-90 thus became a major catalyst for the divestment of tanker ownership by oil companies.

Other cargo interests have taken to carrying oil in their own double-hull vessels, enjoying greater control over their operations and reducing the appertaining risks of pollution.[881] Several owners have even resorted to corporate restructuring of their businesses in order to create one-ship companies. While this strategy might avoid liability by shielding the parent companies from claims, it is unlikely that it will be successful in the long term. This is because most charterers are now deterred from using vessels owned by one-ship companies given the

---

[877] This is a worldwide concern which has been raised at IMO. A common view is that under international law, a criminal action against the master can only be undertaken by the flag state or the state of which the master is a national, see Edgar Gold, as quoted in Lloyd's List, *Time Behind Bars: A New Barrier for Those Earning a Living at Sea*, 10 Aug. 2004. See also J. Giffin, *Developments Concerning Criminal Charges Against Vessel Owners and Corporate Officers for Oil Spills in US Waters*, 5 INT'L MAR. L. 91 (1999).
[878] PETROLEUM INDUSTRY RESOURCES FOUNDATION, TRANSPORTING US OIL IMPORTS: THE IMPACT OF OIL LEGISLATION ON THE TANKER MARKET 63 (1992), cited in DE LA RUE & ANDERSON, *supra* note 777, at 68.
[879] DE LA RUE & ANDERSON, *ibid.* at 68.
[880] Anderson & de la Rue, *supra* note 98, at 44. Many such charterers forget, however, that they can still be sued by the shipowner in a recourse action to an unlimited amount, see *Aegean Sea Traders Corp. (Aegean Sea)* v. *Repsol Petroleo S.A.*, [1998] Lloyd's Rep. 39, at 49 and Anderson & de la Rue, *ibid.* at 46–7.
[881] In 2000, 43 per cent of all tankers calling at US ports were double-hulled, see INTERTANKO, *supra* note 14, at 53.

risk that US courts might extend liability to any party closely associated with the operation of these vessels.

Another point of interest is that although OPA-90 does not pre-empt individual states from enacting rules which go beyond federal standards,[882] state laws enacted in the aftermath of OPA-90 have generally displayed consistency with federal law. This is true even for the most stringent states such as California, Washington and Maine. By and large, the laws of these states go beyond pre-*Exxon Valdez* standards but come fairly within OPA-90 limits. In any event, many of the stringent state laws had been in existence even before OPA-90 was legislated. The passage of OPA-90 never changed this but only served to highlight it.

Overall, it is believed in the US that the impact of OPA-90 has been positive.[883] The Act has certainly led to higher operating costs and stringent operational and CDEM requirements such as double hulls on vessels entering US waters. The associated deterrent effects are believed to have led to a decline in sub-standard vessels operating to the US. There has also been a reported reduction in the amount of oil spilled into US waters.[884]

Despite its achievements, OPA-90 is still some way from delivering its promise of a clearer and more predictable regulatory system. For one thing, OPA-90 did not fully repeal existing federal legislation and case law. These laws, together with the vast array of state legislation permitted by OPA-90, still present a formidable challenge to any ship operator wishing to fully understand the US regulatory system. While the shipowning and oil industries have since grudgingly accepted OPA-90, it is also undeniable that the unilateral US regime has substantially increased the costs of transporting oil and other substances.[885] That the shipping industry has not abandoned the US market is less a testimony to OPA-90's acceptability than to the fact that most owners could not avoid trading to the world's largest economy.

---

[882] OPA-90, 33 U.S.C. 2718(a)(1). See generally DE LA RUE & ANDERSON, *supra* note 777, at 1163–77.
[883] Personal interviews. See also DE LA RUE & ANDERSON, *ibid*. at 68–9.
[884] The average annual spill of oil declined from 6.3 million gallons for the period 1986 to 1990 to 0.9 million gallons for the period 1991 to 1995, see MARITIME ADMINISTRATION AND US COAST GUARD, MARITIME TRADE AND TRANSPORTATION 1999, at 63 (C. Moore ed., 1999).
[885] The costs of implementing the eleven principal regulations of OPA-90 have been estimated at US$11 billion, see Lloyd's List, *Enforcement Cost of OPA 90 Regulations Put at $11 bn*, 18 May 2001.

The unilateral imposition of stringent measures under OPA-90 has also had regulatory effects on other trading regions in the world. There are now fears that lower-quality vessels deterred from operating to the US will simply be re-assigned to regions where enforcement action is weaker.[886] This introduces increased safety and environmental hazards for the developing countries. In any event, the provisions of OPA-90 fail to address the root causes of sub-standard shipping. In particular, the phasing out of single-hull vessels and the imposition of high liability limits do not address systemic problems inherent in the ship transportation industry such as the lack of incentives to use quality vessels and to provide adequate maintenance and crew training.

6. The 1992 Protocols to the CLC and FUND Conventions

The future of the inter-governmental liability and compensation regimes was thrown into serious doubt by the US decision to proceed unilaterally with OPA-90. IMO was thus forced to consider ways of bringing the 1984 Protocols into effect without US participation. To this end, an urgent diplomatic conference was convened by IMO in November 1992 to modify the entry into force requirements of the two Protocols.[887] The 1992 amendments thus reduced the tonnage and contributing oil thresholds necessary for entry into force, effectively dispensing with US acceptance of the Protocols.

The opportunity also arose for other improvements to be made. Without US participation, the Japanese oil industry came to bear a large proportion of contributions to the IOPC Fund.[888] Like many other countries, Japan had agreed to the higher limits in the 1984 Protocols on the assumption that the US would eventually join the system. As a condition for its own acceptance of the Protocols, Japan insisted on a formula which would ease the burden shouldered by its oil industry. A compromise was thus reached in 1992 to the effect that the

---

[886] Personal interviews.

[887] Urgency was also provided by the large *Haven* spill in the Italian port of Genoa in April 1991. On CLC/FUND 92 generally, see e.g. W. Chao, Pollution from the Carriage of Oil by Sea: Liability and Compensation (1996); Liability for Damage to the Marine Environment (C. de la Rue ed., 1993); G. Gauci, Oil Pollution at Sea: Civil Liability and Compensation for Damage (1997); and N. Gaskell, *Compensation for Oil Pollution Damage: 1992 Protocols to the Civil Liability Convention and the Fund Convention*, 8 Int'l J. Marine & Coastal L. 286 (1993).

[888] The biggest oil receivers who are currently in the FUND 92 regime are, in decreasing order, Japan, Italy, Republic of Korea, the Netherlands, France, the UK and Singapore.

contributions of any one state would be capped, for an interim period, at a maximum level of 27.5 per cent of overall levies.

With these issues settled, the substance of the 1984 agreement was re-cast in the form of the 1992 Protocols to the CLC and FUND Conventions. These Protocols thus brought into being the 1992 Civil Liability Convention (hereinafter 'CLC 92') and the 1992 FUND Convention (hereinafter 'FUND 92'). In relation to limits of liability, the 1992 Conventions adopted the same figures which the 1984 Protocols had proposed. Other substantive changes originally adopted in 1984 were re-introduced. These included the new 'intentional or reckless conduct' test for barring the shipowner's right to limitation.[889] This was not only a more stringent test for conduct barring limitation but it also unequivocally imposed the onus on the claimant to prove the gravity of the owner's conduct.[890] This generally pro-shipowner provision contrasts sharply with the relative ease with which OPA-90 limitation can be broken.

As compared to OPA-90, CLC 92 also channels liability more narrowly toward the shipowner. This reduces the scope for claimants in CLC 92 states to employ non-CLC regimes against other parties such as the servants or agents of the owner, the crew members, pilots, charterers and salvors.[891] Other provisions originally adopted in 1984 include the extension of coverage to bunker pollution caused by empty tankers on ballast voyages.[892] The cost of preventive measures taken in the wake of a casualty threatening grave or imminent risk of pollution would also

---

[889] CLC 92, art. V(2); LLMC 76, art. 4, *supra* note 881.

[890] On limitation, see generally P. GRIGGS ET AL., LIMITATION OF LIABILITY FOR MARITIME CLAIMS (2004).

[891] CLC 92, art. III(4), *supra* note 791. This was in response to the *Amoco Cadiz* and *Haven* litigations which sought to bring claims against non-shipowner parties, see N. Soisson, *International Oil Spill Compensation Systems*, 9 INT'L MAR. L. 273, at 275 (1997). Note that the exemption of non-owner liability from non-CLC proceedings is subject to conditions, see CLC 92, art. III(4). Exemption is lost if the same conduct which would have barred the owner's right to limitation can be proven on the part of these parties. This is in contrast to the position of servants or agents under CLC 69, whose exemption from liability is unqualified.

[892] It remains doubtful, however, whether an operational discharge of slops from a tanker in ballast would be covered. This is because it is often difficult to identify the cause of an operational discharge. Such identification is still needed under the CLC/FUND 92 regime, *supra* note 824. In any event, it is uncertain if slops can be considered as 'cargo'. Since 'oil' is defined by CLC 92, art. I(5) as 'persistent hydrocarbon mineral oil ... whether carried on board a ship as cargo or in the bunkers of such a ship', residues, tank washings and slops must be considered as part of 'cargo' before the conventions can apply, see DE LA RUE & ANDERSON, *supra* 777, at 84 and 136.

be recoverable even if no actual discharge of oil occurred.[893] Thus, CLC 92 and FUND 92 provide compensation for preventive measures taken anywhere either within or outside the geographic scope of the conventions as long as damage is caused or threatened to be caused to the areas within the geographic scope.

The definition of 'pollution damage' restricts compensation for impairment of the environment (other than loss of profit arising from such impairment) to the costs of reasonable measures of reinstatement actually undertaken or to be undertaken.[894] Thus, the costs of clean-up operations and property damage as well as consequential and pure economic losses can generally be compensated. However, the scope of environmental damage claims is explicitly confined to the costs of reasonable reinstatement measures. Accordingly, the 1992 conventions affirm the position that assessments of damage to the environment's intrinsic value arrived at by using abstract mathematical models or contingent valuation cannot be compensated.[895] Again, this is in stark contrast to the position under OPA-90.

That said, there remains the problem that the wording in the 1992 Conventions do not appear to preclude states from introducing domestic legislation permitting recovery in respect of matters which fall outside the definition of 'pollution damage'.[896] As such, states may retain the competence to prescribe domestic legislation pertaining to natural resource damage claims. Given that domestic courts are increasingly sympathetic to wide interpretations of 'pollution damage', the IOPC Fund may well have to review its conservative position on compensating natural resource damage claims as more of such claims arise.

The 1992 Protocols came into effect on 30 May 1996, bringing into force the CLC 92 and FUND 92 Conventions. A new IOPC Fund – known as the 1992 Fund – thus commenced operation. The 1992 Fund's Secretariat is staffed by the same London-based administrators who had been running the 1971 Fund. As the number of states ratifying the

---

[893] CLC 92, arts. I(8) and II(b).
[894] CLC 92, art. I(6). See generally C. Redgwell, *Compensation for Oil Pollution Damage – Quantifying Environmental Harm*, 16 MARINE POL'Y 90, 91 (1992) and DE LA RUE & ANDERSON, *supra* note 777, at 507–12.
[895] This is also the general position taken by the IOPC Funds' member states, see IOPC FUNDS, CLAIMS MANUAL 30 (2002). Note that the Funds decided in 2002 that the costs of post-spill environmental studies may be compensated.
[896] CLC 92, art. III(4). See the P&I Clubs' concerns over similar provisions in the 2001 Bunkers Convention, LEG Docs. 80/4/2 (1999) and 81/4/2 (2000).

1992 Conventions increased, the shipowning and oil industries announced in November 1995 that the TOVALOP/CRISTAL industry arrangements would not be renewed beyond 20 February 1997.[897]

In subsequent years, the incentive for oil-receiving states to abandon FUND 71 became especially great because any state which remained behind in that regime assumed the burden of proportionately larger contributions as other states left for the 1992 Fund. Thus, in the event of a devastating incident occurring in a FUND 71 member state, the claims will be concentrated on the remaining oil-receiving states, irrespective of how small their actual oil imports may be. Given this scenario, most major oil-receiving states lost no time in switching to FUND 92. In September 2000, IMO took the critical step of adopting a Protocol that amended FUND 71 to the effect that the convention would cease to be in force when certain conditions were met.[898] These conditions were fulfilled at the end of 2001 and, on 24 May 2002, the FUND 71 Convention was wound up.

In the meantime, there remain major oil-receiving states like China which have still not ratified FUND 92.[899] These states presumably feel that the costs of their oil receivers having to contribute to the 1992 Fund far outweigh whatever benefits the fund might bring.[900] In essence, these states are taking a calculated choice to self-insure against major oil pollution damage arising within their waters. Pollution claims in developing countries are invariably smaller and less costly, so these states reckon. Yet, the contribution per ton of oil received is the same for all oil-receiving states. Given that the largest claims in the IOPC Funds' history have arisen in the developed states such as Japan, France, Spain, and the UK, developing states like China may well believe

---

[897] See C. de la Rue, *TOVALOP and CRISTAL – A Purpose Fulfilled*, INT'L J. SHIPPING L. 285 (1996).

[898] These were either when the number of member states falls below twenty-five or one year after the 1971 Fund Assembly or the Administrative Council notes that the total quantity of contributing oil has fallen below 100 million tonnes, whichever is the earlier. This represents the first time that a tacit acceptance procedure was used to terminate a convention. The traditional way of winding up FUND 71 would have required the number of contracting states to fall below three, see FUND 71, art. 43. This was not realistically possible because the remaining state parties were small oil importers (and thus non-contributors to the fund) which had no incentive nor interest to denounce the convention.

[899] China is the world's third largest oil consumer, although its share of world oil demand (6.7 per cent) is far below that of the US. China is expected to surpass Japan as the second largest consumer within the next decade, see INTERTANKO, *supra* note 14, at 60.

[900] Personal interviews.

that they will end up subsidising the developed states if they accept FUND 92.

In response to the *Erika* incident in December 1999, France and the European Commission insisted on a revision of the CLC/FUND 92 limits. This formed part of a package of proposals which included the accelerated phase-out of single-hull tankers.[901] In October 2000, IMO duly adopted amendments to increase the maximum limits by 50.37 per cent.[902] The amendments entered into force by tacit acceptance on 1 November 2003 and enhanced the maximum amount of compensation available under CLC 92 from 59.7 million SDRs to 89.77 million SDRs (US$123 million). For ships smaller than 5,000 gross tons, the CLC minimum limit was raised to 4.5 million SDRs. The total amount of compensation available under the 1992 Conventions (including CLC 92) was thus raised from 135 million SDRs to 203 million SDRs (US$273 million).[903]

Following the *Erika*, proposals were also made in Europe to create a third tier of liability for oil pollution damage amounting to EUR 1 billion.[904] Known as COPE (Fund for the Compensation of Oil Pollution Damage in European Waters), the scheme was conceived as a 'top-up' fund in the event that FUND 92 became breached. In essence, the European states were concerned that there was now a risk of damage exceeding the limits payable under CLC/FUND 92, and that even the 50.37 per cent increase approved in 2000 might not be able to keep up with inflation. These fears were compounded by the occurrence of the *Prestige* incident in November 2002.

Most EU states, however, were averse to financing a third-tier fund which might burden their oil receivers and the benefits of which were likely to accrue to claimants from other states.[905] The decision was thus made to pursue the matter multilaterally at IMO. After negotiations at the IOPC Fund were conducted, IMO convened a conference in May 2003 to adopt a brand new supplementary protocol to FUND 92.[906] This

---

[901] See Ch. 3.
[902] These revisions were adopted through a formula already existing in the conventions, see CLC 92, art. 15, final clauses, and FUND 92, art. 33, final clauses.
[903] If three states contributing to the fund receive more than 600 million tonnes of oil a year, the maximum amount can be raised to 300.7 million SDRs.
[904] See Anderson & de la Rue, *supra* note 98, at 54 and the proposal for the *Erika* II package, *supra* note 377.
[905] Anderson & de la Rue, *ibid.* at 54.
[906] The text of the 2003 Protocol can be found at Doc. LEG/CONF.14/20 (2003).

protocol established an optional third-tier fund to provide new maximum compensation limits supplementing the amounts payable under CLC/FUND 92.

The third-tier fund will only pay for pollution damage in states which are parties to the new Protocol, and will be financed by cargo interests in these states. New maximum limits were set at 750 million SDRs (US$1.25 billion), inclusive of the amounts payable under CLC/FUND 92.[907] The new Protocol will enter into force three months after being accepted by eight states accounting for 450 million tonnes of oil receipts.[908] At the insistence of Japan, a cap for contributions was set at 20 per cent of total receipts.[909]

To address the oil companies' recurring concerns over small tankers,[910] a Small Tanker Oil Pollution Indemnification Agreement (STOPIA) was created alongside the new Protocol. Under STOPIA, the P&I Clubs voluntarily offered to raise the minimum limit for smaller ships under CLC 92 to 20 million SDRs (US$27 million). This limit will apply to all damage claims in states which are parties to the third tier, irrespective of the flag or ownership of the cargo. In essence, STOPIA is a *quid pro quo* offered by the shipowners for the oil companies' assumption of full liability under the third tier.[911] With STOPIA, the frequency of small ship claims will thus be balanced against the relatively infrequent but possibly huge claims under the third tier.

Looking forward, it is unlikely that the Supplementary Fund will attract support from the developing countries.[912] Practically, it is improbable that oil spill claims in developing countries will ever reach the high limits contemplated by the third tier. Another disincentive is the provision in the new Protocol for states to assume

---

[907] Spain (victim of the *Prestige*) had proposed 800 million SDRs, while OCIMF had lobbied for 400 million SDRs.

[908] This requirement was fulfilled on 3 December 2004 with the ratification by Spain. The Protocol thus entered into force on 3 March 2005. As at December 2004, Denmark, Finland, France, Germany, Ireland, Japan, Norway and Spain have accepted the Protocol.

[909] This cap will be in place until at least 1 billion tonnes of oil are received annually, or for ten years from the Protocol's entry into force, whichever is earlier.

[910] *Supra* note 838.

[911] The oil companies had attempted to involve the shipowners in the third tier and to introduce a proposal for all ships (regardless of size or capacity) to have a flat CLC limit of 90 million SDRs (US$123 million). These proposals were eventually rejected at IMO. For details on STOPIA, see Doc. LEG/CONF.14/12 (2003).

[912] Even FUND 92 itself has problems attracting ratifications by major developing oil receivers, *supra* notes 899–900.

contributions to the fund, under certain conditions, if no liable person exists for the total aggregated quantities received in that state.[913] Small developing states are thus likely to be concerned that this will place the burden of contributions on national governments as opposed to industrial interests like oil companies.

The Conference which adopted the 2003 Protocol also adopted a resolution providing for future revision of the CLC and FUND Conventions. This sets the stage for a fundamental re-assessment of the conventions, especially in relation to the maximum limit for shipowners. The oil companies had forcefully argued during the 2003 Conference that any supplementary protocol funded by the oil industry alone could end up insulating the low-quality shipowner, who would have no incentives to upgrade standards.[914] Discussions have thus commenced at the IOPC Fund to revise CLC 92 so as to introduce greater equity in contributions between shipowners/insurers and cargo interests.[915]

Clearly, the oil interests see the revision of CLC 92 as a *quid pro quo* for their accepting the Supplementary Fund. In addition, states such as Canada and the UK want the compensation instruments to provide explicit cost disincentives such as higher liability limits for owners and insurers of sub-standard vessels.[916] There are also proposals to deny limitation to shipowners and to provide for fund recourse action against charterers if damage arises from the ship's structural condition.[917] The oil companies have also proposed, *inter alia*, that the test for conduct barring limitation should revert to the less stringent 'actual fault and privity' standard, and that a flat tranche for shipowner liability (dispensing with tonnage-pegged limitation) be introduced.[918] Meanwhile, a Japanese proposal is seeking to make owners of sub-standard ships

---

[913] 2003 Protocol, art. 14.
[914] Submission of OCIMF to the Diplomatic Conference on the IOPC Supplementary Fund, Doc. LEG/CONF.14/13 (2003).
[915] See Reports on the Seventh and Eighth Meetings of the IOPC Fund's Third Inter-Sessional Working Group, *Review of the International Compensation Regime*, Docs. 92FUND/WGR.3/20 (2004) and 92FUND/WGR.3/23 (2004).
[916] Submission of Australia, Canada, Finland, France, the Netherlands, Russia and the UK, Doc. 92FUND/WGR.3/19/1 (2004). See also Doc. 92FUND/WGR.3/20 (2004), *ibid.* at 4.
[917] Position of France, see Doc. 92FUND/WGR.3/20 (2004), *ibid.* at 4–5.
[918] Position of OCIMF, see Doc. 92FUND/WGR.3/20 (2004), *ibid.* at 4–5 and 11–13. This will resurrect the original 'minimum tranche' idea advocated during the 1984 Conference, see Section 4.3 above. There is also a proposal to extend the requirement for compulsory insurance or equivalent financial security to *all* ships carrying oil in bulk as cargo (CLC 92 currently has a 2,000-ton threshold), see Doc. 92FUND/WGR.3/23 (2004), *supra* note 915, at 26.

pay more for damage caused if their ship has been chartered by a receiver in a Supplementary Fund state.[919]

These measures are all aimed at imposing pollution costs on the actors (including owners, charterers and oil receivers) who are directly implicated in a pollution incident caused by a sub-standard vessel. In this way, the measures seek to insulate the fund (comprising oil receivers in all fund states) from having to underwrite pollution incidents caused by sub-standard vessels and operators. Of course, these proposals are being resisted by the P&I Clubs, who point to the difficulty in defining which ships are 'sub-standard'. At the same time, there are states who feel strongly that safety and quality ideals should not be pursued in a compensation regime, but should instead be promoted by tightening instruments such as MARPOL 73/78 and SOLAS.[920]

The current proposed revisions do not necessarily seek to increase the maximum limits of CLC/FUND 92. Instead, they appear to be calling for a further recalibration of liability among the respective industry actors, with the laudable ideal being that the sub-standard operators should not continue to be effectively subsidised by other actors. Yet, there have been concerns among some states that the revision process may see the FUND 92 limits being upped, leading effectively to less contributions by developed state parties to the Supplementary Protocol and more burdens falling on the general FUND 92 membership.[921] On their part, the P&I Clubs appear willing to share the Supplementary Fund's burden with the oil industry, on condition that the CLC/FUND 92 limits remain unchanged. Overall, consistent with the trends identified in this work, the shipowners are on the defensive yet again and will likely be forced to accept greater liability limits, particularly for incidents involving sub-standard vessels.

7. Pollution by Hazardous and Noxious Substances (HNS)

In the aftermath of the *Torrey Canyon* incident in 1967, it had been envisaged that the new CLC 69 proposed by IMCO for oil pollution would embrace pollution caused by hazardous and noxious substances

---

[919] Doc. 92FUND/WGR.3/20 (2004), *ibid.* at 5.
[920] *Ibid.* at 16. See Anderson & de la Rue, *supra* note 98, at 59–60, for a similar view. Yet, one cannot discount the possibility that imposing greater liability on cargo interests will reduce or eliminate the *demand* for sub-standard shipping.
[921] Position of the Republic of Korea, see Doc. 92FUND/WGR.3/23 (2004), *supra* note 915, at 14.

(HNS) as well. However, it was readily acknowledged by IMCO at the time that the carriage of chemical substances by sea entailed far more difficulties and complexities than oil transportation. For one thing, HNS encompassed an extremely wide range of chemicals and substances with varying degrees of toxicity and risks to the marine environment. The differing types and sizes of ships used to carry HNS also posed difficulties for the uniform imposition of compulsory insurance requirements. Moreover, since the different types of HNS cargoes were received in port by different receiving parties, it was extremely difficult to devise any compensation system which could effectively levy contributions from the cargo interests.

In the result, IMCO decided in the late 1960s that the HNS issue would have to be deferred for future consideration and that the immediate priority for IMCO was oil pollution. In the meantime, HNS matters would have to be left to general principles of domestic tort law. However, the general absence within domestic laws of such critical concepts like compulsory insurance and strict liability for HNS damage soon revealed the inadequacies of national regimes in dealing with the subject.

At the 1984 IMO Conference, an attempt was made to adopt a convention relating to HNS damage alongside the negotiations over the CLC/FUND Protocols. However, the complexities of the HNS subject again hindered consensus on a convention.[922] The major points of disagreements included the extent of the cargo shipper's obligation to effect insurance and to assume liability for HNS-related damage, the question of whether limits of liability should 'stand alone' or reflect the provisions of LLMC 76, and whether HNS carried in packaged (as opposed to bulk) form should be covered. In essence, the major cargo-owning nations and their associated interests resisted any attempts to impose a share of liability upon them for HNS-related damages.

Following this abortive attempt, threats of unilateral action by states (particularly in Europe) led to efforts within IMO's Legal Committee to reconsider the HNS issue. After more than a decade's worth of fresh negotiations, agreement was finally reached in 1996 on an International Convention on Liability and Compensation for Damage

---

[922] This was the first diplomatic conference to be convened by IMO which failed to achieve its desired objective, see generally A. DeBievre, *Liability and Compensation for Damage in Connection with the Carriage of Hazardous and Noxious Substances by Sea*, 17 J. Mar. L. & Com. 61 (1986).

in Connection with the Carriage of Hazardous and Noxious Substances by Sea (hereinafter HNSC).[923] The HNSC's successful (albeit overdue) adoption represented a pro-active regulatory effort on IMO's part, given that it was adopted before any catastrophic HNS incident had occurred.

Pursuant to the compromise reached at the 1996 Conference, the HNSC adopted a two-tier compensation system largely similar to that employed by the CLC/FUND regime. Thus, the HNSC provided for the imposition of strict first-tier liability on the shipowner, the requirement of compulsory insurance and certificates evidencing such insurance, direct action against insurers, channelling of liability to owners and their insurers, free-standing liability limits separate from those under LLMC 57 and LLMC 76, limitation funds to be constituted by the shipowner, conduct barring limitation and the establishment of a second-tier HNS Fund financed by the cargo interests. In addition to compensating for pollution damage caused by HNS, the convention also extends to non-pollution damage resulting from incidents such as fires or explosions.

The term 'hazardous and noxious substances' was defined by reference to a comprehensive list of substances and materials which, when carried as cargo or as residues from their previous carriage in bulk,[924] triggers the applicability of the convention. The number of substances covered by the list (estimated to exceed 6,000) represents one of the most difficult aspects of the convention in terms of its implementation. The inclusion of oil in this list is to provide for the risks of fire and explosion (i.e. non-pollution) damage arising from the carriage of oil as well as for pollution damage caused by non-persistent oil.[925]

At the same time, the HNSC was crafted to exclude the carriage of coal. This is despite the fact that coal cargoes could present fire and explosion risks as well.[926] The coal-related interests had argued that since coal was usually carried in large quantities at relatively low risk, its inclusion would lead to high transport costs for coal exporters and a disproportionate second-tier burden for importers. The strong objections of the major coal importers (such as Japan, Italy, Canada, the US and Sweden) and the developing coal producers (including Mexico,

---

[923] *Supra* note 95.   [924] HNSC, art. 1(5).
[925] Pollution damage arising from the carriage of persistent oil is covered by CLC/FUND and is therefore excluded from HNSC, see art. 4(3).
[926] Submission of Belgium, Denmark, Finland, Germany, Ireland, the Netherlands, Spain, Sweden and the UK, LEG/CONF.10/CW/WP.13 (1996). These were the states which desired the inclusion of coal.

South Africa, Chile, Bangladesh and Brazil) thus resulted in its being excluded from the HNSC altogether. Similarly, fishmeal, woodchip and other high-volume, low-hazard solid substances were excluded. Damage arising from the carriage of these substances would thus fall to be covered under the applicable LLMC or national law regimes.

Apart from situations where claims are excluded, several exceptions to the owner's strict liability are provided. Most of these are identical to those applicable under CLC 92. An exception unique to the HNSC relates to the failure of the shipper or any other person to furnish information on the hazardous and noxious nature of the cargo. If this failure to furnish information causes the damage, wholly or partly, or leads the owner not to obtain insurance for the cargo, the owner is wholly exempted from liability, provided that neither the owner nor its servants or agents knew or ought reasonably to have known of the hazardous and noxious nature of the cargo.[927] This exception was adopted in recognition of the fact that unlike oil carried in bulk, the carriage of HNS typically entails the shipment of substances in various forms of packaging and stowage without adequate description of the contents being supplied to the carrier. Where damage arises from such situations, compensation will have to be obtained from the HNS Fund.

As regards limitation, the HNSC conferred the right to limit upon shipowners in recognition of their submission to strict liability as well as to apportion the burden of compensation between the shipping and cargo interests. The prevailing limits applicable in many states – primarily LLMC 57 or 76 – were thought to be too low to deal with the potentially large HNS claims. Hence, the Conference settled on provisions inspired by CLC 92 – independent first-tier limits for the shipowner, with second-tier liability borne by an HNS Fund financed by cargo interests.

In relation to small ships, it will be recalled that this concern had previously arisen with oil pollution claims under CLC. Since serious damage could conceivably result even from small quantities of HNS cargoes carried by small ships, it was decided that the owner's limits of liability had to be pegged at a minimum level of 10 million SDRs for all ships of up to 2,000 tons. As a compromise for owners of small ships, the HNSC allowed contracting states to wholly exempt from the convention (by way of an opting-out procedure) ships which do not exceed 200 gross tons and which carry HNS only in packaged form while being

---

[927] HNSC, art. 7(2)(d).

engaged on entirely domestic voyages.[928] This provision was inserted at the insistence of countries such as Japan which had significant domestic trade carried by small ships.

For ships above 2,000 tons, the limit increases from the baseline 10 million SDRs level by 1,500 SDRs for each ton from 2,001 to 50,000 tons; beyond that, a further 360 SDRs per ton would be applicable up to an overall ceiling of 100 million SDRs.[929] The maximum amount of compensation available under the HNS Fund was set at 250 million SDRs, inclusive of the amount actually recovered from the shipowner or his insurer. Overall, the limits imposed were considered to be very high, at least in the eyes of shipowning interests such as ICS, Greece and China. These relatively high limits mean that the second-tier HNS Fund would effectively apply only to catastrophic incidents. This was insisted upon by the representatives of the chemical cargo interests such as the European Chemical Industry Council (CEFIC).

Due to the varied nature of HNS cargoes and their respective receivers, the system of levies and contributions for the HNS Fund is much more complex than is the case for the IOPC Fund. In this regard, the HNS Fund maintains a general account as well as three separate independent accounts. The latter hold 'fenced-off' contributions paid for by the three largest categories of HNS cargoes – oil, liquefied natural gases (LNG) and liquefied petroleum gases (LPG).

The objective of separate accounts is to reflect the different levels of volumes, risks and contributions associated with certain cargoes. This way, high-volume cargoes with low transportation risks (i.e. those cargoes with outstanding safety records and low frequency of incidents) would not be made to cross-subsidise higher-risk cargoes. This was at the insistence of major LNG producers such as Indonesia, Malaysia and Brunei, which feared that without separate accounts, they would end up subsidising the chemical industries of the developed states.[930]

The inherent difficulties in implementing the HNSC have led to extremely low acceptance of the convention, with only seven states having ratified as of December 2004. The entry into force requirements are fairly stringent; the convention will enter into force eighteen months after at least twelve states, including four with not less than two million units of gross tonnage, have ratified it. In addition, HNS receivers in the

---

[928] HNSC, art. 5(1).   [929] HNSC, art. 9(1).
[930] See submissions of Indonesia, LEG Docs. 66/4/5 (1992) and 67/3/11 (1992); of Malaysia, LEG Docs. 67/3/8 (1992) and 68/4/13 (1993); and of Brunei, LEG Doc. 67/3/9 (1992).

ratifying states must have received a total quantity of at least 40 million tonnes of contributing cargo in the preceding calendar year.[931]

While it appears that the Western European states are collectively able to fulfil such conditions, they are naturally reluctant to impose the substantial costs of acceptance on their industries without the participation of other major chemical importers, principally Japan. US participation is ruled out, given the existence of its own CERCLA legislation.[932] Recently, there have been indications from the UK, Ireland, Finland, Sweden, Denmark and Norway as to their willingness to accept the HNSC.[933] The UK, in particular, is playing a leading role to prepare for the HNSC's eventual implementation, and is currently working on a system to facilitate the reporting of contributing cargo. It is thus likely that the HNSC will enter into force reasonably soon, but negotiations between Europe and Japan are likely to occur first to get the latter to come on board. For now, resort to the LLMC and national law regimes will be needed should an incident involving HNS substances occur.

8. Pollution by Bunker Fuel Oils

As far back as the 1960s when CLC 69 was first mooted, many states had already called for claims arising from bunker fuel pollution to be compensated along with those from oil cargo pollution. Despite these efforts, CLC 69 was eventually restricted to cargo and bunker pollution from laden tankers only. On their part, the 1984 CLC/FUND Protocols covered cargo and bunker pollution from all oil tankers, whether laden or in ballast. However, bunker pollution from non-tankers remained uncovered.

The exclusion of non-tankers was a result of insistence by industry interests that bunker pollution was not a serious enough problem which needed international attention. By the early 1990s, however, the maritime world had become aware of the hazards posed by heavy bunker oils. In most instances, the damage caused by bunker fuel pollution exceeded the limits of compensation available under the applicable LLMC or national regimes.[934] The problem was especially

---

[931] HNSC, art. 46.
[932] On CERCLA, see DE LA RUE & ANDERSON, *supra* note 777, at 307–69.
[933] Submission of the UK, LEG Doc. 86/7 (2003).
[934] According to ITOPF estimates, about 50 per cent of oil spills attended to in recent years involved bunker fuel spilled from non-tankers, see I. White, *Oil Spill Response – Experience, Trends and Challenges*, ITOPF Paper (2000), *available at* http://www.itopf.com/spillcon.pdf (last accessed 31 Dec. 2004).

acute in relation to small ships with low tonnage-based limitation amounts. In essence, as long as ships continued to use low-quality heavy fuel oil, the threat of bunker discharges causing serious environmental impact was always present.

With the CLC/FUND avenue being shut, states such as the UK suggested that the proposed new HNSC should provide for compulsory insurance and higher compensation limits in relation to bunker fuel damage from non-tankers. However, the shipping and insurance interests continued to resist strict liability and compulsory insurance for bunker spills, arguing that these would impose administrative burdens for enforcement and policing. It was contended that since all ships carry bunker fuel, any insurance requirement for bunker spills would have to be imposed on virtually every ship in the world, even passenger liners, fishing vessels and pleasure craft. This, together with the fact that many insurers apart from the P&I Clubs offered cover for bunker spills, would make enforcement almost impossible.

It was also argued that the HNSC regime, like CLC/FUND, was fundamentally tied to cargo carriage and could not thus be extended to bunkers. In other words, bunker fuels could never practically be considered as 'contributing cargo' for the purposes of contribution levies and second-tier liability. There was also the issue of principle as to whether the HNS Fund should compensate for bunker damage caused by a ship not carrying any contributing cargo.

The insurers claimed that P&I insurance already covered bunker spills, albeit without the advantages of compulsory insurance and direct action. In this regard, the Clubs were open to a requirement for compulsory insurance but strongly resisted extending direct action to bunker spills. In their view, allowing direct action would be prejudicial to the owners and their insurers given that there existed no *quid pro quo* requirement for second-tier cargo liability (as exists with oil and HNS pollution). Consequently, when the HNSC was finally adopted in 1996, it, too, excluded consideration of the non-tanker bunker problem.

In subsequent years, proposals emerged at IMO for the adoption of a convention dedicated to non-tanker bunker fuel damage. Interest in the matter was ignited by several bunker pollution incidents involving uninsured or under-insured ships. In almost all these cases, the full clean-up costs could not be recovered from the owners. The incident which garnered the greatest attention was the bunker spill caused by the bulk carrier *Iron Baron* off the coast of Tasmania, Australia in July

1995. Following the incident, the Australian government canvassed IMO to plug the last remaining gap in the compensation regime for vessel-source oil pollution.

The Australian initiatives at IMO were supported by delegations such as the UK, which had also faced problems in recovering clean-up costs from owners or insurers which could not be detected.[935] In March 2001, IMO successfully concluded the International Convention on Liability and Compensation for Bunker Oil Spills (hereinafter 'Bunkers Convention').[936] The Bunkers Convention contains standard features such as strict but limited liability for pollution damage caused by bunker spills from non-tankers. Against resistance from the shipowners and P&I Clubs, a requirement for compulsory insurance cover was adopted along with a right of direct action against insurers.

Unlike the CLC/FUND and HNSC regimes, the Bunkers Convention does not establish independent limitation amounts, but merely pegs limitation to the relevant existing regime in state parties (i.e. either LLMC or national law).[937] In addition, the convention does not provide for second-tier cargo liability.[938] This was one reason why the owners and insurers had fought so hard to resist direct action. The convention applies to ships over 1,000 gross tons, and will enter into force one year after eighteen states, including five with ships whose combined gross tonnage exceeds one million gross tons, have either signed it without reservation or ratified it.[939] While the administrative difficulties of implementing the convention are clear, it is nonetheless a welcome development that after decades of equivocation, the international regulatory system has finally reached agreement on a regime for compensating pollution damage arising from non-tanker bunker spills.[940]

---

[935] E.g. the *Borodinskoye Polye* and *Pionersk* incidents in 1994, involving fish factory vessels causing spills for which clean-up costs could not be recovered. The US faced similar problems with the *Kure* (1997) and *New Carrissa* (1999) incidents.

[936] The text can be found at Doc. LEG/CONF.12/19 (2001). On the convention, see W. Chao, *Liability and Compensation for Bunker Pollution*, 33 J. Mar. L. & Com. 553 (2002).

[937] For national law and other regimes, see DE LA RUE & ANDERSON, *supra* note 777, at 263-75.

[938] The definition of 'shipowner' in the convention is also broader than in the CLC - this embraces 'the owner, including the registered owner, bareboat charterer, manager and operators of the ship'. A larger group of persons is thus exposed to liability for pollution damage caused by bunker oil.

[939] As of December 2004, only five states - Jamaica, Samoa, Slovenia, Spain and Tonga - are parties.

[940] In terms of further regulation, there are indications from IMO that double hulls could be introduced for non-tankers' bunker fuel tanks.

9. The Liability and Compensation Regimes: Concluding Analysis

The true worth of the CLC/FUND, HNSC and Bunkers Convention regimes lies in their creation of a uniform international system providing incentives for compliance with standardised rules. For most cases, this guarantees the consolidation of pollution claims under one jurisdiction, the ease of administering limitation funds and the mutual recognition and enforcement of judgments in all contracting states. From the perspective of oil spill victims, the regimes guarantee prompt and adequate compensation with direct action against insurers. In particular, claims can be brought in the courts of the victims' own countries without their having to pursue the shipowner elsewhere.

The regimes also render it unnecessary for claimants to bear the expenses of arresting vessels and enforcing judgments following spill incidents. This benefits not only claimants but also shipowners who can avoid delays to their trading schedules. In addition, the regimes provide for the application of strict liability; this allows for amicable resolution of cases without the expense and delay of litigating fault. Moreover, the operation of the second-tier IOPC Fund (and the proposed HNS Fund when the HNSC enters into force) has greatly facilitated claims settlement, often without resort to litigation. In sum, features such as strict liability, compulsory insurance, limitation funds, direct action against insurers and cargo-financed supplemental funds have all benefited pollution victims immensely.

As examined, most of the CLC/FUND regime's weaknesses relate to CLC 69 and FUND 71. These have now been largely redressed by the 1992 Conventions. Pollution damage in the EEZ is now covered, as are preventive measures in 'pure threat' situations and damage caused by tankers in ballast. However, the continued exemption of non-persistent oils is problematic given that such oils are equally capable of causing serious damage to the marine environment. Also, the exemption of unidentified operational spills causes especial concern for coastal states, given that such incidents remain major sources of pollution.

The channelling of liability to the shipowner has also proven too rigid in some cases with the result that joint and several liability cannot be imposed on other parties who may be equally responsible for pollution incidents. In this regard, the imposition of civil liability on actors such as charterers may actually be desirable if it can deter these actors from using sub-standard ships. Thus, there is a case for the CLC/FUND, HNSC and Bunkers Convention regimes – originally meant for compensation purposes – to be redesigned to promote deterrence, behavioural change and incentives for compliance. This is consistent with the thesis that a more widely distributed burden-sharing regime (both in relation to pollution control equipment as well as liability for claims) can better foster an industry-wide ethos for quality shipping.

As seen above, in the wake of the recent oil spill disasters in Europe, the European Commission has begun to question the efficacy of the CLC/FUND regime in deterring negligent practices which cause serious pollution incidents. In the Commission's view, the current focus of the regime is too much on the compensation of victims, as opposed to the liability of the actual polluter.[941] Thus, liability can almost always be avoided by virtue of the owner's right to limitation, the difficulty in breaking this right and the general immunity of non-owner actors.[942] In the forthcoming revision of the CLC and FUND Conventions, it can be expected that the Commission will press for unlimited shipowner liability in cases of gross or serious negligence and the removal of immunity for non-owner actors such as charterers and ship managers, particularly when sub-standard vessels are implicated.[943]

Another challenge for the international regimes appears to be the increasing tendency of national legislatures and courts to widen the scope of 'pollution damage'. This is not helped by drafting weaknesses in CLC 92 which do not seem to preclude domestic legislation allowing recovery for matters falling outside the convention's definition of 'pollution damage'.[944] Already, jurisdictions including the US and some European countries have begun to recognise claims such as 'natural resource damage' or 'harm to the environment', the assessment of which may be conducted using theoretical models leading to substantial judgment sums.[945] Consequently, the IOPC Fund's established practice of excluding speculative claims in respect of natural resource damage assessment, i.e. claims that fall outside recovery in respect of restoration or reinstatement, may soon have to be reviewed.

The liability and compensation regimes have also had significant cost impact on the shipowning, insurance and cargo-owning industries. In

---

[941] Commission Proposal for a Directive on Sanctions, *supra* note 394, at 5-7.
[942] *Ibid.* at 6.   [943] *Ibid.*
[944] CLC 92, art. III(4), *supra* note 791. See the P&I Clubs' concerns, *supra* note 896.
[945] See OPA-90's NRDA provisions, 33 U.S.C. 2702(b)(2)(A), *supra* note 875.

particular, the imposition of strict liability, the requirement for compulsory insurance and the entrenchment of direct action against insurers must rank as among the most dramatic changes to affect the shipowners and P&I Clubs in the past 50 years. On its part, the second-tier liability funds financed by the cargo interests can be seen as an attempt to ameliorate the primary burden on shipowners. Yet, the fact that the Supplementary Funds are designed to 'kick in' only in the more serious pollution incidents testifies to the greater relative influence of the cargo interests. The same is true in relation to minimum liability thresholds on small tankers.

Based on the trends at IMO over the years, it is likely that with increasing environmental concerns in the developed states and the growing invocation of the 'polluter pays' principle, greater costs will progressively be imposed on the shipping industry. Along with stricter discharge and CDEM standards and more vigilant port state enforcement, stronger liability and compensation regimes mark an increasing erosion of the traditional right of free and unhindered navigation. At the same time, the impending imposition of liability on the non-shipowning interests is likely to provide greater incentives for these actors to promote the use of well-maintained ships and to suppress the market for sub-standard ones. To such extent, there exist prospects for more equitable burden-sharing arrangements to be instituted among all maritime actors.

PART C

The Future of Regulation

7 Challenges and Prescriptions

1. Improving Institutional Responses

One of the most pressing issues facing IMO today is the need to demonstrate its effectiveness in promulgating and implementing harmonised international regulations so as to avert unilateral action by states. Throughout this work, references have been made to the shipping community's concerns over the threat of unilateral or regional action by states or groups of states – collectively referred to here as 'unilateralism'. Indeed, the resort to unilateral measures arrived at independent of international agreement represents a serious challenge to the decision-making authority of multilateral institutions such as IMO.

As things stand, the traditional right of the maritime interests to free navigation is already facing progressive erosion by coastal state action. If instances of unilateralism or regionalism occur with increasing frequency, not only will the delicate balance struck by the UN Law of the Sea Convention between the freedom of navigation and coastal state jurisdiction be further shaken, but there is a risk that IMO's authority will be compromised. This will have serious repercussions for the uniformity and stability of the global maritime trading system.

In the maritime arena, the systemic costs of unilateralism can be significant – these include a multiplicity of rules across different jurisdictions and an increase in transportation costs which have to be passed on to the consumer. In addition, unilateral controls by states or regions invariably have the effect of exporting safety and pollution risks to less developed regions of the world. For their part, unilateralist actors who remain outside the ambit of international agreement forgo the opportunity to lead and influence global policies.

In the aggregate, few states in the world can afford the political and financial costs of unilateral action apart from the obvious actors such as the US and the EU. That said, the potential for unilateral action by any state cannot be discounted in an age of growing concern for ship safety, environmental protection and maritime security. Often, such action becomes likely if a state actor perceives that the international system is unable to respond in the manner or speed desired by domestic demands. The need to appease media and popular agitation following a particular pollution event typically fuels the unilateralist mood. Thus, it has been seen how the US and EU responses to serious pollution incidents were dictated primarily by the perceived inefficacy of IMO to deal with serious pollution incidents.

In the event, if unilateralism is to be averted or minimised at all, several systemic deficiencies which fuel unilateralist tendencies must be addressed. These are: the reactive, 'knee-jerk' approach to rule-making at IMO; the slow entry into force of IMO conventions once these are enacted; the inadequate implementation of these conventions even after entry into force; and the overall impotence of IMO in enforcing compliance with the relevant rules. These systemic defects can be addressed by the following measures, each of which is examined below: pro-active rule-making by IMO; securing prompt entry into force for conventions; ensuring effective compliance; and strengthening IMO's enforcement capacity.

1.1 Pro-active Rule-Making by IMO

For the past half century or so, the international regulatory system's response to marine environmental concerns has characteristically been reactive, as opposed to pro-active, in nature. The catalysts for action have invariably been vessel accidents involving calamitous loss of lives or serious environmental pollution, often with the attendant media and public outcry. The IMO legislation book is filled with instruments enacted in response to high-profile incidents such as the *Torrey Canyon*, *Amoco Cadiz*, *Argo Merchant*, *Exxon Valdez*, *Herald of Free Enterprise*, *Estonia* and, most recently, the *Erika* and *Prestige*.

As much as these incidents help to highlight issues of concern, it is also fair to say that they promote a culture of legislative opportunism among states and their politicians. In the aftermath of vessel accidents, discussions typically become clouded by political demands emanating out of state capitals, often with threats of unilateralism being wielded to compel IMO action. In such a climate, the regulatory system consistently fails to enact appropriate, long-term responses which would best meet the root causes of the relevant accidents. Instead, short-term 'quick fixes' which are readily understood by impatient politicians and the general public become fashionable.[946]

Thus, it has been seen how the US Congress and IMO rushed to adopt the 'double hull' requirement in response to the *Exxon Valdez* grounding even though it remained unclear whether double hulls could have prevented such accidents in the first place. Indeed, the probable true cause of the *Exxon Valdez* incident – negligent navigation – did not receive as much regulatory attention. Similarly, while the political response to the *Erika* and *Prestige* incidents triggered demands to accelerate the phasing out of single-hull tankers and to ban the carriage of heavy grades of oil in these tankers, it failed to grant adequate credence to the fact that structural failure caused by improper repairs, maintenance and operation was the likely cause of the accidents. In all these cases, critical measures such as enhanced surveys and inspections were approved only as incidental responses.

It is thus unfortunate that the regulatory system constantly misses the opportunity to address the fundamental and systemic causes of vessel accidents. Indeed, human-related causes such as negligence, fatigue, poor maintenance and inadequate training continue to be highlighted as the main causes of accidents but nevertheless fail to attract sustained regulatory action. At the same time, the systemic deficiencies in the underlying structure of ship registration, ownership and management continue to evade rectification. In the heat of recriminations following vessel accidents, it is common for intangible 'software' factors such as the human element to become sidelined by attention to equipment and 'hardware' standards.

In order to reduce the risks of future vessel accidents and the threats of unilateralism which typically follow, IMO member states must address the root causes of vessel-source pollution in a more dispassionate yet pro-active manner. In particular, more resources should be dedicated to the 'human element' in order to redress systemic weaknesses such as inadequate seafarer training, improper supervision by classification societies and poor enforcement by flag states. In all fairness, anticipatory approaches to decision-making are not new to IMO. It was precisely due to the need to avoid reactive, 'knee-jerk' responses that IMO undertook deliberations on anti-fouling paints and harmful

---

[946] See e.g. Lloyd's List, *Lyras Hits Out at 'Accident-led' Response to Shipping's Woes*, 4 June 2002.

aquatic organisms. In both cases, IMO member states keenly invoked the precautionary approach to justify regulation even when scientific evidence on the issues remained inconclusive.[947] Similarly, a decision was made to negotiate a regime on compensation for victims of pollution by hazardous and noxious substances even before a major incident involving these substances had occurred.[948]

However, these positive examples were largely initiated on an *ad hoc* basis by the needs of self-interested states. While they did help to harmonise international rules and avert unilateral action, the fact remains that decision-making at IMO continues to be dictated by the political choices of a select group of actors – the wealthy, developed states. This may not be optimal for a democratic organisation of more than 160 states, the majority of whom are silent participants by circumstance, not choice.

What would benefit the regulatory system more is to have the IMO Secretariat *institutionalise* the practice of anticipatory response. In this regard, an advisory board comprising selected scientific, government and industry experts should be constituted to advise the Secretariat on the contemporary challenges which need addressing. Thus, a body similar in inspiration to GESAMP[949] may be contemplated, even though it should have to play a much more active role beyond that performed by GESAMP. In particular, it is to be noted that GESAMP, as presently constituted, does not serve to evaluate legislative proposals by states.

What IMO needs is a body which is qualified to lay down guidelines for legislative proposals and to vet such proposals for their urgency, practicability and cost-effectiveness. This way, proposals can be filtered in order to identify those that are most pressing given the needs and resources of the Organization. The vetting process can thus employ sound scientific bases together with a precautionary approach to produce a more realistic, balanced and responsive legislative agenda. Very importantly, such mechanisms can serve to temper state demands for selective attention to 'pet' issues while allowing the Secretariat to formulate pro-active policies.

To these ends, both the member states as well as the IMO Secretariat should be allowed to initiate rule-making. All policy initiatives should be guided by pro-active and rational approaches to problem-solving in

---

[947] See Ch. 3.
[948] There had been some 65 smaller incidents, see LEG Doc. 85/INF.2 (2002).
[949] *Supra* note 1.

order to minimise 'sabre-rattling' inclinations following vessel accidents. This way, the tendency to resort to or to threaten unilateral action may be somewhat alleviated, if not diminished. Of course, such enhancement of the IMO Secretariat's powers demands a re-consideration of its erstwhile limited role in initiating policies. It will be recalled that in the past, the developed maritime states resisted enlarged powers for the Secretariat for fear of compromising their own latitude in the Organization. However, those were the days when these actors dominated the ranks of the top shipowning states. With the decline in their shipping registries and the concomitant growth in environmental concerns, it is in these states' interest to support enhanced powers for the Secretariat to pursue more pro-active environmental causes.

On their part, it may be expected that the developing and open registry states which form the largest shipowning states today will resist enhanced powers for the Secretariat. However, given that these interests are currently powerless to resist the proliferation of legislative proposals brought about by the environmentalist states, it might actually benefit them to have IMO play an arbiter's role in developing a more balanced policy agenda. Consequently, there *is* enough common ground for all the interests concerned to agree to an enlargement of competence for the IMO Secretariat. This will ultimately benefit not only the marine environment but the overall stability of decision-making as well.

1.2 Prompt Entry into Force for Conventions

As examined in Chapter 2, the IMO conventions typically employ a formula predicating entry into force upon the acceptance of a minimum number of state parties accounting for a minimum percentage of world shipping tonnage. Such stipulations originated from the days when the traditional maritime states dominated the ranks of shipowning states, both in terms of ship registration and beneficial ownership. The conventions were thus designed to entrench the interests of these states and to condition entry into force upon their acceptance.

With the progressive decline of the developed state flags, the biggest ship registries today are to be found in the developing countries, primarily the open registries. For so long as the traditional formula is upheld, these states will now hold the key to prompt entry into force of conventions. Since ecological consciousness is at best nascent in many of these states, they often lack the incentives to accept and implement conventions relating to environmental protection. This has greatly alarmed the environmentalists who see the open registries' reticence as a potential veto over the expeditious entry into force and implementation of new conventions.

In response, the environmentally motivated states have recently insisted on lower entry into force thresholds for newer IMO conventions. The basic idea is to eliminate altogether or diminish greatly the minimum tonnage requirement in the traditional formula. Emphasis is now placed upon the simple acceptance by a minimum number of states with negligible regard to tonnage. Such a formula was first used for the 1990 OPRC Convention which required the acceptance of a minimum number of fifteen states regardless of their tonnage holdings. This development had not been seriously challenged by the open registries as the OPRC was not particularly controversial. However, it signified a major change in the way entry into force requirements would henceforth be crafted.

For instance, the recent 2001 Bunkers Convention adopted a formula which dilutes the minimum tonnage requirement significantly but increases slightly the number of required state ratifications. Thus, the convention will enter into force upon the acceptance of eighteen states, five of which must each have fleets of 1.1 million gross tons. On its part, the 2001 Anti-Fouling Systems (AFS) Convention predicates entry into force upon the acceptances of twenty-five states representing among them 25 per cent of global shipping tonnage.

In effect, such formulae seek to circumvent the open registry states. For instance, the Bunkers Convention's requirement for five states each with 1.1 million gross tons of shipping tonnage can quite easily be fulfilled by many Western European countries or even small maritime powers like Australia. Given the current global shipping tonnage of some 605 million gross tons, it effectively means that states with a cumulative holding of less than 1 per cent of global shipping tonnage can impose their will on the rest of the maritime community! This is a drastic change from MARPOL 73/78's insistence on at least 50 per cent of world tonnage.

In principle, the reform of entry into force requirements is laudable. In line with responsible environmental behaviour, all states must do their utmost to bring conventions into force as expeditiously as possible. From a practical perspective, new conventions risk obsolescence if their provisions do not enter into force promptly. These conventions will then have to be amended almost immediately after entry into force should their provisions prove to be technically outdated or overtaken by developments. Such was the case in the 1980s with Annexes I and II of MARPOL 73/78, and more recently with Annex IV.

More ominously, delayed entry into force encourages impatient states to resort to early implementation of the relevant rules. This may still be tolerable compared with cases of outright unilateralism whereby a state prescribes and enforces its own rules independent of international negotiation. Nevertheless, early implementation ahead of entry into force remains prejudicial to the goals of the multilateral trading system which seek to ensure both uniform rule-making and rule-application.

Despite its advantages, it must be recognised that the reform of entry into force provisions through the drastic whittling down of the minimum tonnage requirement remains fundamentally undemocratic. Clearly, the minimum tonnage requirement served the interests of the developed states when they were the largest shipping registries. Now that they are no longer so, it seems opportunistic to remove or weaken the tonnage requirement to the disadvantage of the open registries. While it can be argued that the environmental motives are noble and that whatever means adopted to protect the marine environment are justified, there must be considerations of how such a move may damage the long-term credibility of IMO in the eyes of the vast majority of developing states.

For these states, the minimum tonnage requirement represents the last bastion of influence wielded at IMO given that substantive leadership and agenda-setting are already dominated by the developed states. Thus, even if the entry into force requirements should be amended, they should not be diluted to such an extreme extent that the shipowning states become effectively marginalised. A more imaginative and equitable formula should be found, perhaps a 'sliding scale' variant that reduces the minimum tonnage requirement either with time or as more states ratify a convention. Alternatively, a fairer minimum tonnage figure such as 30 per cent should be adopted.

On their part, the environmental interests should not be too quick to blame the slow entry into force of recent IMO conventions on the minimum tonnage requirement and the open registries. Some of the best-known examples of languishing (or formerly so) IMO instruments – the HNS Convention, Annex IV to MARPOL 73/78 on sewage and Annex VI on air pollution – are or have been as much victims of developed state reticence. The HNS Convention, for example, is plagued by the complexities inherent in regulating different forms of hazardous pollutants owned and carried by myriad actors. At the same time, the US – the world's largest chemicals importer – has its own HNS compensation regime and will not accept the convention. The entry into force and viability of the convention thus depend critically on the acceptance of major chemical importers such as Japan and Western Europe, *not* the shipowning states.

On its part, Annex IV to MARPOL 73/78 was ignored for a long time because states – both developed and developing – resisted its requirement for reception facilities. After nearly three decades on the rule books, Annex IV only recently entered into force in September 2003 after amendments were adopted in 2000 to relax its requirements.[950] As for Annex VI, many of the developed states found that the 4.5 per cent sulphur cap was too lenient to be politically acceptable.[951] Consequently, it is not only the open registries and shipowning actors who have held up the entry into force of IMO conventions.

In principle, any convention which is brought into force without the participation of a large segment of shipowning states (or cargo-owning states where relevant) can only be compromised in its universality. In this regard, the basic strategy of the developed pro-environment states is to achieve quick entry into force and then to compel adherence by other actors through measures such as national or regional port state control. Such action detracts from the spirit of consensus which IMO has been building in the past few decades, and can only lead to a patchwork of inconsistent regimes for different parts of the globe. Moreover, conventions which are brought into force using means which override the views of the most relevant stakeholders run the serious risk of ineffective implementation.

While it is undeniable that the shipping interests are generally not enamoured of conventions which impose environmental costs on shipping, the key to securing expeditious entry into force does not lie in tampering with the minimum tonnage requirement. Instead, efforts should be directed more at the beneficial owners of vessels registered in the open registries and the developing states. In the first place, many of these owners are nationals of the developed states such as Greece, Norway, Japan, the US and the UK. Therefore, if indeed shipowning

---

[950] IMO is now urging states to apply the revised version, see MEPC Doc. 44/20 (2000), Annex 10. Note that Annexes I and II were also recently amended and revised, with entry into force provided for 1 January 2007.
[951] There are now signs that more European states will accept Annex VI (which entered into force in May 2005), since it does not preclude them from adopting stricter standards within SO_x Emission Control Areas, *supra* text accompanying note 420.

interests lack the incentive to secure prompt entry into force of IMO conventions, the developed states should bring pressure to bear upon their own shipowner nationals and compel them to influence the behaviour of the flag states they are using.

In turn, the open registries – all along sensitive to the demands of their shipowner clients – can be pressured into ratifying conventions promptly. Indeed, apart from being responsive to the views of their clients, it is a fact that the major open registries strive to present an environmentally friendly image. As a result of the constant negative publicity over their safety and pollution records, these actors are typically willing to ratify IMO conventions, even those which they resisted in the negotiating process. Whether or not they subsequently seek to implement these conventions is, of course, a different matter. The fact remains that they would be more likely to embrace a convention which they had had some incentive in supporting rather than one which had been willed into effect without their assent. In this regard, an outright assault on the minimum tonnage requirement can only be counterproductive in the long run.

1.3 Ensuring Effective Enforcement and Compliance

The most obvious weakness of the IMO regulatory system is its failure to ensure effective enforcement of rules and standards. In spite of the numerous regulations which exist, sub-standard ships still ply the oceans posing significant risks to human lives and the environment. In this regard, the previous chapters have already detailed how substandard shipping thrives within an extremely cost-conscious industry whose actors continue to lack the incentives to curb the operation and employment of poor quality ships.

The challenge of eradicating sub-standard shipping and of ensuring safer shipping and cleaner oceans will thus have to be met with greater enforcement rigour. Otherwise, it can be expected that more states will follow the lead of the US and the European Commission in resorting to or threatening unilateral action to deal with the problem. In this regard, effective compliance with IMO rules and standards can be promoted and improved by the following prescriptions:

(i) concerted efforts by all maritime actors to discriminate against sub-standard shipping;
(ii) liability for non-owner actors such as cargo owners and classification societies;

(iii) re-flagging to developed states for greater flag state control;
(iv) continuing attention to the role of flag states in supervising their vessels;
(v) progressive strengthening of port state control on a global and harmonised basis; and
(vi) greater enforcement powers for IMO.

1.3.1 Market Discrimination Against Sub-standard Shipping

To overcome the maritime industry's compliance deficiencies, co-ordinated efforts are needed to foster market conditions favouring the quality operator and in turn, discriminating against sub-standard shipping. Since it is practically impossible for each segment of the maritime industry to generate these conditions by itself, concerted efforts are needed to compel all industry actors to adhere to higher standards simultaneously. Such efforts can come from within the industry itself (e.g. through market forces) or from external regulation such as by IMO or individual states. Thus, instead of just prescribing discharge and equipment standards for ships, IMO could seek to regulate the performance of individual owners, classification societies, charterers and insurers. Ultimately, a pervasive culture of responsible ship operation must be inculcated among all actors forming the maritime safety and pollution control chains.

Initially, IMO may face difficulties in extending its mandate over non-owner actors. In the short term, the regulatory system will have to rely upon port state control to highlight deficiencies in the practices of classification societies and charterers. Already, the Paris and Tokyo MOUs on Port State Control and the US Coast Guard have established target lists of not only deficient ships and their flags but also of classification societies and charterers of such ships.[952] These moves will serve to expose the non-compliant behaviour of non-owner actors and to pressure them to become more transparent in their dealings with owners.

In the wake of the *Exxon Valdez*, *Erika* and *Prestige* incidents, much has been said about the ill effects of US and European unilateralism. However, it must be acknowledged that some significant benefits have arisen out of the measures taken, particularly in the creation of a fledgling two-tier market for ships.[953] In this regard, the threats of stringent port state control against sub-standard ships and the prospect of immense negative publicity attaching to any association with such

---

[952] See Ch. 5.
[953] With the measures adopted in recent years to phase out aging tankers, the world tanker fleet is today greatly modernised, see INTERTANKO, *supra* note 14, at 12.

ships have discernibly changed the behaviour of many maritime actors. Thus, charterers are now preferring to hire newer, double-hull ships to the advantage of the quality operators.[954]

The adoption of legislation to phase out older, single-hull vessels has also led to a higher scrapping rate for such ships, again favouring the responsible operator. In addition, insurance premia for poor quality ships have escalated to reflect their greater risk in the current market. Cargo insurers have also inserted contractual clauses requiring cargo owners to use ships associated with quality flags and classification societies.[955] At the same time, the societies – through IACS – have been forced to tighten their inspection procedures and to restrain the shady practice of 'class-hopping' among owners, particularly since anti-hopping rules are now mandatory in the EU.[956] All these measures effectively discourage charterers and cargo owners from utilising sub-standard ships.

Positive incentives should also be given to quality owners and operators – these may include allowing those with good track records to self-regulate and undertake parts of their own supervisions, inspections and surveys.[957] Preferential port dues and charges can also be given to these operators. The 'points' system currently practiced by port state control authorities already reward quality operators by exempting them from future inspections. Such measures should be further bolstered as they not only provide incentives for operators to behave responsibly but free up classification societies and port state control inspectors to concentrate on the sub-standard ships.

Market differentiation in favour of high-quality ships had never quite materialised in the past simply because owners, insurers and classification societies competed aggressively by lowering operating standards. It would thus be a pity if the current market momentum favouring quality ships cannot be sustained – indeed, it should preferably be followed up by multilateral responses designed to institutionalise tangible incentives for safer and cleaner shipping. If this can be done, the political uproar over the *Erika* and *Prestige* may have some benefits after all.

---

[954] Personal interviews.
[955] For the view that such clauses are difficult to enforce because goods are often transshipped, consigned to the next available ship or consolidated with other cargo for on-carriage, see REMOVAL OF INSURANCE, *supra* note 5, at 65–6. Cargo insurers and their practices are thus believed to have minimal impact on sub-standard shipping.
[956] Directive 2001/105/EC, 2002 OJ (L 19) 9, *supra* note 237.
[957] See Payer, *supra* note 91, at 297.

1.3.2 Liability of Non-Owner Interests

One effect of the recent tanker spills such as the *Erika* and *Prestige* is the intensifying spotlight thrown on the charterer's and cargo owner's liability for employing tankers of sub-standard quality.[958] Increasingly, a criterion for assessing the worth of a civil liability and compensation regime is whether it adequately discourages ship operators and cargo interests from operating and employing sub-standard vessels.[959] Thus, as part of efforts to create market disincentives for chartering sub-standard vessels, specific liability should be imposed upon cargo interests whose negligence can be linked to a vessel accident and pollution incident. In this regard, the rules on the liability of cargo interests should be reconsidered to enhance the exposure of these actors to pollution claims and to reduce the scope of their immunities and defences.

Under the current international compensation regimes, the cargo interests incur potential liability only for secondary compensation payable under the CLC/FUND and HNSC regimes. By virtue of the channelling of strict liability to the shipowners, no primary liability is attached to the charterer of the vessel or the owner of the particular cargo involved in the incident for any damage caused.[960] Moreover, the second-tier compensation under the respective funds is a burden borne collectively by all industry contributors,[961] levied at a fixed rate which does not reflect the particular cargo receiver's level of care or culpability. In the result, there exist inadequate incentives for cargo receivers to behave responsibly in hiring vessels, particularly because the costs of financing the funds are passed on to the consumer.

The channelling provisions may not avail the cargo interests in situations where claims are brought for loss or damage other than that covered by the relevant international conventions, or where claims are brought under national law in non-convention states,[962] or where

---

[958] The major oil companies are typically both charterers of tankers as well as owners of the cargo carried on board.
[959] See Ch. 6.   [960] See CLC 69, art. III; CLC 92, art. III(4)(c); FUND 71, art. 3; HNSC, art. 7(5).
[961] See FUND 71, art. 10(1); FUND 92, art. 10(1); HNSC, art. 10. There is now third-tier liability under the 2003 Supplementary Protocol to FUND 92, payable by oil receivers in Protocol contracting states, see Ch. 6.
[962] See e.g. the provisions in OPA-90 and the state laws in the US imposing liability on charterers and cargo owners under certain circumstances. For details, see DE LA RUE & ANDERSON, *supra* note 777, at 613–16 and 626–9.

damage results from an intentional or reckless act on the part of the charterer or cargo owner.[963] In addition, the cargo interests may be liable in an action brought against them by the shipowner or by third parties such as the IOPC Funds by way of recourse.[964] Yet, these are all extremely limited circumstances, and it remains generally difficult and uncommon for the liability of the charterer or the cargo owner to be incurred.[965]

The relative infrequency of such claims and the legal difficulty in proving them raise the question of whether there exist adequate incentives to influence the behaviour of charterers and cargo owners in their choice of vessels. The upcoming revision of the CLC/FUND 92 regime thus provides a timely opportunity for reviewing the channelling provisions which generally insulate the cargo interests from CLC 92 liability and to possibly institute greater responsibility for these actors on account of their employing sub-standard vessels. For example, cargo interests who persist in using sub-standard vessels should be made to pay a greater portion of the cost of oil spills in the form of higher contributions to the IOPC Funds.[966]

To make their chartering practices more transparent, the oil majors had introduced the Ship Inspection Report Exchange (SIRE) programme, designed to vet tankers in the market for compliance with international safety and pollution standards.[967] In recent times, the oil industry has developed a complementary Tanker Management and Self-Assessment (TMSA) programme,[968] which is aimed at getting ship operators to conduct their own self-assessments to improve management systems. The results of such programmes go toward collating lists of vessels approved (and disapproved) for charter.

While helpful in removing the market for sub-standard tankers, such vetting programmes may themselves prove to be a source of liability for charterers. In holding a charterer-defendant to a particular standard of

---

[963] CLC 92, art. III(4), *supra* note 791.
[964] CLC 92, art. III(5); HNSC, art. 7(6). The common form of recourse action against the charterer is not through the conventions, but a *contractual* claim by the shipowner for damages or indemnity under the relevant charterparty (a claim not precluded by the conventions), see DE LA RUE & ANDERSON, *supra* note 777, at 644-53.
[965] See generally Anderson & de la Rue, *supra* note 98, at 7-56.
[966] See Ch. 6 in relation to the European proposal to revise the CLC/FUND 92 regime.
[967] See Ch. 2. The chemical industry operates a similar vetting scheme under the aegis of the Chemical Distribution Institute.
[968] Unlike SIRE, TMSA is not administered by the oil industry, but appeals to the interest of the shipowner to benchmark his own standards against industry best practice.

care, courts of law may examine whether vettings have been properly conducted and recommendations adhered to. A failure to meet such industry standards may thus be construed as a lack of due diligence on the charterer's part.[969] It follows that if a charterer's vetting programme does not conform to prevailing industry standards, or if a charterer employs a vessel that SIRE has already thrown up to be sub-standard, national courts could (and should) impose liability on that charterer in the event of a spill involving the vessel.

Such potential liability will have positive effects on the shipowners' and charterers' behaviour, and it will also compel the cargo interests to be prudent and insist on the use of responsible classification societies and insurers. It is also consistent with the proposed imposition of higher FUND liability for cargo interests who employ sub-standard ships, the 'black-listing' of charterers of sub-standard vessels by port state control authorities and the sanctions proposed in Europe for non-owner actors contributing to pollution by grossly or seriously negligent conduct.[970] In sum, shifting attention to the users of ships may prove to be more effective in curbing sub-standard shipping than the current unsatisfactory practice of highlighting only the flags and owners of vessels.

Under the prevailing system, it is similarly difficult to attach legal liability on the classification societies for losses arising from a pollution incident caused by a ship. The legal position in most countries is that owners remain responsible for the seaworthiness of their ships.[971] Moreover, the IMO conventions make it clear that the duty of seaworthiness remains the owner's and cannot be delegated to classification societies. The societies are also often contractually covered by release and indemnity clauses in their contracts with shipowners, which protect them against claims by the shipowner and third parties respectively.[972] In addition, some major flag states provide legislative

---

[969] Anderson & de la Rue, *supra* note 98, at 41.
[970] Commission Proposal for a Directive on Sanctions, *supra* note 394.
[971] See e.g. the cases of *The Nicholas H*, 2 Lloyd's Rep. 299 (H.L. 1995) and *Sundance Cruises Corp. v. American Bureau of Shipping (The Sundancer)*, 7 F.3d 1077 (US 2nd Cir. 1993), 1 Lloyd's Rep. 183 (1994). It is outside the scope of this work to analyse contractual and tortious liability for vessel pollution under national law. Suffice it to highlight from a regulatory perspective that the reluctance under national law to impose liability on classification societies does not augur well for efforts to create incentives for more responsible behaviour among these actors.
[972] Honka, *supra* note 99, at 9.

immunity under their domestic laws for classification societies appointed by the state to issue statutory certificates.[973]

While administrative measures are in place in many national systems to regulate the activities of classification societies, clear liability provisions do not commonly exist. As with the cargo interests, the question has often been asked whether adequate incentives (or disincentives) exist to influence the behaviour of classification societies in their inspections of vessels. It remains true that the physical control over the safety of a ship lies with the shipowner and not a classification society. As such, a classification society cannot be viewed as an insurer who warrants the seaworthiness of the vessel.[974] However, where the evidence in a case clearly shows that the classification society (through its surveyors) has certified a ship in blatant disregard of its actual substandard condition, there must arise a case for at least joint liability on the part of the society. Imposing liability on classification societies in appropriate cases will compel these actors to behave more responsibly and professionally.[975]

Of course, there are serious issues to consider here, not least of which is the cost of insurance to cover the liability of classification societies and the fundamental integrity of the whole classification system. Ultimately, however, it is conceivable that placing some amount of liability on the societies or having them assume a form of limited liability by way of contract will have the effect of furthering safety and pollution prevention at sea.[976] Recent developments in Europe have pointed the way toward greater responsibility on the part of classification societies. These have been catalysed by a string of pollution incidents in European waters involving sub-standard vessels whose condition had been allegedly overlooked or ignored by their classification societies. Thus, in the wake of the *Erika* and the *Prestige*, the rules in the European Directive concerning classification societies have been strengthened to include, *inter alia*, stricter quality criteria in relation to

---

[973] Ibid. at 18. [974] Cane, *supra* note 98, at 368–75.
[975] See Honka, *supra* note 99, at 33–4, referring to the need for a 'preventive effect' of liability, i.e. liability that would compel classification societies to be more diligent in inspecting vessels and thus avoiding casualties at sea.
[976] The scope of this work does not permit a comprehensive assessment of the nature of liability for classification societies. The point made here is that the fundamental rules on apportioning liability should be reconsidered so as to provide more incentives for responsible (or disincentives for irresponsible) behaviour among all actors in the maritime trading system.

switch of class and enhancement of Community powers to suspend recognition of societies which fail to meet the relevant standards.[977]

In addition to these administrative measures, the liability of classification societies following ship accidents has been enhanced in Europe. Thus, there is now the possibility of unlimited liability where death, personal injury or property damage is caused by the wilful acts or omissions or gross negligence of the classification society, and limited liability for negligence or recklessness.[978] This may open the way for other states to consider instituting more stringent liability systems for classification societies in order to bring about a stronger preventive or deterrent effect. In this regard, a multilateral treaty solution negotiated at IMO may be preferable, given the imperative to harmonise national laws across states.

In time, national court attitudes toward the negligence of classification societies may change, and it is likely that the traditional defences and immunities afforded to these actors may increasingly become irrelevant or watered down. To illustrate, the recent sinking of the *Prestige* has seen the Spanish government instituting legal proceedings in New York against the vessel's classification society, the American Bureau of Shipping (ABS). Spain has alleged that ABS's 'negligent, reckless, wilful and wanton conduct was the proximate cause of the injuries suffered'.[979] More specifically, it charged that ABS was negligent in passing as seaworthy a ship 'unfit and unsuitable' for carrying oil, resulting in its loss and an environmental disaster. If successful, the suit will signal a growing movement to hold classification societies responsible for their acts and omissions in relation to supervising standards on board ships.

The logic in extending liability to cargo interests and classification societies can conceivably be applied to other non-shipowner interests as well.[980] Thus, insurers should be made to shoulder greater legal liability for knowingly underwriting sub-standard ships. They should also be compelled not to pay the fines of shipowners found guilty of safety or

---

[977] Directive 2001/105/EC, *supra* note 237.
[978] There is a minimum penalty of EUR 4 million in case of injury or personal death and EUR 2 million in case of loss or damage to property, see art. 6, Directive 2001/105/EC, *Ibid*. See also Lloyd's List, *Question of Societies' Liability Continues to Bubble Away*, 4 Feb. 2002.
[979] Lloyd's List, *ABS Backlash Puts Spain in the Dock for Prestige*, 1 July 2003. ABS is expected to defend its case vigorously and to counter-claim with its own allegations that Spain acted 'recklessly, negligently and grossly negligently' in refusing refuge in its ports to the *Prestige*, and that this had been the proximate cause of the environmental disaster.
[980] See generally INTERNATIONAL COMMISSION ON SHIPPING (ICONS), SHIPS, SLAVES AND COMPETITION (2001).

pollution-related offences.[981] At the same time, more co-operation and information-sharing should be promoted between classification societies and insurers. More effective measures must also be instituted to prevent or reduce the practice of class- and insurer-hopping.

In many countries, banks and financing institutions are increasingly facing due diligence tests designed to assess if they should share liability for environmental damage caused by the projects or clients which they finance.[982] The same approach may be taken in the marine environmental field with respect to financiers or mortgagees of ships. In general, 'due diligence' rules which dictate the behaviour of shore-based shipowners such as those currently found in the ISM Code[983] should be extended to the other actors. In all these respects, what may possibly begin as domestic law initiatives should be replicated at the international level through harmonisation efforts conducted by bodies such as CMI or IMO.

In essence, the current tendency to look to non-shipowner actors is growing because of third party victims' disenchantment with the right of limitation enjoyed by shipowners.[984] The fact that shipowners' liabilities are pooled among the P&I Clubs and reinsured typically results in individual shipowners not possessing adequate incentives for responsible behaviour. This feature of the liability system, coupled with the ready availability of second- and third-tier funds payable by the cargo interests, effectively insulate the shipowner from the consequences of his actions and are seen to be inconsistent with the 'polluter pays' principle. As analysed above, the impending revision of CLC/FUND 92 is expected to introduce concrete disincentives against sub-standard shipping by reviewing the shipowner's right of limitation, the cargo interests' liability for employing sub-standard vessels causing serious pollution and the non-shipowner actors' *de facto* immunity from compensation claims.[985]

1.3.3 Return of the Developed State Flags

A related measure which should be pursued is to make flag states compete on quality. In Chapter 2, it was explained how the developed

---

[981] Lloyd's List, *OECD in Crackdown on Substandard Shipping*, 15 Apr. 2002. The current P&I Club practice is to reimburse the fines for accidental, but not intentional discharges, *supra* note 398.

[982] See generally DE LA RUE & ANDERSON, *supra* note 777, at 671–96. [983] *Infra* note 1002.

[984] See COM(2002) 681, *supra* note 384, at 10 and Commission Proposal for a Directive on Sanctions, *supra* note 394, at 6.

[985] COM(2002) 681, *ibid*. If adopted, this will bring the international position closer to that of OPA-90.

states have in recent years tried to rebuild their national ship registries after decades of neglect and decline. Thus, several Western European countries have introduced favourable regulatory and tonnage tax regimes in order to attract their shipowners back to the national flags. This has proven to be fairly successful for some flags. By and large, however, the majority of tonnage still resides in the open registries.

In this regard, if the environmentally minded developed states are serious about eradicating sub-standard shipping in their waters, they should re-double efforts to make their own flags more competitive. The more ships they attract back, the greater the control they can exert as flag states. If the developed states want to take the battle further, they may even contemplate providing tax or other disincentives for their shipowner nationals who persist in using suspect foreign flags. This emphasis on quality might then introduce competition for the other flags which would have to respond similarly. It would also be consistent with IMO's familiar stand that flag state control should remain as the primary tool in the campaign against sub-standard shipping.

On their part, the largest shipowners should also be directly persuaded to re-flag. After all, being flagged in a reputable state provides a more solid guarantee against port state harassment. The reality of the matter is that port state control regimes worldwide can be politically motivated. Thus, they may have the tendency to target ships flying certain flags, primarily those of the open registries and developing countries. In an atmosphere where public opinion toward shipowners has turned hostile, it might make more strategic and economic sense for owners to use developed state flags despite their higher overall costs.

Such considerations may not have been relevant just a few decades ago when environmental concerns were less critical and economic costs paramount. Today, however, owners and charterers suffer grave repercussions if their ships are involved in pollution incidents. In any event, responsible owners who use open registries are already expending vast amounts of money to ensure that their ships are well maintained to pass port state control and charterer checks. Consequently, it may actually make better sense for these owners to use developed state flags in the first place. In other words, contemporary cost-benefit analyses may actually favour the use of reputable but more expensive flags.

In advocating re-flagging to raise standards, it is not meant to suggest that ships flagged in open registries are *necessarily* sub-standard or that their administrations are lenient on transgressions. Neither is the argument meant to deprive the developing states of a much-needed source of revenue. Rather, what is contended here is that since the developed states have for so long grumbled about poor enforcement by the open registries, they should now take up the challenge of showing how proper flag state control should be conducted. This can only have a positive 'cascade' effect on the standards of open registries as a whole. Moreover, since the nationals of the developed states remain the largest shipowners, cargo owners and charterers, these states should be obliged to redress the problem at its source – beginning with their own nationals. Again, much blame has been placed on the open registry flags – it is time for the developed states to lead by example and to take concrete action.

1.3.4 Tightening Flag State Obligations

The prescriptions in the previous paragraphs are not meant to relieve flag states of their primary obligation to ensure safer and cleaner shipping. On the contrary, all flag states – including the open registries and developing states – must continue to adhere to their duties and obligations under the LOSC and IMO conventions. After all, the open registry phenomenon is so entrenched in maritime practice today that it is unlikely to be overtaken any time soon by re-flagging to developed states. Due also to the prevalence of open registries, port state control cannot be expected to fully supplant flag state control and will thus remain a secondary line of defence at best.[986]

Hence, steps should be taken to tighten further the implementation of rules and standards by flag states. While seeking to create market disincentives for sub-standard shipping, the regulatory system should aim to reward the quality flags. To this end, recent proposals for a network of accredited quality registers should be pursued with greater intensity. Such proposals seek to lay down criteria for the assessment of ship registries and to identify a list or network of quality registers which charterers will be encouraged to use. This is entirely in line with other efforts being undertaken to ensure responsible behaviour among non-owner actors such as charterers, classification societies and insurers. At the same time, shipowners and industry actors that maintain high standards should be rewarded with other incentives such as reduced classification fees, cheaper insurance premia, fewer and less time-consuming port state inspections and lower port charges.

---

[986] Sinan, *supra* note 135, at 103.

Practical problems remain, however, as to which authority will determine the quality flags and what criteria will be used to define 'quality'. Understandably, the proposals for a network of quality registers have met with resistance from the open registries which fear that subjective and politicised criteria will be used to eliminate certain flags from the network. In this regard, the relevant assessment authority (perhaps the IMO-constituted body of experts advocated above)[987] must come up with principles which can accurately and equitably assess flag state performance. Criteria such as casualty rates, port state control detention rates, age and profile of ships on the registry as well as the classification society entrusted with statutory certification will be relevant even if they are likely to excite more controversy than they can resolve.

Ultimately, it may be up to the maritime industry itself, and not IMO, to produce market intelligence as to which are the quality flags. Such information already exists in the market; it is simply up to the industry actors to act upon it.[988] The current IMO efforts to persuade flag states to conduct self-assessments on their own capacity and performance may also be reinforced. However, undue optimism should not be placed on self-assessment given current discouraging signs that many flag states are not taking the exercise seriously.[989]

What is needed is continuous pressure from states, industry and IMO alike to persuade flag states to improve on their performance. With the continued emphases on quality and responsible supervision, it is hoped that all flag states and operators will settle into an environment in which competition is one that relates to quality and not the lack of it.[990] Simultaneously, the market pressure on owners to use only quality flags and the move by the developed states to attract tonnage back to

---

[987] See Section 1.1.
[988] Personal interviews. Note the existence of the round table of international shipping associations (comprising BIMCO, INTERCARGO, ICS/ISF and INTERTANKO), which releases an annual Shipping Industry Flag State Performance Table. This is intended to help shipping companies assess the performance and credibility of some 100 flag states.
[989] As of April 2004, only 54 IMO member states (responsible for 79 per cent of world tonnage) had submitted self-assessment reports, *supra* note 766. However, the US Coast Guard's insistence on self-assessment records as a pre-condition to including ships in its Qualship 21 preference programme, *infra* note 996, appears likely to compel more flags to conduct self-assessment, see Lloyd's List, *Qualship 21 to Stay Tough on Flag States*, 21 Jan. 2002.
[990] See VOGEL, *supra* note 18, at 248-70, on how stricter regulation in the trade realm, particularly by the powerful states, can lead to firms worldwide competing to raise, rather than lower standards.

their registries should also serve to increase the overall standards of open registry fleets. However, in order for this to be achieved, political pressure by the developed states must be brought to bear not only on the operators, but also the users of shipping such as charterers and cargo owners, most of whom are nationals of these states to begin with.[991]

1.3.5 Enhancing Port State Control

For so long as the majority of flag states remain ineffective in ensuring compliance with IMO rules, port state control must continue to play a complementary role in maintaining high shipping standards. Indeed, port state control has emerged as a political priority in environmentally minded countries which view foreign-flagged shipping as a threat to their coasts and waters. In this regard, a balanced port state control regime which upholds IMO rules, standards and practices can help to commit coastal and port states to a discipline of uniform conduct. This diffuses the pressure and inclination to resort to rules that go beyond international standards.[992]

There remain fundamental concerns over port states abusing their right to inspect and detain ships. Indeed, some states have been known to apply port state control in a subjective and arbitrary manner. This is where the establishment of regional port state control MOUs enforcing IMO standards may foster a fairer and more uniform enforcement system. For one thing, the fact that member port states are obliged to submit enforcement reports to the relevant MOU Secretariats will help promote a culture of accountability and transparency.[993] Port state control officers must also be adequately trained and supervised in order to minimise instances of capricious, politically motivated or arbitrary action.[994] Clear procedures for handling appeals against detention are desirable given that many owners have complained about the lack of access to appeal mechanisms.

The various regional MOUs should also continue to refine the targeting system pioneered by the Paris and Tokyo MOUs and the US Coast

---

[991] On the role of rich states in driving standards upwards, see Vogel, *ibid.* at 268-70.
[992] Lowe, *supra* note 124, at 642.   [993] See Ch. 5.
[994] Anderson, *supra* note 19, at 169. There are reports of port states (both in developed and developing countries) charging excessively for inspections as a means of obtaining revenue. In addition, allegations abound of corrupt inspectors extracting bribes from ships and of inspectors conducting checks even on quality ships simply for the sake of generating inspection statistics (source: personal interviews).

Guard. A more accurate targeting procedure will help to weed out substandard ships for enhanced inspections, reward those ships with good maintenance records and reduce instances of multiple inspections.[995] In this regard, more groups of maritime actors should be included in the published lists of targeted ships. Thus, not only should the owners, flags and classification societies of deficient ships be identified, the charterers, insurers and even financiers should be made known as well. At the same time, positive incentives should be given to quality ships, as is being practised by the US Coast Guard's Qualship 21 programme.[996] Again, the emphasis is on creating strong market incentives for quality shipping and disincentives for sub-standard operators.

An all-embracing targeting system relies heavily on the existence of an accurate, comprehensive and frequently updated information database. In this regard, it is encouraging that the various port state control authorities are already sharing information with each other. The EU has also recently collaborated with several maritime authorities worldwide to create an electronic information database known as Equasis, which makes use of the latest Internet technology.[997] The database collates information pertaining to matters such as ship safety records and inspection history and is accessible not only to MOU authorities but also charterers and insurers wishing to obtain information on ships. The Equasis website also makes public the comments submitted by flag states following detentions of their vessels in port states. Such initiatives are making up for the current low reporting rates to IMO and the lack of analyses conducted on information submitted to IMO.[998]

While the regional port state control MOUs are instrumental in harmonising the practices of member state authorities, the next step forward should be to unify standards and increase co-operation among the

---

[995] Some owners claim to have been inspected more than thirty-five times a year, Lloyd's List, *Tankers Dogged by Over-inspection*, 29 Jan. 2002.

[996] The Port State Control Quality Shipping (Qualship 21) programme rewards quality foreign-flagged ships with incentives such as less frequent inspections in the US and possibly, in future, reduced port charges, see submission of the US, FSI Doc. 9/6/5 (2001). The ships are identified based on specific eligibility criteria – among other factors, they must be registered in flag states with 'superior port state control' and which have submitted flag state self-assessment reports to IMO and the Coast Guard. The UK is also proposing a 'reward scheme', to be initiated in conjunction with Lloyd's Register, see Lloyd's List, *Credit Where Credit's Due*, 2 Nov. 2001. Similarly, the Paris MOU states are planning a reward programme for implementation in 2005.

[997] See the Equasis website at http://www.equasis.org (last accessed 8 Nov. 2004).

[998] See Ch. 5.

regional MOUs.⁹⁹⁹ Otherwise, sub-standard ships turned away from regions with stringent controls may relocate to those with lax supervision.¹⁰⁰⁰ This will severely affect the interests of the developing states which can hardly afford to deal with increased safety and pollution risks. The harmonisation of standards across different regions will naturally be difficult given the huge disparity in resources and expertise possessed by the various countries. IMO will thus have to work closer with the MOU authorities in Western Europe and the US to effect a meaningful transfer of financial resources and technical expertise to the developing maritime administrations so as to enhance their training and operational capacity.

1.4 Enforcement Powers for IMO

Related to the above proposals is the need to ensure a strong central enforcement agency for maritime safety and pollution matters. It will be recalled that the IMO Secretariat's powers have traditionally been circumscribed. Indeed, the Secretariat has rarely initiated policies, leaving it to the member states to dictate the content and pace of decision-making. This state of affairs originated in the 1950s when the maritime states were averse to surrendering their sovereignty to a newly constituted multilateral agency.

In an age when economic, competitive and security concerns were paramount, it was originally felt that an agency increasingly dominated by the developing states could severely prejudice the commercial interests of the developed maritime states. Today, however, a new political and social consciousness has arisen in most countries. With the traditional notions of free navigation and flag state primacy being increasingly qualified, the idea that IMO's competence should remain hobbled appears to be outdated, at least in relation to environmental governance.

It has been proposed above that the IMO Secretariat should be allowed to initiate new rules in a more pro-active and anticipatory manner. Similarly, the Secretariat must be accorded greater powers in enforcing compliance with its conventions. While it was fashionable in the last few decades to decry IMO as an agency with no real 'teeth' to

---

⁹⁹⁹ In March 1998, the Paris and Tokyo MOU parties signed a joint declaration to strengthen inter-regional action. Such moves should be extended to the other MOUs in less developed regions.
¹⁰⁰⁰ Anderson, *supra* note 19, at 168 and Sinan, *supra* note 135, at 103.

enforce its rules, it behoves the member states today to rectify the situation in a meaningful manner. Indeed, it is critical for IMO's own credibility in the next few years that it is seen to possess greater enforcement powers. That IMO's perceived weakness in enforcement was a catalyst for US and European unilateralism in the past few years seems undeniable.

A promising start was made in the mid-1990s when IMO was given the power by its members to enforce compliance with the 1995 Protocol to the Convention on Standards of Training, Certification and Watchkeeping for Seafarers (STCW). In this regard, IMO was empowered to supervise the compliance systems of labour-providing states to ensure that their seafarers meet the requisite standards for training and certification prescribed under STCW. IMO was thus authorised to oversee and assess the performance of states and to pronounce upon which states would appear in a 'white-list' of approved labour-providing countries, signifying compliance with STCW.

While the STCW Protocol initiative was a significant milestone for IMO, it would appear that the proposal met with minimal opposition largely because of the weak bargaining positions of the major labour-providing states. Thus, actors such as the Philippines, India and Bangladesh were effectively compelled to accept the demands of the developed states for greater supervision over the training of seafarers. The situation would have been very different if IMO's enhanced enforcement powers had impinged upon the interests of the more powerful states. Yet, there remains optimism that the STCW experience may point the way forward in developing greater responsibilities for IMO organs.[1001]

Another positive development in this regard is the adoption of the International Safety Management (ISM) Code[1002] in 1998 as a mandatory part of the SOLAS Convention. The ISM Code imposes responsibility for the activities of a ship on its shore-bound owners and managers. Pursuant to the Code's requirements, a Safety Management System is to be established by owners, and a Document of Compliance issued by the flag state administration for every company complying with the Code's requirements. In addition, a Safety Management Certificate is to

---

[1001] For proposals to build on and expand the 'white-list' approach of eliciting compliance, see submission of the UK, Australia and Canada, FSI Doc. 6/3/3 (1998).
[1002] *Supra* note 151. See generally P. ANDERSON, ISM CODE: A PRACTICAL GUIDE TO THE LEGAL AND INSURANCE IMPLICATIONS (1998) and P. ANDERSON, CRACKING THE CODE: THE RELEVANCE OF THE ISM CODE AND ITS IMPACT ON SHIPPING PRACTICES (2003).

be issued to each individual ship by the administration or a recognised classification society. This certificate will provide the basis of port state control inspections.

From a compliance perspective, the ISM Code's promise lies in its provision of a ready legal benchmark to evaluate whether due diligence has been exercised or the minimum standard of supervision and management applied by the shipowner over his/its vessels.[1003] Thus, in litigious cases, the owner's liability for providing an unseaworthy ship which results in loss of lives or property or damage to the environment can be more easily established. As regards enforcement, the ISM Code and its certification system feature as yet another control requirement insisted upon by the port state control authorities.

That said, the integrity of the system rests with the certification provided by the flag state administration and/or its recognised classification societies. If owners persist in using indulgent flag states and classification societies which are willing to overlook management deficiencies and issue certificates which do not correspond to the true condition of the ships, the ultimate task of enforcing the benefits of the ISM system must fall on port state control. Indeed, industry observers have expressed concern that despite its technical merits, the ISM Code risks becoming another 'paper' exercise which can be easily circumvented by irresponsible flag states and classification societies.[1004]

It follows that one obvious area where greater compliance enforcement is needed is in assessing the performance of flag states and the delegation of flag state supervisory functions to classification societies. Indeed, IMO has recognised the need to shore up flag state implementation; to this end, the IMO Council has approved in principle a Voluntary Member State Audit Scheme[1005] similar to the Safety Oversight Programme implemented by the International Civil Aviation Organisation (ICAO). The proposed

---

[1003] See IMO Assembly Resolution A.913(22) (2001) on Revised Guidelines for the Implementation of the ISM Code and G. P. Pamborides, *The ISM Code: Potential Legal Implications*, INT'L MAR. L. 52 (Feb. 1996).

[1004] Personal interviews.

[1005] The scheme was originally proposed in 2002 as a 'Model Audit Scheme' by a group of mainly developed countries, see Council Doc. C88/13/2 (2002). Note the objections of Brazil and the Bahamas, questioning the need for the scheme and the mechanics of funding it, Council Docs. C88/13/3 (2002) and C88/13/4 (2002). In 2003, the scheme was renamed the 'Voluntary IMO Member State Audit Scheme' to emphasise its voluntary nature, see IMO Assembly Resolution A.946(23) (2003). A related Code for the Implementation of IMO Instruments is also being drafted, with both schemes being scheduled for adoption in 2005.

scheme is voluntary in nature and will entail an independent body of experts assessing flag states' implementation and enforcement of IMO conventions and providing feedback, advice and corrective action plans to improve on their performance.

The establishment of such a scheme is to be welcomed. Indeed, it would be even better if IMO can set up a permanent advisory body of auditors which comprise representatives from states, industry as well as the MOU Secretariats. This could be the same body proposed above for evaluating legislative proposals. In discharging its enforcement mandate, the said body will first have to be given access to the information databases which currently exist (such as Equasis) as well as to industry intelligence about sub-standard ships. The results of the audit should preferably be made public, even though the proposal to IMO has recommended that this be confidential and available only to the audited state.

In auditing states' performance, the body should perform tasks such as assessing the reports submitted by flag states pursuant to their reporting obligations under MARPOL 73/78 and comparing these to their actual performance as reflected by port state control detention statistics and industry reports. Based on the evidence garnered, the IMO body should be authorised to pronounce upon those flag states which have demonstrated satisfactory compliance with their obligations under MARPOL 73/78. Thus, instead of publishing a black-list of non-compliant flags (a controversial move which will be politically difficult to achieve), IMO could instead produce a reverse 'white-list' of compliant flags, similar to the list of STCW-compliant countries currently being produced.

This proposal resembles the 'network of quality registers' model mooted in recent years, only in that it bears IMO's stamp and involves the Organization in the direct assessment of compliance behaviour.[1006] In time, the same strategy can be adopted to produce white-lists of compliant classification societies as well as charterers, P&I Clubs, insurers and other relevant actors. Thus, while the proposed audit scheme is a good start, its mandate and objectives can certainly be broadened to encompass a wider and more effective enforcement role. It will be difficult, though, to make the audit

---

[1006] It also resembles the US Coast Guard's Qualship 21 scheme for quality ships, *supra* note 996.

mandatory, given that flag states will actively resist any such moves on grounds of sovereignty.[1007]

On a more fundamental level, the reporting obligations under MARPOL 73/78 should be strengthened by having IMO conduct more comprehensive analyses on the information reported by states. This way, states can derive more value from reporting and would thus have more incentives to submit proper reports. As things stand, many states do not take the reporting requirement seriously precisely because IMO does so little with the reports it receives.[1008] By undertaking analyses of reports and publication of 'lists' of compliant actors, there is greater hope for IMO to maintain its credibility in the eyes of its member states.

In addition to the audit scheme, IMO is also seeking to ensure proper monitoring of the work carried out by 'recognised organisations' (i.e. classification societies) on behalf of flag state authorities. Here, a major concern is the issue of transfer of class between societies. IMO has also recently discussed new powers to set uniform minimum standards for ship construction and equipment.[1009] Under current practice, the fact that no uniform standards exist means that each classification society is free to develop and modify its own standards as it deems fit. The IMO proposal thus promises to erode the exclusive authority of classification societies in this regard. Overall, it represents a new role for IMO in setting and enforcing compliance with benchmark standards.[1010]

2. Enhancing Equity in Representation and Responsibilities

The other critical issue is that of ensuring equity in discharging the obligations to promote maritime safety and the protection of the marine environment. In accommodating the developed states' demands for ever greater regulation, the international regulatory system risks marginalising the other participants, particularly the developing states and the shipowning community. Perhaps the most critical challenge in this regard is to reform IMO's decision-making architecture which

---

[1007] In fact, Spain had proposed a mandatory scheme, but there was little support at IMO for this.
[1008] See Ch. 5.   [1009] This arose out of a joint proposal by Greece and the Bahamas.
[1010] There are concerns that IMO may be taking on more than it can handle, in that it has no technical capacity to assume or oversee the functions exercised by the classification societies.

continues to be perceived by many states as being heavily tilted in favour of the developed state interests.

Structural reform aside, the states and cargo-owning interests must also be prepared to assume greater *operational* and *financial* responsibilities in combating sub-standard shipping and marine pollution. Thus, state commitments to construct reception facilities must be fulfilled while charterers and cargo owners should bear greater costs in promoting quality shipping. At the same time, shipowners and operators must themselves cultivate greater transparency and co-operation within their own industry to discourage harmful competition and to maintain viable freight rates.

2.1 Reforming IMO

2.1.1 Institutional and Financial Equity

One feature of IMO's structure that needs reform is the constitution of its Council. Currently, a few large states monopolise the Categories A and B seats which are designated for those states with the largest interest in international shipping services and seaborne trade. This leaves the rest of the states – including the major open registries – to clamber for the Category C seats which are intended to reflect diverse geographical representation. Amidst the campaigning and electioneering at the IMO Assembly's biannual sessions, important maritime states may be left out of the Council (e.g. Liberia during the 1999, 2001 and 2003 elections). In addition, Category C's geographical diversity criterion occasionally fails to deliver on equitable representation; in the 1999 elections, for instance, no Central or Southern African countries were elected to the Council.

The 1993 amendment to the IMO Constitution (which entered into force in November 2002) had increased the number of Council representatives to forty from the previous number of thirty-two, with twenty seats going to the states with the largest shipping and trading interests and twenty to the rest of the world. However, increasing the number of seats does not address the problem by itself. For one thing, the open registries derive no guarantee of Council representation even if the seats have been increased.[1011] In this regard, the developed states must realise that there could be a backlash against IMO if the major open registries' representation is not secured in the Council. After all, it

---

[1011] See Lloyd's List, *Power Shift at IMO*, 27 Nov. 2001, detailing the orchestration at the IMO Assembly for filling up Council seats.

is extremely aggravating for the biggest contributors to the budget not to be represented in the very body determining the Organization's spending policies.[1012] Furthermore, engaging the open registries is critical if effective flag state implementation is ever to be achieved.

For these reasons, an amendment to the IMO Constitution should be considered to provide at least two or three guaranteed seats for the top contributors to the IMO budget. This will accord due recognition to the major flag states for their critical role in maritime affairs. This does not amount to permanent representation for any state; far from it, the top shipowning states should contest these seats among themselves. It is no answer to suggest that these states can always contest the Category C seats because, as explained above, the process of election for these seats leaves open the possibility of major open registries being excluded.

At the same time, election to Category C may perhaps be improved by adding a more explicit regional representation clause specifying a quota for the various continents or regions of the world. This will ensure that no region or sub-region is left out. In addition, the states which have hitherto filled the Categories A and B seats unopposed should adopt a more progressive and democratic attitude of offering these seats up for free election.[1013] Ultimately, a more representative Council which more accurately reflects the contemporary realities of shipowning and operation will be better placed to address the modern challenges of maritime safety and environmental protection. Otherwise, the shipping interests and the poorer states will continue to be under-represented at IMO as compared to the coastal and environmental interests.

Reform is also crucially needed in relation to financial contributions by member states. At present, contributions are calculated based on two components: the tonnage of the merchant fleet (87.5 per cent) and the state's ability to pay as determined by an established UN procedure (12.5 per cent).[1014] Given that the bulk of IMO's agenda is currently being dictated by the rich states with minimal direct shipping interests, it is eminently more sensible to de-emphasise the tonnage component and to increase the 'ability to pay' component correspondingly. This will more accurately and equitably reflect the extent to which IMO decision-making is driven to meet the demands of certain state interests.

[1012] The open registries are the biggest paymasters of IMO, with the top contributors in 2003 being Panama, Liberia and the Bahamas.
[1013] The current practice is for these seats to be filled by an elite group of states without election.
[1014] See Ch. 2.

In this regard, a third component could possibly be added to ensure that developed states which initiate regulatory proposals in a given year or period should contribute a proportionately larger sum in order to defray the costs and expenses of IMO meetings. This is consistent with a 'user-pays' concept and will ensure greater equity since it avoids having the developing states effectively subsidise the costs of regulation. Existing procedural rules which minimise the marginalisation of small delegations should also be reinforced. Thus, IMO should strictly enforce the restriction on the number of Working and Drafting Groups meeting outside the plenary. Correspondence group activities in between IMO sessions should be monitored closely lest they determine outcomes which should rightfully be decided with greater participation.[1015]

This is not to suggest that legislative activity at IMO should be impeded or slowed down; far from it, the demands of the ecological age rightly dictate that increased attention and resources must be directed toward meeting new environmental challenges. What is advocated here is a more efficient and equitable allocation of IMO resources. Indeed, prioritisation and balance are critical in ensuring that regulatory challenges are met without sacrificing democratic ideals such as equitable representation for all relevant interests.

2.1.2 Discipline in Agenda-Setting

A sliding-scale principle that pegs member states' financial contributions to their initiation of policies will also compel states to exercise greater discipline in agenda-setting. With the proliferation of rules in recent years and the consequent difficulties faced by states in implementing them, IMO will have to begin ensuring legislative priority for the more important and pressing matters.[1016] Overall, IMO's credibility will be damaged if a vast proportion of its rules are not ratified or implemented by member states and remain good only on paper.

[1015] However, recent MSC and MEPC discussions on reform seem to indicate that IMO will continue to rely on inter-sessional correspondence and working groups, Lloyd's List, *Keeping IMO Reform on the Straight and Narrow*, 19 Apr. 2002.

[1016] In this regard, a proposal by Brazil to subject all work programme items to prior endorsement by at least one-fifth of member states was rejected in 2002, see Council Doc. C88/29(a) (2002) and MEPC Doc. 48/18/2 (2002). IMO itself recognises that its committees are coming under severe workload pressures, see Lloyd's List, *IMO under Strain from Green Rules*, 29 Apr. 2003.

In addition, the severe difficulties faced by developing states in keeping up with IMO legislation should be redressed immediately by a more comprehensive technical assistance programme. Otherwise, the international regulatory system risks being swamped with excessive legislation. Worse, the system could turn into a two-tier implementation structure with developed states pursuing effective enforcement and poorer states languishing behind. This will be greatly detrimental to the over-arching goals of promoting a uniform regulatory regime.

As suggested above,[1017] an advisory body set up within IMO may be able to ensure legislative discipline by vetting state as well as Secretariat initiatives based on proper scientific bases tempered by a precautionary approach. Discipline in agenda-setting will also mean that states must exercise restraint in demanding reactive responses to specific vessel incidents. At the same time, it will ensure that states do not use the platform of IMO decision-making to advance self-interested concerns without thinking through their repercussions for the wider community. From an equity perspective, this will prevent the vast majority of states from being dictated to by a small number of states with narrow sectoral interests and which pay negligible sums for IMO's upkeep.

Again, this is not to say that the pace of decision-making at IMO should be slowed down. Indeed, it would be prejudicial to the marine environment if *bona fide* proposals for regulation become bogged down by the majority's insistence on inflexible assessment thresholds.[1018] Rather, what is being suggested here is a more refined appraisal system which is better able to evaluate state initiatives for regulation and to

---

[1017] See Section 1.1.
[1018] As things stand, more and more issues are likely to arise at IMO, many of them hugely controversial. These include the potential liability of states in relation to offering or denying refuge to ships in distress, a concern raised by the *Prestige*. Another difficult issue relates to ship scrapping or recycling and the associated environmental, safety and occupational health risks, particularly in developing countries. Having recently adopted Guidelines on Recycling of Ships *vide* Assembly Resolution A. 962(23) (2003), IMO is now considering making certain parts of the Guidelines mandatory. The Guidelines merely impose responsibilities on the state of recycling and will thus have to be reconciled with the 1989 Basel Convention on the Control of Transboundary Movement of Hazardous Wastes and their Disposal, 28 I.L.M. 652 (1989), which holds waste producers accountable as well. Perhaps the most contentious emerging issue is that of greenhouse gas (GHG) emissions from ships, which is not covered by Annex VI to MARPOL 73/78. Since the Kyoto Protocol to the Convention on Climate Change, 37 I.L.M. 22 (1998) (in force 16 Feb. 2005) only obliges the so-called 'Annex I' developed countries to reduce GHG emissions, a major issue for shipping will be the obligations of the developing open registry states which register the bulk of world shipping. In this regard, any extension of GHG emission obligations to all states is being resisted

balance equitably the competing demands of the various interests. This way, the most optimal response can be found to meet environmental challenges without necessarily subjugating the interests of the many to that of the few.

Overall, the implementation of existing rules should be emphasised while the enactment of new rules subjected to greater scrutiny based on need. Admittedly, such balance will be exceedingly difficult to achieve given the often diametrically opposed demands of the state, shipping and environmental interests. Yet IMO must continue to seek that elusive balance between commitment to environmental policy-making on the one hand, and discipline in agenda-setting on the other.[1019]

2.2 States and the Provision of Reception Facilities

The intractable, age-old problem of reception facilities must be resolved once and for all. This is not to say that a simplistic and quick solution can be found to force states to provide them. Decades of negotiations have demonstrated the futility of expecting states to succumb to treaty prescriptions for reception facilities. Rather, states must continue to be persuaded and given the requisite incentives to provide such facilities.

Consequently, IMO should promote stronger state–industry dialogue to foster market incentives for providing reception facilities. In particular, innovative burden-sharing arrangements between states and industry should be explored. At the same time, IMO could be empowered to produce white-lists of ports which meet the requirement for adequate facilities and black-lists of ports which do not. Given that states do not usually have the incentive to report on their own or other ports' reception facilities, it necessarily falls on the industry actors to provide such information to IMO.[1020]

While this is already being done, what has not been attempted to date is a detailed analysis by IMO of the industry information provided so as

---

by non-Annex I parties such as China, India, Saudi Arabia, Bangladesh and Pakistan, see MEPC Doc. 49/22 (2003). These states insist that the international community must respect the principle of common but differentiated responsibilities, as entrenched in the 1992 Framework Convention on Climate Change, 31 I.L.M. 848 (1992) (in force 21 Mar. 1994) and IMO Assembly Resolution A.963(23) (2003) on IMO Policies and Practices on GHG Emissions from Ships. Major disagreements on such issues can thus be expected in the coming years.

[1019] Achieving this balance will also help alleviate the budget difficulties caused by the zero-nominal growth policy imposed upon IMO by its member states, see Lloyd's List, *IMO Budget Policy 'is not Viable'*, 18 June 2001.

[1020] See Ch. 5.

to compile authoritative lists of compliant and non-compliant ports. IMO should then publicise such lists, together with the reasons for the absence or inadequacy of facilities. Such modest forms of IMO enforcement powers could go a long way in catalysing ports to provide reception facilities. For one thing, ports and states are largely immune to criticism by industry actors for failing to comply with treaty obligations; criticism by IMO, however, cannot be so easily ignored.

Hence, IMO should endorse the information provided by industry on port reception facilities so as to imbue it with some legitimacy. At the same time, it must be ensured that the criteria used by industry actors to identify deficient ports are consistent and fair. Indeed, IMO may even spearhead the formulation of such criteria and use the industry actors as its enforcing 'agents'. By targeting individual ports for mention (as opposed to states), IMO may also be able to avoid political difficulties with states.

In time, IMO may even contemplate stronger measures against non-compliant ports and states such as conditioning a state's candidacy for Council membership upon satisfactory provision of reception facilities. Financial incentives should also be used – for example, a member state's dues to IMO (which is collected from shipowners using the state's shipping registry) may enjoy a discount if the state agrees to commit the corresponding sum toward the provision of reception facilities. Ultimately, just as market incentives and disincentives can be created for owners, charterers, classification societies and insurers, similar measures should be adopted in dealing with ports and states found lacking in the provision of reception facilities.

2.3 The Cargo Interests and Burden-Sharing

Burden-sharing among maritime actors has already been assessed in detail. It bears reiteration that refined cost-sharing arrangements should be worked out between the carriers and owners of cargo so as to create a more equitable system of apportioning regulatory burdens. In other words, the 'polluter pays' principle should be construed more widely to encompass not only the direct polluter but also other indirect agents contributing to the problem of vessel-source pollution. As explored earlier, while cargo owners already bear some post-event exposure to liability, they must do more to demonstrate commitment to preventive, pre-accident measures. For example, they should absorb some of the costs of new equipment and construction measures. This can be effected either by direct payment for these measures or more indirectly, the paying of higher freight charges. At the same time, greater cargo interest responsibility for compensating pollution damage victims should be instituted.

In general, cargo owners must be prepared to charter quality ships which conform to IMO rules and to pay correspondingly higher freight for these ships. Attempts to drive down freight rates by favouring sub-standard ships in the 'spot' market should be curtailed. This will go a long way toward creating a two-tier market capable of differentiating between quality and sub-standard ships. In turn, higher freight will enable responsible shipowners to embark on proper fleet maintenance and renewal. This will have positive all-round effects on shipping in general.

In particular, double-hull vessels with modern stability and pollution control equipment should be systematically favoured by cargo owners and charterers. Short of actually legislating the use of quality ships, the regulatory system can create market conditions which favour the employment of such ships. For instance, port state control regimes should seek to identify errant charterers who persist in using sub-standard ships. The delays that will be caused to these ships as well as the negative publicity incurred will conceivably serve as disincentives for sub-standard owners and charterers alike.

Furthermore, legal rules should be crafted to impose negligence or criminal liability on charterers of sub-standard ships which pollute the marine environment, whether volitionally or otherwise.[1021] This will compel the cargo interests to exercise greater prudence in checking the condition of the ships they use. Indeed, strong disincentives to use ships of questionable quality might well have prevented accidents such as the *Erika* and *Prestige*. Given that the majority of cargo owners are nationals of the developed states, these states should legislate domestic laws imposing penalties for knowingly chartering sub-standard vessels. Such moves will demonstrate the sincerity of the developed coastal states in eradicating sub-standard shipping. Otherwise, by continuing to target only the shipowners (who are frequently foreigners), these states stand accused of ignoring the role of their own cargo-owning interests.

The developed states should thus capitalise on the present political and legislative momentum generated by the *Erika* and *Prestige* to demand greater responsibility on the part of their cargo interests. In

---

[1021] See e.g. Commission Proposal for a Directive on Sanctions, art. 6, *supra* note 394.

the meantime, the threat of European unilateralism and IMO's accelerated phasing out of single-hull tankers have demonstrably lifted the freight market somewhat, leading to charterers having to pay more for quality, double-hull ships. However, this effect may only be temporary, and long-term measures are needed to entrench greater cargo interest responsibility. Ultimately, the behaviour of users of shipping *does* have a huge bearing on ship safety and pollution risks. Imposing greater costs on these actors – whether through market forces or legal sanctions or a combination of both – will have significant effects on the quality of shipping worldwide.

2.4 Shipowners and Intra-Industry Co-operation

On their part, the shipowners and operators must strive for greater co-operation and transparency within their own industry. Otherwise, the cargo-owning interests will continue to exploit systemic weaknesses such as the fragmentation of the industry and the lack of unity among owners.[1022] For far too long, shipowners have hurt their own industry by resorting to short-term profit-maximising measures whenever freight rates showed signs of the slightest improvement. For example, owners typically rush to order new vessels and to delay scrapping old ones whenever freight rates rise, only to contribute to a glut in supply a few years down the road.[1023]

Owners have also not been able to agree on the desirability of new pollution control equipment. Up until the *Erika* incident, for instance, owners who had renewed their fleets sang praises of double hulls while those who chose to retrofit their vessels with hydrostatic balancing continued to resist double hulls. The whole climate of secrecy and suspicion in the industry further exacerbates competition among owners, often leading to under-cutting of freight rates and neglect of safety and pollution standards. In the result, it is hardly surprising that the shipping industry continues to attract negative publicity. In essence, shipowners can hardly complain about the opportunistic behaviour of charterers seeking the lowest freight rates when they themselves have not sought to present a united and responsible front.

[1022] The passivity of the shipping industry and its chronic lack of leadership remain huge problems, see Lloyd's List, *Leading the Fight in the Shipping Arena*, 10 Mar. 2001, quoting Peter Morris, Chairman of the International Commission on Shipping (ICONS).

[1023] INTERTANKO, *supra* note 14, at 26.

The obvious solution for the shipping industry is to work harder toward greater co-operation. This will be a difficult task for the industry, given its traditionally fragmented and competitive nature. Industry bodies such as INTERTANKO, ICS and BIMCO have tried for many years to present a common voice at IMO. Often, however, they are reduced to ambiguous positions reflecting the lowest common denominators of agreement among the respective shipowners. The difficulty resides in the fact that there are so many owners in different countries with fleets differing in size, tonnage, flag, age, nature and function of vessel and level of maintenance. At the same time, there exist many unscrupulous owners operating out of states and regions with minimal supervision over shipping.

Despite these difficulties, the industry must continue to strive for greater transparency, co-operation and unity. Shipowners and P&I Clubs must begin to recognise the benefits of sharing information on the sub-standard practices of their own members. For instance, the Clubs should inform each other on inspection results of sub-standard ships, and owners should be made to disclose the results of previous inspections when applying for cover with a new Club.[1024] The Clubs should also institute measures such as unifying their standards for coverage and disqualifying sub-standard ships from being accepted into pooling arrangements. This way, they can check on the practices of their own members and enforce a measure of internal discipline. At a broader level, greater information sharing should be promoted with other industry actors which conduct ship vettings such as the cargo interests and classification societies, as well as port state control authorities and the Equasis administrators.

In the absence of incentives for the industry to conduct self-regulation, the imposition of pressure from external sources such as port state control and the threat of coastal state unilateralism may actually have positive effects for the responsible owner. As mentioned above, such owners may ironically find the regulatory fervour arising out of incidents such as the *Erika* and *Prestige* to be a blessing in disguise given its effects on charterer behaviour and freight rates and on the targeting of sub-standard competitors by port state control authorities.

However, these 'benefits' are largely incident-dependent and may be short-term at best. It would be more desirable for responsible owners to

---

[1024] REMOVAL OF INSURANCE, *supra* note 5, at 42. There could, however, be competition law implications for such information sharing.

support greater IMO activism in promoting long-term differentiation between quality and sub-standard shipping. At the same time, if responsible owners wish to increase their bargaining positions at IMO, they might consider re-flagging their fleets to the developed states. Otherwise, they will continue to be frustrated by the relative lack of influence of their open registry proxies.

3. Final Thoughts

At first glance, some of the prescriptions outlined above may appear mutually incompatible. For instance, according greater representation to the shipping and developing state interests may seem retrogressive if their resistance to regulation actually increases the risk of coastal state unilateralism. Similarly, discipline in agenda-setting may be interpreted as impeding the enactment of rules to meet new challenges. Yet, these prescriptions need not be mutually exclusive. In the climate of contemporary regulation today, it is incontestable that navigational safety, maritime security and environmental protection have become dominant concerns. Indeed, it would appear that ever-increasing regulation over shipping is imminent in the years to come, leading to further erosion of the traditional right of free and unhindered navigation.

That this is occurring is conceded to even by the most ardent proponents of maritime freedom. This trend will substantially affect actors such as the shipowners, the open registries and the developing states, who might be expected to come under ever-increasing pressure to respond to safety, security and environmental concerns, to demonstrate compliance with the relevant rules, and to bear the associated costs of regulation. In such a climate, equity in representation and burden-sharing as well as discipline in agenda-setting become all the more critical if IMO is not to lose its credibility among the developing state and shipping interests. In a truly global industry such as shipping, the agreement or acquiescence of as many relevant stakeholders as possible is needed to ensure uniform applicability of rules. In this respect, any decision-making process that marginalises a substantial proportion of its participants can only be deficient.

Hence, the IMO regulatory process must continue to find that balance between accommodating the environmentalists' demands, on the one hand, and according the opposing interests some platform to voice their concerns, on the other. As much as the developed states may wish to accelerate the pace of regulation, they must be acutely sensitive to the needs and demands of the shipping interests. It follows that the more activist IMO becomes in pursuing safety and environmental goals, the more it must strive to avoid alienating its shipping and developing state constituents.

In this regard, it would be desirable if, on their part, the maritime actors can come around to the realisation that environmental obligations need not be hostile to their interests. Indeed, the respective aspirations of the shipping and environmental communities – namely, profitability and ecological responsibility – are not necessarily irreconcilable. In practical terms, the shipping industry itself derives benefits from exhibiting responsible environmental behaviour. Where the protection of the marine environment can be made politically and economically worthwhile, industry commitment to the ecological ideal can only reinforce the goals of the environmentalists.

The prime obstacle to this complementarity is, of course, the free-riding practice of sub-standard shipping. Consequently, the regulatory process as well as market forces need to be co-ordinated in order to deter those actors who persist in operating sub-standard ships to the detriment of both quality owners and the environment. To this end, enforcement efforts such as port state control and flag state implementation will have to be enhanced. Critically, the other actors in the maritime chain – including the cargo owners, classification societies, insurers, financiers, shipbuilders as well as states themselves – will have to share in a larger proportion of the owner's burden in seeking to foster quality standards.

For all these reasons, it is imperative that the shipping interests be treated as partners – not targets or adversaries – in the regulation of vessel activities. Hence, the international regulatory process must continue to engage, co-operate with and co-opt the shipping interests in its quest to stamp out sub-standard shipping practices and to formulate effective policies for marine environmental protection. An interlocking and mutually accountable network of actors behaving responsibly is the only effective means of eradicating sub-standard shipping and of ensuring greater safety at sea and protection of the marine environment.

Ultimately, it is entirely possible that through equitable representation, participation and burden-sharing, the various state and industry actors can find the requisite incentives to achieve the goals of international maritime regulation, namely safer shipping and cleaner seas. There is surely enough room in the maritime realm for such optimism.

Bibliography

Treatises

ABECASSIS, D. W., THE LAW AND PRACTICE RELATING TO OIL POLLUTION FROM SHIPS (Butterworths, London, Boston, 1978)

ABECASSIS, D. W. & JARASHOW, R., OIL POLLUTION FROM SHIPS (2nd edn, Stevens, London, 1985)

ADEMUNI-ODEKE, BAREBOAT CHARTER (SHIP) REGISTRATION (Kluwer Law International, Boston, 1998)

ANDERSON, P., ISM CODE: A PRACTICAL GUIDE TO THE LEGAL AND INSURANCE IMPLICATIONS (LLP, London, 1998)

    CRACKING THE CODE: THE RELEVANCE OF THE ISM CODE AND ITS IMPACT ON SHIPPING PRACTICES (Nautical Institute, London, 2003)

ATTARD, D., THE EXCLUSIVE ECONOMIC ZONE IN INTERNATIONAL LAW (Clarendon Press, Oxford; Oxford University Press, New York, 1987)

BIRNIE, P. & BOYLE A., INTERNATIONAL LAW AND THE ENVIRONMENT (2nd edn, Oxford University Press, London, 2002)

BOCZEK, B. A., FLAGS OF CONVENIENCE: AN INTERNATIONAL LEGAL STUDY (Harvard University Press, Cambridge, MA, 1962)

BOISSON, P., SAFETY AT SEA – POLICIES, REGULATIONS AND INTERNATIONAL LAW (D. Mahaffey trans., Edition Bureau Veritas, Paris, 1999)

BROWN, E. D., THE LEGAL REGIME OF HYDROSPACE (Stevens, London, 1971)

    THE INTERNATIONAL LAW OF THE SEA (Dartmouth, Brookfield, VT, 1994)

BRUBAKER, D., MARINE POLLUTION AND INTERNATIONAL LAW: PRINCIPLES AND PRACTICE (Belhaven Press, London, 1993)

BURGER, J., OIL SPILLS (Rutgers University Press, New Brunswick, NJ, 1997)

BUTLER, W. E. (ed.), THE LAW OF THE SEA AND INTERNATIONAL SHIPPING: ANGLO-SOVIET POST-UNCLOS PERSPECTIVES (Oceana Publications, New York, 1985)

CARLISLE, R. P., SOVEREIGNTY FOR SALE: THE ORIGINS AND EVOLUTION OF THE PANAMANIAN AND LIBERIAN FLAGS OF CONVENIENCE (Naval Institute Press, Annapolis, MD, 1981)

CHAO, W., POLLUTION FROM THE CARRIAGE OF OIL BY SEA: LIABILITY AND COMPENSATION (Kluwer, London, 1996)

CHAYES, A. & CHAYES, A. H., THE NEW SOVEREIGNTY: COMPLIANCE WITH INTERNATIONAL REGULATORY AGREEMENTS (Harvard University Press, Cambridge, MA, 1995)
CHURCHILL R. R. & LOWE, A. V., THE LAW OF THE SEA (3rd edn, Manchester University Press, Manchester, 1999)
CHURCHILL, R. R. et al. (eds.), 3 NEW DIRECTIONS IN THE LAW OF THE SEA (Oceana Publications, London, New York, 1973-5)
CICIN-SAIN, B. & KNECHT, R. W., THE FUTURE OF U.S. OCEAN POLICY: CHOICES FOR THE NEW CENTURY (Island Press, Washington, D.C., 2000)
CLARK, R. B., MARINE POLLUTION (4th edn, Clarendon Press, Oxford, 1997)
COLES, R. & READY, N. P. (eds.), SHIP REGISTRATION: LAW AND PRACTICE (LLP, London, 2002)
CRAWFORD, J., THE INTERNATIONAL LAW COMMISSION'S ARTICLES ON STATE RESPONSIBILITY: INTRODUCTION, TEXT AND COMMENTARIES (Cambridge University Press, Cambridge, 2002)
CRAWFORD, J. & ROTHWELL, D. (eds.), THE LAW OF THE SEA IN THE ASIAN PACIFIC REGION (Martinus Nijhoff, Dordrecht, Boston, 1995)
DE LA RUE, C. & ANDERSON, C. B., SHIPPING AND THE ENVIRONMENT: LAW AND PRACTICE (LLP, London, 1998)
DE LA RUE, C (ed.), LIABILITY FOR DAMAGE TO THE MARINE ENVIRONMENT (LLP, London, 1993)
ESTY, D. & GERADIN, D. (eds.), REGULATORY COMPETITION AND ECONOMIC INTEGRATION: COMPARATIVE PERSPECTIVES (Oxford University Press, Oxford, 2001)
FRANCKX, E. (ed.), VESSEL-SOURCE POLLUTION AND COASTAL STATE JURISDICTION: THE WORK OF THE ILA COMMITTEE ON COASTAL STATE JURISDICTION RELATING TO MARINE POLLUTION (1991-2000) (Kluwer Law International, The Hague, 2001)
FREESTONE, D. & HEY, E. (eds.), THE PRECAUTIONARY PRINCIPLE AND INTERNATIONAL LAW: THE CHALLENGE OF IMPLEMENTATION (Kluwer Law International, Boston, 1996)
FREESTONE, D. & IJLSTRA, T. (eds.), THE NORTH SEA: PERSPECTIVES ON REGIONAL ENVIRONMENTAL CO-OPERATION (Graham & Trotman, London, Boston, 1990)
GAUCI, G., OIL POLLUTION AT SEA: CIVIL LIABILITY AND COMPENSATION FOR DAMAGE (John Wiley, Chichester, 1997)
GOLD, E., MARITIME TRANSPORT: THE EVOLUTION OF INTERNATIONAL MARINE POLICY AND SHIPPING LAW (Lexington Books, Lexington, MA, 1981)
GARD HANDBOOK ON MARINE POLLUTION (2nd edn, Assuranceforeningen Gard, Arendal, Norway, 1997)
GRIGGS, P. & WILLIAMS, R., LIMITATION OF LIABILITY FOR MARITIME CLAIMS (3rd edn, LLP, London, 1998)
GRIGGS, P. et al., LIMITATION OF LIABILITY FOR MARITIME CLAIMS (LLP, London, 2004)
GROTIUS, H., THE FREEDOM OF THE SEAS (1608) (R. Van Deman Magoffin trans., J. B. Scott (ed.), Oxford University Press, Oxford, 1916)
HAKAPÄÄ, K., MARINE POLLUTION IN INTERNATIONAL LAW: MATERIAL OBLIGATIONS AND JURISDICTION (Suomalainen Tiedeakatemia, Helsinki, 1981)
HARDIN, G., EXPLORING NEW ETHICS FOR SURVIVAL (Viking Press, New York, 1972)
JOHNSTON, D. M. (ed.), THE ENVIRONMENTAL LAW OF THE SEA (E. Schmidt, Berlin, 1981)
KASOULIDES, G. C., PORT STATE CONTROL AND JURISDICTION: EVOLUTION OF THE PORT STATE REGIME (Martinus Nijhoff, Dordrecht, Boston, 1993)
KINDT, J. W., MARINE POLLUTION AND THE LAW OF THE SEA (W. S. Hein, Buffalo, NY, 1986)

Kiss, A. C. & Shelton, D., International Environmental Law (2nd edn, Transnational Publishers, Ardsley, NY, 2000)
Koers, A. W. & Oxman, B. H. (eds.), The 1982 Convention on the Law of the Sea (Law of the Sea Institute, University of Hawaii, 1984)
Kriwoken, L. et al. (eds.), Oceans Law and Policy in the post-UNCED Era: Australian and Canadian Perspectives (Kluwer Law International, London, 1996)
Kwiatkowska, B., The 200-Mile Exclusive Economic Zone in the New Law of the Sea (Martinus Nijhoff, Dordrecht, Boston, 1989)
Mahmoudi, S., The Law of Deep Sea Bed Mining (Almqvist & Wiksell International, Stockholm, 1987)
Mankabady, S., The International Maritime Organization (Croom Helm, London, Wolfeboro, NH, 1986)
McDorman, T. et al., The Marine Environment and the Caracas Convention on the Law of the Sea (Dalhousie Ocean Studies Programme, Canada, 1981)
McDougal, M. S. & Burke, W. T., The Public Order of the Oceans: A Contemporary International Law of the Sea (Yale University Press, New Haven, 1962)
Meng, Q.-N., Land-Based Marine Pollution (Graham & Trotman, London, Boston, 1987)
Metaxas, B. N., Flag of Convenience: A Study of Internationalisation (Gower, Aldershot, Brookfield, VT, 1985)
Meyers, H., The Nationality of Ships (Martinus Nijhoff, The Hague, 1967)
M'Gonigle, R. M. & Zacher, M. W., Pollution, Politics and International Law: Tankers at Sea (University of California Press, Berkeley, 1979)
Miles, E. L., Global Ocean Politics: The Decision Process at the Third United Nations Conference on the Law of the Sea, 1973–1982 (Martinus Nijhoff, Boston, 1998)
Mitchell, R. B., Intentional Oil Pollution at Sea – Environmental Policy and Treaty Compliance (MIT Press, Cambridge, MA, 1994)
Molenaar, E. J., Coastal State Jurisdiction over Vessel-Source Pollution (Kluwer Law International, The Hague, 1998)
Naess, E. D., The Great PanLibHon Controversy – The Fight over the Flags of Shipping (Gower Press, Epping, 1972)
Nandan, S., Rosenne, S. & Nordquist, M. H. (eds.), 2 United Nations Convention on the Law of the Sea 1982: A Commentary (Martinus Nijhoff, Dordrecht, Boston, 1993)
  (eds.), 3 United Nations Convention on the Law of the Sea 1982: A Commentary (Martinus Nijhoff, Dordrecht, Boston, 1995)
Northrup, H. R. & Rowan, R. L., The International Transport Workers' Federation and Flag of Convenience Shipping (University of Pennsylvania, Philadelphia, 1983)
O'Connell, D. P., The Influence of Law on Sea Power (Manchester University Press, Manchester, 1975)
  The International Law of the Sea (2 vols., Clarendon Press, Oxford, 1982, 1984)
Özçayır, Z. O., Port State Control (LLP, London, 2004)
Payoyo, P. B., Port State Control in the Asia-Pacific: An International Legal Study of Port State Jurisdiction (University of the Philippines Law Center, Manila, 1993)

PEET, G., OPERATIONAL DISCHARGES FROM SHIPS: AN EVALUATION OF THE APPLICATION OF THE DISCHARGE PROVISIONS OF THE MARPOL CONVENTION BY ITS CONTRACTING PARTIES (AIDEnvironment, Amsterdam, 1992)
PRITCHARD, S. Z., OIL POLLUTION CONTROL (Croom Helm, London, Wolfeboro, NH, 1987)
REISMAN, W. M. & WESTON, B. H. (eds.), TOWARDS WORLD ORDER AND HUMAN DIGNITY: ESSAYS IN HONOR OF MYRES S. MCDOUGAL (Free Press, New York, 1976)
RIENOW, R., THE TEST OF NATIONALITY OF A MERCHANT VESSEL (New York, 1937)
ROACH, J. A. & SMITH, R. W., EXCESSIVE MARITIME CLAIMS (2nd edn, Martinus Nijhoff, Boston, 1996)
ROSS, W. M., OIL POLLUTION AS AN INTERNATIONAL PROBLEM (University of Washington Press, Seattle, 1973)
SADLER, P. & KING, J., STUDY ON MECHANISMS FOR THE FINANCING OF FACILITIES IN PORTS FOR THE RECEPTION OF WASTES FROM SHIPS, *attached to* MEPC Doc. 30/INF.32 (International Maritime Organization, London, 1990).
SAND, P. H., TRANSNATIONAL ENVIRONMENTAL LAW: LESSONS IN GLOBAL CHANGE (Kluwer Law International, London, 1999)
SHAW, M. N., INTERNATIONAL LAW (3rd edn, Grotius Publications, Cambridge, 1991)
INTERNATIONAL LAW (5th edn, Cambridge University Press, Cambridge, 2003)
SHINN, R. A., THE INTERNATIONAL POLITICS OF MARINE POLLUTION CONTROL (Praeger, New York, 1974)
SIBENIUS, J. K., NEGOTIATING THE LAW OF THE SEA (Harvard University Press, Cambridge, MA, 1984)
SILVERSTEIN, H., SUPERSHIPS AND NATION STATES: THE TRANSNATIONAL PROBLEM OF OIL POLLUTION (Westview Press, Boulder, CO, 1978)
SIMMONDS, K. R., THE INTERNATIONAL MARITIME ORGANIZATION (Simmonds & Hill, London, 1994)
SINGH, N., MARITIME FLAG AND INTERNATIONAL LAW (Thomason Press, Haryana, 1978)
SMITH, B. D., STATE RESPONSIBILITY AND THE MARINE ENVIRONMENT: THE RULES OF DECISION (Oxford University Press, 1988)
STOOP, M., OLIEVERONTREINIGING DOOR SCHEPEN OP DER NOORDZEE OVER DE PERIODE 1982–1987: OPSPORING EN VERVOLGING (Werkgroep Nordzee, Amsterdam, 1989)
TIMAGENIS, G., INTERNATIONAL CONTROL OF MARINE POLLUTION (Oceana Publications, NY, 1980)
TOLOFARI, S. R., OPEN REGISTRY SHIPPING: A COMPARATIVE STUDY OF COSTS AND FREIGHT RATES (Gordon & Breach Science Publishers, New York, NY, 1989)
VALOIS, P., TANKERS – AN INTRODUCTION TO THE TRANSPORT OF OIL BY SEA (Witherby & Co., London, 1997)
VOGEL, D., TRADING UP: CONSUMER AND ENVIRONMENTAL REGULATION IN A GLOBAL ECONOMY (Harvard University Press, Cambridge, MA, 1995)
WATERS II, W. G. et al., OIL POLLUTION FROM TANKER OPERATIONS – CAUSES, COSTS, CONTROLS (University of British Columbia, Vancouver, 1980)
WEISS, E. B. & JACOBSON, H. (eds.), ENGAGING COUNTRIES: STRENGTHENING COMPLIANCE WITH INTERNATIONAL ACCORDS (MIT Press, Cambridge, MA, 1998)
WILLINGALE, M., SHIP MANAGEMENT (3rd edn, LLP, London, 1998)

YOUNG, O., COMPLIANCE AND PUBLIC AUTHORITY: A THEORY WITH INTERNATIONAL APPLICATION (Johns Hopkins University Press, Baltimore, MD, 1979)
(ed.), THE EFFECTIVENESS OF INTERNATIONAL ENVIRONMENTAL REGIMES: CAUSAL CONNECTIONS AND BEHAVIORAL MECHANISMS (MIT Press, Cambridge, MA, 1999)

Articles in Periodicals

Abecassis, D. W., *Marine Oil Pollution Laws: The View of Shell International Marine Limited*, 8 INT'L BUS. L. 3 (1980).
Ademuni-Odeke, *Port State Control and U.K. Law*, 28 J. MAR. L. & COM. 657 (1997)
Alcantara, L. F. & Cox, M. A., *OPA 90 Certificates of Financial Responsibility*, 23 J. MAR. L. & COM. 369 (1992)
Alcock, T. M., *'Ecology' Tankers and the Oil Pollution Act of 1990: A History of Efforts to Require Double Hulls on Oil Tankers*, 19 ECOLOGY L. Q. 97 (1992)
Allen, C. H., *Federalism in the Era of International Standards: Federal and State Government Regulation of Merchant Vessels in the United States* (Part III), 30 J. MAR. L. & COM. 85 (1999)
Anderson, C. B. & de la Rue, C., *Liability of Charterers and Cargo Owners for Pollution from Ships*, 26 MAR. LAW. 42 (2001)
Anderson, D. W., *National and International Efforts to Prevent Traumatic Vessel Source Oil Pollution*, 30 U. MIAMI L. REV. 985 (1976)
Anderson III, H. E., *The Nationality of Ships and Flags of Convenience: Economics, Politics and Alternatives*, 21 TUL. MAR. L. J. 139 (1996)
Ayorinde, A. A., *Inconsistencies Between OPA 90 and MARPOL 73/78: What is the Effect on Legal Rights and Obligations of the United States and Other Parties to MARPOL 73/78?*, 25 J. MAR. L. & COM. 55 (1994)
Baldwin, M. et al., *Recent Developments: A Review of Developments in Ocean and Coastal Law 1999-2000*, 5 OCEAN & COASTAL L. J. 367 (2000)
Becker, G. L., *A Short Cruise on the Good Ships TOVALOP and CRISTAL*, 5 J. MAR. L. & COM. 609 (1974)
Bederman, D. J., *Dead in the Water: International Law, Diplomacy and Compensation for Chemical Pollution at Sea*, 26 VA. J. INT'L. L. 485 (1986)
  International Control of Marine 'Pollution' by Exotic Species, 18 ECOLOGY L. Q. 677 (1991)
Bernhardt, J. P. A., *A Schematic Analysis of Vessel-Source Pollution: Prescriptive and Enforcement Regimes in the Law of the Sea Conference*, 20 VA. J. INT'L L. 265 (1980)
Bilder, R., *The Canadian Arctic Waters Pollution Prevention Act: New Stresses on the Law of the Sea*, 69 MICH. L. REV. 1 (1970)
Birnie, P., *Reflagging of Fishing Vessels on the High Seas*, 2 RECIEL 270 (1993)
Bodansky, D. M., *Protecting the Marine Environment from Vessel-Source Pollution: UNCLOS III and Beyond*, 18 ECOLOGY L. Q. 719 (1991)
Boehmer-Christiansen, S., *Marine Pollution Control: UNCLOS III as the Partial Codification of International Practice*, 7 ENVTL. POL'Y & L. 71 (1981)

Boos, M., *The Oil Pollution Act of 1990: Striking the Flags of Convenience?*, 2 COLO. J. INT'L ENVTL. L. & POL'Y 407 (1991)

Boyle, A. E., *Marine Pollution under the Law of the Sea Convention*, 79 AM. J. INT'L L. 347 (1987)

Land-Based Sources of Marine Pollution: Current Legal Regime, 16 MARINE POL'Y 20 (1992)

Dispute Settlement and the Law of the Sea Convention: Problems of Fragmentation and Jurisdiction, 46 INT'L & COMP. L. Q. 37 (1997)

Bradshaw, R. E., *The Politics of Soviet Maritime Security*, 10 J. MAR. L. & COM. 411 (1979)

Bryant, D. L., *Port State Control as Practiced by the U.S. Coast Guard*, 10 INT'L MAR. L. 303 (1997)

Buzan, B., *Negotiating by Consensus: Developments in Technique at the United Nations Conference on the Law of the Sea*, 75 AM. J. INT'L L. 324 (1981)

Cane, P. F., *The Liability of Classification Societies*, 3 LLOYD'S MAR. & COM. L. Q. 363 (1994)

Chao, W., *Liability and Compensation for Bunker Pollution*, 33 J. MAR. L. & COM. 553 (2002)

Charney, J. I., *The Marine Environment and the 1982 United Nations Convention on the Law of the Sea*, 28 INT'L LAW. 879 (1994)

U.S. Provisional Application of the 1994 Deep Seabed Agreement, 88 AM. J. INT'L L. 705 (1994)

The Protection of the Marine Environment by the 1982 United Nations Convention on the Law of the Sea, 7 GEO. INT'L ENVTL. L. REV. 731 (1995)

Entry into Force of the 1982 Convention on the Law of the Sea, 35 VA. J. INT'L L. 381 (1995)

Chayes, A. & Chayes, A. H., *Compliance Without Enforcement: State Behavior under Regulatory Treaties*, 7 NEGOTIATION J. 311 (1991)

Churchill, R. R., *The Meaning of the 'Genuine Link' Requirement in Relation to the Nationality of Ships*, A Report for the International Transport Workers' Federation (2000), *available at* http://www.oceanlaw.net/hedley/pubs/ITF-Oct2000.pdf

Clarke, A., *Port State Control or Sub-Standard Ships: Who is to Blame? What is the Cure?*, LLOYD'S MAR. & COMM. L. Q. 202 (1994)

Cohen, L. G., *Revisions of TOVALOP and CRISTAL: Strong Ships for Stormy Seas*, 18 J. MAR. L. & COM. 525 (1987)

Cooney, M. K., *The Stormy Seas of Oil Pollution Liability: Will Protection and Indemnity Clubs Survive?*, 16 HOUS. J. INT'L L 343 (1993)

Curtis, J. B., *Vessel-Source Oil Pollution and MARPOL 73/78: An International Success Story?*, 15 ENVTL. L. 679 (1985)

Cuttler, M., *Incentives for Reducing Oil Pollution from Ships: The Case for Enhanced Port State Control*, GEO. INT'L ENVTL. L. REV. 175 (1995)

DeBievre, A. F. M., *Liability and Compensation for Damage in Connection with the Carriage of Hazardous and Noxious Substances by Sea*, 17 J. MAR. L. & COM. 61 (1986)

Degan, V. D., *Internal Waters*, 17 NETH. Y.B. INT'L L. 3 (1986)
de Gennaro, M., *Oil Pollution Liability and Control under International Maritime Law: Market Incentives as an Alternative to Government Regulation*, 37 VAND. J. TRANSNAT'L L. 265 (2004)
de la Fayette, L., *Access to Ports in International Law*, 11 INT'L J. MARINE & COASTAL L. 1, at 22 (1996)
de la Rue, C., *TOVALOP and CRISTAL - A Purpose Fulfilled*, INT'L J. SHIPPING L. 285 (1996)
Dehner, J. S., *Vessel-Source Pollution and Public Vessels: Sovereign Immunity v. Compliance - Implications for International Environmental Law*, 9 EMORY INT'L L. REV. 508 (1995)
Dempsey, P. S., *Compliance and Enforcement in International Law - Oil Pollution of the Marine Environment by Ocean Vessels*, 6 NW. J. INT'L L. & BUS. 459 (1984)
Dempsey, P. S. & Helling, L., *Oil Pollution by Ocean Vessels - Environmental Tragedy: The Legal Regime of Flags of Convenience, Multilateral Conventions and Coastal States*, 10 DENV. J. INT'L L. & POL'Y 37 (1980).
DeSombre, E., *Flags of Convenience and the Implementation of International Environmental, Safety, and Labor Standards at Sea*, 37 INT'L POL. 213 (2000)
Dinstein, Y., *Oil Pollution by Ships and Freedom of the High Seas*, 3 J. MAR. L. & COM. 363 (1972)
Duruigbo, E., *Multinational Corporations and Compliance with International Regulations Relating to the Petroleum Industry*, 7 ANN. SURV. INT'L & COMP. L. 101 (2001).
Dzidzornu, D. M., *Coastal State Obligations and Powers Respecting EEZ Environmental Protection under Part XII of the UNCLOS: A Descriptive Analysis*, 8 COLO. J. INT'L ENVTL. L. & POL'Y 283 (1997)
Dzidzornu, D. M. & Tsamenyi, B. M., *Enhancing International Control of Vessel-Source Oil Pollution under the Law of the Sea Convention, 1982: A Reassessment*, 10 U. TASM. L. REV. 270 (1991)
Ehlers, P., *The Helsinki Convention: Improving the Baltic Sea Environment*, 8 INT'L J. MARINE & COASTAL L. 191 (1993)
Ellis, E. J., *International Law and Oily Waters: A Critical Analysis*, 6 COLO. J. INT'L ENVTL. L. & POL'Y 32 (1995)
Eskenazi, N. J., *Forum Non Conveniens and Choice of Law In Re: The Amoco Cadiz Oil Spill*, 24 J. MAR. L. & COM. 371 (1993)
Franckx, E., *Coastal State Jurisdiction with Respect to Marine Pollution - Some Recent Developments and Future Challenges*, 10 INT'L J. MARINE & COASTAL L. 253 (1995)
Garick, J. A., *Crisis in the Oil Industry - Certificates of Financial Responsibility and the OPA 1990*, 17 MARINE POL'Y 272 (1993)
Gaskell, N., *Compensation for Oil Pollution Damage: 1992 Protocols to the Civil Liability Convention and the Fund Convention*, 8 INT'L J. MARINE & COASTAL L. 286 (1993)
Giffin, J., *Developments Concerning Criminal Charges Against Vessel Owners and Corporate Officers for Oil Spills in U.S. Waters*, 5 INT'L MAR. L. 91 (1999)
Gjerde, K. & Freestone, D. (eds.), *Particularly Sensitive Sea Areas - An Important Environmental Concept at a Turning Point*, 9 INT'L J. MARINE & COASTAL L. 431 (1994)

Gold, E., *Learning from Disaster: Lessons in Regulatory Enforcement in the Maritime Sector*, 8 RECIEL 16 (1999)

Goldie, L. F. E., *Recognition and Dual Nationality – A Problem of Flags of Convenience*, 39 BRIT. Y.B. INT'L L. 220 (1963)

Environmental Catastrophes and Flags of Convenience – Does the Present Law Pose Special Liability Issues?, 3 PACE Y. B. INT'L L. 63 (1991)

Gordan III, J. D., *The Liability of Marine Surveyors and Ship Classification Societies*, 19 J. MAR. L. & COM. 301 (1988)

Griffin, A., *MARPOL 73/78 and Vessel Pollution: A Glass Half Full or Half Empty?*, 1 IND. J. GLOBAL LEGAL STUD. 489 (1994)

Handl, G., *International Liability of States for Marine Pollution*, 21 CAN. Y.B. INT'L L. 85 (1983)

Controlling Implementation of and Compliance with International Environmental Agreements: The Rocky Road from Rio, 5 COLO. J. INT'L ENVTL L. & POL'Y 305, at 330 (1994)

Hardin, G., *The Tragedy of the Commons*, 162 SCI. 1243 (1968)

Hare, J., *Port State Control: Strong Medicine to Cure a Sick Industry*, 26 GA. J. INT'L & COMP. L. 571 (1997)

Harling, R., *The Liability of Classification Societies to Cargo Owners*, 1 MAR. & COM. L. Q. 1 (1993)

Healy, N. J., *The CMI and IMCO Draft Conventions on Civil Liability for Oil Pollution*, 1 J. MAR. L. & COM. 93 (1970)

Henkin, L., *Arctic Antipollution: Does Canada Make or Break International Law?*, AM. J. INT'L L. 131 (1971)

Hey, E., IJlstra, T. & Nollkaemper, A., *The 1992 Paris Convention for the Protection of the Marine Environment of the North-East Atlantic: A Critical Analysis*, 8 INT'L J. MARINE & COASTAL L. 1 (1993)

Honka, H., *The Classification System and its Problems with Special Reference to the Liability of Classification Societies*, TUL. MAR. L. J. 1 (1994)

Jacobsen, D. A. & Yellen, J. D., *Oil Pollution: The 1984 Protocols and Amoco Cadiz*, 15 J. MAR. L. & COM. 467 (1984)

Jacobsson, M. & Trotz, N., *The Definition of Pollution Damage in the 1984 Protocols to the 1969 Civil Liability Convention and the 1971 Fund Convention*, 17 J. MAR. L. & COM. 467 (1986)

Johnson, D. H. N., *The Nationality of Ships*, 8 INDIAN Y.B. INT'L AFF. 3 (1959)

Joyner, C. C., *Biodiversity in the Marine Environment: Resource Implications for the Law of the Sea*, 28 VAND. J. TRANSNAT'L L. 635 (1995)

Juda, L., *IMCO and the Regulation of Ocean Pollution from Ships*, 26 INT'L & COMP. L. Q. 558 (1977)

Kasoulides, G. C., *The 1986 United Nations Convention for the Conditions for the Registration of Vessels and the Question of Open Registry*, 20 OCEAN DEV. & INT'L L. 543 (1989)

Keselj, T., *Port State Jurisdiction in Respect of Pollution from Ships: The 1982 United Nations Convention on the Law of the Sea and the Memorandum of Understanding*, 30 OCEAN DEV. & INT'L L. J. 127 (1999)

Kiehne, G., *Investigation, Detention and Release of Ships under the Paris MOU on Port State Control: A View from Practice*, 11 INT'L J. MARINE & COASTAL L. 217 (1996)
Kimball, L., *The Law of the Sea Convention and Marine Environmental Protection*, 7 GEO. INT'L ENVTL. L. REV. 745 (1995)
Kindt, J. W., *The Effect of Claims by Developing Countries on LOS International Marine Pollution Negotiations*, 20 VA. J. INT'L L. 313 (1980)
Koroleva, N. D. & Kiesev, V. A., *Soviet Marine Pollution Legislation: Prevention of Pollution from Ships and the LOS Convention*, 15 MARINE POL'Y 49 (1991)
Kwiatkowska, B., *Marine Pollution from Land-Based Sources: Current Problems and Prospects*, 14 OCEAN DEV. & INT'L L. 315 (1984)
  Creeping Jurisdiction Beyond 200 Miles in the Light of the 1982 Law of the Sea Convention, 22 OCEAN DEV. & INT'L L. 153 (1991)
Lapidoth, R., *Freedom of Navigation – Its Legal History and Its Normative Basis*, 6 J. MAR. L & COM. 259 (1975)
Lee, L. T., *The Law of the Sea Convention and Third Parties*, 77 AM. J. INT'L L. 541 (1983)
Legatski, R., *Port State Jurisdiction over Vessel-Source Pollution*, 2 HARV. ENVTL. L. REV. 448 (1977)
Legault, L., *The Freedom of the Oceans: A License to Pollute?*, 21 U. TORONTO L. J. 39 (1971)
Li, K. X. & Wonham, J., *New Developments in Ship Registration*, 14 INT'L J. MARINE & COASTAL L. 137 (1999)
Lotilla, R. P., *The Efficacy of the Anti-Pollution Legislation Provisions in the 1982 Convention on the Law of the Sea*, 41 INT'L. & COMP. L. Q. 137 (1992)
Lowe, A. V., *The Enforcement of Marine Pollution Regulations*, 12 SAN DIEGO L. REV. 624 (1975)
Marion, M. A., *OPA 1990 Revisited*, INT'L J. SHIPPING L. 188 (1997)
Marston, G., *The U.N. Convention on Registration of Ships*, 20 J. WORLD TRADE L. 575 (1986)
Matlin, D. F., *Re-evaluating the Status of Flags of Convenience Under International Law*, 23 VAND. J. TRANSNAT'L L. 1017 (1991).
McConnell, M. L., *'... Darkening Confusion Mounted Upon Darkening Confusion': The Search for the Elusive Genuine Link*, 16 J. MAR. L. & COM. 365 (1985)
  'Business as Usual': An Evaluation of the 1986 UNCCRS, 18 J. MAR. L. & COM. 435 (1986)
McDorman, T., *Port State Enforcement: A Comment on Article 218 of the 1982 Law of the Sea Convention*, 28 J. MAR. L. & COM. 305 (1997)
  Regional Port State Control Agreements: Some Issues of International Law, OCEAN & COASTAL L. J. 207 (2000)
McDougal, M. S., Burke, W. T. & Vlasic, I. A., *The Maintenance of Public Order at Sea and the Nationality of Ships*, 54 AM. J. INT'L L. 25 (1960)
McRae, D. & Goundrey, D., *Environmental Jurisdiction in Arctic Waters: The Extent of Article 234*, 16 U. BR. COL. L. REV. 197 (1982)
Meese, S. A., *When Jurisdictional Interests Collide: International, Domestic and State Efforts to Prevent Vessel-Source Oil Pollution*, 12 OCEAN DEV. & INT'L L. 71 (1982)
Mendelsohn, A. I., *Ocean Pollution and the 1972 United Nations Conference on the Environment*, 3 J. MAR. L. & COM. 385 (1972)

Mensah, T. A., *International Environmental Law: International Conventions Concerning Oil Pollution at Sea*, 8 Case W. Res. J. Int'l L. 110 (1976)

Mitchell, G., *Preservation of State and Federal Authority Under the Oil Pollution Act of 1990*, 21 Envtl. L. 237 (1991)

Molenaar, E. J., *EC Directive on Port State Control in Context*, 11 Int'l J. Marine & Coastal L. 241 (1996)

Mooradian, C., *Protecting 'Sovereign Rights': The Case for Increased Coastal State Jurisdiction Over Vessel-Source Pollution in the Exclusive Economic Zone*, 82 B.U. L. Rev. 767 (2002)

Moore, J. N., *The Regime of Straits and the Third United Nations Conference on the Law of the Sea*, 74 Am. J. Int'l L. 77 (1980)

Morgan, J., *The Oil Pollution Act of 1990: A Look at its Impact on the Oil Industry*, 6 Fordham Envtl. L. J. 1 (1994)

Nagelmackers, H.-G., *Aftermath of the Amoco Cadiz – Why Must the European Community Act?*, 4 Marine Pol'y 3 (1980)

Nanda, V. P., *The Torrey Canyon Disaster: Some Legal Aspects*, 44 Denv. L. J. 400 (1967)

Nandan, S. N. & Anderson, D. H., *Straits Used for International Navigation: A Commentary on Part III of the United Nations Convention on the Law of the Sea 1982*, 60 Brit. Y.B. Int'l L. 159 (1989)

Nelson, L. D. M., *The New Deep Seabed Mining Regime*, 10 Int'l J. Marine & Coastal L. 189 (1995)

Ng, J. M., *International Maritime Conventions: Seafarers' Safety and Human Rights*, 33 J. Mar. L. & Com. 381 (2002)

Nollkaemper, A. & Hey, E., *Implementation of the LOS Convention at Regional Level: European Community Competence in Regulating Safety and Environmental Aspects of Shipping*, 10 Int'l J. Marine & Coastal L. 281 (1995)

Northrup, H. R. & Scrase, P. B., *The International Transport Workers' Federation Flag of Convenience Shipping Campaign: 1983–95*, 23 U. Denv. Transp. L. J. 369 (1996)

Oda, S., *The Concept of the Contiguous Zone*, 11 Int'l & Comp. L. Q. 131 (1962)

Dispute Settlement Prospects in the Law of the Sea, 44 Int'l & Comp. L. Q. 863 (1995)

Okamura, B., *Proposed IMO Regulations for the Prevention of Air Pollution from Ships*, 26 J. Mar. L. & Com. 183 (1995)

Osieke, E., *Flags of Convenience Vessels: Recent Developments*, 73 Am. J. Int'l L. 604 (1979)

The International Labour Organization and the Control of Sub-standard Merchant Vessels, 30 Int'l & Comp. L. Q. 497 (1981)

Oxman, B. H., *The New Law of the Sea*, 69 A.B.A. J. 157 (1983)

The Regime of Warships Under the United Nations Convention on the Law of the Sea, 24 Va. J. Int'l L. 809 (1984)

The Duty to Respect Generally Accepted International Standards, 24 N.Y.U. J. Int'l L. & Pol. 109 (1991)

Environmental Protection in Archipelagic Waters and International Straits – The Role of the International Maritime Organization, 10 Int'l J. Marine & Coastal L. 467 (1995)

United States Interests in the Law of the Sea, 88 AM. J. INT'L L. 167 (1994)
Oxman, B. H. & Bantz, V., *Case Note on the Saiga Case*, 94 AM. J. INT'L L. 140 (2000)
Pamborides, G. P., *The ISM Code: Potential Legal Implications*, INT'L MAR. L. 52 (1996)
Payne, R., *Flags of Convenience and Oil Pollution: A Threat to National Security*, 3 HOUS. J. INT'L L. 67 (1980)
Payoyo, P. B., *Implementation of International Conventions Through Port State Control: An Assessment*, 18 MARINE POL'Y 379 (1994)
Peet, G., *Particularly Sensitive Sea Areas – A Documentary History*, 9 INT'L J. MARINE & COASTAL L. 469 (1994)
Plant, G., *International Legal Aspects of Vessel Traffic Services*, 14 MARINE POL'Y 71 (1990)
A European Lawyer's View of the Government Response to the Donaldson Report, 19 MARINE POL'Y 453 (1995)
Pritchard, S. Z., *Load on Top – From the Sublime to the Absurd*, 9 J. MAR. L. & COM. 185 (1978)
Rauscher, S., *Raising the Stakes for Environmental Polluters: The Exxon Valdez Criminal Prosecution*, 19 ECOLOGY L. Q. 147 (1992)
Redgwell, C., *Compensation for Oil Pollution Damage – Quantifying Environmental Harm*, 16 MARINE POL'Y 90 (1992)
Reisman, W. M., *The Regime of Straits and National Security: An Appraisal of International Lawmaking*, 74 AM. J. INT'L L. 48 (1980)
Ringbom, H., *Preventing Pollution from Ships – Reflections on the 'Adequacy' of Existing Rules*, 1 RECIEL 21 (1999)
Rosencranz, A., *The ECE Convention of 1979 on Long-Range Transboundary Air Pollution*, 75 AM. J. INT'L L. 975 (1981)
Salvarani, R., *The EC Directive on Port State Control: A Policy Statement*, 11 INT'L J. MARINE & COASTAL L. 225 (1996)
Schachter, O. & Serwer, D., *Marine Pollution Problems and Remedies*, 65 AM. J. INT'L L. 84 (1971)
Schneider, J., *Something Old, Something New: Some Thoughts on Grotius and the Marine Environment*, 18 VA. J. INT'L L. 147 (1977)
Shaw, B., Winslett, B. & Cross, F., *The Global Environment: A Proposal to Eliminate Marine Oil Pollution*, 27 NAT. RESOURCES J. 157 (1987)
Shearer, I., *Problems of Jurisdiction and Law Enforcement Against Delinquent Vessels*, 35 INT'L & COMP. L. Q. 320 (1986)
Simmonds, K. R., *The Constitution of the Maritime Safety Committee of IMCO*, 12 INT'L & COMP. L. Q. 56 (1963)
Sinan, I. M., *UNCTAD and Flags of Convenience*, 18 J. WORLD TRADE L. 95 (1984)
Sletmo, G. K. & Holste, S., *Shipping as the Competitive Advantage of Nations: The Role of International Ship Registers*, 20 MAR. POL'Y MGMT. 243 (1993)
Smith, B., *Innocent Passage as a Rule of Decision: Navigation v. Environmental Protection*, 21 COLUM. J. TRANSNAT'L L. 49 (1983)
Smith, J. T., *Natural Resource Damages Under CERCLA and OPA: Some Basics for Maritime Operators*, 18 TUL. MAR. L. J. 1 (1993)
Smith, S. T., *An Analysis of the Pollution Act of 1990 and the 1984 Protocols on Civil Liability for Oil Pollution Damage*, 14 HOUS. J. INT'L L. 115 (1991)

Sohn, L. B., *The Stockholm Declaration on the Human Environment*, 14 HARV. INT'L L. J. 423 (1973)

'*Generally Accepted' International Rules*, 61 WASH. L. REV. 1073 (1986)

Soisson, N., *International Oil Spill Compensation Systems*, 9 INT'L MAR. L. 273 (1997)

Sperling, G., *The New Convention on Standards of Training, Certification and Watchkeeping: What, if Anything, Does it Mean?* 22 TUL. MAR. L. J. 595 (1998)

Srivastava, C. P., *The Role of the International Maritime Organization*, 14 MARINE POL'Y 243 (1990)

Stevenson, J. R. & Oxman, B. H., *The Future of the United Nations Convention on the Law of the Sea*, 88 AM. J. INT'L L. 488 (1994)

Sturmey, S. G., *The United Nations Convention on Conditions for Registration of Ships*, LLOYD'S MAR. & COMM. L. Q. 97 (1987)

Sweeney, J. C., *Oil Pollution of the Oceans*, 37 FORDHAM L. REV. 115 (1968)

Tache, S. W., *The Nationality of Ships: The Definitional Controversy and Enforcement of Genuine Link*, 16 INT'L LAWYER 301 (1982)

Tetley, W., *The Law of the Flag, 'Flag Shopping' and the Choice of Law*, 17 TUL. MAR. L. J. 175 (1992)

Tharpes, Y. L., *International Environmental Law: Turning the Tide on Marine Pollution*, 20 U. MIAMI INTER-AM. L. REV. 579 (1989)

Tilley, M., *The Origin and Development of the Mutual Shipowners' Protection and Indemnity Associations*, 17 J. MAR. L. & COM. 261 (1986)

Tomczak, M., *Defining Marine Pollution: A Comparison of Definitions Used by International Conventions*, 8 MARINE POL'Y 311 (1984)

Van Dyke, J. M., *Sea Shipment of Japanese Plutonium and International Law*, 24 OCEAN DEV. & INT'L L. 399, (1993)

van Reenen, W., *Rules of Reference in the New Convention on the Law of the Sea, in Particular in Connection with the Pollution of the Sea by Oil Tankers*, 12 NETH. Y.B. INT'L L. 3 (1981)

Wagner, T. J., *The Oil Pollution Act of 1990: An Analysis*, 21 J. MAR. L. & COM. 569 (1990)

Walker, G. K. & Noyes, J. E., *Definitions for the 1982 Law of the Sea Convention*, 32 CAL. W. INT'L L. J. 343 (2002)

Wallace, M. W., *Safer Ships, Cleaner Seas: The Report of the Donaldson Inquiry into the Prevention of Pollution from Merchant Shipping*, LLOYD'S MAR. & COMM. L. Q. 404 (1995)

Wang, C.-P., *A Review of the Enforcement Regime for Vessel-Source Oil Pollution Control*, 16 OCEAN DEV. & INT'L L. 305 (1986)

Warner-Kramer, D., *Control Begins at Home: Tackling Flags of Convenience and IUU Fishing*, 34 GOLDEN GATE U. L. REV. 497 (2004)

Wefers Bettink, H., *Open Registry, the Genuine Link and the 1986 Convention on Registration Conditions for Ships*, 18 NETH. Y.B. INT'L L. 68 (1987)

Wolfrum, R., *Reflagging and Escort Operation in the Persian Gulf: An International Law Perspective*, 29 VA. J. INT'L L. 387 (1989)

Yankov, A., *The International Tribunal for the Law of the Sea: Its Place Within the Dispute Settlement System of the U.N. Law of the Sea Convention*, 37 INDIAN J. INT'L L. 356 (1997)

Yuzon, F. J., *Full Speed Ahead: International Law Concerning Marine Pollution and the United States Navy - Steaming Towards State Responsibility and Compliance*, PACE INT'L L. REV. 57 (1997)

Chapters in Treatises

Angelo, J., *The International Maritime Organization and Protection of the Marine Environment*, in NORDQUIST, M. H. & MOORE, J. N. (eds.), CURRENT MARITIME ISSUES AND THE INTERNATIONAL MARITIME ORGANIZATION 105 (Martinus Nijhoff, The Hague, 1999)
  Erika Aftermath: Developments at IMO on Double Hulls (A U.S. Perspective), in NORDQUIST, M. H. & MOORE, J. N., CURRENT MARINE ENVIRONMENTAL ISSUES AND THE INTERNATIONAL TRIBUNAL FOR THE LAW OF THE SEA 309 (Martinus Nijhoff, The Hague, 2001)
Birnie, P. W., *Enforcement of the International Laws for the Prevention of Oil Pollution from Vessels*, in CUSINE, D. J. & GRANT, J. P. (eds.), THE IMPACT OF MARINE POLLUTION 95 (Croom Helm, London, 1980)
  The Status of Environmental 'Soft Law': Trends and Examples with Special Focus on IMO Norms, in RINGBOM, H. (ed.), COMPETING NORMS IN THE LAW OF MARINE ENVIRONMENTAL PROTECTION - FOCUS ON SHIP SAFETY AND POLLUTION PREVENTION 31 (Kluwer Law International, London, 1997)
Boyle, A. E., Freestone, D., Krummer, K. & Ong, D., *Marine Environment and Marine Pollution*, in ROBINSON, N. (ed.), AGENDA 21 AND THE UNCED PROCEEDINGS 1207 (Oceana Publications, New York 1992)
Churchill, R. R., *Levels of Implementation of the Law of the Sea Convention: An Overview*, in VIDAS, D. & ØSTRENG, W. (eds.), ORDER FOR THE OCEANS AT THE TURN OF THE CENTURY 318 (Kluwer Law International, The Hague, 1999)
Clingan, T. A., *Vessel-Source Pollution, Problems of Hazardous Cargo, and Port State Jurisdiction*, in VAN DYKE, J., ALEXANDER, L. & MORGAN, J. (eds.), INTERNATIONAL NAVIGATION: ROCKS AND SHOALS AHEAD? 227 (Law of the Sea Institute, University of Hawaii, 1988)
Falk, R. & Elver, H., *Comparing Global Perspectives: The 1982 UNCLOS and the 1992 UNCED*, in VIDAS, D. & ØSTRENG, W. (eds.), ORDER FOR THE OCEANS AT THE TURN OF THE CENTURY 145 (Kluwer Law International, The Hague, 1999)
Gold, E., *From Process to Reality: Adopting Domestic Legislation for the Implementation of the Law of the Sea Convention*, in VIDAS, D. & ØSTRENG, W. (eds.), ORDER FOR THE OCEANS AT THE TURN OF THE CENTURY 375 (Kluwer Law International, The Hague, 1999)
Göransson, M., *The 1984 and 1992 Protocols to the Civil Liability Convention 1969 and the Fund Convention 1971*, in DE LA RUE, C. (ed.), LIABILITY FOR DAMAGE TO THE MARINE ENVIRONMENT (LLP, London, 1993)
Hargrove, J., *Environment and the Third Conference on the Law of the Sea*, in HARGROVE, J. (ed.), WHO PROTECTS THE OCEANS? 191 (West Pub. Co., St. Paul, MN, 1975)

Howe, N., *ITLOS - A Practitioner's Perspective*, in NORDQUIST, M. H. & MOORE, J. N., CURRENT MARINE ENVIRONMENTAL ISSUES AND THE INTERNATIONAL TRIBUNAL FOR THE LAW OF THE SEA 159 (Martinus Nijhoff, The Hague, 2001)

Koh, T. T. B., *A Constitution for the Oceans*, in THE LAW OF THE SEA - UNITED NATIONS CONVENTION ON THE LAW OF THE SEA, U.N. Pub. Sales No. E.83. V.5 xxiii (UN, 1983)

Kolossovsky, I. K., *The Future of the U.N. Law of the Sea Convention and Maintenance of Legal Order and Peace in the Oceans in the 21st Century*, in HONG, S. Y. et al. (eds.), THE ROLE OF THE OCEANS IN THE 21ST CENTURY 321 (Law of the Sea Institute, University of Hawaii, 1995)

McDougal, M. S. et al., *The World Constitutive Process of Authoritative Decision*, in BLACK, C. & FALK, R. (eds.), THE FUTURE OF THE INTERNATIONAL LEGAL ORDER 73 (Princeton University Press, Princeton, NJ, 1969)

Miles, E. L., *Implementation of International Regimes: A Typology*, in VIDAS, D. & ØSTRENG, W. (eds.), ORDER FOR THE OCEANS AT THE TURN OF THE CENTURY 327 (Kluwer Law International, The Hague, 1999)

Payer, H., *Insurer and Class and Marine Accidents*, in NORDQUIST, M. H. & MOORE, J. N., CURRENT MARINE ENVIRONMENTAL ISSUES AND THE INTERNATIONAL TRIBUNAL FOR THE LAW OF THE SEA 294 (Martinus Nijhoff, The Hague, 2001)

Pineschi, L., *The Transit of Ships Carrying Hazardous Wastes Through Foreign Coastal Zones*, in FRANCIONI, F. & SCOVAZZI, T. (eds.), INTERNATIONAL RESPONSIBILITY FOR ENVIRONMENTAL HARM 299 (Graham & Trotman, London, Boston, 1991)

The EEC, Safety of Navigation and Vessel-Source Pollution, in MILES, E. L. & TREVES, T. (eds.), THE LAW OF THE SEA: NEW WORLDS, NEW DISCOVERIES 526 (Law of the Sea Institute, University of Hawaii, 1993)

Plant, G., *The Relationship Between International Navigation Rights and Environmental Protection: A Legal Analysis of Mandatory Ship Traffic Systems*, in RINGBOM, H. (ed.), COMPETING NORMS IN THE LAW OF MARINE ENVIRONMENTAL PROTECTION - FOCUS ON SHIP SAFETY AND POLLUTION PREVENTION 27 (Kluwer Law International, London, 1997)

Reisman, W. M., *Sanctions and Enforcement*, in BLACK, C. & FALK, R. (eds.), 3 CONFLICT MANAGEMENT: THE FUTURE OF THE INTERNATIONAL LEGAL ORDER 273 (Princeton University Press, Princeton, NJ, 1971)

Ringbom, H., *The Erika Accident and Its Effects on EU Maritime Regulation*, in NORDQUIST, M. H. & MOORE, J. N., CURRENT MARINE ENVIRONMENTAL ISSUES AND THE INTERNATIONAL TRIBUNAL FOR THE LAW OF THE SEA 265 (Martinus Nijhoff, The Hague, 2001)

Roach, J. A., *Alternatives for Achieving Flag State Implementation and Quality Shipping*, in NORDQUIST, M. H. & MOORE, J. N. (eds.), CURRENT MARITIME ISSUES AND THE INTERNATIONAL MARITIME ORGANIZATION 151 (Martinus Nijhoff, The Hague, 1999)

Salient Issues in the Implementation of Regimes under the Law of the Sea Convention: An Overview, in VIDAS, D. & ØSTRENG, W. (eds.), ORDER FOR THE OCEANS AT THE TURN OF THE CENTURY 435 (Kluwer Law International, The Hague, 1999)

Roseanne, S., *The International Maritime Organization Interface with the Law of the Sea Convention*, in NORDQUIST, M. H. & MOORE, J. N. (eds.), CURRENT MARITIME ISSUES AND THE INTERNATIONAL MARITIME ORGANIZATION 251 (Martinus Nijhoff, The Hague, 1999)

Schachte, Jr., W. L., *The Value of the 1982 U.N. Convention on the Law of the Sea: Preserving Our Freedoms and Protecting the Environment*, in COUPER, A. & GOLD, E. (eds.), THE MARINE ENVIRONMENT AND SUSTAINABLE DEVELOPMENT: LAW, POLICY AND SCIENCE 105 (Law of the Sea Institute, University of Hawaii, 1993)

Sielen, A. B. & McManus, R. J., *IMCO and the Politics of Ship Pollution*, in KAY, D. & JACOBSON, H. (eds.), ENVIRONMENTAL PROTECTION: THE INTERNATIONAL DIMENSION (Allanheld, Osmun & Co., Totowa, NJ, 1983)

Sohn, L. B., *Implications of the Law of the Sea Convention Regarding the Protection and Preservation of the Marine Environment*, in KRUEGER, R. & RIESENFELD, S. (eds.), THE DEVELOPING ORDER OF THE OCEANS 106 (Law of the Sea Institute, University of Hawaii, 1985)

Stairs, K. & Taylor, P., *Non-Governmental Organisations and the Legal Protection of the Oceans: A Case Study*, in HURRELL, A. & KINGSBURY, B. (eds.), THE INTERNATIONAL POLITICS OF THE ENVIRONMENT: ACTORS, INTERESTS AND INSTITUTIONS 110 (Clarendon Press, Oxford, 1992)

Teclaff, L. A., *International Law and the Protection of the Oceans from Pollution*, in TECLAFF, L. A. & UTTON, A. (eds.), INTERNATIONAL ENVIRONMENTAL LAW 104 (Praeger, New York, 1974)

Valenzuela, M., *IMO: Public International Law and Regulation*, in JOHNSTON, D. M. & LETALIK, N. (eds.), THE LAW OF THE SEA AND OCEAN INDUSTRY: NEW OPPORTUNITIES AND RESTRAINTS 141 (Law of the Sea Institute, University of Hawaii, 1984)

Enforcing Rules against Vessel-Source Degradation of the Marine Environment: Coastal, Flag and Port State Jurisdiction, in VIDAS, D. & ØSTRENG, W. (eds.), ORDER FOR THE OCEANS AT THE TURN OF THE CENTURY 485 (Kluwer Law International, The Hague, 1999)

VanderZwaag, D., *Shipping and Marine Environmental Protection in Canada: Rocking the Boat and Riding a Restless Sea*, in ROTHWELL, D. & BATEMAN, S. (eds.), NAVIGATIONAL RIGHTS AND FREEDOMS AND THE NEW LAW OF THE SEA 209 (Kluwer Law International, The Hague, 2000)

Vukas, B., *Generally Accepted International Rules and Standards*, in SOONS, A. H. A. (ed.), IMPLEMENTATION OF THE LAW OF THE SEA CONVENTION THROUGH INTERNATIONAL INSTITUTIONS 405 (Law of the Sea Institute, University of Hawaii, 1990)

Vukas, B. & Vidas, D., *Flags of Convenience and High Seas Fishing: The Emergence of a Legal Framework*, in STOKKE, O. (ed.), GOVERNING HIGH SEAS FISHERIES: THE INTERPLAY OF GLOBAL AND REGIONAL REGIMES 53 (Oxford University Press, New York, 2001)

Wolfrum, R., *IMO Interface with the Law of the Sea Convention*, in NORDQUIST, M. H. & MOORE, J. N. (eds.), CURRENT MARITIME ISSUES AND THE INTERNATIONAL MARITIME ORGANIZATION 223 (Martinus Nijhoff, The Hague, 1999)

Reports by Governmental, Inter-Governmental, Industry and Miscellaneous Bodies

Churchill, R. R., *The Meaning of the 'Genuine Link' Requirement in Relation to the Nationality of Ships*, 2000, A Report for the International Transport Workers'

Federation (ITF), available at http://www.oceanlaw.net/hedley/pubs/ITF-Oct2000.pdf

CLARKSON, THE TANKER REGISTER (1994)

DREWRY SHIPPING CONSULTANTS, SAFER SHIPS (1992)

DREWRY SHIPPING CONSULTANTS, COST OF QUALITY IN SHIPPING: THE FINANCIAL IMPLICATIONS OF THE CURRENT REGULATORY ENVIRONMENT (1998)

EUROPEAN COMMISSION DIRECTORATE GENERAL FOR ENERGY AND TRANSPORT, MEMORANDUM: ERIKA – TWO YEARS ON (2001)

HER MAJESTY'S STATIONERY OFFICE, REPORT OF THE COMMITTEE OF INQUIRY INTO SHIPPING, Cmnd. 4337 (1970)

HER MAJESTY'S STATIONERY OFFICE, SAFER SHIPS, CLEANER SEAS – REPORT OF LORD DONALDSON'S INQUIRY INTO THE PREVENTION OF POLLUTION FROM MERCHANT SHIPPING, Cm. 2560 (1994) and Cm. 2766 (1995)

IMO/FAO/UNESCO/WMO/WHO/IAEA/UN/UNEP JOINT GROUP OF EXPERTS ON THE SCIENTIFIC ASPECTS OF MARINE POLLUTION (GESAMP), THE STATE OF THE MARINE ENVIRONMENT, REP. STUD. GESAMP NO. 39 (1990)

IMO/FAO/UNESCO/WMO/WHO/IAEA/UN/UNEP JOINT GROUP OF EXPERTS ON THE SCIENTIFIC ASPECTS OF MARINE POLLUTION (GESAMP), IMPACT OF OIL AND RELATED CHEMICALS AND WASTES ON THE MARINE ENVIRONMENT, REP. STUD. GESAMP NO. 50 (1993)

INTERNATIONAL COMMISSION ON SHIPPING (ICONS), SHIPS, SLAVES AND COMPETITION (2001)

INTERTANKO, TANKER TRENDS AND ECONOMICS (2002)

IOPC FUNDS, CLAIMS MANUAL (2002)

JACOBS & PARTNERS, WORLD OIL TANKER TRENDS (1998)

JAPAN MARITIME RESEARCH INSTITUTE, IMO REGULATIONS RELATING TO DOUBLE-HULL STRUCTURE AND THEIR EFFECTS ON EXISTING TANKERS, REPORT NO. 45 (1993)

MARITIME ADMINISTRATION AND US COAST GUARD, MARITIME TRADE AND TRANSPORTATION 1999 (C. Moore, ed., 1999)

NATIONAL ACADEMY OF SCIENCES, PETROLEUM IN THE MARINE ENVIRONMENT, attached to MEPC Doc. 30/INF.13 (1990), International Maritime Organization (IMO), London

NATIONAL ACADEMY OF SCIENCES, OIL IN THE SEA III: INPUTS, FATES AND EFFECTS (2002)

ORGANIZATION FOR ECONOMIC CO-OPERATION AND DEVELOPMENT (OECD), OECD STUDY ON FLAGS OF CONVENIENCE (1973), reprinted in 4 J. MAR. L. & COM. 231 (1973)

ORGANIZATION FOR ECONOMIC CO-OPERATION AND DEVELOPMENT (OECD), NON-OBSERVANCE OF INTERNATIONAL RULES AND STANDARDS: COMPETITIVE ADVANTAGES (1996), OCDE/GD(96)4, attached to MSC Doc. 66/12/1 (1996), International Maritime Organization (IMO), London

ORGANIZATION FOR ECONOMIC CO-OPERATION AND DEVELOPMENT (OECD), SAFETY AND ENVIRONMENTAL PROTECTION: DISCUSSION PAPER ON POSSIBLE ACTIONS TO COMBAT SUBSTANDARD SHIPPING BY INVOLVING PLAYERS OTHER THAN THE SHIPOWNER IN THE SHIPPING MARKET, OECD Doc. DSTI/DOT/MTC(98)10/final (1998)

ORGANIZATION FOR ECONOMIC CO-OPERATION AND DEVELOPMENT (OECD), THE COST TO USERS OF SUBSTANDARD SHIPPING (2001)

ORGANIZATION FOR ECONOMIC CO-OPERATION AND DEVELOPMENT (OECD), REPORT ON SHIP SCRAPPING, OECD Doc. DSTI/DOT/MTC(2001)12 (2001), attached to MEPC Doc. 48/INF.2 (2002), International Maritime Organization (IMO), London

ORGANIZATION FOR ECONOMIC CO-OPERATION AND DEVELOPMENT (OECD), COST SAVINGS STEMMING FROM NON-COMPLIANCE WITH INTERNATIONAL ENVIRONMENTAL REGULATIONS IN THE MARITIME SECTOR, DST/DOT/MTC/(2002)/8/final, *attached to* MEPC Doc. 49/INF.7 (2003), International Maritime Organization (IMO), London

ORGANIZATION FOR ECONOMIC CO-OPERATION AND DEVELOPMENT (OECD), OWNERSHIP AND CONTROL OF SHIPS (2003)

ORGANIZATION FOR ECONOMIC CO-OPERATION AND DEVELOPMENT (OECD), MARITIME TRANSPORT COMMITTEE REPORT ON THE REMOVAL OF INSURANCE FROM SUBSTANDARD SHIPPING (2004)

Oude Elferink, A. G., *The Genuine Link Concept: Time for a Post Mortem?*, Netherlands Institute of the Law of the Sea Paper, available at http://www.uu.nl/content/genuine%20link.pdf

PARLIAMENT OF THE COMMONWEALTH OF AUSTRALIA, SHIPS OF SHAME: INQUIRY INTO SHIP SAFETY (1992)

PETROLEUM INDUSTRY RESOURCES FOUNDATION, TRANSPORTING U.S. OIL IMPORTS: THE IMPACT OF OIL LEGISLATION ON THE TANKER MARKET (1992)

PREPARATORY COMMITTEE FOR THE UNITED NATIONS CONFERENCE ON ENVIRONMENT AND DEVELOPMENT, PROTECTION OF OCEANS, ALL KINDS OF SEAS INCLUDING ENCLOSED AND SEMI-ENCLOSED SEAS, COASTAL AREAS AND THE PROTECTION, RATIONAL USE AND DEVELOPMENT OF THEIR LIVING RESOURCES, UN Doc. A/CONF.151/PC/100/Add.21 (1991)

REPORT OF IMO COMPARATIVE STUDY ON OIL TANKER DESIGNS, *attached to* MEPC Docs. 32/7/15 (1992) and 32/7/17/Add.1 (1992), International Maritime Organization (IMO), London

RESTATEMENT (THIRD) OF THE FOREIGN RELATIONS LAW OF THE UNITED STATES (1987)

White, I., *Oil Spill Response – Experience, Trends and Challenges*, ITOPF Paper (2000), *available at* http://www.itopf.com/spillcon.pdf

Articles in Newspapers

Lloyd's List, *Scathing Attack on SCA Article*, 24 Feb. 1992
Lloyd's List, *Shell Urges Tanker Crackdown*, 21 Jan. 1993
Lloyd's List, *ITF Says Greek Owners are Among Most Exploitative*, 4 Dec. 1997
Lloyd's List, *Greek Owners Set to Reject ITF Claims*, 5 Dec. 1997
Lloyd's List, *Oiling the Wheels of Misfortune*, 27 Jan. 2000
Lloyd's List, *Asia-Pacific Alert on Substandard Ships*, 9 Mar. 2001
Lloyd's List, *Leading the Fight in the Shipping Arena*, 10 Mar. 2001
Lloyd's List, *A Ship for Whose Convenience?*, 12 Mar. 2001
Lloyd's List, *Rule Out the Culture to Cut Corners*, 26 Apr. 2001
Lloyd's List, *Enforcement Cost of OPA 90 Regulations Put at $11 bn*, 18 May 2001
Lloyd's List, *IMO Budget Policy 'is Not Viable'*, 18 June 2001
Lloyd's List, *Court Threat to EU States over Safety*, 19 July 2001
Lloyd's List, *TBT Manufacturers Lobby Diplomats Against Ban*, 1 Oct. 2001
Lloyd's List, *Credit Where Credit's Due*, 2 Nov. 2001
Lloyd's List, *Shipboard Solution 'the Only Option' for Ballast Contamination*, 8 Nov. 2001
Lloyd's List, *Power Shift at IMO*, 27 Nov. 2001

Lloyd's List, *Qualship 21 to Stay Tough on Flag States*, 21 Jan. 2002
Lloyd's List, *Tankers Dogged by Over-inspection*, 29 Jan. 2002
Lloyd's List, *Question of Societies' Liability Continues to Bubble Away*, 4 Feb. 2002
Lloyd's List, *USCG Dismisses Pleas for Secrecy*, 27 Mar. 2002
Lloyd's List, *OECD in Crackdown on Substandard Shipping*, 15 Apr. 2002
Lloyd's List, *Keeping IMO Reform on the Straight and Narrow*, 19 Apr. 2002
Lloyd's List, *IMO Buries Ownership Check*, 1 May 2002
Lloyd's List, *Lyras Hits Out at 'Accident-led' Response to Shipping's Woes*, 4 June 2002
Lloyd's List, *IMO Under Strain from Green Rules*, 29 Apr. 2003
Lloyd's List, *French Tanker Ban Stays until IMO Deal*, 1 May 2003
Lloyd's List, *ABS Backlash Puts Spain in the Dock for Prestige*, 1 July 2003
Lloyd's List, *Chorus of Disapproval for EU Directive on Handling Ship Waste*, 30 Apr. 2004
Lloyd's List, *Time Behind Bars: A New Barrier for Those Earning a Living at Sea*, 10 Aug. 2004

Personal Interviews

Zafrul Alam, Permanent Mission of Singapore to IMO
Rosalie Balkin, International Maritime Organization
Lawrence Barchue, Sr., Permanent Mission of Liberia to IMO
Agustín Blanco-Bazán, International Maritime Organization
Michael Boock, Office of the Judge Advocate General, United States Navy
Alan Boyle, British Institute of International and Comparative Law
Andreas Chrysostomou, Permanent Mission of Cyprus to IMO
Patrick Chun, Permanent Mission of Hong Kong to IMO
James Cowley, Permanent Mission of Vanuatu to IMO
John De Rose, International Association of Classification Societies (IACS)
Kristina Gjerde, World Wide Fund for Nature (WWF)
Edgar Gold, Dalhousie University
Michael Grey, Lloyd's List
Patrick Griggs, Comité Maritime International (CMI)
Chris Horrocks, International Chamber of Shipping (ICS)
Måns Jacobsson, International Oil Pollution Compensation (IOPF) Funds
Douglas Johnston, University of Victoria
James Joyce, International Chamber of Shipping (ICS)
Sally Lentz, Friends of the Earth International (FOEI)
Nigel Maude, Permanent Mission of the Marshall Islands to IMO
Trygve Meyer, International Association of Independent Tanker Owners (INTERTANKO)
Anthony Nunn, International Union of Marine Insurers (IUMI)
Birgit Olsen, Permanent Mission of Denmark to IMO
William O'Neill, Secretary-General, International Maritime Organization
Stephen Pan, Worldwide Shipping, Singapore

Erik Røsæg, Permanent Mission of Norway to IMO
Jean-Claude Sainlos, International Maritime Organization
Yoshio Sasamura, Permanent Mission of Japan to IMO
Koji Sekimizu, International Maritime Organization
Richard Shaw, Comité Maritime International (CMI)
Joseph Slater, International Maritime Organization
Wayne Stuart, Permanent Mission of Australia to IMO
Teh Kong Leong, Neptune Orient Lines (Singapore) Limited
John Vercoe, Oil Companies International Marine Forum (OCIMF)
Lloyd Watkins, International Group of Protection and Indemnity Clubs
Ian White, International Tanker Owners Pollution Federation (ITOPF)
Tim Wilkins, International Association of Independent Tanker Owners (INTERTANKO)
John Wren, Permanent Mission of the United Kingdom to IMO

Index

accidents
   causes, 82, 154, 349-50
   collisions, effect, 21
   decline, 17
   frequency, 5
   v. operational pollution, 20
   and public opinion, 69-71
   reactive regulation, 348-9
   reputable actors, 8
acid rain, 155-6
actors
   cargo owners. *See* cargo owners/charterers
   classification societies. *See* classification societies
   coastal interests, 67-73
   developing countries. *See* developing countries
   flag states. *See* flag states
   insurers. *See* insurance
   interaction, 9, 98-104
   key actors, 25, 34-74
   maritime interests, 34-67
   media, 69-71
   military interests, 46-7
   NGOs, 67-9, 102, 158
   political choices, 350
   public opinion, 69-71
   shipowners. *See* shipowners
   treaty-making process, 25, 34-74
Adams, Brock, 135
Aden, Gulf of, 83, 265
Adriatic Sea, 116
African West Coast, 82
air pollution, 33, 155-62
Albania, 57, 250
Algeria, 57, 250, 262
American Bureau of Shipping, 362
American Trader, 141

Amoco Cadiz, 70, 90, 97, 311-12, 314, 319
anti-fouling paints, 16, 22
   AFS Convention, 167-8, 352
   alternatives, 165-6
   TBT regulation, 161, 162-8
archipelagic waters, 211
arenas. *See* fora
Argentina, 74
Argo Merchant, 135, 319
Arrow, 183
Australia
   and ballast water, 103, 169-70
   coastal incidents, 97
   coastal interests, 68, 72
   environmentalist state, 32
   and *Iron Baron* incident, 340
   reporting diligence, 278
   special area designation, 116
   TBT regulation, 163
   UNCLOS positions, 200

Bahamas, 60, 61, 65, 158, 161, 278
ballast water
   ballast water management plans, 173
   BWMC, 172-4
   IMO guidelines, 171, 173
   International Ballast Water Management Certificates, 173
   management, 169
   pollution, 16, 21, 22
   regulation initiatives, 103
Baltic Sea, 85, 132, 156, 262
Bangladesh, 336, 370
bareboat charters, 59, 288, 292
Barracuda, 288, 292
Belgium, 295
Belize, 60, 250
Bermuda, 58
bilge wastes, 21, 22
BIMCO, 37-8, 382

black listing, 372
Black Sea, 93, 132, 262
Bolivia, 57, 60, 250
BP, 116
Braer incident, 91, 96
Brazil, 32, 74, 101, 187, 336
Brunei, 338
Brussels Conference 1969, 293-300
bunker fuel oils
   civil liability, 339-41
   Convention, 341, 352
   limits on liability, 341

Cambodia, 60, 250
Canada
   Arctic region, 215
   Brussels Conference 1969, 183, 294
   coal imports, 336
   coastal interests, 68, 72
   coastal state jurisdiction, 186-7
   early negotiations, 116
   environmentalist state, 32
   Fund Conference 1971, 303
   Great Lakes contamination, 169
   MARPOL 73, 186-7, 189, 190
   and sub-standard ships, 333
   UNCLOS positions, 200, 215, 228
Canary Islands, 58
cargo owners/ charterers
   burden-sharing, 379-81
   civil liability, 288, 358-60
   interests, 38-40
   representatives, 40
   spot charters, 40, 380
   targeting regime, 92
   US liability, 322
Caribbean, 82, 93
Carter Initiatives, 135, 319
CDEM standards
   2001 MARPOL amendments, 147-50
   2003 MARPOL amendments, 150-5
   double hull requirement, 139-55
   enforcement record, 237-9, 283
   enforcement regime, 189
   exclusive economic zones, 213
   internal waters, 204
   MARPOL 78, 191
   mid-deck tanker design, 144, 146
   port state jurisdiction, 218, 221
   purpose, 22
   SBTs, 126-32, 134-9
   territorial seas, 205-6
Central Africa, agreements, 93
chemicals
   HNS. *See* hazardous and noxious substances
   MARPOL 73, 133

pollution, 22
waste reception facilities, 263
Chile, 336
China, 32, 66, 74, 147, 278, 330-1
civil liability
   1992 Fund, 329
   1992 Protocols, 327-34
   Amoco Cadiz, 311-12, 314
   apportionment of liability, 288, 302, 313, 318, 322, 358-63
   assessment, 342-4
   bunker fuel oils, 339-41
   cargo owners/ charterers, 288, 358-60
   classification societies, 360-2
   CLC 69, 288-300
   compulsory insurance, 287, 300
   conventions, 286-7
   COPE, 331
   CRISTAL, 301-2, 310-11, 315, 330
   definition of pollution damage, 324, 329, 343
   direct action against insurers, 297
   exemptions, 299-300, 304
   financial capacity, 305-6
   financial institutions, 363
   Fund Convention 1971, 300-9, 330
   funds, 298, 300
   hazardous and noxious substances, 334-9
   IMO Conference 1984, 313-15
   International Oil Pollution Compensation (IOPC) Fund, 303-7, 312, 327, 342
   issues, 293-4
   jurisdiction, 298
   limits
      bunker fuel oil pollution, 341
      HNS, 337-8
      national limits, 289
      oil pollution, 287, 293, 297, 298, 302, 303, 313, 317, 331
   national laws, 287, 297, 329
   non-owner interests, 358-63
   oil pollution, 42-3
   operational discharges, 304-5
   pre-1969 developments, 288-93
   preventive measures, 328-9
   restriction of claims, 298-9
   shipowner indemnification, 306-9, 310, 314
   shipowners, 288, 296-7, 302, 315, 328, 342-3
   small tankers, 313, 316, 332
   STOPIA, 332
   strict liability, 287, 297-8, 344
   sub-standard ships, 333-4
   territorial restrictions, 299-300

civil liability (*cont.*)
  and *Torrey Canyon*, 288-90
  tortious liability, 289, 290, 311-12
  TOVALOP, 291-3, 309-10, 315, 330
  US regime, 287, 318-27
Civil Liability Convention 1969
  1992 Protocol, 327-34, 333
  Brussels Conference 1969, 293-300
  extension, 314-15
  and Fund Convention 1971, 302-6
  future revisions, 333
  generally, 288-300
  jurisdiction, 312
  pre-1969 developments, 288-93
Civil Liability Protocol 1992
  commencement, 329
  generally, 327-34
  revisions, 333
class-hopping, 45, 357
classification societies
  class-hopping, 45, 357
  improving procedures, 56
  insurance, 361
  interests, 43-5
  legal liability, 360-2
  lowering of standards, 6, 44-5
  monitoring, 373
  statutory certification, 44-5
  targeting regime, 92
clean-seas clauses, 263-4
coal, 336-7
coastal interests
  environmental NGOs, 67-9
  and Fund Convention 1971, 309
  generally, 67-73
  media, 69-71
  public opinion, 69-71
  states with coastal interests, 71-3
coastal states
  activism, 229
  jurisdiction, 24-5, 179-80
    archipelagic waters, 211
    contiguous zones, 211-12
    creeping jurisdiction, 199
    early attempts to extend, 181-4
    exclusive economic zones, 212-17
    high seas, 217
    internal waters, 204-5
    limits, 180
    LOSC, 199-201, 204-17
    MARPOL 73, 185-7, 188-9
    straits, 209-11
    territorial seas, 205-9
  meaning, 23, 30
  terminology, 31, 32
Comité Maritime International (CMI), 290, 295

commons, tragedy of the commons, 11
compliance
  assessment, 282-5
  CDEM standards, 237-9
  discharge standards, 236-7
  enforcement of treaties, 4, 234, 234-5
  factors, 236
  improving, 355-69
  incentives. *See* incentives
  marine pollution standards, 236-51
  meaning, 231
  non-compliance, 4
  non-owner interests, 284
  port control, 284-5
  records, 232
  reporting, 269-82
  sanctions, 266
  waste reception facilities, 251-68
contiguous zones, 211-12
conventions. *See* treaties
co-operation, intra-industry co-operation, 381-3
COPE, 331
corporate veil, 36
cost-cutting, 6-7
criminal liability
  negligent discharges in EU countries, 152-3, 154
  sub-standard ships, 380
  United States, 324-5
CRISTAL
  amendments, 310-11, 315
  scheme, 301-2
  termination, 330
Croatia, 278
crude oil washing (COW)
  compliance, 238
  enforcement jurisdiction, 191
  MARPOL, 133-9, 191
  method, 136
customary law, 30-1
Cyprus, 60, 61, 88, 89, 149, 153, 251

deep seabed, 53, 193, 194, 197
Denmark
  and 2001 MARPOL amendments, 148
  and civil liability regime, 290
  and criminal sanctions for negligent discharge, 153
  Fund Conference 1971, 308
  HNSC ratification, 339
  maritime interests, 67
  registration of ships, 59
developing countries
  Brussels Conference 1969, 296
  and compensation funds, 332-3
  and deep seabed, 197

and IMO, 73-4, 99-101, 351
incorporation of treaties, 234, 234-5
New International Economic Order, 53
non-enforcement of treaties, 235
open registry states, 101, 351
and SBTs, 130
UNCLOS positions, 200-1
waste reception facilities, 261, 264, 267
discharge standards
early regulation, 107-9
enforcement record, 236-7
internal waters, 204
London Conference 1962, 115-18
LOT, 120-6
MARPOL 73, 190
MARPOL 78, 126-39
OILPOL regime, 110
purpose, 22
dispute settlement, LOSC, 214, 229
domestic fora, 94-8
Donaldson Report, 91, 96, 97, 217, 267
double hulls
compliance, 239, 380
effect, 128
reaction to accidents, 349
regulation history, 139-55
US policy, 135, 349
due diligence, 363

East African region, 83
ecological unity, 224-5
Egypt, 121
enforcement
AFS Convention, 167
BWMC, 173
IMO powers, 369-73
improving, 355-69
London Conference 1962, 117-18
marine pollution standards, 236-51
MARPOL 73, 189
OILPOL, 112-13, 125
practice, 234, 234-5
reasons for non-enforcement, 4, 235
reporting on enforcement actions, 273-82
state enforcement of pollution control, 239-51, 285
state obligations, 236-82
environmental interests. *See* coastal interests
Equasis, 368, 382
Equatorial Guinea, 60
equity
cargo interests, 379-81
IMO finances, 375-6
IMO structure, 374-5
Erika, 71, 87, 88, 97, 147-50, 331, 349, 380

errors, human errors, 16, 82, 349
Estonia, 278
Europe, political developments, 83-9
European Council of Chemical Manufacturers' Federations (CEFIC), 166
European Maritime Safety Agency, 88
European Union
and CLC/FUND regime, 343
coastal interests, 71
compensation fund, 331-2
control of classification societies, 361-2
COPE, 331
Equasis, 368, 382
IMO membership, 88
and MARPOL 2001 amendments, 147
and MARPOL 2003 amendments, 150
political dynamics, 86-9
port state control, 92-3, 152-5
reporting requirements, 154
sulphur regulation, 161
TBT regulation, 163
treaty-making politics, 33
unilateralism, 356-7
waste reception facilities, 266-7
exclusive economic zones
acceptance of concept, 314
coastal state jurisdiction, 203, 204, 206-7, 212-17
extent, 212
special areas, 215
state practice, 223
UNCLOS issue, 201
Exxon Valdez, 65, 71, 139-47, 320, 349

Faulkner Committee, 110-11
financial institutions, liability, 363
Finland, 67, 278, 339
fisheries, 55, 62
fishmeal, 337
flag states
black listing, 253, 285
and coastal state jurisdiction, 74
collusion, 5
competition, 363-5
developed state flags, return, 363-5
enforcement of treaties, 113, 237, 245
genuine link, 50-8
implementation of treaties, 232
investigation practice, 222
jurisdiction, 18-19, 23
extent, 178-9
LOSC, 201-3
MARPOL 73, 185, 188, 191
OILPOL, 112
meaning, 23
national sovereignty, 118

flag states (*cont.*)
  open registries. *See* open registries
  quality flags, 366, 372
  re-flagging, 363-5
  reports, 244-5
  and ship nationality, 34
  standards, 24
  tightening obligations, 365-7
  white listing, 55, 282, 370, 372-3
Food and Agriculture Organization (FAO), 62, 80
fora
  domestic fora, 94-8
  IMO. *See* International Maritime Organization (IMO)
  regional fora, 83-94
  regulation of pollution, 75-98
  UN bodies, 80-3
France
  ban on single hulls, 151-2
  Brussels Conference 1969, 294
  and civil liability regime, 290
  coastal incidents, 97-8
  and double hulls, 144
  and early regulation, 109
  and *Erika* incident, 89, 147, 331
  failure to report enforcement activities, 278
  Fund Conference 1971, 308
  IOPC claims, 330
  Kerguelen registry, 59
  London Conference 1962, 115, 117, 274
  maritime interests, 67
  OILPOL conference, 125
  port state jurisdiction, 189
  post-OILPOL policy, 123
  and SBTs, 129
  TBT regulation, 163
freedom of navigation
  bans on single hulls, 152
  and coastal jurisdiction, 180
  erosion, 4, 25
  military interests, 46
  principle, 17-19
  transit rights, 198
Friends of the Earth, 69, 144
FUND 71
  1971 Conference, 302-9
  1992 Protocol, 327-34
  and CLC 69, 302-6
  entry into force, 311
  extension, 314-15
  future revisions, 333
  generally, 300-9
  pre-1971 developments, 300-2
  switch to FUND 92, 330
FUND 92
  commencement, 329
  generally, 327-34
  non-ratifications, 330-1
G77, 52, 197, 200-1
GAIRS, 195-7, 225-6, 229
garbage, 22, 133, 263
Gard and Skuld, 67
generally accepted international rules and standards, 195-7, 225-6, 229
Germany
  1997 MARPOL Protocol, 161
  Brussels Conference 1969, 294
  and civil liability regime, 290
  Fund Conference 1971, 308
  maritime interests, 67
  post-OILPOL policy, 123
  registration of ships, 59, 60
  reporting diligence, 278
GESAMP, 3, 350
Greece
  1997 MARPOL Protocol, 161
  and criminal sanctions, 153
  Fund Conference 1971, 306, 308
  maritime interests, 67
  MARPOL 78, 137
  reporting diligence, 278
  shipping interests, 88, 89, 134
Green parties, 67
Greenpeace, 69
Grenadines, 250
Grotius, Hugo, 18

harmful aquatic organisms, 169
hazardous and noxious substances
  civil liability, 334-9
  coal, 336-7
  definition, 336
  exemptions from liability, 337
  HNS Fund, 337-8, 342
  HNSC, 336-9
    entry into force, 338-9, 353-4
    ratification, 338
  information requirements, 337
  limits on liability, 337-8
  liquid natural gas, 338
  list, 336-7
  MARPOL 73, 133
  pollution, 22
  small ships, 337-8
HELCOM, 85
high seas
  coastal state jurisdiction, 217, 222, 223
  port state jurisdiction, 218-19
Honduras, 250
Hong Kong, 66

INDEX 409

IMO
  agenda discipline, 376-8
  Assembly, 77
  Assembly resolutions, 78
  beginnings, 75-6
  committees, 76
  constitutional equity, 374-5
  conventions, 77-80
  Council, 77, 374-5
  dominance, 25
  enforcement powers, 369-73
  equity, 374-6
  finances, 77
  financial equity, 375-6
  Flag State Implementation Sub-
    Committee, 55, 282
  generally, 75-80
  Legal Committee, 70, 289
  membership, 77
  MEPC, 69, 269, 275
  monitoring procedures, 8
  pro-active rule-making, 348-51
  reactive regulation, 348-9
  reform, 374-8
  regulatory weakness, 8
  seat in London, 66
  Secretariat, 33, 77, 350-1, 369-70
  structure, 76-7, 350-1
  treaty-making process, 98-102
  Voluntary Member State Audit Scheme, 371
IMO Conference 1984
  generally, 313-15
  HNS issue, 335
  pre-1984 developments, 311-12
implementation
  before treaty commencement, 353
  generally, 232-6
  incorporation into domestic law, 234
  meaning, 230
  ratification, 233
  reporting, 269-82
incentives
  against sub-standard ships, 357
  and compliance, 8, 232, 236-7, 283-4
  environmental protection by developing countries, 351-2
  flag states, 245
  reporting by port states, 281
  reporting enforcement, 282
  waste reception facilities, 264-5, 268
incidents. *See* accidents
India, 66, 74, 370
Indian Ocean, agreements, 93
individuals, and treaty-making process, 32-3
Indonesia, 262, 338

information
  databases, 372
  hazardous and noxious substances, 337
  sharing, 363, 381-3
inspection. *See* ship inspections
Institute of London Underwriters (ILU), 41
insurance
  bunker fuel oil pollution, 341
  classification societies, 361
  CLC 69, 183
  competition, 6, 42
  compulsory insurance, 287, 300, 341, 343-4
  direct action against insurers, 297
  hull and machinery (H&M), 40
  interests, 40, 40-3
  P&I Clubs, 41-3, 291, 340, 363, 382
  pay-to-be-paid rule, 43, 287
  representatives, 41-2
  sub-standard ships, 237, 362
  TOVALOP scheme, 292
Inter-Governmental Maritime Consultative Organization (IMCO), 110, 115
internal waters, jurisdiction, 204-5
International Association of Classification Societies (IACS), 43, 357
International Chamber of Shipping (ICS), 37, 40-3, 158, 290, 301, 382
International Conference on Tanker Safety and Pollution Prevention 1978, 135-9
International Group of P&I Clubs, 41, 323-4
International Labour Organization (ILO), 80, 81-2
international law
  conventions. *See* treaties
  customary law, 30-1
  generally accepted international rules and standards, 195-7, 225-6, 229
International Law Commission, 51
International Maritime Organization. *See* IMO
International Maritime Organization (IMO) Legal Committee, 70, 289
International Oil Pollution Compensation (IOPC) Fund, 303-7, 312, 327, 342
International Oil Pollution Prevention Certificates (IOPPC), 188, 246, 247
International Safety Management (ISM) Code, 55, 78, 221, 370-1
International Tanker Owners Pollution Federation (ITOPF), 291, 292
International Transport Workers Federation (ITF), 57
International Union for the Conservation of Nature (IUCN), 69
International Union of Marine Insurers, 41

INTERTANKO, 37-8, 382
Iran, 187, 262
Iraq, 262
Ireland, 72, 339
Iron Baron, 340
Isle of Man, 59
ISM Code, 55, 78, 221, 363, 370-1
Italy, 67, 115, 134, 294, 336
Ixtoc I, 319

Jacobson, H., 9
Japan
　1973 Conference, 129
　Brussels Conference 1969, 294
　coal imports, 336
　and double hulls, 144
　Fund Conference 1971, 308
　IOPC claims, 330
　IOPC contributions, 327-8
　maritime interests, 66
　MARPOL 73, 189
　port state jurisdiction, 190
　post-OILPOL policy, 123
　reporting diligence, 278
　and SBTs, 129
　shipbuilding, 120
　and sub-standard ships, 333
　TBT regulation, 163
jurisdiction. *See* state jurisdiction

Kirki, 97

labour
　blue certificates, 57
　cost-cutting, 6
　crew nationality, 54
　human errors, 16, 82, 349
　and second registries, 60
　STCW Protocol, 370
　'White List' certification, 55
Latin America, agreements, 93
Law of the Sea Convention (LOSC)
　See also UNCLOS conferences
　adoption, 194
　assessment, 229
　compromises, 198-9
　dispute settlement, 214, 229
　and ecological unity of seas, 224-5
　and GAIRS, 195-7, 225-6, 229
　marine environment, 192-201
　seabed regime, 197
　state jurisdiction, 178, 192-221
　　archipelagic waters, 211
　　coastal states, 204-17
　　contiguous zones, 211-12
　　exclusive economic zones, 212-17
　　flag states, 201-3
　　high seas, 217
　　internal waters, 204-5
　　port states, 217-21
　　straits, 209-11
　　territorial seas, 205-9
　status, 192
　violations, 229
　zones of the sea, 194-5
League of Nations, 109
Lebanon, 250
liability. *See* civil liability
Liberia
　1997 MARPOL Protocol, 161
　American ship registration, 65
　Brussels Conference 1969, 295
　flag of convenience, 60, 61
　Fund Conference 1971, 306, 308
　reporting diligence, 278
　shipping interests, 32
　and special areas, 158
Libya, 262
Lloyd's, 41
load-on-top (LOT)
　adoption, 120-6
　compliance, 236-7
　criticisms, 126-9
　MARPOL 73, 131
London Conference 1962, 115-18,
　272, 274
LOSC. *See* Law of the Sea Convention
　(LOSC); UNCLOS conferences
low sulphur fuel, 156-62
Luxembourg, 59

Madagascar, 116
Malaysia, 338
Malta, 60, 61, 88, 89, 149, 153, 251
Manhattan, 183
marine fuel oil
　low-sulphur fuel, 156-62
　standards, 156
marine pollution
　crisis points, 11
　definition of pollution damage, 324,
　　329, 343
　incidents. *See* accidents
　land-based sources, 12, 13-14
　vessel-source. *See* vessel-source marine
　　pollution
maritime interests
　cargo owners. *See* cargo
　　owners/charterers
　classification societies. *See* classification
　　societies
　flag states. *See* flag states
　insurers. *See* insurance
　military, 46-7

shipowners. *See* shipowners
states with maritime interests, 62-7
treaty-making process, 34-67
maritime states
  meaning, 30
  terminology, 31, 32
MARPOL
  1978 amendments, 133-9
  1992 amendments, 139-47
  1997 Protocol, 160, 160-2
  2001 amendments, 147-50
  2003 amendments, 150-5
  annexes, 129
  crude oil washing, 133-9, 191
  and double hulls, 139-47
  enforcement obligations, 234-5
  Protocols, 130
  reporting requirements, 269, 274-5
  segregated ballast tanks (SBTs), 126-32, 134-9
  state jurisdiction, 178, 184-92
Marshall Islands, 60
Mauritius, 60
media role, 69-71
Mediterranean Sea, 82, 93, 116, 132, 262
memoranda of understanding
  Asia-Pacific MOU, 247
  co-operation, 368
  Paris MOU, 90-4, 153, 248-51, 356, 367
  port state control, 90-4, 356, 367-9
  reporting practice, 281-2
  Tokyo MOU, 93, 252, 253, 356, 367
Mexico, 336
mid-deck tanker design, 144, 146
military interests, 46-7
Mitchell, George, 320
Mongolia, 60
monitoring
  classification societies, 373
  discharges, 236
  IMO procedures, 8
  OILPOL regime, 113

national fora, 94-8
national security, 223
national sovereignty, 118
nationality
  crews, 54
  and flag states, 34
natural resources, 53
navigation standards, 22
Netherlands, 60, 67, 148, 163, 186, 187, 308
New International Economic Order, 53, 81
New Zealand, 72, 163
NGOs
  environmental NGOs, 67-9
  IMO activism, 102

and special areas, 158
Nigeria, 262
non-state actors
  IMO treaty process, 102
  individuals, 32-3
  influence, 23, 29
  and international law, 31
North Korea, 250
North Sea, 33, 86, 155, 157, 262
North-East Atlantic, 85
Norway
  1997 MARPOL Protocol, 161
  Brussels Conference 1969, 294
  and civil liability regime, 290
  and double hulls, 144
  Fund Conference 1971, 308
  HNSC ratification, 339
  maritime interests, 66
  MARPOL 78, 137
  North Sea Conferences, 155
  registration of ships, 59, 60
  shipping interests, 88, 134
  TBT regulation, 163

OCIMF, 40, 301, 313
OECD, 134
oil companies
  divestment of tanker ownership, 39
  interests, 39-40
  oil majors, 39
  representatives, 40
Oil Companies Institute for Marine Pollution Compensation Ltd, 301
oil crisis 1970s, 52, 121, 199
oil pollution
  bunker fuel oils, 339-41
  civil liability. *See* civil liability
  fuel oil, 22
  history of regulation, 107-55
  operational pollution, 20-2
  v. other pollutants, 20
  statistics, 12
OILPOL
  1969 amendments, 124-5
  discharge standards, 110
  enforcement, 112-13
  London Conference 1962, 115-18, 272, 274
  and LOT, 120-6
  reporting requirements, 273-4
  state jurisdiction, 178
  weaknesses, 126
Oman, 262
Oman, Gulf of, 82
one-ship companies, 34, 35, 48, 50-8, 289, 325-6
open registries
  debate, 47-62

open registries (cont.)
  flags of convenience, 24, 35, 47
  phasing out, 48, 50-8
  states
    developing countries, 101, 351
    IMO activism, 101
    non-compliance, 251
    ratification of treaties, 355
    UNCLOS conferences, 74
ORB, 113, 117, 124, 246

Pacific, agreements, 93
paints. *See* anti-fouling paints
Palacio, Loyola de, 71
Panama, 32, 60, 61, 158, 161, 251, 278
Paris MOU, 90-4, 153, 248-51, 356, 367
Particularly Sensitive Sea Areas (PSSAs), 154, 225, 226-8, 229
Persian Gulf, 82, 116, 132, 157, 262, 265
phantom ships, 62
Philippines, 101, 370
P&I Clubs
  and bunker fuel oil pollution, 340
  information sharing, 382
  interests, 40, 40-3
  pooling of liabilities, 363
  and TOVALOP, 291
PLATO, 316
politics
  IMO dynamics, 102-4
  treaty-making process, 29-30, 31-4
  wealthy state dominance, 350
polluter pays principle, 35, 68, 168-74, 265, 344, 379
pollution damage, definition, 324, 343
port shopping, 94
port state control
  1969 proposals, 125
  abuse, 367
  and compliance, 284-5
  detention, 238
  domestic legislation, 9
  enforcement record, 245-51
  enhancing, 367-9
  entry denial, 238
  EU regulation, 92-3, 152-5
  inspections. *See* ship inspections
  London Conference 1962, 117
  memoranda of understanding, 90-4, 356, 367-9
  OILPOL, 113
  points system, 357
  political targets, 364
  reports, 242-3, 252
  weaknesses, 6-7
port states

incentives to report enforcement, 281
jurisdiction, 24, 180-1, 189-91, 217-21
meaning, 23
Portugal, 59, 152
precautionary principle, 68-9, 174, 224
Prestige, 71, 87, 89, 97, 150-5, 209, 349, 362, 380
Principe, 250
public opinion, 69-71
public vessels, immunity, 20, 46-7, 214

Qatar, 262

ratification of treaties, 233
reception facilities. *See* waste reception facilities
Red Sea, 83, 116, 132, 262, 265
regional agreements
  Europe, 83-9
  fora, 83-94
  MOUs on port state control, 90-4
  and UNEP, 82-3
registration of ships
  bareboat charters, 59
  change, 58-62, 80
  closed registries, 48
  conditions, 53-5
  developing countries, 351
  fishing vessels, 62
  flag states. *See* flag states
  international registries, 59-60
  offshore registries, 58-9
  open registries. *See* open registries
  second registries, 59-60
regulation of pollution sources
  actors. *See* actors
  arenas. *See* fora
  equity, 373-83
  generally, 10-17
  improving institutional responses, 347-73
reporting
  enforcement actions, 273-82
  EU regulation, 154
  flag states, 244-5
  IMO surveys, 269-71
  implementation activities, 269-82
  incentives, 281, 282
  industry surveys, 273
  MOU system, 248-51, 281-2
  port states, 242-3
  provision of reception facilities, 269-73
  reporting on others, 272-3
  self-reporting, 188, 269-72
  Ship Inspection Report Exchange, 56, 359, 360
  ship inspections, 240-1

state practice, 246-7
strengthening obligations, 373
Tokyo MOU, 252, 253
Rio Declaration, 68
Rio Summit, 67
Rochdale Report, 48

Samoa, 60
São Tomé, 250
Saudi Arabia, 262
security, and flags of convenience, 62
segregated ballast tanks (SBTs)
  compliance, 238
  flag state jurisdiction, 188
  MARPOL 73, 126-32
  MARPOL 78, 134-9
separators, 111-13, 118, 122
sewage, 22, 133, 263
Seychelles, 60
Shell, 116, 121
ship inspections
  1969 proposals, 125
  EU regulation, 153
  flag state obligations, 202
  incentives, 237
  London Conference 1962, 117
  MARPOL 73, 189
  port control, 61, 91-2
  port state jurisdiction, 218
  reports, 240-1
  Ship Inspection Report Exchange, 56, 359, 360
ship operators. *See* shipowners
shipbuilding
  high-tensile steel, 6
  VLCCs, 120
shipowners
  1992 liability Protocols, 328
  civil liability, 288, 296-7, 302, 315, 328, 342-3
  competition, 35
  and European Union, 88
  and FUND Convention, 309
  indemnification, 306-9, 310, 314
  independents, 38-9, 291-2
  interests, 34-8
  intra-industry co-operation, 381-3
  ownership secrecy, 34-5, 36-7
  political power, 67
  representatives, 37-8
shipping industry
  co-operation, 381-3
  features, 9, 10
  lobbying power, 35
  old ships, 16-17
  resistance to regulation, 10
Singapore, 66, 101, 161

SIRE, 56, 359, 360
Small Tanker Oil Pollution Indemnification Agreement (STOPIA), 332
South Africa, 336
South Korea, 66, 101, 147
South-East Pacific, 83
sovereign immunity, 20, 46-7
Soviet Union, 123, 130, 187, 295, 308
Spain
  1997 MARPOL Protocol, 161
  and criminal sanctions, 153
  IOPC claims, 330
  maritime interests, 67
  offshore ship registration, 58
  Prestige incident, 150, 362
  and single hulls, 151-2
special areas
  chemical discharges, 133
  London Conference 1962, 116
  MARPOL 73, 131-2
  sulphur emissions, 156, 157-9
  waste reception facilities, 262
spot market, 40, 380
St Vincent, 250
standards. *See* technical standards
state enterprises, 284
state jurisdiction
  adjudicative jurisdiction, 176
  civil liability, 298
  coastal states, 179-80
    archipelagic waters, 211
    contiguous zones, 211-12
    early attempts to extend, 181-4
    exclusive economic zones, 212-17
    high seas, 217
    internal waters, 204-5
    straits, 209-11
    territorial seas, 205-9
  enforcement jurisdiction, 176
  flag states, 18-19, 23, 112, 178-9, 201-3
  internal waters, 204-5
  international law, 23-5, 177-8
  LOSC, 192-221
    coastal states, 204-17
    flag states, 201-3
    port states, 217-21
  marine pollution regimes, 176-81
  MARPOL 73
    enforcement jurisdiction, 187-91
    prescriptive jurisdiction, 184-7
  MARPOL 78, 191-2
  port states, 180-1
  territorialist states, 185
  and *Torrey Canyon*, 289
states
  coastal. *See* coastal states

states (cont.)
  enforcement of pollution control, 239-51, 285
  flag. See flag states
  interests, 32
  ports. See port states
  territorialist states, 185
  with coastal interests, 71-3
  with maritime interests, 62-7
statutory certification, 44-5
Stockholm Conference 1972, 82, 126-8
straits, jurisdiction, 209-11
sub-standard shipping
  causes, 4, 5, 35
  civil liability, 333-4
  criminal liability, 380
  eradication, 8
  EU blacklists, 92
  and flags of convenience, 57
  insurance, 237, 362
  market discrimination against, 356-7
  regional trades, 7
  subsisting problem, 15-16
Suez crisis, 118
Sweden, 67, 122, 137, 336, 339

tacit acceptance procedures, 196
Taiwan, 66
Tanio, 70, 97, 312
tank washings, 21
Tanker Management and Self-Assessment (TMSA), 359
TBTs
  AFS Convention, 167-8
  alternatives, 165-6
  regulation, 161, 162-8
technical standards
  categories, 22-3
  CDEM. See CDEM standards
  discharge. See discharge standards
  discharge v. equipment standards, 238-9
  early regulation, 107-9
  enforcement practice, 236-51
  marine fuel oil, 156
  marine pollution, 107-55
territorial seas, jurisdiction, 203, 205-9
Tokyo MOU, 93, 252, 253, 356, 367
Tonga, 250
Torrey Canyon, 40, 70, 76, 84, 97, 120, 288-90
tortious liability, 289, 290, 311-12
TOVALOP
  amendments, 309-10, 315
  ceiling, 293
  and CRISTAL, 301-2
  scheme, 291-3
  termination, 330
tragedy of the commons, 11

transit rights, 198, 209-11
transparency
  port state control, 92
  shipowning, 36-7, 57, 381-3
treaties
  compliance. See compliance
  effectiveness, 231-2, 238-9
  enforcement. See enforcement
  IMO conventions, 77-80
  implementation. See implementation
  incorporation into domestic law, 234
  minimum tonnage requirement, 352-4
  preferred regulation method, 13
  ratification, 233
  speed of entry into force, 351-5
treaty-making process
  actors. See actors
  arenas. See fora
  consultative status, 102
  and developing countries, 99-101
  and effectiveness, 231
  equity, 373-83
  IMO conventions, 77-80, 98-102
  interplay of interests, 9, 98-104
  politics, 29-30, 31-4, 102-4
  weaknesses, 8
Tunisia, 250
two-dollar companies, 34

UNCED, 224
UNCLOS conferences
  Canadian role, 72
  compromises, 198-9
  deep seabed, 53
  developing countries' positions, 73-4
  EEZ issue, 201
  flag states, 53
  generally, 83
  history, 115
  LOSC. See Law of the Sea Convention
  negotiations, 193-4
  open registry states, 74
  voting procedures, 193
UNCTAD, 52-3, 80-1
UNEP, 80, 82-3, 126
unilateralism
  and IMO weakness, 370
  issue, 347-8
  threats, 348, 351, 356-7
  United States, 65, 94
Union Oil, 288-9, 292
United Arab Emirates, 262
United Kingdom
  1969 Brussels Conference, 294, 295
  1969 proposals, 125
  1971 Fund Conference, 306, 308
  1997 MARPOL Protocol, 161

2001 MARPOL amendments, 148
bunker fuel oils, 340, 341
and civil liability regime, 290
and criminal sanctions for negligent discharge, 153
domestic legislation, 96-7
and early regulation, 107-9
HNSC ratification, 339
IOPC claims, 330
Isle of Man registry, 59
London Conference 1962, 115, 117-18, 274
LOT regulation, 122
maritime interests, 65-6
MARPOL 73, 186, 187
MARPOL 78, 136
off-shore ship registration, 58
oil industry, 308
OILPOL 54, 110-11, 113-15
port state jurisdiction, 189
post-OILPOL policy, 122-3
registration of ships, 60
reporting diligence, 278
ship inspections, 91
shipping interests, 88
and sub-standard ships, 333
TBT regulation, 163
waste management plans, 267-8
United Nations agencies, 80-3
United States
  and 1970s treaties, 33
  ballast water discharge, regulation, 103
  ballast water regulation, 170
  Brussels Conference 1969, 294
  Carter Initiatives, 135
  certificates of financial responsibility, 323
  civil liability regime, 287, 318-27
  coal imports, 336
  criminal liability, 324-5
  domestic regulation, 94-6
  and double hulls, 129, 131, 135, 140-7, 349
  ecological awareness, 128-9
  Exxon Valdez impact, 320
  Fund Conference 1971, 303, 306, 308
  Great Lakes contamination, 169
  hazardous substances, 353
  HNSC, 339
  IMO Conference 1984, 313, 315-16, 318, 320
  maritime interests, 63-5
  MARPOL 73, 186-7, 188, 189
  MARPOL 78, 134-9, 191
  MARPOL 1992 Protocol, 146
  non-ratification of liability conventions, 318-19, 327-34

OILPOL Conference 1962, 272
OPA 1990, 320-7
political influence, 107-9
port state control, 93-4, 190, 254-5, 356, 367
post-OILPOL policy, 123
pre-1990 regime, 318
Qualship 21, 368
reception facilities, 116
and reporting requirements, 272
and shipownership secrecy, 36
state legislation, 326
TBT regulation, 163
tortious liability, 312
treaty-making politics, 33
unilateralism, 65, 94, 356-7
Uruguay, 187
USRR. *See* Soviet Union

Vanuatu, 60, 161, 278
Venezuela, 262
vessel-source marine pollution
  accidental pollution, 20
  air pollution. *See* air pollution
  ballast water. *See* ballast water
  bunker fuel oils, 339-41
  international focus, 12-13
  liability. *See* civil liability
  meaning, 3
  oil. *See* oil pollution
  operational pollution, 20, 20-2
  paints. *See* anti-fouling paints
  standards. *See* technical standards
  statistics, 13-15
  technical issues, 19
VLCCs, 120, 143, 296

warships, 20, 46-7, 214
Washington Conference 1926, 107-9
waste reception facilities
  compliance record, 8, 251-68
  developing countries, 261, 264, 267
  early regulation, 108-9
  European Union, 266-7
  Fund for Reception Facilities, 267
  improvement, 378-9
  incentive deficit, 264-5, 268
  inefficiency, 263
  lack of sanctions, 266
  liability for costs, 256, 264, 265, 268
  London Conference 1962, 118
  and LOT, 120, 121, 122
  MARPOL 73, 132
  OILPOL, 111-26, 116-17
  oil-producing countries, 262, 264-5
  reporting on provision, 269-73
  special areas, 262

waste reception facilities (*cont.*)
  surveys, 257-62, 267, 269-71, 273
  waste management plans, 267
  white listing, 268
Weiss, E. B., 9
West Africa, agreements, 93

white listing, 55, 282, 370, 372-3, 378
wing ballast tanks, 139
woodchip, 337
World Meteorological Organization
  (WMO), 81
World Wide Fund for Nature (WWF), 69

CAMBRIDGE STUDIES IN INTERNATIONAL AND COMPARATIVE LAW

Books in the series

Law in Times of Crisis
Emergency Powers in Theory and Practice
Oren Gross and Fionnuala Ní Aoláin

Vessel-Source Marine Pollution
The Law and Politics of International Regulation
Alan Tan

Enforcing Obligations Erga Omnes *in International Law*
Christian J. Tams

Non-Governmental Organisations in International Law
Anna-Karin Lindblom

Democracy, Minorities and International Law
Steven Wheatley

Prosecuting International Crimes
Selectivity and the International Law Regime
Robert Cryer

Compensation for Personal Injury in English, German and Italian Law
A Comparative Outline
Basil Markesinis, Michael Coester, Guido Alpa,
Augustus Ullstein

Dispute Settlement in the UN Convention on the Law of the Sea
Natalie Klein

The International Protection of Internally Displaced Persons
Catherine Phuong

Imperialism, Sovereignty and the Making of International Law
Antony Anghie

Necessity, Proportionality and the Use of Force by States
Judith Gardam

International Legal Argument in the Permanent Court of International Justice
The Rise of the International Judiciary
Ole Spiermann

Great Powers and Outlaw States
Unequal Sovereigns in the International Legal Order
Gerry Simpson

Local Remedies in International Law
C. F. Amerasinghe

Reading Humanitarian Intervention
Human Rights and the Use of Force in International Law
Anne Orford

Conflict of Norms in Public International Law
How WTO Law Relates to Other Rules of Law
Joost Pauwelyn

Transboundary Damage in International Law
Hanqin Xue

European Criminal Procedures
Edited by Mireille Delmas-Marty and John Spencer

The Accountability of Armed Opposition Groups in International Law
Liesbeth Zegveld

Sharing Transboundary Resources
International Law and Optimal Resource Use
Eyal Benvenisti

International Human Rights and Humanitarian Law
René Provost

Remedies Against International Organisations
Karel Wellens

Diversity and Self-Determination in International Law
Karen Knop

The Law of Internal Armed Conflict
Lindsay Moir

International Commercial Arbitration and African States
Practice, Participation and Institutional Development
Amazu A. Asouzu

The Enforceability of Promises in European Contract Law
James Gordley

International Law in Antiquity
David J. Bederman

Money Laundering
A New International Law Enforcement Model
Guy Stessens

Good Faith in European Contract Law
Reinhard Zimmerman and Simon Whittaker

On Civil Procedure
J. A. Jolowicz

Trusts
A Comparative Study
Maurizio Lupoi

The Right to Property in Commonwealth Constitutions
Tom Allen

International Organizations Before National Courts
August Reinisch

The Changing International Law of High Seas Fisheries
Francisco Orrego Vicuña

Trade and the Environment
A Comparative Study of EC and US Law
Damien Geradin

Unjust Enrichment
A Study of Private Law and Public Values
Hanoch Dagan

Religious Liberty and International Law in Europe
Malcolm D. Evans

Ethics and Authority in International Law
Alfred P. Rubin

Sovereignty Over Natural Resources
Balancing Rights and Duties
Nico Schrijver

The Polar Regions and the Development of International Law
Donald R. Rothwell

Fragmentation and the International Relations of Micro-States
Self-determination and Statehood
Jorri Duursma

Principles of the Institutional Law of International Organizations
C. F. Amerasinghe

For EU product safety concerns, contact us at Calle de José Abascal, 56–1°, 28003 Madrid, Spain or eugpsr@cambridge.org.